PARERGA AND

Arthur Schopenhauer in April 1859

Parerga and Paralipomena

Short Philosophical Essays

by
ARTHUR SCHOPENHAUER

Translated from the German
by
E. F. J. PAYNE

VOLUME ONE

CLARENDON PRESS · OXFORD

OXFORD
UNIVERSITY PRESS

Great Clarendon Street, Oxford OX2 6DP

Oxford University Press is a department of the University of Oxford.
It furthers the University's objective of excellence in research, scholarship,
and education by publishing worldwide in

Oxford New York

Auckland   Cape Town Dar es Salaam   Hong Kong   Karachi
Kuala Lumpur Madrid Melbourne Mexico City   Nairobi
New Delhi Shanghai Taipei Toronto
With offices in
Argentina Austria Brazil Chile Czech Republic France Greece
Guatemala Hungary Italy Japan South Korea Poland Portugal
Singapore Switzerland Thailand Turkey Ukraine Vietnam

ISBN 978-0-19-924220-7

Printed in the United Kingdom by
Lightning Source UK Ltd., Milton Keynes

Vitam impendere vero
Juvenal, *Sat.* IV. 91
["Dedicate one's life to truth"]

Contents

VOLUME ONE

Translator's Introduction

COVERING more than the first half of the nineteenth century Schopenhauer's original and unorthodox opinions inevitably provoked a vigorous reaction of the scholars, thinkers, and theologians who at that time were the representatives of culture, art, science, and religion. More than any other philosopher of modern times he had to contend with fractious contemporaries who were ever ready to denigrate and denounce him, to secrete and suppress his works by the simple expedient of silence, and who did not scruple to misquote him blatantly and unblushingly from his own writings. Such denunciation over several decades was bound to result in a distorted image of the philosopher and a perverted presentation of his views even in the academic circles of the early years of the present century—a presentation that has often been founded on a perfunctory acquaintance with the main tenets of his system.

But the pace and pressure of events in the first half of the twentieth century during which, in spite of an impressive advance in many branches of technology, there has been a steady decline in culture, have imposed on Western man the necessity to re-examine the thoughts of serious philosophers in general and those of Schopenhauer in particular. The easy and agreeable optimism of the years before 1914 with its confident belief in the perfectibility of man and in his steady advance to the millennium was rudely shaken by the outbreak of the First World War and finally shattered by the terrible episodes prior to and during the second war.

By 1945 all melioristic dreams had been dispelled and men in the Western hemisphere were constrained to reappraise the unpalatable truths of philosophical pessimism. In a mood of despair the present generation is evincing a growing interest in those systems of thought which do not shrink from presenting the stark realities of existence, but nevertheless offer a long-term prospect of final emancipation and salvation from the eternal thraldom of birth, life, suffering, death, and rebirth. It is therefore hardly surprising that in the quarter of a century since 1945 many have become increasingly concerned with realistic thinking, and all who have witnessed and experienced barbarism and brutality on a global scale are athirst for a philosophy of life which will facilitate a reconciliation between their rational and logical outlook and the sombre and ineluctable truths and precepts of New Testament Christianity and indeed of all genuine religion. A similar revulsion of feeling a century before may well have ushered in a revival of interest in serious philosophy after the momentous events of 1848, that year of revolutionary rumblings. In 1851 the *Parerga and Paralipomena* were published at a time when Europe was passing through a period of despondency and disillusionment.

Arthur Schopenhauer was born in Danzig in 1788 and at the early age of twenty-five published his first work *On the Fourfold Root of the Principle of Sufficient Reason*, for which the University of Jena awarded him a doctor's degree. This essay soon attained the rank of a philosophical classic and even today is probably one of the best treatises on epistemology. In 1816 he wrote a short essay *On Vision and Colours*, and in 1819 his chief work, *The World as Will and Representation*, was published in one volume in which he expounded his whole philosophical system and included in an appendix a masterly criticism of Kant's three *Critiques*. In 1830 he published in Latin a second essay on the theory of colours and in 1836 there appeared the essay *On the Will in Nature*, in which he discussed the corroborations which his philosophy had obtained from the empirical sciences since its first appearance. In 1839 and 1840 Schopenhauer wrote two prize-essays: (1) on the freedom of the human will and (2) on the basis of ethics. The first was awarded a prize by a Norwegian academy, but the second was rejected by a Danish academy, although Schopenhauer's was the only essay submitted. In 1841 the two essays, preceded by a long and caustic preface, were published in one volume with the title *The Two Fundamental Problems of Ethics*.

From his earliest years Schopenhauer was in the habit of noting down the many different observations and reflections which occurred to him during his frequent meditations on the mystery and riddle of existence. By 1844 he had amassed enough material and hoped that Brockhaus, the publisher of 1819, would accede to the proposal to publish a second and enlarged edition of *The World as Will and Representation*. But in view of the failure of the first edition of 1819 to impress the learned world of that year, the publisher showed little enthusiasm, but finally agreed reluctantly to publish in two volumes an augmented edition of the chief work, for which Schopenhauer received no honorarium. These two volumes likewise failed to stimulate any interest. Undaunted by such discouragement, Schopenhauer steadily pursued the dreary path of truth and turned his attention to other important subjects which had hitherto not come within the framework of his systematic writings. The elaboration and compilation of the many notes and drafts which had accumulated over more than a generation occupied some six years of unremitting daily toil. From Schopenhauer's posthumous notes we learn that these supplementary essays and observations do not enable the reader to become fully acquainted with the main tenets of his philosophical system. On the contrary, they were written for those readers who already subscribed to his earlier and more important works, and so he assumed an acquaintance with his teaching and addressed himself to those already conversant with it.

It may be stated generally that the first volume of *Parerga and Paralipomena* contains the parerga (supplementary works) whereas the second comprises the paralipomena (matters omitted from the main structure of Schopenhauer's ideas). These paralipomena were regarded by him as complementary to the supplements to his chief work, and this is especially true of chapters I–XIV of the second *Parerga* volume which therefore assume a knowledge of the author's philosophy. On the other hand, the remainder of the second *Parerga* volume together with the whole of the first can be understood without any such previous knowledge; yet those already familiar with the main tenets of his philosophy will discern many references to these and observe that they throw additional light on many of his arguments.

At the end of 1850 Schopenhauer was ready to approach a publisher with the manuscript of his last major work in two volumes. But only after long delay and much disappointment was Julius Frauenstädt, his close friend and disciple, able to persuade Hayn of Berlin to publish the two volumes in 1851 in an edition of 750 copies of which Schopenhauer received ten but no honorarium.

Shortly after their publication, the *Parerga and Paralipomena* came to the notice of John Oxenford, the translator of Goethe's conversations with Eckermann, who in 1852 wrote a review for the *Westminster and Foreign Quarterly Review* and in 1853 for the same journal an article entitled 'Iconoclasm in German Philosophy'. This article was read by Ernst Otto Lindner, a friend of Schopenhauer's, who arranged for the publication of a German translation in the *Vossische Zeitung*. The effect was dramatic and almost overnight Schopenhauer in his own country passed from obscurity to fame and from then till his death in 1860 he basked in the sunshine of belated recognition and eminence. This sudden interest in his philosophy called for new editions of his other published works and the old sage's obvious pleasure at final acknowledgement was naïve and childlike and in some measure compensated him for the many years of frustration and bitterness.

Of the early English translators of the *Parerga and Paralipomena* Thomas Bailey Saunders (1860–1928) and Ernest Belfort Bax (1854–1926) are the best-known who before the turn of the century had begun to make selections from the more popular essays. There was no collaboration between the two and a certain amount of duplication was therefore inevitable. Moreover, their styles and terminology were idiosyncratic, a factor which precluded the compilation of their combined efforts into a uniform and homogeneous translation. Bailey Saunders's renderings had indeed caught the piquancy and pungency of Schopenhauer's style, but in some instances they border on paraphrase, a practice of which the philosopher himself disapproved. Nevertheless these two distinguished scholars succeeded in introducing to English readers the many gems of Schopenhauer's genius at a time when it was fashionable to dismiss the philosopher as a crotchety, woman-hating old pessimist. Using the German text of the old and long since discarded Frauenstädt edition of Schopenhauer's works, they inevitably suffered from handicaps which do not burden the modern translator able to avail himself of a more accurate and scholarly text. The present translation is the first complete English rendering of the *Parerga and Paralipomena* and has been made from the German text of the Hübscher–Brockhaus edition, itself the outcome of more than a century of textual research and emendation. The immense range of Schopenhauer's erudition is reflected in the many quotations from Greek, Latin, English, French, German, Italian, and Spanish authors; translations of all foreign-language quotations are given in footnotes in the text.

No introduction can end without an expression of gratitude to the many friends who through their help and encouragement have greatly contributed to the completion of a long and arduous undertaking. In particular Arthur Hübscher, President of the Schopenhauer-Gesellschaft and the most eminent living authority on Schopenhauer and his philosophy, has for many years generously given valuable advice. Professor Richard Taylor of Rochester University, New York State has sedulously used his influence to bring Schopenhauer's philosophy to the notice of American readers, whilst Bryan Magee has rendered a similar service to students in this country. Finally to his wife Eileen the translator is grateful for her inexhaustible fund of patience and inspiration. Without the very real help and interest of these and many other friends, this translation could not have come to fruition.

Preface

THESE additional writings, that are subsidiary to my more important and systematic works, consist partly of a few essays on a wide variety of special topics and partly of isolated ideas on an even greater range of subjects. All have been brought together here since, by reason largely of the subject-matter, they could not find a place in those systematic works; some, however, are included here merely because they came too late for inclusion in their proper place in those works.

Here, of course, I have primarily had in mind those readers who are acquainted with my systematic and more comprehensive works, for perhaps they too will here find many a desired explanation. But on the whole, the contents of these volumes will, with the exception of a few passages, be intelligible and interesting even to those who are unacquainted with my philosophy. But whoever is familiar with this, will yet have an advantage, since this always reflects its light, however remotely, on all that I think and write, just as, on the other hand, that philosophy itself always receives some further elucidation from everything that emanates from my mind.

Frankfurt am Main,
(December 1850)

SKETCH OF A HISTORY OF THE DOCTRINE OF THE IDEAL AND THE REAL

Plurimi pertransibunt, et multiplex erit scientia.

['Many shall run to and fro, and knowledge shall be increased.' Daniel 12:4.]

Sketch of a History of the Doctrine of the Ideal and the Real

DESCARTES is rightly regarded as the father of modern philosophy primarily and generally because he helped the faculty of reason to stand on its own feet by teaching men to use their brains in place whereof the Bible, on the one hand, and Aristotle, on the other, had previously served. But he is the father in a special and narrower sense because he was the first to bring to our consciousness the problem whereon all philosophizing has since mainly turned, namely that of the ideal and the real. This is the question concerning what in our knowledge is objective and what subjective, and hence what eventually is to be ascribed by us to things different from us and what is to be attributed to ourselves. Thus in our head images arise not arbitrarily, as it were, from within, nor do they proceed from the connection of ideas; consequently, they arise from an external cause. But such images alone are what is immediately known to us, what is given. Now what relation may they have to things which exist quite separately from and independently of us and which would somehow become the cause of those images? Are we certain that such things generally exist at all, and in this case do the images give us any information as to their nature? This is the problem and in consequence thereof the main endeavour of philosophers for the last two hundred years has been clearly to separate by a line of cleavage correctly drawn the ideal, in other words, what belongs to our knowledge solely and as such, from the real, that is to say, what exists independently of our knowledge, and thus to determine the relation of the two to each other.

Neither the philosophers of antiquity nor even the Schoolmen really appear to have become clearly aware of this fundamental philosophical problem, although we find a trace of it, as idealism and even as the doctrine of the ideality of time, in Plotinus, and in fact in *Enneads*, lib. VII, c. 10, where he tells us that the soul made the world by emerging from eternity into time. He says there, for instance: οὐ γάρ τις αὐτοῦ τούτου τοῦ παντὸς τόπος, ἢ ψυχή. (neque datur alius hujus universi locus, quam anima.)[1] as also: δεῖ δὲ οὐκ ἔξωθεν τῆς ψυχῆς λαμβάνειν τὸν χρόνον, ὥσπερ οὐδὲ τὸν αἰῶνα ἐκεῖ ἔξω τοῦ ὄντος. (oportet autem nequaquam extra animam tempus accipere, quemadmodum neque aeternitatem ibi extra id, quod ens appellatur);[2] here is really expressed Kant's ideality of time. And in the following chapter: οὗτος ὁ βίος τὸν χρόνον γεννᾷ διὸ καὶ εἴρηται ἅμα τῷδε τῷ παντὶ γεγονέναι, ὅτι ψυχὴ αὐτὸν μετὰ τοῦδε τοῦ παντὸς ἐγέννησεν. (haec vita nostra tempus gignit: quamobrem dictum est, tempus simul cum hoc universo factum esse; quia anima tempus una cum hoc universo progenuit.)[3] Yet the clearly recognized and clearly expressed problem continues to be the characteristic theme of *modern* philosophy, after the necessary reflectiveness had first been awakened in Descartes. He was struck by the truth that we are above all restricted to our own consciousness and that the world is given to us only as *representation* or *mental picture* [*Vorstellung*]. Through his well-known *dubito, cogito, ergo sum*,[4] he tried to lay stress on the only certain thing of subjective consciousness in contrast to the problematical nature of everything else, and to express the great truth that self-consciousness is the only thing really and unconditionally *given*. Closely considered, his famous proposition is the equivalent of that from which I started, namely: 'The world is my representation'. The only difference is that his proposition stresses the immediateness of the subject, whereas mine stresses the mediateness of the object. Both propositions express the same thing from two points of view. They are the reverse each other and therefore stand in the same relation as the laws of inertia and causality, according to my discussion in the preface to my ethics. [*The Two Fundamental Problems of Ethics treated in two academical prize-essays by Dr. Arthur Schopenhauer*. Frankfurt am Main, 1841, p. xxiv; 2nd edn., Leipzig, 1860, pp. xxivf.] Since the days of Descartes his

---

[1] ['For there is for this universe no other place than the mind.']

[2] ['But we should not accept time outside the mind; and also we should not accept the eternity of the Beyond outside Being (i.e. the world of Ideas).']

[3] ['This life produces time, which also means that time arose simultaneously with this universe; for the mind has produced it simultaneously with this universe.']

[4] ['I doubt, that is to say, I think, consequently I am.']

proposition has been repeated innumerable times from a mere feeling of its importance and without a clear understanding of its real meaning and purport. (See *Meditationes*, Med. II, p. 15.) And so it was he who discovered the gulf between the subjective or ideal and the objective or real. He clothed this insight in the form of a doubt concerning the existence of the external world; but by his inadequate solution of such doubt, namely that God Almighty would surely not deceive us, he has shown how profound the problem is and how difficult it is to solve. Meanwhile through him this scruple had come into philosophy and was bound to continue to have a disturbing effect until it was thoroughly disposed of. The consciousness that, without thorough knowledge and an explanation of the distinction that had been discovered, no sure and satisfactory system was possible, had since existed and the question could no longer be shirked.

To dispose of it, Malebranche first devised the system of occasional causes. He grasped the problem itself in its whole range more clearly, seriously, and deeply than did Descartes. (*Recherches de la vérité*, Livre III, seconde partie.) The latter had assumed the reality of the external world on the credit of God; and here, of course, it seems strange that, whereas the other theistic philosophers endeavour to demonstrate the existence of God from that of the world, Descartes, on the contrary, proves the existence of the world first from the existence and trustworthiness of God; it is the cosmological proof the other way round. Here too Malebranche goes a step farther and teaches that we see all things immediately in God himself. This certainly is equivalent to explaining something unknown by something even more unknown. Moreover, according to him, we not only see all things in God, but God is also the sole activity therein, so that physical causes are so only apparently; they are mere *causes occasionnelles*. (*Recherches de la vérité*, Livre VI, seconde partie, chap. 3.) And so here we have essentially the pantheism of Spinoza who appears to have learnt more from Malebranche than from Descartes.

On the whole, one might be surprised that even in the seventeenth century pantheism did not gain a complete victory over theism; for the most original, finest, and most thorough European expositions of it (none of them, of course, will bear comparison with the *Upanishads* of the *Vedas*) all came to light at that period, namely through Bruno, Malebranche, Spinoza, and Scotus Erigena. After Scotus Erigena had been lost and forgotten for many centuries, he was again discovered at Oxford and in 1681, thus four years after Spinoza's death, his work first saw the light in print. This seems to prove that the insight of individuals cannot make itself felt so long as the spirit of the age is not ripe to receive it. On the other hand, in our day pantheism, although presented only in Schelling's eclectic and confused revival thereof, has become the dominant mode of thought of scholars and even of educated people. This is because Kant had preceded it with his overthrow of theistic dogmatism and had cleared the way for it, whereby the spirit of the age was ready for it, just as a ploughed field is ready for the seed. In the seventeenth century, on the contrary, philosophy again forsook that path and accordingly arrived at Locke, on the one hand, for whom Bacon and Hobbes had paved the way, and at Christian Wolff, on the other, through Leibniz. These two were then dominant in the eighteenth century, especially in Germany, although ultimately only in so far as they had been initiated into syncretistic eclecticism.

Malebranche's profound ideas, however, first gave rise to Leibniz's system of *harmonia praestabilita*, and the widespread fame and high repute of this in his day furnish a proof of the fact that in the world the absurd most easily succeeds. Although I cannot boast of having a clear notion of Leibniz's monads, which are at the same time mathematical points, material atoms, and souls, yet it seems to me beyond doubt that such an assumption once settled could help to save us from all further hypotheses for explaining the connection between the ideal and the real, and to dispose of the question by the fact that both are already fully identified in the monads. (For this reason Schelling in our day, as the originator of the system of identity, has again relished it.) However, it did not please the famous philosophizing mathematician, polyhistor, and politician to employ them for this purpose, but to this end he expressly formulated the pre-established harmony. This now furnishes us with two entirely different worlds, each incapable of acting in any way on the other (*Principia philos.*, § 84, and *Examen du sentiment du P. Malebranche*, pp. 500 ff. of the *Oeuvres de Leibniz*, publ.

by Raspe), each the wholly superfluous duplicate of the other. But yet the two are now supposed to exist once for all, to run exactly parallel to each other, and to keep time with each other to a hair. Therefore at the very beginning, the originator of both established between them the precisest harmony wherein they now continue most beautifully to run side by side. Incidentally, the *harmonia praestabilita* might perhaps be best rendered comprehensible by a comparison with the stage. Here very often the *influxus physicus*[5] only apparently exists, since cause and effect are connected merely by means of a pre-established harmony of the stage manager, for example, when the one shoots and the other falls *a tempo*. In §§ 62, 63 of his *Théodicée*, Leibniz has presented the matter in its monstrous absurdity in the crassest manner and in brief. And yet with the whole dogma he has not even the merit of originality, since Spinoza had already presented the *harmonia praestabilita* clearly enough in the second part of his *Ethics*, thus in the sixth and seventh propositions together with their corollaries, and again in the fifth part, first proposition, after he had expressed, in his own way in the fifth proposition of the second part, the very closely related doctrine of Malebranche, that we see everything in God.* Therefore Malebranche alone is the originator of this whole line of thought which both Spinoza and Leibniz have utilized and modified, each in his own way. Leibniz could very well have dispensed with the

---

* [Footnotes with an asterisk or dagger represent additions made by Schopenhauer in his interleaved copy between 1851 and his death in 1860.]
Ethics, Pt. II, prop. 7: *Ordo et connexio idearum idem est, ac ordo et connexio rerum.*—Pt. v, prop. 1: *Prout cogitationes rerumque ideae concatenantur in Mente, ita corporis affectiones, seu rerum imagines ad amussim ordinantur et concatenantur in Corpore.*—Pt. II, prop. 5: *Esse formale idearum Deum, quatenus tantum ut res cogitans consideratur, pro causa agnoscit, et non quatenus alio attributo explicatur. Hoc est tam Dei attributorum, quam rerum singularium ideae non ipsa ideata, sive res perceptas pro causa efficiente agnoscunt: sed ipsum Deum, quatenus est res cogitans.*
['The order and connection of ideas are the same as the order and connection of things. . . Just as the thoughts and ideas of things are linked in the mind, so are the affections of the body or the images of things arranged and linked in the body.
. . . The formal existence of ideas has God as its cause, in so far as he is considered as a thinking being, and not in so far as he is evolved by another attribute. That is to say: the ideas of the attributes of God, as of individual things, have as their cause, not the objects of these ideas, i.e. perceived things, but God himself, in so far as he is a thinking being.']

[5] ['Physical influence'. (Term used by Descartes.)]

thing altogether, for here he had already given up the mere fact, constituting the problem, namely that the world is immediately given to us merely as our representation, in order to substitute for it the dogma of a corporeal world and a spiritual world between which no bridge is possible. For he interweaves the question concerning the relation of representations to things-in-themselves with that concerning the possibility of the movements of the body through the will, and now solves both together by means of his *harmonia praestabilita*. (See *Système nouveau de la nature*, in Leibniz's *Works*, ed. Erdmann, p. 125—Brucker, *Hist. Ph.*, Tom. iv, Pt. II, p. 425.) The monstrous absurdity of his assumption was placed in the clearest light even by some of his contemporaries, especially by Bayle, who showed the consequences resulting from it. (See also in Leibniz's short works, translated by Huth, 1740, the note on page 79, where Leibniz himself is compelled to expose the revolting consequences of his contention.) Nevertheless, the very absurdity of the assumption, to which a thinking mind was driven by the problem before us, shows its magnitude, difficulty, and perplexity, and also how little we are able to brush it aside and thus cut the knot by merely repudiating it, as some in our day have ventured to do.

Spinoza starts again directly from Descartes; therefore, in his capacity as a Cartesian, he at first retained even the dualism of his teacher and accordingly assumed a *substantia cogitans* and a *substantia extensa*,[6] the former as subject, the latter as object, of knowledge. Later, however, when he stood on his own feet, he found that both were one and the same substance, viewed from different sides, and hence at one time conceived as *substantia extensa*, at another as *substantia cogitans*. Now this is really equivalent to saying that the distinction between the thinking and the extended, or between mind and body, is unfounded and therefore inadmissible, and hence that nothing more should have been said about it. But nevertheless he still retains it in so far as he is never tired of repeating that the two are one. Now in addition to this, he says by a mere *sic etiam* that *modus extensionis et idea illius modi una eademque est res*[7] (*Ethics*, Pt. II, prop. 7,

---

6 ['A thinking substance' and 'an extended substance'.]
7 ['Likewise a mode of extension and the idea of this mode are also one and the same.']

schol.), by which is meant that our representation of bodies and these bodies themselves are one and the same. However, the *sic etiam*[8] is an insufficient transition to this, for although the distinction between mind and body or between what represents and what is exended is unfounded, it by no means follows that the distinction between our representation and something objective and real existing outside this, that fundamental problem raised by Descartes, is also unfounded. What represents and what is represented may still be homogeneous, yet the question remains whether I can infer with certainty from representations in my head the existence of entities, in themselves different from me, that is to say, entities that are independent of those representations. The difficulty is not the one into which Leibniz would prefer to distort it (e.g. *Théodicée*, Pt. I, § 59), namely that between the assumed souls or minds and the corporeal world, as between two wholly heterogeneous kinds of substances, absolutely no action and connection can take place, for which reason he denied physical influence. For this difficulty is merely a consequence of rational psychology and, therefore, needs only to be discarded as a fiction, as is done by Spinoza. Moreover, there is, as the *argumentum ad hominem*[9] against the upholders of rational psychology, their dogma that God, who is indeed a spirit, created the corporeal world and continues to govern it; and so a spirit can act immediately on bodies. On the contrary, the difficulty is and remains merely the Cartesian, namely that the world, which alone is given immediately to us, is only ideal, in other words, one that consists of mere representations in our head; whereas, over and above this, we undertake to judge of a real world, in other words, one that exists independently of our representations. Therefore by abolishing the difference between *substantia cogitans* and *substantia extensa*, Spinoza has still not solved this problem, but has at most again rendered physical influence admissible. This, however, does not suffice to solve the difficulty, for the law of causality is demonstrably of subjective origin. But even if that law sprang conversely from external experience, it would still belong to that world in question which is given to us only ideally. Hence in no case can the law of causality

8 ['Likewise'.]
9 [An irrelevant or malicious appeal to personal circumstances.]

furnish a bridge between the absolutely objective and the subjective; on the contrary, it is merely the bond that connects phenomena with one another. (See *World as Will and Representation*, vol. II, chap. 1.)

But to explain more fully the above-mentioned identity of extension and of the representation thereof, Spinoza furnishes something that at the same time includes the views of Malebranche and Leibniz. Thus, wholly in accordance with Malebranche, we see all things in God: *rerum singularium ideae non ipsa ideata, sive res perceptas, pro causa agnoscunt, sed ipsum Deum, quatenus est res cogitans.*[10] *Ethics*, Pt. II, prop. 5; and this God is also at the same time the real and active principle in them, just as he is with Malebranche. In the last resort, however, nothing is explained by Spinoza's designation of the world with the name *Deus*. But at the same time there is with him, as with Leibniz, an exact parallelism between the extended and the represented worlds: *ordo et connexio idearum idem est, ac ordo et connexio rerum,*[11] Pt. II, prop. 7 and many similar passages. This is the *harmonia praestabilita* of Leibniz; only that here the represented world and the objectively existing world do not remain wholly separated, as with Leibniz, corresponding to each other merely by virtue of a *harmonia*, regulated in advance and from without, but actually they are one and the same. Therefore we have here in the first place a complete and absolute *realism*, in so far as the existence of things corresponds exactly to their representation in us, since indeed both are one.* Accordingly, we know the things-in-themselves; they are in themselves *extensa*, just as they also manifest themselves as *extensa*, in so far as they appear as *cogitata*, that is to say, in our representation of them. (Incidentally, here is the origin of Schelling's identity of the real and the ideal.) Now all this, properly speaking, is based only on mere assertion.

---

* In the *Treatise on the Improvement of the Understanding*, pp. 414/25 he evinces a decided realism and indeed in such a way that *idea vera est diversum quid a suo ideato;* etc. ['A true idea is something different from its object.'] Nevertheless, this treatise is undoubtedly older than his *Ethics*.

[10] ['The ideas of particular things do not have as their cause the objects of these ideas, in other words, perceived things, but God himself, in so far as he is a thinking being.']

[11] ['The order and connection of ideas are the same as the order and connection of things.']

The exposition is difficult to understand through the ambiguity of the word *Deus* that is used in a wholly improper sense; and so it loses itself in obscurity and in the end amounts to saying: *nec impraesentiarum haec clarius possum explicare.*[12] But obscurity in the exposition always arises from obscurity of a philosopher's own understanding and study of his works. Vauvenargues has very aptly said: *La clarté est la bonne foi des philosophes.*[13] (See *Revue des deux mondes*, 15 August 1853, p. 635.) What in music is the 'pure phrase or movement' is in philosophy perfect clearness, in so far as it is the *conditio sine qua non*,[14] and without the fulfilment of this, everything loses its value and we have to say: *quodcunque ostendis mihi sic incredulus odi.*[15] If even in the affairs of ordinary practical life we have through clearness carefully to guard against possible misunderstandings, how can we dare to express ourselves indefinitely, or even unintelligently, in the most difficult, abstruse, and wellnigh impenetrable subject of thought, in the problems of philosophy? The obscurity I have censured in Spinoza's doctrine arises from his not proceeding impartially from the nature of things as he finds them, but from Cartesianism, and accordingly from all kinds of traditional concepts, such as *Deus, substantia, perfectio*, and so on, which he attempted in roundabout ways to bring into harmony with his notion of truth. Very often he expresses the best things only indirectly, especially in the second part of the *Ethics*, since he always speaks *per ambages*[16] and almost allegorically. On the other hand, Spinoza again evinces an unmistakable *transcendental idealism*, namely a knowledge, although only general, of the truths expounded by Locke and particularly by Kant, hence a real distinction between the phenomenon and the thing-in-itself, and a recognition that only the phenomenon is accessible to us. See, for example, *Ethics*, Pt. II, prop. 16, with the second corollary; prop. 17, schol.; prop. 18, schol.; prop. 19; prop. 23, which extends it to self-knowledge; prop. 25, which expresses it clearly,; and finally, as a *résumé*, the corollary to prop. 29, which clearly states that

---

[12] ['And for the present I cannot explain this more clearly.']
[13] ['Lucidity is the good faith of philosophers.']
[14] ['Indispensable condition'.]
[15] ['All that you show me is to me incredible and repulsive.' (Horace, *Ars poetica*, 188)]
[16] ['Through circumlocutions'.]

we do not know either ourselves or things as they are in themselves, but merely as they appear. The demonstration of Pt. III, prop. 27, expresses the matter most clearly at the very beginning. With regard to the relation of Spinoza's doctrine to Descartes's, I here recall what I have said in the *World as Will and Representation*, vol. ii, chap. 50. But by starting from the concepts of the Cartesian philosophy, Spinoza in his exposition not only gave rise to much obscurity and misunderstanding, but he was also led into many flagrant paradoxes, obvious fallacies, and indeed absurdities and contradictions. In this way, much that is true and admirable in his teaching has acquired an extremely unwelcome admixture of positively indigestible matter, and the reader is tossed between admiration and annoyance. But in the aspect here to be considered, Spinoza's fundamental fault is that from the wrong point he drew his line of intersection between the ideal and the real, or between the subjective and objective worlds. Thus *extension* is by no means the opposite of *representation*, but lies wholly within this. We represent things as extended and, in so far as they are extended, they are our representation. But the question and the original problem is whether, independently of our representing, anything is extended, or indeed whether anything exists at all. This problem was later solved by Kant, and so far with undeniable accuracy, by his stating that extension or spatiality lies simply and solely in the representation and hence that it is closely connected with and dependent on this, since the whole of space is the mere form of the representation; and, therefore, independently of our representing, nothing extended can exist and also quite certainly nothing does exist. Accordingly, Spinoza's line of intersection has been drawn entirely on the ideal side and he has stopped at the *represented* world. Indicated by its form of extension, this world is, therefore, regarded by him as the real and consequently as existing independently of its being represented in our heads, in other words, as existing in itself. He is then, of course, quite right in saying that what is extended and what is represented, in other words our representation of bodies and these bodies themselves, are one and the same (Pt. II, prop. 7, schol.). For naturally only as represented are things extended, and only as extended are they capable of representation; the world as representation and the world in space are *una eademque res*;[17] this we can fully admit. Now if extension were a quality of things-in-themselves, then our intuitive perception would be a knowledge of things-in-themselves. This is what he assumes, and therein consists his realism. But since he does not establish realism and does not prove that, corresponding to our intuitive perception of a spatial world, there is a spatial world independent of that perception, the fundamental problem remains unsolved. This, however, is simply due to the fact that the line of intersection is not correctly drawn between the real and the ideal, the objective and the subjective, the thing-in-itself and the phenomenon. On the contrary, he carries the intersection, as I have said, through the middle of the ideal, subjective, phenomenal side of the world and hence through the world as representation. He splits this world into the extended or spatial and our representation of the extended, and then takes a great deal of trouble to show that the two are identical, as in fact they are. Just because Spinoza remains entirely on the ideal side of the world, for he thought he would find the real in what is extended and belongs to the world; and as, in consequence, the world of intuitive perception is the sole reality *outside* us, and that which knows (*cogitans*) the sole reality *within* us, so, on the other hand, he shifts the only truly real, namely the will, into the ideal, for he represents it as being a mere *modus cogitandi*; in fact, he identifies it with the *judgement*. See *Ethics*, Pt II, the proofs of the propositions 48 and 49, where it says: *per VOLUNTATEM intelligo affirmandi et negandi facultatem*, and again: *concipiamus singularem aliquam VOLITIONEM, nempe modum cogitandi, quo mens affirmat, tres angulos trianguli aequales esse duobus rectis*, whereupon the corollary follows: *Voluntas et intellectus unum et idem sunt.*[18] In general Spinoza has the great fault of purposely misusing words for expressing concepts that in the entire world go by other names, and, on the other hand, of depriving them of the meaning which they everywhere have. Thus he calls 'God' that which is everywhere called 'the world'; 'justice' that which is everywhere called 'power'; and 'will' that which

[17] ['One and the same thing'.]

[18] ['By *will* I understand the ability to affirm and deny. . . . Let us take a definite *act of will*, namely the mode of thought whereby the mind affirms that the three angles of a triangle are equal to two right angles . . . Will and intellect are one and the same.']

is everywhere called 'judgement'. Here we are fully justified in recalling the Hetman of the Cossacks in Kotzebue's *Graf Benjowsky*.[19]

Although coming later and already with the knowledge of Locke, Berkeley consistently went farther on this path of the Cartesians, and thus became the originator of the proper and true *idealism*, that is, of the knowledge that what is extended in and fills space, and thus the world of intuitive perception generally, can have its existence as such absolutely only in our *representation*, and that it is absurd and even contradictory to attribute to it, as such, another existence outside all representation and independently of the knowing subject, and accordingly to assume a matter existing in itself.* This is a very true and deep insight, but his whole philosophy consists in nothing but this. He had hit upon and clearly separated the ideal; but he did not know how to find the real, about which he did not trouble himself very much and expressed himself only occasionally, piecemeal, and incompletely. With him God's will and omnipotence are directly the cause of all the phenomena in the world of intuitive perception, that is to say, of all our representations. Real existence belongs only to knowing and willing beings, such as we ourselves are: hence these, together with God, constitute the real. They are spirits, that is, just knowing and willing beings; for willing and knowing are regarded by him as absolutely inseparable. Also in common with his predecessors, he regards God as better known than the actual world before us; and he therefore regards a reduction to him as an explanation. Speaking generally, his clerical and even episcopal position cramped and fettered him, and restricted him to a narrow circle of ideas against which he

---

* The uninitiated in philosophy, who include many doctors thereof, should be wholly deprived of the word *Idealism* because they do not know what it means and with it are up to all sorts of mischief. By idealism they understand first spiritualism, and then possibly the opposite of Philistinism, and in this view they are strengthened and confirmed by vulgar men of letters. The words 'idealism' and 'realism' are not ownerless and unappropriated, but have their fixed philosophical meaning. Those who mean something else, should simply use another word. The contrast between *idealism* and *realism* concerns what is *known*, the object; on the other hand, that between *spiritualism* and *materialism* concerns the *knower*, the subject. (The ignorant scribblers of today confuse idealism and spiritualism.)

[19] [Kotzebue, A. F. F. v. (1761–1819). This early play has long since been forgotten.]

could never offend. He could, therefore, go no further, but in his head the true and the false had to learn as best they could to be compatible with each other. These remarks may be extended even to the works of all these philosophers, with the exception of Spinoza. They are all marred by that Jewish theism which is impervious to any investigation, dead to all research, and thus actually appears as a fixed idea. At every step, it plants itself in the path of truth, so that the harm it does here in the theoretical sphere appears as a counterpart to that which it has done in the practical in the course of a thousand years; I mean in religious wars, inquisitions, and conversions of nations by the sword.

The closest affinity between Malebranche, Spinoza, and Berkeley is unmistakable. We see them all start from Descartes in so far as they retain and try to solve the fundamental problem that is presented by him in the form of a doubt concerning the existence of the external world. For they are concerned to investigate the separation and connection of the ideal subjective world, given solely in our representation, and the real objective world, existing independently thereof and thus in itself. Therefore this problem is, as I have said, the axis on which the whole of modern philosophy turns.

Now Locke differs from those philosophers in that, probably because he is under the influence of Hobbes and Bacon, he attaches himself as closely as possible to experience and common sense, avoiding as far as possible hyperphysical hypotheses. For him the *real* is *matter*, and without paying any regard to Leibniz's scruple as to the impossibility of a causal connection between the immaterial thinking substance and the material extended substance, he at once assumes physical influence between matter and the knowing subject. Here, however, with rare deliberation and honesty, he goes so far as to confess that possibly that which knows and thinks can also be matter (*On the Human Understanding*, lib. IV, c. 3, § 6). Later this won for him the repeated praise of the great Voltaire; on the other hand, in his own day it exposed him to the malicious attacks of an artful Anglican priest, the Bishop of Worcester.[20] Now

[20] There is no Church that dreads the light more than does the English just because no other has at stake such great pecuniary interests, its income amounting to £5,000,000 sterling, which is said to be £40,000 more than the income of the

with him the *real*, i.e. matter, generates in the knower representations or the *ideal* through 'impulse', i.e. through push or thrust. (Ibid., lib. I, c. 8; § 11.) Thus here we have a thoroughly massive realism which by its very exorbitance called forth contradiction and gave rise to Berkeley's idealism. The special point of origin of this is perhaps what Locke states at the end of § 2 of chapter 21 of the second book with so surprisingly little reflection. Among other things he says that 'solidity, extension, figure, motion and rest, would be really in the world, as they are, whether there were any sensible being to perceive them or not'. Thus as soon as we reflect on this, we are bound to recognize it as false; but then Berkeleyan idealism stands there and is undeniable. However, even Locke does not overlook that fundamental problem, namely the gulf between the representations within us and the things existing independently of us and thus the distinction between the ideal and the real. But speaking generally, he disposes of it with arguments of sound but rough common sense, and by reference to the adequacy of our knowledge of things for practical purposes (ibid., lib. IV, c. 4 and 9), which obviously has nothing to do with the case and only shows how very inadequate to the problem empiricism remains. But now it is just his realism that

whole of the remaining Christian clergy of both hemispheres taken together. On the other hand, there is no nation which it is so painful to see methodically stupefied by the most degrading blind faith than the English who surpass all others in intelligence. The root of the evil is that there is no ministry of public instruction and hence that this has hitherto remained entirely in the hands of the parsons. These have taken good care that two-thirds of the nation shall not be able to read and write; in fact, from time to time, they even have the audacity with the most ludicrous presumption to yelp at the natural sciences. It is, therefore, a human duty to smuggle into England, through every conceivable channel, light, liberal-mindedness, and science, so that those best-fed of all priests may have their business brought to an end. When Englishmen of education display on the Continent their Jewish sabbatarian superstition and other stupid bigotry, they should be treated with undisguised derision, *until they be shamed into common sense* [Schopenhauer's own English]. For such things are a scandal to Europe and should no longer be tolerated. Therefore even in the ordinary course of life, we should never make the least concession to the superstition of the English Church, but should at once stand up to it in the most caustic and trenchant manner wherever it puts in an appearance. For no arrogance exceeds that of Anglican parsons; on the Continent, therefore, this must suffer enough humiliation, so that a portion thereof is taken home, where there is a lack of it. For the audacity of Anglican parsons and of their slavish followers is quite incredible, even at the present time; it should, therefore, be confined to its island and, when it ventures to show itself on the Continent, it should at once be made to play the role of the owl by day.

leads him to restrict what corresponds to the *real* in our knowledge to qualities inherent in things, *as they are in themselves*, and
to distinguish these qualities from those that are connected
merely with our *knowledge* of them, and thus only with the *ideal*.
Accordingly, he calls the latter *secondary* qualities but the
former *primary*. This is the origin of the distinction between
thing-in-itself and phenomenon, which later on in the Kantian
philosophy becomes so very important. Here, then, is the true
genetic point of contact between the Kantian teaching and the
earlier philosophy, namely in Locke. The former was provoked,
and more immediately occasioned, by Hume's sceptical
objections to Locke's teaching; on the other hand, it has only a
polemical relation to the philosophy of Leibniz and Wolff.

Now those *primary* qualities, which are said to be exclusively
determinations of things-in-themselves and consequently to
belong thereto, even outside and independently of our representation, prove to be merely such as *cannot be thought away*,
namely extension, impenetrability, form, motion or rest, and
number. All the rest are recognized as *secondary*, that is, as
creations of the action of those primary qualities on our organs
of sense, consequently as mere sensations therein; such qualities
are colour, tone, taste, smell, hardness, softness, smoothness,
roughness, and so on. Accordingly, these have not the least resemblance to that quality in the *things-in-themselves* which
excites them, but are reducible to those primary qualities as
their causes, and these alone are purely objective and actually
exist in things. (Ibid., lib. 1, c. 8, §§ 7 *seqq.*) Our representations
of these are, therefore, actually faithful copies of them, which
reproduce exactly the qualities present in the things-in-themselves (loc. cit., § 15. I wish the reader luck who actually
perceives here how ludicrous realism becomes). We see,
therefore, that Locke takes away from the nature of things-in-
themselves, whose representations we receive from without, that
which is an action of the nerves of the *sense organs*, an easy,
comprehensible, and indisputable observation. But on this
path, Kant later took the immeasurably greater step of also
taking away that which is an action of our *brain* (this incomparably greater mass of nerves). Thus all those ostensibly
primary qualities sink into secondary ones, and the assumed
things-in-themselves into mere phenomena. The real thing-in-

itself, however, now divested even of those qualities, remains over as an entirely unknown quantity, a mere *x*. Now this, of course, called for a difficult and deep analysis that was long to be defended against the attacks of misunderstanding and of a want of understanding.

Locke does not deduce his primary qualities of things, nor does he state any further reason why just these and no others are purely objective, except to say that they are ineradicable. Now if we ourselves investigate why he declares as *not* objectively present those qualities of things which act immediately on sensation and which consequently come directly from without, whereas he concedes objective existence to those qualities which (as we have since recognized) spring from our intellect's own special functions, then the reason for this is that the objectively perceiving consciousness (the consciousness of other things) necessarily requires a complicated apparatus, and as the function of this it appears; consequently, its most essential fundamental determinations are already fixed from within. Therefore the universal form, i.e. the mode, of intuitive perception, from which alone the *a priori* knowable can result, presents itself as the basic fabric of the intuitively perceived world and accordingly appears as the absolutely necessary factor that is without exception and cannot in any way be removed so that, already in advance, it stands firm as the condition of all other things and of their manifold variety. We know that this is first of all time and space, and what follows from them and is possible only through them. In themselves, time and space are empty; if anything is to come into them, it must appear as *matter*, in other words, as something *acting* and consequently as causality; for matter is through and through pure causality. Its being consists in its acting and vice versa; it is simply the objectively apprehended form of the understanding for causality itself. (*On the Fourfold Root of the Principle of Sufficient Reason*, §21; as also *World as Will and Representation*, vol. i, § 4, and vol. ii, chap. 4.) Hence it follows that Locke's primary qualities are merely such as cannot be thought away; and this indicates clearly enough their subjective origin, since they result directly from the nature and constitution of the perception-apparatus itself. Conseqently, it follows that he regards as absolutely objective just that which, as a function of the brain, is much more subjective than is the sensation that is occasioned directly from without, or is at any rate more fully determined.

Meanwhile, it is fine to see how, through all these different conceptions and explanations, the problem, raised by Descartes, of the relation between the ideal and the real is ever more developed and clarified and thus truth is advanced. This, of course, took place under the favourable circumstances of the times or more correctly of nature which, in the brief interval of two centuries, gave birth to, and allowed to mature in Europe, half a dozen thinking minds. Moreover, as a gift from fate, they were permitted, in a vulgar-minded world that was slavishly abandoned to profit and pleasure, to follow their eminent and exalted calling, indifferent as they were to the yelping of priests and to the twaddle or deliberate activities of the contemporary professors of philosophy.

Now as, in accordance with his strict empiricism, Locke enabled us to know even the relation of causality only through experience, Hume did not dispute this false assumption, which would have been the correct thing to do. On the contrary, he at once overshot the mark, the reality of the causality relation itself, and in fact did this by the observation, correct in itself, that experience can never give, sensuously and directly, more than a mere succession of things, not an ensuing and effecting in the real sense, namely a necessary connection. We all know how this sceptical objection of Hume's gave rise to Kant's incomparably deeper investigations of the matter, which led him to the result that causality, and indeed also space and time, are known by us *a priori*, that is to say, lie within us prior to all experience, and hence belong to the *subjective* part of knowledge. From this it further follows that all those primary, i.e. absolute, qualities of things, which had been determined by Locke, cannot be peculiar to things-in-themselves, but are inherent in our way of knowing these, for all such qualities are composed of pure determinations of time, space, and causality, and consequently are to be reckoned as belonging not to the real, but to the ideal. Finally, it follows from this that we know things in no respect as they are *in themselves*, but simply and solely in their *phenomenal appearance*. But then the real, the thing-in-itself, remains as something wholly unknown, a mere x, and the whole world of intuitive perception accrues to the ideal as a mere representation, a phenomenon, to which, however, as such a real, a thing-in-itself, must somehow correspond.

From this point I have finally made a step that I believe will be the last because I have solved the problem whereon all philosophizing since Descartes has turned. Thus I have reduced all being and knowing to the two elements of our self-consciousness and hence to something beyond which there can no longer be any principle of explanation, since it is that which is most immediate and therefore ultimate. I have thus called to mind, as follows from the investigations of all my predecessors which are here discussed, that the absolutely real, or the thing-in-itself, can never be given to us directly from without on the path of the mere *representation* because it is inevitably in the nature of such representation always to furnish only the ideal. On the other hand, since we ourselves are indisputably real, it must be possible in some way to draw a knowledge of the real from the interior of our own true nature. In fact, it now appears here in an immediate way in consciousness, namely as *will*. Accordingly, with me the line of intersection now falls between the real and the ideal in such a way that the whole world of intuitive perception, presenting itself objectively, including everyone's own body, together with space, time, and causality, and consequently together with the extended of Spinoza and the matter of Locke, belongs as *representation* to the *ideal*. But in this case, only the *will* is left as the real and all my predecessors, thoughtlessly and without reflection, had cast this into the ideal, as a mere result of representation and thought; in fact, Descartes and Spinoza even identified it with the judgement.[21] Thus with me *ethics* is now directly and incomparably more closely connected with metaphysics than it is in any other system, and so the moral significance of the world and existence is more firmly established than ever. *Will and representation* alone are fundamentally different in so far as they constitute the ultimate and basic contrast in all things in the world and leave no remainder. The represented thing and the representation thereof are the same; but only the *represented* thing, not the thing-*in-itself*. The latter is always *will*, whatever be the form in which it appears in the representation.

21 Spinoza, loc. cit.—Descartes, *Meditationes de prima philosophia*, Med. IV, p. 28.

APPENDIX

Readers who are acquainted with what has passed for philosophy in Germany in the course of this [nineteenth] century, might perhaps wonder why they do not see mentioned in the interval between Kant and me either the idealism of Fichte, or the system of the absolute identity of the real and the ideal, as they quite properly appear to belong to our subject But I have not been able to include them because Fichte, Schelling, and Hegel are in my opinion not philosophers; for they lack the first requirement of a philosopher, namely a seriousness and honesty of inquiry. They are merely sophists who wanted to appear to be rather than to be something. They sought not truth, but their own interest and advancement in the world. Appointments from governments, fees and royalties from students and publishers, and, as a means to this end, the greatest possible show and sensation in their sham philosophy—such were the guiding stars and inspiring genii of those disciples of wisdom. And so they have not passed the entrance examination and cannot be admitted into the venerable company of thinkers for the human race.

Nevertheless they have excelled in one thing, in the art of beguiling the public and of passing themselves off for what they are not; and this undoubtedly requires talent, yet not philosophical. On the other hand, that they were unable to achieve in philosophy anything substantial was ultimately due to the fact that *their intellect had not become free*, but had remained in the service of their *will*. For it is true that the intellect can achieve an extraordinary amount for the will and its aims, yet it can do nothing for philosophy, any more than it can for art. For these lay down, as their very first condition, that the intellect acts only spontaneously and of its own accord and that, during the time of this activity, it ceases to submit to the will, that is, to have in view one's own personal aims. But when the intellect itself is of its own accord active, by its nature it knows of no other aim than truth. Hence to be a philosopher, that is to say, a lover of wisdom (for wisdom is nothing but truth), it is not enough for a man to love truth, in so far as it is compatible with his own interest, with the will of his superiors, with the dogmas of the Church, or with the prejudices and tastes of contemporaries; so long as he rests content with this position, he is only a φίλαυτος, not a φιλόσοφος.[1] For this title of honour is well and wisely conceived precisely by its stating

[1] ['A friend of his own ego, not a friend of wisdom'.]

that one should love the truth earnestly and with one's whole heart, and thus unconditionally and unreservedly, above all else, and, if need be, in defiance of all else. Now the reason for this is the one previously stated that the intellect has become *free*, and in this state it does not even know or understand any other interest than that of truth. The consequence, however, is that we then conceive an implacable hatred of all lying and deception, in whatever garb they may appear. In this way, of course, we shall not get on very well in the world, but we shall in philosophy. On the other hand, the auspices for philosophy are bad if, when proceeding ostensibly on the investigation of truth, we start saying farewell to all uprightness, honesty, and sincerity, and are intent only on passing ourselves off for what we are not. We then assume, like those three sophists, first a false pathos, then an affected and lofty earnestness, then an air of infinite superiority, in order to impose where we despair of ever being able to convince. One writes carelessly because, thinking only in order to write, one had saved up one's thoughts till the moment of writing. The attempt is made to smuggle in palpable sophisms as proofs, to give out hollow and senseless verbiage for profound ideas. A reference is made to intellectual intuition or to absolute thought and the self-movement of concepts. One expressly challenges the standpoint of 'reflection', in other words, of rational deliberation, impartial consideration, and honest presentation, and thus the proper and normal use of the faculty of reason generally. Accordingly, an infinite contempt is expressed for the 'philosophy of reflection', by which name is designated every course of thought that deduces consequents from grounds, such as constitutes all previous philosophizing. If, therefore, one is provided with sufficient audacity and is encouraged by the pitiable spirit of the times, one will hold forth somewhat as follows: 'It is not difficult to see that the *manner* of stating a proposition, of adducing grounds or reasons for it, and likewise of refuting its opposite through grounds or reasons, is not the form in which truth can appear. Truth is the movement of itself within itself', and so on. (Hegel, Preface to the *Phenomenology of the Mind*, p. lvii, in the complete edition, p.36.) I do not think that it is difficult to see that whoever puts forward anything like this is a shameless charlatan who wants to fool simpletons and observes that he has found his people in the Germans of the nineteenth century.

Accordingly if, while hurrying ostensibly to the temple of truth, we hand the reins over to our personal interests which look aside at very different guiding stars, for instance at the tastes and foibles of contemporaries, at the established religion, but in particular at the hints and suggestions of those at the head of affairs, then how shall we ever reach the high, precipitous, bare rock whereon stands the temple of truth? Then we may well attach to ourselves, through the sure bond of interest, a host of genuinely hopeful disciples, hopeful, that is, of protection and posts. These form in appearance a sect but in reality a faction, and by their united stentorian voices one is now proclaimed to all the four winds as a sage without parallel; the interest of the person is satisfied, that of truth betrayed.

All this explains the painful impression with which we are seized when, after studying the above-discussed genuine thinkers, we come to the writings of Fichte and Schelling, or even to the presumptuously scribbled nonsense of Hegel, produced as it was with a boundless, though justified, confidence in German stupidity.[2] With those genuine thinkers one always found an *honest* investigation of truth and just as *honest* an attempt to communicate their ideas to others. Therefore whoever reads Kant, Locke, Hume, Malebranche, Spinoza, and Descartes feels elevated and agreeably impressed. This is produced through communion with a noble mind which has and awakens ideas and which thinks and sets one thinking. The reverse of all this takes place when we read the above-mentioned three German sophists. An unbiased reader, opening one of their books and then asking himself whether this is the tone of a thinker wanting to instruct or that of a charlatan wanting to impress, cannot be five minutes in any doubt; here everything breathes so much of *dishonesty*. The tone of calm investigation, which had characterized all previous philosophy, is exchanged for that of unshakable certainty, such as is peculiar to charlatanry of every kind and at all times. Here, however, this certainty claims to rest on immediate intellectual intuition or on thought that is absolute, in other words, independent of the subject and thus of the fallibility thereof. From every page and every line, there speaks an endeavour to beguile and deceive the reader, first by producing an effect to dumbfound him, then by incomprehensible phrases and even sheer nonsense to stun and stupefy him, and again by audacity of assertion to puzzle him, in short, to throw dust in his eyes and mystify him as much as possible.

[2] The Hegelian sham wisdom is really that millstone in the student's head in *Faust*. If our intention is to make a youth stupid and wholly incapable of all thinking, there is no means more approved than the laborious study of Hegel's original works. For these monstrous articulations of words that cancel and contradict one another, so that the mind vainly torments itself in trying through them to think of anything till it finally collapses with exhaustion, gradually destroy so completely his ability to think, that henceforth hollow, empty flourishes and phrases are regarded by him as thoughts. Now add to this the presumption, confirmed for the youth by the word and example of all in authority, that that hollow verbiage is true and lofty wisdom! If at any time a guardian should ever be afraid that his wards might become too clever for his plans, then such a misfortune could be prevented by a sedulous study of the Hegelian philosophy.

Thus the impression felt by a man in the case of the transition in question as regards the theoretical, can be compared with that which he may have as regards the practical, if he found himself in a den of swindlers after coming from a community of men of honour. What an estimable man is Christian Wolff in comparison with them, a man so disparaged and ridiculed precisely by those three sophists! He had real thoughts and furnished them; they, on the other hand, had mere word structures and phrases for the purpose of deceiving. Accordingly, the true distinguishing character of the philosophy of the whole of this so-called post-Kantian school is *dishonesty*, its element mist and smoke, and its goal personal aims. Its exponents were concerned *to appear*, not *to be*; they are, therefore, sophists, not philosophers. The ridicule of posterity, extending to their admirers, and then oblivion awaits them. Incidentally, associated with the above-mentioned tendency of these men is the bickering and abusive tone which everywhere pervades Schelling's writings as an obligato accompaniment. Now if all this were not the case, and if Schelling had gone to work with honesty instead of with bluff and humbug, then, as being decidedly the most gifted of the three, he might at least have occupied in philosophy the subordinate position of an eclectic, useful for the time being. The amalgam prepared by him from the doctrines of Plotinus, Spinoza, Jacob Boehme, Kant, and of the natural sciences of modern times, could to this extent fill for the time being the great gap produced by the negative results of the Kantian philosophy, until a really new philosophy came along and properly afforded the satisfaction demanded by the former. In particular, he has used the natural science of our century to revive Spinoza's abstract pantheism. Thus without any knowledge of nature, Spinoza had philosophized at random merely from abstract concepts and, without properly knowing the things themselves, he had erected the structure of his system. To have clothed this bare skeleton with flesh and blood and to have imparted life and movement to it, as well as might be, by applying natural science that had in the meantime developed, although this was often falsely applied, is the undeniable merit of Schelling in his *Naturphilosophie*, which is also the best of his many different attempts and new departures.

Just as children play with weapons intended for serious purposes or with other implements belonging to adults, so have the three sophists we are considering dealt with the subject here discussed, in that they have furnished the grotesque pendant of two centuries of laborious investigations on the part of musing and meditating philosophers. Thus after Kant had more than ever accentuated the great problem of the relation between what exists in-itself and our representations, and so had brought it a great deal nearer to solution, Fichte came forward with the assertion that there is nothing more behind the representations and that these are simply products of the knowing subject, of the ego. While attempting in this way to outdo Kant, he produced merely a caricature of that philosopher's system since, by constantly applying the method of those three pseudo-philosophers which was already much vaunted, he entirely abolished the real and left over nothing but the ideal. Then came Schelling who, in his system of the absolute identity of the real and the ideal, declared that whole difference to be of no account and maintained that the ideal is also the real and that the two are identical. In this way, he attempted again to throw into confusion that which had been so laboriously separated by means of a slow and gradually developing process of reflection, and to mix up everything. (Schelling, *Vom Verhältniss der Naturphilosophie zur Fichte'schen*, pp. 14–21.) The distinction of the ideal and the real is just boldly denied in imitation of the above-censured errors of Spinoza. At the same time, even the monads of Leibniz, that monstrous identification of two absurdities, thus of the atoms and of the indivisible, originally and essentially knowing individuals called souls, are again fetched out, solemnly apotheosized, and made use of. (Schelling, *Ideen zur Naturphilosophie*, 2nd edn., pp. 38 and 82.) Schelling's philosophy of nature bears the name of the philosophy of identity because, following in Spinoza's footsteps, it abolishes three distinctions which he too had abolished, namely that between God and the world, that between body and soul, and finally also that between the ideal and the real in the intuitively perceived world. This last distinction, however, as was previously shown when we considered Spinoza, does not by any means depend on those other two. On the contrary, the more it was brought into prominence, the more were those other two rendered doubtful; for they are based on dogmatic proofs (overthrown by Kant), whereas it is based on a simple act of reflection. In keeping with all this, metaphysics was by Schelling identified with physics and accordingly the lofty title *Von der Weltseele* was given to a merely physico-chemical diatribe. All really metaphysical problems that untiringly force themselves on human consciousness were to be silenced through a flat denial by means of peremptory assertions. Nature is here just because it is, out of itself and through itself; we bestow on it the title of God, and with this it is disposed of; whoever asks for more is a fool. The distinction between subjective and objective is a mere trick of the schools, like the whole Kantian philosophy, and this philosophy's distinction of *a priori* and *a posteriori* is of no account. Our empirical intuitive perception quite properly furnishes us with the things-in-themselves, and so on. Let us see *Ueber das Verhältniss der Natur-philosophie zur Fichte'schen*, pp. 51 and 67 and also p. 61, where those are expressly ridiculed 'who are really astonished that there is not nothing and who cannot be surprised enough that anything actually exists'. Thus to Herr von Schelling everything seems to be a matter of course. At bottom, however, such talk as this is a veiled appeal, in pompous phrases, to the so-called sound, i.e. crude, common sense. For the rest, I recall here what was said at the very beginning of chapter seventeen in the second volume of my chief work. Significant for our subject, and very naïve, is the passage on page 69 of Schelling's, above-quoted book: 'If empiricism had completely attained its object, its opposition to philosophy, and therewith philosophy itself, would disappear as a particular sphere or species of science. All abstractions would dissolve themselves into direct, "friendly" intuitive perception; the highest would be a sport of pleasure and *innocence*; the most difficult would be easy, the most immaterial material, and man would be able to read gladly and freely in the book of nature.' That would, of course, be most delightful! But with us it is not like that; thinking cannot be shown the door in this way. The serious old sphinx with its riddle lies there motionless, and it does not plunge down from the rock because you declare it to be a ghost. Therefore when Schelling himself later observed that meta-physical problems cannot be dismissed by peremptory assertions, he gave us a really metaphysical essay in his treatise on freedom. This, however, is a mere piece of the imagination, a *conte bleu*,[3] a fairy-tale; and so it is that whenever the style assumes the tone of demonstra-tion (e.g. pp. 453ff.), it has a decidedly comical effect.

Through his doctrine of the identity of the real and the ideal, Schelling had accordingly tried to solve the problem that was started by Descartes, dealt with by all great thinkers, and finally brought to a head by Kant. He attempted to solve this problem by cutting the knot, in that he denied the antithesis between the real and the ideal. In this way he really came into direct contradiction with Kant from whom he professed to start. Meanwhile he had firmly kept at any rate the original and proper meaning of the problem which concerns the relation between our *intuitive perception* and the being and essence-in-itself of the things that present them-selves in that perception. But since he drew his doctrine mainly from Spinoza, he soon adopted from him the expressions *thinking* and *being* which state very badly the problem we are discussing and later gave rise to the absurdest monstrosities. With his doctrine that *substantia cogitans et substantia extensa una eademque est substantia, quae*

---

[3] ['Fairy-tale'.]

am sub hoc jam sub illo attributo comprehenditur (*Ethics*, Pt. II, prop. 7, schol.); or *scilicet mens et corpus una eademque est res, quae jam sub cogitationis, jam sub extensionis attributo concipitur*[4] (*Ethics*, Pt. III, prop. 2, schol.), Spinoza had first tried to abolish the Cartesian antithesis of body and soul. He may also have recognized that the empirical object is not different from our representation thereof. Schelling now received from him the expressions *thinking* and *being*, which he gradually substituted for those of *perceiving*, or rather perceived and thing-in-itself. (*Neue Zeitschrift für spekulative Physik*, vol. i, first article: 'Further expositions' and so on.) For the relation of our *intuitive perception* of things to their *being* and *essence-in-itself* is the great problem whose history I am here sketching; not, however, the relation of our *thoughts or ideas*, that is, of *concepts*. For quite obviously and undeniably these are mere abstractions from what is known through intuitive perception, and they have arisen from our arbitrarily thinking away or dropping of some qualities and our retention of others. To doubt this can never occur to any reasonable man.[5] Therefore these *concepts* and *thoughts*, constituting the class of *non-perceptive* representations, never have an immediate relation to the *essence and being-in-itself* of things. On the contrary, they have always only a *mediate* relation, that is, through the mediation of *intuitive perception*. It is this, that, on the one hand, furnishes them with the material and, on the other, stands in relation to the things-in-themselves, in other words, to the unknown, real, and true essence of things that objectifies itself in intuitive perception.

Now the inaccurate expression, borrowed by Schelling from Spinoza, was later used by that insipid and inane charlatan Hegel, who in this respect appears as Schelling's buffoon, and it was so distorted that *thinking* itself in the proper sense and hence *concepts* were to be identical with the essence-in-itself of things. Therefore what is thought *in abstracto*, as such and directly, was to be identical with what is objectively present in itself, and accordingly logic was at the same time to be the true metaphysics. In that case, we should need only to think, or put our trust in concepts, in order to know how the world outside is absolutely constituted. According to this, everything haunting a skull would at once be true and real. Now since 'the madder the better' was the motto of the philosophasters of this period, this absurdity was supported by a second, namely that *we* did not think, but the concepts, alone and without our

---

[4] ['The thinking substance and the extended substance are one and the same substance which is comprehended now under this attribute, now under that. . . . namely that mind and body are one and the same thing which is conceived at one moment under the attribute of thinking, at another under that of extension.']

[5] *On the Fourfold Root of the Principle of Sufficient Reason*, 2nd edn., §26.

assistance, completed the thought process, which was, therefore, called the dialectical self-movement of the concept, and was now to be a revelation of all things *in et extra naturam*. But this buffoonery was really based on yet another that likewise rested on a misuse of words, and indeed was never clearly expressed, although it is undoubtedly at the bottom thereof. After the manner of Spinoza, Schelling had given the world the title of *God*. Hegel took this in the literal sense. Now as the word really signifies a personal being who, together with other qualities absolutely incompatible with the world, has also that of *omniscience*, *this* too was now transferred by Hegel to the *world*. Naturally it could not find any other place than the simple mind of man, whereupon he needed only to give free play to his thoughts (dialectical self-movement) in order to reveal all the mysteries of heaven and earth, namely in the absolute gibberish of the Hegelian dialectic. There is one art that Hegel has really understood, and that is how to lead Germans by the nose. But it is not a great art; indeed, we see with what rubbish and nonsense he was able for thirty years to keep in its proper place the learned world of Germany. The professors of philosophy still take these three sophists seriously and consider it important to assign to them a place in the history of philosophy. This is only because it belongs to their *gagne-pain*,[6] since here they have material for elaborate dissertations, verbal and written, on the history of the so-called post-Kantian philosophy wherein the tenets and dogmas of these sophists are expounded in detail and seriously considered. But from a rational point of view, we should not bother about what these men brought to market in order to appear to be something, unless it were the intention to regard Hegel's scribblings as medicinal to be kept in chemists' shops as a psychically effective vomitive, for the disgust they excite is really quite specific. But enough of them and their author whose veneration we will leave to the Danish Academy of Scientific Studies. In him it recognized a *summus philosophus* in its sense of the term and therefore demands deference to him in its judgement that is appended as a lasting memorial to my prize-essay *On the Basis of Ethics*. This judgement merited rescue from oblivion no less on account of its discernment than of its remarkable honesty and also because it furnishes a striking confirmation of La Bruyère's fine saying: *Du même fonds dont on néglige un homme de mérite, l'on sait encore admirer un sot.*[7]

6 ['Livelihood'.]
7 ['For the same reason that we neglect a man of merit we are capable of admiring a fool.' (La Bruyère, *Les Caractères*.)]

FRAGMENTS FOR THE
HISTORY OF PHILOSOPHY

Fragments for the History of Philosophy

Concerning the History of Philosophy

To read all kinds of expositions of the doctrines of philosophers, or generally the history of philosophy instead of their own original works, is as if we wanted to have our food masticated by someone else. Would anyone read the history of the world if he were free to behold with his own eyes the interesting events of ancient times? Now as regards the history of philosophy, such an autopsy of its subject is actually accessible to him, thus in the original writings of philosophers wherein he may still limit himself, for the sake of brevity, to the main and well-chosen chapters, the more so as they all teem with repetitions which he can spare himself. In this way, he will become acquainted with the essentials of their doctrines in an authentic and unadulterated form, whereas from the half-dozen histories of philosophy that appear annually he obtains merely what has entered the head of a professor of philosophy, and indeed in the form in which it there appears. Now it is obvious that the thoughts of a great mind are bound to shrink considerably in order to find room in the three-pound brain of such a parasite of philosophy whence they are to emerge once more clothed in the particular jargon of the day and accompanied by his serious and solemn criticisms. Moreover, it may be reckoned that such a money-making writer of the history of philosophy can have read scarcely a tithe of the writings about which he furnishes a report. Their real study demands all of a long and studious life, such as the stout-hearted Brucker formerly devoted to them in the industrious times of old. On the other hand, what can have been thoroughly investigated by such little men who, detained by constant lecturing, official business, holiday tours, and amusements, appear for the most part in their early years with histories of philosophy? But in addition, they wish to be pragmatical and claim to have fathomed and to expound the necessity of the origin and sequence of systems, and even to criticize, correct, and find fault with the serious and genuine philosophers of antiquity. How can it be otherwise than that they copy the older ones and one another, but then, to conceal this, make matters worse by endeavouring to give them the modern cast of the current quinquennium, likewise pronouncing judgement on them in the spirit of this? On the other hand, a collection of the important passages and essential chapters of all the principal philosophers, made by honest scholars of insight conscientiously and in common, would be very appropriate. Such a collection could be arranged in a chronological pragmatical order, much in the same way first as Gedicke and later Ritter and Preller did with the philosophy of antiquity, yet in much greater detail; thus it would be a great and universal anthology, prepared with care and a knowledge of the subject.

The fragments, here given, are at any rate not traditional, that is, they are not copied down; on the contrary, they are ideas occasioned by my own study of the original works.

§ 2

Pre-Socratic Philosophy

The *Eleatic philosophers* were indeed the first to become aware of the contrast between the intuitively perceived and the conceived, between φαινόμενα and νοούμενα. The latter alone was for them the truly existing, the ὄντως ὄν. Of this they asserted that it is one, unalterable, and immovable; but not so of the φαινόμενα, i.e. of the intuitively perceived, that which appears, the empirically given. To assert of this anything of the kind would have been positively ludicrous; and so the proposition, so misunderstood, was once refuted by Diogenes in the well-known way. Thus they really distinguished between appearance [*Erscheinung*], φαινόμενον, and thing-in-itself, ὄντως ὄν. The latter could not be perceived sensuously, but only comprehended through thought; accordingly it was νοούμενον. (Aristotle, *Metaphysics*, I, 5, p. 986 et schol., Berlin edn., pp. 429, 430, and 509.) In the scholia to Aristotle (pp. 460, 536, 544, and 798), the work of Parmenides, τὰ κατὰ δόξαν,[1] is mentioned; and so this would have been the doctrine of the *phenomenon* and thus physics. In keeping with this, there would undoubtedly have

[1] ['The doctrine of meaning'.]

been another work, τὰ κατ' ἀλήθειαν,[2] the doctrine of the *thing-in-itself* and thus metaphysics. A scholium of Philoponus positively says of Melissus: ἐν τοῖς πρὸς ἀλήθειαν ἐν εἶναι λέγων τὸ ὄν, ἐν τοῖς πρὸς δόξαν δύο (should be πολλὰ) φησὶν εἶναι.[3] In contrast to the Eleatics, and probably provoked by them, was Heraclitus, in so far as he taught the ceaseless movement of all things, whereas *they* taught their absolute immobility; he accordingly confined himself to the φαινόμενον. (Aristotle, *De coelo*, III, 1, p. 298, Berlin edition.) Now in this way, he again evoked as *his* antithesis Plato's doctrine of Ideas, as follows from the statement of Aristotle (*Metaphysics*, p. 1078).

It is noteworthy that we find repeated innumerable times in the writings of the ancients, yet very little beyond them, the comparatively few main propositions of the pre-Socratic philosophers. Thus, for example, we have the doctrines of Anaxagoras of the νοῦς and the ὁμοιομέρειαι;[4] those of Empedocles of φιλία καὶ νεῖκος[5] and of the four elements; those of Democritus and Leucippus of the atoms and the εἴδωλα;[6] those of Heraclitus of the continuous flux of things; those of the Eleatics as previously explained; those of the Pythagoreans of numbers, metempsychosis, and so on. However, it may well be that this was the sum total of all their philosophizing, for we also find in the works of the moderns, for example in those of Descartes, Spinoza, Leibniz, and even Kant, the few fundamental propositions of their philosophies repeated innumerable times; so that all these philosophers seem to have adopted the motto of Empedocles who may also have been a lover of the sign of repetition, δὶς καὶ τρὶς τὰ καλά.[7] (See Sturz, *Empedocles of Agrigentum*, p. 504.)

Moreover, the above two dogmas of Anaxagoras are closely connected. Thus πάντα ἐν πᾶσιν[8] is his symbolic description of the dogma of the homoeomeries. Accordingly, in the primal chaotic mass the *partes similares* (in the physiological sense) of all things were present and complete. To separate them out and

---

[2] ['The doctrine of truth'.]
[3] ['Whereas in the doctrine of truth he (Melissus) declares that what exists is one, in the doctrine of meaning he asserts that there are two (many) of them.']
[4] ['Mind' and 'homogeneous elements of things'.]
[5] ['Love and hatred'.]   [6] ['Copies, likenesses'.]
[7] ['The good can be spoken twice and also thrice.' (Proverb.)]
[8] ['Something of everything is to be found in everything.']

combine, arrange, and form them into specifically different things (*partes dissimilares*), a νοῦς was needed which, by selecting the constituents, reduced confusion to order; for indeed the chaos contained the most complete mixture of all substances (schol. in Aristotle, p. 337). Yet the νοῦς had not completely brought about this first separation, and so in each thing there were still to be found the constituents of everything else, although to a lesser degree: πάλιν γὰρ πᾶν ἐν παντὶ μέμικται[9] (ibid.).

On the other hand, Empedocles had, instead of innumerable homoeomeries, only four elements whence things were now said to emerge as products, not as educts as with Anaxagoras. But the uniting and separating and hence regulating role of the νοῦς is with him played by φιλία καὶ νεῖκος, love and hatred. Both these are very much more sensible. Thus he assigns the ordering of things not to the *intellect* (νοῦς), but to the *will* (φιλία καὶ νεῖκος), and the different kinds of substances are not, as with Anaxagoras, mere educts, but actual products. Whereas Anaxagoras represented them as being brought about by an understanding that separates, Empedocles represents them as being produced by a blind impulse, i.e. by a will that is devoid of knowledge.

On the whole, Empedocles is a thorough man and, underlying his φιλία καὶ νεῖκος there is a profound and true *aperçu*. Even in inorganic nature we see the elements seeking and avoiding one another, uniting and separating, according to the laws of elective affinity. But those that show the strongest tendency to unite chemically, a tendency that can be satisfied only in the state of fluidity, enter into the most definite electrical opposition when they come into contact with one another in the solid state; they now separate into opposite and hostile polarities in order again to seek and embrace one another. What else is that polar contrast, appearing generally in the whole of nature under the most varied forms, but a constantly renewed discord or variance on which the ardently desired reconciliation follows? Thus φιλία καὶ νεῖκος are actually present everywhere, and only according to the circumstances will one or the other appear at any time. And so even we ourselves can be instantly friendly or hostile; the disposition

9 ['Everything is indeed blended with everything.']

to be either exists and awaits the circumstances. Only prudence bids us stop at the point of indifference, of unconcern, although this is at the same time the freezing-point. In the same way, a strange dog, approached by us, is at once ready to adopt a friendly or hostile tone and changes easily from barking and growling to tail-wagging and vice-versa. What lies at the basis of this universal phenomenon of the φιλία καὶ νεῖκος is, of course, ultimately the great primal contrast between the unity of all beings according to their essence-in-itself and their complete diversity and variety in the phenomenon, which has for its form the *principium individuationis*. Similarly, Empedocles recognized as false the doctrine of atoms that was already known to him and, on the other hand, taught the infinite divisibility of bodies, as we are told by Lucretius, lib. i, vv. 749 *seqq.*

But above all, the decided pessimism of Empedocles is noticeable in his doctrines. He fully recognized the misery of our existence and for him, as for true Christians, the world is a vale of tears, Ἄτης λειμών.[10] He compares it, as did Plato later, to a dark cave wherein we are confined. In our earthly existence he sees a state of exile and misery and the body is the prison of the soul. These souls were once in a state of infinite bliss and reached the present perdition through their own fault and sins. Through sinful conduct they become ever more ensnared in this perdition and are involved in the circle of metempsychosis. On the other hand, through virtue and moral purity, which also included abstinence from animal food, and by turning away from earthly pleasures and desires, they can again reach their previous state. Hence the same fundamental wisdom, constituting the basic idea of Brahmanism and Buddhism and indeed of true Christianity (by which is not to be understood optimistic, Jewish–Protestant rationalism) was also brought home to us by this ancient Greek, whereby the *consensus gentium*[11] concerning it was rendered complete. It is probable that Empedocles, whom the ancients generally describe as a Pythagorean, obtained this view from Pythagoras, especially as at bottom it is shared even by Plato, who is likewise under the influence of Pythagoras. Empedocles adheres most definitely to the doctrine of metempsychosis which is associated with this view of the world. The

[10] ['A vast field of evil'.]   [11] ['Agreement of all peoples'.]

passages of the ancients which, together with his own verses, bear witness to that world conception of Empedocles, are found collected with great industry in Sturz's *Empedocles Agrigentinus*, pp. 448–58. The view that the body is a prison and life a condition of suffering and purification, from which we are released by death if we are quit of the transmigration of souls, is shared by Egyptians, Pythagoreans, Empedocles, along with Hindus and Buddhists. With the exception of metempsychosis, it is also contained in Christianity. Diodorus Siculus, Cicero, and others (see Wernsdorf, *De metempsychosi veterum*, p. 31, and Cicero, *Fragmenta de philosophia*, p. 299 (*Somnium Scipionis*) 316, 319, *ed. Bip.*)[12] bear witness to that view of the ancients. In these passages Cicero does not state to what school of philosophers they belong; yet they appear to be remnants of Pythagorean wisdom.

In the remaining dogmas of these pre-Socratic philosophers, there is also much that can be demonstrated as true, and of this I will give a few examples.

According to the cosmogony of Kant and Laplace, which has actually been confirmed *a posteriori* by Herschel's observations and which Lord Rosse with his giant telescope is trying again to render doubtful for the consolation of the English clergy, planetary systems are formed through condensation from luminous nebulae that slowly coagulate and then revolve. Thus after thousands of years, Anaximenes was right after all when he declared air and vapour to be the fundamental substance of all things (schol. in Aristotle, p. 514). But at the same time, Empedocles and Democritus also obtain confirmation; for, like Laplace, they explained the origin and constitution of the world from a vortex, δίνη (Aristotle, *Opera*, Berlin edition, p. 295, et schol., p. 351). Even Aristophanes (*Nubes*, l. 820) mocks at this as godlessness, just as the English parsons of today ridicule the theory of Laplace; for here, as with all truth that comes to light, they feel ill at ease, that is to say, they are concerned about their livings. Indeed, even our chemical stoicheiometry to a certain extent leads back to the Pythagorean philosophy of numbers: τὰ γὰρ πάθη καὶ αἱ ἕξεις τῶν ἀριθμῶν τῶν ἐν τοῖς οὖσι παθῶν τε καὶ ἕξεων αἴτια, οἶον τὸ διπλάσιον, τὸ ἐπίτριτον, καὶ

---

12 [The Editiones Bipontinae were editions, mainly of the Greek and Latin classics, published in Zweibrücken in Germany, from 1779 onwards.]

ἡμιόλιον.[13] (Schol. in Aristotle, pp. 543 et 829.) It is well known that the Copernican system had been anticipated by the *Pythagoreans*; indeed it was known to Copernicus himself who drew his fundamental idea straight from the well-known passage on *Hicetas* in Cicero's *Academicae quaestiones* (II. 39), and on *Philolaus* in Plutarch, *De placitis philosophorum*,[14] lib. III, c. 13 (according to Maclaurin, *On Newton*, p. 45). This old and important knowledge was afterwards rejected by Aristotle so that in its place he could put his own humbug about which I shall have something to say in § 5. (Cf. *World as Will and Representation*, vol. ii, chap. 26 end.) But even Fourier's and Cordier's discoveries concerning the heat in the interior of the earth are confirmations of the doctrine of the ancients: ἔλεγον δὲ Πυθαγόρειοι πῦρ εἶναι δημιουργικὸν·περὶ τὸ μέσον καὶ κέντρον τῆς γῆς, τὸ ἀναθάλπον τὴν γῆν καὶ ζωοποιοῦν. Schol. in Aristotle, p. 504.[15] If, in consequence of those very discoveries, the earth's crust is today regarded as a thin layer between two media (atmosphere and hot molten metals and metalloids), contact between which must occasion a conflagration destroying that crust, then this confirms the opinion that the world will ultimately be consumed by fire, an opinion wherein all the ancient philosophers agree and which is shared by the *Hindus* (*Lettres édifiantes et curieuses*, 1819 edn., vol. vii, p. 114). It is also worth noting that, as can be seen from Aristotle (*Metaphysics*, I. 5, p. 986), the Pythagoreans had correctly interpreted under the name δέκα ἀρχαί[16] the *Yin* and *Yang* of the Chinese.

That the metaphysics of music, as I have explained in my chief work (vol. i, § 52 and vol. ii, chap. 39), can be regarded as an exposition of the Pythagorean philosophy of numbers, has already been briefly alluded to by me in that work. Here I will explain the matter somewhat more fully, but assume that the reader has before him the foregoing passages. According to these, *melody* expresses all movements of the will as it makes itself known in man's self-consciousness; in other words, it

[13] ['For the properties and proportions of numbers are the basis for the properties and relations of things, as for example, the double, one and a third, one and a half.']
[14] [This work was not written by Plutarch.]
[15] ['The Pythagoreans said that an active fire is to be found in the middle and centre of the earth which gives warmth and life to the earth.']
[16] ['The ten principles' (of the Pythagoreans).]

expresses all emotions, feelings, and so on. *Harmony*, on the other hand, indicates the scale of the will's objectification in the rest of nature. In this sense, music is a second reality that runs entirely parallel with the first, yet it is of quite a different nature and character therefrom so that, while it has complete analogy, it has absolutely no similarity with it. But now, *as such*, music exists only in our auditory nerve and brain; apart from these or *in itself* (understood in the *Lockean* sense), it consists of mere numerical relations, first, according to their quantity, as regards measure or beat, and then, according to their quality, as regards the intervals of the scale, which rest on the arithmetical relations of vibrations. In other words, music consists of numerical relations in its rhythmic as well as its harmonic element. Accordingly, the whole nature of the world, both as microcosm and macrocosm, may certainly be expressed by mere numerical relations and thus to a certain extent be reduced thereto. In this sense, Pythagoras had been right in placing the true nature of things in numbers. But what are numbers? Relations of succession whose possibility rests on *time*.

When we read what is said in the scholia to Aristotle (p. 829, Berlin edition) about the Pythagoreans' philosophy of numbers, we may be led to suppose that the use of the word λόγος at the beginning of the gospel ascribed to John, a use so strange, mysterious, and verging on the absurd, and also the earlier analogues thereof in Philo, are derived from the Pythagorean philosophy of numbers, that is, from the meaning of the word λόγος in the arithmetical sense as numerical relation, *ratio numerica*. For according to the Pythagoreans, such a relation constitutes the innermost and indestructible essence of every being and hence is its first and original principle, ἀρχή; whereupon ἐν ἀρχῇ ἦν ὁ λόγος[17] might be true of everything. It should also be noted that Aristotle says (*De anima*, I. 1): τὰ πάθη λόγοι ἔνυλοί εἰσι, *et mox:* ὁ μὲν γὰρ λόγος εἶδος τοῦ πράγματος.[18] One is also reminded here of the λόγος σπερματικός[19] of the Stoics to which I shall shortly return.

According to the biography of Pythagoras by Jamblichus,

---

[17] ['In the beginning was the word.']

[18] ['"The emotions are material numerical relations;" and shortly after, "for the numerical relation is the form of the thing."']

[19] ['Creative reason' (containing the germs of all things).]

the former obtained his education mainly in Egypt where he stayed from his twenty-second to his fifty-sixth year, and indeed from the priests of that country. Returning in his fifty-sixth year, he really intended to found a kind of priest state in imitation of the Egyptian temple hierarchies, although with modifications necessary for the Greeks; in this he did not succeed in his native land Samos, but to some extent did in Croton. Now since Egyptian culture and religion undoubtedly came from India, as is proved by the sacredness of the cow and by a hundred other things (Herodotus, lib. II, c. 41), this explains Pythagoras' precept to abstain from animal food, especially the order not to slaughter horned cattle (Jamblichus, *Life of Pythagoras*, c. 28, § 150), as also the gentle treatment of all animals which is enjoined; similarly his doctrine of metempsychosis, his white robes, his eternal mysterious conduct giving rise to symbolic utterances and extending even to mathematical theorems; again the establishment of a kind of priestly caste with strict discipline and much ceremonial, worship of the sun (c. 35, § 256), and many other things. Even the more important of his fundamental astronomical conceptions were obtained from the Egyptians. Hence the prior claim of his doctrine of the obliquity of the ecliptic was disputed by Oenopides who had been with him in Egypt. (Concerning this, see the end of the twenty-fourth chapter of the first book of the *Eclogues* of Stobaeus with Heeren's note from Diodorus.) In general, when we look through the elementary conceptions of astronomy that have been gathered by Stobaeus from all the Greek philosophers (especially lib. I, cc. 25 *seqq.*), we find that they have usually produced absurdities, with the single exception of the Pythagoreans, who, as a rule, are quite right. There is no doubt that this comes not from their own resources but from Egypt.

The well-known prohibition of Pythagoras regarding beans is of purely Egyptian origin and is merely a superstition coming from that country, for Herodotus (lib. II, c. 37) relates that in Egypt the bean is considered unclean and is abhorred, so that the priests could not even bear the sight of it.

Moreover, that the doctrine of Pythagoras was a decided pantheism is testified, both conclusively and concisely, by a sentence of the Pythagoreans, preserved for us by Clement of

Alexandria in the *Cohortatio ad gentes* whose Doric dialect points to its genuineness. It runs as follows: Οὐκ ἀποκρυπτέον οὐδὲ τοὺς ἀμφὶ τὸν Πυθαγόραν, οἳ φασιν· Ὁ μὲν θεὸς εἷς· χ᾽ οὗτος δὲ οὐχ, ὥς τινες ὑπονοοῦσιν, ἐκτὸς τᾶς διακοσμήσιος, ἀλλ᾽ ἐν αὐτᾷ, ὅλος ἐν ὅλῳ τῷ κύκλῳ ἐπίσκοπος πάσας γενέσιος, κρᾶσις τῶν ὅλων· ἀεὶ ὤν, καὶ ἐργάτας τῶν αὐτοῦ δυνάμιων καὶ ἔργων ἁπάντων ἐν οὐράνῳ φωστήρ, καὶ πάντων πατὴρ, νοῦς καὶ ψύχωσις τῷ ὅλῳ κύκλῳ πάντων κίνασις[20] (See Clement of Alexandria, *Opera*, Tom. i, p. 118 *in Sanctorum Patrum opera polemica* vol. iv, Würzburg, 1778). Thus it is a good thing at every opportunity to convince ourselves that theism proper and Judaism are convertible terms.

According to Apuleius, Pythagoras may have travelled as far as India and have been instructed even by the Brahmans themselves. (See Apuleius, *Florida*, p. 130, *ed. Bip.*) Accordingly, I believe that the wisdom and knowledge of Pythagoras, which are certainly to be highly rated, consisted not so much in what he thought as in what he had learnt and hence that they were less his own than that of others. This is confirmed by a saying of Heraclitus concerning him. (Diogenes Laërtius, lib. VIII, c. 1, § 5.) Otherwise he would have written them down in order to preserve his ideas from extinction; on the other hand, what had been learnt from others remained secure at the source.

§ 3

Socrates

The wisdom of Socrates is a philosophical article of faith. It is clear that the Socrates of Plato is an ideal and is therefore poetical, expressing Platonic thoughts, whereas in the Socrates of Xenophon there is not exactly much wisdom to be found. According to Lucian (*Philopseudes*, 24), Socrates had a fat belly, which is not one of the distinguishing marks of genius. Yet as regards high intellectual abilities, it is just as doubtful with all who have not written, and so too with Pythagoras. A great

---

[20] ['However, we cannot pass over in silence the followers of Pythagoras when they say: God is one; but he is not, as some imagine, outside the universe, but inside it. He is the entire sphere as overlord of all origin, as pervading everything. He exists eternally and is a master of all his own forces and works, a light in the heavens, father of the universe, spirit and inspiration of the whole world-orbit, movement of the universe.']

mind must gradually recognize his vocation and attitude to mankind; consequently, he is bound to become conscious of belonging not to the flock but to the shepherds, I mean to the educators of the human race. From this, however, it will clearly become his duty not to restrict his immediate and assured influence to the few whom chance brings near to him, but to extend it to humanity, so that it is able to reach the exceptions, the elect and hence the rare ones among mankind. But the organ whereby one speaks *to humanity* is only writing; verbally one addresses only a number of individuals, and so what is thus said remains in relation to the human race a private matter. For such individuals generally are a poor soil for a rich and noble seed; in such soil either it does not thrive at all, or it rapidly degenerates in what it produces; and so the seed itself must be preserved. Yet this is not done through tradition that is falsified at every step, but solely through writing, this one and only faithful preserver of thoughts. Moreover, every profound thinker necessarily has the impulse, for his own satisfaction, to fix and retain his ideas and to reduce them to the greatest possible clearness and precision, and consequently to embody them in words. But this is done to perfection only by writing; for the written report is essentially different from the verbal, since it alone admits of the highest precision, concision, and pregnant brevity, and consequently becomes the pure ectype of the thought. As a result of all this, it would be a strange presumption in a thinker to want to leave unused the most important invention of the human race. Accordingly, it is hard for me to believe in the really great intellect of those who have not written; on the contrary, I am inclined to regard them mainly as practical heroes who effected more by their character than by their brains. The sublime authors of the *Upanishads* of the *Vedas* have written, although the *Sanhita* of the *Vedas*, consisting of mere prayers, were at first propagated only verbally.

Very many parallels can be pointed out between Socrates and Kant. Both reject all dogmatism; both profess a complete ignorance in metaphysical matters, and their special characteristic lies in the clear awareness of such ignorance. On the other hand, both maintain that the practical, that which man has to do and suffer, is of itself perfectly certain without any further theoretical foundation. Both had the same fate in that their immediate successors and declared disciples nevertheless differed from them in those very principles and, elaborating metaphysics, established wholly dogmatic systems. Further, these systems proved to be utterly different and yet all agreed in maintaining that they had started from the doctrine of Socrates or Kant, as the case may be. As I am myself a Kantian, I wish here to express in a few words my relation to Kant. He teaches that we cannot know anything beyond experience and its possibility. I admit this, yet I maintain that in its totality experience itself is capable of an explanation, and I have endeavoured to give this by deciphering it like a handwriting, but not, like all previous philosophers, by undertaking to go beyond it by means of its mere forms, a method that Kant had shown to be inadmissible.

The advantage of the *Socratic method*, as we come to know it from Plato, consists in the fact that we arrange for the grounds of the propositions we intend to demonstrate to be admitted one at a time by the collocutor or opponent before he has surveyed their consequents. For from a didactic delivery in continuous speech he would have an opportunity to recognize at once consequents and grounds as such, and would thus attack them if they did not suit him. Meanwhile, one of the things that Plato might impose on us is that, by means of an application of this method, the sophists and other fools would quite calmly have let Socrates demonstrate to them that they were so. This is inconceivable; on the contrary, at about the last quarter of the way, or generally as soon as they noticed where it would lead to, they would have spoilt the cleverly planned game of Socrates and would have torn his net by digressions, or by denying what was previously said, by intentional misunderstandings, and by whatever else is instinctively applied as tricks and dodges by dogmatical dishonesty. Or again, they would have become so impolite and insulting that he would have found it prudent to save his skin betimes. For how could even the sophists fail to know the means whereby anyone can make himself the equal of anyone else and instantly remove even the greatest intellectual inequality, namely insult? A low and ignoble nature, therefore, feels even an instinctive urge to insult as soon as it begins to detect intellectual superiority.

§ 4

Plato

In Plato we find the origin of a certain false dianoiology that is put forward with a secret metaphysical intention, namely for the purpose of a rational psychology and of a doctrine of immortality attaching thereto. It afterwards proved itself to be a deceptive doctrine of the toughest vitality, for it prolonged its existence throughout the whole of ancient, mediaeval, and modern philosophy, until Kant, the crusher of everything, finally knocked it on the head. The doctrine, here referred to, is the rationalism of the theory of knowledge, with a metaphysical ultimate aim. It may briefly be summarized as follows. What knows in us is an immaterial substance, fundamentally different from the body and called soul; the body, on the other hand, is an obstacle to knowledge. Hence all knowledge brought about through the senses is deceptive; the only true, accurate, and sure knowledge, on the other hand, is that which is free and removed from all sensibility (thus from all intuitive perception), consequently *pure thought*, i.e. an operation exclusively with abstract concepts. For this is performed by the *soul* entirely from its own resources; consequently, it will succeed best after the soul is separated from the body and so when we are dead. In this way, therefore, dianoiology here plays into the hands of rational psychology for the purpose of its doctrine of immortality. This doctrine which I have here summarized, is found fully and clearly expounded in the *Phaedo*, chap. 10. It is conceived somewhat differently in the *Timaeus*, from which Sextus Empiricus expounds it very precisely and clearly in the following words: Παλαιά τις παρὰ τοῖς φυσικοῖς κυλίεται δόξα περὶ τοῦ τὰ ὅμοια τῶν ὁμοίων εἶναι γνωριστικά. Μοχ: Πλατὼν δέ, ἐν τῷ Τιμαίῳ, πρὸς παράστασιν τοῦ ἀσώματον εἶναι τὴν ψυχήν, τῷ αὐτῷ γένει τῆς ἀποδείξεως κέχρηται. Εἰ γὰρ ἡ μὲν ὅρασις, φησί, φωτὸς ἀντιλαμβανομένη, εὐθύς ἐστι φωτοειδής, ἡ δὲ ἀκοὴ ἀέρα πεπληγμένον κρίνουσα, ὅπερ ἐστι τὴν φωνήν, εὐθὺς ἀεροειδὴς θεωρεῖται, ἡ δὲ ὄσφρησις ἀτμοὺς γνωρίζουσα πάντως ἐστὶ ἀτμοειδής, καὶ ἡ γεῦσις, χυλούς, χυλοειδής· κατ᾽ ἀνάγκην καὶ ἡ ψυχὴ τὰς ἀσωμάτους ἰδέας λαμβάνουσα, καθάπερ τὰς ἐν τοῖς ἀριθμοῖς καὶ τὰς ἐν τοῖς πέρασι τῶν σωμάτων (hence pure mathematics) γίνεταί τις ἀσώματος (*Adversus mathematicos*, VII. 116 et

119). (*vetus quaedam, a physicis usque probata, versatur opinio quod similia similibus cognoscantur.—Mox: Plato, in Timaeo, ad probandum, animam esse incorpoream, usus est eodem genere demonstrationis:* ' *nam si visio*', *inquit,* ' *apprehendens lucem statim est luminosa, auditus autem aërem percussum judicans, nempe vocem, protinus cernitur ad aëris accedens speciem, odoratus autem cognoscens vapores, est omnino vaporis aliquam habens formam, et gustus, qui humores, humoris habens speciem; necessario et anima, ideas suscipiens incorporeas, ut quae sunt in numeris et in finibus corporum, est incorporea.*')[21]

Even Aristotle admits this argument, at any rate hypothetically, for in the first book of *De anima* (c. 1) he says that the separate existence of the soul could be determined accordingly if there accrued to it some manifestation in which the body had no part, and that first and foremost thinking appeared to be such a manifestation. But if even *this* should not be possible without intuitive perception and imagination, then it also cannot take place without the body. (εἰ δέ ἐστι καὶ τὸ νοεῖν φαντασία τις, ἢ μὴ ἄνευ φαντασίας, οὐκ ἐνδέχοιτ' ἂν οὐδὲ τοῦτο ἄνευ σώματος εἶναι.)[22] But now Aristotle does not admit the condition previously laid down and thus the premisses of the argument, namely in so far as he teaches what was later formulated in the proposition: *nihil est in intellectu, quod non prius fuerit in sensibus.*[23] (As to this, see *De anima,* III. 8.) Therefore even he saw that everything purely and abstractly conceived had borrowed the whole of its material and content first from the intuitively perceived. This also disturbed the Schoolmen and so, even in the Middle Ages, attempts were made to prove that there are *pure cognitions of reason,* that is to say, thoughts that have no reference to any images and hence a thinking that draws all its material from itself. The

[21] ["An old opinion finds favour with the natural philosophers that the homogeneous is knowable for the homogeneous." Shortly afterwards: "But in the *Timaeus* Plato makes use of this very method of proof to demonstrate the incorporeal nature of the soul. For if, he says, the face is adapted to light because it is susceptible to light, and hearing is aerially conditioned because it perceives the concussion of the air, namely the tone, and smell because it experiences fumes and vapours, is at all events so conditioned, and taste is similarly adapted because it tastes juices, then the soul must also be of necessity an incorporeal essence because it knows incorporeal ideas as, for example, those in numbers and those to be found in the forms of bodies."']

[22] ['But if thought is a kind of imagination, or takes place not without imagination, then something of the kind cannot take place without body.']

[23] ['In the intellect there is nothing that has not previously existed in the senses.']

efforts and controversies on this point are found in Pomponatius, *De immortalitate animi*, for he derives his main argument therefrom. Now to satisfy the aforesaid requirement, the *universalia* and the cognitions *a priori*, conceived as *aeternae veritates*,[24] had to be used. The development the matter received through Descartes and his school has already been discussed in the detailed observation appended to § 6 of my prize-essay *On the Basis of Ethics*, where I quoted the original words of the Cartesian de la Forge, which are worth reading. For, as a rule, we find precisely the false doctrines of every philosopher expressed most clearly by his disciples because they are not, like the master himself, concerned with keeping as dark as possible those aspects of his system which might betray its weakness; for here they act in good faith and have nothing to fear. Now Spinoza already opposed to the whole Cartesian dualism his doctrine that *substantia cogitans et substantia extensa una eademque est substantia, quae jam sub hoc, jam sub illo attributo comprehenditur*,[25] thereby showing his great superiority. Leibniz, on the other hand, remained astutely on the path of Descartes and orthodoxy. But then this evoked the endeavour of the admirable Locke which was so thoroughly wholesome for philosophy; he finally insisted on investigating the *origin of concepts* and made the sentence '*no innate ideas*' the basis of his philosophy, after he had discussed it at length. The French, for whom his philosophy was elaborated by Condillac, soon went too far in the matter, although for the same reason, since they put forward and urged the sentence *penser est sentir*.[26] Taken absolutely, this is false; yet in it is to be found the truth that all thinking partly presupposes feeling, as an ingredient of the intuitive perception that furnishes it with its material, and that thinking, like feeling, is itself partly conditioned by bodily organs. And thus just as feeling is conditioned by the nerves of sense, so is thinking by the brain, and the two are nervous activity. Now even the French school did not stick so firmly to this sentence for its own sake, but again with a metaphysical, and indeed a materialistic, purpose. In the same way, the Platonic, Cartesian, Leibnizian opponents

---

[24] ['Eternal truths'.]

[25] ['The thinking substance and the extended substance are one and the same substance which is comprehended now under this attribute, now under that.']

[26] ['To think is to perceive.']

had stuck to the false proposition that the only correct knowledge of things consists in pure thinking, likewise with a
metaphysical intention, namely to prove from it the immaterial-
ity of the soul. Kant alone leads us to the truth from these two
false paths and from a dispute wherein both parties do not
really go to work honestly. For both profess dianoiology but are
directed to metaphysics, and thus they falsify dianoiology. And
so Kant says: 'Certainly there is a pure knowledge of reason
[*Vernunft*], that is, cognitions *a priori* that precede all experience
and consequently a thinking that does not owe its material to
any knowledge that is produced by means of the senses.' But
although not drawn *from* experience, this very knowledge *a
priori* has value and validity only *for the purpose of* experience.
For it is nothing but the awareness of our own *knowledge-
apparatus* and of the structure and mechanism thereof (brain-
function) or, as Kant expresses it, the *form* of the knowing consciousness itself. This form obtains its *material* primarily through
empirical knowledge that is added by means of sensation; but
without such knowledge it is empty and useless. Precisely on
this account, his philosophy is called the *Critique of Pure Reason*.
Now through this, all that metaphysical psychology falls down
and with it all Plato's pure activity of the soul. For we see that
knowledge without the intuitive perception that is brought
about by the body has no material, and consequently that the
knower as such, without the presupposition of the body, is
nothing but an empty form; not to mention that all thinking
is a physiological function of the brain, just as digestion is of
the stomach.

Accordingly, if Plato's doctrine of withdrawing knowledge
and keeping it clear from all connection with the body, the
senses, and intuitive perception, proves to be purposeless,
mistaken, and even impossible, we can nevertheless regard my
doctrine as its corrected analogue. This doctrine says that
only the intuitive knowledge, that is kept clear of all connection
with the *will*, reaches the highest objectivity and hence perfection. With regard to this, I refer to the third book of my chief
work.

§ 5
Aristotle

The fundamental characteristic of Aristotle might be said to be the greatest shrewdness and sagacity combined with circumspection, power of observation, versatility, and want of depth. His view of the world is shallow, although ingeniously elaborated. Depth of thought finds its material within ourselves; sagacity must obtain its material from without in order to have data. Now at that time, empirical data were to some extent scanty and poor and in part even false. Nowadays the study of Aristotle is, therefore, not very profitable, whereas that of Plato remains so in the highest degree. The want of depth, complained of in Aristotle, is naturally most obvious in the *Metaphysics*, where mere keenness is not sufficient, as it is elsewhere; and so in this work he is least satisfactory. His *Metaphysics* is for the most part a mere talk on the philosophemes of his predecessors whom he criticizes and refutes from his point of view, mostly in accordance with isolated utterances, without really penetrating their meaning; on the contrary, he is like a man who breaks windows from outside. He advances few or no dogmas of his own, at any rate not consistently. It is an accidental merit that we are indebted to his polemic for most of our knowledge of the older philosophemes. He is most hostile to Plato precisely where Plato is entirely right. Plato's 'Ideas' are always coming back in his mouth like something he cannot digest; he is resolved not to admit their validity. Keenness and ingenuity are adequate in the sciences of experience, and so Aristotle has a predominantly empirical turn of mind. But since his day empirical science has made such progress that its state at that time is related to it as the child to the adult. And so today the sciences of experience cannot be directly advanced very much by a study of him; but they can be indirectly by the method and the really scientific attitude which characterize him and were introduced by him. In zoology, however, he is still of direct use, at any rate in some respects. Now generally speaking, his empirical turn of mind gives him a tendency always to become prolix and diffuse. In this way, he digresses so readily and often from the line of thought taken up by him that he is almost incapable of pursuing any line for any length of time and to the end; but it is precisely in this that *deep* thinking consists. On the contrary, he starts up problems everywhere, but only touches on them; and without solving them or even thoroughly discussing them, he at once passes on to something else. Therefore his reader so often thinks 'now it will come', but nothing comes; and so when he has raised a problem and has pursued it for a short distance, the truth so often appears to be on the tip of his tongue; but suddenly he is on to something else and leaves us in doubt. For he cannot stick to anything, but jumps from what he has in hand to something else that occurs to him, just as a child drops one toy in order to seize another that it has just seen. This is the weak side of his intellect; it is the vivacity of superficiality. This explains why, although Aristotle had an extremely systematic mind, for he originated the separation and classification of the sciences, his exposition nevertheless always lacks systematic arrangement and in it we miss the methodical progress, indeed the separation of the heterogeneous and the classification of the homogeneous. He discusses things as they occur to him, without having thought them out beforehand and sketched a clear scheme; he thinks with a pen in his hand, which is, of course, a great relief for the author but a great hardship for the reader. Hence the planlessness and inadequacy of his presentation; thus he comes back a hundred times to the same thing because something heterogeneous to it had come in between; and so he cannot stick to a subject, but goes from the hundredth to the thousandth; and hence, as I have previously described, he leads by the nose the reader who is anxious to have the solution to the problems raised. Therefore, after devoting several pages to a subject, he suddenly begins his investigation thereof at the beginning with λάβωμεν οὖν ἄλλην ἀρχὴν τῆς σκέψεως,[27] and this six times in one work; hence the motto *quid feret hic tanto dignum promissor hiatu*[28] applies to so many exordiums of his books and chapters; in a word, he is so often confusing and unsatisfactory. As an exception, he has, of course, acted differently; for instance, the three books of *Rhetoric* are in every way a model of scientific method; indeed they show an architectonic symmetry that may have been the original of the Kantian.

[27] ['Therefore let us take another starting-point for our consideration.']
[28] ['What matter of importance can be promised by this opening of the mouth?']

The radical antithesis of Aristotle, both in his mode of thought and presentation, is Plato. This philosopher sticks to his main idea as with an iron hand, pursues its thread, however slender, in all its ramifications, through the labyrinths of the longest dialogues, and again finds it after all the episodes. We see here that, before he started to write, he had thoroughly and maturely thought out his subject and had planned an artistic arrangement for its presentation. Hence every dialogue is a planned work of art all of whose parts have a well-thought-out connection, often intentionally concealed for a time, and whose frequent episodes lead back automatically and often unexpectedly to the main idea that is now made clear by them. Plato always knew, in the full sense of the word, what he wanted and what he intended, although in most cases he does not bring the problems to a definite solution, but rests content with their thorough discussion. Therefore we need not be very surprised if, as some accounts state, especially in Aelian (*Variae historiae*, III. 19, IV. 9, etc.), considerable want of personal harmony was displayed between Plato and Aristotle; also here and there Plato may have spoken somewhat disparagingly of Aristotle, whose wanderings, vagaries, and digressions connected with his polymathy, were quite antipathetic to Plato. Schiller's poem *Breite und Tiefe* can also be applied to the antithesis between Aristotle and Plato.

In spite of this empirical turn of mind, Aristotle was nevertheless no consistent and methodical empiricist; and so he had to be overthrown and driven out by the true father of empiricism, Bacon. Whoever really wants to understand in what sense and why Bacon is the opponent and subduer of Aristotle and his method should read the books of Aristotle *De generatione et corruptione*. Here he will find a reasoned *a priori* statement on nature, which endeavours to understand and explain her processes from mere concepts; a particularly glaring example is furnished in lib. II, c. 4, where a chemistry is constructed *a priori*. Bacon, on the other hand, appeared with the advice to make not abstract, but perceptual, experience the source of a knowledge of nature. The brilliant result of this is the present high state of the natural sciences whence we look down with a charitable smile on these Aristotelian vexations and annoyances. In this respect, it is noteworthy that the above-mentioned books of Aristotle quite clearly disclose even the origin of Scholasticism; indeed its hair-splitting, word-juggling method is already to be met with in them. For the same purpose, the books *De coelo* are also very useful and therefore worth reading. The very first chapters are a good specimen of the method of trying to know and determine the essence of nature from mere concepts, and here the failure to do so is obvious. There in chap. 8 it is demonstrated from mere concepts and *loci communes*[29] that there are not several worlds; and in chap. 12 there is likewise a speculation on the course of the stars. It is a consistent subtle reasoning from false concepts, a quite special nature-dialectic, undertaking to decide *a priori* from certain universal axioms that are supposed to express the rational and proper, how nature must exist and act. Now while we see such a great and indeed stupendous intellect, such as Aristotle had in spite of everything, so deeply ensnared in errors of this kind which maintained their validity till a few hundred years ago, it becomes pre-eminently plain how very much mankind owes to Copernicus, Kepler, Galileo, Bacon, Robert Hooke, and Newton. In chapters seven and eight of the second book, Aristotle expounds the whole of his absurd arrangement of the heavens. Thus he states that the stars are firmly attached to the revolving hollow sphere, sun and planets to similar nearer ones; that the friction of revolution causes light and heat; and that the earth positively stands still. All this might pass if previously there had not been something better. But when he himself in chap. 13 presents us with the entirely correct views of the Pythagoreans on the shape, position, and motion of the earth in order to reject them, this inevitably rouses our indignation. This will occur when from his frequent polemics against Empedocles, Heraclitus, and Democritus we see how all these had a very much more correct insight into nature and had also paid more attention to experience than had the shallow prattler now before us. Empedocles had indeed already taught about a tangential force arising from rotation and acting in opposition to gravity (II. 1 et. 13, and also schol. p. 491.) Far from being able to estimate such things at their true value, Aristotle does not even admit the correct views of those older philosophers concerning the true significance of above and below, but here

29 ['Commonplaces, platitudes'.]

he also takes his stand on the opinion of the common herd which follows the superficial appearance (IV. 2). But now it must be borne in mind that these views of his met with recognition and dissemination, superseded all that was earlier and better, and so later became the foundation of Hipparchus, and then of the Ptolemaic system of astronomy. Mankind had to be burdened with this system until the beginning of the sixteenth century, doubtless to the great advantage of the Jewish-Christian religious dogmas that are at bottom incompatible with the Copernican system of astronomy; for how can there be a God in heaven when no heaven exists? *Theism* seriously meant necessarily presupposes that the world is divided into *heaven* and *earth*; on the *latter* human beings run about, in the *former* sits the God who governs them. Now if astronomy takes away heaven, then with it it has taken away God; thus it has so extended the world that there is no room left for God. But a personal being, as every God inevitably is, who has no *place*, but is everywhere and nowhere, can merely be spoken of, not imagined, and thus not believed in. Accordingly, in so far as physical astronomy becomes popularized, theism must disappear, however firmly it may have been impressed on men by an incessant and most pompous preaching. The Catholic Church rightly recognized this at once and accordingly persecuted the Copernican system; and so as regards this, it is foolish to wonder at, and raise such an outcry over, the crushing of Galileo; for *omnis natura vult esse conservatrix sui.*[30] Who knows whether some secret knowledge or at any rate an inkling of this congeniality of Aristotle to the doctrine of the Church and of the danger averted by him has not contributed to the excessive admiration of him in the Middle Ages?* Who knows whether many a man, stimulated by Aristotle's accounts of the older astronomical systems, did not secretly examine these truths long before Copernicus? After many years of hesitation, and when on the point of quitting the world, Copernicus finally ventured to proclaim them.

---

* The older authors who ascribe to Aristotle actual *theism*, take their proofs from the books *De mundo* which are definitely not by him. This, of course, is now generally accepted.

[30] ['Every being of nature strives to preserve itself.']

§ 6
Stoics

A very fine and profound conception with the *Stoics* is that of the λόγος σπερματικός,[31] although we should like to have fuller accounts of it than those that have come down to us. (Diogenes Laërtius, lib. vii, c. 136; Plutarch, *De placitis philosophorum*, i. 7; Stobaeus, *Eclogues*, lib. i, c. 372.) Yet this much is clear, that through it we think of that which in the successive individuals of a species asserts and preserves the identical form thereof, since it passes from one individual to another; hence the concept of the species embodied in the seed, so to speak. Accordingly, the λόγος σπερματικός is the indestructible element in the individual; it is that whereby the individual is one with the species, representing and maintaining it. It is that which prevents death, the destroyer of the individual, from attacking the species. By virtue of the species, the individual exists again and again, in spite of death. Hence λόγος σπερματικός might be translated as the magical formula that at all times summons this form into the phenomenon. Very closely akin to it is the concept of the *forma substantialis* of the Schoolmen, by which is thought the inner principle of the complex of all the qualities of every natural being. Its antithesis is the *materia prima*, pure matter, without any form and quality. The soul of man is just his *forma substantialis*. What distinguishes both concepts is that the λόγος σπερματικός accrues merely to living and propagating beings, but the *forma substantialis* also to inorganic bodies. Similarly, the *forma substantialis* is concerned primarily with the individual, the λόγος σπερματικός with the species; yet both are obviously related to the Platonic Idea. Explanations of the *forma substantialis* are found in Scotus Erigena, *De divisione naturae*, lib. iii, p. 139 of the Oxford edition; in Giordano Bruno, *Della causa*, Dial. 3, pp. 252ff.; and at great length in the *Disputationes metaphysicae* of Suarez (Disp. 15, sect. 1), that genuine compendium of the whole of scholastic wisdom. An acquaintance thereof must be sought in that work rather than in the bombastic chatter of inane German professors of philo-, sophy who are the quintessence of all platitudes and tediousness.

A principal source of our knowledge of Stoic ethics is its very

---

31 ['Creative reason' (containing the germs of all things).]

detailed description preserved for us by Stobaeus (*Eclogae ethicae*, lib. II, c. 7) in which we flatter ourselves that we possess for the most part verbal extracts from Zeno and Chrysippus. If such be the case, this description is not calculated to give us a high opinion of the spirit and intellect of these philosophers. On the contrary, it is a pedantic, schoolmasterly, thoroughly diffuse, incredibly dreary, flat, and spiritless exposition of the Stoic morality without force and life and without any valuable, striking, or penetrating ideas. In it everything is derived from mere concepts; nothing is drawn from reality and experience. Accordingly, mankind is divided into σπουδαῖοι and φαῦλοι, virtuous and vicious. Everything good is attributed to the former, and everything bad to the latter; and so all things appear black and white, like a Prussian sentry box. These shallow school exercises, therefore, will not bear comparison with the energetic, spirited, and well-thought-out works of Seneca.

The dissertations of Arrian on the *philosophy of Epictetus*, which were written some four hundred years after the origin of the Stoa, do not give any sound information as to the true spirit and the real principles of the *Stoic morality*; on the contrary, this book in form and content is unsatisfactory. First as regards form, we miss in the book every trace of method, systematic treatment, and even orderly progress. In chapters that are tacked on to one another without any order and connection, it is incessantly repeated that we should think nothing of all that is not the expression of our own will and that, in consequence, we should regard with complete indifference all that usually moves man; this is the Stoic ἀταραξία.[32] Namely that which is not ἐφ' ἡμῖν[33] would also not be πρὸς ἡμᾶς.[34] This colossal paradox, however, is not derived from any principles, but the most extraordinary opinion of the world is expected of us without any reason being stated for this. Instead of it we find endless declamations in constantly recurring expressions and turns of phrase. For the conclusions and deductions from those strange maxims are expounded most fully and vividly, and accordingly many descriptions are given of how the Stoics make something out of absolutely nothing. Meanwhile, everyone

[32] ['Calmness', 'serenity', 'equanimity'.]   [33] ['From us'.]
[34] ['Of concern to us'.]

who is of a different opinion is called a slave and a fool. But in vain do we hope for the statement of any clear and cogent reason for assuming that strange mode of thought; for such a reason would be much more effective than all the declamations and words of abuse in the whole bulky book. Yet with its hyperbolic descriptions of Stoic equanimity, its tirelessly repeated panegyrics of the patron saints Cleanthes, Chrysippus, Zeno, Crates, Diogenes, and Socrates, and its abuse of all who think differently, this book is a veritable capuchin's sermon. The planless and desultory nature of the whole exposition is, of course, in keeping with such a book. What the title of a chapter states is only the subject-matter of its beginning; at the first opportunity a digression is made and, according to the *nexus idearum*,[35] one passes from the hundredth to the thousandth. So much for the *form*.

Now as to the *content*, it is the same, even apart from the fact that the foundation is entirely lacking; it is by no means genuine and purely Stoic; on the contrary, there is a strong foreign admixture that smacks of a Christian-Jewish source. The most undeniable proof of this is the theism which is to be found on all sides and is also the supporter of morality. Here the Cynic and Stoic act on behalf of God whose will is their guidance; they submit to him, put their trust in him, and so on. Such things are quite foreign to the genuine original Stoa; here God and the world are one and there is absolutely no knowledge of a God who is a thinking, willing, commanding, and provident person. Not only in Arrian, however, but in most of the pagan philosophical authors of the first century of the Christian era, we see Jewish theism already shining dimly, which was soon to become the popular creed as Christianity, just as today there dimly shines in the writings of scholars the pantheism native to India, which is also destined later to pass into the popular creed. *Ex oriente lux.*[36]

For the reason stated, the morality itself here expounded is also not purely Stoic. Many of its precepts are even mutually incompatible; and so, of course, no common fundamental principles of it could be laid down. In the same way, Cynicism is also completely falsified by the doctrine that the Cynic should be such mainly for the sake of others, namely to act on

[35] ['Sequence of ideas'.]   [36] ['Out of the East comes the light.']

them by his example as a messenger of God, and to guide them by intervening in their affairs. Hence it is said: 'In a city of none but sages, no Cynic would be necessary'; likewise that he should be healthy, strong, and cleanly in order not to repel people. How far removed this is from the self-sufficiency of the old genuine Cynics! Diogenes and Crates were certainly the friends and advisers of many families; but this was secondary and accidental and by no means the purpose of Cynicism.

Arrian has, therefore, entirely missed the really main idea of Cynicism as also of Stoic ethics; indeed he does not even appear to have felt the need for them. He preaches self-renunciation just because it pleases him; and possibly it pleases him merely because it is difficult and contrary to human nature, whereas preaching is easy. He did not look for the grounds of self-renunciation; and so we imagine we are listening now to a Christian ascetic and then again to a Stoic. For the maxims of both often coincide, it is true, but the principles whereon they rest are quite different. In this connection, I refer to my chief work, vol. i, § 16, and vol. ii, chap. 16, where the true spirit of Cynicism and the Stoa is thoroughly discussed, and indeed for the first time.

Arrian's inconsistency appears even in a ridiculous way since in his description of the perfect Stoic which is repeated innumerable times, he always says: 'he blames no one, complains neither of gods nor men, rebukes no one', and yet his whole book is for the most part couched in scolding terms that often descend to abusive language.

In spite of all this, genuine Stoic ideas are to be met with here and there in the book, which Arrian or Epictetus drew from the ancient Stoics; and in the same way, Cynicism is clearly and vividly described in some of its features. In places there is likewise much sound common sense and there are also striking descriptions drawn from life of men and their actions. The style is easy and fluent, but very diffuse and prolix.

I do not believe that the *Encheiridion* of Epictetus is composed by Arrian, as F. A. Wolf assured us in his lectures. It has much more spirit in fewer words than have the dissertations; it has sound sense throughout, no empty declamations, and no ostentation; it is concise and to the point and is also written in the tone of a well-meaning friend who is giving advice. The dissertations, on the other hand, speak mostly in a scolding and reproachful tone. The contents of the two books are on the whole the same, only that the *Encheiridion* has extremely little of the theism that is found in the dissertations. Perhaps the *Encheiridion* was Epictetus' own compendium that he dictated to his hearers, whereas the dissertations were the notes, taken down by Arrian, of the free discourses that serve as a commentary to that work.

§ 7
Neoplatonists

Reading the *Neoplatonists* calls for much patience because they all lack form and style. Yet in this respect, Porphyry is far better than the rest, for he is the only one who writes clearly and coherently so that we read him without aversion.

On the other hand, the worst is Jamblichus in his book *De mysteriis Aegyptiorum*; he is full of crass superstition and gross demonology and is also obstinate and headstrong. It is true that he has a different, as it were, esoteric view on magic and theurgy, yet his explanations thereof are shallow and insignificant. On the whole, he is an inferior and vexatious writer, narrow, perverse, grossly superstitious, confused, and vague. We see clearly that what he teaches has not sprung at all from his own reflection, but that it consists of the dogmas of others which are often only half-understood but are the more obstinately asserted; and so he is full of contradictions. But the book in question is now said to be not by Jamblichus, and I am inclined to agree with this view when I read the long extracts from his lost works which have been preserved by Stobaeus and are incomparably better than that book *De mysteriis*, containing as they do many a good thought of the Neoplatonic school.

Again, Proclus is a shallow, diffuse, and insipid talker. His commentary to Plato's *Alcibiades*, one of the worst of the Platonic dialogues which may also not be genuine, is the most diffuse and prolix chatter in the world. For there is endless talk on every word of Plato, even the most insignificant, wherein a deep meaning is sought. What Plato said mythically and allegorically is taken in its real sense and strictly dogmatically, and everything is distorted into the superstitious and theosophical. Yet there is no denying that, in the first half of that commentary, some very good ideas are to be found which, of course, may belong to the school rather than to Proclus. It is an extremely important proposition that concludes the *fasciculus primus partis primae*: αἱ τῶν ψυχῶν ἐφέσεις τὰ μέγιστα συντελοῦσι πρὸς τοὺς βίους, καὶ οὐ πλαττομένοις ἔξωθεν ἐοίκαμεν, ἀλλ' ἐφ' ἑαυτῶν προβάλλομεν τὰς αἱρέσεις, καθ' ἃς διαζῶμεν (*animorum appetitus (ante hanc vitam concepti) plurimam vim habent in vitas eligendas, nec extrinsecus fictis similes sumus, sed nostra sponte facimus electiones, secundum quas deinde vitas transigimus*).[37] This, of course, has its root in Plato, but also approaches Kant's doctrine of the intelligible character. It stands far above the shallow and narrow doctrines of the freedom of the individual will that can always do one thing and likewise another. Even at the present time, our professors of philosophy, who always have in mind the catechism, labour under such doctrines. For their part, Augustine and Luther with predestination or election by grace had found a way out of the difficulty. That was good enough for those devout times, for one was still ready, if it pleased God, to go to the devil in God's name. But in our times refuge can be found only in the aseity[38] of the will, and it must be acknowledged that, as Proclus has it, οὐ πλαττομένοις ἔξωθεν ἐοίκαμεν.[39]

Finally Plotinus, the most important of all, is changeable and inconsistent, and the individual *Enneads* are of extremely different value and content; the fourth is excellent. Yet even with him presentation and style are for the most part bad. His ideas are not arranged or previously considered, but have been written down at random just as they came. In his biography Porphyry speaks of the careless and inaccurate way in which Plotinus set to work. And so his diffuse and tedious prolixity and confusion often cause us to lose all patience, and we wonder how such stuff could have come down to posterity. He often has the style of a pulpit orator, and just as the latter preaches the gospel, so he sets forth Platonic doctrines. At the same time, what Plato has said mythically or indeed half metaphorically, is dragged down by him to positive prosaic

---

[37] ['The desires of souls (before their birth) contribute most to the shaping of their course of life, and we do not look as if we had been formed from without, but from out of ourselves we come across the elective decisions whereby we live.']

[38] [Being by and of itself. All other being are *ab alio*, dependent in their existence on a creator (God).]

[39] ['We do not look as if we had been formed from without.']

seriousness. He chews for hours at the same idea without adding anything from his own resources. Here he proceeds as one who reveals without demonstrating; and thus he speaks throughout *ex tripode* and relates things as he imagines them to be, without undertaking to provide any foundation. Nevertheless, great, important, and profound truths are to be found in his works which he himself certainly understood, for he is by no means without insight. He, therefore, thoroughly deserves to be read and richly rewards the patience necessary for this.

I find the explanation for these contradictory characteristics of Plotinus in the fact that he and the Neoplatonists generally are not philosophers in the proper sense, are not original thinkers. On the contrary, what they expound is the teaching of others which was handed down to them, but was in most cases well digested and assimilated by them. Thus it is Indo-Egyptian wisdom which they tried to embody in Greek philosophy and, as a suitable connecting link, a means of transmission, or *menstruum* for this, they use the Platonic philosophy, especially that part which inclines to the mystical. The whole of the All-One doctrine of Plotinus primarily and undeniably testifies to this Indian origin, through Egypt, of the Neoplatonic dogmas, and we find this admirably presented in the fourth *Ennead*. The very first chapter of its first book, περὶ οὐσίας ψυχῆς,[40] gives very briefly the fundamental teaching of his whole philosophy of a ψυχή that is originally one and is split up into many only by means of the corporeal world. Of special interest is the eighth book of this *Ennead* which explains how that ψυχή fell into this state of plurality through a sinful striving; accordingly, it bears a double guilt, namely that of its having descended into this world, and also of its sinful deeds therein. For the former guilt it atones through temporal existence in general; for the latter, which is less important, it atones through metempsychosis or the transmigration of souls (c. 5). This is obviously the same idea as the Christian original sin and particular sin. But the most readable of all is the ninth book, where in c. 3, εἰ πᾶσαι αἱ ψυχαὶ μία,[41] from the unity of that world-soul, among other things, the marvels of animal magnetism are explained, especially the phenomenon, to be

[40] ['On the essential nature of the soul.']
[41] ['Whether all souls are one.']

met with even now, where the somnambulist hears at the greatest distance a softly spoken word. This, of course, must be effected by means of a chain of persons standing in contact with her. With Plotinus there even appears, probably for the first time in Western philosophy, *idealism* that had long been current in the East even at that time, for it is taught (*Enneads*, iii, lib. VII, c. 10) that the soul has made the world by stepping from eternity into time, with the explanation: οὐ γάρ τις αὐτοῦ τοῦδε τοῦ παντὸς τόπος, ἢ ψυχή (*neque est alter hujus universi locus quam anima*),[42] indeed the ideality of time is expressed in the words: δεῖ δὲ οὐκ ἔξωθεν τῆς ψυχῆς λαμβάνειν τὸν χρόνον, ὥσπερ οὐδὲ τὸν αἰῶνα ἐκεῖ ἔξω τοῦ ὄντος (*oportet autem nequaquam extra animam tempus accipere*).[43] That ἐκεῖ (the life hereafter) is the opposite of the ἐνθάδε (this life), and is a concept very familiar to him, which he explains more fully by κόσμος νοητός and κόσμος αἰσθητός, *mundus intelligibilis et sensibilis*,[44] also by τὰ ἄνω καὶ τὰ κάτω.[45] In chapters 11 and 12 very good explanations are given for the ideality of time. Connected therewith is the fine explanation that in our temporal condition, we are not what we ought to be and might be. Thus we expect from the future always better things and look forward to the fulfilment of our shortcomings; and from this arise the future and its condition, namely time (c. 2 et c. 3). A further proof of the Indian origin is afforded by Jamblichus (*De mysteriis*, sect. 4, c. 4 et c. 5) in his exposition of the doctrine of metempsychosis, and also by the doctrine (sect. 5, c. 6) of the ultimate liberation and salvation from the bonds of birth and death, ψυχῆς κάθαρσις, καὶ τελείωσις, καὶ ἡ ἀπὸ τῆς γενέσεως ἀπαλλαγή, and (c.12) τὸ ἐν ταῖς θυσίαις πῦρ ἡμᾶς ἀπολύει τῶν τῆς γενέσεως δεσμῶν,[46] and hence that promise, stated in all Indian religious books and expressed in English as *final emancipation* or salvation. Finally, we have in addition (op. cit., sect. 7, c. 2) the account of the Egyptian symbol that shows a creative God sitting on the lotus. This is obviously the world-creating Brahma sitting on the lotus blossom that springs from the navel of Vishnu, as he is frequently depicted, for example

---

[42] ['For there is for this universe no other place than the soul or mind.']
[43] ['We should not accept time outside the soul or mind.']
[44] ['The world of Ideas and the world of the senses'.]
[45] ['Up there and here below'.]
[46] ['The purification and perfection of the soul and the liberation from becoming; ... the fire at the sacrifice delivers us from the fetters of becoming.']

in Langlès, *Monuments de l'Hindoustan*, vol. i, p. 175; in Coleman's *Mythology of the Hindus*, Plate 5, and others. This symbol is extremely important as a sure proof of the Indian origin of the Egyptian religion, as is also in the same respect the account given by Porphyry, *De abstinentia*, lib. II, that in Egypt the cow was sacred and no one was allowed to slaughter it. It is related by Porphyry in his life of Plotinus that, after being for several years the disciple of Ammonius Saccus, Plotinus wanted to go to Persia and India with Gordian's army, but was prevented from so doing by the defeat and death of Gordian. Even this circumstance indicates that the doctrine of Ammonius was of Indian origin, and that Plotinus now intended to draw it more purely from its source. The same Porphyry furnished a detailed theory of metempsychosis which is wholly in the Indian spirit, although adorned with Platonic psychology. It is found in the *Eclogues* of Stobaeus, lib. I, c. 52, § 54.

§ 8

Gnostics

The *Cabalistic* and *Gnostic philosophies* with whose founders, as Jews and Christians, monotheism stood firmly in the forefront, are attempts to eliminate the flagrant contradiction between the production of the world by an almighty, infinitely good, and wise being and the dreary and defective state of this same world. Therefore between the world and that world-cause they introduce a series of intermediate beings through whose fault a decline occurred and thus the world first originated. And so they take the blame, as it were, off the shoulders of the sovereign and lay it on those of his ministers. Of course, this proceeding was already suggested by the myth of the Fall of Man which is generally the culminating point of Judaism. With the Gnostics, therefore, those beings are now the πλήρωμα, the aeons, the ὕλη, the demiurge, and so on. The series was lengthened at the discretion of each Gnostic.

The whole proceeding is analogous to that wherein physiological philosophers sought to interpose intermediate essences, such as nerve fluid, nerve ether, vital spirits, and the like, in order to lessen the contradiction entailed by the assumed connection and mutual influence in man of a material and an immaterial substance. Both cover up what they are unable to abolish.

§ 9
Scotus Erigena

This remarkable man affords the interesting spectacle of the struggle between the truth he has recognized and seen for himself, and local dogmas, fixed by early inculcation and grown beyond all doubt or at any rate beyond all direct attack, side by side with the endeavour, arising therefrom, of a noble nature somehow to reduce to harmony the dissonance that had thus resulted. This, of course, can be done only by his turning, twisting, and where necessary, distorting the dogmas until, *nolentes volentes*,[47] they conform to the truth that he has recognized for himself. Such truth remains the dominating principle, yet it is forced to go about in a strange and even cumbersome attire. In his great work, *De divisione naturae*, Erigena knows how to carry out this method everywhere with success until at last he tries to square accounts with the origin of evil and sin together with the threatened tortures of hell. Here the method comes to grief, and indeed in the optimism that is a consequence of Jewish monotheism. In the fifth book he teaches the return of all things to God and the metaphysical unity and indivisibility of all mankind and even of all nature. The question now arises: where does sin remain? It cannot rest with God. Where is hell with its endless tortures, such as have been promised? Who is to go there? Mankind is saved, and indeed the whole of mankind. Here the dogma remains insurmountable. Erigena wriggles miserably through lengthy and diffuse sophisms that turn out to be mere words. In the end, he is forced into contradictions and absurdities, especially since the question concerning the origin of sin has inevitably crept in. But such origin cannot lie either in God or even in the will created by him, since God would otherwise be the originator of sin, a point that he understands perfectly (see p. 287 of the Oxford *editio princeps* of 1681). He is now driven to absurdities, for sin is not to have either a cause or a subject: *malum incausale est, . . . penitus incausale et insubstantiale est*:[48] ibid. The deeper reason

---

[47] ['Willy-nilly'.]
[48] ['Sin is causeless . . . it is entirely causeless and insubstantial.']

for these drawbacks is that the doctrine of the *redemption* of mankind and the world, which is obviously of Indian origin, also presupposes the Indian teaching according to which the origin of the world (this Samsara of the Buddhists) is itself based already on evil; that is to say, it is a sinful act of Brahma. Now we ourselves are again this Brahma, for Indian mythology is everywhere transparent. In Christianity, on the other hand, that doctrine of the redemption of the world had to be grafted on to Jewish theism, where the Lord not only made the world, but afterwards found it to be excellent: πάντα καλὰ λίαν. *Hinc illae lacrimae.*[49] From this arise the difficulties, fully recognized by Erigena, although in his day he did not dare to attack the evil at its root. However, he has Indian mildness; he rejects the eternal damnation and punishment laid down by Christianity. All creatures, rational, animal, vegetable, and inanimate, must, according to their inner essence, attain to eternal bliss through the necessary course of nature, for they have come from eternal goodness. But complete unity with God, *Deificatio*, is only for the saintly and righteous. For the rest, Erigena is honest enough not to conceal the great embarrassment in which he is placed by the origin of evil; he expounds it clearly in the above-quoted passage of the fifth book. In fact, the origin of evil is the rock whereon theism and pantheism split, for both imply optimism. Now evil and sin in their frightful magnitude are incontestable and cannot be argued away; indeed, the threatened punishments for the latter only increase the amount of the former. Now whence comes all this in a world that is either itself a God or is the well-meant work of a God? If the theistic opponents of pantheism cry out against it: 'What! are all the wicked, terrible, and hideous beings supposed to be God?' then the pantheists can answer: 'Why not? all those wicked, terrible, and hideous beings are supposed to have been created by a God *de gaieté de coeur.*'[50] We also find Erigena in the same difficulty in his other work that has come down to us, namely the book *De praedestinatione* which, however, is far inferior to the work *De divisione naturae* and in which he also appears not as a philosopher but as a theologian. Therefore here too he worries himself miserably with those contradictions which have

[49] ['Everything was very good.' 'Hence those tears.']
[50] ['From sheer wantonness'.]

as their ultimate ground the fact that Christianity is grafted on to Judaism. But his attempts merely put such contradictions in an even clearer light. God is said to have made everything, all and all in all; this is fixed; 'therefore wickedness and evil as well'. This inevitable consequence has to be removed and Erigena sees himself forced to put forward miserable cavilling and hair-splitting. For evil and wickedness are said not to *exist* at all; and so they are supposed to be nothing, even the devil is! Or else *free will* is to blame; thus God has, it is true, created this will, yet he has created it *free*; he is, therefore, not concerned with what it afterwards decides to do; for it was free, that is to say, it could do this and also that and so could be good as well as bad. Excellent! However, the truth is that to be free and to be created are two mutually eliminating and therefore contradictory qualities; and hence the assertion that God has created beings and has at the same time given them freedom of the will is really equivalent to saying that he has created and at the same time has not created them. For *operari sequitur esse*, in other words, the effects or actions of any possible thing can never be anything but the consequence of its nature and constitution, and only in such actions is its nature known. For to be free in the sense here demanded, a being would have to have no nature at all; in other words, it would have to be *nothing* at all, and so would have to be and not to be at the same time. For what *is* must be *something*; an existence without an essence cannot even be conceived. Now if a being is *created*, then it is created as it is *constituted*; and so it is badly *created* if it is badly *constituted*, and it is badly *constituted* if it acts badly, in other words, if its effects are bad. Consequently, the *guilt* of the world as well as its *evil*, which is just as undeniable, is always shifted back on to the shoulders of the originator of the world and, like Augustine before him, Scotus Erigena wears himself out in an endeavour to exonerate the creator.

If, on the other hand, a being is to be morally *free*, it cannot be created but must have aseity, that is to say, it must be something original that exists by virtue of its own primary force and absolute power; and it must not refer to anything else. Its existence is then its own act of creation and this act unfolds and spreads itself in time, revealing once for all a decided character or disposition of that being. Nevertheless, such character or disposition is its own work and so the responsibility for all the manifestations of that character rests on the being itself. Now if a being is to be *responsible* for its actions, if it is to be *accountable*, it must be *free*. Therefore from the responsibility and imputability, which our conscience states, it certainly follows that the will is free; but from this again it follows that the will is the original thing itself. Consequently, not merely the actions, but also the existence and essence of man are his own work. Concerning all this, I refer to my essay 'On the Freedom of the Will', where it is to be found fully and irrefutably discussed. For this reason, the professors of philosophy have tried by the most inviolable silence to boycott this essay that was awarded a prize. The guilt of sin and evil always comes back from nature on to her creator. Now if that creator is the *will* itself, manifesting itself in all the phenomena of nature, that guilt has reached the right man; if, on the other hand, it is said to be a God, then the authorship of sin and evil contradict his divinity.

In reading Dionysius the Areopagite to whom Erigena so often refers, I have found that the former was in every respect the model of the latter. The pantheism of Erigena and also his theory of wickedness and evil are, as regards their main features, to be found in Dionysius; but of course he has only indicated what Erigena has developed, expressed with boldness, and discussed with fire. Erigena has infinitely more spirit and genius than has Dionysius, but the material and course of his reflections were given to him by Dionysius, who thus did for him an immense amount of preparatory work. That Dionysius is ungenuine does not affect the case; it is immaterial what was the name of the author of the book *De divinis nominibus*. But as he probably lived in Alexandria, I believe that, in some other way unknown to us, he was also the channel whereby a drop of Indian wisdom may have reached Erigena. For, as Colebrooke has observed in his essay on the philosophy of the Hindus (in Colebrooke's *Miscellaneous Essays*, vol. i, p. 244), proposition 3 of the *Karika of Kapila* is to be found in Erigena.

§ 10

Scholasticism

I should look for the really distinctive characteristic of *Scholasticism* in the fact that for it the supreme criterion of truth is

Holy Scripture to which we can, therefore, always appeal from every rational conclusion. One of its peculiarities is that its style has throughout a polemical character. Every investigation is soon transformed into a controversy whose *pro et contra* produce new *pro et contra* and thereby furnish it with the material that for it would otherwise soon run short. The hidden ultimate root of this peculiarity, however, is to be found in the antagonism between reason [*Vernunft*] and revelation.

The mutual claim of *realism* and *nominalism* and thus the possibility of so long and obstinate a dispute over them can be clearly understood from the following remarks.

I call the most heterogeneous things *red* if they have this colour. Obviously *red* is a mere name whereby I designate that phenomenon, no matter where it is to be found. Now in the same way, all common concepts are mere names for designating qualities that occur in different things. These things, however, are what is actual and real, so that *nominalism* is obviously right.

On the other hand, when we observe that all those actual things, to which alone reality was just now attributed, are temporal and consequently soon pass away, whereas qualities such as red, hard, soft, alive, plant, horse, human being, which are designated by those names, continue to exist regardless of this and accordingly are present at all times, we find that these qualities which are thought of precisely through common concepts whose designation are those names, have, by virtue of their ineradicable existence, much more reality. Consequently, such reality is to be attributed to *concepts*, not to individual entities; and so *realism* is right.

Nominalism really leads to materialism; for, after the elimination of all qualities, only matter in the last resort is left. Now if concepts are mere names, but individual things are real, their qualities being individually transient, then matter alone remains as that which continues to exist, and consequently as the real.

But strictly speaking, the above-mentioned claim of realism does not really belong to it, but to the Platonic doctrine of Ideas whereof it is the extension. The eternal forms and qualities of natural things, εἴδη, continue to exist, in spite of all change. Thus there is attributable to them a reality of a higher kind than to the individuals in which they manifest themselves. On the other hand, this is not to be conceded to mere abstractions that cannot be supported by intuitive perception. For example, what is the real element in such concepts as 'relation, difference, separation, disadvantage, indefiniteness', and so on?

A certain affinity or at any rate a parallelism of contrasts is evident when we match Plato with Aristotle, Augustine with Pelagius, the realists with the nominalists. One could maintain that, to a certain extent, a polar divergence in the human way of thinking here shows itself. This has expressed itself in a most extraordinary way, for the first time and most definitely, in two very great men who lived at the same time and near to each other.

§ 11
Francis Bacon

In another and more specially definite sense than that just indicated, the express and deliberate antithesis to Aristotle was Bacon. Thus Aristotle had been the first to give a thorough exposition of the correct method for arriving at particular from universal truths and hence the way downwards; this is syllogistic reasoning, the *Organum Aristotelis*. On the other hand, Bacon exhibited the way upwards, in that he expounded the method for arriving at universal from particular truths; this is induction, as distinct from deduction, and its exposition is the *Novum organum*. This expression, chosen in opposition to Aristotle, says in effect: 'quite a different manner of attacking'. The error of Aristotle, or rather of Aristotelians, lay in the assumption that they really possessed all truth. Thus they asserted that the truth was contained in their axioms and so axioms in certain *a priori* propositions or in those regarded as such, and that, to obtain particular truths, only deduction from such propositions was needed. An Aristotelian example of this was given by the books *De coelo*. On the other hand, Bacon quite rightly showed that those axioms had no such content at all; that the truth was not to be found at all in the system of human knowledge at that time, but rather outside it; and hence that the truth could not be developed from that system, but had to be introduced into it; and that, in consequence, universal and true propositions of great and rich content had to be gained first through *induction*.

The Schoolmen, led by Aristotle, thought: first we wish to establish the universal: the particular will flow therefrom, or generally may afterwards find a place thereunder as best it can. Accordingly, we will first of all settle what accrues to the *ens*, to the *thing in general*. What is peculiar to particular things may afterwards be added gradually, possibly even through experience: this can never alter anything in the universal. Bacon, on the other hand, said: we will first become acquainted as thoroughly as possible with individual things: we shall then ultimately know what the thing in general is.

Nevertheless, Bacon is inferior to Aristotle in that his method, leading upwards, is by no means so correct, certain, and infallible as is Aristotle's that leads downwards. Indeed, in his physical investigations Bacon himself has set aside the rules of his method that are given in the *New Organon*.

Bacon turned his attention mainly to physics. What he did for this, namely to begin at the beginning, was done immediately afterwards for metaphysics by Descartes.

§ 12
The Philosophy of the Moderns

In books on arithmetic the correctness of the solution of an example usually shows itself through the balancing of the result, in other words, by the fact that no remainder is left. The position is similar with regard to the solution of the riddle of the world. All systems are sums that do not balance out; they leave a remainder, or if a chemical simile be preferred, an insoluble precipitate. Such remainder consists in the fact that, if we logically draw conclusions from their propositions, the results do not fit, do not harmonize with, the real world lying before us; on the contrary, many aspects thereof remain quite inexplicable. For instance with materialistic systems that represent the world as arising out of a matter endowed with merely mechanical properties and in accordance with the laws of such matter, neither the universal and marvellous appropriateness of nature, nor the existence of knowledge wherein even that matter is first exhibited, is in agreement; and so this is their remainder. Again with the theistic, and equally with the pantheistic, systems, the overwhelming physical evils and moral depravity of the world cannot be brought into harmony. Therefore these are left as a remainder or as an insoluble precipitate. It is true that, in such cases, there is no lack of sophisms or, where necessary, even of mere words and phrases, for covering up such remainders; but in the long run they are of no use. As the sum does not balance out, individual errors in the calculation are looked for until in the end it has to be admitted that the preliminary statement itself of the problem was wrong. On the other hand, if the general consistency and harmony of all the propositions of a system are accompanied at every step by just as universal an agreement with the world of experience, without any discord ever being heard between the two—then this is the criterion of its truth, the required balancing out of the arithmetical sum. Similarly, the preliminary statement of the problem was wrong, equivalent to saying that, even from the beginning, the matter had not been attacked from the right end, whereby one was afterwards led from error to error. For it is with philosophy as with very many things; everything depends on whether it is tackled at the right end. Now the phenomenon of the world to be explained presents innumerable ends of which only one can be right. It is like a tangled mass of thread with many false ends hanging therefrom. Only the man who discovers the actual end is able to unravel the whole. But then one thing is easily developed from another, and from this we know that it was the right end. It can also be compared to a labyrinth that presents a hundred entrances opening into corridors all of which, after various long and intricate windings, finally lead out again with the exception of a single one, whose windings actually lead to the centre where the idol stands. If we have hit upon this entrance, we shall not miss the way; but by no other path can we ever reach the goal. I do not conceal the fact that I am of the opinion that only the will in us is the right end of the tangle, the true entrance to the labyrinth.

On the other hand, Descartes started on the example of Aristotle's metaphysics from the concept of *substance*, and we also see all his successors burdened therewith. But he assumed two kinds of substance, the thinking and the extended. Now these were supposed to act on each other through *influxus*

physicus,[51] which soon proved to be his remainder. This took place, namely not merely from without inwards in the representation of the corporeal world, but also from within outwards between the will (which was unhesitatingly assigned to thought) and the actions of the body. The closer relation between these two kinds of substance now became the main problem, whereby such great difficulties arose that in consequence thereof men were driven to the system of *causes occasionnelles* and of *harmonia praestabilita,* after the *spiritus animales,* which had settled the matter with Descartes himself, could be of no further use.*
Thus Malebranche considered the *influxus physicus* to be unthinkable, yet here he did not take into consideration that this *influxus physicus* is assumed without question in the creation and direction of the corporeal world by a God who is a spirit. He therefore puts in its place the *causes occasionnelles* and *nous voyons tout en Dieu;*[52] here is to be found his remainder. Spinoza, following in the footsteps of his teacher, also started from that concept of *substance* just as though it were something given. Yet he declared the two kinds of substance, the thinking and the extended, to be one and the same, whereby the above-mentioned difficulty was avoided. But his philosophy now became in this way mainly negative, thus amounting to a mere negation of the two great Cartesian antitheses; for he also extended his identification to the other antithesis set up by Descartes, namely that of God and the world. This, however, was really a mere method of teaching or form of presentation. Thus it would have been much too offensive to say outright: 'It is not true that a God has made this world, but it exists by its own absolute power;' he therefore chose an indirect turn of phrase and said: 'The world itself is God;' and this would never have occurred to him if, instead of starting from Judaism, he had been able to start dispassionately from nature herself. This turn of phrase at the same time helps to give his doctrines the appearance of being positive, whereas at bottom they are merely negative. He therefore leaves the world really unexplained,

---

* For the rest, the *spiritus animales* occur as something well known in Vanini, *De naturae Arcanis,* Dial. 49. Their originator is possibly Willisius (*De anatome cerebri; De anima brutorum,* Geneva, 1680, pp. 35 ff.) Flourens, *De la vie et de l'intelligence,* vol. ii, p. 72, ascribes them to Galen. Indeed even Jamblichus in Stobaeus (*Eclogues,* lib. I, c. 52, § 29) mentions them pretty clearly as a doctrine of the Stoics.

[51] ['Physical influence'.]   [52] ['We see everything in God.']

since his teaching amounts to saying: 'The world is because it is; and it is as it is because it is so.' (With this phrase Fichte used to mystify his students.) Yet the deification of the world that arose in the above manner did not admit of any true ethics; moreover, it was in flagrant contradiction with the physical evils and moral wickedness of this world. Here, then, is Spinoza's remainder.

As I have said, the concept of *substance* from which Spinoza also starts is taken by him as something given. It is true that he defines it in accordance with his purpose, but he does not concern himself as to its origin. For it was Locke who, shortly after him, propounded the great doctrine that a philosopher who wants to deduce or demonstrate anything from concepts has first to investigate the *origin* of every such concept, since its content and what may follow therefrom are determined entirely by its origin, as the source of all knowledge that is attainable by means of it. But if Spinoza had inquired into the origin of that concept of substance, he was bound ultimately to have found that this was simply and solely *matter*, and that the true content of the concept was nothing but just the essential and *a priori* assignable qualities of matter. Indeed everything attributed by Spinoza to his substance finds its confirmation in matter and only there; it is without origin and hence causeless, eternal, singular, and unique, and its modifications are extension and knowledge; the latter, of course, as the exclusive quality of the brain that is material. Accordingly, Spinoza is an unconscious materialist; yet when we go into the question, the matter that realizes and empirically confirms his concept is not the falsely understood and atomistic matter of Democritus and of the later French materialists which has none but mechanical properties, but the correctly understood matter that is endowed with all its inexplicable qualities. As regards this distinction, I refer to my chief work, vol. II, chap. 24. But even with the *Eleatics* we find this method of taking up unexamined the concept of *substance* in order to make it the starting-point, as can be seen particularly from the Aristotelian book *De Xenophane*, and so on. Thus Xenophanes also starts from the ὄν, i.e. from substance, and its properties are demonstrated without its being previously asked or stated whence he obtains his knowledge of such a thing. If this were done, one would clearly see what he was really talking about, in other words, what intuitive perception it ultimately was that was the basis of his concept and imparted reality thereto; and then in the end the result would be only matter, and all that he says is true of this. In the following chapters on Zeno, the agreement with Spinoza extends even to the style and expressions. And so we can scarcely refrain from assuming that Spinoza knew and used this work; for in his day Aristotle, although attacked by Bacon, was still always held in high esteem and good editions in Latin were available. Accordingly, Spinoza was a mere reviver of the Eleatics, as Gassendi was of Epicurus. Again, we see how extremely rare is the really new and wholly original in all branches of thought and knowledge.

Moreover, and especially in a formal respect, that starting from the concept of *substance* on the part of Spinoza rests on a false fundamental idea that he obtained from his teacher Descartes, who in turn had obtained it from Anselm of Canterbury. This idea is that *existentia* could result from *essentia*, in other words, that from a mere concept there could be inferred an existence which would accordingly be a necessary one; or again that, by virtue of the nature or definition of a thing merely *thought*, it becomes necessary for the thing to be no longer merely thought, but actually to exist. Descartes had applied this false fundamental idea to the concept of the *ens perfectissimum*;[53] but Spinoza took that of *substantia* or *causa sui*,[54] (this latter expresses a *contradictio in adjecto*);[55] see his first definition which is his πρῶτον ψεῦδος[56] in the introduction to the *Ethics*, and then proposition 7 of the first book. The difference between the fundamental concepts of the two philosophers consists almost entirely in the expression; but underlying their use as starting-points, and hence as something given, there is with the one as with the other the mistake of making a representation of intuitive perception arise out of an abstract representation; whereas, in point of fact, every abstract representation arises out of the representation of intuitive

---

[53] ['The most perfect of all beings'.]

[54] ['Cause of itself': that whose nature cannot be conceived as not existing.]

[55] [A logical inconsistency between a noun and its modifying adjective, such as 'round square', 'wooden iron', 'cold fire', 'hot snow'.]

[56] ['The first false step', i.e. the fault in a premiss which is the cause of the conclusion's also being false.]

perception and so is based thereon. Thus we have here a fundamental ὕστερον πρότερον.[57]

Spinoza burdened himself with a difficulty of a special kind by calling his one and only substance *Deus*; for this word was already used to designate quite a different concept, and he had continually to fight against misunderstandings that arose from the fact that the reader always associated with the word the concept usually designated thereby instead of the concept it was supposed to designate according to Spinoza's first explanations. If he had not used the word, he would have been spared long and distressing disquisitions in the first book. But he did this so that his teaching would meet with less opposition, an object in which he nevertheless failed. But then a certain ambiguity pervades his whole exposition which might, therefore, to some extent be called allegorical especially as he adopts the same course with one or two other concepts, as was previously observed (in the first essay). How much clearer and consequently better would his so-called *Ethics* have proved to be had he frankly expressed what was in his mind and had called things by their proper name! How much better it would have been if in general he had presented his ideas, together with their grounds, sincerely and naturally, instead of letting them appear laced up in the Spanish boots of propositions, demonstrations, scholia, and corollaries, in this garb borrowed from geometry. Instead of giving to philosophy the certainty of geometry, this garb rather loses all significance as soon as geometry with its constructions of concepts itself ceases to stand inside it. Hence the proverb also applies here: *cucullus non facit monachum.*[58]

In the second book he expounds the two modes of his one and only substance as extension and representation (*extensio et cogitatio*), which is obviously a false division, for extension exists simply and solely for and in the representation; and therefore it should not have been opposed but subordinated thereto.

Spinoza everywhere expressly and emphatically extols *laetitia* and sets it up as the condition and sign of every praiseworthy action, whereas he rejects absolutely all *tristitia*, although his Old Testament might have told him: 'Sorrow is

---

[57] ['Confusion of ground and consequent'.]
[58] ['The cowl does not make a monk.']

better than laughter: for by the sadness of the countenance the heart is made better' (Ecclesiastes 7:3). All this he does merely out of love for consistency; for if this world is a God it is an end in itself and must glorify and rejoice at its own existence, hence *saute Marquis! semper* gay, *nunquam* sad! Pantheism is essentially and necessarily optimism. This obligatory optimism forces Spinoza to many other false conclusions, the most conspicuous being the absurd and often revolting propositions of his moral philosophy, which in the sixteen chapter of his *Tractatus theologico-politicus* rise to real infamies. On the other hand, he occasionally loses sight of the conclusion where it would have led to correct views, for instance in his propositions regarding animals, which are as unworthy as they are false. (*Ethics*, Pt. IV, *Appendicis*, c. 26, et ejusdem Partis prop. 37, schol.) Here he speaks in accordance with the first and ninth chapters of Genesis, just as a Jew knows how to, so that we others, who are accustomed to purer and worthier doctrines, are here overcome by the *foetor judaicus*. He appears not to have known dogs at all. The revolting proposition with which the above-mentioned twenty-sixth chapter begins: *Praeter homines nihil singulare in natura novimus, cujus mente gaudere et quod nobis amicitia, aut aliquo consuetudinis genere jungere possumus,*[59] is best answered by a Spanish man of letters of our day (Larra, pseudonym Figaro, in *Doncel*, c. 33): *El que no ha tenido un perro, no sabe lo que es querer y ser querido.* (Whoever has never kept a dog does not know what it is to love and to be loved.) The deeds of cruelty which, according to Colerus, Spinoza was accustomed to practise on spiders and flies, for his own amusement and amid hearty laughter, correspond only too closely to his propositions that are here censured as well as to the aforesaid chapters of Genesis. By virtue of all this, Spinoza's *Ethica* is throughout a mixture of the false and the true, the admirable and the bad. Towards the end, in the second half of the last part, we see him vainly endeavouring to make things clear to himself. This he is unable to do, and so there is nothing left for him but to become *mystical*, as happens here. Not to be unjust to this undoubtedly great man, we must accordingly bear in

---

[59] ['Besides human beings, we know of no individual being in nature whose mentality could give us pleasure, and with whom we could be united through friendship or through any kind of association.']

mind that he still had too little at his disposal, hardly more than Descartes, Malebranche, Hobbes, and Giordano Bruno. The basic concepts of philosophy were not yet adequately elaborated, the problems not properly ventilated.

Leibniz too started from the concept of *substance* as something given, yet he kept mainly in view the fact that such a substance must be *indestructible*. For this purpose it had to be *simple*, since everything extended would be divisible and hence destructible; consequently it was without extension and thus immaterial. There remained, then, no other predicates for his substance than the immaterial or spiritual and hence perception, thinking, and desiring. He now assumed an immense number of such simple immaterial substances. Although these themselves were not extended, they were supposed to be the basis of the phenomenon of extension. He therefore defines them as *formal atoms* and *simple substances* (*Opera*, ed. Erdmann, pp. 124, 676), and gives them the name *monads*. And so these are supposed to be the basis of the phenomenon of the corporeal world and accordingly this phenomenon is a mere *appearance* without proper and immediate reality, such reality belonging merely to the monads that are to be found in and behind it. On the other hand, that phenomenon of the corporeal world is now brought about in the perception of the monads (namely of those that actually perceive which are very few, the majority being always asleep) by virtue of the pre-established harmony which the central monad produces entirely alone and at its own expense. Here we are somewhat involved in obscurity; but be that as it may, the mediation between the mere thoughts of these substances and that which is really and in itself extended is effected through a harmony that is pre-established by the central monad. Here it might be said that all is remainder. But to do justice to Leibniz, we must call to mind the method of regarding *matter* which was at the time put forward by Locke and Newton and according to which matter exists as absolutely dead, purely passive and will-less, endowed merely with mechanical forces, and subject only to mathematical laws. On the other hand, Leibniz rejects *atoms* and purely *mechanical* physics in order to put in its place a *dynamic* physics, in all of which he prepared the way for Kant. (See *Opera*, ed. Erdmann, p. 694.) In the first place (*Opera*, p. 124), re recalled the *formae substantiales* of the Schoolmen and accordingly arrived at the view that even the merely mechanical forces of matter, besides which scarcely any others were known or admitted at that time, must have something spiritual or immaterial underlying them. But he did not know how to make this clear to himself except through the extremely awkward fiction that matter consists of nothing but little souls that are at the same time formal atoms and exist for the most part in a state of stupor and yet possess an analogue of *perceptio* and *appetitus*. Here he was led astray, for, like all the others, he made knowledge instead of the will the basis and *conditio sine qua non*[60] of everything spiritual. I was the first to vindicate for the will the primacy due to it and in this way everything in philosophy was transformed. However, the attempt of Leibniz to base spirit and matter on one and the same principle merits recognition. We might even find in it a presentiment of my own teaching as well as of the Kantian, but *quas velut trans nebulam vidit.*[61] For underlying his monadology is the idea that matter is not a thing-in-itself, but a mere phenomenon, and therefore that the ultimate ground of even its mechanical action must be sought not in the purely geometrical, that is to say, in what belongs merely to the phenomenon, such as extension, motion, form, and hence that impenetrability is not a merely *negative* quality, but the manifestation of a positive *force*. The fundamental view of Leibniz which is here commended is most clearly expressed in some shorter French works, such as *Système nouveau de la nature*, and others that are taken from the *Journal des savans* and the edition of Dutens into the Erdmann edition, and in the letters etc., Erdmann, *Opera*, pp. 681–95. There is also a choice collection of Leibniz's relevant passages on pages 335–40 of his *Kleinere philosophische Schriften* translated by Köhler and revised by Huth, Jena, 1740.

On the whole, we always see in connection with this entire concatenation of strange dogmatic theories one fiction dragging in another as its support, just as in practical life one lie renders many others necessary. At the root of all this is the Cartesian division of all that exists into God and the world, and of man into spirit and matter; accruing to the latter division

---

[60] ['Indispensable condition'.]
[61] ['Which he saw through the mist as it were'.]

is everything else. Moreover, there is the error, common to these philosophers and to all who have ever lived, of placing our fundamental nature in knowledge instead of in the will, and hence of representing the will as secondary and knowledge as primary. These, then, were the fundamental errors against which nature and the reality of things protested at every step and to save which the *spiritus animales*, the materiality of animals, the occasional cause, the seeing of all things in God, pre-established harmony, monads, optimism, and all the rest of it, had then to be invented. With me, on the other hand, where things are tackled at the right end, everything fits in automatically, each thing appears in its proper light, no fictions are required, and *simplex sigillum veri*.[62]

Kant was not directly concerned with the problem of substance; he went beyond it. With him the concept of substance is a category and hence a mere form of thought *a priori*. In the necessary application of this form to sensuous intuitive perception, nothing is known as it is in itself; therefore the fundamental essence at the root of bodies as of souls may in itself be one and the same. This is his teaching. For me it paved the way to the insight that everyone's own body is only the intuitive perception of his will, a perception arising in his brain. Extended afterwards to all bodies, this relation resulted in the analysis of the world into will and representation.

Now that concept of *substance*, which had been made the principal concept of philosophy by Descartes, true to Aristotle, and with the definition of which Spinoza accordingly begins, although after the manner of the Eleatics, appears on close and honest investigation to be a higher yet unjustified abstraction of the concept *matter*. Such abstraction together with matter was supposed also to include the supposititious child, *immaterial substance*, as I have explained in detail in my 'Criticism of the Kantian Philosophy' at the end of the first volume of my chief work. But apart from this, the concept of *substance* is useless as the starting-point of philosophy because in any case it is *objective*. Thus everything objective is for us always only mediate; the subjective alone is the immediate; and so this must not be passed over, but must be made the absolute starting-point. Now this has also been done by Descartes; indeed he was the

[62] ['Simplicity is the stamp of truth.']

first to recognize and do it, and for this reason with him a new main epoch of philosophy begins. But he does this only as a preliminary at the very first rush, after which he at once assumes the objective absolute reality of the world on the credit of the trustworthiness of God, and from now on he philosophizes in a wholly objective manner. Moreover, in this respect he really makes himself guilty of a serious *circulus vitiosus*.[63] Thus he demonstrates the objective reality of the objects of all our representations of intuitive perception from the existence of God as their author whose trustworthiness does not admit of his deceiving us. But he demonstrates the existence of God himself from the innate representation we are supposed to have of him as the all-perfect being. *Il commence par douter de tout, et finit par tout croire*,[64] says one of his countrymen of him.

Berkeley was, therefore, the first to treat the subjective starting-point really seriously and to demonstrate irrefutably its absolute necessity. He is the father of idealism; but this is the foundation of all true philosophy which has since been retained generally, at any rate as the starting-point, although every subsequent philosopher has attempted different modulations and variations of it. Thus even Locke started from the subjective in that he conceded a great part of the properties of bodies to our sense-impression. It must be noted, however, that his reduction of all *qualitative* differences, as secondary qualities, to merely *quantitative*, namely of size, shape, position, and so on, as the only primary, i.e. objective qualities, is still basically the doctrine of Democritus, who likewise reduced all qualities to the form, composition, and position of atoms. This can be seen with special clearness from Aristotle's *Metaphysics*, Book I, chap. 4, and from the *De sensu* of Theophrastus, cc. 61–5. To this extent, Locke was a reviver of the Democritean philosophy, as Spinoza was of that of the Eleatics. He too really paved the way for the subsequent French materialism. Yet through this preliminary distinction of the subjective element from the objective in intuitive perception, he led directly up to Kant who, following his direction and track in a much higher sense, managed clearly to separate the subjective from the objective. In this process, of course, so much now accrued to the subjective, that the

---

[63] ['Vicious circle'.]
[64] ['He begins by doubting everything and ends by believing everything'.]

objective remained only as a wholly obscure point, as something that could not be further known—a thing-in-itself. Now I have again reduced this to the essential reality that we come across in our self-consciousness as the will; thus here also I have again returned to the subjective source of knowledge. But it could not have turned out otherwise just because, as I have said, everything objective is always only secondary, that is to say, a representation. Therefore we must look for the innermost kernel of beings, namely the thing-in-itself, certainly not outside us, but only within ourselves and hence in the subjective as that which alone is immediate. Moreover there is the fact that, with the objective, we can never reach a point of rest, something ultimate and original, because there we are in the domain of *representations*. But these all have as their essential form the *principle of sufficient reason* in its four aspects, whereupon every object at once falls under and submits to the demand of that principle. For example, an assumed objective absolute is at once besieged with the destructive questions Whence? and Why? before which it must give way and fall. It is different when we are immersed in the silent, though obscure, depths of the subject. But here, of course, we are threatened with the danger of falling into mysticism. We can, therefore, draw from this source only what is in fact true, accessible to each and all, and consequently absolutely undeniable.

The *dianoiology* which, as the result of investigations since Descartes, was current until Kant, is found *en résumé* presented with naïve distinctness in Muratori, *Della fantasia*, chaps. 1–4 and 13. Locke there appears as a heretic. The whole is a nest of errors whereby it can be seen how very differently I conceived and presented it after having Kant and Cabanis as predecessors. The whole of that dianoiology and psychology is built on the false Cartesian dualism; in the whole work everything must now be reduced to this dualism, *per fas et nefas*,[65] including many correct and interesting facts that are introduced. The whole procedure as a type is interesting.

§ 13
Some further Elucidations of the Kantian Philosophy
As the motto for the *Critique of Pure Reason* a passage from Pope

[65] ['By hook or by crook'.]

would be very appropriate (*Works*, vol. vi, p. 374, Basel edn.). It was written some eighty years earlier and says: 'Since 'tis reasonable to doubt most things, we should most of all doubt that reason of ours which would demonstrate all things.'

The real spirit of the Kantian philosophy, its fundamental idea and true meaning, may be conceived and presented in many different ways. Such different turns of phrase and expressions of the matter will be suitable, some more than others according to the diversity of minds, for disclosing to this or that man a true understanding of that profound and therefore difficult teaching. The following is one more attempt of this kind wherein I undertake to shed some light on Kant's profundity.[66]

Mathematics is based on *intuitive perceptions* on which its proofs are supported; yet because such perceptions are not empirical but *a priori*, its theories are apodictic. Philosophy, on the other hand, has mere *concepts* as the given element from which it starts and which is to impart necessity (apodicticity) to its proofs. For it cannot rely directly on merely *empirical* intuitive perception because it undertakes to explain the universal of things not the particular, its purpose being to lead beyond what is empirically given. Now there remains for it nothing but universal concepts since these, of course, are not what appertains to intuitive perception and are not purely empirical. Such concepts must, therefore, furnish the foundation of its theories and proofs, and a start must be made from them as something present and given. Accordingly, philosophy is now a science from mere *concepts*, whereas mathematics is a science from the *construction* (intuitive presentation) of its concepts. Strictly speaking, however, it is only the demonstration or argumentation of philosophy that starts from mere *concepts*. Thus this demonstration cannot start, like the mathematical, from an *intuitive perception* because such would have to be either purely *a priori* or empirical; the latter gives no apodicticity and the former furnishes only mathematics. If,

---

[66] Here I observe once for all that the pagination of the first edition of the *Critique of Pure Reason*, from which I usually quote, is also appended to Rosenkranz's edition.

[The page numbering of the German first edition is given in square brackets in the text of Prof. Max Müller's English translation (1881: repr. with additions, 1896) of the *Critique of Pure Reason*.]

therefore, it tries somehow to support its doctrines by demonstration or argumentation, this must consist in the correct logical inference from concepts that are taken as a basis. Things had gone on quite well in this direction throughout the long period of Scholasticism and even in the new epoch established by Descartes, so that we see even Spinoza and Leibniz follow this method. But at last it had occurred to Locke to investigate the *origin* of concepts, and the result had been that all universal concepts, however, abstract they may be, are drawn from experience, in other words, from the actual existing, sensuously perceivable, empirically real world, or else from inner experience such as is afforded to everyone by empirical self-observation. Consequently, those concepts derive their whole content only from these two; and so they can never furnish more than what outer or inner experience has put there. Strictly speaking, it should have been inferred from this that they never lead beyond experience, that is, they never lead to the goal; but with the principles drawn from experience Locke went beyond experience.

In further opposition to his predecessors and for the purpose of correcting Locke's doctrine, Kant showed that there are in fact some concepts which form an exception to the above rule and therefore do *not* originate from experience. But at the same time, he also showed that these are drawn partly from the pure, i.e. *a priori*, given intuitive perception of space and time, and that in part they constitute the peculiar functions of our understanding itself for the purpose of their use in experience that is regulated by them. Consequently, he demonstrated that their validity extends only to possible experience which is to be produced at all times through the medium of the senses, since they themselves are merely destined, on the stimulation of sensation, to generate in us that experience, together with all its events that conform to law. In themselves devoid of content, they therefore obtain all their material and content solely from *sensibility* in order then to produce therewith experience. Apart from this, however, they have no content or significance since they are valid only on the assumption of an intuitive perception that rests on sensation and refer essentially to this. Now from this it follows that they cannot furnish us with the guides to lead us beyond all possibility of experience; and again that *metaphysics is impossible* as being the science of that which lies beyond nature, that is, beyond the possibility of experience.

Now as the one element of experience, namely the universal, the formal, and the one that conforms to law, is knowable *a priori*, but for that very reason depends on the essential and regular functions of our intellect, whereas the other element, namely the particular, the material, and the contingent, springs from sensation, it follows that both are of *subjective* origin. From this it follows that the whole of experience together with the world presenting itself therein is a mere *phenomenon*, in other words, something existing primarily and directly only for the subject that knows it. Yet this phenomenon points to a *thing-in-itself* that underlies it and, as such, is nevertheless absolutely unknowable. These, then, are the negative results of the Kantian philosophy.

Here I must call attention to the fact that Kant speaks as though we were merely knowing beings and thus had absolutely no datum except the *representation*, whereas we certainly possess another in the *will* within us that is *toto genere* different from the representation. It is true that he also took into consideration the will, yet not in theoretical but only in practical philosophy, which with him is quite separate from the former. This he did simply and solely to establish the fact of the purely moral significance of our conduct and to set up thereon a moral faith as a counterpoise to the theoretical ignorance and thus to the impossibility of all theology, to which we revert in virtue of the foregoing.

Kant's philosophy, as distinct from, and indeed opposed to all others, is also characterized as *transcendental philosophy*, or more accurately as *transcendental idealism*. The expression 'transcendent' is not of mathematical but philosophical origin, for it was already familiar to the Schoolmen. It was first introduced into mathematics by Leibniz in order to express *quod Algebrae vires transcendit*,[67] and so all operations that cannot be carried out by ordinary arithmetic and algebra, as for example finding the logarithm of a number or vice versa; or finding the trigonometrical functions of an arc purely arithmetically, or vice versa; and generally all problems that can be solved only by a calculus carried to infinity. The Schoolmen,

[67] ['What transcends the power of algebra'.]

however, characterized as *transcendent* the highest of all concepts, namely those that were even more universal than the ten categories of Aristotle; even Spinoza uses the word in this sense. Giordano Bruno (*Della causa*, etc., Dial. 4), describes as *transcendent* the predicates that are more universal than the distinction between corporeal and incorporeal substance and belong therefore to substance in general. According to him they concern that common root in which the corporeal is one with the incorporeal and which is the true original substance; in fact he even sees therein a proof that there must be such a substance. Now in the first place, Kant understands by *transcendental* the recognition of the *a priori* and thus merely formal element in our knowledge *as such*, in other words, the insight that such knowledge is independent of experience, indeed prescribes for this even the unalterable rule whereby it must turn out. Such insight is bound up with the understanding why such knowledge is this and has this power, namely because it constitutes the *form* of our intellect, and thus in consequence of its subjective origin. Therefore, properly speaking, only the *Critique of Pure Reason* is transcendental. In contrast thereto he describes as *transcendent* the use, or rather misuse, of that purely formal element in our knowledge beyond the possibility of experience; this he also terms hyperphysical. Accordingly, *transcendental* means briefly 'prior to all experience'; *transcendent*, on the other hand, means 'beyond all experience'. Therefore Kant approves of metaphysics only as transcendental philosophy, that is to say, as the doctrine of the formal, *as such*, that is contained in our knowing consciousness, and of the limitation thereby entailed by virtue whereof the knowledge of things-in-themselves is for us impossible, since experience can furnish nothing but mere phenomena. Yet the word '*metaphysical*' is with him not entirely synonymous with 'transcendental'. Thus everything that is *a priori* certain but concerns experience is called by him *metaphysical*, whereas the teaching that it is *a priori* certain only on account of its subjective origin and as purely formal, is alone called *transcendental*. *Transcendental* is the philosophy that makes us aware of the fact that the first and essential laws of this world that are presented to us are rooted in our brain and are therefore known *a priori*. It is called *transcendental* because it *goes beyond* the whole given phantasmagoria to the origin thereof. Therefore, as I have said, only the *Critique of Pure Reason* and generally the critical (that is to say, Kantian) philosophy are transcendental.* On the other hand, the *Anfangsgründe der Naturwissenschaft* as well as the *Tugendlehre* and others are *metaphysical*.

However, the notion of a transcendental philosophy may be taken in an even deeper sense if we undertake to concentrate therein the innermost spirit of the Kantian philosophy, somewhat in the following way. The whole world is given to us only in a *secondary* manner as representation, as a picture in our head, as a brain phenomenon, whereas our own will is given to us immediately in self-consciousness. Accordingly, there occurs a separation, indeed a contrast, between our own existence and that of the world. All this is a mere consequence of our individual and animal existence with the abolition of which it therefore falls away. But until then, it is for us impossible to eliminate in thought that fundamental and original form of our consciousness, which is what is described as the division into subject and object, since all thinking and representing presuppose it. We therefore always accept and leave untouched that form as the primarily essential and fundamental constitution of the world, whereas it is in fact only the form of our animal consciousness and of the phenomena brought about by means thereof. But from this there arise all those questions concerning the beginning, end, limits, and origin of the world, our own continued existence after death, and others. Accordingly, they all rest on a false assumption that attributes to the thing-in-itself, and thus proclaims as the primary and fundamental nature of the world, that which is only the form of the *phenomenon*, that is, of *representations* produced by means of an animal cerebral consciousness. This is the meaning of the Kantian expression 'all such questions are *transcendent*.' They are, therefore, absolutely incapable of any answer not merely subjectively, but in and by themselves, that is to say, objectively. For they are problems that disappear entirely with the abolition of our cerebral consciousness and of the antithesis resting thereon; and yet they were raised as though they were independent of it. For instance, whoever asks whether he continues to exist after his death, abolishes *in hypothesi* his animal brain-consciousness; yet

---

* The *Critique of Pure Reason* has transformed ontology into dianoiology.

he asks about something that exists only on the assumption thereof, since that something rests on the form of consciousness, thus on subject, object, space, and time; and so he asks about his individual existence. Now a philosophy that brings to distinct consciousness all these conditions and limitations *as such*, is *transcendental* and, in so far as it vindicates for the subject the universal fundamental determinations of the objective world, it is *transcendental idealism*. It will gradually be seen that the problems of metaphysics are insoluble only in so far as a contradiction is already contained in the questions themselves.

Nevertheless, transcendental idealism does not by any means question the *empirical reality* of the world actually before us. On the contrary, it states merely that it is not unconditioned, since it has as its condition our brain-functions whence the forms of intuitive perception, time, space, and causality, arise; consequently, it states that this empirical reality itself is only that of a phenomenal appearance. Now if in this appearance a plurality of beings manifest themselves to us one of which is always passing away and another arising, yet we know that plurality is possible only by means of the intuitive form of space, and arising and passing away are possible only by means of the intuitive form of time, then we recognize that such a source of events has no *absolute* reality. In other words, we recognize that this course does not belong to the essence-in-itself that manifests itself in that phenomenal appearance. On the contrary, if we could withdraw those forms of knowledge like the glass from the kaleidoscope, we should have to our astonishment that essence-in-itself before us as something single, unique, enduring, imperishable, unchangeable, and identical, in spite of all apparent change, perhaps even down to quite individual determinations. In accordance with this view, the following three propositions may be stated:

(1) The sole form of reality is the present; only in this is the real to be met with directly and is contained always entirely and completely.

(2) The truly real is independent of time and hence is one and the same in every point of time.

(3) Time is the intuitive form of our intellect and is, therefore, foreign to the thing-in-itself.

These three propositions are at bottom identical. Whoever clearly sees their truth as well as their identity has made great progress in philosophy, since he has grasped the spirit of transcendental idealism.

How pregnant in general is Kant's doctrine of the ideality of space and time which he has expounded so dryly and baldly! On the other hand, absolutely nothing results from the pompous, pretentious, and purposely incomprehensible twaddle of the three notorious sophists who have drawn from Kant on to themselves the attention of a public that is unworthy of him. Before Kant, it may be said, we were in time; now time is in us. In the first case, time is *real* and, like everything lying in time, we are consumed by it. In the second case, time is *ideal*; it lies within us. First of all, then, the question concerning the future after death falls to the ground. For if I am not, then time also is no more. It is only a deceptive delusion that shows me a time which after my death proceeds without me. All three divisions of time, past, present, and future, are likewise my product, belong to me, but not I to any one of them in preference to another. Again another conclusion which might be drawn from the proposition that time does not belong to the essence-in-itself of things, is that, in some sense, the past is *not* past, but that everything, which has ever really and truly existed, must at bottom still exist, since time indeed is only like a stage waterfall that appears to flow downwards, whereas, being a mere wheel, it does not move from its place. Long ago in my chief work, I compared space analogously to a glass cut with many facets which enables us to see in countless reproduction that which exists singly. Indeed if at the risk of indulging in extravagant fancies we go still more deeply into the matter, it might appear to us as though, by a very vivid representation of our own very remote past, we were immediately convinced of the fact that time does not touch the real essence of things, but is only interpolated between this essence and ourselves, as a mere medium of perception after the removal of which all would again be there. On the other hand, our true and living faculty of memory wherein that remote past maintains an imperishable existence, testifies also to the fact that there is likewise in us something that does not grow old and consequently does not lie within the domain of time.

The main tendency of the Kantian philosophy is to demonstrate the complete *diversity of the real and the ideal*, after Locke had already made a start in this direction. Incidentally, we can say that the *ideal* is the form of intuitive perception that presents itself in space with all the qualities that are perceivable in it; whereas the *real* is the thing in and by itself, independent of its being represented in the head of another or in our own head. But the boundary between the two is difficult to draw, and yet it is precisely that whereon the question turns. Locke had shown that everything in that form which is colour, sound, smoothness, roughness, hardness, softness, cold, heat, and so on (secondary qualities), is merely *ideal* and hence does not belong to the thing-in-itself, since in those secondary qualities we are given not the being and essence, but merely the *action* of the thing. Indeed it is a very one-sided definite action, namely that on the quite specifically determined receptivity of our five sense-organs, by virtue whereof, for example, sound does not affect the eye, nor does light the ear. In fact, the action of bodies on the sense-organs consists merely in its putting them into a state of activity that is peculiar to them, almost in the same way as when I pull a thread that makes a musical clock play. On the other hand, Locke still left untouched extension, form, impenetrability, motion or rest, and number, as the real that belonged to the thing-in-itself—and he therefore called these primary qualities. Now with infinitely superior insight, Kant subsequently showed that even these qualities do not belong to the purely objective nature of things or to the thing-in-itself, and so cannot be absolutely *real*, since they are conditioned by space, time, and causality. But by their whole constitution and conformity to law, space, time and causality are given to us *prior* to all experience and are precisely known; and so they must lie preformed within us, as does the specific kind of receptivity and activity of each of our senses, Accordingly, I have stated plainly that those forms are the *brain's* share in intuitive perception, just as the specific sensations are the share of the receptive sense-organs.* And so according to Kant, the purely objective nature of things, which is independent of our representation

---

* Just as our eye produces green, red, and blue, so does *our brain* produce, *time, space,* and *causality* (whose objectified abstraction is *matter*). My *intuitive perception* of a body in space is the product of my sense-function and brain-function with *x*.

and our representing apparatus and which he calls the thing-in-itself and hence the truly real as distinct from the ideal, is already something utterly different from the form that presents itself to us in intuitive perception. For, properly speaking, neither extension nor duration can be attributed to the thing-in-itself, as it is supposed to be independent of space and time, although it imparts the power to exist to everything that has extension and duration. Even Spinoza has comprehended the matter as a whole, as can be seen from *Ethics*, Pt. ii, prop. 16 with the second corollary, also prop. 18, schol.

Locke's real as opposed to the ideal is at bottom *matter*, stripped it is true of all the qualities that he eliminates as secondary, that is to say, as conditioned through our sense-organs. But yet it is something, existing in and by itself as extended and so on, whose mere reflex or copy is the representation within us. Here I recall the *Fourfold Root*, para. 21, and the *World as Will and Representation*, vol. i, § 4, and vol. ii, chap. 4, the latter work in less detail, where I have explained that the essential nature of matter consists simply in its *action* and consequently that matter is through and through causality, and that, as every particular quality and hence every specific way of acting is disregarded when it is conceived as such, it is action or pure causality deprived of all specific determinations, causality *in abstracto*. For a thorough comprehension of this I ask the reader to refer to the above-quoted passages. But now Kant had already taught, although I was the first to give the correct proof of it, that all causality is only a form of our understanding and hence that it exists only for the understanding and in the understanding. Accordingly, we now see Locke's alleged real, namely matter, retreating in this way entirely into the ideal and thus into the subject, in other words, existing solely in the representation and for the representation. By his presentation Kant certainly deprived the real or thing-in-itself of materiality, but for him it also remained only a wholly unknown *x*. But I have at last demonstrated the truly *real*, the thing-in-itself, which alone has a real existence independent of the representation and its forms, to be the *will* within us, whereas hitherto this had been classed unquestionably with the *ideal*. Accordingly, it will be seen that Locke, Kant, and I are closely connected since in the interval of almost two hundred years we present the gradual development of a coherent, consistent, and uniform train of thought. David Hume may also be considered as a connecting link in this chain although, properly speaking, only with regard to the law of *causality*. With reference to him and his influence, I have to supplement the above discussion with the following remarks.

Locke, as well as Condillac and his disciples following in his footsteps, argue and indicate that a sensation entering a sense-organ must correspond to its cause outside our body, and also that the differences of such effect (sense-impression) must correspond to those of the causes, whatever these may ultimately be; from this results the distinction between primary and secondary qualities previously alluded to. With this they end and for them an objective world now stands out in space, a world consisting of nothing but things-in-themselves which are indeed colourless, odourless, noiseless, neither warm nor cold, and so on, but which are nevertheless extended, formed, impenetrable, movable, and countable. But the axiom itself, by virtue whereof that transition from the inner to the outer and that whole derivation and installation of things-in-themselves have taken place, thus the *law of causality*, has been assumed by them, as by all previous philosophers, to be self-evident, and its validity has been subjected to no investigation. Now Hume directed on to this his sceptical attack by doubting the validity of that law. For he stated that experience whence, according to that very philosophy, all our cognitions were said to be derived, could never furnish us with the causal connection itself but always only with the mere succession of states in time and thus never with a consequence but only with a mere sequence which, precisely as such, would always prove to be only contingent or accidental and never necessary. Now this argument, so opposed to common sense yet not easy to refute, induced Kant to investigate the true *origin* of the concept of causality. He found this to reside in the essential and innate form of our understanding itself and hence in the subject not the object, for it was not first brought to us from without. Now in this way, the whole of that objective world of Locke and Condillac was drawn back again into the subject, for Kant had shown the clue to it to be of subjective origin. For now the rule also is just as subjective as is the sense-impression and, in consequence of it, that impression is to be conceived as the effect of a cause; yet it is this cause alone that is intuitively perceived as the objective world. For the subject assumes an object outside itself merely in consequence of the peculiar characteristic of its intellect, namely that of presupposing a cause for every change. Thus the subject projects the object really out of itself into a space ready for the purpose, such space itself being likewise a product of the intellect's own and original constitution, and also the specific sensation in the sense-organs, at the instance of which the whole process occurs. Accordingly, Locke's objective world of things-in-themselves had been changed by Kant into a world of mere phenomena in our cognitive apparatus, and this the more completely in that the space in which they present themselves and also the time in which they pass were shown by him to be undeniably of subjective origin.

But in spite of all this, both Kant and Locke still allowed the thing-in-itself to continue, that is to say, something which would exist independently of our representations that furnish us with mere phenomena, and which would form the basis of such phenomena. Now to this extent Kant was here quite right; yet his justification for taking this view was not to be derived from principles laid down by him. Here, then, was the Achilles' heel of his philosophy, and when that inconsistency was demonstrated, it again had to forfeit the recognition it had obtained of absolute validity and truth; yet in the last resort it was in this respect unjustly treated. For it is quite certain that the assumption of a thing-in-itself behind phenomena, of a real kernel under so many shells, is by no means untrue; on the contrary, its denial would be absurd. It is only the way in which Kant introduced such a thing-in-itself and sought to unite it with his principles that was faulty. At bottom, therefore, it was only his presentation of the case (this word taken in the widest sense) and not the case itself that was overthrown by his opponents. In this sense, it could be asserted that the arguments used against him were really only *ad hominem* and not *ad rem*. In any case, the Indian proverb here again finds application: no lotus without a stem. Kant was guided by the truth certainly felt that there lies behind every phenomenon a being-in-itself whence such phenomenon obtains its existence; thus behind the representation there lies something represented. But he undertook to derive this from the given representation itself by the addition of its laws that are known to us *a priori*. Yet just because these are *a priori*, they cannot lead to something independent of, and different from, the phenomenon or representation; and so for this purpose we have to pursue an entirely different course. The inconsistencies in which Kant was involved through the faulty course taken by him in this respect were demonstrated to him by G. E. Schultze who in his ponderous and diffuse manner expounded the matter first anonymously in *Aenesidemus* (especially pp. 374–81), and then in his *Kritik der theoretischen Philosophie* (vol. II, pp. 205ff.). Against this Reinhold conducted Kant's defence, yet without any particular success so that the matter had to rest with the *haec potuisse dici, et non potuisse refelli.*[68]

Here I will clearly set forth once for all in my own way that which underlies the whole controversy and is really essential to the matter, independently of Schultze's conception thereof. A strict deduction of the thing-in-itself has never been given by Kant; on the contrary, he took it over from his predecessors, especially Locke, and retained it as something whose existence was not to be doubted since it was really self-evident; indeed to a certain extent, he had to do this. According to Kant's discoveries, therefore, our empirical knowledge contains one element that is demonstrably of subjective origin, and another whereof this is not the case. The latter element thus remains objective because there is no ground for regarding it as subjective.* Accordingly, Kant's transcendental idealism denies the objective essence of things or their reality that is independent of our apprehension in so far, of course, as the *a priori* in our knowledge extends yet no farther, just because the ground for denying does not go farther. Accordingly, he allows what lies beyond to remain and hence all such properties of things as cannot be constructed *a priori*. For the whole essential nature of the given phenomena, that is, of the corporeal world, is by no means *a priori* determinable by us; on the contrary, it is merely

---

* Everything has *two kinds of properties*, those that can be known *a priori*, and those that can be known only *a posteriori*. The former spring from the intellect that apprehends them, the latter from the essence-in-itself of the thing which is what we find in ourselves as will.

[68] ['This could be asserted and could not be refuted.']

the universal form of its phenomenal appearance, and this may be reduced to space, time, and causality, together with the entire conformity to law of those three forms. On the other hand, what is left undetermined by all those *a priori* existing forms and thus is contingent or accidental with regard to them, is just the manifestation of the thing-in-itself. Now the *empirical* content of the phenomena, that is to say, every closer determination thereof, every physical quality appearing therein, cannot be known otherwise than *a posteriori*. These empirical qualities (or rather their common source) are accordingly left to the thing-in-itself, as manifestations of its own essential nature through the medium of all those *a priori* forms. This *a posteriori* which appears in every phenomenon shrouded as it were in the *a priori* but yet imparts to every being its special and individual character, is accordingly the *material or substance* [*Stoff*] of the phenomenal world as opposed to its *form*. Now this material is in no way to be derived from the *forms* of the phenomenon which attach to the subject; for these were most carefully investigated by Kant and were definitely shown to be *a priori*. On the contrary it is still left over after the abstraction of everything that flows from those forms, and so it is found as a second wholly distinct element of the empirical phenomenon and as an addition that is foreign to them. On the other hand, it by no means comes from the caprice of the knowing subject; indeed it often stands in opposition to this. And so in view of all this, Kant did not hesitate to leave this *material or substance* of the phenomenon to the thing-in-itself and thus to regard it as coming entirely from without, because it must come from somewhere or, as Kant expresses it, it must have some ground. Now as we cannot possibly isolate such qualities as are knowable only *a posteriori*, and conceive them as separated from and purified of those that are *a priori* certain, but they always appear enveloped in the latter, Kant teaches that we know the *existence* of things-in-themselves, but nothing beyond this. Thus we know only *that* they are, not *what* they are; and so the *essential nature* of things-in-themselves remains with him an unknown quantity, an *x*. For the *form* of the phenomenon everywhere clothes and conceals the essential nature of the thing-in-itself. At best we can say that those *a priori* forms belong without distinction to all things as phenomena since they come from our intellect, but that things at the same time show a very considerable diversity. Therefore what determines these differences and hence the specific variety of things is the thing-in-itself.

Looked at in this way, therefore, Kant's assumption and presupposition of things-in-themselves, notwithstanding the subjective nature of all our forms of knowledge, seem to be perfectly justified and well grounded. Yet this assumption is shown to be untenable when its only argument, namely the empirical content in all phenomena, is closely examined and traced back to its origin. Thus in empirical knowledge and its source, namely the representation of intuitive perception, there certainly exists a *material or substance* that is independent of the form of that knowledge, a form that is known to us *a priori*. The next question is whether this substance is of objective or subjective origin, since only in the first case can it guarantee the thing-in-itself. And so if we pursue it to its origin, we find this to be nowhere but in our *sense-impression*. For it is change that occurs in the retina of the eye, in the auditory nerve, or in the tips of the fingers, and it brings about the representation of intuitive perception; in other words, it first sets in motion the whole apparatus of our forms of knowledge which lie ready *a priori*, the result of this play being the perception of an external object. To that change that is felt in the sense-organ the *law of causality* is first applied by means of a necessary and infallible *a priori* function of the understanding. With its *a priori* sureness and certainty, that law leads to a *cause* of that change and as such a cause is not within the arbitrary power of the subject, it now presents itself as something *external* thereto. This quality obtains its significance first by means of the form of *space*; but for this purpose such form is also added immediately by our own intellect. In this way, that cause which is necessarily to be assumed, at once presents itself in intuitive perception as an *object* in space; and this object bears as its intrinsic properties those changes that are effected in our sense-organs by the cause. The reader will find this whole process thoroughly and fully discussed in § 21 of the second edition of my essay *On the Principle of Sufficient Reason*. But now the sense-impression that provides the starting-point for this process and unquestionably the whole *material* for empirical intuitive perception, is something entirely subjective. All the *forms* of knowledge by means

whereof the objective representation of intuitive perception
arises from that material and is projected outwards, according
to Kant's absolutely correct demonstration, are also of subjective
origin. It is clear, therefore, that both the material and the
form of the representation of intuitive perception spring from
the subject. Accordingly, the whole of our empirical knowledge
is now resolved into two components both of which have their
origin *in ourselves*; namely the sense-impression and the forms
time, space, causality that are given *a priori* and hence are
embedded in the functions of our intellect or brain. Kant,
however, had added to these forms eleven other categories of the
understanding which were shown by me to be superfluous and
inadmissible. Consequently, the representation of intuitive
perception and our empirical knowledge resting thereon really
furnish no data for inferring things-in-themselves, and Kant
was not entitled to assume such in accordance with his principles. Like all previous philosophies, Locke's had also taken the
law of causality as absolute and so was justified in inferring from
the sense-impression external things that actually exist independently of us. This passage from the effect to the cause,
however, is the only way to reach directly from the internal
and subjectively given to the external and objectively existing.
But after Kant had conceded the law of causality to the
subject's form of knowledge, this way was no longer left open
to him. Moreover, he himself warned us often enough against
making a transcendent use of the category of causality, that is
to say, a use that goes beyond experience and its possibility.

In fact, the thing-in-itself is never to be arrived at in this
way, and not at all on the path of purely *objective* knowledge.
Such knowledge always remains representation, but as such it
is rooted in the subject and can never furnish anything really
different from the representation. But we can reach the
thing-in-itself only by our *shifting* once for all *the standpoint*, that
is to say, by starting from what *is represented* instead of, as hitherto, always merely from what *represents*. But for everyone this is
possible with one thing only which is also accessible to him
from within and is thus given to him in a twofold way. I refer
to his own body which stands out in the objective world
precisely as representation in space, but which at the same time
proclaims itself to his own *self-consciousness* as *will*. But in this

way, the will hands over the key first to a comprehension of all
its actions and movements that are produced by external causes
(here motives). Without that inner and direct insight into their
essence, such actions and movements would remain just as
incomprehensible and inexplicable to us as are the changes
that occur in accordance with natural laws and as manifestations of natural forces in all the bodies that are given to us in
objective intuitive perception alone. The will then furnishes
the key to an understanding of the permanent *substratum* of all
these actions in which all the forces for them are rooted, and
hence to the body itself. This direct knowledge which everyone
has of the inner essence of his own phenomenon, a phenomenon
that is otherwise given to him, like all others, only in objective
intuitive perception, must afterwards be transferred by analogy
to all the other phenomena that are given in the latter way
alone. Such knowledge then becomes the key to that of the
inner essence of things, that is, of things-in-themselves. And
so we can reach that knowledge only on a path that is entirely
different from the purely *objective* knowledge that remains mere
representation. Thus we can do so by availing ourselves of the
self-consciousness of the subject of knowledge that appears always
only as an animal individual, and by making it the exponent
of the *consciousness of other things*, i.e. of the intuitively perceiving
intellect. This is the path taken by me and is the only correct
one, the narrow portal to truth.

Now instead of pursuing this course, men confused Kant's
presentation with the essence of the matter; they believed that
with the former the latter was refuted; they regarded as
argumenta ad rem what were only *argumenta ad hominem*; and
accordingly, as a result of Schultze's attacks, they declared
Kant's philosophy to be untenable. Thus the field was now free
for sophists and humbugs. The first of this class to appear on
the scene was Fichte who, because the thing-in-itself had just
been discredited, at once prepared a system without any
thing-in-itself. Consequently, he rejected the assumption of
anything that was not through and through merely our
representation, and therefore let the knowing subject be all in
all or at any rate produce everything from its own resources.
For this purpose, he at once did away with the essential and
most meritorious part of the Kantian doctrine, the distinction

between *a priori* and *a posteriori* and thus that between the phenomenon and the thing-in-itself. For he declared everything to be *a priori*, naturally without any proofs for such a monstrous assertion; instead of these, he gave sophisms and even crazy sham demonstrations whose absurdity was concealed under the mask of profundity and of the incomprehensibility ostensibly arising therefrom. Moreover, he appealed boldly and openly to intellectual intuition, that is, really to inspiration. This, of course, sufficed for a public that lacked all power of judgement and was unworthy of Kant. It regarded excess as excellence and accordingly declared Fichte to be a philosopher far greater even than Kant. Indeed even today there is no lack of philosophical authors who endeavour to foist on to the new generation the false fame of Fichte which has now become traditional. They quite seriously assure us that what Kant merely attempted had been achieved by Fichte, and that *he* was really the right man. By their Midas-judgement in the second instance, these gentlemen betray their utter incapacity to understand anything of Kant. Indeed they reveal so palpably and clearly their deplorable want of understanding that it is to be hoped the rising and finally disillusioned generation will guard against wasting their time and ruining their minds on their numerous histories of philosophy and other writings. I wish to take this opportunity to call to mind a short work from which we can see the impression made on impartial and unprejudiced contemporaries by Fichte's personal appearance and conduct. It is called *Kabinet Berliner Charactere* and appeared in 1808 without indicating where it was printed; it is said to be by Buchholz, but of this I am not certain. We may compare this with what the lawyer Anselm von Feuerbach says about Fichte in the letters edited by his son in 1852, and also with *Schillers und Fichtes Briefwechsel*, 1847, and we shall obtain a more correct picture of this sham philosopher.

It was not long before Schelling, worthy of his predecessor, followed in Fichte's footsteps which, however, he forsook in order to proclaim his own invention, the absolute identity of the subjective and the objective, or of the ideal and the real. This implies that everything that rare minds like Locke and Kant had separated after an incredible amount of reflection and judgement, was to be again poured into the pap of that absolute identity. For the teaching of these two thinkers may be very appropriately described as the doctrine of the *absolute diversity of the ideal and the real, or of the subjective and the objective.* But now matters went farther from aberrations to aberrations. When once incomprehensibility of speech was introduced by Fichte and the semblance of profundity was put in place of thought, the seeds were scattered which were to result in one corruption after another and finally in the complete demoralization of philosophy and thus of the whole of literature, which has arisen in our day.*

Schelling was followed by a philosophical ministerial creature, to wit Hegel, who for political and indeed mistaken purposes was from above dubbed a great philosopher—a commonplace, inane, loathsome, repulsive, and ignorant charlatan, who with unparalleled effrontery compiled a system of crazy nonsense that was trumpeted abroad as immortal wisdom by his mercenary followers, and was actually regarded as such by blockheads, whereby such a complete chorus of admiration arose as had never before been known.[69] The extensive intellectual activity that was forcibly usurped by such a man resulted in the mental ruin of a whole generation of scholars. The admirer of this pseudo-philosophy has in store for him the ridicule of posterity, which is already preluded by the delightfully audible derision of *neighbours.* Or ought it not to sound melodious to my ears when the nation, whose learned caste has for thirty years thought nothing and less than nothing of my achievements and deemed them not worth a glance, obtains from neighbours the reputation of having throughout thirty years revered and even deified as the highest and most unheard-of wisdom, that which is thoroughly bad, absurd, and senseless and at the same time serves material ends? As a good patriot, I suppose I should indulge in praise of the Germans and of things German and be delighted at having belonged to this nation and to no other. But it is as the Spanish proverb says: *cada uno cuenta*

---

* Nowadays the study of the Kantian philosophy is still specially useful in showing us how low philosophical literature in Germany has sunk since the *Critique of Pure Reason* was written. Kant's profound investigations are in such striking contrast with the crude twaddle of today; and in connection with this we imagine we see, on the one hand, hopeful candidates and, on the other, barbers' assistants.

[69] See the preface to my *Fundamental Problems of Ethics.*

de la feria, como le va en ella. (Everyone reports about the fair according as it fared with him.) Go to the Democolacs and get praised! Solid, unwieldy, ministerially puffed-up charlatans and scribblers of nonsense, without mind and without merit, are what belong to the Germans, not men like myself. This is the testimony I have to give to them on parting. Wieland (*Briefe an Merck*, p. 239) calls it a misfortune to be born a German; Bürger, Mozart, Beethoven, and many others would have agreed with him; I also. It rests on the fact that σοφὸν εἶναι δεῖ τὸν ἐπιγνωσόμενον τὸν σοφόν,[70] or *il n'y a que l'esprit qui sente l'esprit.*[71]

One of the most brilliant and meritorious sides of the Kantian philosophy is unquestionably the *Transcendental Dialectic* whereby Kant undermined speculative theology and psychology to such an extent that no one has since been able, even with the best will in the world, to set them up again. What a benefit to the human mind! Or do we not see how, during the whole period from the revival of the sciences down to Kant, the thoughts of even the greatest men receive a twist and indeed are often put completely out of joint, as a consequence of those two absolutely inviolable assumptions that paralyse the whole mind, and are withdrawn from, and so are dead to, all investigation? Are not the primary and most essential views of ourselves and of all things confused and falsified when we start with the assumption that all this is produced and arranged from without according to notions and well-reflected designs by a personal and thus individual being? In the same way, man's fundamental essence is supposed to be one that thinks and he is said to consist of two wholly heterogeneous parts which have come together and have been welded without our knowing how, and which must now get on with each other as best they can in order soon to be separated again for ever *nolentes volentes.*[72] The powerful effect of Kant's critique of these notions and their grounds on all branches of knowledge is evident from the fact that, since then, at any rate in superior German literature, those assumptions appear at most only in a figurative sense and are no longer seriously made, being left for popular writings

---

[70] ['One must be a sage to recognize a sage.']
[71] ['The mind alone is capable of understanding the mind.']
[72] ['Willy-nilly'.]

and professors of philosophy who earn their living by them. In particular, our works on natural science keep free from such things, whereas in our view the English works are degraded by their modes of expression and diatribes alluding to them, or by their apologies.* Immediately before Kant, things were, of course, in this respect quite different. Thus we see even the eminent Lichtenberg, whose early education was pre-Kantian, stick in his essay on physiognomy to that antithesis of soul and body earnestly and with conviction, and thereby mar his case.

Whoever reflects on this high value of the *Transcendental Dialectic*, will not find it superfluous if here I go into it somewhat more specifically. In the first instance, therefore, I present connoisseurs and admirers of the *Critique of Reason* with the following attempt to conceive quite differently and thus to criticize the argument in the critique of rational psychology, for only in the first edition does this appear complete, whereas in subsequent editions it appears castrated. On pages 361ff., this argument is criticized under the title 'Paralogism of Personality'. For Kant's undoubtedly profound presentation thereof is not only extremely subtle and difficult to understand, but it can also be reproached with assuming, suddenly and without further justification, the object of self-consciousness, or in Kant's language of the inner sense, to be the object of a foreign consciousness, even of an outer intuitive perception, in order then to judge it in accordance with the laws and analogies of the corporeal world. On page 363 it ventures to assume two different times, one in the consciousness of the judged and one in that of the judging subject, which do not harmonize. I should, therefore, give quite a different turn to the aforesaid argument of personality and accordingly present it in the two following propositions.

* Since the above was written, things with us have changed. In consequence of the resurrection of time-honoured and ten-times-exploded materialism, philosophers have appeared from the druggist's shop and the dispensary, men who have learnt nothing but what belongs to their profession, and who now quite innocently and honestly lecture on their old-women's speculation and dispute over 'body and soul' and their relation to each other, as though Kant had just been born. Indeed (*credite posteri!* ['believe it, posterity!']), they show that the seat of the aforesaid soul is in the brain. Their audacity merits the reprimand that one must have learnt something to be allowed to join in the discussion and that they would be wiser not to expose themselves to the unpleasant allusions to apothecaries and the catechism.

(1) With regard to all motion generally, whatever its nature, we can establish *a priori* that it is primarily perceivable by comparison with anything at rest. From this it follows that even the course of time with everything therein could not be perceived unless there were something having no part in it, whose rest or repose we compare with the motion of that course. Here we naturally judge in accordance with the analogy of motion in space; but space and time must always serve mutually to elucidate each other. We must, therefore, represent to ourselves even time under the image of a straight line in order to construct it *a priori* by apprehending it in intuitive perception. Consequently, we cannot imagine that, if everything in our consciousness moved forward simultaneously and together in the flux of time, this forward movement would nevertheless be perceivable, but for this purpose we must assume something fixed past which time with its content would flow. For the intuitive perception of the outer sense, this is done by matter as the permanent substance under the change of accidents, as Kant also explains in the proof to the 'first analogy of experience', p. 183 of the first edition. Yet it is precisely in this passage that he makes the intolerable mistake, elsewhere censured by me and contradicting his own doctrine, of saying that it is not time itself that flows but only the phenomena therein. That this is fundamentally false is proved by the absolute certainty, implanted in us all, that, even if all things in heaven and on earth suddenly stood still, time would nevertheless continue its course undisturbed thereby; so that if nature were later on again set in motion, the question of the length of the previously existing pause would in itself be capable of a perfectly precise answer. If it were otherwise, time would also have to stop with the clock or have to go with the clock when this goes. But it is precisely these facts, together with our *a priori* certainty about them, that incontestably prove that time has its course and hence its essence in our heads, not outside. In the sphere of outer intuitive perception, as I have said, matter is that which persists and endures. With our argument of personality, on the other hand, it is a question merely of the perception of the *inner* sense, and into such perception that of the outer sense is also again taken up. I therefore said that, if our consciousness with its entire content moved

forward uniformly in the stream of time, we could not become conscious of this motion. For this, therefore, there must be in consciousness itself something that is immovable; yet this cannot be anything but the knowing subject itself which, unmoved and unaltered, contemplates the course of time and the change of its content. Before the eye of the knowing subject, life like a drama pursues its course to the end. We even feel how small a part the knowing subject itself has in this course when in old age we vividly conjure up in our minds the scenes of youth and childhood.

(2) Inwardly in self-consciousness, or in Kant's language through the inner sense, I know myself in *time* alone. Now *objectively* considered, there cannot be anything permanent and enduring in mere time alone because such a thing presupposes a duration, but this is simultaneity, and this again *space*. (The establishment of this proposition is found in my essay *On the Principle of Sufficient Reason*, § 18, and again in the *World as Will and Representation*, vol. i, § 4, and in my criticism of the Kantian philosophy.) Despite all this, however, I find myself actually as the permanent substratum of my representations which endures for ever, notwithstanding all the changes therein. This substratum is related to those representations precisely as matter is to its changing accidents, consequently it merits the name of *substance* just as does matter and, as it is not spatial and thus is not extended, it merits the name of *simple substance*. Now, as I have said, in mere time alone, nothing permanent can take place; yet on the other hand, the substance in question is perceived not by the outer sense and consequently not in *space*. Therefore to conceive this substance as something enduring in face of the flux of time, we must assume it as lying outside time and accordingly say that all object lies in time whereas the knowing subject proper does not. Now as there is also no cessation or end outside time, we should have in the knowing subject within us an enduring substance that is yet neither spatial nor temporal and consequently is indestructible.

Now to establish as a paralogism this argument of personality thus understood, we should have to say that its second proposition makes use of an empirical fact to which this other may be opposed, namely that the knowing subject is bound up with life and even with wakefulness, and that therefore its continuance during both these by no means proves that it can also exist apart therefrom. This actual permanence for the duration of the conscious state is still far removed, indeed *toto genere* different, from the permanence of matter (this source and sole realization of the concept *substance*). We know matter in intuitive perception and see *a priori* not merely its actual duration, but its necessary indestructibility and the impossibility of its annihilation. Yet it is on the analogy of this truly indestructible substance that we would fain assume in ourselves a *thinking substance* that would then be certain of an endless duration. Now apart from the fact that this latter would be the analogy with a mere phenomenon (with matter), the mistake, made by the dialectical reason in the above proof, consists in the fact that this reason now treats the permanence of the subject, in spite of the change of all the latter's representations in time, just like the permanence of matter that is given to us in intuitive perception and accordingly includes both under the concept of substance. This it does in order now to attribute to that so-called immaterial substance all that it can state of matter *a priori*, although under the conditions of intuitive perception, especially permanence throughout all time. Yet the permanence of this immaterial substance rather depends merely on the fact that it itself is assumed to exist in absolutely no time, let alone in all time, whereby the conditions of intuitive perception in consequence whereof the indestructibility of matter is stated *a priori*, are here expressly abolished, especially that of space. But precisely on this rests (according to the above-quoted passages in my works) the permanence of matter.

As regards the proofs of the immortality of the soul from its assumed *simplicity* and consequent *indissolubility* whereby the only possible kind of decay, the dissolution of the parts, is excluded, it may be said generally that all the laws concerning arising, passing away, change, permanence, and so on, which we know either *a priori* or *a posteriori*, apply solely to the *corporeal world* that is given to us objectively and is moreover conditioned by our intellect. Therefore as soon as we depart from this world and talk of *immaterial* beings or essences, we are no longer justified in applying those laws and rules in order to assert how the arising and passing away of such beings is possible or not, for here we lack all clues. Thus all such proofs of immortality from the simplicity of the thinking substance are ruled out. For the amphiboly lies in the fact that we talk of an immaterial substance and then introduce the laws of the material substance in order to apply them to it.

Nevertheless, the paralogism of personality, as I have conceived it, gives in its first argument the proof *a priori* that something permanent must reside in our consciousness, and in the second it demonstrates the same thing *a posteriori*. On the whole, the truth, as a rule underlying every error and also that of rational psychology, appears to have its root here. This truth is that, even in our empirical consciousness, an eternal point can certainly be shown, yet only a point, and moreover only shown and no more, without our obtaining therefrom material for further demonstration. Here I refer to my own teaching according to which the knowing subject is that which knows all but is not known. And so we regard it as the fixed point past which time with all the representations flows, since the very course of time can certainly be known only in contrast with something permanent. I have called this the point of contact of the object with the subject. With me the subject of knowledge, like the body, is a phenomenon of the will, and it objectively manifests itself as the brain-function of the body. As the sole thing-in-itself, the will is here the substratum of the correlative of all phenomena, i.e. of the subject of knowledge.

If we now turn to *rational cosmology*, we find in its antinomies pregnant expressions of the perplexity which arises from the principle of sufficient reason and has from time immemorial urged men to philosophize. Now the purpose of the following discussion is to emphasize this more clearly and plainly in a way somewhat different from that of Kant. Unlike the Kantian, this discussion does not operate merely dialectically with abstract concepts, but appeals directly to the intuitively perceiving consciousness.

Time can have no beginning and no *cause* can be the first. Both these are *a priori* certain and hence unquestionable; for all beginning is in time and therefore presupposes this; and every cause must have behind it one previous whereof it is the effect. How, then, could a first beginning of the world and things have ever taken place? (Accordingly, the first verse of the Pentateuch naturally appears to be a *petitio principii*,[73] and this in the most literal meaning of the term.) If, on the other hand, there had *not* been a first beginning, the actual present could not be *just now*, but would have already existed *long ago*; for between it and the first beginning we must assume some interval of time, yet definite and limited. But if we deny the beginning, that is to say, move it back into infinity, the interval of time also moves back. Yet even *if* we assume a first beginning, this in the last resort does not help us, for in this way we have arbitrarily cut off the causal chain and mere time will at once prove to be a difficulty. Thus the ever-renewed question: 'Why did not that first beginning occur even earlier?' will push it back more and more in beginningless time, whereby the chain of causes lying between it and us is then drawn up to such an extent that it can never become long enough to reach down to the actual present; accordingly, it would *never yet* have reached this. Now this is contradicted by the fact that the present actually *exists* now and even constitutes our only datum for the calculation. But the justification for the above very inconvenient question arises from the fact that the first beginning as such assumes no cause that preceded it and that for this reason it might just as well have occurred trillions of years earlier. Thus if the first beginning required no cause for its occurrence, it also did not have to wait for any; accordingly it was bound to have occurred infinitely earlier since nothing existed to prevent it. For as nothing need precede the first beginning as its cause, so nothing need precede it as its hindrance; and so it has absolutely nothing to wait for and never comes soon enough. Therefore in whatever point of time we put it, we can never see why it should not have existed much earlier. And so this pushes it back ever farther, and since time itself can have absolutely no beginning, an infinite time, an eternity, has always elapsed down to the present moment. Hence the pushing back of the world's beginning is also endless, so that every causal chain from it to us turns out to be too short, the result being that we never reach from it to the present moment. This comes from our

[73] ['Begging of the question'; a fallacy involving the assumption, as premises, of one or more propositions that are identical with (or equivalent to) the conclusion to be proved.]

lacking a given and fixed point of departure (*point d'attache*), and thus from our arbitrarily assuming somewhere such a point which, however, always retreats before our hands back into infinity. The result, then, is that, if we assume a *first beginning* and start therefrom, we never reach from it *down to the present moment*.

If, on the other hand, we start from the actually given *present*, then, as already stated, we never reach back to the *first beginning*. For every cause to which we proceed must always have been the effect of a previous cause which is again in the same case, and this cannot possibly come to an end. Therefore for us the world is now beginningless just as is infinite time itself; here our power of imagination is exhausted and our understanding obtains no satisfaction.

These two opposite views may accordingly be compared to a stick whose either end may be conveniently grasped while the other is prolonged for ever to infinity. However, the essence of the matter may be summed up in a sentence by saying that time, as being absolutely infinite, proves to be far too great for there to be in it a world that is assumed to be *finite*. But here at bottom the truth of the 'antithesis' in the Kantian antinomy is again confirmed; for if we start from what is alone certain and actually given, the real present, the beginninglessness of time is the result. On the other hand, the first beginning is merely an arbitrary assumption which as such cannot be reconciled with what we have said is the only certain and actual thing, namely the present. For the rest, we have to regard these considerations as disclosing the absurdities that result from an assumption of the absolute reality of time, and consequently as confirming Kant's fundamental teaching.

The question whether the world is limited or unlimited in *space* is not absolutely transcendent, but rather in itself empirical. For the matter still always lies within the realm of possible experience, and it is only our own physical mode of existence that prevents us from reducing it to reality. *A priori* there is no demonstrably certain argument here either for the one alternative or the other, so that the matter really resembles an antinomy in so far as considerable drawbacks present themselves with the one assumption as with the other. Thus a limited world in unlimited space vanishes to an infinitely small size, be it ever so large, and we ask for what purpose the remaining space exists. On the other hand, we cannot conceive that no fixed star[74] should be the remotest in space. Incidentally, the planets of such a star would have at night a starry heaven during only one-half of their year, but one without stars during the other half; and this would inevitably make a very weird and uncanny impression on the inhabitants. Accordingly, that question may also be expressed by asking: 'Is there a fixed star whose planets are in this predicament or not?' Here it appears to be obviously empirical.

In my criticism of the Kantian philosophy, I have shown to be false and illusory the whole assumption of the antinomies. With due reflection, however, everyone will at once recognize as impossible that concepts which are correctly drawn from phenomena and from the *a priori* certain laws thereof, but are then combined into judgements and conclusions according to the laws of logic, should lead to contradictions. For in the phenomenon itself that is given in intuitive perception or in the regulative connection of its links, there would inevitably be contradictions; and this is an impossible assumption. For that which relates to intuitive perception as such knows no contradiction at all; with reference to it, the term contradiction has no meaning or significance. Such a term exists merely in the abstract knowledge of reflection; thus either openly or covertly we can simultaneously assume and not assume something, in other words, we can contradict ourselves; but something actual and real cannot simultaneously be and not be. Zeno the Eleatic with his well-known sophisms and Kant also with his antinomies naturally tried to demonstrate the opposite of the foregoing. I therefore refer the reader to my criticism of the Kantian philosophy.

Kant's service to *speculative theology* has already been touched on in general. To emphasize this still more, I will now attempt to make the essence of the matter comprehensible as briefly as possible and in my own way.

In the Christian religion the existence of God is an established

---

[74] [It is possible that 'ein Fixstern', rather than 'kein Fixstern' should be the reading here. On this point the Translator consulted Arthur Hübscher, the editor of the German edition. Since 'kein Fixstern' does make sense, and since it is the reading of all the earlier editions from the first onwards, neither felt justified in making this emendation.]

fact beyond and above all investigation. This is as it should be; for here it properly belongs and is established by revelation. I therefore regard it as a mistake on the part of the rationalists, when they attempt in their dogmas to demonstrate the existence of God otherwise than from the Scriptures. In their innocence they do not know how dangerous is this pastime. Philosophy, on the other hand, is a science and as such has no articles of faith; accordingly in it nothing can be assumed as existing except what is either positively given empirically or demonstrated through indubitable conclusions. Now men naturally imagined that they had long been in possession of these when Kant disillusioned the world on this point and demonstrated so decisively even the impossibility of such proofs that no philosopher in Germany has again attempted to advance anything of the kind. Kant was perfectly justified in doing this; in fact he did something that was highly meritorious; for a dogma that presumes to stamp as a rogue everyone who refuses to accept it deserves once for all to be seriously put to the test.

Now as regards those so-called proofs, the position is as follows. Since the *reality* of the existence of God cannot be shown by empirical proof or evidence, the next step would really have been to establish its *possibility* in the course of which we should have encountered difficulties enough. Instead of this, the attempt was made to prove even its *necessity* and thus to demonstrate God as a *necessary being*. Now as I have shown often enough, *necessity* is never anything but the dependence of a consequent on its ground and hence the appearance or establishment of the consequents because the ground is given. Accordingly, for this purpose the choice lay between the four forms of the principle of sufficient reason, demonstrated by me, and it was found that only the first two could be used. Thus there arose two theological proofs, the cosmological and ontological, the one according to the principle of sufficient reason of becoming (cause), and the other according to the principle of sufficient reason of knowing. The first proof attempts to show that that *necessity* is *physical* according to the law of *causality* since it regards the world as an *effect* that must have a *cause*. This cosmological proof is then assisted and supported by the physico-theological. The cosmological argument is most strongly expressed in Wolff's version thereof which is as follows: 'If anything exists, there also exists an absolutely necessary being', by which is to be understood either the given thing itself or the first of the causes whereby it has attained to existence; the latter is then assumed. In the first place, this proof has the weakness of being a conclusion from the consequent to the ground, and to this form of conclusion logic denies all claims to certainty. It then ignores the fact, often pointed out by me, that we can think of something as *necessary* only in so far as it is the consequent and not the ground of another given thing. Moreover, applied in this way, the law of causality proves too much; for if it has had to carry us from the world back to the cause thereof, it does not allow us to stop here, but leads us further back to the cause of that cause, and so remorselessly on and on *in infinitum*. This is entailed in its very nature. Here we are in the same position as that of the magician's apprentice in Goethe, whose creature begins by order, it is true, but does not again stop. In addition, there is the fact that the force and validity of the law of causality extends only to the *form* of things, not to their matter. It is the clue to the change of forms and nothing more; matter remains untouched by all the arising and passing away of forms, a fact which we discern prior to all experience and therefore know with certainty. Finally, the cosmological proof is overthrown by the transcendental argument that the law of causality is demonstrably of subjective origin and is therefore applicable merely to *phenomena* for our intellect and not to the essence of *things-in-themselves*.* As I have

---

* If things are considered quite realistically and objectively, it is as clear as daylight that the world *maintains itself*. Organic beings subsist and propagate by virtue of their own inner and original vital force. Inorganic bodies bear within themselves forces whereof physics and chemistry are the mere description; and the planets proceed in their courses from inner forces by virtue of their inertia and gravitation. Hence for its subsistence the world needs no one outside itself. For this is *Vishnu*.

But to say that at some point in time this world with all its indwelling forces did not exist at all, but was produced out of nothing by a foreign force lying outside it, is a wholly vain and futile notion that is incapable of any proof or support, more especially as all its forces are bound up with matter, whose arising or passing away cannot even be conceived by us.

This conception of the world will do for *Spinozism*. It is very natural for men in their extreme anguish to have conceived everywhere beings who control the forces of nature and the course thereof in order to be able to invoke them. The Greeks and Romans, however, were content to let the matter rest with the control exercised by each being in its own sphere. It never occurred to them to say that one of them had made the world and the forces of nature.

said, the *physico-theological* proof is given as a subsidiary aid to the cosmological, and at the same time it tries to afford support, confirmation, plausibility, colour, and form to the assumption that is introduced by the cosmological proof. But it can always appear only on the assumption of that first proof of which it is the elucidation and amplification. Its method, then, consists in its raising that assumed first cause of the world to a being that knows and wills, since from the many consequents that might be explained by such a ground, it seeks to establish this ground by induction. But induction can at best give strong probability, never certainty; moreover, as I have said, the whole proof is one that is conditioned by the first. But now if we go into this favourite physico-theology more closely and seriously and test it in the light of my philosophy, it proves to be the working out of a fundamentally false view of nature. Such a view degrades and reduces the *immediate* phenomenon or objectification of the will to one that is merely *mediate*. Hence instead of recognizing in the beings of nature the original and primarily powerful action of the will which is without know-ledge and is for that very reason infallibly certain, it explains it as something merely secondary that has happened only in the light of knowledge and on the clue of motives. Accordingly, it conceives that which has been urged outwards from within as something that has been cut, constructed, and modelled from without. For if, as a thing-in-itself which is certaintly *not* representation, the will in the act of its objectification enters from its original nature into the representation, and we now proceed with the assumption that what exhibits itself in the representation is something brought about in the world of representation itself and thus in consequence of *knowledge*, then, of course, it presents itself as something possible only by means of an immeasurably perfect knowledge that takes in at a glance all objects and their concatenations, that is to say, as a work of supreme wisdom. On this point I refer to my essay *On the Will in Nature*, especially the chapter 'Comparative Ana-tomy', and to my chief work, vol. ii, chap. 26 at the beginning.

The second theological proof, the *ontological*, does not take, as I have said, the law of causality as its clue, but the principle of the ground or reason of knowing whereby the necessity of God's existence is here a *logical* one. Thus through a merely analytical judgement God's existence is here supposed to result from the concept of *God*, so that we cannot make this concept the subject of a proposition wherein he would be denied existence, namely because this would contradict the subject of the proposition. This is logically correct, but it is also very natural and a conjuring trick that is easily seen through. Thus after introducing the predicate of existence into the subject by means of the handle of the concept 'perfection' or even 'reality', which we used as *terminus medius*, we cannot fail subsequently to find it there again and now to expose it by an analytical judgement. But the justification for putting forward the whole concept is by no means demonstrated thereby; on the contrary, it was either invented quite arbitrarily, or was introduced by the cosmological proof whereby everything is reduced to physical necessity. Christian Wolff appears to have clearly seen this, for in his metaphysics he makes use of the cosmological argument alone and expressly mentions this. The ontological proof is found closely examined and assessed in the second edition of my essay *On the Fourfold Root of the Principle of Sufficient Reason*, § 7, and to this I therefore refer.

The two theological proofs certainly support each other, but yet do not stand on that account. The cosmological has the advantage of giving an account of how it arrived at the concept of a God, and now by its adjunct, the physico-theological proof, it makes this plausible. The ontological, on the other hand, cannot prove at all how it arrived at its concept of the most real of all beings. Therefore either it alleges that this concept is innate, or it borrows it from the cosmological proof, and then tries to support it by lofty-sounding sentences about the being that cannot be conceived except as existing, whose existence lies already in its concept, and so on. However, we shall not deny the invention of the ontological proof the merit of ingenuity and subtlety if we consider the following. To explain a given existence, we indicate its cause in reference to which it then shows itself to be a necessary existence; and this is considered to be an explanation. But, as I have shown often enough, this way leads to a *regressus in infinitum* and can, therefore, never reach anything final that would furnish a fundamental ground of explanation. Now the case would be different if the *existence* of any being could be actually inferred from its *essence* and thus from its mere concept or definition. Thus it would then be known as something *necessary* (which here, as everywhere, simply says 'something following from its ground') without being tied thereby to anything other than its own concept and consequently without its necessity being merely transitory and momentary, namely one that is itself again conditioned and accordingly leads to an endless series, as is always the case with *causal* necessity. On the contrary, the mere reason or ground of knowledge would then have transformed itself into a ground of reality and so into a cause, being thus admirably suitable now to serve as the ultimate and therefore firm point of departure for all causal series; we should then have what we are looking for. But we have already seen that all this is illusory and it actually looks as if even Aristotle wished to avoid such a sophism when he said: τὸ δὲ εἶναι οὐκ οὐσία οὐδένι *ad nullius rei essentiam pertinet existentia*[75] (*Posterior Analytics*, II. 7). Unconcerned about this, Descartes later advanced the concept of God as one that fulfilled all that was required, after Anselm of Canterbury had paved the way to a similar line of thought. Spinoza, however, produced the concept of the world as the only existing substance, which would accordingly exist *causa sui*, i.e. *quae per se est et per se concipitur, quamobrem nulla alia re eget ad existendum.*[76] He then confers on this world that is so established the title *Deus, honoris causa*, in order to make everyone satisfied. But it is still always the same *tour de passe-passe*[77] that tries to smuggle into our hands the *logically* necessary as something *really* necessary. Together with other similar deceptions, it finally gave rise to Locke's great investigation of the *origin* of concepts whereby the foundation of critical philosophy was now laid. A more detailed description of the method of those two dogmatists is contained in my essay *On the Principle of Sufficient Reason*, second edition, §§ 7 and 8.

Now after Kant had given the death-blow to speculative theology by his criticism thereof, he had to attempt to mitigate the impression thereby produced and thus to apply a palliative as an anodyne. This was analogous to the method of Hume who,

[75] ['Existence does not pertain to the essence of anything.']
[76] ['Cause of itself, i.e. which exists by and through itself and is conceived through itself; hence it requires nothing else in order to exist.']
[77] ['Conjuring trick'.]

in the last of his *Dialogues on Natural Religion,* as readable as they are inexorable, informs us that all this had been merely a joke, a mere *exercitium logicum.* Accordingly, Kant gave, as a substitute for the proofs of God's existence, his postulate of practical reason [*Vernunft*] and the moral theology resulting therefrom which, without any claim to objective validity for knowledge or theoretical reason, was to have complete validity in respect of conduct or for practical reason, whereby a faith without knowledge was then established so that people would at any rate have something in their hands. Properly understood, his exposition states merely that the assumption of a just God who rewards and punishes after death, is a useful and adequate *regulative scheme* for the purpose of explaining the serious, deeply felt, and ethical significance of our conduct and also of directing this conduct itself. And so to a certain extent, he set up an allegory of the truth so that in this respect, which alone is ultimately the main point, that assumption can take the place of truth, although theoretically or objectively it cannot be justified. An analogous scheme of similar tendency, but containing very much more truth, of greater plausibility, and therefore of more immediate value, is the dogma of Brahmanism, of a rewarding and punishing metempsychosis. According to this, we must be reborn at some time in the form of every being that has been injured by us so that we may suffer the same injury. Therefore Kant's moral theology has to be taken in the sense indicated, since we must here bear in mind that he himself dare not speak as plainly as is done here about the real state of affairs. On the contrary, by setting up the monstrosity of a *theoretical* doctrine of merely practical validity, he reckoned on the *granum salis*[78] of the more intelligent and judicious. The theological and philosophical writers of this later period, which is far removed from the Kantian philosophy, have therefore usually tried to make it appear as though Kant's moral theology were a real dogmatic theism, a new proof of the existence of God. But Kant's moral theology is not so at all; on the contrary, it is valid solely within morality, merely for the purpose of morality, and not a hair's-breadth beyond.

Not even the professors of philosophy rested content with this for long, although they were greatly embarrassed by Kant's

[78] ['Grain of salt'.]

criticism of speculative theology. For they had recognized from early times that speculative theology was their special vocation for demonstrating the existence and attributes of God and for making him the main subject of their philosophizing. And so when the Scriptures tell us that God feeds the ravens in the field, I must add that he feeds also the professors of philosophy in their chairs. Indeed even at the present day, they boldly assert that the Absolute (well known as the new-fangled title for God) and its relation to the world are the proper theme of philosophy, and now, as always, they are concerned with more closely defining this and with amplifying it in their imagination. For naturally governments, who provide the money for such philosophizing, would like to see coming from the philosophical lecture-rooms good Christians and keen church-goers. How, then, were the gentlemen of the lucrative philosophy bound to feel when Kant had so completely upset their concept by his demonstration that all the proofs of speculative theology are untenable, and that all cognitions concerning their chosen theme are absolutely inaccessible to our intellect? At first they had tried to help themselves by their well-known familiar method of ignoring and then of disputing; but in the long run this did not work. They then eagerly took up the assertion that the existence of God is assuredly incapable of any proof, nor is it in need of any; for, they said, it was self-evident, the most settled affair in the world which we could not possibly doubt since we had a 'divine consciousness'.* They asserted that our faculty of reason [*Vernunft*] was the organ for a direct knowledge of supramundane things, and that information concerning them was immediately *discerned* [*vernommen*] by that faculty which was therefore called *discernment* or *reason* [*Vernunft*]! (Here I earnestly request the reader to refer to my essay *On the Principle of Sufficient Reason*, 2nd edn., § 34, also to my *Fundamental Problems of Ethics*, 'Basis of Ethics', para. 6 at end, and finally also to my 'Criticism of the Kantian Philosophy' at the end of the first

---

* As regards the *genesis* of this divine consciousness, we recently had a remarkable pictorial illustration, namely a copper engraving depicting a mother and her three-year-old child kneeling on the bed with hands folded, whom she is teaching to pray. This certainly is a frequent occurrence constituting the genesis of the divine consciousnesss; for there is no doubt that after the brain has been moulded in this way at the tenderest age and in the first stage of its development, the divine consciousness has become as firmly embedded as if it were actually inborn.

volume of my chief work.) Yet according to others, the faculty of reason furnished mere surmises or presentiments; on the other hand, others again had even intellectual intuitions! Yet again others invented absolute thought, i.e. one by which man need not look round at things, but in divine omniscience settles how they are once for all. This is unquestionably the most convenient of all those inventions. They one and all seized on the word 'Absolute', which is simply nothing but the cosmological proof *in nuce*, or rather so greatly contracted that, having become microscopic, it escapes the eye, slips through unnoticed, and is now palmed off as something self-evident. For since the Kantian *examen rigorosum*, it dare not appear again in its true form, as I have discussed at greater length in the second edition of my essay *On the Principle of Sufficient Reason*, para. 20 and also in my 'Criticism of the Kantian Philosophy' at the end of the first volume of my chief work. I am no longer able to state who was the first, some fifty years ago, to use the trick of smuggling in *incognito*, under this exclusive word *absolute*, the exploded and proscribed cosmological proof. The trick, however, was wholly in keeping with the abilities of the public, for even at the present time the word 'absolute' passes current as true coin. In short, despite the *Critique of Reason* and its proofs, the professors of philosophy have never yet lacked authentic accounts of God's existence and of his relation to the world. According to these men, philosophizing is really said to consist in a detailed statement of such accounts. But as we say, 'copper money, copper wares', so too is this self-evident God of theirs; he has neither hand nor foot. Therefore they keep him hidden behind a mountain or rather behind a noisy edifice of words, so that hardly a sign of him is visible. If only they could be compelled clearly to explain themselves as to what is really to be understood by the word God, we should then see whether he is self-evident. Not even a *natura naturans*[79] (into which their God often threatens to pass) is self-evident, for we see Leucippus, Democritus, Epicurus, and Lucretius construct the world without it. But despite all their errors, these men were much more estimable than a legion of weathercocks whose trade-philosophy turns with the wind. But a *natura naturans* is still far from being a

[79] ['Nature naturing', 'creative nature'; the term is used by Spinoza and other philosophers.]

God; on the contrary, there is contained in the concept of this simply the knowledge that, behind the ever-fleeting and restlessly changing phenomena of the *natura naturata*,[80] there must lie concealed an imperishable and untiring force by virtue whereof they constantly renewed themselves, since this force itself would not be affected by their decline and extinction. Just as the *natura naturata* is the subject of physics, so is the *natura naturans* that of metaphysics. This will ultimately lead us to see that even we ourselves form a part of nature and consequently possess in ourselves not only the nearest and clearest specimen of *natura naturata* as well as of *natura naturans*, but even the only one accessible to us *from within*. Now as a serious and careful reflection of ourselves discloses to us the *will* as the core of our true being, in this we have an immediate revelation of the *natura naturans* and are therefore justified in transferring this to all other beings that are only one-sidedly known to us. We thus arrive at the great truth that the *natura naturans* or thing-in-itself is the will in our heart, whereas the *natura naturata* or the phenomenon is the representation in our head. Yet even apart from this result, it is sufficiently obvious that the mere distinction between a *natura naturans* and a *natura naturata* is still far from being theism; indeed it is not even pantheism. For the addition of certain moral qualities to pantheism would be necessary (if this is not to be a mere mode of expression), qualities such as goodness, wisdom, bliss, and so on, which obviously do not belong to the world. Moreover, pantheism is a concept that invalidates itself, since the concept of a God presupposes as its essential correlative a world different from him. If, on the other hand, the world itself is to take over his role, there remains simply an absolute world without God, and so pantheism is only a euphemism for atheism. But this last expression in its turn contains something underhand since it assumes in advance that theism is self-evident, whereby it cunningly evades the *affirmanti incumbit probatio*,[81] whereas it is rather so-called atheism which has the *jus primi occupantis*[82] and has first to be driven from the field by theism. Here I venture to remark that men come into the world uncircumcised and thus not as Jews. But

[80] ['Nature natured', 'created nature'; the complex of all created things; the term is used by Spinoza and other philosophers.]

[81] ['Proof is incumbent on the man who makes a positive assertion.']

[82] ['The right of first occupancy'.]

even the assumption of some cause of the world different therefrom is still not theism. For this demands a world-cause that is not only different from the world, but is intelligent, that is to say, knows and wills, and so is personal and consequently also individual; it is only such a cause that is indicated by the word God. An impersonal God is no God at all, but merely a word wrongly used, a misconception, a *contradictio in adjecto*,[83] a shibboleth for professors of philosophy, who, having had to give up the thing, are anxious to slip through with the word. On the other hand, personality, in other words, self-conscious individuality, which first *knows* and then *wills* in accordance with what is known, is a phenomenon known solely from the animal nature that exists on our small planet. It is so intimately associated with such nature that we are not only not justified in, but are also not even capable of, conceiving it as separate from, and independent of, that nature. But to assume a being of such a kind as the origin of nature herself, indeed of all existence generally, is a colossal and extremely bold idea. We should be astonished at it if we heard it for the first time and it had not become familiar indeed second nature to us, I might almost say a fixed idea, by dint of the earliest inculcation and constant repetition. And so I may mention incidentally that for me nothing has testified to the genuineness of Caspar Hauser[84] so much as the statement that so-called natural theology, as expounded to him, did not appear to enlighten him as much as had been expected. Moreover (according to the *Brief des Grafen Stanhope an den Schullehrer Meyer*), he professed a peculiar awe for the sun. Now to teach in philosophy that that fundamental theological idea is self-evident and that the faculty of reason is merely the ability directly to grasp it and to recognize it as true, is a bold and shameless pretence. Not only have we no right, without the most valid proof, to assume such an idea in philosophy, but it is by no means essential even to religion. This is attested by the religion that has the greatest number of followers on earth, Buddhism, which is very ancient and now numbers three hundred and seventy million followers. It is a highly

[83] [A logical inconsistency between a noun and its modifying adjective, such as 'round square', 'wooden iron', 'cold fire', 'hot snow'.]

[84] Caspar Hauser (1812?–33) was a German foundling youth of mysterious and controversial origins.

moral and even ascetic religion and supports the most numerous body of clergy; yet it does not accept such an idea at all; on the contrary, it expressly rejects this out of hand and is thus according to our notions *ex professo* atheistic.[85]

According to the foregoing, anthropomorphism is in every way an essential characteristic of theism. Indeed such anthropomorphism consists not merely in the human form or even only in human emotions and passions, but in the fundamental phenomenon itself, namely that of a will that is equipped with an intellect for its guidance. As I have said, such a phenomenon is known to us only from animal nature and most completely from human nature, and it is conceivable solely as individuality which, when it is rational, is called personality. This is also confirmed by the expression 'as true as God lives'; he is just a living being, that is, one who wills with knowledge. Precisely on this account, a God needs a heaven wherein he is enthroned and reigns. Much more for this reason than on account of the expression in the Book of Joshua was the Copernican system of the universe at once received by the Church with rage and anger; and accordingly a hundred years later, we find Giordano Bruno as the champion both of that system and of pantheism. Those who attempt to clear theism of anthropomorphism, while imagining that they touch only the shell, really strike at its

[85] In an essay on his religion given by him to a Catholic bishop, the Zaradobura, the Chief Rahan (High Priest) of the Buddhists in Ava, reckons as one of the six damnable heresies the doctrine that a being exists who created the world and all things therein and is alone worthy of worship; Francis Buchanan, *On the Religion of the Burmas*, in the *Asiatic Researches*, vol. vi, p. 268. Here it is also worth mentioning what is said in the same series, vol. xv, p. 148, namely that the Buddhists do not bow down before any idol, giving as their reason the fact that the primary being permeates the whole of nature and consequently is also in their heads. Similarly, I. J. Schmidt, the profoundly erudite orientalist of St. Petersburg Academy, says in his *Forschungen im Gebiete der älteren Bildungsgeschichte Mittelasiens*, St. Petersburg, 1824, p. 180: 'The system of Buddhism knows no eternal, uncreated, single, divine being who existed prior to all time and created everything visible and invisible. This idea is quite foreign to it, and not the slightest trace of it is found in Buddhist books. Just as little is there a creation', and so on. Where, then, is the 'divine consciousness' of the professors of philosophy who have been embarrassed by Kant and the truth? How is this to be reconciled with the fact that the language of the Chinese, who constitute about two-fifths of the human race, has no expressions at all for *God* and *Creation*? Thus the first verse of the Pentateuch cannot be translated into Chinese, to the great perplexity of the missionaries whom Sir George Staunton wished to help with his book entitled: *An Inquiry into the proper mode of rendering the word God in translating the Sacred Scriptures into the Chinese Language*, London, 1848.

innermost core. In their efforts to conceive its object in the abstract, they sublimate it to a vague, hazy form whose outline gradually vanishes entirely in the endeavour to avoid the human figure. In this way, the fundamental childlike idea itself is finally evaporated to nothing. But in addition to this, the rationalist theologians who are given to making such attempts can be reproached with flatly contradicting Holy Writ which says: 'God created man in his own image; in the image of God created he him.' Hence away with the jargon of the professors of philosophy! There is no other God than God, and the Old Testament is his revelation in particular the Book of Joshua.*

With Kant we could, of course, in a certain sense call theism a practical postulate, yet in a sense quite different from that meant by him. Thus theism is in fact a product not of *knowledge* but of the *will*. If it were originally *theoretical* how could all its proofs be so untenable? But it springs from the will in the following way. The constant need, now gravely oppressing and then violently agitating man's heart (will), keeps him in a permanent state of fearing and hoping, whereas the things *about* which he hopes and fears are not in his power; indeed the connection of the causal chains whereon such things are produced can be traced by his knowledge for only a short distance. This need, this constant fearing and hoping, cause him to hypostasize personal beings on whom everything depends. Of such it may now be assumed that, like other persons, they will be susceptible to entreaty and flattery, service and gift, and will therefore be more tractable than the rigid necessity, the inexorable and unfeeling forces of nature, and the mysterious powers of the course of the world. Now to begin with, as is natural and was very appropriately carried out by the ancients, there were several of these gods, according to the diversity of circumstances. Later on, through the need for bringing into knowledge consistency, order, and unity, these gods were subordinated or even reduced to one and, as Goethe once remarked to me, this one is very undramatic, for with only one person we can do nothing. The essential thing, however, is the intense desire of tormented man to throw himself down and cry out for help in his frequent, woeful, and great distress, and also in regard to his

* From God, who was originally Jehovah, philosophers and theologians have stripped off one covering after another until in the end nothing is left but the word.

eternal happiness. A man relies rather on the grace of another than on his own merit. This is one of the main supports of theism. And so in order that his heart (will) may have the relief of prayer and the consolation of hope, his intellect must create for him a God; but not conversely, that is, he does not pray because his intellect has correctly and logically deduced a God. Let him be without needs, desires, and requirements, a merely intellectual will-less being, then he needs no God and makes none. In its grave affliction the heart, i.e. the will, needs to call for almighty and consequently supernatural assistance. And so because a prayer is to be offered up, a God is hypostasized and not conversely. Hence the theoretical element in the theology of all nations is very different as regards the number and nature of the gods; but they all have in common the fact that they can and do help when they are served and worshipped because this is the point on which everything depends. But this is at the same time the birthmark whereby we recognize the descent of all theology, namely that it has sprung from the *will*, from the heart not from the head or knowledge, as is pretended. In conformity with this, is also the fact that Constantine the Great and Chlodowig, King of the Franks, changed their religion because they hoped from the new god for better support in war. There are a few races who, as it were, prefer the minor key to the major and have, instead of gods, merely evil spirits; through sacrifice and prayer these are persuaded not to do harm. Speaking generally, there is no great difference in the result. Similar races appear also to have been the original inhabitants of the Indian peninsula and Ceylon before the introduction of Brahmanism and Buddhism; and even now their descendants are said to have to some extent such a cacodemonological religion, just as do many savage races. Hence springs the Cappuism that is mixed with Sinhalese Buddhism. Similarly the devil-worshippers of Mesopotamia visited by Layard belong to this category.

Intimately connected with the true origin, here discussed, of all theism and likewise proceeding from man's nature, is the impulse to make *sacrifices* to his gods in order to purchase their favour or, if they have already shown this, to ensure its continuance, or to buy off evils from them. (See Sanchuniathon's *Fragmenta*, ed. Orelli, Leipzig, 1826, p. 42.) This is the meaning

of every sacrifice and thus the origin and support of the existence of all gods, so that it can be truly said that gods live on
sacrifice. For just because the impulse to call and purchase the
assistance of supernatural beings, although an offspring of want
and intellectual narrowness, is natural to man and its satisfaction is a need, he creates gods for himself. Hence the universal nature of sacrifice in all ages and among the most diverse
races and the identity of the thing in spite of the greatest
difference in circumstances and degrees of culture. Thus
Herodotus (lib. IV, c. 152) relates that a ship from Samos had
acquired an unprecedented fortune through the extremely
profitable sale of its cargo in Tartessus. These Samians then
spent a tenth part of this fortune, amounting to six talents, on a
large, brazen, and artistically worked vase and presented it to
Hera in her temple. As a counterpart to those Greeks, we see
in our own day the miserable, nomad, reindeer-breeding
Laplander, with figure shrunk to that of a dwarf, hide his
savings in various secret recesses of the rocks and ravines. He
does not divulge these to anyone except to his heir in the hour
of his dying; and even from this man he conceals one place
because the money there deposited has been sacrificed by him
to the *genius loci*, the tutelary god of his district. (See Albrecht
Pancritius, *Hägringar, Reise durch Schweden, Lappland, Norwegen,
und Dänemark im Jahre 1850*, Königsberg, 1852, p. 162.) The
belief in gods is thus rooted in egoism. Only in Christianity
has the sacrifice proper disappeared, although it still exists in
the form of masses for the dead and in the building of cloisters,
churches, and chapels. For the rest and particularly with
Protestants, praise, glory, and thanks have to serve as a substitute for sacrifice and these are, therefore, carried to the most
extreme superlatives, even on occasions which to an impartial
man seem little suited to them. This is analogous to the case
where the State does not always reward merit with gifts but
with mere testimonials of honour, and thus maintains its
continuance. In this connection it is well worth recalling what
the great David Hume has to say: 'Whether this god, therefore,
be considered as their peculiar patron, or as the general
sovereign of heaven, his votaries will endeavour, by every art,
to insinuate themselves into his favour; and supposing him to
be pleased, like themselves, with praise and flattery, there is no

eulogy or exaggeration, which will be spared in their addresses to him. In proportion as men's fears or distresses become more urgent, they will invent new strains of adulation; and even he who outdoes his predecessors in swelling up the titles of his divinity, is sure to be outdone by his successors in newer and more pompous epithets of praise. Thus they proceed; till at last they arrive at infinity itself beyond which there is no further progress.' (*Essays and Treatises on Several Subjects*, London, 1777, vol. ii, p. 429.) And again: 'It appears certain that, though the original notions of the vulgar represent the Divinity as a limited being, and consider him only as a particular cause of health or sickness; plenty or want; prosperity or adversity; yet when more magnificent ideas are urged upon them, they esteem it *dangerous to refuse their assent*. Will you say that your deity is finite and bounded in his perfections; may be overcome by a greater force; is subject to human passions, pains, and infirmities; has a beginning and may have an end? This they dare not affirm; but thinking it *safest to comply with the higher encomiums, they endeavour, by an affected ravishment and devotion to ingratiate themselves* with him. As a confirmation of this, we may observe that the assent of the vulgar is, in this case, merely verbal, and that they are incapable of conceiving those sublime qualities which they seemingly attribute to the Deity. Their real idea of him, notwithstanding their pompous language, is still as poor and frivolous as ever.' (Ibid., p. 432.)

In order to mitigate the objectionable aspect of his criticism of all speculative theology, Kant added to it not only moral theology, but also the assurance that, although God's existence must remain unproved, it is also just as impossible to prove the opposite. Many acquiesced in this, for they did not notice that, with pretended simplicity, he ignored the *affirmanti incumbit probatio*.[86] They also failed to notice that the number of things whose non-existence cannot be proved is infinite. Naturally he has been even more careful not to indicate the arguments that could actually be employed for an apagogic counter-proof, if one no longer wanted to maintain a merely defensive attitude, but wished to become aggressive. The following would be somewhat of this nature:

(1) In the first place, the melancholy constitution of a world

[86] ['Proof is incumbent on the man who makes a positive assertion.']

whose living beings subsist by devouring one another, the consequent distress and dread of all that lives, the multitude and colossal magnitude of evils, the variety and inevitability of sufferings often swelling to the dreadful, the burden of life itself hurrying forward to the bitterness of death, all this cannot honestly be reconciled with the idea that the world is supposed to be the work of a united infinite goodness, wisdom, and power. To raise an outcry against what is here said is just as easy as it is difficult to meet the case with solid and convincing arguments.

(2) There are two points which not only concern every thinking man, but which also the followers of every religion have most at heart, and thus on which the strength and stability of religions rest. They are first the transcendent moral significance of our conduct, and secondly our continued existence after death. If a religion has taken care of these two points, everything else is secondary. I shall, therefore, test theism here in respect of the first point, but later in respect of the second.

Thus theism has a double connection with the morality of our conduct, one *a parte ante* and one *a parte post*, in other words, as regards the grounds and as regards the consequences of our actions. To take the last point first; theism, it is true, gives morality a support, yet one of the crudest kind, indeed one whereby the true and pure morality of conduct is fundamentally abolished, since every disinterested action is at once transformed into an interested by means of a very long-dated but safe bill of exchange that is received as payment for it. Thus the God who, to begin with, was the creator in the end appears as avenger and as one who repays. Regard for such a God can, of course, call forth virtuous actions, but these will not be purely moral, as fear of punishment or hope of reward is their motive. On the contrary, the essence of such a virtue will amount to a prudent and carefully calculating egoism. In the last resort, it is a question solely of the firmness of faith in indemonstrable things. If this exists, then we shall certainly not hesitate to accept a short period of suffering for an eternity of joy, and the really guiding principle of morality will be: 'we can wait.' But everyone seeking a reward for his deeds either in this or in a future world is an egoist. If the hoped-for reward escapes him, then it is immaterial whether this happens through chance that rules this world or through the emptiness of the illusion that built for him the future world. Properly speaking, this is why Kant's moral theology undermines morality.

Again *a parte ante*, theism is likewise in conflict with morality since it abolishes freedom and accountability. For neither guilt nor merit is conceivable in a being which, as regards its *existentia* and *essentia*, is the work of another. Vauvenargues very rightly says: *Un être qui a tout reçu ne peut agir que par ce qui lui a été donné; et toute la puissance divine qui est infinie ne saurait le rendre indépendant.*[87] (*Discours sur la liberté.* See *Oeuvres complètes*, Paris, 1823, Tom. ii, p. 331.) Like every other conceivable being, it cannot act except in accordance with its *nature or disposition*, and thereby make this known; but here it is created just as it is conditioned. If it acts badly, this comes from its *being* bad, and then the fault is not its, but of him who made it. The originator of its existence and of its nature, as well as of the circumstances in which it has been placed, is inevitably the author of its action and deeds; and these are determined by all this just as certainly as is the triangle by two angles and a line. The correctness of this argument has been fully acknowledged and admitted by St. Augustine, Hume, and Kant, while others have cunningly and timidly ignored it, a matter fully discussed by me in my prize-essay 'On the Freedom of the Will', chap. 4. Just to elude this terrible and exterminating difficulty, the freedom of the will, the *liberum arbitrium indifferentiae*,[88] was invented. This contains an utterly monstrous fiction and was therefore always disputed and discarded long ago by all thinking minds, but perhaps nowhere is it refuted so systematically and thoroughly as in the above-quoted work. Let the mob labour under the freedom of the will if it likes; even the literary, the philosophical mob; what does it matter to us? The assertion that a given being is *free*, that is to say, can act under given circumstances thus and also otherwise, implies that it has an *existentia* without any *essentia*, in other words, that it merely *is* without being *something* and hence that it is *nothing*, but yet *is*, consequently that it simultaneously is and is not. Therefore this is the height of absurdity, yet it is nevertheless good enough for

[87] ['A being who has received everything can act only in keeping with what has been given to him; and all the power of God which is infinite could not make him independent.']

[88] ['The will's free decision, uninfluenced by any antecedent determination.']

those who are seeking not the truth but their fodder, and so will never admit anything that does not fit in with their stuff, the *fable convenue* by which they live. Their impotence is better served by ignoring than by refuting. And ought we to attach any importance to the opinions of such βοσκήματα, *in terram prona et ventri obedientia?*[89] All that *is*, is also *something*, has an essence, a nature, a character; it must operate in accordance therewith, it must act (which means operate according to motives) when the external occasions arise that draw out its particular manifestations. Now it gets its character, its constitution, its *essentia* from the same quarter whence it obtains its *existentia*, since both are distinguishable in conception, it is true, yet not separable in reality. But that which has an *essentia*, that is to say, a nature, a character, a disposition, can always act only in accordance therewith and never otherwise. It is merely the point of time and the precise form and nature of the individual actions that are here determined each time by the motives that present themselves. That the creator created man *free* implies an impossibility, namely that he endowed him with an *existentia* without *essentia* and thus gave him *existence* merely *in abstracto*, in that man was left to be what he wanted to be. On this point I request the reader to refer to § 20 of my essay 'On the Basis of Ethics'. Moral freedom and responsibility or accountability absolutely presuppose *aseity*.[90] Actions always arise from the character, i.e. from the peculiar and therefore unalterable constitution of a being, and they do so with necessity in accordance with, and under the influence of, the motives. If, therefore, it is to be responsible, it must exist originally and by virtue of its own absolute power. As regards its *existentia* and *essentia*, it must be its own work and the creator of itself, if it is to be the true creator of its *deeds*. Or, as I have expressed it in my two prize-essays, freedom cannot lie in the *operari*; it must therefore reside in the *esse*, for it certainly exists.

Now all this is not only demonstrable *a priori*, but even daily experience clearly teaches us that everyone brings with him into the world his moral character ready complete, and to the end

---

[89] ['Of such animals that incline to the earth and serve their bellies'. (Sallust, *Catilina*, c. 1.)]

[90] [Being by and of itself. All other beings are *ab alio*, dependent in their existence on a creator (God).]

remains unalterably true thereto. Moreover, this truth is tacitly but certainly assumed in real practical life, since every man bases his trust or mistrust in another once for all on the traits of character that are manifested by the other man. In view of all this, one might wonder how for some sixteen hundred years the opposite was theoretically asserted and accordingly taught, namely that from a moral point of view, all men are originally quite equal, and that the great difference in their conduct springs not from an original inborn difference of disposition and character, and just as little from the circumstances and occasions that occur, but really from nothing at all, such absolute nothing then receiving the name of 'free will'. But this absurd doctrine is rendered necessary by another assumption, also purely theoretical, with which it is closely connected, namely that man's birth is the absolute beginning of his existence, since he is *created* out of nothing (a *terminus ad hoc*). Now if on this assumption life is still to retain a moral significance and tendency, these must naturally find their origin in its course and indeed from nothing, just as this entire man thus conceived is from nothing. For every reference to a preceding condition, a previous existence, or an act outside time, to which the immeasurable, original, and inborn difference of moral characters nevertheless clearly points, is here excluded once for all. Hence the absurd fiction of a free will. It is well known that all truths are connected with one another, but errors also render one another necessary, just as one lie requires a second, or two cards on edge mutually support each other, so long as nothing upsets the two.

(3) On the assumption of theism, things are not much better with our continuance after death than they are with the freedom of the will. That which is created by another has a beginning to its existence. Now that this should henceforth continue to exist to all eternity after not having existed at all for an infinite time, is an exceedingly bold assumption. If at my birth I have first come from nothing and have been created out of nothing, then it is highly probable that at my death I shall again become nothing. Endless duration *a parte post* and nothing *a parte ante* do not go together. Only that which is itself original, eternal, and uncreated, can be indestructible. (See Aristotle, *De coelo*, I, c. 12, pp. 281–3, and Priestley, *On Matter and Spirit*,

Birmingham, 1782, vol. I, p. 234.) And so perhaps those may be anxious in death who believe that thirty or sixty years ago they were a pure nothing and then came out of that nothing as the work of another. For they now have the difficult task of assuming that an existence so arisen will yet be of endless duration, despite its late beginning which came about after the lapse of an infinite time. On the other hand, how could anyone fear death who recognizes himself as the original and eternal essence, the source, of all existence itself, and knows that outside him nothing really exists, he who ends his individual existence with the words of the sacred *Upanishad* on his lips or even in his heart: *hae omnes creaturae in totum ego sum, et praeter me aliud ens non est?*[91] And so only he can with logical consistency die calmly and serenely. For, as I have said, *aseity* is the condition of immortality as also of accountability. In keeping with all this, contempt for death and the most complete calm and even joy in dying are thoroughly at home in India. Judaism, on the other hand, originally the one and only purely monotheistic religion that teaches an actual God creator of heaven and earth, has with perfect consistency no doctrine of immortality. Thus it has no reward or punishment after death, but only temporal punishments and rewards whereby it is distinguished from all other religions, though not to its advantage. The two religions that sprang from Judaism really became inconsistent, because they took up immortality that had become known to them from other and better doctrines, and yet retained the God creator.*

[91] ['I am all these creatures, every one of them, and besides me no other being exists.']

* The real *religion of the Jews*, as presented and taught in *Genesis* and all the historical books up to the end of *Chronicles*, is the crudest of all religions because it is the only one that has absolutely no doctrine of immortality, not even a trace thereof. When he dies, each king, each hero or prophet, is buried with his fathers and with this everything is finished. There is no trace of any existence after death; indeed every idea of this kind seems to be purposely dismissed. For example, Jehovah delivers a long eulogy to King Josiah and ends it with the promise of a reward. It says: ἰδοὺ προστίθημί σε πρὸς τοὺς πατέρας σου, καὶ προστεθήσῃ πρὸς τὰ μνήματά σου ἐν εἰρήνῃ ['Behold, I will gather thee to thy fathers, and thou shalt be gathered to thy grave in peace.' 2 Chronicles 34:28]; thus he shall not live to see Nebuchadnezzar. But there is no idea of another existence after death and with it of a positive reward instead of the merely negative one of dying and of suffering no further sorrows. On the contrary, when Jehovah has sufficiently used up and tormented his handiwork and plaything, he throws it away into the ditch; that is the reward for it. Just because the religion of the Jews knows no immortality and

consequently no punishments after death, Jehovah can threaten the sinner, the one who prospers on earth, only with punishing his misdeeds in the persons of his children and children's children unto the fourth generation, as may be seen in Exodus 34:7, and Numbers 14:18. This proves the absence of any doctrine of immortality. Likewise the passage in Tobias, 3:6, where the latter begs Jehovah to let him die, ὅπως ἀπολυθῶ καὶ γένωμαι γῆ ['that I may be saved, and return to dust']; nothing more, no notion of an existence after death. In the Old Testament the reward promised to virtue is to live a really long time on earth (e.g. Deuteronomy 5:16 and 33); in the *Veda*, on the other hand, it is not to be born again. The contempt in which the Jews were always held by contemporary peoples may have been due in great measure to the poor character of their religion. What is said in Ecclesiastes 3:19, 20 is the true sentiment of the *Jews' religion*. If immortality is alluded to, as in Daniel 12:2, it is as an imported foreign doctrine, as is evident from Daniel, 1:4 and 6. In the second book of Maccabees, chapter 7, the doctrine of immortality appears clearly to be of Babylonian origin. All other religions, those of the Indians, both Brahmans and Buddhists, of the Egyptians, Persians, and even of the Druids, teach immortality and, with the exception of the Persians in the *Zendavesta*, metempsychosis as well. D. G. v. Ekendahl establishes in his review of the *Svenska Siare och Skalder* of Atterbom, in the *Blätter für litter. Unterhaltung*, 25 August 1843, that the Edda, especially the *Voluspa*, teaches transmigration of souls. Even Greeks and Romans had something *post letum* ['after death'], namely Tartarus and Elysium, and said:

Sunt aliquid manes, letum non omnia finit:
Luridaque evictos effugit umbra rogos.
Propertius, IV. 7.

['The shades of the departed are still something, death does not end all: the lurid shadow rises triumphant from the fiery flames.']

Speaking generally, the really essential element in a religion as such consists in the conviction it gives that our existence proper is not limited to our life, but is infinite. Now this wretched religion of the Jews does not do this at all, in fact it does not even attempt it. It is, therefore, the crudest and poorest of all religions and consists merely in an absurd and revolting theism. It amounts to this that the κύριος ['Lord'], who has created the world, desires to be worshipped and adored; and so above all he is jealous, is envious of his colleagues, of all the other gods; if sacrifices are made to them he is furious and his Jews have a bad time. All these other religions and their gods are stigmatized in the Septuagint as βδέλυγμα ['abomination']; but it is crude Judaism without any immortality that really merits this description. It is most deplorable that this religion has become the basis of the prevailing religion of Europe; for it is a religion without any metaphysical tendency. While all other religions endeavour to explain to the people by symbols and parables the metaphysical significance of life, the religion of the Jews is entirely immanent and furnishes nothing but a mere war-cry in the struggle with other nations. Lessing's *Erziehung des Menschengeschlechts* should be called education of the Jewish race, for the whole of the human race with the exception of these elect of God was convinced of that truth. The Jews are the chosen people of their *God* and he is the chosen God of his people. And this need not trouble anyone else. Ἔσομαι αὐτῶν θεός, καὶ αὐτοὶ ἔσονται μου λαός ['I will be their God, and they shall be my people'] is a passage from one of the prophets, according to Clement of Alexandria. But when I observe that the present nations of Europe to a certain extent regard themselves as the heirs to that chosen people of God, I cannot conceal my regret. On the other hand, Judaism cannot be denied the reputation of being the only really monotheistic religion on earth; for no other religion can boast of an objective God, creator of heaven and earth.

That Judaism is, as already stated, the only purely monotheistic religion, that is, one that teaches a God creator as the
origin of all things, is a merit which, for reasons unknown, men
have tried to conceal by always maintaining and teaching
that all nations worshipped the true God, although under
other names. Yet in this they are not only greatly mistaken, but
quite wrong. Through the agreement of all genuine testimonies
and original documents, it is put beyond all doubt that Buddhism, the religion that is the foremost on earth by virtue of the
overwhelming number of its adherents, is absolutely and
expressly atheistic. The *Vedas* also teach no God creator, but a
world-soul called *Brahm* (in the neuter). *Brahma*, sprung from
the navel of Vishnu with the four faces and as part of the
Trimurti, is merely a popular personification of Brahm in the
extremely transparent Indian mythology. He obviously
represents the generation, the origin, of beings just as Vishnu
does their acme, and Shiva their destruction and extinction.
Moreover, his production of the world is a sinful act, just as is
the world incarnation of Brahm. Then Ormuzd of the Zendavesta is, as we know, the compeer of Ahriman, and the two
have emerged from immeasurable time, Zervane Akerene (if
the statement is founded on fact). Similarly in the very fine
and extremely readable cosmogony of the Phoenicians,
written by Sanchuniathon and preserved for us by Philo
Byblius, which is perhaps the prototype of the Mosaic cosmogony, we find no trace of theism or of world creation by a
personal being. Thus here we also see, as in the Mosaic Genesis,
the original chaos submerged in night; but no God appears
commanding 'Let there be light! let there be this, and let there
be that!' Oh no! but ἠράσθη τὸ πνεῦμα τῶν ἰδίων ἀρχῶν.[92] The
spirit, fermenting in the mass, falls in love with its own essence
or being, whereby a mixture of those primary constituents or
elements of the world arises. From this is developed the primeval
slime or ooze, and indeed very effectively and significantly, in
consequence of that very longing or πόθος which, as the com-
mentator rightly observes, is the Eros of the Greeks. Finally
from this slime plants proceed and last of all knowing beings,
i.e. animals. For hitherto, as is expressly observed, everything
occurred without knowledge: αὐτὸ δὲ οὐκ ἐγίγνωσκε τὴν ἑαυτοῦ

[92] ['The spirit fell in love with its own origin.']

κτίσιν.[93] (It is thus, adds Sanchuniathon, in the cosmogony written by Taaut, the Egyptian.) His *cosmogony* is then followed by the more detailed *zoogony*. Certain atmospheric and terrestrial events are described which actually suggest the logical assumptions of our modern geology. At last thunder and lightning follow torrential rains and, startled by the crashing, animals with knowledge are awakened into existence, and 'now there move on the earth and in the sea *male and female*.' Accordingly, Eusebius, to whom we are indebted for these fragments of Philo Byblius (See *Praeparatio evangelica*, lib. II, c. 10), quite rightly accuses this cosmogony of atheism; and this it unquestionably is, as are all theories of the origin of the world with the single exception of the Jewish. In the mythology of the Greeks and Romans, it is true that we find gods as fathers of gods and incidentally of men (although these are originally the potter's work of Prometheus), yet we find no God creator. For the fact that one or two philosophers, who had become acquainted with Judaism, later tried to regard Father Zeus as such a creator does not affect the matter which is also as little affected by the fact that Dante in his *Inferno*, without having sought his permission, summarily tries to identify him with *Domeneddio*, whose unheard-of thirst for vengeance and cruelty are there celebrated and depicted; e.g. can. 14, st. 70; can 31, st. 92. Finally (for everything has been grasped at), the endlessly repeated statement is quite wrong, that the North American savages worshipped God, the creator of heaven and earth, under the name of the *Great Spirit*, and were consequently pure theists. This error has recently been refuted in a paper on the North American savages which John Scouler read at a meeting of the London Ethnographical Society held in 1846, and of which *l'Institut, Journal des sociétés savantes*, sect. 2, July 1847, gives an extract. He says: 'When in reports on the superstitions of the Indians we are told about the *Great Spirit*, we are apt to assume that this expression indicates a conception consistent with the one we associate with it, and that their belief is a simple natural *theism*. But this interpretation is very far from correct; on the contrary, the religion of those Indians is a pure *fetishism*, consisting in charms, spells, and sorcery. In the report of Tanner who from childhood lived among them, the

[93] ['But it did not itself recognize its own creation.']

details are reliable and remarkable, yet far different from the inventions of certain authors. Thus from this we see that the religion of those Indians is really only a fetishism, similar to that formerly met with among the Finns and even now to be found among tribes in Siberia. Among the Indians dwelling east of the mountains the fetish consists merely of any object to which mysterious qualities are attributed', and so on.

In consequence of all this, the opinion here discussed should rather give way to its opposite, namely that only a unique, indeed very small and insignificant race, despised by all contemporary nations and living quite alone among them all without any belief in a continued existence after death but yet predestined for the purpose, has had pure monotheism or knowledge of the true God. Moreover, this it has not through philosophy, but simply through revelation, as is indeed appropriate; for what would be the value of a revelation that taught only what one knew without it? That no other nation has ever conceived such an idea must accordingly contribute to our regard for revelation.

§ 14
Some Observations on my own Philosophy

There is scarcely a philsophical system so simple and composed of so few elements as is mine; and so it can be taken in and comprehended at a glance. This is due ultimately to the complete unity and agreement of its fundamental ideas and is generally a favourable indication of its truth; indeed truth is akin to simplicity: ἁπλοῦς ὁ τῆς ἀληθείας λόγος ἔφυ, *simplex sigillum veri.*[94] My system might be described as *immanent dogmatism*, for its doctrines are indeed dogmatic, yet they do not go beyond the world that is given in experience. On the contrary, by analysing it into its ultimate elements, they explain merely *what the world is.* Thus the old dogmatism that was overthrown by Kant (and likewise the blarney and humbug of the three modern university sophists) is *transcendent* since it goes beyond the world in order to explain it from something different; it makes the world the consequent of a ground, such ground being inferred from the consequent itself. My philosophy, on

[94] ['Whoever has truth to tell expresses himself simply. Simplicity is the seal of truth.']

the other hand, began with the proposition that there are grounds and consequents solely *within* the world and on the assumption thereof, since the principle of sufficient reason or ground in its four aspects is merely the most universal form of the intellect, but that in this intellect alone, as the true *locus mundi*, the objective world exists.

In other philosophical systems, consistency is effected by inferring one proposition from another. But this necessarily demands that the real content of the system exists already in the very first propositions, whereby the remainder, as derived therefrom, can hardly prove to be other than monotonous, poor, empty, and tedious, since it merely develops and repeats what was already stated in the basic propositions. This dismal consequence of demonstrative deduction is most noticeable in Christian Wolff; but even Spinoza, who strictly followed this method, was unable entirely to escape its drawback, although through his intellect he was able to compensate for it. My propositions, on the other hand, for the most part do not rest on chains of reasoning, but directly on the world of intuitive perception itself, and the strict consistency to be found in my system as much as in any other is, as a rule, not obtained on the merely logical path. On the contrary, it is that natural agreement of the propositions which inevitably results from the fact that all are based on the same intuitive knowledge, that is to say, on the intuitive apprehension of the same object that is successively contemplated from different points of view and hence of the real world in all its phenomena, by virtue of the consciousness wherein it presents itself. And so I was never concerned about the harmony and agreement of my propositions, not even when some of them seemed to me to be inconsistent, as was occasionally the case for a time. For agreement subsequently appeared automatically according as the propositions all came together numerically complete, since with me such harmony or consistency is simply nothing more than the agreement of reality with itself, which of course can never go wrong. This is analogous to our sometimes not understanding the continuity and connection of a building's parts when we look at it for the first time and from only one direction; yet we are certain that such continuity is not wanting and that it will appear as soon as we have walked right round the building. But this kind of consistency is perfectly certain by virtue of its original nature and because it is constantly under the control of experience. On the other hand, the deduced consistency that is brought about solely by the syllogism can easily prove to be false in some particular, that is to say, as soon as some link in the long chain is not genuine, is loosely fitted, or is otherwise of a faulty nature. Accordingly, my philosophy has a wide basis whereon everything stands directly and thus securely; whereas other systems are like tall towers where, if one support breaks, the whole edifice collapses. All that I have said here may be summarized by saying that my philosophy has arisen and is presented on the analytical path, not on the synthetical.

I may mention, as a special characteristic of my philosophizing, that I try everywhere *to go to the very root of things*, since I continue to pursue them up to the ultimate given reality. This happens by virtue of a natural disposition that makes it wellnigh impossible for me to rest content with any general and abstract knowledge that is therefore still indefinite, with mere concepts, not to mention words. On the contrary, I am urged forward until I have plainly before me the ultimate basis of all concepts and propositions which is at all times intuitive. I must then let this stand as the primary phenomenon, or, if possible, I still resolve it into its elements, but in any case I follow out to the utmost the essential nature of the matter. It will, therefore, be recognized one day (though naturally not in my lifetime) that the treatment of the same subject by any previous philosopher appears shallow and superficial when compared with mine. Thus mankind has learned much from me that will never be forgotten and my works will not sink into oblivion.

Even theism represents the world as proceeding from a *will*; the planets are represented as being guided in their orbits by a will, and a nature as being produced on their surface. But theism childishly puts this will outside the universe and causes it to act on things only indirectly, through the intervention of knowledge and matter, in human fashion. With me, on the other hand, the will acts not so much on things as in them; indeed they themselves are simply nothing but the very visibility of the will. However, in this agreement we see that we cannot conceive the original of things as anything but a *will*.

Pantheism calls the will that operates in things a God and the absurdity of this has been censured by me often and severely enough. I call it the *will-to-live* because this expresses what is ultimately knowable therein. This same relation of mediateness to immediateness appears once again in morality. The theists want a reconciliation between what a man does and what he suffers; so do I. But they assume such a reconciliation first by means of time and of a judge and avenger; whereas I do this directly, since I point out the same essential nature in the doer and the sufferer. The moral results of Christianity up to the most extreme asceticism are found in my works based on reason and the connection and continuity of things, whereas in Christianity they are founded on mere fables. Belief in these is daily disappearing and people will, therefore, have to turn to my philosophy. The *pantheists* cannot have any seriously meant morality, for with them everything is divine and excellent.

I have often been criticized for having represented, in philosophy and thus theoretically, life as wretched, full of misery, and by no means worth desiring. Yet whoever shows practically the most decided disregard and contempt for life is praised and even admired, whereas the man who is carefully concerned over its preservation is despised.

My works had scarcely excited the attention of a few, when the dispute as to priority arose with regard to my fundamental idea, and it was stated that Schelling had once said 'willing is original and primary being', and anything else of this kind that could be adduced. With regard to the matter itself, it may be observed that the root of my philosophy is to be found already in the Kantian, especially in Kant's doctrine of the empirical and intelligible characters, but generally in the fact that, whenever Kant brings the thing-in-itself somewhat nearer to the light, it always appears through its veil as *will*. I have expressly drawn attention to this in my 'Criticism of the Kantian Philosophy', and accordingly have said that my philosophy is only his thought out to the end. Therefore we need not wonder if the philosophemes of Fichte and Schelling, which also start from Kant, show traces of the same fundamental idea, although they there appear without sequence, continuity, or development, and accordingly may be regarded as a mere foreshadowing of my doctrine. In general, however, it may be said on this point that, before every great truth has been discovered, a previous feeling, a presentiment, a faint outline thereof, as in a fog, is proclaimed, and there is a vain attempt to grasp it just because the progress of the times prepared the way for it. Accordingly, it is preluded by isolated utterances; but he alone is the author of a truth who has recognized it from its grounds and has thought it out to its consequents; who has developed its whole content and has surveyed the extent of its domain; and who, fully aware of its value and importance, has therefore expounded it clearly and coherently. On the other hand, in ancient and modern times, one has expressed a truth on some occasion, semi-consciously and almost like talking in sleep; and accordingly it can be found there if it is expressly looked for. Yet this does not signify much more than if such a truth were before us *totidem litteris*,[95] even although it may exist *totidem verbis*.[96] In the same way, the finder of a thing is only the man who, knowing its value, picked it up and kept it, not he who once accidentally took it up in his hand and dropped it again. Or again Columbus is the discoverer of America, not the first shipwrecked sailor there cast up by the waves. This is precisely the meaning of the saying of Donatus: *pereant qui ante nos nostra dixerunt*.[97] If, on the other hand, opponents wanted to admit such chance utterances as priorities against me, they could have gone back much further and quoted, for example, what Clement of Alexandria said (*Stromata*, lib. II, c. 17): προηγεῖται τοίνυν πάντων τὸ βούλεσθαι· αἱ γὰρ λογικαὶ δυνάμεις τοῦ βούλεσθαι διάκονοι πεφύκασι (*Velle ergo omnia antecedit: rationales enim facultates sunt voluntatis ministrae*.[98] See *Sanctorum patrum opera polemica*, vol. v, Würzburg, 1779: Clement of Alexandria, *Opera*, Tom. ii, p. 304). Spinoza also said: *Cupiditas est ipsa unius cujusque natura seu essentia*[99] (*Ethics*, Pt. III, prop. 57, demonstr.) and previously: *Hic conatus, cum ad mentem solam refertur, Voluntas appellatur; sed cum ad mentem et corpus simul refertur, vocatur Appetitus, qui proinde nihil aliud est,*

---

[95] ['With just so many letters'.]
[96] ['With just so many words'.]
[97] ['Down with those who, prior to us, have expressed our ideas.']
[98] ['Therefore willing precedes everything; for the forces of reason are the handmaidens of willing.']
[99] ['Cupidity is precisely that which constitutes everyone's nature or true essence.']

quam IPSA HOMINIS ESSENTIA.[1] (Pt. III, prop. 9, schol.,
and finally Pt. III, Defin. 1, explic.) Helvétius quite rightly
says: *Il n'est point de moyens que l'envieux sous l'apparence de la
justice n'emploie pour dégrader le mérite . . . C'est l'envie seule qui nous
fait trouver dans les anciens toutes les découvertes modernes. Une phrase
vide de sens ou du moins inintelligible avant ces découvertes, suffit pour
faire crier au plagiat.*[2] (*De l'esprit,* IV, 7.) On this point I make so
bold as to recall yet another passage from Helvétius; but I ask
the reader not to ascribe my quotation to vanity and presumption, but simply to bear in mind the correctness of the idea
expressed in it and to leave it an open question whether or
not anything contained in it could apply to me. *Quiconque se
plaît à considérer l'esprit humain voit dans chaque siècle cinq ou six
hommes d'esprit tourner autour de la découverte que fait l'homme de
génie. Si l'honneur en reste à ce dernier, c'est que cette découverte est,
entre ses mains, plus féconde que dans les mains de tout autre; c'est qu'il
rend ses idées avec plus de force et de netteté; et qu'enfin on voit toujours à
la manière différente, dont les hommes tirent parti d'un principe ou
d'une découverte, à qui ce principe ou cette découverte appartient*[3] (*De
l'esprit,* IV, 1).

In consequence of the old and implacable war that is always
and everywhere waged by incapacity and stupidity against
intellect and understanding—by legions on the one side against
individuals on the other—anyone producing anything valuable and genuine has to fight a hard battle against want of
understanding, dullness, depraved taste, private interests, and
envy, all in worthy alliance, of which Chamfort says: *en
examinant la ligue des sots contre les gens d'esprit, on croirait voir une*

---

[1] ['This impulse is called will when it is referred to the mind alone; it is called
appetite when it is referred simultaneously to mind and body; and it is nothing but
man's *real essence.*']

[2] ['There are no means which an envious man, in the guise of justice,
will not employ to belittle merit . . . It is mere envy which makes us find among
the ancients every modern discovery. A phrase devoid of meaning, or at any
rate unintelligible prior to those discoveries, suffices to bring an accusation of
plagiarism.']

[3] ['Whoever takes pleasure in observing the human mind sees how in every
century five or six men of intellect wander round the discovery that is made by a
man of genius. If the honour of that discovery rests with the latter, this is because
the discovery is in his hands more fruitful than in those of everyone else; because he
expresses his ideas with greater force and precision; and finally because we can
always see from the different ways in which men make use of a principle or discovery to whom that principle or discovery belongs.']

conjuration de valets pour écarter les maîtres.[4] For me there was in addition an unusual adversary; the majority of those whose business and occasion it was to guide public opinion in my branch of knowledge were appointed and paid to propagate, laud, and even extol to the skies, the worst of all systems, namely *Hegelry.* But this cannot succeed if at the same time we are willing to accept the good even only to some extent. This may explain to later readers the fact, otherwise so puzzling to them, that to my contemporaries I have remained as strange and unknown as the man in the moon. Yet a system of thought which, even in spite of an absence of any co-operation on the part of others, is capable of ardently and incessantly engaging its author throughout a long life, and of spurring him on to unremitting and unrewarded labour, possesses in this very fact a testimony as to its value and truth. Without any encouragement from outside, love for my work alone sustained my efforts and did not let me grow weary throughout the many days of my life during which I looked down with contempt on the noisy trumpeting of the bad. For when I entered life, my genius offered me the choice either of recognizing truth but then of pleasing no one, or with others of teaching the false with encouragement and approbation; and for me the choice had not been difficult. Accordingly, the fate of my philosophy was so entirely the opposite of that enjoyed by Hegelry that we can regard the two as the opposite sides of the same sheet, corresponding to the nature and character of the two philosophies. Hegelry, devoid of truth, clearness, intelligence, and even of common sense, appearing moreover in the cloak of the most nauseous nonsense ever heard of, was a subsidized and privileged chair-philosophy and consequently a species of nonsense that nourished its man. Appearing simultaneously with it, my philosophy indeed had all the qualities which it lacked; but such a philosophy was not cut out for any ulterior aims, was not at all suited for the chair at that time, and hence, as we say, there was nothing to be made out of it. It then followed, as day follows night, that Hegelry became the banner to which all flocked, whereas my philosophy met with neither approbation nor followers. On the contrary, it was universally and

4 ['When we see the league of blockheads against men of intelligence, we think we are witnessing a conspiracy of servants to overthrow their masters.']

deliberately ignored, suppressed, and, where possible, smothered because through its presence that fine old game would have been upset, as is the shadow-play on the wall by the incoming light of day. Accordingly, I became the iron mask or, as the noble Dorguth says, the Caspar Hauser[5] of the professors of philosophy, secluded from air and light so that no one would see me and my natural claims might not gain authority. But now the man who was killed by the silence of the professors of philosophy, has risen again from the dead, to their great consternation, for they do not know at all what expression they should now assume.

[5] [Caspar Hauser (1812?–33), a German foundling youth of mysterious and controversial origins, claimed to have spent most of his life in solitary confinement.]

ON PHILOSOPHY AT
THE UNIVERSITIES

Ἡ ἀτιμία φιλοσοφίᾳ διὰ ταῦτα προσπέπτωκεν. ὅτι οὐ κατ᾽ ἀξίαν αὐτῆς ἅπτονται· οὐ γὰρ νόθους ἔδει ἅπτεσθαι, ἀλλὰ γνησίους.

Plato, *The Republic*, Book VII.

['Philosophy has fallen into contempt because people are not engaged in it to the extent that it merits; for not spurious, but genuine, philosophers should devote themselves to it.']

On Philosophy at the Universities

THE teaching of philosophy at universities certainly benefits it in various ways. Thus it obtains an official existence and its standard is raised before the eyes of men whereby its existence is constantly brought to mind and men are made aware of it. But the main advantage from this will be that many a young and capable mind is made acquainted with it and is encouraged to study it. Yet it must be admitted that, whoever is capable and thus in need of it, would also come across it and make its acquaintance in other ways. For those who cherish one another, and are born for one another, readily come together; kindred souls already greet one another from afar. Thus such a man will be more powerfully and effectively stirred by every work of any genuine philosopher which happens to come into his hands than is possible through the lectures of a chair-philosopher, such as are given by the day. Plato should also be carefully read on the classical side of schools because he is the most effective means for stimulating the philosophical mind. But, in general, I have gradually formed the opinion that the above-mentioned use of the chair-philosophy is burdened with the disadvantage which philosophy as a profession imposes on philosophy as the free investigation of truth, or which philosophy by government order imposes on philosophy in the name of nature and mankind.

In the first place, a government will not pay people to contradict directly, or even only indirectly, what it has had promulgated from all the pulpits by thousands of its appointed priests or religious teachers; for in so far as such a proceeding were effective, it would inevitably render ineffective the former organization. For it is well known that judgements cancel one another not merely through contradictory, but also through merely contrary, opposites. Thus for example, the judgement 'the rose is red' is contradicted not merely by 'it is not red', but also by 'it is yellow', a judgement that in this respect achieves just as much or even more. Hence the maxim *improbant secus docentes*.[1] But through this circumstance university

[1] ['We reject and condemn the man who teaches something different.']

philosophers land themselves in a very curious position whose open secret may here receive a few words. In all the other branches of knowledge the professors are obliged only to teach as far as possible and to the best of their ability what is true and correct. But only in the case of professors of philosophy are we to understand the matter *cum grano salis*.[2] Thus we have here a curious state of affairs due to the fact that the problem of their science is the same as that about which religion also in its way gives us information. I have, therefore, described religion as the metaphysics of the people. Accordingly, the professors of philosophy are also, of course, supposed to teach what is true and correct; but this must be fundamentally and essentially the same as that which is also taught by the established religion that is likewise true and correct. This is the origin of that naïve utterance, already quoted in my 'Criticism of the Kantian Philosophy', which was made in 1840 by quite a reputable professor of philosophy. He said: 'If a philosophy denies the fundamental ideas of Christianity, then either it is false, or, *even if true, it is of no use.*' From this we see that in philosophy at the universities truth occupies only a secondary place and, if called upon, she must get up and make room for another attribute. And so at universities it is this that distinguishes philosophy from all other branches of knowledge that are taught there.

In consequence of this, university authorities will always permit only such a philosophy to be taught so long as the Church lasts. Framed with general regard to the established religion, this philosophy runs essentially parallel thereto; and so, being perhaps intricately composed, curiously trimmed, and thus rendered difficult to understand, it is always at bottom and in the main nothing but a paraphrase and apology of the established religion. Accordingly, for those teaching under these restrictions, there is nothing left but to look for new turns of phrase and forms of speech by which they arrange the contents of the established religion. Disguised in abstract expressions and thereby rendered dry and dull, they then go by the name of philosophy. Yet if someone or other wants to do anything besides this, he will either wander off into neighbouring branches of knowledge or have recourse to all kinds of

2 ['With a grain of salt'.]

innocent fudge, such as carrying out difficult analytical computations on the equilibrium of mental pictures in the human head, and similar jests. Meanwhile, university philosophers, restricted in this way, are quite happy about the matter, for their real concern is to earn with credit an honest livelihood for themselves and also for their wives and children and moreover to enjoy a certain prestige in the eyes of the public. On the other hand, the deeply stirred mind of the real philosopher, whose whole concern is to look for the key to our existence, as mysterious as it is precarious, is regarded by them as something mythological, if indeed the man so affected does not even appear to them to be obsessed by a monomania, should he ever be met with among them. For that a man could really be in dead earnest about philosophy does not as a rule occur to anyone, least of all to a lecturer thereon; just as the most sceptical Christian is usually the Pope. It has, therefore, been one of the rarest events for a genuine philosopher to be at the same time a lecturer on philosophy.* In the second volume of my chief work, chap. 17, I have already discussed with reasons and results why Kant himself presented this exceptional case. Moreover, Fichte's well-known fate affords proof of the conditional existence of all university philosophy which I have just revealed, although at bottom this man was a mere sophist and not a real philosopher. Thus in his philosophizing he had dared to disregard the doctrines of the established religion with the result that he was dismissed and, in addition, insulted by the mob. In his case the punishment proved to be effective since, after his subsequent appointment in Berlin, the absolute Ego or I was most obediently converted into the good Lord, and the whole doctrine generally assumed an extremely Christian complexion; evidence of this is furnished in particular by

---

* It is quite natural that the more godliness, the less erudition is required of a professor, just as in Altenstein's day it was enough for a man to be acquainted with Hegel's nonsense. But since in the appointment to professorships godliness can be substituted for erudition, these gentlemen do not trouble themselves about the latter. The *Tartuffes* or sanctimonious hypocrites should restrain themselves and ask: 'who will believe us when we say that we believe this?' That *these gentlemen* are professors is a matter of interest to those who appointed them; I know them to be simply bad authors against whose influence I am working. I have been looking for *truth*, not for a professorship. On this rests, in the last resort, the difference between me and the so-called post-Kantian philosophers. This will be more and more recognized with the passing of time.

'Instructions on how to live a happy life'. It is a remarkable circumstance of his case that he was charged mainly with saying that God is nothing but the moral world-order itself; whereas such a statement differs only slightly from the utterance of St. John: 'God is love'. In 1853 a similar fate befell Dr. Fischer, a privat docent[3] of Heidelberg, who had his *jus legendi* withdrawn because he taught pantheism. Hence the solution is: 'eat up thy pudding, slave, and give out as philosophy Jewish mythology!' But the jest of the matter is that these men call themselves philosophers and as such pass judgement on me; in fact with an air of superiority they cut a dash at my expense. For forty years they did not deign to look down at me, regarding me as not worth their notice. But the State must protect its own people and should, therefore, pass a law forbidding anyone to make fun of professors of philosophy.

Accordingly, it is easy for us to see that, under such circumstances, the chair-philosophy cannot very well help acting like

> A long-legged grasshopper appears to be,
> That springing flies, and flying springs;
> And in the grass the same old ditty sings.[4]

The hazardous part of the business is also the mere possibility, still to be admitted, that the ultimate insight into the nature of things attainable by man, into his very being and that of the world, might not coincide exactly with the doctrines which were in part made known to the former little race of the Jews and in part appeared in Jerusalem eighteen hundred years ago. In order to dispel this doubt once for all, the professor of philosophy called Hegel invented the expression 'absolute religion' with which he also attained his object, for he knew his public. For the chair-philosophy it is also actually and really absolute, in other words, such as should and must be absolutely and positively true, or else ... ! Again, others of these investigators of the truth weld philosophy and religion into one centaur which they call philosophy of religion; they too are in the habit of teaching that religion and philosophy are really the same thing. Such a statement, however, appears to be true only in the sense in which Francis I is supposed to have said in a very

---

3 [A privat docent is an unsalaried lecturer at a German university.]
4 [Goethe's *Faust*, Pt. 1, Bayard Taylor's translation.]

conciliatory tone with reference to Charles V: 'what my brother Charles wants is also what I want', namely Milan. Others again do not stand on such ceremony, but talk bluntly about a Christian philosophy, which is much the same as if we were to speak of a Christian arithmetic, and this would be stretching a point. Moreover, epithets taken from such dogmas are obviously unbecoming of philosophy, for it is devoted to the attempt of the faculty of reason to solve by its own means and independently of all authority the problem of existence. As a science, philosophy has nothing whatever to do with what may or should or must be *believed*, but merely with what can be *known*. Now if this should turn out to be something quite different from what we have to believe, then even so faith would not be impaired, for it is so by virtue of its containing what we *cannot* know. If we could also know this, then faith would appear as something quite useless and even ridiculous, just as if a dogma were set up over the themes of mathematics. If, however, we are convinced that the truth, whole and entire, is contained and expressed in the established religion, then we should restrain ourselves and give up all philosophizing; for we should not pretend to be what we are not. The pretence of the impartial investigation of truth, with the resolve to make the established religion the result, indeed the measure and control, of truth, is intolerable and such a philosophy, tied to the established religion like a dog to a chain, is only the vexatious caricature of the highest and noblest endeavour of mankind. Meanwhile, that very philosophy of religion, described as being like a centaur, is one of the principal articles offered for sale by university philosophers. In its way, it really amounts to a kind of gnosis or knowledge, to a philosophizing on certain favourite assumptions that are not confirmed at all. Programme-titles such as *De verae philosophiae erga religionem pietate*,[5] a suitable inscription over such a philosophical sheepfold, clearly indicate the tendency and motives of professorial philosophy. It is true that these tame philosophers occasionally make a dash that appears to be perilous; but we can with composure bide our time, convinced that they will arrive at the goal they have fixed once for all. Indeed at times we feel tempted to think that they had finished with their seriously meant philosophical

[5] ['On the piety of true philosophy compared with religion'.]

investigations even before their twelfth year and that at that age they had for the rest of their lives settled their view on the nature of the world and on everything pertaining thereto. We feel so tempted because after all the philosophical discussions and dangerous deviations under venturesome leaders, they always come back to what is usually made plausible to us at that tender age and appear to accept this even as the criterion of truth. All heterodox philosophical doctrines, with which they must at times be concerned in the course of their lives, appear to them to exist merely to be refuted and thus to establish those others the more firmly. We are bound even to admire the way in which they have managed to retain so unsullied their inner philosophical innocence, spending their lives as they do among so many mischievous heresies.

Anyone who, after all this, is still in doubt concerning the spirit and aim of university philosophy, should consider the fate of Hegel's pretended wisdom. Has it in any way been discredited by virtue of the fact that its fundamental ideas were the absurdest fancy, a world turned upside down, a philosophical buffoonery,[6] or by virtue of its contents being the hollowest and most senseless display of words ever lapped up by blockheads, and its presentation, as seen in the works of the author himself, being the most repulsive and nonsensical gibberish, recalling the rantings of a bedlamite? No, not in the least! On the contrary, it has flourished these twenty years as the most brilliant chair-philosophy that has ever brought in fees and emoluments; it has grown fat and been proclaimed throughout Germany in hundreds of books as the final pinnacle of human wisdom and the philosophy of philosophies; in fact it has been lauded to the skies. Students were examined in it and professors appointed to teach it. Anyone not wishing to go with the rest was declared to be a 'fool on his own responsibility'[7] by the impudent tutor of its author, as docile as he is dull; and even the few who ventured a feeble opposition against such mischief, were diffident and shy in face of the recognition and acknowledgement of the 'great mind and boundless genius'—that preposterous philosophaster. Proof of what is here said is

---

[6] See my 'Criticism of the Kantian Philosophy' at the end of the first volume of my chief work.

[7] [From Goethe, *Den Originalen.*]

furnished by the whole literature of this pretty business which, now as completed documents, passes through the outer court of sneering and mocking neighbours to that seat of judgement where we all meet again, to the tribunal of posterity. Among other weapons wielded by that tribunal, a bell of infamy is tolled which can be rung even for a whole age. Now what has finally happened to bring that glory so suddenly to an end, to occasion the fall of the *bestia trionfante*, and to disperse a whole host of its mercenaries and simpletons, except a few remnants who, herded together as stragglers and marauders under the banner of the *Halle'sche Jahrbücher*, were still permitted for a while to carry on their mischief, to the extent of a public scandal, and with the exception of a few miserable duffers who even today believe in and hawk round what was imposed on them in the years of their youth? Simply that someone had the mischievous idea to point out that this is a university philosophy agreeing with the established religion only apparently and in the letter, but not actually and in a real sense. By itself this reproach was well founded, for it was this that *Neo-Catholicism* subsequently demonstrated. *German or Neo-Catholicism* is thus nothing but popularized *Hegelry*. Like this, it leaves unexplained the world which is just there without any further information. The world merely receives the name *God*, and mankind the name *Christ*. Both are an 'end in itself', in other words, they exist so that one can have a good time as long as this brief life lasts. *Gaudeamus igitur!*[8] And the Hegelian apotheosis of the State further leads to communism. A very complete description of Neo-Catholicism in this sense is given by F. Kampe, in his *Geschichte der religiösen Bewegung neuerer Zeit*, vol. iii, 1856.

But that such a reproach could be the Achilles' heel of a prevailing philosophical system, shows us

> You know the quality that can
> Decide the choice, and elevate the man,[9]

or what is the real criterion of truth and the admissibility of a philosophy at German universities and on what it depends. Moreover, an attack of this kind, even apart from the

---

[8] ['Therefore let us rejoice!']
[9] [Goethe's *Faust*, Bayard Taylor's translation.]

contemptible nature of every charge of heresy, was bound to have been quite briefly disposed of with οὐδὲν πρὸς Διόνυσον.[10]

Whoever requires yet further proofs of the same view, should consider the sequel to the great Hegel farce, namely Herr v. Schelling's immediately following and extremely well-timed conversion from Spinozism to bigotry and his subsequent transfer from Munich to Berlin, accompanied by the trumpetings of all the newspapers. According to their hints and allusions, one might imagine that he was bringing the personal God in his pocket for whom there was such a great demand; whereupon the throng of students became so great that they even climbed through the windows into the lecture-room. Then at the end of the course, the great diploma for men was most submissively handed to him by a number of professors of the university who had attended his lectures; and altogether he kept up without a blush the whole of the extremely brilliant, and no less lucrative, role in Berlin; and this in his old age when in nobler natures concern over the reputation a man leaves behind outweighs every other. At anything like this, one might in the ordinary way feel depressed; indeed one might almost imagine that the professors of philosophy themselves ought to raise a blush, yet that would be expecting too much. Now anyone who, after considering such a consummation, has not had his eyes opened to the chair-philosophy and its heroes, is past help.

Fairness, however, demands that we should judge university philosophy not merely as here, from the standpoint of its alleged purpose, but also from that of its true and proper aim. In fact, it comes to this that the junior barristers, solicitors, doctors, probationers, and pedagogues of the future should maintain, even in their innermost conviction, the same line of thought in keeping with the aims and intentions that the State and its government have in common with them. I have no objection to this and so in this respect have nothing to say. For I do not consider myself competent to judge of the necessity or needlessness of such a State expedient, but rather leave it to those who have the difficult task of governing *men*, that is to say, of maintaining law and order, peace and quiet among many

---

[10] ['Does not concern Dionysus' (i.e. the dramatic performance got up in his honour; a frequent exclamation at the festival of Dionysus).]

millions of a boundlessly egoistical, unjust, unfair, dishonest, envious, malicious, perverse, and narrow-minded race, to judge from the great majority, and of protecting the few who have acquired property from the immense number of those who have nothing but their physical strength. The task is so difficult that I certainly do not presume to argue with them over the means to be employed in this case; for my motto has always been: 'Thank God, each morning, therefore, that you have not the Roman realm to care for!'[11] But it was these constitutional aims of university philosophy which procured for *Hegelry* such unprecedented ministerial favour. For to it the *State* was 'the absolute perfect ethical organism', and it represented as originating in the *State* the whole aim of human existence. Could there be for future junior barristers and thus for state officials a better preparation than this, in consequence whereof their whole substance and being, their body and soul, were entirely forfeited to the *State*, like bees in a beehive, and they had nothing else to work for, either in this world or the next, except to become efficient wheels, co-operating for the purpose of keeping in motion the great State machine, that *ultimus finis bonorum*?[12] The junior barrister and man were accordingly one and the same. It was a real apotheosis of philistinism.

But the relation of such a university philosophy to the State is one thing and its relation to philosophy proper is another. In this connection, it might as *pure* philosophy be distinguished from the former as *applied*. Thus pure philosophy knows no other aim than truth; and then it might follow that every other aim, aspired to by means thereof, would tend to prove fatal to this. Its lofty goal is the satisfaction of that noble need, called by me the *metaphysical*, which at all times among men makes itself deeply and ardently felt, but which asserts itself most strongly when, as at the present time, the prestige and authority of dogma have been ever more on the decline. Thus dogma is intended for, and suited to, the great mass of the human race; and as such it can contain merely *allegorical* truth that it nevertheless has to pass off as truth *sensu proprio*. Now with the ever-greater extension of every kind of historical, physical, and even philosophical knowledge, the number of those whom

---

[11] [Goethe's *Faust*, Bayard Taylor's translation.]
[12] ['The ultimate goal of good things'.]

dogma can no longer satisfy becomes ever greater and they will press more and more for truth *sensu proprio*. But then in view of this demand, what can such a *nervis alienis mobile*[13] chair-puppet do? And yet how far shall we get with the subsidized petticoat-philosophy, with hollow word-structures, with fine flourishes that mean nothing and render unintelligible by a torrent of words the commonest and most obvious truths, or even with Hegel's absolute nonsense? On the other hand, if from the wilderness the righteous and honest John were actually to come who, clothed in skins and living on locusts and untouched by all the terrible mischief, were meanwhile to apply himself with a pure heart and in all seriousness to the investigation of truth and to offer the fruits thereof, what kind of a reception would he have to expect from those businessmen of the chair, who are hired for State purposes and with wife and family have to live on philosophy, and whose watchword is, therefore, *primum vivere, deinde philosophari*?[14] These men have accordingly taken possession of the market and have already seen to it that here nothing is of value except what they allow; consequently merit exists only in so far as they and their mediocrity are pleased to acknowledge it. They thus have on a leading rein the attention of that small public, such as it is, that is concerned with philosophy. For on matters that do not promise, like the productions of poetry, amusement and entertainment but only instruction, and financially unprofitable instruction at that, that public will certainly not waste its time, effort, and energy, without first being thoroughly assured that such efforts will be richly rewarded. Now by virtue of its inherited belief that whoever lives by a business knows all about it, this public expects an assurance from the professional men who from professor's chairs and in compendiums, journals, and literary periodicals, confidently behave as if they were the real masters of the subject. Accordingly, the public allows them to sample and select for it whatever is worth noting and what can be ignored. My poor John from the wilderness, how will you fare if, as is to be expected, what you bring is not drafted in accordance with the tacit convention of the gentlemen of the

---

[13] ['A wooden doll that is moved by extraneous forces' (Horace, *Satires*, II. 7 82).]

[14] ['First live and then philosophize.']

lucrative philosophy? They will regard you as one who has not entered into the spirit of the game and thus threatens to spoil the fun for all of them; consequently, they will regard you as their common enemy and antagonist. Now even if what you bring were the greatest masterpiece of the human mind, it could never find favour in their eyes. For it would not be drawn up *ad normam conventionis*;[15] and so it would not be such as to enable them to make it the subject of their lectures from the chair in order to make a living *from* it. It never occurs to a professor of philosophy to examine a new system that appears to see whether it is true; but he at once tests it merely to see whether it can be brought into harmony with the doctrines of the established religion, with government plans, and with the prevailing views of the times. After all this he decides its fate. But if it were yet to carry its point and proved to be instructive and to contain information; even if it attracted the attention of the public and were worth studying, then to this extent it would inevitably deprive the chair-philosophy of that same attention, in fact of its credit and, worse still, of its sale. *Di meliora?*[16] Therefore such a thing must not be allowed to happen and all must resist it to a man. The method and tactics for this are furnished by a happy instinct, such as is readily given to every being for its self-preservation. Thus to challenge and refute a philosophy that runs counter to the *norma conventionis*, especially where one detects merits and certain qualities that are not conferred by a professor's diploma, is often a risky business on which, in the last resort, one should certainly not venture. For in this way, works whose suppression is indicated would acquire notoriety and be sought after by the inquisitive; but then extremely unwelcome comparisons might be drawn and the result might be critical and precarious. On the contrary, as brothers of the same turn of mind and also of like ability, they unanimously regard such an inconvenient piece of work as *non avenu*.[17] In order to suppress and smother it, they regard with the greatest unconcern the most important as quite unimportant and what has been thoroughly thought out and has existed for centuries as not worth talking about. They maliciously compress their lips and remain silent, yes silent

---

[15] ['According to the current pattern'.]   [16] ['God forbid!']
[17] ['Not having occurred'.]

with that *silentium quod livor indixerit*[18] that is denounced even by old Seneca (*Epistulae*, 79). At times, they crow the more loudly over the abortive intellectual offspring and monsters of the fraternity, comforted by the thought that what no one knows is as good as non-existent, and that things in the world pass for what they seem to be and for what they are called, not for what they are. This is the safest and least dangerous method against merit and accordingly I might recommend it as the best for all shallow minds who seek their livelihood from things that call for higher talent and ability, yet without my vouching for the ultimate consequences of this.

However, the gods should certainly not be invoked here over an *inauditum nefas*.[19] All this is only a scene from the play which we have before us at all times and in all arts and sciences, that is to say, the old conflict between those who live *for* the cause and those who live *by* it, or between those who *are* it and those who *represent* it. To some it is the end in view to which their life is the mere means; to others it is the means, indeed the irksome condition, for life, well-being, enjoyment, and domestic happiness in which alone their true earnestness lies, since it is here that nature has drawn the boundary to their sphere of activity. Whoever wishes to see examples of this and become more closely acquainted therewith, should study the history of literature and read the biographies of great masters of every kind and in every art. He will then see that it has been so at all times and will understand that it will always remain so. Everyone recognizes it in the past, hardly anyone in the present. The illustrious pages of the history of literature are at the same time almost invariably the tragic. In all branches of knowledge they show us how, as a rule, merit has had to wait till the fools had stopped fooling, the merry-making had come to an end, and all had gone to bed. It then arose, like a ghost in the dead of night, to occupy the place of honour that was withheld from it, yet ultimately still as a shadow.

Here, however, we are concerned solely with philosophy and its advocates. In the first place, we now find that very few philosophers have ever been professors of philosophy, and even relatively fewer professors of philosophy have been philosophers. Therefore it might be said that, just as idioelectrical bodies are

---

[18] ['The silence imposed by envy'.]   [19] ['Unheard-of transgression'.]

non-conductors of electricity, so philosophers are not professors of philosophy. In fact this appointment, almost more than any other, obstructs the independent thinker. For the philosophical chair is to a certain extent a public confessional, where a man makes his confession of faith *coram populo*.[20] Again, hardly anything is so obstructive to the actual attainment of a thorough or very deep insight and thus of true wisdom, as the constant obligation to appear wise, the showing off of so-called knowledge in the presence of pupils eager to learn and the readiness to answer every conceivable question. Worst of all, however, is that a man in such a position is seized with anxiety when any idea occurs to him, whether such will fit in with the aims and intentions of his superiors. This paralyses his thinking to such an extent that such ideas themselves no longer dare occur. The atmosphere of freedom is indispensable to truth. I have already mentioned what is necessary concerning the *exceptio quae firmat regulam*[21] that Kant was a professor. Here I merely add that even his philosophy would have been more remarkable, firmer, purer, and finer had he not been invested with that professorship. Nevertheless, as far as possible, he very wisely drew a distinction between the philosopher and the professor, since from the chair he did not lecture on his own doctrine (See Rosenkranz, *Geschichte der Kantischen Philosophie*, p. 148).

Now if I look back at the so-called philosophers who have appeared in the half-century that has elapsed since Kant's activities, I am afraid I see no one of whom I could say to his credit that he was really and seriously concerned with the investigation of truth. On the contrary, I find them all, although not always clearly conscious of this, zealously bent on the mere semblance of the business, on producing an effect, on imposing and even mystifying in order to obtain the approbation of their superiors and subsequently of their students. In this connection, the ultimate aim is always to spend the proceeds of the business on living comfortably with wife and family. But it is also really in keeping with human nature which, like the animal, knows as its immediate aims only eating, drinking, and the care of offspring, that it has obtained in addition, as its special apanage, a mania for shining and showing off. On the other hand, the first condition of real and genuine achievements in philosophy,

[20] ['In public'.]   [21] ['The exception that confirms the rule'.]

as in poetry and the fine arts, is a wholly abnormal disposition which, contrary to the rule of human nature, puts in the place of the subjective striving for the well-being of one's own person, a wholly *objective* striving, directed to an *achievement* that is foreign to one's own person and precisely on this account is very appropriately called *eccentric* and sometimes even ridiculed as quixotic. But even Aristotle said: οὐ χρὴ δέ, κατὰ τοὺς παραινοῦντας, ἀνθρώπινα φρονεῖν ἄνθρωπον ὄντα, οὐδὲ θνητὰ τὸν θνητόν, ἀλλ' ἐφ' ὅσον ἐνδέχεται, ἀθανατίζειν, καὶ πάντα ποιεῖν πρὸς τὸ ζῆν κατὰ τὸ κράτιστον τῶν ἐν αὐτῷ (*Neque vero nos oportet humana sapere ac sentire, ut quidam monent, quum simus homines; neque mortalia, quum mortales; sed nos ipsos, quoad ejus fieri potest, a mortalitate vindicare, atque omnia facere, ut ei nostri parti, quae in nobis est optima, convenienter vivamus.*[22] *Nicomachean Ethics*, x. 7). Such an intellectual tendency is certainly an extremely rare anomaly; but precisely on that account its fruits in the course of time benefit the whole of mankind, since fortunately they are such as can be preserved. On further consideration, we can divide thinkers into those who think *for themselves* and those who think *for others*; the latter are the rule, the former the exception. Accordingly, the former are original and independent thinkers in a double sense and egoists in the noblest sense of the word; it is they alone from whom the world obtains instruction. For it is only the light that a man kindles for himself which afterwards radiates for others so that the converse of what Seneca asserts in a moral regard, namely *alteri vivas oportet, si vis tibi vivere*[23] (*Epistulae*, 48) is true from an intellectual point of view: *tibi cogites oportet, si omnibus cogitasse volueris.*[24] But this is precisely that rare anomaly which is not to be enforced by any resolution and good will, yet without which no real progress in philosophy is possible. For others or generally for indirect aims, a man never undergoes the greatest mental exertion which is required for this purpose and which demands just the forgetting of self and of all aims; on the contrary, he stops at the mere semblance and pretence of things. Possibly a few concepts are found and com-

---

[22] ['But we should not, as the poets remind us, ponder as human beings over human things and as mortals over mortal things; but we should, as far as possible, aspire to the immortal and should do everything in order to live in accordance with what is noblest in us.']

[23] ['You must live for others if you wish to live for yourself.']

[24] ['You must think for yourself if you wish to have thought for all.']

bined in several different ways so that out of them is fashioned a house of cards, as it were; but in this way nothing new and genuine comes into the world. Moreover, there is the fact that those whose real aim is their own wellbeing, thinking being merely the means thereto, must always keep in view the passing needs and inclinations of contemporaries, the aims and intentions of those in authority, and so on. Here one cannot aim at the truth which, even when honestly looked for, is infinitely difficult to come across.

But speaking generally, how is anyone who seeks an honest living for himself and his family to devote himself simultaneously to *truth*, which has at all times been a dangerous companion and everywhere an unwelcome guest? Presumably it appears naked because it brings nothing and has nothing to bestow, but is sought merely for its own sake. We cannot at the same time serve two such different masters as the world and truth which have nothing in common but the same initial letter;[25] such an undertaking leads to hypocrisy, toadyism, and opportunism. For it can happen that a priest of truth becomes a champion of fraud and deception who earnestly teaches what he himself does not believe, and thus wastes the time and ruins the minds of trusting and gullible youth. Renouncing all literary conscience, he devotes himself to the praising and crying up of influential blunderers and sanctimonious blockheads, or makes a point of deifying the State, of making it the pinnacle of all human efforts and all things because he is paid by the State for State purposes. In this way, he not only turns the philosophical lecture-room into a school of the shallowest philistinism, but in the end, like Hegel for instance, he arrives at the revolting doctrine that man's destiny is identified with the *State*, somewhat like that of bees in a beehive; whereby the highest goal of our existence is entirely withdrawn from view.

In his descriptions of the Sophists whom he contrasts with Socrates, Plato has shown that philosophy is not suitable for breadwinning; but at the beginning of the *Protagoras* he has described, delightfully and with matchless humour, the activities and successes of these men. With the ancients money-making with philosophy was always the sign that distinguished the sophist from the philosopher. The relation between the two

[25] [The two words in German are *Welt* and *Wahrheit*.]

was, therefore, entirely analogous to that between girls inspired by true love and paid prostitutes. I have already shown in my chief work, vol. ii, chap. 17, that on this account Socrates put Aristippus among the sophists and even Aristotle reckoned him to be one. Stobaeus reports that the Stoics also held similar views (*Eclogae ethicae*, lib. II, c. 7): τῶν μὲν αὐτὸ τοῦτο λεγόντων σοφιστεύειν, τὸ ἐπὶ μισθῷ μεταδιδόναι τῶν τῆς φιλοσοφίας δογμάτων· τῶν δ' ὑποτοπησάντων ἐν τῷ σοφιστεύειν περιέχεσθαί τι φαῦλον, οἱονεὶ λόγους καπηλεύειν, οὐ φαμένων δεῖν ἀπὸ παιδείας παρὰ τῶν ἐπιτυχόντων χρηματίζεσθαι, καταδεέστερον γὰρ εἶναι τὸν πρόπον τοῦτον τοῦ χρηματισμοῦ τοῦ τῆς φιλοσοφίας ἀξιώματος.²⁶ (See Stobaeus, *Eclogae physicae et ethicae*, ed. Heeren, 2nd Pt., vol. i, p. 226.) The passage in Xenophon, quoted by Stobaeus in the *Florilegium*, vol. i, p. 57, also runs according to the original (*Memorabilia*, I. 6. 17): τοὺς μὲν τὴν σοφίαν ἀργυρίου τῷ βουλομένῳ πωλοῦντας, σοφιστὰς ἀποκαλοῦσιν.²⁷ Ulpian also puts the question: *An et philosophi PROFESSORUM numero sint? Et non putem, non quia non religiosa res est, sed quia hoc primum PROFITERI eos oportet, MERCENARIAM OPERAM SPERNERE.*²⁸ (*Lex*, I, §4, *Digesta de extraordinaria cognitione*, 50. 13.) Opinion on this point was so unshakeable that we find it in full force even under the later emperors; for even in Philostratus (lib. I, c. 13), Apollonius of Tyana reproaches his opponent Euphrates mainly with τὴν σοφίαν καπηλεύειν (*sapientiam cauponari*),²⁹ and also in his fifty-first epistle he writes to this very man: ἐπιτιμῶσί σοί τινες, ὡς εἰληφότι χρήματα παρὰ τοῦ βασιλέως· ὅπερ οὐκ ἄτοπον, εἰ μὴ φαίνοιο φιλοσοφίας εἰληφέναι μισθόν, καὶ τοσαυτάκις, καὶ ἐπὶ τοσοῦτον, καὶ παρά τοῦ πεπιστευκότος, εἶναί σε φιλόσοφον. (*Reprehendunt te quidam, quod pecuniam ab imperatore acceperis: quod absonum non esset, nisi videreris philosophiae mercedem accepisse,*

---

²⁶ ['A difference is to be drawn between those who confess that they just teach as sophists, namely impart for money the doctrines of philosophy, and those who think that to teach as a sophist merits a rebuke, since it is a peddling and bartering of ideas, and who declare that it is not permitted to take money for the education of those in search of knowledge, as this kind of money-making is not conducive to the dignity of philosophy.']

²⁷ ['Those who sell wisdom for money to anyone wanting it are called sophists.']

²⁸ ['Are philosophers also to be included among the *professors*? I think not; not because it is not here a question of something carried out with conscientious care, but because it behoves them above all publicly to confess that they *disdain to work for reward*.']

²⁹ ['To barter with wisdom'.]

et toties, et tam magnam, et ab illo, qui te philosophum esse putabat.)[30] In keeping with this, he says of himself in the forty-second epistle that he would accept alms in case of necessity, but never a reward for philosophy, not even in case of destitution: '*Ἐάν τις Ἀπολλωνίῳ χρήματα διδῷ, καὶ ὁ διδοὺς ἄξιος νομίζηται, λήψεται δεόμενος· φιλοσοφίας δὲ μισθὸν οὐ λήψεται, κἂν δέηται* (Si quis Apollonio pecunias dederit et qui dat dignus judicatus fuerit ab eo; si opus habuerit, accipiet. Philosophiae vero mercedem, ne si indigeat quidem, accipiet).*[31] This time-honoured view is well founded and is based on the fact that philosophy has very many points of contact with human life, both public and private. And so if profit is being derived from it, intention at once gains an ascendancy over insight and from self-styled philosophers we get mere parasites of philosophy. But such men will by hostile obstruction oppose the activities of genuine philosophers; in fact they will plot against them merely to assert what their cause is promoting. For as soon as it is a case of profit, it may easily happen that, where interest and advantage demand it, every kind of mean and low device, every form of connivance and coalition and so on, are employed in order to procure for material ends a favourable reception and acceptance for the false and the inferior. It therefore becomes necessary to suppress the true, the genuine, and the valuable that are opposed to them. But no man is less a match for such stratagems than the genuine philosopher who with his cause might have come under the activities of these tradesmen. Little harm is done to the fine arts, even to poetry, by their serving for gain; for each of their works has by itself a separate existence, and the bad can no more supplant the good than it can eclipse it. But philosophy is a whole and thus a unity; it is directed to truth, not to beauty. There are many kinds of beauty but only one truth; many Muses but only one Minerva. For this reason, the poet may cheerfully disdain to censure what is bad, but the philosopher may find himself in the predicament of having to

---

[30] ['Some reproach you with having taken money from the king. This would not be inadmissible, if you did not give the impression of having taken it for philosophy, indeed so often and in such large sums, and moreover from one who was bound to think that you were a philosopher.']

[31] ['If anyone offers money to Apollonius and is deemed worthy to give it, then Apollonius will accept it if he needs it; but he will take no reward for philosophy, not even if he were in need of the money.']

do so. For now the bad that has found favour opposes the good with downright hostility and the luxuriant weed chokes the useful plant. By its very nature, philosophy is exclusive; in fact it is the basis of the manner of thought of the age; and so the prevailing system, like the sons of sultans, will not tolerate beside it any other. Add to this the fact that judgement is extremely difficult, indeed the procuring of data for it is arduous and laborious. Now if by tricks and stratagems the false is brought into circulation and is everywhere noised abroad by paid stentorian voices as the true and genuine, then the spirit of the times is poisoned, all branches of literature are ruined, all higher flights of the mind are at a standstill, and a bulwark is set up against all that is really good and genuine, and it lasts for a long time. These are the fruits of the φιλοσοφία μισθοφόρος.[32] Let us see, by way of illustration, the mischief that has been done to philosophy since Kant's time and what has come of it. But it is only the true story of Hegelian charlatanry and of the ways in which it has been spread about which will one day afford a fitting illustration of what has been said.

In consequence of all this, the man who is concerned not with State and comic philosophy, but with knowledge and hence with the investigation of truth that is meant seriously and without regard for others, will have to look for it anywhere but at the universities, where its sister, the philosophy *ad normam conventionis*,[33] is in command and writes the bill of fare. Indeed I am more and more inclined to the view that for philosophy it would be more wholesome if it ceased to be a money-making business and no longer appeared in ordinary life and represented by professors. It is a plant which, like the rhododendron and flowers that grow on precipices, thrives only in free mountain air, but which with artificial cultivation degenerates. Those who represent philosophy in ordinary life do so in much the same way as an actor represents the king. Were the sophists, whom Socrates challenged so indefatigably and Plato made the theme of his derision, in any way different from the professors of philosophy and rhetoric? Is it not really that very old feud which I am still carrying on at the present time, since it is has never entirely ceased to exist? The highest efforts of the human

---

[32] ['Philosophy serving for remuneration'.]
[33] ['According to the current pattern'.]

mind are at once incompatible with profit; their noble nature cannot be amalgamated therewith. Perhaps philosophy at the universities might still pass muster if its appointed teachers, after the manner of other professors, thought of satisfying their vocation by passing on to the rising generation the knowledge of their particular subject as it exists and passes for truth at the moment, and thus by truly and accurately explaining to their hearers the system of the most recent genuine philosopher and going over in detail all the points. This, of course, would be the case if only they were to apply to their task enough judgement, or at any rate discernment, not to regard as philosophers mere sophists, such as a Fichte or a Schelling, not to speak of a Hegel. But they not only lack the aforesaid qualities; they also labour under the fatal and erroneous idea that it appertains to their office themselves to play the part of philosopher and to present the world with the fruits of their profound thought. From this erroneous idea there now result those productions, as deplorable as they are numerous, wherein commonplace minds, and indeed such as are not even commonplace, deal with *those* problems on whose solution the greatest efforts of the rarest minds, equipped with extraordinary abilities, have been directed for thousands of years. Forgetting about their own persons through their love for truth, such minds have occasionally been thrown into prison and even driven to the scaffold by their passionate striving for the light. Such minds are so exceedingly rare that the history of philosophy which for two thousand five hundred years has run concurrently with that of nations as its ground-bass can hardly show one-hundredth as many famous philosophers as political history can show famous monarchs. For there are no minds other than those that are wholly isolated wherein nature had come to a clearer consciousness of herself. But these very minds are so remote from the crowd that well-merited recognition comes to most of them only after their death or at best late in life. For instance, Aristotle's really great fame, which later became more widespread than any other, first began, according to all accounts, two hundred years after his death. Epicurus, whose name is known to the vast majority even at the present time, lived in Athens entirely unknown up to his death (Seneca, *Epistulae*, 79). Bruno and Spinoza were accepted and honoured only in the second century after their death. Even so clear and popular a writer as David Hume was fifty years old before people began to pay any attention to him, although he had produced his works many years previously. Kant became famous only after the age of sixty. With our present-day chair-philosophers matters certainly move more quickly, for they have no time to lose. Thus one professor proclaims as the finally attained pinnacle of human wisdom the doctrine of a prosperous colleague at a neighbouring university, and the latter is at once a great philosopher who promptly occupies his place in the history of philosophy, that is to say, in the one that is being prepared by a third colleague for the next fair. Quite unconcerned, he now tacks on to the immortal names of the martyrs of truth from all the centuries the worthy names of his well-appointed colleagues who at the moment are flourishing, as just so many philosophers who can also enter the ranks, for they have filled very many sheets of paper and have met with universal consideration from colleagues. For example, we see written 'Aristotle and Herbart', or 'Spinoza and Hegel', 'Plato and Schleiermacher', and an astonished world cannot fail to see that philosophers, whom parsimonious nature formerly managed to produce only singly in the course of centuries, have during recent decades everywhere shot up like mushrooms among the Germans who, as we know, are so highly gifted. Naturally, this glory of the age is pushed forward in every way; and so whether in literary journals or even in his own works, one professor of philosophy will not fail to take into careful consideration the absurd and preposterous notions of another, and will do this with weighty countenance and official gravity so that it quite looks as though we were actually dealing here with real advances in human knowledge. In return for this, his own abortive efforts soon receive the same honour and indeed we know that *nihil officiosius quam cum mutuum muli scabunt.*[34] But seriously speaking, a thoroughly deplorable spectacle is presented by so many ordinary minds who, for the sake of office and profession, think themselves obliged to represent what nature had least of all intended them to do, and to assume burdens that require the shoulders of intellectual giants. It is painful for the hoarse to listen to singing and for the lame

---

[34] ['Nothing is more dignified than when two mules scratch each other.']

to watch dancing, but it is intolerable to watch a limited intellect philosophize. Now, to conceal a want of real ideas, many make for themselves an imposing apparatus of long compound words, intricate flourishes and phrases, immense periods, new and unheard-of expressions, all of which together furnish an extremely difficult jargon that sounds very learned. Yet with all this they say—just nothing; we obtain no new ideas and do not feel our insight increased, but are bound to sigh: 'We hear quite well the clattering of the mill, but do not see the flour.' Indeed we see only too clearly what paltry, common, shallow, and crude views are hidden behind this high-sounding bombast. If only we could give such comic philosophers a notion of the real and terrible seriousness with which the problem of existence grips the thinker and stirs his innermost being! Then they could no longer be comic philosophers; no longer concoct with composure frivolous rubbish about the absolute thought or the contradiction that is said to be found in all fundamental concepts, or enjoy with enviable satisfaction such hollow nuts as 'the world is the existence of the infinite in the finite', and 'the mind is the reflection of the infinite in the finite', and so on. It would be hard on them, for now they want to be philosophers and at the same time quite original thinkers. Now it would be just as likely for a common mind to have uncommon ideas as for an oak to bear apricots. On the other hand, everyone already has *ordinary* ideas and does not need them for lecturing; consequently nothing can ever be achieved here by ordinary minds, since in philosophy it is merely a question of ideas, not of experiences and facts. Conscious of the drawback, some have laid in a store of strange ideas that are most imperfectly and always superficially understood; and in their heads, of course, such ideas are always in danger of evaporating into mere phrases and words. They shift these about and perhaps try to fit them to one another like dominoes; thus they compare what one has said with what another has said, and again a third with a fourth, and from all this they try to appear clever and smart. In such men we should look in vain for a firm and fundamental view of things and the world, one based on intuitive perception and therefore thoroughly consistent and coherent. For this reason, they have no decided opinion or fixed and definite judgement about anything, but with the ideas, views, and exceptions learnt by them, they grope about as in a fog. Properly speaking, they have directed their efforts to knowledge and learning for the purpose of imparting further instruction. That might be so; but then they should not play the part of philosophers, but should learn how to distinguish the oats from the chaff.

The real thinkers have aimed at *insight*, and indeed for its own sake, since they ardently desired in some way to render comprehensible the world in which they happened to be; but this they did not do in order to teach and talk. And so, in consequence of constant meditation, there gradually grows in them a fixed, coherent, and fundamental view which always has as its basis the apprehension of the world through *intuitive perception*. From this paths radiate to all special truths which again reflect light on to the fundamental view. It follows also from this that they have at any rate a definite, well understood, and coherent opinion concerning every problem of life and the world; and so they do not need to square anyone with empty phrases, as do thinkers of the other kind. We always find the latter occupied with a comparison and consideration of the opinions of others instead of with things themselves. Accordingly, it might be imagined that it was a question of far countries about which we had to make a critical comparison of the accounts written by the few travellers who had been there, and not one of the real world that is spread out and clearly lies before their eyes. But with them it is a case of:

> Pour nous, Messieurs, nous avons l'habitude
> De rédiger au long de point en point,
> Ce qu'on pensa, mais nous ne pensons point.[35]
> Voltaire

But the worst feature of the whole business, which otherwise might be allowed to continue for the curious dilettante, is that it is in their interest that the shallow and insipid pass for something. But this it cannot do, if the genuine, the great, and the profound make their appearance and at once come into their own. Thus to stifle the good and to let the bad take its course unhindered, they get together, as do all the feeble and

[35] ['With regard to ourselves, gentlemen, we are accustomed to criticize at length and in detail what others have thought, but we do not think for ourselves at all.']

impotent, and form themselves into cliques and parties. They take possession of the literary journals in which, as also in their own books, they discuss their respective masterly achievements with profound reverence and an air of gravity, and in this way a short-sighted public is led by the nose. Their relation to real philosophers is somewhat like that of former master-singers to poets. By way of illustration of what has been said, one has only to see the scribblings of the chair-philosophers which regularly appear along with the literary journals that play their tune. Whoever is conversant therewith should consider the cunning with which the latter, should the occasion arise, are at pains to gloss over and hush up the significant as something insignificant, and should note the tricks employed by them for diverting the public's attention from it, mindful of the aphorism of Publilius Syrus: *Jacet omnis virtus, fama nisi late patet.*[36] (See *P. Syri et aliorum sententiae*, recension of J. Gruter. Meissen, 1790, l. 266.) Now with such considerations in mind, let us go back on this path to the beginning of the nineteenth century and see how, previously the Schellingites, and then far worse the Hegelians, recklessly sinned in this direction. Let us overcome our reluctance and turn over the pages of the nauseating rubbish, for no man can be expected to read it! Then let us consider and calculate how much time, paper, and money the public must have wasted on these bungling works in the course of half a century. The patience of the public is certainly incomprehensible, for year in year out it reads the endless twaddle of dull and insipid philosophasters, regardless of the tormenting tedium that broods like a thick fog over it, just because one reads and reads without ever gaining possession of an idea. For the writer who has nothing clear and definite in his mind heaps words on words and phrases on phrases; and yet he says nothing because he has nothing to say, knows nothing, and thinks of nothing. Yet he wants to talk and so chooses his words not in accordance with how they express his ideas and judgements more strikingly, but with how they more skilfully conceal the lack of them. Yet such stuff is printed, bought, and read, and half a century has elapsed without readers being aware that they *papan viento*, as the Spanish say, that is, gulp down mere air. However, in fairness I must mention that, to keep going

---

[36] ['There on the ground lies virtue, deprived of fame.']

this clattering mill, a very peculiar device is often employed whose invention is traceable to Messrs. Fichte and Schelling. I refer to the artful trick of writing abstrusely, that is to say, unintelligibly; here the real subtlety is so to arrange the gibberish that the reader must think he is in the wrong if he does not understand it, whereas the writer knows perfectly well that it is he who is at fault, since he simply has nothing to communicate that is really intelligible, that is to say, has been clearly thought out. Without this device Fichte and Schelling could not have established their pseudo-fame; but we know that no one has practised this same trick so boldly and to such an extent as has Hegel. At the very outset, he should have explained in clear and intelligible words the absurd fundamental idea of his pretended philosophy, namely that of turning the true and natural course of things upside down and accordingly of making *universal concepts* the primary, the original, the truly real thing (the thing-in-itself in Kant's language), concepts which are abstracted from empirical intuitive perception and therefore arise through our thinking away the modifications, and which are in consequence the more void the more universal they are; for only as a result of the truly real or thing-in-itself does the empirically real world first have its existence. He should have clearly explained this monstrous ὕστερον πρότερον,[37] indeed this really crazy notion, adding that such concepts without our assistance think and move by themselves. If he had done this, all would have laughed in his face, or would have shrugged their shoulders and regarded the tomfoolery as not worth their notice. But then even venality and baseness would have sounded the trumpet in vain in order to proclaim to the world as the highest wisdom the absurdest thing ever seen and for ever to compromise with its power of judgement the German learned world. On the contrary, under the veil of incomprehensible grandiloquent nonsense, it passed off and the crazy folly was a success:

> Omnia enim stolidi magis admirantur amantque,
> Inversis quae sub verbis latitantia cernunt.[38]

Lucretius, 1.642.

[37] [Making the consequent an antecedent; inverting the logical order by explaining a thing in terms of something which presupposes it.]

[38] ['Fools admire and love to excess everything that is said to them figuratively and in queer or puzzling words.']

Encouraged by such examples, almost every wretched scribbler has since taken a delight in writing with affected and fastidious abstruseness so that it might look as though no words could express his lofty or profound thoughts. Instead of endeavouring in every way to make himself clear to his reader, he seems to call out tauntingly to him: 'I am sure you cannot guess what is in my mind!' Now if, instead of replying: 'Then I'll go to blazes' and throwing the book away, the reader wearies himself to no purpose, then in the end he thinks it must be something extremely clever, exceeding even his power of comprehension, and with raised eyebrows he now calls his author a profound thinker. One of the consequences of this pretty proceeding is that, when anyone in England wishes to describe something as very obscure or even quite unintelligible, he says *it is like German metaphysics*,[39] in much the same way as the French say: *c'est clair comme la bouteille à l'encre.*[40]

It is perhaps superfluous to mention here, yet it cannot too often be said, that as a contrast good authors always make strenuous efforts to urge the reader to think exactly what they themselves have thought; for the man who has something worth imparting will see to it that it is not lost. And so good style depends mainly on whether a writer really has something to say; it is simply this small matter that most of our present-day authors lack and is responsible for their bad style. But in particular, the generic characteristic of the *philosophical* works of the nineteenth century is that of writing without really having something to say; it is common to them all and can therefore be just as well studied in Salat as in Hegel, in Herbart as in Schleiermacher. Then according to the homoeopathic method, the weak minimum of an idea is diluted with a fifty-page torrent of words and now with boundless confidence in the truly German patience of the reader the author calmly continues the twaddle on page after page. The mind that is condemned to such reading hopes in vain for real, solid, and substantial ideas; it pants and thirsts for any ideas as does a traveller for water in the Arabian desert—and must remain parched. On the other hand, let us take any *genuine* philosopher, no matter from what period or country, be he Plato or

39 [Schopenhauer's own words.]
40 ['There's no making head or tail of it.']

Aristotle, Descartes or Hume, Malebranche or Locke, Spinoza or Kant. We always come across a fine intellect pregnant with ideas which has and produces knowledge, but which in particular always honestly tries to communicate it to others. And so the receptive reader of such a thinker is immediately rewarded for the trouble of reading every line of him. At bottom, what makes the writings of our philosophasters so exceedingly poor in ideas and thus tormentingly tedious, is really the poverty of their intellect, but primarily the fact that their mode of expression generally moves in highly abstract, universal, and extremely wide concepts and thus usually parades only in vague, indefinite, and ambiguous expressions. But they are forced to this aerobatic course because they must guard against touching the earth where, by encountering the real, the definite, the individual, and the clear, they would run on to those dangerous rocks whereon their verbal schooners might be shipwrecked. For instead of firmly and steadily directing the senses and understanding to the world that lies before them in intuitive perception and thus to what is really and truly given, to what is pure, genuine, and in itself not exposed to error, and hence to that by which we have to fathom the essence of things—they know nothing except the highest abstractions, such as being, essence, becoming, absolute, infinite, and so on. They start from these and build systems whose contents ultimately amount to mere words. Thus such words are really only soap-bubbles which can be played with for a while, but cannot touch the ground of reality without bursting.

If, with all this, the harm done to the branches of learning by incompetent interlopers were merely that they achieve nothing therein, as is at present the case with regard to the fine arts, we could console ourselves with the fact and disregard it. But in philosophy they do positive harm, first by all being in a natural league against the good in order to keep up the reputation of the bad, and by exerting every effort to prevent the good from finding favour. For do not let us deceive ourselves; at all times and in all circumstances, all over the globe, there exists a conspiracy, framed by nature herself, of all the mediocre, inferior, and dull minds against intellect and understanding. Against these they all constitute a large body of loyal confederates. Or are we so artless as to believe that they just wait for superiority in order to acknowledge, admire, and proclaim it and thus see themselves rightly set at naught? Not likely! But *tantum quisque laudat, quantum se posse sperat imitari.*[41] 'In the world there shall be bunglers and none but bunglers so that we may be something!' This is their real motto, and preventing capable men from finding favour is an instinct as natural to them as catching mice is to a cat. The fine passage of Chamfort, quoted at the end of the previous essay, may also be recalled here. Let the open secret be once expressed and the moon-calf be brought to light, strange as it may appear therein; narrow-mindedness and stupidity always and everywhere, in all situations and circumstances, detest nothing in the world so heartily and thoroughly as understanding, intellect, and talent. Here mediocrity remains true to itself, as is shown in all the spheres and affairs that relate to life, for it endeavours everywhere to suppress, indeed to eradicate and exterminate, superior qualities in order to exist *alone*. No kindness, no benevolence can reconcile it with intellectual superiority. Thus it is unalterable and will ever remain so; and what a formidable majority it has on its side! This is one of the main obstacles to mankind's progress in every sphere. Now in such circumstances how can there be progress in *that* sphere where not even plenty of brains, diligence, and tenacity of purpose are enough, as in other branches of knowledge, but quite special gifts are required even at the expense of personal happiness? For assuredly the most disinterested sincerity of purpose, the irresistible urge to solve the riddle of existence, the earnestness of deep thinking that strives to fathom the innermost essence of things, and a genuine enthusiasm for truth—these are the first and indispensable conditions for the hazardous enterprise of stepping up once more to the ancient sphinx with another attempt at solving its eternal riddle, at the risk of falling headlong into the dark abyss of oblivion whither so many have already gone.

Further harm that is done in all branches of knowledge by the activities of unauthorized interlopers is that a temple of error is erected, and superior minds and upright characters have to toil and moil at its subsequent demolition, sometimes

---

[41] "Everyone praises only as much as he himself hopes to achieve.']

throughout their lives; and so it is in philosophy, in knowledge that is most general, most important, and most difficult! If we want special proofs of this, let us look at the hideous example of Hegelry, that shameless pretended wisdom, which for one's own careful and honest thought and investigation substituted as a philosophical method the dialectical self-movement of concepts and hence an objective *thought-automaton* that gambols on its own account freely in the air or in empyrean and whose traces and footprints are the scriptures of Hegel and the Hegelians. Such, however, are merely hatched out of very thick and shallow skulls; and far from being something absolutely objective, they are exceedingly subjective and the invention of very mediocre subjects at that. And so let us contemplate the height and duration of this Babel-structure and reflect on the incalculable harm such a philosophy of absolute nonsense, forced on studious youths by strange and extraneous means, was bound to do to the generation that grew up on it, and thus to the whole age. Are not innumerable minds of the present generation of scholars thoroughly distorted and deranged by it? Are they not crammed with corrupt views, and do they not accept hollow phrases, meaningless twaddle, and nauseating Hegel-jargon where thoughts and ideas are expected? Is not their entire view of life crazy and has not the most insipid, philistine, and even vulgar way of thinking supplanted noble and lofty thoughts which were still the inspiration of their immediate predecessors? In short, are not the youths who have grown to maturity in the incubator of Hegelry like men intellectually castrated, incapable of thinking, and full of the most ludicrous presumption? Indeed, they are constituted in mind as were certain heirs to the throne in body who were formerly rendered unfit to govern or even to propagate by attempts to debauch or drug them. They are mentally enervated, robbed of the regular use of their reason, an object of pity, a lasting theme for paternal tears. Now let us hear from the other side what scandalous opinions are spread abroad concerning philosophy itself and generally what groundless reproaches there are against it. On closer examination, it is found that these detractors understand by philosophy nothing but the senseless and purposeless twaddle of that wretched charlatan and its echo in the hollow heads of his silly and absurd admirers; this is what they mean by philosophy! They simply do not know any other. In fact, almost the whole of the younger set has been infected with Hegelry as it has been with venereal disease; and just as this evil poisons all the humours of the body, so has that other ruined all their mental powers. Thus the younger scholars of today are, as a rule, no longer capable of sound thought or even of any natural expression. In their heads there exists not only no single correct notion, but not even one clear and definite idea about anything; the confused and empty verbiage has dissolved and dispersed their powers of thought. Moreover, the evil of Hegelry is just as difficult to eradicate as is the disease just compared to it, when once it has penetrated *in succum et sanguinem*. On the other hand, it was fairly easy to establish it and spread it in the world, for insight and intelligence are soon enough driven from the field when designs and intentions are marshalled against them, in other words, when *material* ways and means are used for the spreading of opinions and the stipulation of judgements. Guileless and unsophisticated young men go to the university full of childlike trust and gaze with awe at the self-styled possessors of all knowledge and now even at the presumptuous investigator of our existence, at the man whose fame they hear enthusiastically proclaimed by a thousand tongues and whose lectures they see attended by elderly statesmen. And so they go there ready to learn, believe, and revere. Now if these innocent youths without judgement are presented, under the name of philosophy, with a complete chaos of thought that is turned upside down, a doctrine of the identity of being and nothing, an assortment of words that cause all thought to vanish from a sound mind, a twaddle recalling bedlam, all this trimmed with touches of crass ignorance and colossal stupidity, as irrefutably and incontestably shown by me from Hegel's compendium for students—this I did in the preface to my *Ethics* in order to cast in the teeth of the Danish Academy, that happily inoculated encomiast of bunglers and patron of philosophical charlatans, its *summus philosophus*—then these youths will revere even such stuff. They will merely think that philosophy must indeed consist in such abracadabra and will go forth with minds paralysed in which henceforth mere words pass for thoughts; thus they will for ever be incapable of producing real ideas and so will be mentally castrated. As a result, there grows up a generation of impotent, perverse, yet excessively pretentious minds, swelling with plans and purposes and intellectually anaemic, such as we have before us at the present time. This is the mental history of thousands whose youth and finest faculties have been infected by that pretended wisdom, whereas they too should have partaken of the benefit which nature prepared for many generations when she succeeded in producing a mind like Kant's. Such abuses could never have been practised with real philosophy that is pursued by free men simply for its own sake and has no other support except that of its own arguments, but only with university philosophy that is primarily a State expediency. We see, therefore, that the State has at all times interfered in the philosophical disputations of the universities and has taken sides, no matter whether it was a question of Realists and Nominalists, or Aristotelians and Ramists, or Cartesians and Aristotelians, of Christian Wolff, Kant, Fichte, Hegel, or anything else.

In addition to the harm done by university philosophy to that which is genuinely and seriously meant, we have in particular the supersession, already mentioned, of the Kantian philosophy by the vapourings of the three trumpeted sophists. First Fichte and then Schelling, both of whom were not without talent, but finally Hegel, that clumsy and nauseating charlatan, that pernicious person, who completely disorganized and ruined the minds of a whole generation, were proclaimed as the men who had carried forward Kant's philosophy, had gone beyond it, and so, by really climbing on to his shoulders, had attained an incomparably higher degree of knowledge and insight. From this height they then looked down almost with pity on the labours of Kant which paved the way to their splendour so that they were the first to be the really great philosophers. It was not to be wondered at that young men, without any judgement of their own and that often very wholesome distrust of teachers which only the exceptional mind brings to the university, that is to say, one endowed with power of judgement and so also with a feeling for this—that these young men just believed what they heard and consequently imagined that they need not waste much time on the heavy preparatory work to the new lofty wisdom and thus on the old and formal Kant. On the contrary, they hastened to the new temple of wisdom where those three windbags accordingly sat in succession on the altar to the song of praise of stultified adepts. But now, unfortunately, there is nothing to be learnt from those three idols of university philosophy; their writings waste time and also ruin minds, Hegel's indeed most of all. The result of this state of affairs has been that those with a real knowledge of the Kantian philosophy have gradually died; and so, to the disgrace of the times, this most important of all the philosophical doctrines ever put forward could not continue its existence as something vivid and sustained in men's minds. It exists only in the lifeless letters of its author's works, to await a wiser, or rather less infatuated and mystified, generation. Accordingly, we shall hardly find a thorough understanding of the Kantian philosophy except among a few of the older scholars. On the other hand, the philosophical authors of our day have shown the most scandalous ignorance of it. This is seen to be most shocking in their descriptions of this doctrine, and it clearly stands out whenever they come to speak on the Kantian philosophy and affect to know something about it. We then become indignant when we see that men who live by philosophy do not really and truly know the most important teaching which has been advanced during the last two thousand years and is almost contemporary with them. In fact, they even go so far as to misquote the titles of Kant's works and occasionally represent him as saying the very opposite of what he did say. They mutilate his *termini technici* to the point of absurdity and use them without having the slightest idea of what he signified by them. Naturally it is not possible, indeed it is a ludicrous presumption, to suppose that we can become acquainted with the teaching of that profound mind by hastily scanning Kant's works, as befits such book scribblers and philosophical tradesmen who, moreover, imagine that they 'got through' all this long ago. Kant's first apostle Reinhold said that he fathomed the real meaning of the *Critique of Pure Reason* only after he had strenuously studied it five times. From the descriptions furnished by such men, an accommodating public led by the nose imagines once more that it can assimilate Kant's philosophy in the shortest time and without any effort! But this is absolutely impossible. Without our own strenuous and frequently repeated study of Kant's chief works, we shall never obtain even a mere notion of these most important of all the philosophical phenomena that have ever existed. For Kant has perhaps the most original mind ever produced by nature. To think with him and in his way is something that cannot possibly be compared with anything else; for he possessed a degree of clear and quite peculiar balance of mind such as has never fallen to the lot of any other mortal. We partake of this enjoyment when, initiated through careful and serious study and by reading the really profound chapters of the *Critique of Pure Reason* and giving our whole attention to the subject, we now succeed in actually thinking with Kant's mind and thus in being elevated far above ourselves. This is the case, for example, when we once again go through the 'Principles of the Pure Understanding'; when we consider especially the 'Analogies of Experience' and now fathom the profound idea of the *Synthetic Unity of Apperception.* We then feel ourselves removed and estranged in a marvellous way from the wholly dream-like existence in which we are submerged. For we take up each of its primary elements by itself and now see how time, space, and causality, connected by the synthetic unity of apperception of all phenomena, render possible this empirical complex of the whole and its course wherein our world, so greatly conditioned by the intellect, consists, being precisely on this account mere phenomenon. The synthetic unity of apperception is thus that connection of the world as a whole which rests on the laws of our intellect and is therefore inviolable. In its description Kant demonstrates the primary and fundamental laws of the world where they converge into one with the laws of intellect and before us he holds them up strung out on one thread. This method of consideration which is exclusively Kant's own, may be described as the most detached view that has ever been cast on the world and has the highest degree of objectivity. To follow this method affords an intellectual pleasure perhaps unequalled by any other. For it is of a higher order than that provided by poets who are, of course, accessible to everyone, whereas the pleasure here described must have been preceded by effort and exertion. But what do our present-day professors of philosophy know about it? Really nothing. Recently I read a psychological diatribe by one of them in which much turned on Kant's 'synthetic apperception' (*sic*); for they love to use Kant's technical expressions although, as here, these have only been half picked up and rendered meaningless. Now he imagined that, by this, concentrated attention was to be understood! These and similar small matters thus constitute the favourite themes of their kindergarten philosophy. In fact, those gentlemen do not have either the time, the inclination, or the urge to study Kant; they are as little concerned with him as they are with me; for their refined taste quite different men are needed. Thus what the acute and discriminating Herbart, the great Schleiermacher, or even 'Hegel himself' has said is the stuff for their meditation and its suits them. Moreover, they are heartily glad to see the 'all-crushing Kant' relegated to oblivion, and hasten to make him a dead historical phenomenon, a corpse, a mummy, whom they can then face without fear. For in all seriousness, he has in philosophy put an end to Jewish theism; but they like to hush this up, to conceal and ignore it because without this theism they cannot *live*—I mean eat and drink.

After such a set-back from the greatest advance ever made in philosophy, we need not wonder why the so-called philosophizing of these days has fallen into a wholly uncritical method, an incredible coarseness concealed behind high-sounding phrases and a naturalistic fumbling far worse than it had ever been before Kant. For instance, with an impudence born of ignorance, men everywhere summarily speak of *moral freedom*, as though it were a settled affair, indeed as something absolutely certain, and likewise of the existence and essence of God as things that are self-evident, and of the '*soul*' as a person known to all. Even the expression 'inborn ideas', which since Locke's time had had to slink into a corner, again ventures forth. Here may also be mentioned the gross impudence with which Hegelians in all their works talk at great length without ceremony or introduction about the so-called 'spirit'. They rely on our being far too dumbfounded by their grandiloquent nonsense to tackle the professor, as would be right and proper, with the question: 'Spirit? who is the fellow? Whence do you obtain your knowledge of him? Is he not rather an arbitrary and convenient hypostasis which you do not even define, let alone deduce or demonstrate? Do you think you have before you a public of old women?' This would be the language appropriate to such a philosophaster.

In connection with 'synthetic apperception', I have shown an amusing characteristic of the philosophizing of these tradesmen that, although they do not use Kant's philosophy as being very inconvenient and also much too serious for them and because they can no longer really understand it, they like to make lavish use of the expressions thereof, to give their twaddle a scientific touch, in much the same way as children like to play with papa's hat, stick, and sword. For instance, the Hegelians do this with the word 'categories' with which they express all kinds of wide and universal concepts, blissfully innocent of and unconcerned about Aristotle and Kant. Further, the important question in the Kantian philosophy concerns the *immanent and transcendent* uses, together with the validity, of our knowledge or cognitions. To embark on such dangerous distinctions would not, of course, be advisable for our comic philosophers; but yet they would have liked the expressions very much because they sound so learned. In fact, since their philosophy always has as its main subject only the good Lord, who now appears as a good old acquaintance needing no introduction, they employ these expressions, and now argue as to whether he is within the world or remains outside, that is to say, resides in a space where there is no world. In the former case, they call him *immanent*, and in the latter *transcendent*; and naturally they do all this very seriously and learnedly and talk Hegel jargon as well. It is a delightful jest that reminds the older ones among us of the copper engraving in Falk's satirical almanac that shows Kant ascending to heaven in a balloon, casting to earth all the articles of his wardrobe including his hat and wig, and monkeys picking them up and putting them on.

There is no doubt that the supplanting of Kant's serious, profound, and honest philosophy by the vapourings of mere sophists who are guided by personal aims, has had a most pernicious influence on the culture of the age. The eulogy of so utterly worthless, indeed so mischievous, a mind as Hegel's, as the first philosopher of this or any age, has certainly been the cause of the complete degradation of philosophy and, in consequence thereof, of the decline generally during the last thirty years of superior literature. Woe to the time when in philosophy impudence and nonsense supplant insight and understanding, for the fruits assume the taste of the soil in which they have grown. What is loudly, publicly, and universally praised, is read and is thus the mental pabulum of the generation that is arriving at maturity; but this has the most decided influence on its lifeblood and subsequently on its creations. Thus the prevailing philosophy of an age determines its spirit, and so if there now prevails a philosophy of absolute nonsense; if absurdities invented and advanced under bedlamite twaddle pass for great thoughts, then the result of such sowing is the pretty race of men such as we now have before us. They are without intellect, love of truth, honesty, taste, and are devoid of any noble impulse or of an urge for anything lying beyond material, including political, interests. From this we can explain how the age when Kant philosophized, Goethe wrote, and Mozart composed, could be followed by the present one of political poets and even more political philosophers, of hungry men of letters who earn a living in literature by falsehood and imposture, and of ink-slingers of all kinds who wantonly ruin the language. It calls itself with one of its home-made words, as characteristic as it is euphonious, the 'present time';[42] present time indeed, in other words, because one thinks only of the Now and does not venture to glance at the time that will come and condemn. I wish I could show this 'present time' in a magic mirror what it will look like in the eyes of posterity. Yet this present time calls that past age, just eulogized, the 'age of pigtails'; but attached to those tails were *heads*;[43] it now seems as though the fruit has also vanished with the stalk.

Hegel's followers are accordingly quite right when they assert that their master's influence on his contemporaries was immense. To have completely paralysed mentally a whole generation of scholars, to have rendered them incapable of all thought, indeed to have brought them to such a pass that they no longer know what thinking is, but regard as philosophical thinking the most wanton, as well as the most absurd, playing with words and concepts, or the most thoughtless rubbish on the stereotyped themes of philosophy with fabricated assertions,

---

[42] [The German word is *Jetztzeit*, one of many which Schopenhauer in an essay on the mutilation of the German language condemned as cacophonous.]

[43] [Schopenhauer plays on the words *Zopf* (tail) and *Kopf* (head).]

or with propositions wholly devoid of sense and even consisting of contradictions—all this has been the boasted influence of Hegel. Let us for once compare the textbooks of the Hegelians, which they have the audacity to publish even today, with those of an age that is disparaged but especially regarded with infinite contempt by them and all post-Kantian philosophers, the so-called eclectic period shortly before Kant. We shall then find that the latter are always related to the former not as gold to copper, but as gold to dung. For in those works by Feder, Platner, and others, we invariably find a rich store of real, partially true, and even valuable ideas and striking remarks, an honest ventilation of philosophical problems, a stimulation to individual reflection, a guide to philosophizing, but above all an honest method of treatment throughout. On the other hand, in a similar product of the Hegelian school, we search in vain for any real idea—it does not contain a single one: for any trace of serious and sincere thinking—this is foreign to its business. We find nothing but audacious word combinations which seem to have a meaning, indeed a profound one, but which, when examined, are unmasked as absolutely hollow shells and flourishes of words that are entirely devoid of sense and ideas. With them the writer certainly does not try to instruct his reader, but merely to mislead him, and the latter believes he is dealing with a thinker, whereas the former is a person who does not know what thinking is, a transgressor without any insight and moreover without knowledge. This is the consequence of the fact that, whereas other sophists, charlatans, and obscurantists adulterated and corrupted only *knowledge*, Hegel ruined even the *organ* thereof, the understanding itself. Through his forcing misguided men to cram into their heads, as rational knowledge, a farrago of the grossest nonsense, a tissue of *contradictiones in adjecto*,[44] a babbling from a madhouse, the brains of the poor young men who read such stuff with faithful devotion, and tried to assimilate it as the highest wisdom, were so deranged that they for ever remained incapable of real thought. Accordingly, we see them going round, even at the present time, talking in the nauseating Hegel jargon, praising the master, and quite

---

[44] [Logical inconsistencies between nouns and their modifying adjectives, e.g. 'round square', 'hot snow', 'cold fire'.]

seriously imagining that sentences like 'Nature is the idea in its other being' mean something. Thus to disorganize fresh young minds is really a sin meriting neither forgiveness nor forbearance. This, then, has been Hegel's boasted influence on his contemporaries, and unfortunately it has really spread far and wide; for here too the consequence was commensurate with the cause. Just as the worst that can befall a State is for the most depraved class, the dregs of society, to come into office, so nothing worse can befall philosophy and everything dependent thereon, and thus mankind's whole knowledge and intellectual life, than for a commonplace mind that is distinguished, on the one hand, merely by its obsequiousness and, on the other, by its effrontery to write nonsense, consequently for a Hegel to be proclaimed, with the strongest and most unprecedented emphasis, as the greatest genius and the man in whom philosophy has attained, finally and for all time, its long-pursued goal. For the consequence of such high treason against the noblest of mankind is eventually a state of affairs such as that of philosophy and thus of literature generally at the present time in Germany. Ignorance at the top fraternizing with impudence, cliquishness in place of merit, utter chaos of all fundamental concepts, totally wrong orientation and disorganization of philosophy, flat-heads as reformers of religion, the impudent appearance of materialism and bestiality, ignorance of the ancient languages, mutilation of our own by senseless word clippings and the infamous counting of letters at the discretion of duffers and blockheads, and so on, and so on— look round for yourselves! Even as the external symptom of the coarseness that is gaining the upper hand, you see its constant concomitant, the long beard, that sign of sex in the middle of the face which states that a man prefers the masculinity he has in common with the animals to *humanity*, since he wants first to be a *male* (*mas*), and only subsequently a *human being*. Shaving off beards in all highly civilized ages and countries is the result of a correct feeling to the contrary by virtue whereof one would like to be first of all a *human being*, to some extent a human being *in abstracto*, setting aside the animal sexual difference. On the other hand, length of beard has always kept pace with barbarism, which its name seems to imply. Thus beards flourished in the *Middle Ages*, that millennium of coarseness and ignorance whose style and fashion our noble present-timers [*Jetztzeitler*] strive to imitate.* Also we cannot omit to mention the further and secondary consequence of the treachery to philosophy which we are here discussing, namely contempt for the nation on the part of neighbours and for the age on the part of posterity. For as we make our bed so must we lie on it, and we shall not be spared.

I have already spoken of the powerful influence of intellectual nourishment on the age. Now this is based on the fact that such nourishment determines the form as well as the material of thought; and so very much depends on what is praised and therefore read. For thinking with a genuinely great mind strengthens our own, gives it regular exercise, and puts it in the right frame. It works in much the same way as does the writing-master's hand when guiding the child's. On the other hand, to think with men who have really aimed at mere pretence and hence at deceiving the reader, men like Fichte, Schelling, and Hegel, ruins the mind to an equal extent; this is no less true of thinking with cranks or with those who, like Herbart for instance, have turned their intellect inside out. Speaking generally, however, it is a deplorable waste of time and energy to read the writings of only ordinary minds in those branches of knowledge where it is not a question of facts or their discovery, but an author's own ideas constitute the subject-matter. For what such men think can also be thought by anyone else. The fact that they have expressly adjusted and applied themselves to thinking does not improve matters at all; for it

* It is said that the beard is natural to man; certainly, and so it is quite suitable to him in a state of nature, just as, on the contrary, shaving is suitable to him in the civilized state, since it indicates that the rough brutal power, whose distinctive mark is that excrescence characteristic of the male sex and palpable to everyone, has had to yield to law, order, and civilization.

The beard exaggerates and renders conspicuous the animal part of the face and thus gives it a strikingly brutal appearance. We have only to contemplate the profile of such a bearded man while he is eating!

They would like to pretend that the beard is an *ornament*. For two hundred years we have been accustomed to see this only on Jews, Cossacks, Capuchins, prisoners, and highwaymen.

The atrocious ferocity, given to the countenance by the beard, is due to the fact that a relatively *inanimate* mass occupies half the face, and moreover the morally expressive half. Besides, all hairiness is brutal. Shaving is the symbol (standard token) of higher civilization. In addition, the police are authorized to forbid beards since they are half-masks that make it difficult for them to recognize their man again, and thus encourage all kinds of mischief.

does not enhance their powers and, when a man expressly turns to thinking, he often does the minimum. Moreover, their intellect remains true to its natural destiny of working in the service of the will, for this is just the normal thing. And so an *intention or purpose* always underlies their thoughts and actions; at all times they have an *aim or end in view* and recognize only what relates and thus corresponds thereto. Activity of the intellect that is freed from the will is the condition of pure objectivity and thus of all great achievements, but it remains eternally foreign to ordinary men and is in their hearts a fiction. Only aims and ends are of interest to them and have for them any reality; for in them willing remains predominant. It is, therefore, doubly foolish to waste time on their productions. But the *aristocracy of nature* is what the public never recognizes and understands because it has good reasons for not wanting to. It therefore soon lays aside the rare and the few to whom nature, in the course of centuries, had entrusted the noble mission of reflecting on her or even of presenting the spirit of her works, in order to make itself acquainted with the productions of the latest bungler. If a hero has ever existed, the public soon puts some miserable wretch beside him, as being similar to him. When in her most propitious mood nature has once allowed to proceed from her hands the rarest of her creations, a mind really gifted above the average; when fate in a generous vein has allowed it to be developed; indeed when its works have finally 'triumphed over the opposition of a stupid world',[45] and are acknowledged and recommended as the standard, then it is not long before men come along with a clod who is dragged from their own coterie in order to put him on the altar beside the gifted intellect simply because they do not understand, or even suspect, how *aristocratic nature is*. She is so to such an extent that not one truly great mind is to be found in three hundred millions of her manufactured articles. We should, therefore, become thoroughly acquainted with that mind and regard its works as a kind of revelation; we should read them assiduously and wear them out *diurna nocturnaque manu*.[46] On the other hand, we should have nothing to do with all the commonplace minds and should regard them as what they are, as something just as common and ordinary as flies on a wall.

[45] [From Goethe's *Epilog zu Schiller's Glocke*.]   [46] ['Day and night'.]

In philosophy the state of affairs just described has arisen in a most deplorable way. Fichte is invariably mentioned with Kant and is described as just like him; 'Kant and Fichte' has become a standing phrase. 'See how we apples swim!'[47] said the—. Schelling meets with a similar honour and, *proh pudor!*[48] even Hegel, that scribbler of nonsense and destroyer of minds! The summit of this Parnassus was ever more widely trodden. To such a public we should like to exclaim what Hamlet said to his infamous mother: 'Have you eyes? have you eyes?' Alas! they have none. They are always the same. Everywhere and at all times, they have allowed genuine merit to perish in order to pay homage to mimics and mannerists of all kinds. Thus they imagine they are studying philosophy when they read the extensive creations of minds in whose dull consciousness even the mere problems of philosophy make as little sound as does a bell in a receptacle that is exhausted of air. Strictly speaking, such minds were made and equipped by nature for nothing but quietly earning an honest living like the rest, or for cultivating the field and providing for an increase in the human race; yet they imagine they must be 'jingling fools'[49] on account of their official duty. Their constant butting in and desire to have their say make them like deaf people who join in a conversation. Thus the effect on those who at all times appear only sporadically and naturally have the calling and therefore the real urge to work at the investigation of the loftiest truths, is only like that of a disturbing and bewildering noise, even when it does not, as is very often the case, purposely stifle their voice. For what such isolated minds assert does not serve the purpose of those men for whom there can be nothing serious except intentions and material aims and who, by virtue of their considerable numbers, soon raise such a clamour that a man can no longer hear himself speak. Today they have set themselves the task, in spite of truth and the Kantian philosophy, of teaching speculative theology, rational psychology, freedom of the will, a total and absolute difference between man and the animals by ignoring the gradual shades

---

[47] [A translation of the Latin proverb *ut nos poma natamus.*]
[48] ['What a scandal!']
[49] [From Goethe's *Faust*, Pt. i. *Sei er kein schellenlauter Thor.* (Beware, a jingling fool to be!)]

of intellect in the animal series. In this way, they act only as a remora[50] to the honest investigation of truth. If a man like me speaks, they pretend that they have heard nothing. The trick is good although it is not new. However, I want to see whether or not a badger can be dragged out of his hole.

Now it is obvious that the universities are the centre of all those games that are played with philosophy by purpose and intention. Only by this means could Kant's world-wide epoch-making achievements in philosophy be supplanted by the vapourings of a Fichte which were again supplanted shortly afterwards by fellows like him. This could never have happened with a really philosophical public, that is to say, with one that looks for philosophy merely for its own sake and without any other object, and hence with that public which is, of course, at all times an extremely small number of genuine and earnest thinkers who are deeply impressed by the mysterious nature of our existence. The entire philosophical scandal of the last fifty years has been possible only through the universities with a public that consists of students who religiously take in all that the professor is pleased to tell them. Here the fundamental error is to be found in the fact that the universities, even in matters of philosophy, arrogate to themselves the last word and decisive voice which possibly belong to the three principal faculties each in its own sphere. But the fact is overlooked that in philosophy, as a science that is first to be discovered, matters are different. One also disregards the fact that, with the appointment to chairs of philosophy, not only are the abilities of the candidates taken into consideration, as with other branches of knowledge, but even more so are their views and opinions. Accordingly, the student now thinks that, as the professor of theology is thoroughly conversant with his dogmas, the professor of law with his pandects, and the professor of medicine with his pathology, so too the professor of metaphysics who is appointed to the highest place must be a master of his subject. The student, therefore, attends the course of lectures with childlike trust, and as he finds there a man who, with an air of conscious superiority, looks down on and criticizes all the philosophers who have ever existed, he has no doubt that he has come to the right place and is as faithfully

50 ['Hindrance'.]

impressed by all the bubbling wisdom there as if he were sitting before the tripod of Pythia. Naturally from now on, there is for him no other philosophy but that of his professor. The real philosophers, the instructors of hundreds and even thousands of years, are left unread as being obsolete and refuted, but their works solemnly wait in silence on the shelves of bookcases for those who desire them; like his professor, the student has 'done with' them. On the other hand, he buys the regularly appearing mental offspring of his professor whose frequently repeated editions can be explained only from such a state of affairs. For after his years at the university, every graduate as a rule continues to be faithfully devoted to his professor whose turn of mind he early assumed and whose manner he has adopted. In this way, such philosophical monstrosities obtain an otherwise impossible circulation and their authors a lucrative reputation. How otherwise could such a complex of absurdities, like Herbart's *Einleitung in die Philosophie* for instance, have run through five editions? Thus the fatuous presumption again appears (e.g. on pages 234–5 of the fourth edition) with which this decidedly perverse mind condescendingly looks down on Kant and indulgently puts him right.

Considerations of this kind, and especially a retrospective glance at the whole business of philosophy at the universities since Kant's death, establish ever more firmly in me the opinion that, if there is to be a philosophy at all, that is to say, if it is to be granted to the human mind to devote its loftiest and noblest powers to incomparably the weightiest of all problems, then this can successfully happen only when philosophy is withdrawn from all State influence. Accordingly, the State will do it a great service and sufficiently show its humanity and magnanimity, if it does not pursue philosophy but gives it free play and allows it to exist as a free art, which after all must be its own reward. In return for this, the State can consider itself exempt from spending money on professorships of philosophy, since the men who want to live *on* philosophy will be just those extremely rare ones who really live *for* it, but occasionally there may be even those who furtively plot *against* it.

Official chairs of learning belong by rights only to those branches of knowledge which are already formed and actually exist and which one, therefore, need only have learnt in order to be able to teach. Thus, speaking generally, such branches of knowledge are merely to be passed on, as is implied by the *tradere* in use on the blackboard; yet here it is still open to more capable minds to enrich, correct, and perfect them. But a branch of knowledge which in fact does not yet exist and has not yet attained its goal and which does not even know for certain its path, in fact whose very possibility is still in dispute— to allow such a branch to be taught by professors is really absurd. The natural consequence of this is that each of them thinks his vocation to be the creation of the still missing branch of knowledge, without taking into consideration that such a calling can be entrusted only by nature not by the Ministry of Education. He therefore makes the attempt as best he can, speedily places his abortion in the world, and gives it out as the long-desired wisdom; and there will certainly not be wanting an obliging colleague who at the christening will act as its godfather. These gentlemen, accordingly, become bold enough to call themselves *philosophers* because they live on philosophy; and so they imagine that the last word and decision in philosophical matters rest with them. In the end, they even announce *meetings of philosophers* (a *contradictio in adjecto*,[51] for rarely are there two philosophers simultaneously in the world and hardly ever more than two), and then they flock together to compare notes on the advantage of philosophy!*

Nevertheless, such university philosophers will first of all endeavour to give philosophy that tendency which is in keeping with the aims they have at heart or rather have taken to heart. For this purpose they will, if necessary recast and misrepresent and even falsify the teachings of earlier genuine philosophers, simply in order that the result will be what they need. Now as the public is so childish as to rush after the latest authors whose writings, however, bear the title of philosophy, the result is that,

---

* 'No philosophy having the sole disposal of the means of grace!' exclaims the *meeting of philosophasters at Gotha*, which means in plain language: 'No attempt at objective truth! Long live mediocrity! No intellectual aristocracy, no autocracy of nature's favourites, but mob rule instead! Let each of us speak without the least reserve and let one have as much influence as another!' The rascals then have great fun! Thus even in the history of philosophy they would like to displace the constitutional monarchy hitherto existing and introduce a proletarian republic. But nature lodges a protest; she is severely aristocratic!

[51] [A logical inconsistency between a noun and its modifying adjective, e.g. 'round square', 'hot snow', cold fire'.]

through the absurdity, perversity, senselessness, or at any rate the tormenting tedium thereof, sound minds with a propensity for philosophy are again deterred therefrom whereby it gradually falls into discredit, as is already the case.

But not only are the professors' own productions in a bad way; the period since Kant also shows that it is not even capable of keeping and preserving the achievements of great minds which are acknowledged as such and are accordingly committed to their charge. Have they not allowed the Kantian philosophy to be trifled with at the hands of Fichte and Schelling? Do they not in a most scandalous and defamatory way always mention the windbag Fichte with Kant as being roughly his equal? After the above-mentioned two philosophasters had supplanted and declared obsolete Kant's teaching, did not the most unbridled and fantastic notions take the place of the strict control that was imposed by Kant on all metaphysics? Have they not partly contributed to this and to some extent refrained from firmly setting themselves against this with the *Critique of Reason* in their hands? Was this not because they found it more advisable to make use of the lax observance that had set in either to offer for sale their concocted trivialities, such as Herbart's fudge and Fries's grandmotherly gossip, and generally the whims and fancies of everyone, or even to be able to smuggle in as philosophical conclusions the doctrines of the established religion? Has not all this paved the way to the most scandalous philosophical charlatanry at which the world has ever had to blush, to the activities of Hegel and his miserable fellows? Did not even those who opposed the mischief at the same time always speak with much bowing and scraping about the great genius and powerful intellect of that charlatan and scribbler of nonsense, thereby showing themselves to be simpletons? Are not Krug and Fries alone to be excluded from these (in the interest of truth, be it said) who, resolutely denouncing the mind-destroyer, have merely shown him that forbearance that is now irrevocably shown by every professor of philosophy towards another? Have not the noise and clamour that are raised by the philosophers at German universities in admiration of those three sophists at last attracted general attention even in England and France which on further investigation degenerated into laughter? But they prove to be the perfidious warders and keepers of truths which in the course of centuries were acquired with great difficulty and were finally entrusted to their charge, especially when these do not suit their purpose, that is to say, do not harmonize with the results of a shallow, rationalistic, optimistic theology that is really only Jewish. It is such theology that is the secretly predetermined goal of their whole philosophizing and its lofty phrases. And so they will attempt to obliterate, disguise, suppress, misrepresent, and drag down to the level of what fits in with their plan for educating students and with the aforesaid petticoat philosophy, all those doctrines which serious philosophy, not without great efforts, has managed to bring to light. A shocking instance of this is afforded by the doctrine of the *freedom of the will*. After the strict necessity of all human acts of will had been irrefutably demonstrated by the united and successive efforts of great minds like Hobbes, Spinoza, Priestley, and Hume, even Kant had accepted the matter as already fully established,[52] they suddenly act as if nothing had happened, rely on the ignorance of their public, and in God's name even at the present time assume in almost all their manuals that the freedom of the will is an established and even immediately certain fact. What sort of name does such a method merit? If such a teaching, as firmly established as any by all the philosophers just mentioned, is nevertheless concealed or denied by the professors for the purpose of imposing on students the positive absurdity of free will because it is a necessary ingredient of their petticoat philosophy, are not these gentlemen really the enemies of philosophy? And since (for *conditio optima est ultimi*,[53] Seneca, *Epistulae*, 79) the strict necessity of all acts of will is nowhere demonstrated so thoroughly, clearly, consistently, and completely as in my essay that was fairly awarded a prize by the Norwegian Society for Scientific Studies, we find that, in accordance with their old policy of everywhere meeting me with passive resistance, this essay is not mentioned anywhere either in their books or in their learned journals and literary periodicals. It is most rigorously concealed and is regarded

---

[52] With him his postulate of freedom, based on the categorical imperative, is of merely practical, *not theoretical* validity. See my *Fundamental Problems of Ethics*, 'Freedom of the Will', chap. 4; 'Basis of Ethics', §6.

[53] ['The last man is in the most favourable position.']

comme non avenu,[54] just as is everything that does not serve their contemptible purpose like my ethics generally, indeed like all my works. My philosophy just does not interest those gentlemen; but this is because the investigation of truth does not interest them. On the contrary, what does interest them are their salaries, the guineas they charge, and their titles as privy councillors. It is true that philosophy also interests them in so far as they earn from it their daily bread. They are what Giordano Bruno has already characterized as *sordidi e mercenarii ingegni, che, poco o niente solleciti circa la verità, si contentano saper, secondo che comunmente è stimato il sapere, amici poco di vera sapienza, bramosi di fama e reputazion di quella, vaghi d'apparire, poco curiosi d'essere*.[55] (See *Opere di Giordano Bruno* published by A. Wagner, Leipzig, 1830, vol. ii, p. 83.) And so what would my essay 'On the Freedom of the Will' be to them, even if it had been awarded a prize by ten academies? On the other hand, the drivel that has since been written on the subject by the dullards of their company is puffed up and recommended. Do I need to qualify such conduct? Are these the men who represent philosophy, the rights of reason and freedom of thought? Another instance of the kind is afforded by *speculative theology*. The fact that Kant removed all arguments that constituted its props and completely overthrew it, does not in the least prevent my friends of the lucrative philosophy, even sixty years later, from giving out speculative theology as the real and wholly essential subject of philosophy. However, since they do not attempt to take up once more those exploded arguments, they now talk incessantly without more ado about the *absolute*, a word that is nothing but an enthymeme, a conclusion from premises not expressed. This they do for the purpose of masking and establishing in a cowardly and cunning manner the cosmological proof which, since Kant's time, can no longer appear in its own form and must, therefore, be smuggled in in this disguise. It is as though Kant had had a presentiment of this last trick, for he expressly says: 'Men have at all times talked of the

---

[54] ['As not having occurred'.]

[55] ['Sordid and mercenary fellows who pay little or no heed to truth; they are content with knowledge that is ordinarily regarded as such and have little love for genuine wisdom. They crave for the reputation and prestige that are furnished by wisdom; they desire to appear something and are little concerned at being something.']

absolutely necessary being and have taken the trouble not so much to understand whether and how a thing of this nature could even be conceived, as rather to prove its existence— For to reject by means of the word *unconditioned* all the conditions that are always required by the understanding, in order to regard something as necessary, does not by any means enable me to understand whether through a concept of something unconditionally necessary, I am then thinking of something, or possibly of nothing at all.' (*Critique of Pure Reason*, 1st edn., p. 592; 5th edn., p. 620.) Here I recall once more my doctrine that to be necessary implies absolutely and everywhere nothing but to follow from an existing and given reason or ground, such ground thus being the very *condition* of all necessity. Accordingly, the unconditionally necessary is a *contradictio in adjecto*, and is therefore no thought at all, but a hollow expression, a material that is, of course, frequently used in the structure of professorial philosophy. Further, it may here be mentioned that, in spite of Locke's great epoch-making and fundamental doctrine of the *non-existence of innate ideas* and of all progress since made in philosophy on this basis particularly by Kant, the gentlemen of the φιλοσοφία μισθοφόρος[56] quite coolly impose on their students a 'divine consciousness', in general an immediate knowledge or understanding of metaphysical subjects through the faculty of reason. It is of no avail that Kant demonstrated with a display of the rarest acumen and depth of thought that theoretical reason can never arrive at objects that lie beyond the possibility of all experience. The gentlemen pay no regard to anything of the sort, but for fifty years have summarily taught that the faculty of reason has positively direct and absolute knowledge, that it is really a faculty originally based on metaphysics, one that immediately knows and positively grasps, beyond all possibility of experience, the so-called supersensuous, the absolute, the good Lord, and whatever else there is said to be. But it is obviously a fairy-tale, or more bluntly a palpable lie, that our *reason* is a faculty of such a nature that it knows the required objects of metaphysics not *by means of conclusions or inferences*, but *immediately*. For we need only an honest yet

[56] ['Philosophy serving for remuneration'.]

otherwise not difficult self-examination to convince ourselves of the groundlessness of such an allegation; moreover, the case was bound to be quite different with metaphysics. Yet one of the worst results of philosophy at the universities is that such a lie, which is thoroughly pernicious for philosophy and lacks all motive except confusion and the cunning intentions of its propagator, has for half a century become the regular dogma of the chair, and has been repeated thousands of times and imposed on young students, in spite of the evidence of the greatest thinkers.

However, in keeping with such training, the real and essential theme of metaphysics is for the chair-philosophers the discussion of the relation between God and the world; its most detailed arguments fill their textbooks. Above all, they deem themselves appointed and paid to settle this matter and it is then amusing to see how precociously and learnedly they talk about the Absolute or God, putting on quite serious airs as if they really knew something about it; we are reminded of the seriousness with which children pursue their games. For at every fair a new system of metaphysics appears which consists of a most detailed account of the good Lord and explains how matters really stand with regard to him and moreover how he came to make the world, or give birth to it, or otherwise produce it, so that it seems as if every six months we receive the latest news about him. Yet in this connection, many now come up against a certain difficulty whose effect is extremely comic. Thus they have to teach about a regular personal God as he appears in the Old Testament; this they know. On the other hand, Spinoza's pantheism according to which the word God is synonymous with world has for about forty years been the absolutely predominant and universal mode of thought among scholars and even those of ordinary education. But they would not like to give this up entirely and yet they dare not reach out for this forbidden dish. They now try to extricate themselves, as usual by means of obscure, vague, and confused phrases and hollow verbiage, from a position in which they shuffle and wriggle pitiably. We then see some of them assert in the same breath that God is totally, infinitely, and utterly, really utterly, different from the world, but is at the same time wholly and in every way united and identical with it, in fact is in it up to the ears. This always reminds me of Bottom, the weaver, in *Midsummer Night's Dream*, who promises to roar like a terrible lion, but can at the same time sing as softly as any nightingale. In this performance they encounter the strangest difficulty; for they assert that there is no place for him outside the world and yet they cannot make use of him within the world, and now bandy him about until they fall with him between two stools.*

On the other hand the *Critique of Pure Reason* with its proofs *a priori* of the impossibility of all knowledge of God is to them twaddle by which they do not allow themselves to be confused; for they know the purpose of their existence. To reply to them that nothing more unphilosophical can be imagined than to be for ever talking of something about whose existence we have no knowledge based on any evidence, and of whose real nature we have absolutely no conception, is impertinent interference on our part; for they know the purpose of their existence. They know me as one who is far beneath their notice and attention and through the complete disregard for my works they imagine that they have revealed what kind of man I am (although in precisely this way they have revealed what manner of men *they* are). And so it will be like talking to the winds, as it is with everything I have produced in the last thirty-five years, if I tell them that Kant was not joking when he said that philosophy is really and quite seriously not theology and never can be, but on the contrary is something quite different. In fact we know that, just as every other branch of knowledge is spoilt by an admixture of theology, so too is philosophy, and indeed most of all as is testified by its history. That this is also true even of morality has been very clearly demonstrated by me in my essay 'On the Basis of Ethics'. Therefore the professional gentlemen, true to their tactics of passive resistance, have also been as quiet as mice over this work. Thus theology covers with its veil all the problems of philosophy and so renders impossible not only their solution, but even their comprehension. Hence,

* From an analogous embarrassment comes the praise some of them now give me to save the honour of their good taste, since my light is now no longer hidden under a bushel. But they hasten to add the assurance that in the principal point I am wrong, for they will take care not to agree with a philosophy which is something quite different from Jewish mythology, disguised as this is in high-sounding verbiage and strangely trimmed—a thing that with them is *de rigueur*.

as I have said, the *Critique of Pure Reason* was quite seriously the letter of the retiring *ancilla theologiae*[57] in which once for all she gave notice to her gracious mistress. Theology has since been content with a hireling who occasionally dons the discarded livery of the former servant merely for the sake of appearance; just as in Italy similar substitutes are frequently to be seen especially on Sundays and are, therefore, known by the name of *Domenichini*.

But of course Kant's *Critiques* and arguments were bound to be wrecked on the rocks of university philosophy. For there it says: *sic volo, sic jubeo, sit pro ratione voluntas*.[58] Philosophy *shall* be theology even if twenty Kants were to prove the impossibility of the thing; we know the purpose of our existence; we exist *in majorem Dei gloriam*.[59] Every professor of philosophy is a *defensor fidei*,[60] just as was Henry VIII, and herein he recognizes his primary and principal vocation. Therefore after Kant had so thoroughly dissected the nerve and sinew of every possible argument of speculative theology that no one has since been able to have a hand in them, philosophical effort has consisted, for almost fifty years, in attempts of all kinds to slip in theology quietly and surreptitiously, and philosophical writings are frequently nothing but fruitless attempts to resuscitate a lifeless corpse. For instance, the gentlemen of the lucrative philosophy discovered in man a *divine consciousness* that had so far escaped the whole world and, emboldened by their mutual agreement and by the innocence of their immediate public, they rashly and impudently cast it about and thus in the end led astray even the honest Dutch of Leiden University. Sincerely regarding the tricks and dodges of the professors of philosophy as advances in science, the Dutch quite ingenuously set the following prize-question on 15 February 1844; *Quid statuendum de Sensu Dei, qui dicitur, menti humanae indito*, and so on.[61] By virtue of such a 'divine consciousness', that which all philosophers up to Kant toiled so hard to demonstrate would be something *immediately known*. But what simpletons must all those previous philosophers

---

[57] ['The handmaid of theology'.]
[58] ['I wish that it shall be so; the wish exempts me from giving reasons.' (Juvenal, *Satires*, VI. 223.)]
[59] ['To the greater glory of God'.]   [60] ['Defender of the faith'.]
[61] ['What is the opinion regarding the divine consciousness that is innate in our minds?']

have been who all their lives had exhausted themselves in furnishing proofs of a thing whereof we are directly *conscious*, implying as it does that we know it even more immediately than that twice two are four, which certainly needs reflection. To want to demonstrate such a thing must be like wanting to prove that eyes see, ears hear, and noses smell. And what irrational brutes the Buddhists must be, that is to say, the followers of the principal religion on earth, to judge by the number who profess it. Their religious fervour is so great that in Tibet almost one man in six is in holy orders and submits to the celibacy thereby entailed. Their doctrine supports and sustains an extremely pure, sublime, loving, and strictly ascetic morality (which has not, like Christianity, forgotten the animals). This doctrine is not only decidedly atheistic, but even expressly rejects theism. Thus personality is a phenomenon, known to us only from our animal nature and so, when separated therefrom, is no longer clearly conceivable. Now to make such a phenomenon the origin and principle of the world is always a thesis that will not occur at once to any mind, much less have its roots and residence therein. On the other hand, an impersonal God is a mere subterfuge of professors of philosophy, a *contradictio in adjecto*, an empty expression for silencing those without ideas, or for appeasing the vigilant.

Thus the writings of our university philosophers manifest the liveliest enthusiasm for theology, but very little desire for truth. Without any respect for truth, sophisms, surreptitious methods, misrepresentations, and false assertions are with unheard-of effrontery used and even accumulated. As previously stated, immediate, supersensuous knowledge and hence innate ideas are ascribed, or more correctly falsely imputed, to the faculty of reason, all this simply to bring out theology; only theology, theology at any price! With due deference, I should like to leave the gentlemen to consider that theology may after all be of very great value, but I know of something that in any case is of even greater value, namely honesty; honesty in business as also in thinking and teaching. I would not part with it for all the theology in the world.

But as matters now stand, whoever has taken seriously the *Critique of Pure Reason* and has been quite honest about it, and accordingly has no theology to offer, is of course bound to come off second best *vis-à-vis* those gentlemen. Were he to bring even the most excellent and admirable thing the world has ever seen and serve up all the wisdom of heaven and earth, these men would still avert their eyes and ears if there were no theology. In fact the more merit his case has, the more will it excite not their admiration but their resentment; the more determined will be their passive resistance to it and hence the more malicious will be the silence with which they will attempt to stifle it; at the same time, the more blatantly will they sing encomiums over the delectable intellectual offspring of the fellowship that is so fertile in ideas. This they do merely in order that the voice of insight and sincerity, so hateful to them, may not make itself heard above the others. And so in this age of sceptical theologians and orthodox philosophers, this is demanded by the policy of the gentlemen who with wife and family support themselves on *that* branch of knowledge to which my whole being throughout a long life has sacrificed all its strength. For them the only question is one of theology in accordance with the hints and suggestions of their superiors; everything else is of secondary importance. At the outset each defines, in his own language, turns of phrase and veiled expressions, philosophy as speculative theology, and states quite naïvely that chasing after theology is the essential purpose of philosophy. They know nothing of the fact that we should approach the problem of existence freely and impartially and consider the world, together with the consciousness wherein it exhibits itself, as that which alone is given, as the problem, as the riddle of the old sphinx before whom we have boldly appeared. They cleverly ignore the fact that, if theology wants to be admitted into philosophy, it must first produce its passport, as must all other doctrines, and this is then examined at the office of the *Critique of Pure Reason*, as that which still enjoys the highest prestige among all thinkers, a reputation that has certainly not in the least been impaired by the comic grimaces that the chair-philosophers of the day have tried to make at it. And so without a credential of its own, theology obtains no admission; nor should it either by threats, cunning, or even by an appeal to the fact that the chair may not have anything else for sale. Let them shut up shop! For philosophy is not a church or a religion. It is that tiny spot in the world, accessible to extremely few, where truth, always and everywhere hated and persecuted, shall for once be free from all pressure and coercion; where its saturnalia, permitting as it were free speech even to slaves, shall honour, exalt, and even have the prerogative and final word; where truth shall reign absolutely alone and admit nothing else along with it. Thus the whole world and everything therein is full of *intention*, and often low, mean, and evil intention. Only one tiny spot shall, as a matter of course, remain free therefrom and be open simply to *insight*, indeed to that insight into relations that are of the utmost importance to all. This is philosophy; or are we to understand the matter differently? If so, then everything is a joke and a comedy—'As haply now and then the case may be.'[62] Of course to judge from the compendiums of the chair-philosophers, one would rather imagine that philosophy is a guide to godliness or an institution for training church-goers. For speculative theology is often quite openly assumed to be the essential aim and object of the whole business and to that end is piloted with rudder and full sail. But it is certain that each and every article of faith contributes to the positive ruin of philosophy. Such articles may now be introduced openly and avowedly into philosophy, as was done in Scholasticism, or they are smuggled in by *petitiones principii*,[63] false axioms, fictitious inner sources of knowledge, divine consciousnesses, sham arguments, high-sounding phrases, and grandiloquent nonsense, as is customary at the present time. Everything of this kind ruins philosophy because it renders impossible the clear, impartial, purely objective conception of the world and our existence, this first condition of all investigation of truth.

To lecture on the fundamental dogmas of the established religion under the name of philosophy and in strange guise, dogmas that are then given the title of 'absolute religion' according to one of Hegel's worthy expressions, may be a very profitable business. For it makes students better fitted for the purposes of State and likewise strengthens the reading public in the faith; but to give this out as *philosophy* is really equivalent to

---

[62] [Goethe's *Faust*, Pt. 1, Bayard Taylor's translation.]

[63] ['Begging of the question'. Fallacies that involve the assumption as premises of one or more propositions which are identical with (or in a simple fashion equivalent to) the conclusion to be proved, or which would require the conclusion for their proof.]

selling something for what it is not. If this and all the above-mentioned things continue their course undisturbed, then philosophy at the universities is bound to become more and more a *remora*[64] of the truth. For it is all over with philosophy when something other than pure truth alone is taken as the standard of its criticism or even as the guiding rule of its propositions, the truth that is so hard to arrive at even with a thoroughly honest investigation and the concentration of the highest mental powers. It degenerates into a mere fable that is agreed upon as true, or into a *fable convenue*[65] as Fontenelle called history. If we philosophize in accordance with a pre-arranged goal, we shall never advance even one step in the solution to the problems with which we are confronted on all sides by our infinitely mysterious existence. But, of course, no one will deny that such philosophizing is the generic characteristic of the various species of present-day university philosophy; for it is only too obvious that they all collimate their systems and propositions on to the one target-point. Moreover, this is not even New Testament Christianity proper or the spirit thereof which is too lofty, too ethereal, too eccentric, too little of this world, and thus too pessimistic for them and therefore totally unsuited to the apotheosis of the '*State*'. On the contrary, it is merely Judaism, the doctrine that the world has its existence from a supremely eminent personal being and hence is also a most delightful thing and πάντα καλὰ λίαν.[66] For them this is the kernel of all wisdom to which philosophy should lead, or be led if she shows any resistance. Hence too the war that, since the collapse of Hegelry, is waged by all professors against so-called pantheism in the unanimous condemnation of which they try to outdo one another. Can this zeal have arisen from the discovery of cogent and convincing reasons against it? Or rather do we not see with what embarrassment and alarm they look for reasons against that adversary that calmly stands in its original strength and smiles at them? And so can anyone still doubt that mere incompatibility of that doctrine with 'absolute religion' is the reason why it is not to be true, shall not be, even if the whole of nature proclaimed it from thousands of throats?

---

[64] ['Hindrance'.]   [65] ['A fable that is agreed upon as true.']
[66] ['(And God saw) every thing (that he had made, and, behold, it) was very good.' (Genesis 1:31.)]

Nature is to keep quiet so that Judaism may have its say. Now if there is still anything besides 'absolute religion' which is taken into consideration by them, it will, of course, be the other wishes of an important ministry that has the power to grant and withdraw professorships. This indeed is the Muse that inspires them and directs their lucubrations; and it is, therefore, regularly invoked at the beginning in the form of a dedication. To me these are the men to pull truth out of the well, to tear down the veil of deception, and to challenge all obscurity.

In no branch of learning, by the nature of the case, are men of supreme ability, imbued with a love of knowledge and eagerness for truth, so positively necessary as in the passing on, by word of mouth, to the flower of a new generation the results of the highest exertions of the human mind on the most important of all affairs, or indeed where there should be awakened in this generation the spirit of research. On the other hand, ministries consider that no branch of learning has so much influence on the most intimate views of future scholars and hence of the class that really rules the State and society, as precisely this branch. It must, therefore, be only in the hands of the most devoted men who trim their teaching wholly in accordance with the will and prevailing views of the ministry. Naturally it is the first of these two requirements that must take second place. Now to anyone unacquainted with this state of affairs, it may seem at times as though the most decided dunderheads had strangely devoted themselves to the study of Plato and Aristotle.

Here I cannot refrain from remarking incidentally that situations as private tutors are a very pernicious preparation for a professorship of philosophy; and nearly all who have ever held such situations after their studies at the university have for some years overlooked this fact. For such situations are a suitable training ground for submissiveness and docility. In such a post a man is especially in the habit of entirely subjecting his teachings to the will of his employer and of knowing no other aims than those of his master. This early acquired habit strikes root and becomes second nature so that afterwards, as professor of philosophy, a man finds nothing more natural than to trim and fashion even philosophy exactly in accordance with the wishes of the ministry in charge of professorships. In the end, the results are philosophical views or even systems which seem as though they were made to order. Truth then has a fine game! Here, of course, it is clear that, in order to pay absolute homage to truth and really to philosophize, so many conditions have to be fulfilled, but there is also one that is almost indispensable, namely that we stand on our own feet and recognize no master; accordingly the δός μοι ποῦ στῶ[67] is in a certain sense also applicable here. At any rate, most of those who ever achieved anything great in philosophy were in the same situation. Spinoza was so clearly aware of this that he declined the professorship that was offered to him.

> Ἥμισυ γὰρ τ' ἀρετῆς ἀποαίνυται εὐρύοπα Ζεύς
> Ἀνέρος, εὖτ' ἄν μιν κατὰ δούλιον ἦμαρ ἕλῃσιν.[68]

Real philosophizing demands independence:

> Πᾶς γὰρ ἀνὴρ πενίῃ δεδμημένος οὔτε τι εἰπεῖν,
> Οὔθ' ἔρξαι δύναται, γλῶσσα δέ οἱ δέδεται.[69]
> Theognis.

There is also a passage in Sadi's *Gulistan* (translated by Graf, Leipzig, 1846, p. 185) in which it says that whoever is burdened by the cares of earning a living cannot achieve anything. With reference to this, the genuine philosopher is by nature one who is easily satisfied and does not need much in order to live independently; for his motto will always be Shenstone's remark that 'liberty is a more invigorating cordial than Tokay.'

If, therefore, it were now only a question here of encouraging philosophy and of progressing on the path of truth, the best recommendation I should make would be to stop the prevarication and humbug that are carried on in its name at the universities. For these are really not the place for philosophy that is seriously and honestly meant; only too often is its place there occupied by a puppet dressed up in its clothes which, as a *nervis alienis mobile lignum*,[70] must gesticulate and make a show. Now if such a chair-philosophy still tries to replace genuine

---

[67] ['Give me a foothold' (and I move the earth.)]

[68] ['For thundering Zeus takes away half the excellence of a man as soon as the day of bondage overwhelms him.' (Homer, *Odyssey*, xvii. 322f.)]

[69] ['Everyone oppressed by poverty is unable to say or do what he likes; his tongue is no longer free.' (11. 177–8.)]

[70] ['A wooden doll that is moved by extraneous forces' (Horace, *Satires*, 11. 7. 82).]

ideas by incomprehensible, mind-stupefying phrases, new-fangled words, and unheard-of notions, the absurdities of which are called speculative and transcendental, then it becomes a parody of philosophy, and brings it into discredit; such has been the case in our day. With all this business how can there exist even the mere possibility of that profound seriousness which, together with truth, disregards everything and is the first condition of philosophy? The way to truth is steep and long; and no one will cover the distance with a block tied to his foot; on the contrary, wings would be necessary. Accordingly, I should be in favour of philosophy's ceasing to be a means of livelihood; with this the sublimity of its aspiration is incompatible; indeed this was recognized even by the ancients. It is quite unnecessary for a few shallow talkers to be kept at every university for the purpose of putting young men against philosophy for the rest of their lives. Voltaire is quite right when he says: *les gens de lettres qui ont rendu le plus de services au petit nombre d'êtres pensans répandus dans le monde, sont les lettrés isolés, les vrais savans, renfermés dans leur cabinet, qui n'ont ni argumenté sur les bancs de l'université, ni dit les choses à moitié dans les académies: et ceux-là ont presque toujours été persécutés.*[71] All help that is offered to philosophy from without is, by its nature, suspect. The interest of philosophy is of too lofty a nature for it to be capable of entering into a sincere alliance with the activities of this evilly disposed world. On the contrary, it has its own guiding star that never sets; we should, therefore, give it full play without assistance but also without hindrance. We should not let the serious pilgrim who by nature is endowed and ordained for the elevated temple of truth associate with a fellow who is really concerned only with a meal and a good night's lodging; for it is to be feared that such a man will push an obstacle in the path of the pilgrim in order to be after these amenities himself.

As a result of all this, leaving aside the purposes of State and considering only the interests of philosophy, I regard it as desirable that all instruction therein at the universities be strictly limited to lectures on logic as a complete and accurately

71 ['Those authors who have rendered the greatest service to the small number of world-famous thinkers are the isolated writers, the genuine scholars shut up in their studies, who have neither expounded their arguments from a university chair nor in academies put forward half-truths; and it is they who have almost always been persecuted.']

demonstrable science and to a history of philosophy. The latter should be given quite succinctly in a series of lectures, and should cover in one term of six months the period from Thales to Kant, so that in consequence of its brevity and lucidity of style as little scope as possible is given to the professor's own views and it appears merely as a guide to the student's own future course of study. For only in their own works and certainly not from second-hand accounts can we become really acquainted with philosophers; and I have given the reasons for this in the preface to the second edition of my chief work. Moreover, reading the original works of genuine philosophers in any case has a beneficial and encouraging influence on the mind, since it puts it into immediate touch with a superior and independent thinker. On the other hand, with those histories of philosophy, the mind always receives only the movement that can be imparted to it by the stiff and wooden train of thought of a commonplace intellect, one that has arranged matters in its own way. I should, therefore, like to limit those professorial lectures to a general orientation in the field of philosophical achievements to date and to eliminate from its presentation all arguments and pragmatism that would go further than demonstrate the unmistakable points of contact of successively appearing systems with those previously existing. And so this is in complete contrast with the presumption of Hegelian writers of the history of philosophy who show each system as necessarily taking place, and accordingly construct *a priori* the history of philosophy and demonstrate that every philosopher must have thought exactly what he did think and nothing else. In this connection, the professor very conveniently and haughtily ignores them all, even if he does not smile at them. The sinner! as though all this had not been the work of individual and isolated minds who had to be pushed about for a while in the evil company of this world so that such work would be rescued and saved from coarse and stupid gangs; minds who are as individual as they are rare and hence to each of whom Ariosto's *natura il fece, e poi ruppe la stampa*[72] applies in the fullest sense. And as though another would have written the *Critique of Pure Reason* had Kant died of smallpox, for instance, one of those manu- factured articles of nature with her trade-mark on his forehead,

[72] ['Nature stamped it and then smashed the mould.']

someone with the normal ration of three pounds of coarse brain of pretty tough texture, well preserved in a skull an inch thick, with a facial angle of 70 degrees, feeble pulse, dull inquisitive eyes, strongly developed mouth organs, a stammer, and a heavy slouching gait in keeping with the toad-like agility of his ideas. Yes indeed, you just wait! they will make *Critiques of Pure Reason* and even systems for you whenever the moment that is calculated by the professor arrives and it is their turn, that is to say, when oaks bear apricots. Of course, the gentlemen have good reasons for ascribing as much as possible to upbringing and education, even for flatly denying innate talents as some actually do, and for entrenching themselves in every way against the truth that everything depends on the way in which a man proceeded from the hands of nature, what father begot him and what mother conceived him, and indeed even at what hour. Therefore no man will write *Iliads* whose mother was a goose and whose father was a dullard, even if he has studied at six universities. But still it is no different; nature is aristocratic, more so than any feudal or caste system. Accordingly, her pyramid rises up from a very broad base to a very sharp apex. Even if the mob and rabble who will tolerate nothing over them succeeded in overthrowing all aristocracies, they would still have to allow this one to exist; and for this they shall get no reward; for it is quite properly 'by the grace of God'.

TRANSCENDENT SPECULATION ON THE APPARENT DELIBERATENESS IN THE FATE OF THE INDIVIDUAL

Τὸ εἰκῇ οὔκ ἐστι ἐν τῇ ζωῇ, ἀλλὰ μία ἁρμονία καὶ τάξις.
Plotinus, *Enneads*, IV, lib. 4, c. 35.

['Chance has no place in life, but only
harmony and order reign therein.']

Transcendent Speculation on the Apparent Deliberateness in the Fate of the Individual

ALTHOUGH the ideas to be given here do not lead to any firm result, indeed they might perhaps be termed a mere metaphysical fantasy, I could not bring myself to consign them to oblivion, since to many a man they will be welcome, at any rate as a comparison with his own that he may have entertained on the same subject. Yet such a man should also be reminded that in them everything is dubious and uncertain, not merely the solution but even the problem. Accordingly, here we have to expect anything but definite information; rather the mere ventilation of a very obscure set of facts which have suggested themselves possibly to everyone in the course of his life, or when he has looked back on it. Even our observations on the subject may perhaps not be much more than a fumbling and groping in the dark where we note that something does exist, yet we do not really know where or what it is. If, however, in the course of my remarks I should occasionally adopt a positive or even dogmatic tone, let it be said here and now that this is done merely in order not to become dull and diffuse through the constant repetition of the forms of doubt and conjecture, and that in consequence this is not to be taken seriously.

Belief in a special providence, or else in a supernatural guidance of the events in an individual's life, has at all times been universally popular, and even with thinkers who are averse to all superstition it is occasionally found firm and unshaken and entirely unconnected with any definite dogmas. Opposed to it in the first place is the fact that, like all belief in a God, it has sprung not really from *knowledge*, but from the *will*; thus it is primarily the offspring of our miserable state. The data for this, which might have been furnished merely by *knowledge*, could perhaps be traced to the fact that chance which plays us a hundred cruel and maliciously contrived tricks, does sometimes turn out particularly favourable to us, or indirectly ministers to our great benefit. In all such cases, we recognize therein the hand of providence and this most clearly when it has led us to a fortunate destiny against our own insight and even in ways that we abominate. We then say *tunc bene navigavi, cum naufragium feci*,[1] and the contrast between choice and guidance becomes unmistakably clear, but at the same time in favour of the latter. For this reason, when we meet with misfortunes, we console ourselves with that short maxim that is often proved true 'who knows it may be some good?' This has really sprung from the view that, although *chance* rules the world, *error* is nevertheless its co-regent, since we are as much subject to the one as to the other. Perhaps the very thing that now seems to us a misfortune is a blessing. Thus we shun the blows of one world-tyrant and rush to the other in that we turn from chance and appeal to error.

Apart from this, however, to attribute to pure evident chance a purpose or intention is an idea of unparalleled audacity. Yet I believe that everyone has had at least once in his life a vivid conception of it. It is found among all races and in all faiths, although it is most marked among the Mohammedans. It is an idea that can be the absurdest or profoundest according as it is understood. Nevertheless, striking as the instances may at times be whereby it could be supported, there is always the standing objection to them that it would be the greatest marvel if chance never watched over our affairs as well as, or even better than, our understanding and insight could have done.

Without exception everything that happens takes place with *strict necessity* and this is a truth to be understood *a priori* and consequently to be regarded as irrefutable; here I will call it demonstrable fatalism. In my prize-essay 'On the Freedom of the Will' (chap. 3, at the end) it follows as the result of all previous investigations. It is confirmed empirically and *a posteriori* by the fact, no longer in doubt, that magnetic somnambulists, persons gifted with second sight, and sometimes even the dreams of ordinary sleep directly and accurately predict future events.*

---

[1] ['I then had a good voyage, although I was shipwrecked.']

* In *The Times* of 2 December 1852 the following judicial statement is found: At Newent in Gloucestershire, Mr. Lovegrove the coroner held an inquest on a

This empirical confirmation of my theory of the strict necessity of all that happens is seen most strikingly in *second sight*. For in virtue thereof we afterwards see happen something that was often predicted long previously; it occurs with complete accuracy and with all the attendant circumstances just as they were stated, even when we had purposely made every effort to prevent it or make the event differ, at any rate in some minor circumstance, from the communicated vision. This has always been futile, since the very thing that was to frustrate the predicted event always helped to bring it about. It is precisely the same both in the tragedies and the history of the ancients, the calamity predicted by oracles or dreams is brought about by the very measures that are employed to prevent it. As instances of this, I merely mention from many *Oedipus Rex* and the fine story of Croesus with Adrastus in the first book of Herodotus, cc. 35–43. In keeping with these, we find cases of second sight given by the thoroughly reliable Bende Bendsen in the third part of the eighth volume of the *Archiv für thierischen Magnetismus* by Kieser (especially examples 4, 12, 14, 16), and also a case in Jung-Stilling's *Theorie der Geisterkunde*, § 155. Now if the gift of second sight were as frequent as it is rare, innumerable events predicted would happen exactly, and the undeniable factual proof of the strict necessity of all that happens would be generally evident and accessible to everyone. There would then no longer be any doubt that, however much the course of things was represented as being purely accidental, at bottom it was not so; on the contrary, all these accidents, τα εἰκῇ φέρομενα, are themselves enveloped in a deeply hidden necessity, εἱμαρμένη, whose mere instrument is chance itself. To gain an insight into this has from time immemorial been the endeavour of all *soothsayers*. Now from the divination just mentioned and founded on fact, it follows not merely that all

man named Mark Lane whose body was found in the water. The brother of the deceased stated that, on first hearing that his brother Mark was missing, he at once replied that he had been drowned, for the previous night he had dreamed that he stood in deep water and tried to pull him out. On the following night he again dreamed that his brother had been drowned near the sluice at Oxenhall and that *a trout was swimming close to him*. The next morning he went with his other brother to Oxenhall and there *saw a trout in the water*. At once he was convinced that his brother must be lying there and actually found the body at the spot. Thus something as fleeting as the swimming of a trout was some hours previously foreseen exactly to the second.

events occur with complete necessity, but also that they are in some way determined beforehand and objectively fixed, in that they present themselves to the eye of a seer as something existing. At all events, this could still be traced to the mere necessity of their occurrence in consequence of the course of the causal chain. In any case the insight, or rather the view, that this necessity of all that happens is *not blind* and thus the belief in a connection of events in the course of our lives, as systematic as it is necessary, is a fatalism of a higher order which cannot, like simple fatalism, be demonstrated, but happens possibly to everyone sooner or later and firmly holds him either temporarily or permanently according to his way of thinking. We can call this *transcendent fatalism*, as distinct from that which is ordinary and demonstrable. It does not come, like the latter, from a really theoretical knowledge or from the investigation necessary for this, for which few would be qualified; but it gradually reveals itself from the experiences in the course of a man's own life. Of these certain events become conspicuous to everyone and, by virtue of their being specially and peculiarly appropriate to him, they bear, on the one hand, the stamp of a moral or inner necessity, yet, on the other, they carry the clear impression of an external and wholly accidental nature. The frequent occurrence of this gradually leads to the view, often becoming a conviction, that the course of an individual's life, however confused it appears to be, is a complete whole, in harmony with itself and having a definite tendency and didactic meaning, as profoundly conceived as is the finest epic.* But now the information imparted to him in this way would relate solely to his individual will which in the last resort is his individual error. For plan and totality are to be found not in world history, as professorial philosophy would have us believe, but in the life of the individual. In fact, nations exist merely *in abstracto*; individuals are what is real. Therefore world history is without direct metaphysical significance; it is really only an accidental configuration. Here I remind the reader of what I have said on this point in the *World as Will and Representation*, vol. i, § 35. And so as regards their own individual fate, there

---

* If we very carefully turn over in our minds many of the scenes of the past, everything therein appears to be as well mapped out as in a really systematically planned novel.

arises in many that *transcendent fatalism* which at some time occurs perhaps to everyone through an attentive consideration of his own life after its thread has been spun out to a considerable length. In fact, when he reflects on the details of his life, this may sometimes be presented to him as if everything therein had been mapped out and the human beings appearing on the scene seem to him to be mere performers in a play. This transcendent fatalism has not only much that is consoling, but perhaps much also that is true; and so at all times it has been affirmed even as a dogma.* As being quite unprejudiced, the testimony of an experienced courtier and man of the world, given moreover at a Nestorian age, deserves here to be mentioned, namely that of the ninety-year-old Knebel, who in a letter says: 'On closer observation, we shall find that in the lives of most people there is to be found a certain plan which, through the peculiar nature or circumstances that direct it, is so to speak sketched out for them. The states of their lives may be ever so variable and changeable, yet in the end there appears a totality that enables us to observe thereunder a certain harmony and consistency.——However concealed its action may be, the hand of a definite fate is also strictly in evidence; it may be moved by external influence or inner impulse; indeed contradictory grounds may operate in its direction. However disorganized the course of life, motive and tendency, ground and direction, always make their appearance.' (Knebel's *Litterarischer Nachlass*, 2nd edn., 1840, vol. iii, p. 452.)

The systematic arrangement, here mentioned, in the life of everyone can be explained partly from the immutability and rigid consistency of the inborn character which invariably brings a man back on to the same track. Everyone recognizes immediately and with such certainty what is most appropriate to his character that, as a rule, he by no means receives it in clear reflecting consciousness, but acts according to it at once

---

* Neither our *action* nor our *course of life is our work*, but rather our *essence and existence*, which no one regards as our work. For on the basis of this and of the circumstances that happen in strict causal connection, and also of external events, our action and the course of our life take place with absolute necessity. Accordingly, at his birth the whole course of a man's life is already determined irrevocably down to its details, so that, at the height of her powers, a somnambulist could foretell it exactly. We should bear this great and certain truth in mind when we consider and judge the course of our life, our deeds, and our sufferings.

and, as it were, by instinct. In so far as this kind of knowledge
passes into action without having entered clear consciousness,
it is to be compared to the reflex motions of Marshall Hall.
By virtue thereof everyone pursues and takes up what is appropriate to him as an individual, even without his being able to
give a clear account of it to himself, and the power so to do
does not come to him either from without or from his own
false conceptions and prejudices. In the same way, the turtle
in the sand, that is hatched out by the sun, at once goes straight
to the water, even without being able to see it. And so this is
the inner compass, the mysterious characteristic, that brings
everyone correctly on to *that* path which for him is the only
suitable one; but only after he has covered it does he become
aware of its uniform direction. This, however, seems to be
inadequate in view of the powerful influence and great force
of external circumstances. Here it is very unlikely that the most
important thing in the world, namely the course of a man's
life purchased at the price of so much activity, trouble, and
suffering, should obtain only the other half of its guidance,
namely the part coming from without, simply and solely from
the hand of a really blind chance that is absolutely nothing in
itself and dispenses with all direction and order. On the contrary, we are tempted to believe that, just as there are certain
images or figures called anamorphoses (Pouillet, II. 171) which
reveal to the naked eye only distorted, mutilated, and shapeless
objects, but, on the other hand, show us regular human figures
when seen in a conical mirror, so the purely empirical apprehension of the course of the world is like that intuitive perception of the picture with the naked eye; the pursuit of fate's
purpose, on the other hand, is like the intuitive perception in
the conical mirror which combines and arranges what has there
been scattered apart. Against this view, however, may still
always be opposed the other that the systematic connection we
think we perceive in the events of our lives, is only an unconscious working of our regulating and schematizing imagination similar to that by which we clearly and distinctly discern
on a spotted wall human figures and groups, in that we bring
into systematic connection spots that have been scattered by
the blindest chance. Yet it may be supposed that what in the
highest and truest sense of the word is for us right and beneficial,

cannot really be what was merely projected but never carried into effect and hence has never obtained any other existence than the one in our thoughts—the *vani disegni, che non han' mai loco*[2] of Ariosto—whose frustration by chance we should then have to deplore for the rest of our lives. Rather is it that which is really stamped in the great image of reality and of which we say with conviction after recognizing its appropriateness, *sic erat in fatis*,[3] namely that it was bound to happen. Therefore there had to be some kind of provision for the realization of what is appropriate in this sense through a unity of the accidental and the necessary which lies at the very root of things. In virtue of that unity, the inner necessity showing itself as a kind of instinctive impulse, then rational deliberation, and finally the external operation of circumstances had to assist one another in the course of a man's life in such a way that, at the end thereof when it had been run through, they made it appear like a well-finished and perfected work of art, although previously, when it was still in the making, it had, as in the case of every planned work of art, the appearance of being often without any plan or purpose. But whoever came along after its completion and closely considered it, would inevitably gaze in astonishment at such a course of life as the work of the most deliberate foresight, wisdom, and persistence. Yet on the whole, it would be of significance according as its subject was ordinary or extraordinary. From this point of view, we might conceive the very transcendent idea that, underlying this *mundus phaenomenon* wherein chance reigns, there is generally to be found everywhere a *mundus intelligibilis* that rules over chance itself. Nature, of course, does everything simply for the species and nothing for the mere individual, since for her the former is everything, the latter nothing. But what we here assume as operative is not nature, but the metaphysical that lies beyond nature and exists whole and undivided in every individual to whom, therefore, all this is of importance.

To get to the bottom of these things, we should indeed first have to answer the following questions: is a complete disparity possible between a man's character and fate? or, looking at the main point, does the fate of everyone conform to his

---

[2] ['Vain plans that never have reality'.]
[3] ['Thus it was decreed in fate'.]

character? or finally, does a secret inconceivable necessity, comparable to the author of a drama, actually fit the two together always suitably? But on this very point we are in the dark.

Yet we think that at every moment we are masters of our actions; but if we look back on the course of our lives and in particular bear in mind our unfortunate steps together with their consequences, we often do not understand how we could do this or omit to do that, so that it looks as if a strange power has guided our steps. And so Shakespeare says:

> Fate, show thy force: ourselves we do not owe;
> What is decreed must be, and be this so!
> *Twelfth Night*, Act I, Sc. 5.

In verse and prose the ancients never weary of stressing the omnipotence of fate, showing thereby man's powerlessness by way of contrast. We see everywhere that this is a conviction with which they are imbued, since they suspect a mysterious connection of things which is deeper than the clearly empirical. (See Lucian's *Dialogues of the Dead*, XIX and XXX; Herodotus, lib. I, c. 91 and IX, c. 16.) Hence the many terms in Greek for this concept: πότμος, αἶσα, εἱμαρμένη, πεπρωμένη, μοῖρα, Ἀδράστεια, and possibly others. The word πρόνοια, on the other hand, shifts the concept of the thing in that it starts from νοῦς as something secondary, whereby it naturally becomes plain and intelligible, but also superficial and false.* Even Goethe says in *Götz von Berlichingen* (Act V): 'We human beings do not direct ourselves; power over us is given to evil spirits which practise their mischievous tricks to our undoing.' Also in *Egmont* (Act V, last scene): 'Man thinks he guides his life and directs himself; and his innermost being is irresistibly drawn in accordance with his fate.' Indeed the prophet Jeremiah has said: 'I know that the way of man is not in himself: it is not in man that walketh to direct his steps.' (10: 23). All this is due to our deeds being the necessary product of two factors one of which, our character,

---

* It is extraordinary how much the ancients were inspired and imbued with the notion of an omnipotent fate (εἱμαρμένη, *fatum*). Not only poets especially in tragedies, but also philosophers and historians are evidence of this. In Christian times the idea receded into the background and was less insisted on, since it was superseded by the notion of Providence, πρόνοια, which presupposes an intellectual origin and, starting from a personal being, is not so rigid and unalterable and also not so profoundly conceived and mysterious. Hence it cannot replace the former idea; on the contrary, it has reproached this with infidelity.

is immutably fixed and yet known to us only *a posteriori* and thus gradually; the motives are the other. These reside without, are necessarily brought about by the course of the world, and determine the given character, on the assumption of its fixed nature, with a necessity that is wellnigh mechanical. Now the ego that judges of the ensuing course of things is the subject of knowing; as such it is a stranger to both and is merely the critical spectator of their action. Then, of course, it may at times be astonished.

But if we have once grasped the point of view of that transcendent fatalism and from this aspect now consider the life of an individual, we at times behold the strangest of all spectacles in the contrast between the obvious physical contingency of an event and its moral metaphysical necessity. Yet this can never be demonstrated; on the contrary, it can only be imagined. To get a clear picture of this through a well-known example that, on account of its striking nature, is at the same time suitable as a typical case, let us consider Schiller's *Gang nach dem Eisenhammer*. There we see Fridolin's delay through attendance at mass brought about, on the one hand, just as accidentally as, on the other, it is so extremely important and necessary to him. If we carefully consider the matter, we shall perhaps be able to find analogous cases in our own lives, though not so important or so clear and definite. Many, however, will thus be driven to the assumption that *a secret and inexplicable power* guides all the turns and changes of our lives, indeed often contrary to the intention we had at the time. Yet it does this in such a way as to be appropriate to the objective totality and subjective suitability of our lives and consequently to promote our true and essential welfare. Thus afterwards we often recognize the folly of desires that were entertained in the opposite direction. *Ducunt volentem fata, nolentem trahunt*[4] (Seneca, *Epistulae*, 107). Now such a power that runs through all things with an invisible thread would also have to combine those, which without any mutual connection are allowed by the causal chain, in such a way that they would come together at the required moment. Accordingly, it would be just as complete a master of the events of real life as is the poet of those of his drama. But chance and error which disturb and encroach

[4] ['Fate leads the willing but drags along the unwilling.']

primarily and directly on the regular causal run of things, would be the mere instruments of its invisible hand.

What urges us more than anything to the bold assumption of such an unfathomable power that springs from the unity of the deep-lying root of necessity and contingency, is the consideration that the definite and thoroughly characteristic *individuality* of every man in a physical, moral, and intellectual respect which is all in all to him and must, therefore, have sprung from the highest metaphysical necessity, follows, on the one hand (as I have shown in my chief work, vol. ii, chap. 43), as the necessary result of the father's moral character, of the mother's intellectual capacity, and of the combined corporization of the two. Now, as a rule, the union of these parents has been brought about through obviously accidental circumstances. And so the demand, or metaphysical moral postulate, of an ultimate unity of necessity and contingency here irresistibly forces itself on us. However, I regard it as impossible to arrive at a clear conception of this central root of both; only this much can be said, that it is at the same time what the ancients called fate, εἱμαρμένη, πεπρωμένη, *fatum*, what they understood by the guiding genius of every individual, but equally also what the Christians worship as Providence, πρόνοια. These three, of course, are distinguished by the fact that *fatum* is thought of as blind, whereas the other two are not; but this anthropomorphic distinction falls to the ground and loses all significance with that deeper metaphysical essence of things. In this alone do we have to look for the root of that inexplicable union of the contingent with the necessary which manifests itself as the mysterious disposer of all things human.

The notion of a *genius or guardian angel* that is assigned to every individual and presides over the course of his life, is said to be of Etruscan origin, yet it is widely current among the ancients. Its essential idea is contained in a verse of Menander which has been preserved for us by Plutarch (*De tranquillitate animi*, c. 15, also in Stobaeus, *Eclogues*, lib. i, c. 6, § 4, and Clement of Alexandria, *Stromata*, lib. v, c. 14):

Ἅπαντι δαίμων ἀνδρὶ συμπαραστατεῖ
Εὐθὺς γενομένῳ, μυσταγωγὸς τοῦ βίου
Ἀγαθός.

(*Hominem unumquemque, simul in lucem est editus, sectatur Genius, vitae qui auspicium facit, bonus nimirum.*)⁵ At the end of the *Republic*, Plato describes how before its next rebirth every soul chooses for itself a fate with a personality suited thereto and then says: Ἐπειδὴ δ'οὖν πάσας τὰς ψυχὰς τοὺς βίους ἡρῆσθαι, ὥσπερ ἔλαχον, ἐν τάξει προσιέναι πρὸς τὴν Λάχεσιν, ἐκείνην δ'ἑκάστῳ ὃν εἵλετο δαίμονα, τοῦτον φύλακα ξυμπέμπειν τοῦ βίου καὶ ἀποπληρωτὴν τῶν αἱρεθέντων.⁶ (lib. x, 621.) On this passage Porphyry has furnished a commentary that is well worth reading and is preserved for us by Stobaeus in *Eclogae ethicae*, lib. II, c. 8, § 37 (vol. iii, pp. 368 ff. especially 376.) But Plato had previously said in this connexion: οὐχ ὑμᾶς δαίμων λήξεται, ἀλλ' ὑμεῖς δαίμονα αἱρήσεσθε. πρῶτος δὲ ὁ λαχὼν (fate that determines merely the order of choice) πρῶτος αἱρείσθω βίον, ᾧ συνέσται ἐξ ἀνάγκης.⁷ The matter is very beautifully expressed by Horace:

> *Scit Genius, natale comes qui temperat astrum,*
> *Naturae deus humanae, mortalis in unum-*
> *Quodque caput, vultu mutabilis, albus et ater.*⁸
>
> (*Epistles*, II. 2. 187.)

A passage on this *genius or guardian angel*, well worth reading, is found in Apuleius, *De deo Socratis*, p. 236, 38 ed. Bip. Jamblichus, *On the Egyptian Mysteries*, sect. IX, c. 6, *De proprio daemone*, has a short but important chapter on this. But even more remarkable is the passage of Proclus in his commentary to Plato's *Alcibiades*, p. 77, ed. Creuzer: ὁ γὰρ πᾶσαν ἡμῶν τὴν ζωὴν ἰθύνων καὶ τάς τε αἱρέσεις ἡμῶν ἀποπληρῶν, τὰς πρὸ τῆς γενέσεως, καὶ τὰς τῆς εἱμαρμένης δόσεις καὶ τῶν μοιρηγενετῶν θεῶν, ἔτι δὲ τὰς ἐκ τῆς προνοίας ἐλλάμψεις χορηγῶν καὶ παραμετρῶν, οὗτος ὁ δαίμων ἐστὶ. κ.τ.λ.⁹ Theophrastus Paracelsus has most

---

⁵ ['With a man at his birth is associated a good genius which guides him in the mysteries of life.']

⁶ ['But after all the souls had chosen their courses of life, they stepped in succession by lot before Lachesis. But she associated with each the genius he had chosen to be his guardian through life and to fulfil all his choice.']

⁷ ['No genius will obtain you by lot, but you will select the genius. But the man who has first drawn the lot (that determines the order of succession) shall first choose the course of life, and thereto will he adhere with necessity.']

⁸ ['This is known only by the genius who tempers the fateful oracle of the stars, a mortal god of human nature who to everyone is different and changeable, now of bright and now of sombre form.']

⁹ ['For he who guides our whole life, realizes our elective decisions that took effect before birth, allots the gifts of fate and of the gods born of fate, and also

profoundly expressed the same idea, for he says: 'To understand *fatum* properly, it is that every man has a spirit that dwells outside him and has its seat in the stars above. He uses the bosses* of his master; it is he who presages and shows him forebodings, for they continue to exist after him. These spirits are called *fatum*.' (*Works*, folio, Strasburg, 1603, vol. ii, p. 36.) It is worth noting that this same idea is to be found in Plutarch, for he says that outside that part of the soul which is submerged in the earthly body there remains suspended over man's head another purer part presenting itself as a star which is rightly called his demon or genius and guides him, and which the more prudent man willingly follows. The passage is too long to be quoted; it is found in *De genio Socratis*, c. 22. The principal sentence runs: τὸ μὲν οὖν ὑποβρύχιον ἐν τῷ σώματι φερόμενον Ψυχὴ λέγεται· τὸ δὲ φθορᾶς λειφθέν, οἱ πολλοὶ Νοῦν καλοῦντες, ἐντὸς εἶναι νομίζουσιν αὐτῶν· οἱ δὲ ὀρθῶς ὑπονοοῦντες, ὡς ἐκτὸς ὄντα, Δαίμονα προσαγορεύουσι.[10] Incidentally, I might mention that Christianity which, as we know, readily changed all the gods and demons of the pagans into the devil, appears to have made from this *genius* of the ancients the *spiritus familiaris* of scholars and magicians. The Christian description of Providence is too well known for me to have to dwell on it here. All these things, however, are only figurative, allegorical conceptions of the matter we are considering; for in general it is not granted to us to comprehend the deepest and most hidden truths other than in figures and similes.

In truth, however, that occult power that guides even external influences can ultimately have its root only in our own mysterious inner being; for indeed in the last resort the alpha and omega of all existence lie within us. But even in the most fortunate case we shall be able to obtain only a very remote glimpse of the mere possibility of this and here again only by means of analogies and similes.

---

* *Bossen*, types, protuberances, bumps, from the Italian *bozza, abbozzare, abbozzo*; from this we have *bossieren*, and the French *bosse*.

assigns and apportions the sunshine of Providence—he is the genius or guardian angel.']

[10] ['That which runs in the body in an undercurrent is called soul (ψυχὴ), but the imperishable is called spirit (νοῦς) by the majority who imagine that it resides within them. Those, however, who have the correct opinion assume that it is outside man and call it genius (δαίμων).']

The closest analogy to the sway of that power is seen in the *teleology of nature*, in that it shows us the appropriate and suitable as occurring without knowledge of the end in view, especially where external appropriateness appears, in other words, that which takes place between different and even heterogeneous beings and indeed in inorganic nature. A striking instance of this kind is afforded by driftwood which is carried by the sea in large quantities straight to the treeless polar regions. Another example is that the main mass of land of the planet lies entirely heaped towards the North Pole whose winter for astronomical reasons is eight days shorter and thus again much milder than that of the South. However, the inner suitability that is undeniably evident in the complete and exclusive organism, the surprising harmony, producing such suitability, between the technique and the mere mechanism of nature, or between the *nexus finalis* and the *nexus effectivus* (in this connection I refer to my chief work, vol. ii, chap. 26) enable us to see by analogy how that which proceeds from different and indeed widely remote points and is apparently a stranger to itself, nevertheless conspires to the ultimate end and correctly arrives at that point, guided not by knowledge but by virtue of a necessity of a higher order that precedes all possibility of knowledge. Further, if we conjure up in our minds the theory formulated by Kant and later by Laplace concerning the origin of our planetary system, whose probability amounts almost to a certainty, and arrive at considerations such as I have given in my chief work vol. ii, chap. 25, and thus reflect on how, from the play of blind natural forces that follow their immutable laws, this admirably arranged planetary world was ultimately bound to come about, then here we have an analogy that can serve generally and remotely to show us the possibility that even the course of life of an individual is, so to speak, systematically guided by events that are often the capricious sport of blind chance and in a way that is best suited to the true and ultimate good of the person.* On this assumption, the dogma of *Providence*, as being

---

* Αὐτόματα γὰρ τὰ πράγματ' ἐπὶ τὸ συμφέρον
'Ρεῖ κἂν καθεύδῃς ἢ πάλιν τἀναντία.
Menander in Stobaeus, *Florilegium*, vol. i, p. 363.
['For things continue to develop from themselves, even while you sleep, for your welfare as well as for the opposite thereof.']

thoroughly anthropomorphic, could certainly not pass as true directly and *sensu proprio*; but it might well be the indirect, allegorical, and mythical expression of a truth and so, like all religious myths, would be perfectly adequate for practical purposes and for subjective consolation in the sense, for instance, of Kant's moral theology which is to be understood only as a scheme for finding our bearings, and consequently allegorically; in a word, therefore, such a dogma might not be in fact true, but yet as good as true. In those deep, blind, primary forces of nature, from whose interplay the planetary system results, the will-to-live that subsequently appears in the most perfect phenomena of the world is already the inner operating and guiding principle. In those forces it already works towards its ends by means of strict natural laws and prepares the foundations for the structure and arrangement of the world. For example, the most fortuitous thrust or oscillation determines for all time the obliquity of the ecliptic and the velocity of rotation, and the final result must be the presentation of its entire nature just because such is already active in those original forces themselves. Now in the same way, all the events that determine a man's actions together with the causal connection that brings them about, are likewise only the objectivation of the same will that manifests itself in him. From this it may be seen, although only very obscurely, that they must harmonize and agree even with the special aims of that man. In this sense, they then constitute that mysterious power that guides the fate of the individual and is spoken of allegorically as his genius or his Providence. But considered purely objectively, it is and continues to be the universal causal connection that embraces everything without exception—by virtue whereof everything that happens does so with strict and absolute necessity—a connection that takes the place of the merely mythical control of the world, and indeed has the right to be so called.

The following general consideration can help to make this clearer. 'Accidental' means the concurrence in time of that which is causally not connected. But nothing is *absolutely* accidental; on the contrary, even the most accidental is only something necessary that has come to us on a more distant path, since definite causes lying high up in the causal chain have long ago necessarily determined that that something was bound to occur precisely at this moment and, therefore, simultaneously with something else. Thus every event is the particular link in a chain of causes and effects which proceeds in the direction of time. But in virtue of space, there are numberless such chains side by side; yet they are not entirely foreign to one another and without any interconnection; on the contrary, they are intertwined in many ways. For instance, many causes now operating simultaneously, each of which produces a different effect, have sprung from a common cause higher up and are, therefore, related to one another as great-grandchildren are to their great-grandfather. On the other hand, a particular effect occurring now often requires the coincidence of many different causes which, each as a link in its own chain, have come to us from the past. Accordingly, all those causal chains, that move in the direction of time, now form a large, common, much-interwoven net which with its whole breadth likewise moves forward in the direction of time and constitutes the course of the world. Now if we represent those individual causal chains by meridians that would lie in the direction of time, then that which is simultaneous, and for this reason does not stand in direct causal connection, can be everywhere indicated by parallel circles. Now although all things situated under the same parallel circle do not directly depend on one another, they nevertheless stand indirectly in some connection, though remote, by virtue of the interlacing of the whole net or of the totality of all causes and effects that roll along in the direction of time. Their present co-existence is therefore necessary; and on this rests the accidental coincidence of all the conditions of an event that is necessary in a higher sense, the happening of that which fate has willed. To this is due, for example, the fact that, when in consequence of the migration of the German tribes Europe was overrun with barbarism, the finest master-pieces of Greek sculpture, the Laocoon, the Vatican Apollo, and others disappeared at once as if by a trap-door by finding their way down into the bowels of the earth, there to await unharmed for a thousand years a milder, nobler era that would understand and appreciate the arts. When that time finally arrived at the end of the fifteenth century under Pope Julius II, those masterpieces reappeared as the well-preserved specimens of art and the true type of the human form. In the same way, the arrival at the right moment of the decisive and important occasions and circumstances in the course of an individual's life rests on the same ground; finally even the occurrence of omens, the belief in which is so general and ineradicable that not infrequently it has found a place even in the most superior minds. For nothing is *absolutely* accidental; on the contrary, everything occurs necessarily and even the simultaneity itself of that which is causally *not* connected, and thus what we call chance, is necessary since what is now simultaneous was *as such* already determined by causes in the remotest past. Therefore everything is reflected and echoed in everything else and that well-known utterance of Hippocrates that applies to the co-operation within the organism is applicable also to the totality of things: Ξύρροια μία, σύμπνοια μία, πάντα συμπαθέα.[11] (*De alimento, opp. ed.* Kühn, Tom. ii, p. 20.) Man's ineradicable tendency to observe omens, his *extispicia* and ὀρνιθοσκοπία,[12] his opening of the Bible, his telling of fortunes by cards, his casting of lead for the purpose of foretelling the future, his looking at coffee-grounds, and similar practices testify to his assumption (defying rational explanation) that it is somehow possible to know from what is present and clearly before his eyes that which is hidden by space or time and thus is remote or in the future, so that from the present he could read the future or the remote if only he had the true key to the cipher.

A second analogy that from an entirely different angle can help towards an indirect understanding of the transcendent fatalism we have been considering, is given by the *dream* to which life generally bears a resemblance that has long been recognized and often expressed, so much so that even Kant's transcendental idealism may be conceived as the clearest exposition of this dream-like nature of our conscious existence, as I have observed in my criticism of his philosophy. Indeed it is this analogy with the dream which enables us to observe, although again only remotely and obscurely, how the mysterious power, governing and controlling the external events that affect us with a view to their purpose for us, might yet have its root in the depths of our own unfathomable nature. Thus, even in the dream, circumstances by pure chance coincide and there

---

[11] ['It is only a flowing, only a blowing; all is in sympathy.']
[12] ['Prediction from the entrails of victims and augury from the flight of birds'.]

become the motives of our actions, circumstances that are external to and independent of us and indeed often abhorrent. But yet there is between them a mysterious and appropriate connection since a hidden power that is obeyed by all the incidents in the dream controls and arranges even these circumstances and indeed solely with reference to us. But the strangest thing of all is that this power can ultimately be none other than our own will, yet from a point of view that does not enter our dreaming consciousness. And so it happens that the events in a dream often turn out quite contrary to our wishes therein, cause us astonishment, annoyance, and even mortal terror, without the fate that we secretly direct coming to our rescue. In the same way, we eagerly ask about something and receive an answer whereat we are astonished. Or again, we ourselves are asked, say in an examination, and are incapable of finding the answer, whereupon another, to our shame, gives a perfect answer; whereas in the one case as in the other, the answer can always come only from our own resources. To make even clearer this mysterious guidance of the events in the dream, a guidance that comes from ourselves, and to make its operation more intelligible, there is yet another explanation that alone can do this, but it is necessarily of an obscene nature. I therefore assume that my worthy readers will neither take offence nor treat the matter as a joke. It is well known that there are dreams of which nature avails herself for a material purpose, namely the discharge of the overfilled spermatocysts. Dreams of this kind naturally indicate lascivious scenes. But sometimes the same thing also occurs with other dreams that do not at all have or achieve that purpose. Now here there is a difference that in dreams of the first kind attractive women and the opportunity soon prove favourable to us, whereby nature attains her object. In dreams of the other kind, however, the path to the thing most ardently desired by us is constantly obstructed by fresh obstacles which we vainly attempt to overcome, so that in the end we still do not reach the goal. But what creates these obstacles and constantly frustrates our ardent wish is simply our own will, yet from a region that lies far beyond the representing consciousness in the dream and thus appears therein as inexorable fate. Now might it not be possible for fate in real life and for that systematic planning which perhaps everyone

comes to know from an observation of his own life, to be analogous to the position set forth in the dream?* It sometimes
happens that we have devised and enthusiastically adopted a
plan from which it is evident that it was by no means suited
to our true welfare. Yet while we are eagerly pursuing it we
experience against it a conspiracy of fate, which sets in motion
all its machinery to defeat it. In this way, fate finally thrusts
us back, against our will, on to the path that is truly suited
to us. In view of such opposition that appears intentional,
many a man uses the phrase: 'I note that it *ought* not to be;'
others call it ominous; others again call it a hint from God.
All, however, share the view that, when fate opposes a plan
with such obvious doggedness, we should give it up since, as
it is unsuited to our destiny that to us is unknown, it will not
be realized and by wilfully pursuing it we simply draw down
upon us the harder blows of fate until in the end we are again
on the right track; or because, if we succeeded in forcing the
issue, this would tend merely to our harm and undoing. The
above-mentioned *ducunt volentem fata, nolentem trahunt*[13] is here
fully endorsed. In many cases, it actually turns out subsequently
that the frustration of such a plan has in every way been beneficial to our true welfare. And so this might also be the case
where it is not generally known to us, especially if we regard
as our true welfare the metaphysically moral. Now if from here
we look back to the main result of the whole of my philosophy,
namely that what presents and maintains the phenomenon of
the world is the *will* that also lives and strives in every individual;
and if at the same time we call to mind the universally acknowledged resemblance of life to a dream, then, summing up
all that has been said so far, we can quite generally imagine
as possible that, just as everyone is the secret theatrical manager
of his dreams, so too by analogy that fate that controls the actual
course of our lives ultimately comes in some way from the *will*.
This is our own and yet here, where it appears as fate, it

---

* Objectively considered, the course of an individual's life is of universal and
strict necessity; for all his actions appear just as necessarily as do the movements
of a machine, and all external events appear on the leading line of a causal chain
whose links have a strictly necessary connection. If we adhere to this, we need not
be so surprised when we see the course of an individual's life suitably turn out for
him as if it were systematically planned.

13 ['Fate leads the willing but drags along the unwilling.']

operates from a region that lies far beyond our representing individual consciousness; whereas this furnishes the motives that guide our empirically knowable individual will. Hence such will has often to contend most violently with that will of ours that manifests itself as fate, with our guiding genius, with our 'spirit which dwells outside us and has its seat in the stars above', which surveys the individual consciousness and thus, in relentless opposition thereto, arranges and fixes as external restraint that which it could not leave the consciousness to find out and yet does not wish to see miscarry.

In the first place, a passage from Scotus Erigena may help to reduce the surprising extravagance of this bold sentence where it must be borne in mind that his *Deus* which is without knowledge and of which time, space, and Aristotle's ten categories are not to be predicated, indeed for which generally only one predicate remains, namely *will*—that his *Deus* is obviously nothing but what I call the will-to-live: *Est etiam alia species ignorantiae in Deo, quando ea, quae praescivit et praedestinavit, ignorare dicitur, dum adhuc in rerum factarum cursibus experimento non apparuerint*[14] (*De divisione naturae*, p. 83, Oxford edition). Shortly afterwards he says: *Tertia species divinae ignorantiae est, per quam Deus dicitur ignorare ea, quae nondum experimento actionis et operationis in effectibus manifeste apparent; quorum tamen invisibiles rationes in seipso, a seipso creatas et sibi ipsi cognitas possidet.*[15]

Now if, to make somewhat clearer to ourselves the view we have expounded, we have availed ourselves of the acknowledged similarity of the individual life to a dream, we should nevertheless note the difference that in the mere dream the relation is one-sided, that is to say, only one ego actually wills and feels, whereas the rest are nothing but phantoms. In the great dream of life, on the other hand, a mutual relation occurs, since not only does the one figure in the dream of the other exactly as is necessary, but also that other figures in his dream. Thus by virtue of a real *harmonia praestabilita*, everyone dreams only

[14] ['It is yet another kind of ignorance in God in so far as we say that he does not know that which he foreknows and has predetermined, so long as it has not yet shown itself in the course of the actual things of experience.']

[15] ['A third kind of divine ignorance consists in our saying of God that he does not know that which has not yet come to light in effects through the experience of doing and performing, although in himself he possesses the invisible grounds as such which he himself has created and which are known to himself.']

what is appropriate to him in accordance with his own metaphysical guidance; and all the dreams of life are so ingeniously
interwoven that everyone gets to know what is beneficial to
him and at the same time does for others what is necessary.
Accordingly, some great world event conforms to the fate of
many thousands, to each in an individual way. Consequently,
all the events in a man's life are connected in two fundamentally
different ways; first in the objective causal connection of the
course of nature, secondly in a subjective connection that exists
only in reference to the individual who experiences them. It
is as subjective as his own dreams, yet in him their succession
and content are likewise necessarily determined, but in the
manner in which the succession of the scenes of a drama is
determined by the plan of the poet. Now those two kinds of
connection exist simultaneously and yet the same event, as a
link in two quite different chains, exactly fits them both, in
consequence whereof one man's fate is always in keeping with
another's, and everyone is the hero of his own drama, but at
the same time figures also in that of another. All this, of course,
is something that surpasses all our powers of comprehension
and can be conceived as possible only by virtue of the most
marvellous *harmonia praestabilita*. On the other hand, would it
not be on our part a want of courage to regard it as impossible
that the lives of all men in their mutual dealings should have
just as much *concentus*[16] and harmony as the composer is able to
give to the many apparently confused and stormy parts of his
symphony? Our aversion to that colossal thought will grow
less if we remember that the subject of the great dream of life
is in a certain sense only one thing, the will-to-live, and that
all plurality of phenomena is conditioned by time and space.
It is the great dream that is dreamed by that one entity, but
in such a way that all its persons dream it together. Thus all
things encroach on and are adapted to one another. Now if we
agree to this; if we accept that double chain of all events, by
virtue whereof every being, on the one hand, exists for his
own sake, behaves and acts with necessity according to his own
nature, and pursues his own course, but, on the other, is also
as completely determined and adapted for perceiving another
being and for influencing him as are the pictures in his dreams,

16 ['Harmony, concord'.]

then we shall have to extend this to the whole of nature, and hence to animals and beings without knowledge. Once more, then, we have the prospect of the possibility of *omina, praesagia,* and *portenta,* since that which *necessarily* occurs in the course of nature is again to be regarded, on the other hand, as a mere image or picture for me, as the subject-matter of *my* life-dream, happening and existing merely with reference to *me,* or even as a mere reflection and echo of *my* action and experience. Accordingly, that which in an event is natural and can be causally demonstrated as necessary, does not by any means do away with the ominous element therein; and in the same way, the ominous element does not eliminate the other. And so those people are entirely mistaken who imagine they remove the ominous element of an event by their demonstrating the inevitability of its occurrence, in that they show quite clearly its natural and necessarily operating causes and also, when it is a natural event, do so physically and with an appearance of learning. For no reasonable man doubts these and no one will pretend that the omen is a miracle; but precisely from the fact that the chain of causes and effects that stretches to infinity with the strict necessity and eternal predestination peculiar to it has inevitably established the occurrence of this event at such a significant moment, does the event acquire an ominous element. And so the would-be wise, especially when they become physically minded, should specially remember Shakespeare's words: 'There are more things in heaven and earth than are dreamt of in your philosophy' (*Hamlet,* Act 1, Sc. 5). Yet with the belief in omens we see the doors reopened to astrology; for the most trifling event that is regarded as ominous, the flight of a bird, the meeting of a person, and so on, is conditioned by a chain of causes just as infinitely long and as strictly necessary as is the computable position of the stars at any given time. Of course, the constellation is high enough in the heavens to be seen at the same time by half the inhabitants of the globe, whereas the omen appears only in the sphere of the individual concerned. Moreover, if we wish to picture to ourselves the possibility of the ominous, we can do so by comparing the man who sees a good or bad omen and is thus warned or confirmed at an important step in his life whose consequences are still hidden in the future, to a string which, when struck, does not hear itself and yet hears the sound of another that is emitted in consequence of its vibration.

Kant's distinction of the thing-in-itself from its phenomenon, together with my reference of the former to the will and of the latter to the representation, enables us to see, although only imperfectly and remotely, the compatibility of *three antitheses.* They are:

(1) That between the freedom of the will-in-itself and the universal necessity of all the individual's actions.

(2) That between the mechanism and technique of nature, or between the *nexus effectivus* and the *nexus finalis*, or between the purely causal and the teleological explicability of the products of nature. (In this connection see Kant's *Critique of Judgement*, § 78, and my chief work, vol. ii, chap. 26.)

(3) That between the obvious contingency of all the events in the course of an individual's life and their moral necessity for the shaping thereof in accordance with a transcendent fitness for the individual, or in popular language, between the course of nature and Providence.

The clearness of our insight into the compatibility of each of these three antitheses, although not perfect with any of them, is yet more adequate with the first than with the second, but is least in the case of the third. At the same time, an understanding of the compatibility of each of these antitheses, although imperfect, always sheds light on the other two by serving as their image and simile.

Only in a very general way can it be stated what is really meant ultimately by the whole of this mysterious guidance of the individual's course of life which we have been considering. If we stop at individual cases, it often appears that such guidance has in view only our transient welfare for the time being. Yet this cannot seriously be its ultimate aim, in view of the insignificant, imperfect, futile, and fleeting nature of that welfare. And so we have to look for this ultimate aim in our eternal existence that goes beyond the life of the individual. And then it can be said only quite generally that the course of our life is so regulated by means of that guidance that, from the whole of the knowledge accruing to us in the course of it, there arises metaphysically the most suitable impression on the *will* as being the kernel and essence-in-itself of man. For although the will-to-live obtains its answer generally in the course of the world as the phenomenon of its striving, yet every man is that will-to-live in quite a unique and individual way. He is, so to speak, an individualized act thereof; and so its adequate answer can be only a quite definite shaping of the course of the world, given in events and experiences that are peculiar to him. Now as we have recognized from the results of the serious part of my philosophy (in contrast to mere professorial or comic philosophy) the will's turning away from life as the ultimate aim of temporal existence, we must assume that everyone is gradually led to *this* in a manner that is quite individually suited to him and hence often in a long and roundabout way. Again, as happiness and pleasure militate against that aim, we see, in keeping therewith, misery and suffering inevitably interwoven in the course of every life, although in very unequal measure and only rarely to excess, namely in tragic events where it then looks as if the will should to a certain extent be forcibly driven to turn away from life and to arrive at regeneration by a Caesarian operation so to speak.

Thus that invisible guidance, that shows itself only in a doubtful form, accompanies us to our death, to that real result, and, to this extent, the purpose of life. At the hour of death, all the mysterious forces (although really rooted in ourselves) which determine man's eternal fate, crowd together and come into action. The result of their conflict is the path now to be followed by him; thus his palingenesis is prepared together with all the weal and woe that are included therein and are ever afterwards irrevocably determined. To this is due the extremely serious, important, solemn, and fearful character of the hour of death. It is a crisis in the strongest sense of the word—a day of judgement.

ESSAY ON SPIRIT SEEING AND EVERYTHING CONNECTED THEREWITH

Und lass dir rathen, habe
Die Sonne nicht zu lieb und nicht die Sterne.
Komm, folge mir ins dunkle Reich hinab!
Goethe.

['Take counsel, cherish not the sun and stars; come,
follow me down into the realm of gloom!']

Essay on Spirit Seeing and everything connected therewith

THE apparitions in the past century, over-wise and all-too knowing in spite of all previous ones—apparitions that were everywhere not so much exorcized as outlawed, have during the last twenty-five years been rehabilitated in Germany as was magic a short time before. Perhaps not without good reason; for the proofs against their existence were partly metaphysical, resting as such on uncertain grounds, and partly empirical, proving only that in those cases where no accidental or intentionally arranged deception had been discovered, there also existed nothing that could have acted on the retina by means of the reflection of light-rays, or on the ear-drum by means of vibrations of the air. Yet this argues merely against the presence of bodies whose presence, however, no one had asserted, indeed whose demonstration in the aforesaid physical manner would abolish the truth of a ghostly apparition. For the notion of a spirit or spectre really consists in its presence becoming known to us in a way quite different from that in which we know the presence of a body. What a spirit seer who really knew his own mind and was able to express himself would assert is merely the presence in his intuitively perceiving intellect of a picture perfectly indistinguishable from that caused in his intellect by bodies through the medium of light and his eyes, and yet without the actual presence of such bodies. Similarly in respect of something audibly present, noises, tones, and sounds, exactly like those produced in his ear by vibrating bodies and air, yet without the presence or movement thereof. Here lies the source of the misunderstanding which pervades all that is said for and against the reality of ghostly apparitions, namely that the spirit apparition presents itself wholly like a bodily phenomenon, yet is not and cannot be such. This distinction is difficult and requires special knowledge, indeed philosophical and physiological. For it is a question of understanding that an impression, like that made by a body, does not necessarily presuppose the presence of such.

First of all, then, we must here recall and in all that follows bear in mind what I have often demonstrated in detail (especially in the second edition of my essay *On the Principle of Sufficient Reason*, § 21, and also in my work *On Vision and Colours*, § 1, *Theoria Colorum*, Pt. II, *World as Will and Representation*, vol. i, § 4; vol. ii, chap. 2), namely that our intuitive perception of the external world is not merely a question of the *senses*, but is mainly *intellectual*, in other words, is (objectively expressed) *cerebral*. The senses never give us more than a mere sensation in their organ and thus a material in itself extremely inadequate. From this the *understanding* first builds up this corporeal world through the application of the law of causality that is known to it *a priori* and of the forms of space and time that are just as *a priori* inherent in it. The stimulation of this act of intuitive perception in the waking and normal state definitely starts from sensation since this is the effect to which the understanding refers the cause. But why should it not for once be possible for a stimulation that starts from quite another direction and thus from within, from the organism itself, to reach the brain and there be elaborated like the other by means of the brain's peculiar function and in accordance with the mechanism thereof? But *after* this elaboration it would no longer be possible to detect the difference in the original material, just as in chyle it is no longer possible to recognize the food from which it has been made. In any actual case of this kind, the question would then arise whether even the remoter cause of the phenomenon thus brought about could never be sought farther than within the organism; or whether with the exclusion of all sensation it could nevertheless be an *external* cause which naturally in this case would not have acted physically or corporeally; and if so, what relation the given phenomenon could have to the nature of so remote an external cause; and thus whether it contained evidence of this, or indeed whether the real essence thereof were expressed in it. Accordingly, as in the corporeal world, we should here be brought to the question concerning the relation between the phenomenon and the thing-in-itself. But this is the transcendental standpoint the result of which might possibly be that ideality attached to the spirit apparition neither more nor less than to the bodily phenomenon which, as we know, is inevitably subject to idealism and can, therefore, be traced back to the thing-in-itself, in other words, to the truly real, only in a roundabout way. Now as we have recognized the *will* to be this thing-in-itself, this enables us to suppose that perhaps such a will underlies both spirit and bodily phenomena. All previous explanations of spirit phenomena have been *spiritualistic*; precisely as such, they are the subject of Kant's criticism in the first part of his *Träume eines Geistersehers*. Here I am attempting an *idealistic* explanation.

After this comprehensive and anticipatory introduction to the investigations that now follow, I take the more leisurely course that is appropriate to them. Here I merely observe that I assume the reader to be acquainted with the facts to which they refer. For my business is not to state or expound the facts, but to theorize about them. Moreover, I should have to write a bulky volume if I were to repeat all the cases of magnetic sickness, dream visions, spirit apparitions, and the like that form the basic material of our theme and are already dealt with in many books. Finally, it is not my business to combat the scepticism of ignorance whose over-wise gestures are daily falling out of favour and will soon be current only in England. Whoever at the present time doubts the facts of animal magnetism and its clairvoyance should be called not a sceptic but an ignoramus. But I must take for granted something more, namely an acquaintance with at least some of the works which exist in large numbers on ghostly apparitions, or a knowledge of them that has been acquired in some other way. Even the quotations that refer to such books are given by me only when it is a question of special statements or debatable points. For the rest, I assume on the part of the reader, who, I imagine, is already acquainted with me in some other way, confidence in me, so that when I assume something to be founded on fact, it is known to me from reliable sources or my own experience.

First, then, is the question: whether images or pictures of intuitive perception can actually arise in our intuitively perceiving intellect or brain, complete and indistinguishable from those caused therein by the presence of bodies that act on the external senses, and yet without such influence. Fortunately, a very familiar phenomenon, the *dream*, removes all doubt on this point.

To try to pretend that dreams are mere thought-play, mere pictures of the imagination, testifies to a want of sense or honesty for it is obvious that they are specifically different from these. Pictures of the imagination are feeble, colourless, incomplete, one-sided, and so fleeting that we are barely able to retain for more than a few seconds the picture of one who is absent, and even the most vivid play of the imagination bears no comparison with that palpable reality that is presented to us in the dream. Our graphic ability *in the dream* far and away surpasses our power of imagination. In the dream every object of intuitive perception has a truth, perfection, completeness, and consistent universality down to its most accidental properties, like reality itself, from which the imagination is infinitely remote. And so, if only we could select the object of our dreams, reality would furnish us with the most marvellous spectacles. It is quite wrong to attempt to explain this from the fact that pictures of the imagination would be disturbed and enfeebled by the simultaneous impression of the external world of reality, for even in the deepest silence of the darkest night the imagination is incapable of producing anything that could in any way approach that objective clearness and vivid reality of the dream. Moreover, pictures of the imagination are always produced by the association of ideas or by motives and are attended by an awareness of their arbitrary nature. The dream, on the other hand, stands out as something wholly foreign and extraneous which, like the outside world, forces itself on us without our intervention and even against our will. The totally unexpected nature of its events, even the most insignificant, impresses them with the stamp of objectivity and reality. All its objects appear to be definite and distinct, like reality itself, and to be given not merely in reference to us and thus superficially and from one point of view, or only in the main and in general outline, but worked out exactly down to the smallest and most accidental particulars and attendant circumstances that stand in our path and obstruct us. For every object casts its shadow, every body falls with a heaviness that corresponds exactly to its specific weight, and every obstacle must first be set aside precisely as in real life. Its thoroughly objective nature is further seen in the fact that its events often turn out contrary to our expectation and frequently against our wish and at times even excite our astonishment. The actors in the dream behave towards us with a shocking want of consideration, and in general the objective nature of the dream is seen in the purely objective, dramatic accuracy of the characters and their actions, which has given rise to the pleasant remark that while dreaming everyone is a Shakespeare. For the same omniscience in ourselves, which enables every natural body in the dream to act exactly in accordance with its essential properties, also enables every man to act and speak in complete accord with his character. In consequence of all this, the illusion that is engendered by the dream is so strong that reality itself which stands before us when we wake up often has to struggle at first and needs time before it can put in a word, in order to convince us of the deceptive nature of the dream that now no longer exists. Also as regards memory, we are—in the case of unimportant incidents —sometimes in doubt whether they were dreamed or actually took place. If, on the other hand, anyone doubts whether something took place or was merely *imagined* by him, he is suspected of madness. All this shows that the dream is a thoroughly characteristic function of our brain and is entirely different from the mere power of the imagination and its rumination. Even Aristotle says: τὸ ἐνύπνιόν ἐστιν αἴσθημα, τρόπον τινά (*Somnium quodammodo sensum est*):[1] *De somno et vigilia*, c. 2. He also makes the fine and correct observation that in the dream itself we still picture to ourselves absent things through the imagination. But from this it may be inferred that during the dream the imagination is still available and is, therefore, not itself the medium or organ of the dream.

On the other hand, the dream bears an undeniable resemblance to madness; for what mainly distinguishes dreaming from waking consciousness is a lack of memory or rather of coherent, sensible recollection. In dreams we see ourselves in strange and even impossible situations and circumstances, and it would never occur to us to examine their relations to the absent person and the causes of their appearance. In the dream we do absurd things because we are unmindful of that which opposes them. In our dreams people long since dead figure

---

[1] ['In a certain sense the dream-picture is a perception.']

again and again as living persons because in the dream we do not remember that they are dead. We often see ourselves again in the circumstances of our early years, surrounded by those who were alive at that time and with everything as of old because all the changes and transformations that have since occurred are forgotten. It actually seems, therefore, that in the dream, in spite of the activity of all the mental powers, memory alone is not really available. Its resemblance to madness is due precisely to this, for madness, as I have shown (in the *World as Will and Representation*, vol. i, § 36, and vol. ii, chap. 32), is traceable essentially to a certain derangement of the faculty of recollection. From this point of view, therefore, the dream may be characterized as a brief madness, madness being looked upon as a long dream. On the whole, the intuitive perception of the *present reality* in the dream is, therefore, absolutely perfect and even minute. On the other hand, our intellectual horizon therein is very limited, in as much as the *absent* and the *past*, and even the fictitious, enter consciousness only to a small extent.

Just as in the real world every change can occur solely in consequence of another that preceded it as its cause, so too is the entry of all thoughts and conceptions in our consciousness subject to the principle of sufficient ground or reason in general. Therefore such thoughts must always be called into existence either by an external impression on the senses, or by an idea that precedes them in accordance with the laws of association (see chapter 14 of the second volume of my chief work); otherwise they could not occur. Now, as regards their occurrence, dreams must also be subject in some way to that principle of sufficient reason, for it is the principle of the dependent and conditional nature of all objects existing for us and is without exception. But it is very difficult to determine in what way they are subject to it, for the characteristic of the dream is the condition of sleep essential thereto, in other words, the cessation of the normal activity of the brain and senses. Only when such activity is at rest can the dream occur, just as the pictures of a magic lantern can appear only after the lights of the room have been extinguished. Accordingly, the occurrence and consequently the material of the dream are not brought about in the first instance by external impressions on the senses.

Isolated cases, where during light dozing external sounds and even odours have penetrated the sensorium and influenced the dream, are special exceptions which I here disregard. Now it is very remarkable that dreams are not brought about through the association of ideas; for they arise either during deep sleep when the brain is really at rest, a repose which we have every reason to assume is complete and therefore entirely unconscious; accordingly even the possibility of the association of ideas here falls to the ground; or again they arise while we are passing from waking consciousness to sleep and thus while we are falling asleep. Here they never entirely fail to appear, and in this way they afford us an opportunity of becoming fully convinced that they are not connected through any association of ideas with the mental pictures we have when awake, but leave the thread of these untouched in order to take their material and motive from somewhere quite different, we know not where. These first dream-images of the man who falls asleep are always without any relation to the thoughts he had when falling asleep, as may easily be observed. In fact, they are so strikingly different therefrom that it looks as if, from all the things in the world, they had intentionally selected the very thing about which we thought least of all. And so the man who thinks it over is forced to ask himself in what way their selection and nature could be determined. Moreover, they have the distinctive characteristic (finely and correctly observed by Burdach in the third volume of his *Physiologie*) of not presenting us with any connected event, and in most cases we ourselves do not as actors appear in them as we do in other dreams; on the contrary, they are a purely objective spectacle that consists of isolated pictures suddenly arising when we fall asleep, or they are very simple events. As we often reawake with a start, we can fully convince ourselves that these dreams never have the slightest resemblance, the remotest analogy, or any other relation to the thoughts that existed in our minds just a moment previously, but that they rather surprise us by the wholly unexpected nature of their contents. These are just as foreign to our previous train of thought as is any object of real life which in our state of wakefulness suddenly enters our perception through the merest chance and is indeed fetched from afar and selected so strangely and blindly, as if it had been

determined by fate or by the throwing of dice. Thus the thread
that is put into our hands by the principle of sufficient reason
here seems to be cut off at both ends, the inner and the outer;
but this is impossible and inconceivable. Some cause must necessarily exist which produces and fully determines those dream-
forms so that from this it must be possible to explain exactly
why, for example, there suddenly appears to me, who up to
the moment of dozing off was occupied with quite different
thoughts, a tree in blossom swaying gently in the breeze and
nothing else, at another time, however, a girl with a basket
on her head, or again a line of soldiers, and so on.

Now with the origin of dreams, either when we are falling
or have already fallen asleep, the brain, that sole seat and organ
of all representations or mental pictures, is cut off from the
external excitation through the senses as well as from the internal through ideas. And so we are left with no other assumption than that the brain receives some purely physiological
excitation from within the organism. Two paths to the brain
are open to the influence of this, namely that of the nerves
and that of the blood-vessels. During sleep, that is, during the
cessation of all *animal* functions, the vital force is centred entirely on *organic* life and, with some reduction of breathing,
pulse, warmth, and almost all secretions, it is there mainly
concerned with slow reproduction, the reparation of all waste,
the healing of all injuries, and the elimination of deep-rooted
disorders. Sleep is, therefore, the time during which the *vis
naturae medicatrix*[2] produces in all illnesses the beneficial crises
wherein it then gains a decisive victory over the existing
malady. With the certain feeling of approaching restoration
to health, the patient then wakes up with joy and a sense of
relief. But even in the case of the healthy man, this force
operates in the same way, although to an incomparably lesser
degree, at all points where it is necessary; and so he too on
waking up has a feeling of restored vitality. It is especially
during sleep that the brain receives its nutrition, which is not
feasible when we are awake; and a consequence of this is
a restored clearness of consciousness. All these operations are
under the guidance and control of the plastic nervous system
and thus of all the large ganglia which in the whole length of

---

[2] ['The healing power of nature'.]

the trunk are connected with one another by leading nerve-cords and constitute the *great sympathetic nerve* or *inner* nerve-centre. This is completely separated and isolated from the *outer* nerve-focus, the brain, which is exclusively concerned with the direction of *external* relations and therefore has an outwardly directed nervous apparatus and representations or mental pictures occasioned thereby. Thus in the normal state, the operations of the inner nerve-centre do not enter consciousness and are not felt. However, it has an indirect and feeble connection with the cerebral system through long, attenuated, and inosculating nerves. By way of these that isolation is to some extent broken down in the case of abnormal states or even internal injuries which therefore force their way into consciousness as a dull or distinct pain. In the normal or healthy state, on the other hand, the sensorium receives on this path only an extremely feeble and faint echo of the events and movements in the very complicated and active workshop of organic life, only a stray echo of the easy or difficult development thereof. When we are awake, the brain is fully occupied with its own operations, with receiving external impressions, with intuitive perception when these occur, and with thinking, and that echo is not noticed at all. On the contrary, it has at most a mysterious and unconscious influence, whence arise those changes of disposition whereof no account on objective grounds can be given. Yet when we fall asleep, when the external impressions cease to operate and the activity of ideas gradually dies away in the interior of the sensorium, those feeble impressions that spring in an indirect way from the inner nerve-centre of organic life are then noticed in the same way as every slight modification of the blood circulation is communicated to the brain-cells. This is like the candle that begins to shine when the evening twilight comes, or the murmuring of the spring which is heard at night but was rendered inaudible by the noises of the day. Impressions far too feeble to affect the alert and active brain can, when its own activity is completely suspended, produce a faint stirring of its individual parts and of their powers of representation; just as a harp, while being played, does not re-echo a strange tone, but possibly does when it is not played. Here, then, must be found the cause of the origin and also, by means thereof, the general and fuller determination of those dream-forms that appear when we fall asleep, and likewise the cause of those dreams that spring from the absolute mental calm of deep sleep and have dramatic association. As, however, these occur when the brain is already in a state of profound peace and is wholly taken up with its own nutrition, an appreciably stronger excitation from within is necessary for them. And so it is only these dreams that in isolated and very rare cases have a prophetic or fatidical significance, and Horace rightly says:

post mediam noctem, cum somnia vera.[3]

For in this respect, the last dreams of morning are related to those when we fall asleep in so far as the rested and restored brain is again capable of being easily stimulated.

Therefore it is those feeble echoes from the workshop of organic life which penetrate into the brain's sensory activity (an activity that lapses into or is already in a state of apathy), and which feebly stimulate it, moreover in an unusual way and from a direction different from that when the brain is awake. Nevertheless, as access to all other stimulations is barred, that activity must for its dream-forms seize the occasion and substance from those echoes, however different those forms may be from such impressions. Thus the eye through mechanical shock or internal nervous convulsion may receive sensations of brightness and luminosity exactly like those that are caused by light from without; in consequence of abnormal events taking place in its interior, the ear occasionally hears sounds of all kinds; the olfactory nerve receives quite specifically definite odours without any external cause; and the gustatory nerves are affected in a similar manner. And so sensory nerves can also be stimulated to their characteristic sensations from within as well as from without. In the same way, the brain can be influenced by stimuli coming from the interior of the organism to perform its function of intuitively perceiving forms that fill space. For phenomena that have originated in this way will be quite indistinguishable from those that are occasioned by sensations in the sense-organs which were produced by external causes. Thus, just as the stomach forms chyme from everything it can assimilate and from this the intestines form chyle wherein

[3] ['After midnight when the truth is dreamed'.]

no traces of its original substance are seen, so too does the brain react to all the stimulations that reach it by its carrying out the function that is peculiar to it. This consists first in tracing out pictures in space in all three dimensions, space being the brain's form of intuitive perception; then in moving these pictures in time and on the guiding line of causality, time and causality being likewise functions of the brain's own peculiar activity. For the brain will always speak only its own language; and so in this it interprets those feeble impressions that reach it from within while we are asleep, just as it does the strong and definite impressions coming to it from without in the regular way while we are awake. Thus the former impressions furnish it with the material for pictures that are exactly like those arising from an excitation of the external senses, although between the two kinds of impressions that cause the pictures there may be scarcely any similarity. But here its mode of action is comparable to that of a deaf man who from several vowels that reach his ear composes a complete yet false sentence; or it is comparable even to that of one mentally deranged who, in keeping with his fixed idea, is brought to a state of wild ravings by the chance use of some word. In any case, it is those feeble echoes of certain events in the interior of the organism which disappear right up into the brain and give rise to its dreams. These, then, are more specially determined by the nature of those impressions in that they have at any rate obtained the cue therefrom. In fact, however much they may differ from those impressions, they will nevertheless in some way correspond to them analogously or at least symbolically, and indeed most exactly to impressions that are capable of stimulating the brain during *deep* sleep, for, as I have said, these must already be considerably stronger. Further, as these internal events of organic life also act on the sensorium, regulated as it is for the apprehension of the external world, after the manner of something strange and external to *it*, the intuitive perceptions arising in it on such an occasion will be quite *unexpected* forms, wholly foreign to and different from its train of thought that probably still existed just previously. We have an opportunity for observing this when we fall asleep and again quickly wake up.

At the moment, the whole of this discussion tells us nothing more than the immediate cause or occasion for the appearance of the dream. Such a cause, it is true, must influence the substance of the dream; yet in itself it is bound to be so different therefrom that the nature of its relationship remains a mystery to us. Even more mysterious is the physiological process in the brain itself, in which dreaming really consists. Thus sleep is the resting of the brain, yet the dream is a certain activity thereof; and so to avoid a contradiction, we must declare the former to be merely a relative activity and the latter to be in some way limited and only partial. Again, we do not know in what sense it may be so, whether in accordance with the parts of the brain, with the degree of its excitation, or with the nature of its internal movement, or in what way it really differs from the state of wakefulness. There is no mental power that never proves to be active in the dream; yet the course of the dream as well as our own conduct therein often shows an extraordinary lack of power of judgement as well as of memory, as I have already discussed.

As regards our principal subject, the fact remains that we have a capacity for intuitively representing objects that fill space and for distinguishing and understanding sounds and voices of every kind, both without the external excitation of the sense impressions. These, on the other hand, furnish the occasion, the material, or the empirical basis of our intuitive perception *when we are awake*; yet they are certainly not for that reason identical therewith, for intuitive perception is entirely a matter of the *intellect* and not merely of the senses, as I have often shown and have mentioned above the main relevant passages. Now we must stick to this fact that is not open to any doubt, for it is the *primary and fundamental phenomenon* to which all our further explanations refer, since they will demonstrate only the extensive activity of the faculty we have described. To give it a name, the most descriptive expression would be that very appropriately selected by the Scots for a particular form of its manifestation or application, for they were guided by that correct judgement that is vouchsafed by one's own experience; it is called *second sight*. For the ability to dream, here discussed, is indeed a second faculty of intuitive perception and is unlike the first that is brought about through the medium of the external senses. Yet the objects of that second faculty are the same in kind and form as those of the first and the conclusion to be drawn from this is that, like the first, it is a function of the *brain*. That Scottish term would, therefore, be the most suitable for describing the entire species of phenomena here considered, and for attributing them to a fundamental faculty. As, however, its authors have used it for denoting a particular, rare, and extremely remarkable manifestation of that faculty, I cannot make use of it, much as I would like to, for denoting the whole species of those intuitive perceptions, or more precisely the subjective faculty that manifests itself in all of them. And so for this I am left with no more suitable term than that of *dream-organ* which describes the entire mode of intuitive perception we are discussing by that manifestation of it which is well known and familiar to everyone. I shall, therefore, use it to describe the faculty of intuitive perception which has been shown to be independent of the external impression on the senses.

The objects which this faculty presents to us in the ordinary dream are usually regarded by us as quite illusory, for they vanish when we wake up. This, however, is not always the case and, with regard to our theme it is very important to become acquainted with the exception to this from our own experience. Possibly everyone could do this if he gave adequate attention to the matter. Thus there is a state in which we certainly sleep and dream; yet we dream only the reality itself that surrounds us. We then see our bedroom with everything therein; we become aware of people entering the room; and we know that we are in bed and that everything is correct and in order. And yet we are asleep with our eyes shut; we dream; only what we dream is true and real. It is just as if our skull had then become transparent so that the external world now entered the brain directly and immediately instead of by an indirect path and through the narrow portal of the senses. This state is much more difficult to distinguish from wakefulness than is the ordinary dream because, when we wake up from it, there occurs no transformation of the surroundings and hence no *objective* change at all. But now waking up is the sole criterion between wakefulness and the dream (see *World as Will and Representation*, vol. i, § 5), which accordingly is here abolished as regards its objective and principal half.   Thus when we wake up from a dream of the kind we are discussing, there occurs merely a

subjective change which consists in our suddenly feeling a transformation of the organ of our perception. Yet this is only
slightly perceptible and since it is not accompanied by any
objective change it may easily remain unnoticed. For this
reason, acquaintance with those dreams that present us with
reality will in most cases be made only when forms have been
interposed which do not belong to reality and so vanish when
we wake up; or again when such a dream has received an even
greater intensification about which I shall speak in a moment.
The kind of dream we are describing is that which has been
called *sleep-waking*,[4] not so much because it is an intermediate
state between sleeping and wakefulness, but because it can be
described as becoming awake in the sleep itself. I should, therefore, prefer to call it a dreaming of reality.[5] It is true that in
most cases we shall observe it only in the early morning as also
in the evening some time after falling asleep. This is due merely
to the fact that, only when the sleep was not deep, did the
waking up occur sufficiently easily to leave behind a recollection of what was dreamed. This dreaming certainly occurs
much more frequently during deep sleep, according to the rule
that the somnambulist becomes the more clairvoyant the more
deeply she sleeps; but then no recollection of this is left behind.
On the other hand, that such a recollection sometimes occurs
when the dreaming has taken place during lighter sleep can be
explained from the fact that, even from magnetic sleep, if it was
quite light, a recollection can pass over into wakeful consciousness by way of exception, and an example of this is to be found
in Kieser's *Archiv für thierischen Magnetismus*, vol. iii, Pt. ii, p. 139.
And so according to this, the recollection of such directly and
objectively true dreams remains only when they have occurred
in light sleep, in the morning for example, when we can immediately wake up from them.

Now this kind of dream, whose peculiarity consists in our
dreaming the most immediately present reality, is occasionally
enhanced in its mysterious character by the fact that the range
of the dreamer's vision is somewhat extended so that it goes
beyond the bedroom. Thus the curtains or shutters cease to be
obstacles to vision and the dreamer then perceives quite dis-

---

[4] [The German word is *Schlafwachen*.]
[5] [The German word is *Wahrträumen*.]

tinctly what lies behind them, the yard, the garden, or the
street with the houses opposite. Our astonishment at this will
grow less if we bear in mind that here no physical vision takes
place, but a mere dreaming; yet it is a dreaming of that which
actually exists now and consequently a dreaming of what is
real, and so perception through the dream-organ, which as such
is naturally not tied to the condition of the uninterrupted passage of rays of light. As I said, the skull covering was itself the
first diaphragm through which this strange kind of perception
at first remained unimpeded. Now if it is enhanced still more,
then even curtains, doors, and walls no longer act as barriers
to it. But how this happens is a profound mystery; all we know
is that here the dreamer *dreams what is real* and consequently
that a perception through the dream-organ takes place. Thus
far does this elementary fact take us for our consideration.
What we can do to explain it, in so far as this is possible, is
first to compile and classify properly by grades all the phenomena connected therewith, with the object of discovering
their mutual relationship and in the hope of thus one day
arriving at a closer insight into it.

However, even for the man who in this matter has no experience of his own, the above-mentioned perception through
the dream-organ is irrefutably confirmed by spontaneous
somnambulism proper or sleep-walking. It is quite certain that
the victims of this malady are fast asleep and do not see at all
with their eyes; yet they perceive everything in their immediate
vicinity, avoid every obstacle, go long distances, climb up to the
most dangerous precipices on the narrowest paths, and perform
long jumps without missing their mark. In sleep some of them
accurately carry out their daily domestic affairs while others
draw and write without making mistakes. In the same way,
somnambulists who are artificially put into a magnetic sleep
also perceive their surroundings and, when they become
clairvoyant, even the remotest object. Further, the perception
certain people in a trance have of everything that goes on around
them while they lie rigid and unable to move a limb is undoubtedly of the same nature. They too dream of their present
surroundings and thus bring them to their consciousness on a
path different from that of the senses. Great efforts have been
made to obtain a clue to the physiological organ or seat of this

perception; but so far without success. It is incontestable that, when the state of somnambulism is complete, the external senses have entirely suspended their functions; for even the most subjective of these, namely bodily feeling, has so completely disappeared that the most painful surgical operations have been performed during magnetic sleep without the patient's having betrayed any sensation of them. Here the brain appears to be in a state of the deepest sleep and thus of complete inactivity. This and certain utterances and statements of somnambulists have given rise to the hypothesis that the state of somnambulism consists in the complete removal of the brain's power and in the accumulation of the vital force in the sympathetic nerve. According to this hypothesis, the larger reticula of this nerve, especially the *plexus solaris*, would now be transformed into a sensorium and so, acting as deputy, would take over the functions of the brain which they would now exercise without the aid of external sense-organs and yet with incomparably greater perfection than would the brain. This hypothesis, first advanced by Reil I believe, is not without plausibility and has since been much in vogue. Its mainstay is the statements of almost all clairvoyant somnambulists that their consciousness now has its seat entirely in the pit of the stomach where their thinking and perceiving are carried on as they were previously in the head. Most of them also arrange for objects they wish to examine closely to be laid on the epigastric region. Nevertheless, I consider that the thing is impossible. We have only to look at the solar plexus, this so-called *cerebrum abdominale*, to see how very small is its bulk and how extremely simple its structure, consisting as it does of rings of nerve substance together with some slight protuberances! If such an organ were capable of fulfilling the functions of intuitively perceiving and thinking, then the law *natura nihil facit frustra*[6] which is everywhere else borne out would be overthrown. For what then would be the purpose of the bulk of the brain, weighing usually three pounds and in isolated cases over five, as elaborate as it is protected, with the extremely ingenious structure of its parts? These are so complicated and intricate that it requires several entirely different methods of analysis frequently repeated merely in order to obtain some idea of the structural relation of this organ

6 ['Nature does nothing in vain.']

and to be able to form a tolerably clear picture of the wonderful form and connection of its many parts. Again it must be borne in mind that the steps and movements of a sleep-walker conform with the greatest promptness and precision to the immediate surroundings that are perceived by him through the dream-organ, so that he at once avoids most adroitly every obstacle in a way in which no one could do so in wakefulness; and he also hurries with the same skill towards the goal he has in view. But now the motor nerves spring from the spinal cord that is connected through the *medulla oblongata* with the *cerebellum*, the regulator of movements, this again is connected with the *cerebrum*, the seat of the motives that are representations or mental pictures. In this way it then becomes possible for movements to conform with the greatest promptitude even to the most fleeting perceptions. Now if the representations that, as motives, have to determine movements were shifted to the abdominal ganglionic network for which a difficult, feeble, and indirect communication with the brain is possible only by devious paths (hence in the healthy state we feel absolutely nothing of all the activities that occur so vigorously and restlessly in our organic life); how could the representations or mental pictures there originating guide the perilous footsteps of the sleep-walker and indeed with such lightning speed?* Incidentally, the sleep-walker runs faultlessly and fearlessly along the most perilous paths as he could never do if he were awake, and this is explained by the fact that his intellect is not wholly and positively but only partially active, namely in so far as it is required to guide his footsteps. In this way, reflection and with it all hesitation and irresolution are eliminated. Finally, with regard to the fact that *dreams* are at any rate a function of the brain, the following fact of Treviranus (*Über die Erscheinungen des organischen Lebens*, vol. ii, sect. 2, p. 117), quoted according to Pierquin, gives us even absolute certainty:

---

* With regard to the hypothesis in question, it is always noteworthy that the *Septuagint* usually calls seers and soothsayers ἐγγαστριμύθος [ventriloquist]—in particular also the Witch of Endor. Now this may have been done on the basis of the Hebrew original, or in accordance with the ideas and their expressions that prevailed at that time in Alexandria. The Witch of Endor is obviously a clairvoyante and what is meant by ἐγγαστριμύθος. Saul sees and speaks not to Samuel himself, but through the intercession of the woman who describes to Saul what Samuel looks like. (Cf. Deleuze, *De la prévision*, pp. 147, 148.)

'There was a girl the bones of whose skull were partially destroyed by caries so that her brain was quite exposed. It swelled up when she woke up, and subsided when she fell asleep. During peaceful sleep the depression was at its greatest and with vivid dreaming turgescence took place.' But it is obvious that somnambulism differs only in degree from the dream; *its* perceptions also occur through the dream-organ; it is, as I have said, an immediate dreaming of what is real.*

However, the hypothesis here in dispute could be modified to the extent of saying that the abdominal ganglionic network would not itself become the sensorium, but would take over only the role of the external organs thereof, and thus of the *sense-organs* that have here likewise become powerless, and consequently that it would receive impressions from without which it would then transmit to the brain. This would then elaborate them in accordance with its function and would now shape and build up from them the forms of the external world, as it otherwise does from the sensations in the organs of sense. But here too the difficulty recurs of the lightning transmission of the impressions to the brain that is so completely isolated from this inner nerve-centre. Then, according to its structure, the solar plexus is just as unfit to be the organ of sight and sound as it is to be that of thought; moreover, it is entirely shut off from the impression of light by a thick partition of skin, fat, muscle, peritoneum, and intestines. Therefore, although most somnambulists (like v. Helmont in the passage, quoted by several, *Ortus medicinae*, Leiden, 1667, *demens idea*, § 12, p. 171) state that their seeing and thinking take place in the epigastric region, we have no right at once to assume that this is objectively valid, the less so as several somnambulists expressly deny it. For instance, the well-known Auguste Müller in Karlsruhe states (in the report on her, pp. 53 ff.) that she sees not with the pit of the stomach but with her eyes. She says, however, that most of the other

---

* In the dream we often attempt in vain to cry out or move our limbs, and this is due to the fact that the dream, as a thing of mere representation, is an activity of the *cerebrum* alone that does not extend to the *cerebellum*. Accordingly, the latter remains in the lethargy of sleep, wholly inactive, and cannot fulfil its function, as the regulator of limb movements, of acting on the *medulla*. And so the most urgent commands of the *cerebrum* remain unfulfilled; hence the uneasiness. But if the *cerebrum* breaks through the isolation and becomes master of the *cerebellum*, we then have *somnambulism*.

somnambulists see with the pit of the stomach. To the question whether the power of thought can also be transplanted to the pit of the stomach, she replies that it cannot, but that the power of seeing and hearing can. In keeping with this, is the statement of another somnambulist in Kieser's *Archiv*, vol. x, Pt. II, p. 154; asked whether she thinks with the whole of her brain or with only a part thereof, she replies that she thinks with the whole of it and becomes very tired. The real conclusion from all somnambulistic statements seems to be that the stimulation and material for the intuitively perceiving activity of their brain comes not from without and through the senses as it does when we are awake, but, as was previously explained in connection with dreams, from the interior of the organism whose director and controller are, as we know, the great reticula of the sympathetic nerve. And so with regard to nervous activity, these act on behalf of and represent the whole organism with the exception of the cerebral system. Those statements can be compared with the remarks we make when we imagine we feel the pain in the foot which we actually feel only in the brain and which, therefore, ceases as soon as the nervous connection thereto is interrupted. It is, therefore, an illusion when somnambulists imagine they see and even read with the epigastric region, or assert that in rare cases they can perform this function even with their fingers, toes, or the tips of their noses (for instance the boy Arst in Kieser's *Archiv*, vol. iii, Pt. II; further the somnambulist Koch, vol. x, Pt. III, pp. 8–21; also the girl in Just Kerner's *Geschichte zweier Somnambulen*, 1824, pp. 323–30, who, however, adds that 'the seat of this vision is the brain as in wakefulness'). For although we may try to think of the nervous sensibility of such parts as so greatly enhanced, vision in the real sense, that is, by means of rays of light, remains absolutely impossible in organs that are deprived of every optical apparatus, even if they were not, as is the case, covered with thick coats, but were accessible to light. Indeed it is not merely the high sensibility of the retina which enables it to see, but likewise the extremely ingenious and complicated optical apparatus in the pupil. In the first place, physical vision requires a surface that is sensitive to light; but then the dispersed light-rays outside must again be collected and concentrated on this surface by means of the pupil and of the light-refracting, diaphanous

media that are combined with infinite ingenuity so that a picture, or more correctly a nerve impression exactly corresponding to the external object, arises by which alone the delicate
data are furnished for the understanding. From these the understanding then produces intuitive perception in space and time
through an intellectual process that applies the law of causality.
On the other hand, the pit of the stomach and the tip of the
finger could in any case receive only isolated reflections of light,
even if skin, muscle, and so on were transparent. And so it is
just as impossible to see with them as it is to make a daguerreo-
type in an open *camera obscura* without a convex lens. A further
proof that it is not really these alleged sense-functions of para-
doxical parts and that here there is no seeing by means of the
physical effect of light-rays, is furnished by the circumstance
that the above-mentioned boy of Kieser read with his toes, even
when he was wearing thick woollen stockings, and saw with the
tips of his fingers only when he expressly *willed* this; otherwise
he groped round the room with his hands in front. The same
thing is confirmed by his own statement about these abnormal
perceptions (ibid., p. 128): 'He never called this vision, but to
the question how he knew what was going on there, he replied
that he just knew it to be something new.' In the same way, a
somnambulist in Kieser's *Archiv*, vol. vii, Pt. 1, p. 52. describes
her perception as 'a seeing that is no seeing, an immediate
vision'. In the *Geschichte der hellsehenden Auguste Müller*, Stuttgart,
1818, it is reported on p. 36 that 'she sees perfectly clearly and
perceives all persons and objects in the most impenetrable darkness where it would be impossible for us to see in front of us
our own hand.' The same thing bears out Kieser's statement
with regard to the hearing of somnambulists (*Tellurismus*, vol. ii,
p. 172, 1st edn.) that woollen cords are particularly good conductors of sound, whereas wool is known to be the worst of all
conductors of sound. On this point, however, the following
passage from the above-mentioned work on Auguste Müller is
particularly instructive: 'It is remarkable and yet it is also
observed in the case of other somnambulists that she hears
absolutely nothing at all that is said by people in the room even
when they are quite close to her, if the talking is not definitely
directed to her. On the other hand, every word addressed to
her, however softly, even when several persons are talking to-

gether, is definitely understood and answered. It is much the
same when she is read to; if the person reading to her thinks
of something different from what he is reading, she does not
hear him', p. 40. Again on p. 89; 'Her hearing is not hearing in
the ordinary way through the ear, for this can be tightly closed
without her hearing being impeded.' Similarly in the *Mittheilungen aus dem Schlafleben der Somnambule Auguste K. in Dresden,*
1843, it is repeatedly stated that at times she hears solely
through the palm of her hand and indeed the silent word that
is expressed through the mere movement of the lips. On page 32
she herself warns us not to regard this as a hearing in the literal
sense.

Accordingly, with somnambulists of all kinds it is certainly
not a question of sensuous perceptions in the real meaning of
the word; but their perceiving is an immediate *dreaming of what
is real* [*Wahrträumen*] and therefore takes place through the
very mysterious dream-organ. The fact that the objects to be
perceived are placed on her forehead or the pit of her stomach,
or that, in the individual cases quoted, the somnambulist
directs on to them her outstretched finger-tips, is merely an
expedient for guiding the dream-organ on to these objects
through contact with them in order that they may become the
theme of its dreaming of the real. And so this is done merely to
direct her attention definitely to them or, in technical language,
to put her in closer touch with these objects; whereupon she
then dreams of them and indeed not merely of their visibility,
but also of their audibility, their language, and even their odour.
For many clairvoyants state that *all their senses* are transferred to
the pit of the stomach. (Dupotet, *Traité complet du magnétisme,*
pp. 449–52.) Consequently, it is analogous to the use of the
hands in magnetizing where these do not really act physically,
but that which operates is the *will* of the magnetizer. But it is
just this that obtains its direction and determination through
the application of the hands. For only the insight that is derived from my philosophy can lead to an understanding of the
magnetizer's complete influence through all kinds of gestures,
with and without contact, even from a distance and through
partitions; namely the view that the body is wholly identical
with the will and thus is nothing but the will's image arising
in the brain. The vision of somnambulists is not one in our sense

of the word and is not physically caused through the medium of light. This already follows from the fact that, when enhanced to clairvoyance, it is not impeded by walls; in fact it extends sometimes to distant countries. We are afforded a special illustration of this by the inwardly directed intuitive self-perception that occurs in the higher degrees of clairvoyance. In virtue of it, such somnambulists clearly and precisely perceive all the parts of their own organism, although all the conditions for physical vision are here entirely wanting not only on account of the absence of all light, but also by reason of the many diaphragms that lie between the intuitively perceived part and the brain. Thus we can infer from this the nature of all somnambulistic perception, and so of that which is directed outwards and to a distance, and accordingly of all intuitive perception generally by means of the dream-organ and consequently of all somnambulistic vision of external objects, all dreaming, all visions while we are awake, second sight, the bodily apparition of those who are absent, especially of the dying, and so on. For it is evident that the above-mentioned vision of the internal parts of one's own body results only through an influence on the brain from within, probably through the agency of the ganglionic system. Now, true to its nature, the brain elaborates these inner impressions just as it does those that come to it from without, moulding, as it were, a foreign material into forms that are peculiar and habitual to it. From them just such intuitive perceptions arise similar to those that result from impressions on the external senses, and the former like the latter then correspond in degree and meaning to the things intuitively perceived. Accordingly, every case of vision through the dream-organ is the activity of the intuitively perceiving brain-function that is stimulated by *inner* instead of outer impressions as previously.* That such an activity, however, can have objective reality and truth, even when it relates to *external* and indeed remote things, is a fact whose explanation could be attempted only in a metaphysical way, from the restriction of all individuation and separation to the phenomenon in contrast to the thing-in-itself; and to this we shall

---

* From the doctors' description *catalepsy* appears to be the complete paralysis of the *motor* nerves, whereas *somnambulism* is that of the *sensory* nerves, for which the dream-organ then deputizes.

revert. That the connection between somnambulists and the outer world is in general fundamentally different from that which we have when we are awake is proved in the clearest manner by the circumstance, frequently occurring in the higher degrees, that, whereas the clairvoyante's own senses are inaccessible to any impression, she feels with those of the magnetizer. For example, she sneezes when he takes a pinch of snuff, tastes and determines exactly what he is eating, and hears even the music that is ringing in his ears in a distant room of the house (Kiesers' *Archiv*, vol. i, Pt. i, p. 117.)

The physiological course of events in somnambulistic perception is a difficult riddle to whose solution, however, the first step would be a genuine physiology of the dream, that is, a clear and certain knowledge of the nature of the brain's activity therein, of the way in which this really differs from the activity during wakefulness, and finally of the source of the stimulation to it, consequently a closer definition of the course it takes. So far only this much may be assumed with certainty as regards the whole intuitively perceiving and thinking activity in sleep; first that its material organ, notwithstanding the brain's relative repose, cannot be anything but this brain; and secondly that the stimulation to such intuitive dream perception must take place from the interior of the organism, for it cannot come from without through the senses. But as regards the correct and precise relation, unmistakable in somnambulism, of that intuitive dream perception to the outside world, it remains a riddle to us whose solution I am not undertaking; but later on I shall give only a few general suggestions concerning it. On the other hand, I have worked out in my mind the following hypothesis as the basis of the above-mentioned physiology of the dream and thus for explaining the whole of our intuitive dreaming perception; and in my view this hypothesis is highly probable.

Since during sleep the brain receives its stimulation to the intuitive perception of spatial forms from within, as we have stated instead of from without, as during wakefulness, this impression must affect it in a direction the opposite of the usual one that comes from the senses. In consequence of this, its whole activity and so the inner vibration or agitation of its filaments assume a tendency which is the opposite of the usual one; it begins to move antiperistaltically, so to speak. Thus instead of taking place, as previously, in the direction of the sense impressions and thus from the sense nerves to the interior of the brain, it now occurs in the reverse direction and order; but in this way it is sometimes carried out by different parts. Thus it may not be the lower surface of the brain instead of the upper, but possibly the white medullary substance instead of the grey cortical matter which must function, and *vice versa*. Thus the brain now works the other way round. In the first place it is clear from this why no recollection of the somnambulistic activity passes over into wakefulness, as this is conditioned by a vibration of the brain-filaments in the opposite direction which obliterates every trace of that which previously existed. Incidentally, as a special confirmation of this assumption, the very common but strange fact might be mentioned that, when we at once reawake from the first dozing off, we often experience a complete absence of direction. It is of such a nature that we are forced to look at everything in the reverse sense and thus to imagine that what is on the right of the bed is on the left and what is behind is in front. Moreover, we are so positive about this that in the dark even rational deliberation that things may be the other way round is incapable of obliterating that false imagination, for which purpose touching and feeling are necessary. But in particular, that remarkable liveliness of intuitive dream perception, the above-mentioned apparent reality and corporeality of all objects that are perceived in the dream, is easy to understand from our hypothesis, namely that the stimulation of the brain's activity that comes from the interior of the organism and starts from the centre in a direction contrary to the normal, finally forces its way through and extends ultimately as far as the nerves of the sense-organs, which now become really active, stimulated as they are from within as they previously were from without. Accordingly, we actually have in the dream sensations of light, colour, sound, smell, and taste, only without the external causes that previously stimulated them, merely in virtue of an inner excitation and in consequence of an impression in the opposite direction and in the reverse order of time. Hence from this is explained that corporeality of dreams whereby they differ so powerfully from mere fantasies. The picture of the imagination (in wakefulness) is always merely in the brain; for it is only the reminiscence, although modified, of a previous material excitation of the brain's intuitively perceiving activity that occurs through the senses. On the other hand, the dream apparition is not merely in the brain, but also in the nerves of the senses and has arisen in consequence of a material, actually effective excitation of those nerves which comes from the interior and penetrates the brain. Accordingly, since we actually see in the dream, what Apuleius represents the Grace as saying when she is about to put out the eyes of the sleeping Thrasyllus, is extremely apt, fine, and indeed profoundly conceived: *vivo tibi morientur oculi, nec quidquam videbis, nisi dormiens*[7] (*Metamorphoses*, VIII, p. 172, *ed. Bip.*). The dream-organ is, therefore, the same as the organ of conscious wakefulness and intuitive perception of the external world, only grasped, as it were, from the other end and used in the reverse order. The nerves of the senses which function in both can be rendered active from their inner as well as from their outer end, somewhat like a hollow iron globe which can be made red-hot from within as well as from without. Since, when this occurs, the nerves of the senses are the last to become active, it may happen that such activity has only just begun and is still in progress when the brain is already waking up, in other words, when ordinary intuitive perception is taking the place of intuitive dream perception. Having just woken up, we shall then hear sounds, such as voices, knocks on the door, rifle-shots, and so on, with a clearness and objectivity that *perfectly and completely* resemble reality. We shall then firmly believe that it was sounds of reality, from without, which in the first instance woke us up; or in rarer instances we shall also see forms with complete empirical reality, as is mentioned by Aristotle in *De insomniis*, c. 3 at the end. Now, as I have already adequately explained, it is the dream-organ, here described, whereby somnambulistic intuitive perception, clairvoyance, second sight, and visions of all kinds are brought about.

From these physiological observations, I now return to the previously discussed phenomenon of *dreaming what is real*. This can occur in ordinary sleep at night where it is then at once confirmed by our merely waking up, namely when, as in

---

[7] ['For the rest of your life your eyes will for you be dead and you will no longer see anything except in sleep.']

most cases, it was direct, in other words, extended only to the immediate vicinity, although in rarer instances it goes a little beyond this, to the other side of the nearest partition walls. This extension of the range of vision can, however, go very much farther not only in respect of space, but even of time. The proof of this is given by clairvoyant somnambulists who in the period of the extreme climax of their condition can at once bring into their intuitive dream perception any locality whatsoever to which they are led and can give a correct account of the events there. But occasionally they can even predict that which does not yet exist but still lies hidden in the womb of the future and only in the course of time comes to be realized by means of innumerable intermediate causes that come together by chance. For all clairvoyance in somnambulistic sleep-waking [*Schlafwachen*], both artificially produced and naturally induced, all perception therein that has become possible of the hidden, the absent, the remote, or even the future, is simply nothing but a *true dreaming* thereof whose objects are thus presented to the intellect palpably and plainly like our dreams; and so somnambulists speak of *seeing* them. Meanwhile, we have in these phenomena as also in spontaneous sleep-walking positive proof that that mysterious intuition which is conditioned by no impression from without and is familiar to us through the dream, can stand to the external world of reality in the relation of *perception*, although the connection with that perception which facilitates this remains to us a mystery. What distinguishes the ordinary dream at night from clairvoyance or sleep-waking generally is first the absence of that relation to the outside world and hence to reality, and secondly the fact that very often a recollection of it passes over into wakefulness, whereas such a recollection does not take place from somnambulistic sleep. But these two characteristics might well be connected and related to each other. Thus the ordinary dream leaves behind a recollection only when we have immediately woken up from it. And so it is probably due simply to the fact that waking up results very easily from natural sleep which is not nearly so deep as somnambulistic. For this reason, an immediate and therefore rapid waking up from the latter cannot occur, but a return to conscious wakefulness is possible only by means of a gradual transition. Thus somnambulistic sleep is only one that is incomparably deeper, more highly effective, and more complete in which, therefore, the dream-organ is able to develop its fullest capacity whereby the correct relation to the external world and hence the continuous and coherent dreaming of what is real becomes possible for it. Probably such a dreaming occasionally occurs in ordinary sleep, but precisely only when such sleep is so deep that we do not immediately wake therefrom. On the other hand, the dreams from which we wake up are those of lighter sleep; in the last resort, they have sprung from merely somatic causes that apper-tain to one's own organism and thus have no reference to the outside world. Yet we have already seen that there are excep-tions to this in the dreams that present the immediate environ-ment of the person who is sleeping. Nevertheless, even of dreams that make known the distant or future event, there is, by way of exception, a recollection; and indeed this depends mainly on our immediately waking up from such a dream. For this reason, at all times and among all peoples, it has been assumed that there are dreams of real objective significance and in the whole of ancient history dreams are taken very seriously so that in it they play an important part. However, of the vast number of empty and merely illusory dreams the fatidical have always been regarded only as rare exceptions. Accordingly, Homer tells (*Odyssey*, XIX, 560) of two portals of entry for dreams, one of ivory by which insignificant dreams enter, and one of horn for fatidical dreams. An anatomist might perhaps feel tempted to interpret this in terms of the white and grey matter of the brain. Those dreams that relate to the dreamer's state of health most frequently prove to be prophetic; and indeed in most cases these will predict illnesses and even fatal attacks. (Instances of these have been collected by E. Fabius, *De somniis*, Amsterdam, 1836, pp. 195 ff.) This is analogous to the case where clair-voyant somnambulists foretell with the greatest frequency and certainty the course of their own illness together with its crises and so on. Again external accidents, such as conflagrations, powder explosions, shipwrecks, but particularly deaths, are sometimes presaged through dreams. Finally, other events, sometimes fairly trivial, are dreamed in advance and in minute detail by some people, and of this I am convinced from an unquestionable experience of my own. I will record it here for it also puts in the strongest light the *strict necessity of all that happens*, even of the most accidental. One morning I was preoccupied with writing a long and very important business letter in English. When I had finished the third page, I picked up the ink-bottle instead of the writing-sand and poured all over the letter ink which flowed from the desk on to the floor. The maid who appeared when I rang the bell fetched a pail of water and scrubbed the floor to prevent the stains from soaking in. While doing this she said to me: 'Last night I dreamed that I was here rubbing out ink-stains from the floor.' Whereupon I said: 'That is not true', but she again said: 'It is true and when I woke up I mentioned it to the other maid who was sleeping with me.' At this moment the other maid aged about seventeen happened to enter to call away the one who was scrubbing. I went up to her and asked: 'What did she dream last night?' Her reply was 'I do not know'. But I said 'Yes you do, she told you about it when she woke up.' And the young girl said: 'Oh yes, she dreamed that here she would scrub ink-stains from the floor.' This story which puts theorematic dreams beyond all doubt, since I vouch for its absolute truth, is no less remarkable from the fact that what was dreamed beforehand was the effect of an action that might be called involuntary or automatic in so far as I performed it *without* any intention whatever and it depended on the most trivial slip of my hand. Yet this action was determined beforehand with such strict necessity and inevitability that its effect existed several hours earlier as a dream in the consciousness of another person. Here we see most clearly the truth of my proposition that all that happens necessarily happens. (*The Two Fundamental Problems of Ethics*, 'Freedom of the Will', Pt. III.) For tracing prophetic dreams back to their immediate cause, we have, as we all know, the circumstance that no recollection either of natural or magnetic somnambulism and its events occurs in conscious wakefulness, but that such occasionally passes over into the dreams of natural ordinary sleep and these are subsequently remembered when the person wakes up. And so the dream becomes the connecting link, the bridge, between somnambulistic and waking consciousness. According to this, we must, therefore, first attribute prophetic dreams to the fact that in deep sleep dreaming is enhanced to a somnambulistic clair-

voyance. Now since from dreams of this kind no immediate
waking up and thus no recollection as a rule take place, those
dreams that form an exception to this, and therefore prefigure
the coming event *directly* and *sensu proprio* and have been called
theorematic, are the rarest of all. On the other hand, a man will
often be able to retain a recollection of a dream of this kind,
when its contents are of great importance to him, by his
carrying it over into the dream of lighter sleep from which he
may immediately wake up. Yet this cannot be done directly,
but only by means of a translation of the contents into an
allegory. Clad in this garment, the original prophetic dream
now reaches conscious wakefulness where it still requires
interpretation and explanation. This, then, is the other and
more frequent form of fatidical dreams, the *allegorical*. In his
Oneirocriticon, the oldest book on dreams, Artemidorus drew a
distinction between the two kinds, and called the first *theorematic*.
Man's natural tendency, by no means accidental or artificial, to
brood over the meaning of his dreams has its root in the
consciousness of the ever-present possibility of the above-
mentioned course of events. When this tendency is cultivated
and methodically perfected, it gives rise to oneiromancy. But
this adds the assumption that the events in the dream had a
fixed meaning valid once for all about which a lexicon could
therefore be made. But such is not the case; on the contrary,
the allegory is expressly and individually suited to each and
every object and subject of the theorematic dream that forms
the basis of the allegorical. For this reason, the interpretation of
allegorical fatidical dreams is for the most part so difficult that
in most cases we understand them only after their prediction
has come true. But then we are bound to admire the utterly
strange and demon-like cunning of the wit which is otherwise
quite foreign to the dreamer and with which the allegory has
been constructed and worked out. But till then we retain these
dreams in our memory, and this can be attributed to the fact
that they are through their outstanding clearness and even
vivid reality more deeply impressed than the rest. Practice
and experience will certainly conduce to the art of interpreting
dreams. It is not Schubert's well-known book, however, which
contains nothing of any use except the title, but old Artemidorus from whom we can really become acquainted with the

'*symbolism of the dream*', especially from his last two books. Here in hundreds of examples he renders intelligible the mode, manner, method, and humour that are employed by our dreaming omniscience in order, where possible, to impart something to our lack of knowledge when we are awake. This can be far better learnt from his examples than from his previous theorems and rules on the subject.* That Shakespeare had also perfectly understood the above-mentioned humour[8] of the thing is seen in *Henry VI*, Part II, Act III, Sc. 2, where at the quite unexpected news of the Duke of Gloucester's sudden death, the villainous Cardinal Beaufort who knows best how matters are exclaims:

> God's secret judgement:— I did dream tonight
> The duke was dumb, and could not speak a word.

Here, then, is the place to introduce the important remark that, in the utterances of the ancient Greek oracle, we again find exactly the above-mentioned relation between the theorematic and allegorical fatidical dream that reproduces it. Thus those utterances, like the fatidical dreams, very rarely make a direct statement *sensu proprio*, but veil it in an allegory which requires interpretation and indeed is understood often only after the oracle has come true, like allegorical dreams. I quote from numerous examples merely to illustrate the point; thus, for instance, in Herodotus, lib. III, c. 57 the oracular utterance of Pythia warned the Siphnians of the wooden host and the red herald by which they were to understand a Samian ship painted red and bearing a messenger. The Siphnians, however, did not at once understand this or even after the ship's arrival, but only when it was too late. Further in the fourth book, chapter 163, the oracle of Pythia forewarned King Arcesilaus of Cyrene that, if he should find the kiln full of amphorae, he should not bake these, but send them away. But only after he had burnt the rebels together with the tower to which they had fled did he understand the meaning of the oracle and then became alarmed. The many instances of this kind definitely point to the fact that the utterances of the Delphic oracle were based on ingeniously produced fatidical dreams and that these

---

* In *Aus meinem Leben*, Book I towards the end, Goethe tells us about the allegorical reality-dreams of Textor the magistrate.

[8] [See Shakespeare, *Henry V*, Act II, Sc. I.]

could sometimes be enhanced to the most distinct clairvoyance. The result was then a direct utterance that spoke *sensu proprio*. This is testified by the story of Croesus (Herodotus, lib. I, cc. 47, 48) who put the Pythia to the test by his envoys having to ask what he was doing far away in Lydia at that very moment on the hundredth day after their departure, whereupon the Pythia stated precisely and accurately what no one but the king himself knew, namely that with his own hands he was cooking turtles and mutton in a brazen cauldron with a brazen lid. It is in keeping with the suggested source of the oracular utterances of Pythia that they were consulted medically on account of bodily ailments; Herodotus, lib. IV, c. 155, gives an instance of this.

From what has been said, *theorematic* fatidical dreams are the highest and rarest degree of prophetic vision in natural sleep, *allegorical* dreams the second and lower degree. Now in addition, there is yet the final and feeblest emanation from the same source, namely mere *presentiment* or foreboding. This is more often of a melancholy than a cheerful nature, just because there is in life more misery than mirth. A morose disposition, an uneasy expectation of the coming event, has without any apparent cause taken possession of us after sleep. According to the above description, this can be explained from the fact that that translation of the theorematic true dream, existing in deepest sleep and foreboding evil, into an allegorical dream of lighter sleep was not successful. Therefore nothing of that theorematic dream was left behind in consciousness except its impression on the disposition, that is, the *will* itself, that real and ultimate kernel of man. That impression now re-echoes as a presentiment or gloomy foreboding. Yet this will occasionally take possession of us only when the first circumstances that are connected with the misfortune seen in the theorematic dream appear in reality; for example, when a man is on the point of embarking on a ship that is going to founder; or he approaches a powder-magazine that is going to blow up. Many a man has been saved by obeying the evil presentiment that suddenly occurs to him, or the inner apprehension that comes over him. We have to explain this from the fact that, although the theorematic dream is forgotten, there is nevertheless left over from it a feeble reminiscence, a dull recollection. It is true that this cannot enter clear consciousness, but its clue is renewed by the sight in real life of the very things that affected us so terribly in the forgotten dream. Also of the same nature was the *daimon* of Socrates, that inner warning voice that dissuaded him from anything disadvantageous as soon as he resolved to undertake it; yet it always advised against never in favour of a thing. A direct confirmation of the theory of presentiments here expounded is possible only by means of magnetic somnambulism which divulges the secrets of sleep. And so we find such a confirmation in the well-known *Geschichte der Auguste Müller zu Karlsruhe*, p. 78. 'On 15 December in her nocturnal (magnetic) sleep, the somnambulist became aware of an unpleasant event concerning her which greatly depressed her. At the same time, she remarked that all the next day she would be anxious and uneasy without knowing why.' Further, a confirmation of this case is given by the impression, described in the *Seherin von Prevorst* (1st edn., vol. II, p. 73; 3rd edn., p. 325), which certain verses, relating to somnambulistic events, made during wakefulness on the clairvoyante who knew nothing of them. Also in Kieser's *Tellurismus*, § 271, we find facts that throw light on this point.

As regards all that has been said so far, it is very important to understand and bear in mind the following fundamental truth. Magnetic sleep is only an enhancement of natural sleep, or perhaps a higher potential thereof; it is an incomparably deeper sleep. In keeping with this, clairvoyance is only an enhancement of dreaming; it is a continuous *dreaming of the real* [*Wahrträumen*]; but here such dreaming can be guided from without and directed to what we want. Thirdly, the directly wholesome effect of magnetism, which is verified in so many cases of illness, is also nothing but an enhancement of the natural healing power of sleep in all of them. Indeed sleep is the true and great panacea, for in the first place, by means of it, the vital force is relieved of the animal functions and becomes wholly free, now to appear with all its strength as the *vis naturae medicatrix*,[9] and in this capacity to remove all the disorders that have taken root in the organism. Thus a complete absence of sleep rules out any recovery. Now this is achieved in a much higher degree by the incomparably deeper magnetic sleep; and so when it occurs of itself for the purpose of curing

9 ['The healing power of nature'.]

grave illnesses that have become chronic, it sometimes lasts for
several days, as for instance in the case published by Count
Szapáry (*Ein Wort über den animalischen Magnetismus*, Leipzig,
1840). Once in Russia a consumptive somnambulist in the
omniscient crisis ordered her doctor to put her into a trance for
nine days. During that time her lung had the benefit of complete
rest and was thus restored so that she woke up with health
completely recovered. Now the essence of sleep consists in the
inactivity of the cerebral system and even its wholesomeness
comes precisely from the fact that that system with its animal
life no longer absorbs and consumes any vital force so that this
can now be devoted entirely to organic life. Yet it might appear
to be inconsistent with its main purpose that precisely in
magnetic sleep there sometimes emerges an exceedingly enhanced power of knowledge which by its nature must in some
way be an activity of the brain. But first we must remember that
this case is only a rare exception. Of twenty patients affected
generally by magnetism, only one becomes a somnambulist, in
other words, understands and talks in sleep; and of five somnambulists barely one becomes clairvoyant (according to
Deleuze, *Histoire critique du magnétisme*, Paris, 1813, vol. I, p. 138).
When magnetism acts beneficially without producing sleep,
it does so merely by rousing the healing power of nature and
directing it to the injured part. But in addition, its effect
primarily is only an extremely deep sleep that is dreamless;
in fact the cerebral system is reduced in power to such an
extent that neither sense-impressions nor injuries are felt at all.
It has, therefore, been used with the greatest benefit in surgical
operations, although for this purpose it has been supplanted
by chloroform. Nature really lets it reach clairvoyance, whose
preliminary stage is somnambulism or talking in sleep, only
when her *blindly operating* healing power does not suffice to
remove the disease, but remedies from without are needed
which the patient himself in the clairvoyant stage now correctly
prescribes. Thus for this purpose of self-prescription, nature
brings about clairvoyance, for *natura nihil facit frustra*.[10] Here
her method is analogous and akin to that followed by her on a
large scale with the first production of creatures when she took
the step from the plant to the animal kingdom. Thus for plants

[10] ['Nature does nothing in vain.']

movement on mere *stimuli* had sufficed; but now the more special and complicated needs, whose objects had to be sought, selected, subdued, or even duped, rendered necessary movement on *motives* and therefore *knowledge* in all its many degrees. Accordingly, this is the peculiar characteristic of animal existence, that which is not accidental but really essential to the animal and which we necessarily think under the concept of *animal*. On this point I refer to my chief work, vol. i, § 27; also to my *Ethics*, 'On the Freedom of the Will', Pt. III; and to *On the Will in Nature*, 'Comparative Anatomy and Physiology of Plants'. And so in the one case as in the other, nature kindles for herself a light in order to be able to seek and procure the help that is required by the organism *from without*. Turning the now developed gift of the somnambulist's second sight to things other than her own state of health is merely an accidental use, or really an abuse, thereof. It is also an abuse if we arbitrarily bring on through long-continued magnetization somnambulism and clairvoyance, contrary to nature's purpose. On the other hand, where these are really necessary, nature produces them quite automatically after a brief magnetization indeed sometimes as spontaneous somnambulism. They then appear, as I have said, as a dreaming of what is real [*Wahrträumen*], first only of the immediate environment, then in ever-widening circles, until in the highest degrees of clairvoyance such dreaming can reach all the events on earth to which its attention is directed; and occasionally it penetrates even into the future. The capacity for pathological diagnosis and therapeutic prescription, first for oneself and then by way of abuse for others, is in keeping with these different stages.

With somnambulism in the original and proper sense and hence with morbid *sleep-walking*, such a dreaming of the real occurs, yet here only for direct use and thus extending merely to the immediate surroundings just because in this case nature's end is already attained. In such a state, therefore, the vital force, as *vis medicatrix*,[11] has not suspended animal life as in magnetic sleep, spontaneous somnambulism, and catalepsy in order to be able to apply its whole strength to organic life and to eliminate the disorders that have taken root therein. On the contrary, vital force appears here as an abnormal excess of

[11] ['Healing power'.]

irritability by virtue of a morbid depression to which the age of puberty is most exposed. Nature now endeavours to free herself from this excess and, as we know, in sleep this is done by walking, working, climbing to the most dangerous heights and most perilous leaps. At the same time, nature calls forth that mysterious reality-dreaming as the attendant of those perilous steps. But such dreaming here extends only to the immediate environment, for this suffices to prevent accidents that the released irritability would inevitably cause if it acted blindly. Here, then, this dreaming has only the negative object of preventing harm, whereas in clairvoyance it has the positive one of finding help from without; hence the great difference in the range of vision.

Mysterious as is the effect of magnetization, it is nevertheless clear that it consists primarily in the suspension of animal functions in that the vital force is diverted from the brain, that mere pensioner or parasite of the organism, or rather is driven back to organic life as its primitive function; for now its undivided presence and effectiveness as *vis medicatrix* are required there. But within the nervous system and thus the exclusive seat of all sensuous life, organic life is represented and replaced by the guide and governor of its functions, the sympathetic nerve and its ganglia. Thus the event can also be regarded as a repression of the vital force from the brain to the sympathetic nerve; but generally the two can also be looked upon as mutually opposite poles; and so the brain, with the organs of movement attached thereto, can be regarded as the positive and conscious pole, and the sympathetic nerve, with its ganglionic networks, as the negative and unconscious. Now in this sense, the following hypothesis could be given concerning the course of events in magnetization. It is an action of the magnetizer's brain-pole (and hence of his external nerve-pole) on the *homonymous* pole of the patient; and so it acts on the latter by *repulsion* in accordance with the universal law of polarity, whereby the nervous force is driven back to the other pole of the nervous system, to the inner, the gastric ganglionic system. Therefore men in whom the brain-pole prevails are best fitted for magnetizing, whereas women in whom the ganglionic system predominates are most susceptible to being magnetized and to the consequences thereof. If it were possible for the female ganglionic system to be capable of acting in just the same way on the male and so also by repulsion, then through the reverse process an abnormally enhanced cerebral life, a temporary genius, would inevitably result. This is not feasible because the ganglionic system is not capable of acting outwards. On the other hand, the *magnetizing bucket* might well be regarded as an *attracting* magnetization through the action on each other of *heteronymous or unlike* poles, so that the sympathetic nerves of all the patients sitting round the bucket which are connected thereto by iron rods and woollen cords running to the pit of the stomach and which operate with united force enhanced by the inorganic mass of the bucket, would draw to themselves the individual brainpole of each of the patients, and so lower the potential of animal life, causing it to be submerged in the magnetic sleep of all. This could be compared to the lotus that is submerged every evening in the flood. In keeping also with this is the fact that, when the ladder of the bucket had once been laid on the head instead of on the pit of the stomach, violent congestion and headache were the result (Kieser, *Tellurismus*, 1st edn., Vol. i, p. 439). In the *sidereal* bucket, the bare unmagnetized metals exert the same force. This appears to be connected with the fact that metal is the simplest and most original thing, the lowest grade of the will's objectification, and consequently the very opposite to the brain as being the highest development of that objectification; and hence that it is the thing remotest from the brain. Moreover, metal offers the maximum mass in the minimum space. Accordingly, it recalls the will to its original nature and is related to the ganglionic system as, conversely, light is to the brain, and so somnambulists shun the contact of metals with the organs of the conscious pole. The sensitivity to metals and water of those so disposed can also be explained in this way. With the ordinary magnetized bucket, what operate are the ganglionic systems, connected thereto, of all the patients who are assembled round it and with their united force draw down the brain-poles. This also helps to explain the contagion of somnambulism generally as also the communication, akin to it, of the present activity of second sight through the mutual contact of those endowed with it, and the communication and consequently the communion of visions generally.

But if we wished to venture on an even bolder application of the above hypothesis which concerns the course of events in magnetization and starts from the laws of polarity, then it might be deduced from this, although only schematically, how, in the higher degrees of somnambulism, the relation can go to such lengths that the somnambulist shares all the ideas, knowledge, manners of speaking, and even the sensations of the magnetizer. She is thus present in his brain, whereas his *will*, on the other hand, has a direct influence on her and he is so completely her master that he can fix her by his spell. Thus with the galvanic apparatus, now most commonly used, where the two metals are immersed in two kinds of acids that are separated by earthenware partitions, the positive current flows through these liquids from the zinc to the copper, and then externally in the electrode from the copper back to the zinc. Hence by analogy, the positive current of vital force, as the will of the magnetizer, would flow from his brain to that of the somnambulist, controlling her and driving back to the sympathetic nerve and thus to the epigastric region, to her negative pole, her vital force that produces consciousness in the brain. But then the same current would again flow from here back into the magnetizer, to his positive pole, his brain, where it meets his ideas and sensations; and then in this way does the somnambulist share them. These, of course, are very bold assumptions, but with the extremely obscure matters that here constitute our problem every hypothesis is admissible which leads to some understanding, although such may be only schematic or analogical.

The extremely marvellous and positively incredible feature of somnambulistic clairvoyance, difficult to believe until it was corroborated by the consistency of hundreds of cases of the most trustworthy evidence—a clairvoyance to which are revealed the hidden, the absent, the remote, and even that which still slumbers in the womb of the future—loses at any rate its absolute incomprehensibility if we reflect that, as I have so often said, the objective world is a mere phenomenon of the brain. For the order and conformity to law thereof which are based on space, time, and causality (as brain-functions), are to some extent set aside in somnambulistic clairvoyance. Thus in consequence of the Kantian doctrine of the ideality of space and time, we see that the thing-in-itself, that which alone is the truly real in all phenomena as being free from those two forms of the intellect, knows no distinction between near and remote, between present, past, and future. Therefore the separations that are due to those forms of intuitive perception prove to be not absolute; on the contrary, they no longer offer any insuperable barriers to the method of cognition here discussed which is essentially changed by the transformation of its organ. On the other hand, if time and space were absolutely real and appertained to the essence-in-itself of things, then that prophetic gift of somnambulists, as well as all distance-vision and prevision generally, would certainly be an absolutely incomprehensible miracle. On the other hand, even Kant's doctrine to a certain extent obtains positive confirmation from the facts here discussed. For if time is not a determination of the real nature of things, then, in respect thereof, before and after are without meaning; accordingly, it must be possible for an event to be known just as well before it has happened as after. The art of soothsaying, whether in the dream, somnambulistic prophetic vision, second sight, or anything else, consists only in discovering the path to the freedom of knowledge from the condition of time. The matter can also be made clearer by the following simile. *Thing-in-itself* is the *primum mobile*[12] in the mechanism that imparts motion to the whole complicated and variegated plaything of this world. By its nature and constitution the former must, therefore, be different from the latter. We indeed see the connection of the separate parts of the plaything in the levers and wheels (time-sequence and causality) that are purposely revealed; but that which imparts the *first* motion to all these we do not see. Now when I read how clairvoyant somnambulists foretell the future so far in advance and so accurately, it seems to me as if they had reached that mechanism which is hidden in the background, and from which everything originates. And so that which is seen externally, that is, through our optical lens of time, as merely something that will come in the future, is already at this moment present in that mechanism.

Moreover, the same animal magnetism to which these marvels are due, has for us testified to a direct action of the *will* on

---

[12] ['The prime mover', 'the prime motive' (an expression used by Aristotle).

others and at a distance. But such a thing is precisely the fundamental characteristic of what is described by the notorious name of *magic*. For this is a direct action of our will itself which is freed from the causal conditions of physical action and hence of contact in the widest sense of the word. I have discussed this in a special chapter in my work *On the Will in Nature*. Magical action is, therefore, related to physical as the art of soothsaying is to rational conjecture. It is a real and complete *actio in distans*,[13] in the same way as genuine soothsaying, for example somnambulistic clairvoyance, is *passio a distante*.[14] Just as in the latter the individual isolation of knowledge is abolished, so in the former is the individual isolation of the will. Therefore in both, independently of the limitations imposed by space, time, and causality, we achieve what we can otherwise and ordinarily do only under these limitations. Therefore in them our innermost being, or the thing-in-itself, has cast off those forms of the phenomenon and emerges free therefrom. And so the trustworthiness of the art of soothsaying is akin to that of magic and doubt about both has always come and gone at the same time.

Animal magnetism, sympathetic cures, magic, second sight, dreaming the real, spirit seeing, and visions of all kinds are kindred phenomena, branches of one stem. They afford certain and irrefutable proof of a nexus of entities that rests on an order of things entirely different from *nature*. For her foundation nature has the laws of space, time, and causality, whereas that other order is more deep-seated, original, and immediate. Therefore the first and most universal (because purely formal) laws of *nature* are not applicable to it. Accordingly, time and space no longer separate individuals and their separation and isolation, which are due to those very forms, no longer place insuperable barriers in the way of the communication of thoughts and the direct influence of the will. Thus changes are brought about in a way quite different from that of physical causality with the continuous chain of its links; in other words, they are produced merely by virtue of an act of will that is brought to light in a special manner and thereby intensified to a higher potential beyond the individual. Accordingly, the peculiar characteristic

13 ['Acting at a distance'.]
14 ['Being affected from a distance'.]

of all the animal phenomena here considered is *visio in distans et actio in distans*,[15] both as regards time and space.

Incidentally, the true conception of *actio in distans* is that the space between the causative and the caused, whether full or empty, has absolutely no influence on the effect, but it is quite immaterial whether it amounts to an inch or a billion times the orbit of Uranus. For if the effect is in any way diminished by the distance, then it is either because a matter that already fills space has to transmit it and therefore, by virtue of the constant counter-effect of that matter, the effect is diminished by it in proportion to the distance; or it is because the cause itself consists merely in a material emanation which disperses in space and thus becomes the more attenuated the greater the distance. On the other hand, empty space itself cannot in any way offer resistance to and invalidate causality. And so where the effect grows less in proportion to its distance from the starting-point of the cause, like the effect of light, gravitation, the magnet, and so on, there is no *actio in distans*; and just as little is there where the effect is merely delayed through distance. For matter alone is that which is movable in space; and so it would have to be the bearer of such an effect and cover the distance. Accordingly, it would be compelled to act only after it arrived, consequently first on contact and so not *in distans*.

On the other hand, the phenomena that are here discussed, and were previously enumerated as the branches of one stem, have as their specific characteristic, as I have said, precisely *actio in distans* and *passio a distante*.[16] But in this way, as already mentioned, they first afford a confirmation, as unexpected as it is certain and *factual*, of Kant's fundamental doctrine of the contrast between the phenomenon and the thing-in-itself and of the antithesis between the laws of both. Thus according to Kant, nature and her order are mere phenomenon. As the opposite thereof, we see all the facts that are here considered and can be called magical, rooted directly in the thing-in-itself and in the world of appearance giving rise to phenomena that can never be explained in accordance with the laws thereof. They were, therefore, rightly denied until the experience of

---

15 ['Seeing at a distance and acting at a distance'.]
16 ['Acting at a distance and being affected from a distance'.]

hundreds of cases no longer allowed this. Not only Kant's philosophy, however, but mine also obtains on a closer investigation of these facts important corroboration, namely that in all these phenomena the *will* alone is the real agent, whereby it proclaims itself as the thing-in-itself. Accordingly, touched in his own empirical way by this truth, Count Szapáry, a well-known Hungarian magnetizer, apparently knowing nothing of my philosophy and possibly not much about any other, called the very first essay 'Physical Proofs that the *Will* is the Principle of all Spiritual and Physical Life' in his work *Ein Wort über den animalischen Magnetismus*, Leipzig, 1850.

Now in addition to and quite apart from this, the above-mentioned phenomena furnish in any case an effective and perfectly certain refutation not only of materialism but also of naturalism. In chapter 17 of the second volume of my chief work, I have described materialism as physics installed on the throne of metaphysics. These phenomena show that the order of *nature*, which materialism and naturalism would have us believe to be the absolute and only one, is a purely phenomenal, and therefore merely superficial, order that is based on the essence of things-in-themselves, an essence that is independent of the laws of that order. But the phenomena we are discussing are, at any rate from the philosophical point of view, incomparably the most important of all the facts that are presented to us by the whole of experience. It is, therefore, the duty of every scholar and man of science to become thoroughly acquainted with them.

The following more general observation may help to elucidate this discussion. Belief in ghosts and apparitions is inborn in man; it is found at all times and in all countries, and perhaps no man is entirely free from it. Indeed the great majority at all times and in all countries distinguish between the *natural and the supernatural*, as being two fundamentally different orders of things which nevertheless exist simultaneously. They unhesitatingly attribute to the supernatural miracles, predictions, ghosts, and magic; yet in addition they admit that generally in the last resort there is nothing absolutely natural through and through, but that nature herself rests on something supernatural. It is, therefore, easy to understand ordinary people when they ask whether this or that happens naturally or not.

Now this popular distinction coincides essentially with the Kantian between phenomenon and thing-in-itself, only that this defines the matter more precisely and accurately. Thus the natural and supernatural are not two different and separate kinds of being, but are one and the same which, taken *in itself*, should be called supernatural since only while it *appears*, in other words, comes into the perception of our intellect and thus enters the forms thereof, does it manifest itself as *nature*; and it is precisely nature's merely phenomenal conformity to law which we understand by the term natural. Now for my part I have again elucidated Kant's expression, for I have called the 'phenomenon' [*Erscheinung*] in plain terms *representation or mental picture* [*Vorstellung*]. And now, if we bear in mind that, whenever in the *Critique of Pure Reason* and the *Prolegomena* Kant's thing-in-itself appears even only occasionally from the obscurity in which he keeps it, it makes itself known at once as the morally accountable within us and hence as the *will*, we shall see also that, by showing the *will* to be the thing-in-itself, I have merely elucidated and sustained Kant's idea.

Considered, of course, not from the economical and technological, but the philosophical, point of view, animal magnetism is the most significant and pregnant of all the discoveries that have ever been made, although for the time being it propounds rather than solves riddles. It is really practical metaphysics, as magic was defined by Bacon; to a certain extent it is an experimental metaphysics. For the first and most universal laws of nature are set aside by it and hence it renders possible what was deemed impossible even *a priori*. Now if even in mere *physics* the experiments and facts are still far from showing us a correct insight, but for this purpose their explanation is required which is very often difficult to discover, how much more will this be the case with the mysterious facts of that empirically appearing metaphysics! Rational or theoretical metaphysics will therefore, have to keep abreast with it so that the treasures here discovered may be unearthed. However, a time will come when philosophy, animal magnetism, and natural science, that has made unparalleled progress in all its branches, will shed so bright a light on one another that truths will be discovered at which we could not otherwise hope to arrive. In this connection, we should not pay any attention to the metaphysical utterances and theories of somnambulists, for they are often paltry views which have sprung from the dogmas that were learnt by the somnambulist and are an admixture of these with what she happens to find in the mind of the magnetizer; they are, therefore, not worth considering.

Through magnetism we see also the way opened up to information concerning *spirit apparitions* which have at all times been just as obstinately affirmed as they have been persistently denied. Nevertheless, it will not be easy to come across this path, although it must lie midway between the credulity of our Justin Kerner, so estimable and meritorious in other respects, and the view, still prevalent in England, which admits of no other order of nature than a mechanical, so that everything going beyond this can be brought into line and concentrated the more certainly in a personal being who is quite different from the world and arbitrarily governs it. By opposing with incredible insolence and impudence every form of scientific knowledge so that the matter has gradually become a scandal to our continent, obscurantist English parsondom is mainly guilty of injustice through its encouraging and cherishing all prejudices that favour the 'cold superstition that it calls its religion'[17] and through its hostility to truths that are opposed thereto. Animal magnetism must have suffered such an injustice in England where, after it had been acknowledged in theory and practice in Germany and France for forty years, it was still untested and, with the confidence of ignorance, laughed at and condemned as a clumsy fraud. 'Whoever believes in animal magnetism cannot believe in God' was a remark made to me by a young English parson even in 1850; *hinc illae lacrimae!*[18] Yet even in the island of prejudices and priestly imposture, animal magnetism has at last raised its standard, to the repeated and glorious confirmation of the saying *magna est vis veritatis et praevalebit*,[19] that fine passage from the Bible at which the heart of every Anglican parson rightly quakes for his benefices. On the whole, it is high time that missions of reason, enlightenment, and anti-clericalism were sent to England with v. Bohlen's and Strauss's biblical criticism in the

---

[17] [From Prince Pückler's *Briefe eines Verstorbenen.*]
[18] ['Hence those tears!']
[19] ['Great is the power of truth and it shall prevail.']

one hand and the *Critique of Pure Reason* in the other in order to stop the business of those self-styled *reverend* parsons, the most arrogant and impudent in the world, and to put an end to the scandal. In this respect, however, we may hope for the best from steamships and railways that are just as favourable to the exchange of ideas as to that of goods, whereby they greatly imperil the vulgar bigotry which is nurtured in England with such cunning solicitude and sways even the upper classes. Thus few read but all chatter, and for this purpose those institutions afford opportunity and leisure. That by the crudest bigotry those parsons degrade the most intelligent nation, which is in almost every respect the first in Europe, to the lowest level and thus make it an object of *contempt* is something that should no longer be tolerated, at any rate if we consider the means whereby they attained that end, namely by arranging the education of the masses entrusted to them so that two-thirds of the English nation are unable to read. Here their impudence goes to the length of attacking with wrath, sneers, and shallow ridicule in newspapers even the positive and universal results of *geology*. For they are anxious in all seriousness to uphold the Mosaic myth of creation, oblivious of the fact that in such attacks they are merely hitting an iron pot with an earthenware.* Moreover, the law of primogeniture is the real source of that scandalous English obscurantism that hoaxes the people, namely the law that makes it necessary for the aristocracy (taken in the widest sense) to provide for younger sons. If these are not fit for the Navy or Army, the 'Church Establishment' (characteristic term) with its revenue of five millions a year affords them a *charitable institution*. Thus for the young country gentleman a 'living' is procured (also a very characteristic expression), either through favour or for money. Such livings are very often offered for sale in the newspapers and even for public auction,†

* The English are such a 'matter of fact nation' [Schopenhauer's own words] that when, through recent historical and geological discoveries (for instance, the pyramid of Cheops being a thousand years older than the Great Flood), they are deprived of the factual and historical elements in the Old Testament, their whole religion also falls to the ground.

† In the *Galignani* of 12 May 1855, it is quoted from the *Globe* that the rectory of Pewsey, Wiltshire, was to be publicly auctioned on 13 July 1855; and the *Galignani* of 23 May 1855 gives from the *Leader*, and since then more frequently, a complete list of livings advertised for sale by auction. Appended to each were the income, local amenities, and the age of the present incumbent. For just as

although for decency's sake they do not sell the actual living, but the right of bestowing it once ('the patronage'). But as this transaction must be completed before the actual vacation of the living, appropriate padding is added to the effect that the present incumbent, for instance, is seventy-seven years of age. Also one never fails to praise the fine opportunities for hunting and fishing that attach to the living, and the well-appointed vicarage. It is the most shameless simony in the world. From this it is easy to see why in good, one might say genteel, English society all ridicule of the Church and its cold superstition is regarded as bad taste and rather unseemly, in accordance with the maxim *quand le bon ton arrive, le bon sens se retire.*[20] For this reason, the influence of the parsons in England is so great that, to the *lasting disgrace of the English nation*, Thorwaldsen's statue of Byron, her greatest poet after the incomparable Shakespeare, was not allowed to be set up in Westminster Abbey, her national Pantheon, with other great men. This was simply because Byron had been honest enough not to make any concessions to Anglican parsondom, but went his own way unhampered by them; whereas the mediocre Wordsworth, the frequent target of his ridicule, had his statue suitably installed in Westminster Abbey in 1854. By such baseness do the English write themselves down 'as a stultified and priest-ridden nation'. Europe quite properly laughs at them. Yet it will not always be so; a future and wiser generation will carry Byron's statue in triumph to Westminster Abbey. Voltaire, on the other hand, who wrote against the Church a hundred times more than ever Byron did, gloriously reposes in the French Pantheon, the church of Sainte Geneviève. He was fortunate in belonging to a nation that does not allow itself to be led by the nose and ruled by parsons. The demoralizing effects of this priestly imposture and bigotry naturally are bound to appear. The effect must be demoralizing when parsons tell the people a pack of lies by saying that half the virtues consist in spending Sundays in idleness and blabbing in church, and that one of the greatest vices, paving the way to all the others, is 'Sabbath-breaking',

commissions in the Army can be bought, so also can livings in the Church. The campaign in the Crimea has revealed what manner of men the officers are and experience also tells us something about the parsons.

[20] ['When good form appears, good common sense retires.']

that is, not spending Sundays in idleness. And so in those papers that often give accounts of criminals under sentence of death, they explain that their whole career of crime arose from that shocking vice of 'Sabbath-breaking'. On account of the above-mentioned charitable institution, unhappy Ireland, thousands of whose inhabitants die of starvation, must, in addition to her own Catholic clergy voluntarily paid for from her own resources, maintain an idle army of Protestant clergy with an archbishop, twelve bishops, and a host of deans and rectors, although not directly at the expense of the people, but from Church property.

I have already drawn attention to the fact that the dream, somnambulistic perception, clairvoyance, vision, second sight, and possibly spirit seeing are closely related phenomena. Their common feature is that when we lapse into them, we obtain an intuitive perception that objectively presents itself through an organ quite different from that used in the ordinary state of wakefulness, that is to say, not through the external senses, but yet wholly and exactly as if by means thereof. I have accordingly called such an organ the *dream-organ*. On the other hand, what distinguishes them from one another is the difference of their relation to the empirically real external world that is perceivable through the senses. Thus in the dream that relation is, as a rule, not direct at all, and even in the rare fatidical dreams, it is in most cases only indirect and remote, very rarely direct. On the other hand, in somnambulistic perception and clairvoyance, as also in sleep-walking [*Nachtwandeln*], that relation is direct and quite real; in the vision and possibly in spirit seeing it is problematical. Thus the seeing of objects in the dream is acknowledged to be illusory and hence one that is merely subjective, like that in the imagination. But the same kind of intuitive perception in sleep-waking [*Schlafwachen*] and somnambulism becomes wholly and really objective; in fact, in clairvoyance it even obtains a range of vision that is incomparably greater than that of a man who is awake. Now if it extends here to the phantoms of the departed, it will again be acknowledged as merely a subjective seeing. Yet this does not conform to the analogy of that progressive development, and only this much can be asserted, that objects are now seen whose existence is not verified by the usual intuitive perception of someone who happens to be present and awake; whereas at the immediately preceding stage there were such objects for which the person awake first has to search at a distance or bide his time. Thus from this stage we know clairvoyance to be an intuitive perception which extends also to what is not *immediately* accessible to the brain's waking activity, but which nevertheless really and actually exists. Therefore we have no right at any rate forthwith to deny objective reality to those perceptions that the waking intuition is unable to follow even by covering a distance of space or an interval of time. Indeed by analogy, we might even suppose that a faculty of intuitive perception which extends to what is actually in the future and does not yet exist, might well be capable also of perceiving as present what once existed and now no longer exists. In addition, it is still not certain that the phantoms in question cannot reach even conscious wakefulness. They are perceived most frequently in the state of sleep-waking [*Schlafwachen*], and thus when we correctly see the immediately present environment, although we are dreaming; now as everything that we see is here objectively real, the phantoms appearing therein are presumed to be real primarily *per se*.

Moreover, experience now teaches that the function of the *dream-organ*, which as a rule has as the condition of its activity lighter ordinary sleep or deeper magnetic sleep, can also, by way of exception, be exercised when the brain is awake and hence that that eye with which we see dreams may well be capable of opening once when we are awake. There then stand before us forms so deceptively like those that enter the brain through the senses that they are confused with and mistaken for these, until it is seen that they are not links in the concatenation of experience which connects all those objects, consists in the causal nexus, and is what we understand by the term corporeal world. Now this comes to light either at once by reason of their nature, or only subsequently. A form thus showing itself will now be given the name of hallucination, vision, second sight, or spirit apparition, according to that in which it has its *remoter* cause. For its *nearest* cause must always reside in the interior of the organism since, as was previously shown, it is an impression coming from within which stimulates the brain to an activity of intuitive perception. It wholly permeates the brain and extends as far as the nerves of sense whereby the forms thus manifesting themselves then acquire even the colour and lustre as well as the tone and voice of reality. Nevertheless, in the case where this occurs imperfectly, those forms will appear only feebly coloured, pale, grey, and almost transparent; or by analogy when they exist for hearing, their voice will be abortive and sound hollow, scarcely audible, husky, or squeaky. If anyone who sees these looks at them with keener attention, they usually vanish because the senses that now turn with effort to the *external* impression actually receive this and, as the stronger that takes place in the opposite direction, it overpowers and represses that entire brain activity that comes from *within*. Just to avoid this collision, it sometimes happens that with visions the inner eye projects the forms as far as possible to where the outer eye sees nothing, into dark recesses, behind curtains that suddenly become transparent, and generally into the darkness of night which merely for this reason is the time of ghosts and spirits. For darkness, silence, and solitude eliminate external impressions and allow full scope to that brain activity that starts *from within*. And so in this respect, it can be compared to the phenomenon of phosphorescence which is also conditioned by darkness. Midnight in noisy company with the light of many candles is not the hour for ghosts or spirits, but only the midnight of darkness, silence, and solitude, since here we are instinctively afraid of the appearance of phenomena that manifest themselves as wholly external, although their *immediate* cause lies within ourselves; accordingly we are really afraid of ourselves. Thus whoever fears the appearance of such phenomena takes someone with him.

Now although experience teaches that the phenomena of the whole class we are considering certainly take place in wakefulness and are thereby distinguished from dreams, I am still doubtful whether this wakefulness is complete in the strictest sense. For the necessary division of the brain's power of representation seems to require that, when the dream-organ is very active, this cannot occur without a deduction from the normal activity, and so only under a certain lowering of the power of the waking outwardly directed sense-consciousness. Accordingly, I suspect that, during such a phenomenon, the consciousness that is certainly awake is veiled, as it were, with an extremely light gauze whereby it acquires a certain yet feeble dreamlike tinge. In the first place, it might be explained from this why those who have actually had such phenomena have never died of fright, whereas false and artificially produced spirit apparitions have sometimes had a fatal effect. Indeed actual visions of this kind do not, as a rule, cause any fear at all; but it is only afterwards when we reflect on them that we begin to feel a shudder. This, of course, may be due to the fact that, while they last, they are taken for living persons and only afterwards is it obvious that they could not be. I believe, however, that the absence of fear, which is even a characteristic of actual visions of this kind, is due mainly to the above-mentioned reason since, although we are awake, we are lightly veiled by a kind of dream consciousness. Thus we find ourselves in an element to which the fear of spiritual apparitions is essentially foreign just because in it the objective is not so abruptly separated from the subjective as in the workings of the corporeal world. This is confirmed by the easy and artless way in which the clairvoyante of Prevorst cultivates her spiritual acquaintances, for example, vol. ii, p. 120 (1st edn.), where she quite calmly lets a spirit stand and wait until she has had her soup. J. Kerner himself also says in several places (for example, vol. i, p. 209) that she seemed to be awake, but yet never entirely. At all events it might be possible to reconcile this with her own statement (vol. ii, p. 11, 3rd edn., p. 256) that, whenever she sees spirits she is wide awake.

Of all such intuitive perceptions that occur in the state of wakefulness by means of the dream-organ and present us with wholly objective phenomena similar to intuitive perceptions through the senses, the *immediate* cause, as I have said, must always lie in the interior of the organism. Here, then, it is some unusual change which acts on the brain by means of the vegetative nervous system that is already related to the cerebral system and hence through the sympathetic nerve and its ganglia. Now through this impression the brain can always be stimulated only to the activity that is natural and peculiar to it, namely objective intuitive perception that has space, time, and causality as its forms, precisely as happens through action on the senses that comes from without. And so here also the brain now exercises its normal function. But its perceiving activity that is now stimulated from within even reaches as far as the nerves of sense which accordingly are likewise stimulated to their specific sensations from within as previously they were from without; and they endow the appearing forms with colour, tone, odour, and so on and thus invest them with the complete objectivity and corporeal reality of what is sensuously perceived. This theory obtains a noteworthy corroboration from the following statement of a clairvoyant somnambulist named Heinekens concerning the origin of somnambulistic intuitive perception: 'In the night after a quiet and natural sleep it at once became clear to her that the light develops from the occiput, thence flows to the sinciput and after this comes to the eyes and now renders visible the surrounding objects. Through this light that resembles twilight she clearly saw and recognized everything round her.' (Kieser's *Archiv für den thierischen Magnetismus*, vol. ii, Pt. III, p. 43). The *immediate* cause of such intuitive perceptions that are stimulated in the brain from within must itself again have one which is accordingly its *remoter* cause. Now if we should find that this is not always to be looked for merely in the organism, but sometimes outside, then in the latter case that brain-phenomenon which hitherto manifested itself just as subjectively as mere dreams, indeed as a mere day-dream, would again be assured of real objectivity, that is, of actual causal connection with something existing outside the subject, from an entirely different direction and thus again come in through the back-door, so to speak. Accordingly, I shall now enumerate the *remoter causes* of that phenomenon in so far as they are known to us. In the first place, I here mention that, so long as these reside only *within* the organism, the phenomenon is given the name of *hallucination*; yet it discards this and receives others when a cause lying *outside* the organism is to be demonstrated, or at least must be assumed.

(1) The brain phenomenon in question is most frequently caused by grave and acute illnesses, especially high fevers that bring on delirium, where the aforesaid phenomenon is universally known by the name of fever hallucinations. Obviously this cause resides merely in the organism, although the fever itself may be brought on by external causes.

(2) *Madness* is sometimes, though by no means always,

accompanied by hallucinations. Their cause is to be regarded as the morbid states that give rise to madness in the first instance and frequently exist in the brain, but often in the rest of the organism as well.

(3) In rare cases, fortunately completely verified, hallucinations occur without the presence of fever or any other acute illness not to mention madness, and these appear as human forms that bear a deceptive resemblance to real ones. The best-known case of this kind is that of Nicolai, for in 1799 he lectured on it at the Berlin Academy and had the lecture specially printed. A similar case is found in the *Edinburgh Journal of Science* by Brewster, vol. iv, No. 8, October-April 1831; others are furnished by Brierre de Boismont, *Des hallucinations*, 1845, second edition, 1852, a very useful book for the entire subject of our investigation, to which I shall therefore frequently refer. Of course, it does not by any means give a thorough and detailed explanation of the phenomena in question; unfortunately, it is not even really systematically arranged, but is so only apparently. Nevertheless, it is a very copious compilation, carefully and critically prepared, of all the cases that in some way refer to our theme. In particular, observations 7, 13, 15, 29, 65, 108, 110, 111, 112, 114, 115, 132 relate to the special point we are now considering. But it must be assumed and borne in mind that, of the facts relevant to the whole subject of our present discussion, one that is officially recorded suggests a thousand like it news of which, for various reasons easily understood, has never got beyond the narrow circle of their immediate environment. And so the scientific consideration of this subject has dragged on for hundreds or even thousands of years with a few isolated cases, reality dreams, and spirit narratives, the like of which have since occurred hundreds of thousands of times, but which have not been officially made known and thus incorporated in literature. As instances of those cases that have become typical through endless repetition, I mention merely the reality dream recorded by Cicero in *De divinatione*, 1, 27, the ghost in Pliny's *Epistola ad Suram*, and the spirit apparition of Marsilius Ficinus, according to the stipulation with his friend Mercatus. But as regards the cases considered under the present number of which Nicolai's illness is typical, they all seem to have arisen from purely corporeal abnormal causes that are situated

entirely within the organism itself, not only by virtue of their trifling contents and the periodical nature of their recurrence, but also through the fact that they always yielded to therapeutic remedies, in particular to blood-letting. And so they too come under the category of hallucinations and, properly speaking, should be so called.

(4) After these come certain phenomena (incidentally similar to them) of objectively and externally existing forms which are nevertheless distinguished by a significant and often sinister character that is intended for the person who sees them; and their real significance is frequently placed beyond doubt by the shortly ensuing death of the person to whom they appeared. As an example of this kind, we can consider the case, recorded by Sir Walter Scott in letter 1 of his *On Demonology and Witchcraft*, and also repeated by Brierre de Boismont. It is that of a law-officer who for months always vividly saw first a cat, then a master of ceremonies, and finally a skeleton, whereupon he wasted away and ultimately died. Of exactly the same nature is the vision of Miss Lee to whom her mother's apparition accurately foretold the day and hour of her death. It is narrated first in Beaumont's *Treatise on Spirits* (German translation by Arnold, 1721), then in Hibbert's *Sketches of the Philosophy of Apparitions*, 1824, again in Horace Welby's *Signs before Death*, 1825, likewise in J. C. Henning's *Von Geistern und Geistersehern*, 1780, and finally also in Brierre de Boismont. A third example is furnished by the story of Mrs. Stephens on p. 156 of Welby's above-mentioned book, who on waking saw a corpse lying behind her chair and died a few days later. Also in this category are the cases of self-vision in so far as they occasionally, though certainly not always, augur the death of the person who sees himself. Dr. Formey of Berlin recorded a very remarkable and unusually well-verified case of this kind in his *Heidnischer Philosoph*. It is found fully reproduced in Horst's *Deuteroskopie*, vol. i, p. 115, and also in his *Zauberbibliothek*, vol. i. It should, however, be observed that here the apparition was really seen, not by the man himself who unexpectedly died very soon afterwards, but only by his relations. Of self-vision proper Horst reports a case, guaranteed by himself, in the second part of *Deuteroskopie*, p. 138. Even Goethe relates (*Aus meinem Leben*, eleventh book) that he saw himself on horseback and in a riding

habit in which he actually rode at that very spot eight years later. Incidentally, this apparition really had the object of consoling him since it allowed him to see himself riding in the opposite direction to visit once more after eight years his beloved to whom he had just bidden a very poignant farewell. Thus for a moment it lifted the veil of the future in order to predict for him in his grief a reunion. Apparitions of this kind are now no longer mere hallucinations, but *visions*; for they present us either with something real or refer to actual events in the future. And so they are in the waking state what fatidical dreams are in sleep which, as I have said, refer most frequently to the dreamer's own state of health especially when this is bad; whereas mere hallucinations correspond to the ordinary insignificant dreams.

The origin of these *momentous visions* is to be sought in the fact that that mysterious faculty of knowledge which is concealed within us and is not restricted by relations of space and time and is to that extent omniscient and yet never enters ordinary consciousness, but is for us veiled in mystery—yet casting off its veil in magnetic clairvoyance—that that faculty of knowledge has once espied something of great interest to the individual. Now the will, as the kernel of the whole man, would like to acquaint cerebral knowledge with this matter of interest; but then this is possible only by means of the operation in which it rarely succeeds, namely of once allowing the dream-organ to arise in the *state of wakefulness* and so of communicating this its discovery to cerebral consciousness in the forms of intuitive perception either of direct or allegorical significance. It had succeeded in this in the above briefly mentioned cases. Now all these related to the future; yet even something happening just now can be revealed in this way; however, it naturally cannot concern one's own person, but that of another. For example, the death of my distant friend that takes place at this very moment can become known to me through the sudden appearance of his form, as realistic as that of a living person, without it being necessary for the dying man himself to contribute to this in any way through his vivid thoughts of me. On the other hand, this actually does take place in cases of another kind which will be discussed later. Here I have also introduced this merely by way of illustration, for under this number I am really speaking only of those visions which relate to the man himself who sees them, and which correspond to the fatidical dreams analogous to them.

(5) Again corresponding to those fatidical dreams that relate not to one's own state of health but to quite external events, are certain visions that stand nearest to the above. They presage not dangers that spring from the organism, but those that threaten us from without and naturally often pass over our heads without our being in any way aware of them. In this case, we are unable to establish the external connection of the vision. To be *visible*, visions of this sort require conditions of many kinds, the chief being that the subject in question is peculiarly susceptible to them. On the other hand, if this is the case only in the lower degree, as in most instances, then the declaration will prove to be merely *audible* and will then manifest itself by sounds of different kinds, most frequently by tapping. This usually occurs at night, especially in the early hours of the morning, and it is such that we wake up and immediately afterwards hear a very loud knocking on the bedroom door which has all the distinctness and clearness of reality. It will come to visions that can be seen, and indeed in allegorically significant forms that are indistinguishable from those of reality, only when a very grave danger threatens our lives or we have fortunately escaped such a peril, frequently without knowing this for certain. They then congratulate us, so to speak, and announce that we have still many years to live. Finally visions of this kind will also occur for making known an inevitable misfortune. Of the latter kind was the well-known vision of Brutus before the battle of Philippi that manifested itself as his evil genius, as also the very similar vision of Cassius Parmensis after the battle of Actium which is narrated by Valerius Maximus (lib. I, c. 7, § 7). In general, I imagine that the visions of this category have been a main reason for the myth of the ancients concerning the genius that is assigned to everyone, and also for the *spiritus familiaris* of Christian times. In the Middle Ages the attempt was made to explain them by astral spirits, as is testified by the passage of Theophrastus Paracelsus quoted in the previous essay: 'To understand *fatum* properly, it is that every man has a spirit that dwells outside him and has its seat in the stars above. He uses the bosses'

(fixed types for works in high relief, from which we have the word emboss) 'of his master; it is he who presages and shows him forebodings, for they continue to exist after him. These spirits are called *fatum*.' In the seventeenth and eighteenth centuries, on the other hand, the words *spiritus vitales* were used to explain these and many other phenomena and, as ideas were lacking, these words appeared at the right time. The actual remoter causes of visions of this kind obviously cannot reside simply within the organism, when their relation to external dangers is established. Later on I shall investigate how far we are able to understand the nature of their connection with the external world.

(6) Visions which no longer concern at all the man who sees them and which nevertheless directly present exactly and often in all their details future events occurring soon or some time after them, are peculiar to that rare gift called *second sight* or deuteroscopy. A comprehensive collection of accounts of them is contained in Horst's *Deuteroskopie*, two volumes, 1830. More recent facts of this kind are also found in the different volumes of Kieser's *Archiv für thierischen Magnetismus*. The strange faculty for visions of this kind is by no means to be found exclusively in Scotland and Norway, but occurs also in our country, especially with reference to cases of death. Accounts of it are found in Jung-Stillings' *Theorie der Geisterkunde*, §§ 153 ff. The famous prophecy of Cazotte seems also to depend on something of this kind. Even among the Negroes of the Sahara Desert second sight is frequently met with (see James Richardson's *Narrative of a Mission to Central Africa*, London, 1853). Indeed even in Homer (*Odyssey*, xx, 351–7) we find a description of actual deuteroscopy that bears a strange resemblance to the story of Cazotte. A perfect case of deuteroscopy is likewise reported by Herodotus, lib. viii, c. 65. Thus in this second sight, the vision that here first springs as always from the organism, attains the highest degree of real objective truth and thereby discloses in us a connection with the external world of a kind entirely different from the usual physical one. As a condition of wakefulness, it runs parallel to the highest degrees of somnambulistic clairvoyance. It is really a complete *dreaming of the real in wakefulness* or at any rate in a state that occurs for a few moments at the height of wakefulness. Like the reality-dreams, the vision of

second sight is also in many cases not theorematic, but allegorical or symbolical, yet, what is most remarkable, in accordance with fixed symbols that occur to all clairvoyants with equal significance and are found specified in the above-mentioned book by Horst, vol. i, pp. 63–9, as well as in Kieser's *Archiv*, vol. vi, Pt. iii, pp. 105–8.

(7) Now as a contrast to the visions that are directed to the future and have just been discussed, there are those that bring before the dream-organ appearing in wakefulness the past, especially the forms of those who were once alive. It is pretty certain that they can be brought about by the presence in the vicinity of the deceased person's remains. This very important experience, to which a whole host of spirit apparitions are attributable, has its most solid and certain confirmation in a letter of Professor Ehrmann, son-in-law of the poet Pfeffel, which is given *in extenso* in Kieser's *Archiv*, vol. x, Pt. iii, pp. 151 ff. But extracts are found in many books, for example in F. Fischer's *Somnambulismus*, vol. i, p. 246. Moreover, this experience is confirmed by many cases that are attributable to it, and of these I will here quote only a few. First there is that of Pastor Lindner which is mentioned in that very letter and also comes from a good source and which has likewise been repeated in many books, among others the *Seherin von Prevorst* (vol. ii, p. 98 of the first, and p. 356 of the third edition.) Then there is the narrative of this kind, given by Fischer himself in his abovementioned book (p. 252) from eyewitnesses, which he records for the purpose of correcting a short account of it found in the *Seherin von Prevorst* (p. 358 of the third edition). Then in G. I. Wenzel's *Unterhaltungen über die auffallendesten neuern Geistererscheinungen*, 1800, we find, in the very first chapter, seven such stories of apparitions all of which have their origin in the remains of deceased persons found in the vicinity. The Pfeffel story is the last of them, but the others too are wholly characterized by the stamp of truth and certainly not of invention. They all state only a mere appearance of the form of the deceased person without any further development or even dramatic sequence. And so as regards the theory of these phenomena, they merit every consideration. The rational explanations for them that are given by the author may help to put the utter inadequacy of such solutions in a clear light. Further, the fourth

observation in the above-mentioned book of Brierre de Boismont is to the point, as are also many of the spirit stories that
are handed down to us from some authors of antiquity, for
example, that of the younger Pliny (lib. vii, epist. 27), which is
remarkable for its bearing entirely the same character as that
borne by innumerable stories from modern times. Exactly like
it, and possibly only a different version thereof, is the story
given by Lucian in *Philopseudes*, 31. Then of the same nature is
the narrative of Damo in the first chapter of Plutarch's *Cimo*,
and also what Pausanias (*Attica*, 1. 32) says of the battlefield of
Marathon, which should be compared with what Brierre says
on page 590; finally, there are the statements of Suetonius in
Caligula, chap. 59. In general, almost all the cases might be
attributable to the experience in question, where spirits appear
always in the same place, and the ghost or apparition is confined to a definite locality such as churches, churchyards,
battlefields, places where murders have been committed, central criminal courts, and those houses which for that reason
have acquired an evil reputation and which no one will in-
habit. From time to time one comes across such places, and I
too in the course of my life have met with several. Such localities were the theme of a book by the Jesuit Petrus Thyraeus *De
infestis, ob molestantes daemoniorum et defunctorum spiritus, locis*,
Cologne, 1598. But possibly Brierre de Boismont's 77th observation furnishes the most remarkable fact of this kind. The
vision of a somnambulist, mentioned in Kerner's *Blätter aus
Prevorst*, tenth compilation, p. 61, is to be regarded as a confirmation, well worth considering, of the explanation here given
of so many spirit apparitions, in fact as a middle term leading
to it. Thus this somnambulist suddenly saw a domestic scene
which she described exactly and which might have taken place
there more than a hundred years earlier; for the persons described by her were like existing portraits, although she had
never seen these.

But the important and fundamental experience itself, here
considered, to which all such events are attributable and which
I call 'retrospective second sight', must remain as the primary
phenomenon because till now we still lack the means to explain
it. However, it can be closely associated with another phenomenon which is admittedly just as inexplicable. Yet in this way

much is gained for we then have only one unknown quantity instead of two. This is an advantage, analogous to the well-known one we gain by referring mineral magnetism to electricity. Thus a somnambulist in a high state of clairvoyance is not limited in her perception even by *time*; but occasionally she foresees events actually in the future, and indeed such as occur entirely by chance. The same thing is achieved even more strikingly by those who have second sight and see corpses. And so events that have certainly not yet entered our empirical reality can nevertheless act on such persons and come within their perception out of the darkness of the future. In the same way, events and people, at one time real although no longer so, can act on certain persons who are specially disposed thereto and so can express an after-effect just as those others can express an effect in advance. In fact, this case is less incomprehensible than the other especially when such a perception is initiated and brought about by something material, such as for instance the mortal remains of the perceived persons which still actually exist, or by things that were more specifically connected with them, such as their clothes, the room they occupied, or what they set their heart on, the hidden treasure. Analogous to this is the highly clairvoyant somnambulist who simply through some physical connecting link with the distant persons, such as a piece of cloth worn by the patient on his bare body for a few days (Kieser's *Archiv*, vol. iii, Pt. III, p. 24), or a lock of hair cut off, is said to report on the state of their health, is put in touch with them, and thus obtains their picture or image. This case is closely related to the one under discussion. As a result of this view, the spirit apparitions that are associated with definite localities, or the mortal remains of those who died there, would be only the perceptions of a reversed deuteroscopy which is thus turned to the past—a 'retrospective second sight'. Accordingly, they would be really what the ancients called them (for their whole conception of the realm of shades probably arose from spirit apparitions; see *Odyssey*, He. xxiv), namely shades, *umbrae*, εἴδωλα καμόντων—νεκύων ἀμενηνὰ κάρηνα,[21] *manes* (from *manere*, remnants, vestiges, traces, so to speak), and thus lingering echoes of departed phenomena of this

---

[21] ['The shadow pictures of the deceased'; 'the feeble and impotent heads of the dead'.]

appearance-world of ours which manifests itself in time and space, becomes perceivable to the dream-organ in rare cases during the state of wakefulness, more readily in sleep as mere dreams, but most easily, of course, in deep magnetic sleep when the dream therein has been raised to sleep-waking [*Schlafwachen*] and this to clairvoyance. But they become perceivable also in natural sleep-waking which was mentioned at the very beginning and described as the sleeper's reality dreaming of his immediate surroundings and which precisely through the appearance of such heterogeneous forms first makes itself known as a state different from that of wakefulness. In this sleep-waking the forms of persons, who have just died and whose bodies are still in the house, will most frequently manifest themselves, just as generally, according to the law that this retrospective second sight is initiated by the mortal remains of the dead, the form of a deceased person can appear most easily to one so disposed, even in the state of wakefulness, so long as that deceased person has not yet been buried, although the form is then perceived only by the dream-organ.

From what has been said, it is obvious that the immediate reality of an actually existing object is not to be imputed to a ghost that appears in this way, although indirectly a reality does underlie it. Thus what we see there is certainly not the deceased man himself, but a mere εἴδωλον, a picture of him who once existed which originates in the dream-organ of a man attuned to it and is brought about by some remnant or relic, some trace that was left behind. And so this has no more reality than has the apparition of the man who sees *himself*, or is perceived by others in a place where he does not happen to be. Cases of this kind, however, are known on reliable evidence and some are to be found in Horst's *Deuteroskopie*, vol. ii, Sect. 4. Goethe's case, already mentioned, is also relevant to what we are saying. Similarly, there is the not infrequent case of patients who at death's door imagine that they exist doubly in bed. A doctor recently asked one of his seriously ill patients how he was. 'Better now since we two are in the bed' was the reply; the patient died soon afterwards. Accordingly, a spirit apparition of the kind we are here considering certainly does stand in objective relation to the *former* state of the person who appears, but certainly not to his *present* state, for it does not take any active part therein, and so from this the continued individual existence of the person cannot be inferred. The explanation given is also supported by the fact that the deceased persons appearing in this way are as a rule seen in the clothes they usually wore, and also that a murdered man appears with his murderer, a horse and his rider, and so on. In all probability, most of the ghosts seen by the clairvoyante of Prevorst are also to be reckoned among visions of this kind. But the conversations she carried on with them are to be regarded as the work of her own imagination that furnished the text for this dumb show from its own resources and thus supplied its explanation. Thus by nature man attempts in some way to explain everything that he sees, or at any rate to introduce some connection and sequence and in fact to turn it over in his mind. Therefore children often carry on a dialogue even with inanimate things. Accordingly, without knowing it, the clairvoyante herself was the prompter of those forms that appeared to her. Here her power of imagination was in the same kind of unconscious activity with which we guide and connect the events in the ordinary insignificant dream, indeed with which we sometimes seize the opportunity for this from objective accidental circumstances, such as a pressure felt in bed, or a sound reaching us from without, an odour, and so on, in accordance with which we then dream long stories. To explain this dramaturgy of the clairvoyante, we must see what Bende Bendsen says in Kieser's *Archiv*, vol. xi, Pt. i, p. 121 about his somnambulist to whom her living acquaintances sometimes appeared in magnetic sleep when she then in a loud voice carried on long conversations with them. It says there that 'of the many conversations she had with absent persons, the following is characteristic. While the alleged answers were coming through, she was silent and appeared to be very attentive. During this time, she raised herself in bed and turned her head in a definite direction to listen to the answers of the others, and then put forward her objections to them. She here pictured to herself old Karen with her maid and spoke alternately to the one and to the other.—The apparent splitting of her own personality into three different ones, as is usual in the dream, here went to such lengths that at the time I was quite unable to convince the sleeping woman that she herself created all three.'

Therefore, in my opinion, the spirit conversations of the clairvoyante of Prevorst are also of this nature; and this explanation finds strong confirmation in the unutterable absurdity of the text of those dialogues and dramas that are alone in keeping with the intellectual outlook of an ignorant girl from the hills and with the popular metaphysics that has been drilled into her. To attribute to them an objective reality is possible only on the assumption of a world-order that is so boundlessly absurd and revoltingly stupid that we should have to blush at belonging thereto. Yet if the very prejudiced and gullible Justin Kerner had not secretly had a faint notion of the origin here stated of those spirit conversations, he would not have omitted always and everywhere with such irresponsible levity seriously and zealously to look for the material objects that are made known by the spirits, for example writing materials in church vaults, gold chains in castle vaults, children buried in stables, instead of allowing himself to be deterred from this by the most trifling obstacles. For this would have thrown some light on the facts.

I am generally of the opinion that most of the apparitions of deceased persons which are actually seen belong to this category of visions and that accordingly there corresponds to them a past reality, but certainly not one that is present and positively objective; thus, for instance, the apparition of the President of the Berlin Academy, Maupertuis, that was seen in the hall of the Academy by the botanist Gleditsch. Nicolai mentions this in his lecture, already alluded to, which he gave to that same Academy. Similarly, Sir Walter Scott's narrative in the *Edinburgh Review* and repeated by Horst in the *Deuteroskopie*, vol. i, p. 113, of the bailiff in Switzerland who, on entering the public library, caught sight of his predecessor sitting in the president's chair at a special council meeting and surrounded only by persons who were dead. It also follows from some relevant narratives that the objective cause of visions of this kind is not necessarily bound to be the skeleton or other remnant of a corpse, but that other things, at one time in close contact with the deceased, are also capable of this. Thus, for example, of the seven narratives in the above-mentioned book by G. I. Wenzel, six were concerned with the corpse, but there was one in which the mere coat that was always worn by the deceased was

packed away immediately after his death; when after some
weeks it was fetched out, it gave rise to his living apparition
before his startled widow. Accordingly, it might happen that
even slight traces, hardly perceptible to our senses, such as
drops of blood long since soaked into the floor, or possibly even
the mere locality enclosed by walls where someone under great
fear or despair died a violent death, sufficed to evoke such a
retrospective second sight in the person predisposed to them.
The opinion of the ancients, mentioned by Lucian (*Philopseudes*, 29), that only those who died a violent death could make
an appearance, may be connected with this. A buried treasure
which was always anxiously guarded by the deceased and on
which his last thoughts were fixed, might equally well provide
the objective cause in question for such a vision, and perhaps the
vision might then prove to be even lucrative. With this knowledge of the past that is brought about by means of the
dream-organ, the above-mentioned objective causes fulfil to some
extent the role which the *nexus idearum* assigns to its objects in the
case of normal thinking. Moreover, it is equally true of the perceptions here in question, as of all possible perceptions in wakefulness through the dream-organ, that they enter consciousness
more easily in the audible form than in the visible. Hence the
accounts of sounds that are sometimes heard in one place or
another are much more frequent than those of visible apparitions.

Now if in the case of the few examples of the kind we are
considering it is reported that the apparitions of the dead had
revealed to the man beholding them certain facts hitherto
unknown, this is in the first place to be accepted only on the
most certain evidence and till then should be regarded as doubtful. But then in any case, it could still be explained through
certain analogies with the clairvoyance of somnambulists.
Thus in isolated cases, many somnambulists have told patients
who were brought to them how entirely by chance they had
contracted the disease from which they had long been suffering
and thereby have recalled to their memory an almost entirely
forgotten incident. (Instances of this kind are in Kieser's
Archiv, vol. iii, Art. 3, p. 70, the terror of falling from a ladder
and, in J. Kerner's *Geschichte zweier Somnambulen*, p. 189, the
remark made to the boy that he had previously been sleeping

with an epileptic.) It is also worth noting here that some clair-voyants have correctly recognized the patient and his condition from a lock of hair or a piece of material worn by him, al-though they have never seen him. In Merck's *Reiseerinnerungen aus London und Paris,* Hamburg, 1852, it is related how Alexis accurately knew from a letter the present position of the writer and from an old needle-case the fate of the deceased donor. And so even revelations do not give positive proof of the pre-sence of a deceased person.

Similarly, the fact that the apparition of a dead man has at times been seen and heard by two people may be attributed to the well-known infectious nature not only of somnambulism but also of second sight.

Accordingly, in the present number we have at any rate explained the great majority of authenticated apparitions of dead persons in so far as we have traced them to a common ground, to retrospective second sight, which in many such cases, particularly in those mentioned at the beginning of this number, cannot very well be denied. On the contrary, it is itself an extremely odd and inexplicable fact; but in many things we must be content with an explanation of this kind as, for example, where the whole edifice of the theory of electricity consists merely of a subordination of many different phenomena to a primary phenomenon that remains wholly unexplained.

(8) Another's lively and anxious thought of us can stimulate in our brain the vision of his form not as a mere phantasm, but as something vividly standing before us and indistinguishable from reality. In particular there are those on the point of dying who display this faculty and therefore at the hour of death appear before their absent friends, even to several in different places at the same time. The case has been narrated and veri-fied so often and from such different sources, that I accept it without hesitation as founded on fact. A very fine example, vouched for by distinguished people, is found in Jung-Stilling's *Theorie der Geisterkunde,* § 198. Again, two particularly striking cases are the story of Frau Kahlow in the above-mentioned book by Wenzel, p. 11, and that of the court chaplain in the previously mentioned work by Hennings, p. 329. The following case may here be mentioned as a very recent one. A short time ago, a girl patient died one night at the Jewish hospital here in

Frankfurt. Early the following morning, her sister and niece, one living here and the other about five miles away, arrived on her instructions to inquire after her since in the night she had appeared to both of them. The superintendent of the hospital, on whose report this statement is based, declared that such cases frequently occurred. The *Geschichte der Auguste Müller in Karlsruhe*, previously mentioned, relates that a clairvoyante somnambulist who, during the highest degree of her clairvoyance, invariably fell into a catalepsy resembling a trance appeared before her friend as if in the flesh. It is repeated in Kieser's *Archiv*, vol. iii, Pt. iii, p. 118. Another intentional apparition of the same person is communicated from a thoroughly reliable source in Kieser's *Archiv*, vol. vi, Pt. i, p. 34. On the other hand, it is much rarer for people in perfect health to be able to produce this effect; yet even here there is no lack of trustworthy accounts. The oldest is given by St. Augustine, admittedly at second hand, although he assures us that it is from a very reliable source, *De civitate dei*, XVIII. xviii. 2 in continuation of the words: *Indicavit et alius se domi suae etc.* Thus what one dreams here appears to another in wakefulness as a vision which he regards as reality. The *Spiritual Telegraph* of 23 September 1854, appearing in America, furnishes a case that is wholly analogous to this (apparently without knowing St. Augustine's) and Dupotet gives a French translation of it in his *Traité complet du magnétisme*, 3rd edn., p. 561. A recent case of the kind is added to the last-mentioned account in Kieser's *Archiv*, (vol. vi, Pt. i, p. 35). A wonderful story, bearing on this point, is related by Jung-Stilling in his *Theorie der Geisterkunde*, § 101, yet without stating the source. Several are given by Horst in his *Deuteroskopie*, vol. ii, sect. 4. But a most remarkable instance of the faculty for such appearance, transmitted moreover from father to son and very frequently practised by both even without their intending to do so, is to be found in Kieser's *Archiv*, vol. vii, Pt. iii, p. 158. However, there is an older instance, exactly like it, in Zeibich's *Gedanken von der Erscheinung der Geister*, 1776, p. 29, and repeated in Hennings' *Von Geistern und Geistersehern*, p. 746. As it is certain that the two were independently recorded, they serve to confirm each other in this very remarkable matter. Also in Nasse's *Zeitschrift für Anthropologie*, vol. iv, Pt. ii, p. 111, such a case is recorded by

Professor Grohmann. Likewise in Horace Welby's *Signs before Death*, London, 1825, we find several instances of apparitions of living people in places where they were present only in their thoughts e.g., pp. 45, 88. Cases of this kind, narrated in Kieser's *Archiv*, vol. viii, Pt. iii, p. 120 under the heading 'Second Self' by the thoroughly reliable Bende Bendsen, appear to be particularly trustworthy. Corresponding to the visions which are here considered and take place in wakefulness, are the sympathetic dreams in the state of sleep, that is, dreams that are communicated *in distans* and are accordingly dreamed by two persons at the same time and entirely in the same way. Instances of these are sufficiently well known; a good collection is found in E. Fabius, *De somniis*, § 21, of which there is a particularly good one in Dutch. Further, in Kieser's *Archiv*, vol. vi, Pt. ii, p. 135, there is a very remarkable article by H. M. Wesermann who records five cases where, through his *will*, he deliberately produced in others precisely determined dreams. Now as the person concerned in the last of these cases had not yet gone to bed, she and another who was close to her had the intended apparition *in wakefulness* and it was exactly like reality. Consequently, in such dreams, as also in waking-visions of this class, it is the *dream-organ* that is the medium of intuitive perception. The above-mentioned narrative given by St. Augustine can be regarded as the connecting link between the two kinds in so far as here there appears to one man in wakefulness what another merely dreams he is doing. Two of these cases are of exactly the same nature and are found in Horace Welby's *Signs before Death*, p. 266 and p. 297; later ones are taken from Sinclair's *Invisible World*. Therefore however strikingly lifelike the person appears in visions of this kind, they obviously do not occur at all through an impression on the senses from without, but by virtue of a magic effect of his *will*, whence they emanate, on another person, and thus on the being-in-itself of another's organism that therefore undergoes a change from within. Now by acting on his brain, such change there stimulates just as vivid a picture of the person who acts in such a manner as could be produced only through an impression by means of light-rays reflected from the body of the one on to the eyes of the other.

The 'second selves' or 'doubles' here mentioned wherein the person appearing is obviously alive but absent and, as a rule, does not know of his apparition, suggest to us the correct point of view for the apparitions of the dying and the dead and hence for spirit apparitions proper, in that they teach us that an immediate actual presence, like that of a body acting on the senses, is by no means their necessary assumption. But this very presupposition is the fundamental error of all previous interpretations of spirit apparitions, whether they have been asserted or disputed. Again, that presupposition rests on our having taken up the standpoint of *spiritualism* instead of that of *idealism*.[22] Thus according to spiritualism, a start was made from the wholly unjustified assumption that man consists of two fundamentally different substances, a material substance, the body, and an immaterial substance, the so-called soul. After the severance of the two that occurs at death, the soul, although immaterial, simple, and unextended, was still said to exist in space, thus to move, to go about, and moreover to act on bodies and their senses from without precisely as does a body and accordingly to manifest itself exactly like this. Here, of course, the condition is the same real presence in space which a body seen by us has. All rational denials of spirit apparitions and also Kant's critical elucidation of the matter which constitutes the first or theoretical part of his *Traüme eines Geistersehers, erläutert durch Träume der Metaphysik*, apply to this utterly untenable *spiritualistic* view of such apparitions. And so that view, that assumption of an immaterial yet mobile substance, which moreover acts on bodies as does matter and consequently on their senses as well, has to be entirely given up so that a correct view of all the relevant phenomena may be reached. Instead, we have to gain the idealistic standpoint whence we look at these things in quite a different light, and to obtain quite different criteria as to their possibility. To lay down the basis for this is precisely the purpose of the present essay.

(9) The last case coming under review is where the magic influence that was described under the previous number might still be exercised even after death. In this way, a spirit apparition proper would then take place by means of direct action and so to a certain extent the actual personal presence of someone already dead would occur which would also admit of a retro-

---

[22] Cf. *World as Will and Representation*, vol. ii, chap. 1.

spective effect on him. The *a priori* denial of every possibility
of this kind and the ridicule, in accord therewith, of the opposite
statement can be due to nothing but the conviction that death
is man's absolute annihilation, unless it is based on the belief
of the Protestant Church. According to this, spirits cannot
appear because, in conformity with the belief or unbelief that
was cherished during the few years of earthly existence, they
were for ever consigned immediately after death either to
heaven with its eternal joys or to hell with its eternal torments,
but they cannot come out to us from either. Therefore according
to the Protestant belief, all such apparitions come from devils or
angels, but not from human spirits, as has been thoroughly
and adequately explained by Lavater, *De spectris*, Geneva, 1580,
Pars II, c. 3 et 4. The Catholic Church, on the other hand,
especially through Gregory the Great, in the sixth century had
very prudently rectified this absurd and revolting dogma by
interposing Purgatory between these desperate alternatives. It
permits the apparition of spirits which temporarily reside in
Purgatory and, by way of exception, that of others as well.
This can be seen in detail in the book, already mentioned, *De
locis infestis*, Pars I, cap. 3, *seqq.*, by Petrus Thyraeus. Through
the above dilemma, the Protestants saw themselves compelled
in every way to maintain the existence of the devil merely
because they could not possibly dispense with him when trying
to explain those undeniable spirit apparitions. And so even at
the beginning of the eighteenth century, the deniers of the
devil were called *adaemonistae* with almost the same pious
horror as are the *atheistae* even at the present time. Accordingly,
at the same time, for example, in C. F. Romanus, *Schediasma
polemicum, an dentur spectra, magi et sagae*, Leipzig, 1703, ghosts
were from the very beginning defined as *apparitiones et terri-
tiones DIABOLI externae, quibus corpus, aut aliud, quid in sensus
incurrens sibi assumit, ut homines infestet.*[23] The fact that trials for
witchcraft which, as we know, presuppose a compact with the
devil, were much more frequent with Protestants than with
Catholics, may possibly have something to do with this. Yet,
taking no account of such mythological views, I said just now

[23] ['Apparitions and terrible visions of the *devil* by virtue whereof he assumes a
body or something else perceivable by the senses in order to torment and alarm
men'.]

that the *a priori* rejection of the possibility of an actual apparition of the dead could rest only on the conviction that through death a human being becomes absolutely nothing. For as long as such a conviction is absent, it is impossible to see why one being, in some way still existing, should not also manifest itself somehow and be capable of acting on another, although this other exists in a different state. Therefore, it is as logical as it is naïve when Lucian, after narrating how Democritus had not for one moment allowed himself to be led astray by a spiritual mummery that was arranged to terrify him, added οὕτω βεβαίως ἐπίστευε, μηδὲν εἶναι τὰς ψυχὰς ἔτι, ἔξω γενομένας τῶν σωμάτων (*adeo persuasum habebat, nihil adhuc esse animas a corpore separatas.*)[24] *Philopseudes*, 32. On the other hand, if there is still in man something indestructible besides matter, then it is at any rate *a priori* inconceivable that that something which gave rise to the marvellous phenomenon of life should, after the termination thereof, be absolutely incapable of any influence on those still living. Accordingly, the matter could be decided only *a posteriori* through experience. But this is so much more difficult as, apart from all the intentional and unintentional deceptions of reporters, even the actual vision wherein a dead man reveals himself can quite well belong to one of the eight kinds so far enumerated by me; and so perhaps this may always be the case. In fact, even in the case where such an appearance has revealed things that no one could know, this could, in consequence of the explanation given at the end of number 7, still be taken as the form that the revelation of a spontaneous somnambulistic clairvoyance had here assumed. Of course, the occurrence of such a clairvoyance in wakefulness, or even only with perfect recollection from the somnambulistic state, is not positively demonstrable, but such revelations, as far as I know, have at all events come only through dreams. Yet there may be circumstances that also render impossible such an explanation. Therefore today, when things of this sort are viewed with much more frankness than ever before and are in consequence communicated and discussed with greater confidence, we have a right to hope that positive empirical information on this subject will be forthcoming.

[24] ['So surely was he convinced that souls were no longer anything when they had quitted the body.']

Such, indeed, is the nature of many spirit stories that all explanations of a different kind have great difficulty as soon as they are regarded as not entirely false and untrue. But against this there is in many instances to some extent the character of the original narrator and partly the stamp of honesty and sincerity borne by his description, yet most of all the perfect resemblance in the wholly characteristic course of events and the nature of the alleged apparitions, however widely separated the times and countries may be from which the reports originate. This becomes most striking when it concerns very special circumstances that have been recognized only in recent times in consequence of magnetic somnambulism and of the more precise observation of all these things, such as occasionally takes place in visions. An instance of this kind is to be found in the extremely captious spirit story of 1697 which Brierre de Boismont relates in his 120th observation. It is the circumstance where invariably only the upper half of his friend's spirit was visible to a youth, although he spoke to him for three-quarters of an hour. This partial appearance of human forms has in our time been verified as a peculiarity that sometimes occurs in visions of such a nature. Hence on pages 454 and 474 of his book and without reference to that story Brierre mentions this peculiarity as a not infrequent phenomenon. Kieser (*Archiv*, vol. iii, Pt. ii, p. 139) also reports the same circumstance of the boy Arst; yet he attributes it to the alleged seeing with the tip of the nose. Accordingly, this circumstance in the above-mentioned story furnishes proof that that youth at any rate had not invented the apparition. But then it is difficult to explain this in any other way than as arising from the action, previously promised to him and now carried out, of his friend who the day before was drowned in a remote district. Another circumstance of this kind is the disappearance of apparitions as soon as we deliberately fix our attention on them. This is found in the passage of Pausanias, already mentioned, concerning the audible apparitions on the battlefield of Marathon. These were heard only by those who by chance happened to be there, not by those who had gone there by design. Analogous observations from most recent times are found in several passages of the *Seherin von Prevorst* (e.g. vol. ii, p. 10 and p. 38) where it is explained from the fact that what was perceived through the ganglionic system is again argued away at once by the brain. According to my hypothesis, it could be explained from the sudden reversal in the direction of the vibration of the brain-filaments. Incidentally, I would here like to draw attention to a very striking agreement of that kind. Photius in his article *Damascius* says: γυνὴ ἱερά, θεόμοιραν ἔχουσα φύσιν παραλογοτάτην· ὕδωρ γὰρ ἐγχέουσα ἀκραιφνὲς ποτηρίῳ τινὶ τῶν ὑαλίνων, ἑώρα κατὰ τοῦ ὕδατος εἴσω τοῦ ποτηρίου τὰ φάσματα τῶν ἐσομένων πραγμάτων, καὶ προύλεγεν ἀπὸ τῆς ὄψεως αὐτά, ἅπερ ἔμελλεν ἔσεσθαι πάντως· ἡ δὲ πεῖρα τοῦ πράγματος οὐκ ἔλαθεν ἡμᾶς.[25] Inconceivable as it may be, exactly the same thing is reported from the *Seherin von Prevorst*, page 87 of the third edition. The character and type of spirit apparitions are so absolutely fixed and peculiar that anyone who is versed in the reading of such a narrative can judge whether the vision is invented, rests on an optical illusion, or is really genuine. It is hoped and desired that we shall soon obtain a collection of Chinese ghost-stories, so that we may see whether they too have essentially the very same type and character as our own and show a close agreement even in the attendant circumstances and details. And so this generally would afford strong corroboration of the phenomenon in question, in spite of such a fundamental difference between their customs and dogmas and ours. That the Chinese have exactly the same notion concerning a dead man's apparition and the communications emanating from him as we have, is evident from the spirit apparition in the Chinese tale *Hing-Lo-Tu, ou la peinture mystérieuse*, although here it is only fictitious. It was translated by Stanislas Julien and given in his *Orphelin de la Chine, accompagné de nouvelles et de poésies*, 1834. In this respect, I also draw attention to the fact that most of the phenomena that constitute the characteristic of the spirit phantom, as described in the above-mentioned works of Hennings, Wenzel, Teller, and others, and later of Justin Kerner, Horst, and many more, are to be found just as readily in very old books, for example, in three of the sixteenth century which I have before me, namely Lavater, *De spectris*, Thyraeus, *De locis*

---

[25] ['There was a venerable lady who had an incomprehensible gift bestowed on her by God; for after pouring pure water into a glass tumbler, she saw on the bottom thereof the appearance of future events and, in accordance with what she had seen, she fully predicted them and said how they would come to pass. And the confirmation of the thing did not escape our notice.']

infestis, and *De spectris et apparitionibus,* Book two, *Eisleben,* 1597, anonymous, 500 pages in four volumes. For instance, such phenomena are knocking or tapping; the apparent attempt to force closed doors and also those that are not closed at all; the crashing of a heavy weight on the floor of a room; the noisy flinging about of all the kitchen-utensils, or of wood on the floor which is afterwards found to be at rest and in perfect order; the banging of wine-casks; the distinct nailing of a coffin when someone in the house is about to die; shuffling or fumbling footsteps in a dark room; tugging at the counterpane; the odour of mustiness; the great desire for prayer of the spirits that appear, and many others. On the other hand, it is hardly to be supposed that the authors of these modern statements, who are often very illiterate, had read those rare and ancient works in Latin. Among the arguments for the reality of spirit apparitions, the tone of incredulity is also worth mentioning wherein the learned narrators express themselves at second hand. For, as a rule, this tone bears so clearly the stamp of stiffness, affectation, and hypocrisy that the secret belief behind it can be faintly discerned. I wish to take this opportunity to draw attention to a spirit story of very recent date which merits closer investigation and better acquaintance than is given to it in its description by a very indifferent pen in the *Blätter aus Prevorst,* eighth compilation, p. 166. For, on the one hand, the statements concerning it are judicially recorded and, on the other, there is the very remarkable circumstance that the spirit which appears for several nights was not seen by the person to whom it related and before whose bed it revealed itself because she was asleep, but only by two fellow-prisoners, and then subsequently by her. She was then so greatly perturbed by this that of her own free will she confessed to seven poisonings. The account is in a brochure entitled *Verhandlungen des Assisenhofes in Mainz über die Giftmörderin Margeretha Jäger,* Mainz, 1835. The summary of the verbal statements is printed in *Didascalia,* a Frankfurt daily paper of 5 July 1835.

I have now to take into consideration the metaphysical aspect of the subject, for as regards the physical (here physiological) all that is necessary has already been given. What really stimulates our interest in the case of all visions, that is, of intuitive perceptions through the arising of the dream-organ in wakefulness, is their eventual relation to something empirically objective, that is to say, something that is situated outside and different from us. For only through such a relation do they obtain an analogy and a dignity equal to our ordinary waking intuitive sense-perceptions. Therefore of the nine possible causes of such visions which I have enumerated, it is not the first three resulting merely in hallucinations that are of interest, but rather those that follow. For the perplexity attaching to the consideration of visions and spirit apparitions springs really from the fact that, with these perceptions, the boundary between subject and object, as being the first condition of all knowledge, becomes doubtful, indistinct, and indeed quite blurred. 'Is that outside or inside me?' is asked by everyone—as it was by Macbeth when a dagger floated before him[26]—by everyone who is not deprived of caution and reflectiveness by a vision of such a nature. If one man alone has seen a ghost, it will be declared to be merely subjective, however objectively it stood before him. If, on the other hand, two or more saw or heard it, the reality of a body is at once attributed to it because empirically we know only *one* cause by virtue whereof several persons must necessarily have at the same time the same representation of intuitive perception, and this is where one and the same body, reflecting light in all directions, affects the eyes of them all. But besides this very mechanical cause, there might well be others of simultaneous origin of the same intuitive representation in different persons. Just as sometimes two persons simultaneously dream the same dream (see above under number 8), and therefore while asleep perceive the same thing through the dream-organ, so *in wakefulness* the dream-organ of two (or more) can enter the same activity, whereby a ghost, seen by them simultaneously, then objectively appears like a body. But generally speaking, the difference between subjective and objective is at bottom not absolute, but always relative. For everything objective is again subjective in so far as it is still always conditioned by a subject in general, in fact exists really only in this. And so in the last resort idealism is right. We often imagine we have abolished the reality of a spirit apparition when we show that it was subjectively conditioned. But what weight can this argument have with the man who knows from Kant's

[26] [*Macbeth*, Act II, Sc. I.]

doctrine how large a share the subjective conditions have in the appearance of the corporeal world? Thus that doctrine shows how this world, together with the space in which it exists, the time in which it moves, and the causality in which the essence of matter consists, and hence in accordance with its whole form, is merely a product of the brain-functions, after these have been brought into play by a stimulus in the nerves of the organs of sense, so that here we are left only with the question concerning the thing-in-itself. The *material* reality of bodies acting on our senses from without naturally belongs as little to the spirit apparition as to the dream through whose organ it is in fact perceived; and so, at all events, it can be called a waking dream, *insomnium sine somno*; (cf. Sonntag, *Sicilimentorum academicorum Fasciculus de Spectris et Omnibus morientium*, Altdorf, 1716, p. 11); but at bottom, it does not in this way forfeit its reality. Like the dream, it is, of course, a mere mental picture or representation [*Vorstellung*] and as such exists only in the knowing consciousness. But the same thing may be said of our real external world, for this too is given to us in the first instance and immediately as representation and, as I have said, is a mere brain-phenomenon that has arisen through nerve stimulation and in accordance with the laws of subjective functions (forms of pure sensibility and of the understanding). If we demand for it a further reality, then this is the question of the thing-in-itself which was raised and prematurely settled by Locke, but was then demonstrated by Kant in all its difficulty, in fact was given up by him as insoluble; yet it was answered by me, though under a certain restriction. But just as in any case the thing-in-itself which manifests itself in the phenomenon of an external world is *toto genere* different therefrom, so by analogy may it be related to that which manifests itself in the spirit apparition; in fact, what reveals itself in both may perhaps be ultimately the same thing, namely *will*. In keeping with this view, we find that, in regard to the objective reality of both the corporeal world and spirit apparitions, there is a realism, an idealism, and a scepticism, but finally also a criticism in whose interests we are now concerned. Indeed a positive confirmation of the same view is given even by the following utterance of the most famous and carefully observed clairvoyante, namely of Prevorst (vol. i, p. 12): 'Whether the spirits can render themselves visible only under this form, or whether my eye can see them only under this form, or my sense take them in only in this way; whether they would not be more spiritual for a more spiritual eye, I cannot assert this definitely, but almost divine it.' Is this not entirely on all fours with the Kantian doctrine: 'What things-in-themselves may be we know not, but we know only their phenomenal appearances'—?

The whole demonology and spirit lore of antiquity and the Middle Ages, and also the view of magic associated with them, have as their basis the still undisputed *realism* that was finally overthrown by Descartes. Only *idealism*, which has gradually matured in recent times, leads to the standpoint from which we can arrive at a correct judgement concerning all these things and so also as regards visions and spirit apparitions. On the other hand, on the empirical path, animal magnetism has at the same time brought to light *magic* that previously was always shrouded in obscurity and nervously concealed; and in this way it has made spirit apparitions the subject of dispassionate and searching observation and impartial criticism. In everything criticism always devolves on philosophy, and I hope that, just as mine from the sole reality and omnipotence of the *will* in nature has represented magic as at least conceivable and, when it exists, as intelligible,[27] so has it paved the way to a more correct view even of visions and spirit apparitions through the definite surrender of the objective world to *ideality*.

The positive incredulity with which every thinking man first learns of the facts of clairvoyance on the one hand and of magic, *vulgo* magnetic, influence on the other, and which is only tardily yielding to our own experience or to hundreds of cases of trustworthy evidence, is due to one and the same reason, to the fact that both of them, clairvoyance with its knowledge *in distans* and magic with its action *in distans*, run counter to the laws of space, time, and causality which are known to us *a priori* and in their complex determine the course of events in possible experience. And so in any account of the facts that relate to them, people say not merely 'it is not true', but 'it is not possible' (*a non posse ad non esse*);[28] yet on the other hand, the

---

[27] See the chapter 'Animal Magnetism and Magic' in my work *On the Will in Nature*.
[28] ['From impossibility to unreality'.]

retort is 'but it is so' (*ab esse ad posse*). Now this difference of opinion is due to, and indeed again furnishes a proof of, the fact that those laws, known to us *a priori*, are not absolutely the unconditioned *veritates aeternae* of the Scholastics, are not determinations of things-in-themselves, but spring from mere forms of intuitive perception and understanding and consequently from brain-functions. But the intellect itself, consisting of these, has arisen merely for the purpose of pursuing and attaining the aims and ends of individual phenomena of will, not for grasping and comprehending the absolute nature and constitution of things-in-themselves. Therefore, as I have shown in the *World as Will and Representation*, vol. ii, chaps. 17 and 22, the intellect is a mere superficial force, essentially and everywhere touching only the outer shell, never the inner core of things. The reader who really wants to understand my meaning here, should again read those passages. Now since we ourselves also form part of the inner essence of the world, we succeed for once, by eluding the *principium individuationis*, in getting at things from quite a different direction and on quite a different path, namely directly from within instead of merely from without, and thus in getting possesson of them through knowledge in clairvoyance and action in magic. Just for that cerebral knowledge we then have a result which it was actually unable to reach on its own path and which it is, therefore, determined to dispute. For an effect of this kind can be understood only metaphysically; physically it is an impossibility. On the other hand, a consequence of this is that clairvoyance is a confirmation of the Kantian doctrine of the ideality of space, time, and causality, but that, in addition, magic is also a confirmation of my doctrine of the sole reality of the *will* as the kernel of all things. In this way, Bacon's statement is again confirmed that magic is practical metaphysics.

We now recall once again the explanations given above and the physiological hypothesis there advanced, in consequence whereof all the intuitive perceptions that are carried out by the dream-organ differ from ordinary perception that constitutes wakefulness by the fact that in the latter the brain is stimulated from without through a physical impression on the senses, whereby it simultaneously receives the data and, in accordance therewith, brings about empirical intuitive perception by applying its functions, namely causality, time, and space. On the other hand, with intuitive perception through the dream-organ, the stimulation starts from the interior of the organism and is transmitted from the plastic nervous system to the brain that is thereby induced to make an intuitive perception which wholly resembles that produced in the ordinary way. Since, however, the stimulation to this perception comes from the opposite side and therefore takes place in the opposite direction, it must be assumed that the vibrations or inner movements generally of the brain-filaments also take place in the reverse direction and accordingly in the end extend to the nerves of the senses. These, then, are the last to be stirred here into activity, instead of being the very first as in the case of ordinary intuitive perception. Now if, as is assumed in dreams of reality, prophetic visions, and spirit apparitions, an intuitive perception of this kind is to be related to something actually external, empirically existing and hence wholly independent of the subject, accordingly to something that would to this extent be known through that perception, then this something must have come into some communication with the *interior* of the organism from which the intuitive perception is produced. Yet such a communication cannot possibly be demonstrated empirically; in fact, as it is assumed not to be a spatial one that comes from *without*, it is not even conceivable empirically, that is to say, physically. And so if it does take place, this must be understood only metaphysically. Accordingly, it must be thought of as a communication that is independent of the phenomenon and of all the laws thereof, as something that occurs in the thing-in-itself and is afterwards perceivable in the phenomenon, such thing-in-itself, as the inner essence of things, being everywhere the root of their phenomenal appearance. Now it is such a communication that we understand by the name of a magic influence.

If it is asked what is the path of this magic effect, the like of which is given to us in the sympathetic cure as well as in the influence of the distant magnetizer, then I say that it is that covered by the insect that dies here and again emerges full of vitality out of every egg that has hibernated. It is the path whereby, in a given population, a rise in the number of births follows an unusual increase in the number of deaths. It is the path that does not pass through time and space on the leading string of causality. It is the path through the thing-in-itself.

Now from my philosophy, we know that this thing-in-itself and thus also man's inner being is his *will*, and that everyone's entire organism, as it manifests itself empirically, is merely the objectification of the will, or more precisely the picture or image of this his will that arises in the brain. But the will as thing-in-itself lies outside the *principium individuationis* (time and space) whereby individuals are *separated*; and so the limits that result from that principle do not exist for the will. Now so far as our insight can reach when we step into this region, we can thus explain the possibility of a *direct* influence of individuals on one another, irrespective of their proximity or remoteness in space. Such influence proclaims itself as a fact in some of the nine previously enumerated kinds of waking intuitive perception through the dream-organ and often in sleeping perception. In the same way, from this immediate communication that is grounded in the being-in-itself of things we can explain the possibility of dreaming the real, of our becoming conscious of our immediate environment in somnambulism, and finally of clairvoyance. Since the will of one man is not impeded by any limits of individuation and thus acts on the will of another directly and *in distans*, it has, therefore, operated on the organism of the other man which is only his will itself intuitively perceived in space. Now if such an influence which on this path arrives at the interior of the organism extends to the guide and governor thereof, to the ganglionic system, and thence is transmitted up to the brain by breaking through the isolation, it can be elaborated by that organ, yet always only in a cerebral manner, in other words, it will produce intuitive perceptions exactly like those that come from an external stimulation of the senses. Hence it will produce pictures or images in space in its three dimensions, with movement in time, according to the law of causality, and so on. For the one, like the other, is just the product of the intuitively perceiving brain-function, and the brain is able to speak only its own language. However, an influence of this kind will still always bear the character and stamp of its origin and thus of the person from whom it has come; and it will accordingly impress this stamp on the form that it produces in the brain after so wide a détour, however different its being-in-itself may be from that form. If, for instance, through keen desire or other intention of the will, a dying man affects another at a distance, then, if this influence is very energetic, the form of the dying man will manifest itself in the brain of the other, that is to say, will appear to him exactly like a body in reality. But such influence that occurs through the interior of the organism, will obviously take place in the other man's brain more readily when this is asleep than when it is awake. For in the former case, the filaments of the brain have no opposite movement at all, whereas in the latter they have a movement the opposite of the one they are now to assume. Accordingly, a weaker influence of the kind we are considering will be able to make itself felt only in sleep through the stimulation of dreams. In wakefulness, however, it will possibly rouse ideas, sensations, and restlessness, yet everything always in accordance with its origin and bearing the stamp thereof. Thus, for example, it may produce an inexplicable longing or irresistible impulse to look for the man from whom it has come and, conversely, through a desire not to see him, to frighten away from the threshold of the house the man who wants to come, even when he was summoned and sent for (*experto crede Roberto*).[29] The well-known fact of the contagious nature of visions, second sight, and spirit seeing is also due to this influence which has its ground in the identity of the thing-in-itself in all phenomena. Such contagiousness produces an effect similar in result to that exercised by a corporeal object simultaneously on the senses of several individuals, in that on the strength of it, several at the same time see the same thing which is then quite objectively formed. The frequently observed immediate communication of ideas is also due to the same direct influence. It is so certain that I advise anyone who has to keep a perilous and important secret never to discuss the whole affair to which it refers with another who is not permitted to know it. For while he is discussing the whole affair, he is bound to have in mind the true facts of the case, and so a light may suddenly dawn on the other man in that it will furnish a communication against which neither reserve nor disguise offers

---

[29] ['Believe Robert who experienced it himself.' (From Virgil's *Experto credite*, *Aeneid*, XI. 283. It is found also in Ovid's *Ars amandi*, III. 511.)]

any protection. In the elucidations to the *Westöstlicher Diwan* under the heading 'Exchange of Flowers', Goethe narrates that two loving couples on a pleasure trip set each other charades: 'Very soon not only was each one at once guessed as it was uttered, but ultimately even the word which the other person thought and wanted to transform into the word-puzzle was known and expressed by the most direct divination.' Many years ago, my handsome hostess in Milan asked me in a very animated conversation at the dinner-table what the three numbers were that she had taken as a tern in the lottery. Without thinking, I correctly mentioned the first and second, but then gave the third incorrectly because her merriment confused me; I woke up, as it were, and now reflected. The highest degree of such an influence takes place, as we know, in very clairvoyant somnambulists who describe precisely and accurately to their interrogator his distant native land, his dwelling there, or other remote countries in which he has travelled. The thing-in-itself is the same in all beings and the state of clairvoyance enables the person therein to think with my brain instead of with his own that is fast asleep.

On the other hand, as it is for us quite certain that thc *will*, in so far as it is thing-in-itself, is not destroyed and annihilated by death, we cannot absolutely rule out *a priori* the possibility that a magic effect of the kind just described might not also come from one already dead. Yet such a possibility can as little be clearly understood and thus positively asserted, since, although generally it is not inconceivable, it is nevertheless, on closer examination, open to great difficulties which I now wish briefly to state. Since we have to conceive the inner nature of man, which remained intact in death, as existing outside time and space, its influence on us who are alive could take place only through very many agencies all of which might be on our side, so that it would be difficult to determine how many of them had actually come from the dead man. For such an influence would first have to enter the intuitive perception-forms of the subject perceiving them; consequently, it would have to appear as something spatial, temporal, and materially operative according to the causal law. But in addition, it would also have to enter into association with his abstract thinking, since otherwise he would not know what to make of it. The man appearing to him can be not merely seen, but also to some extent understood in his intentions and in the influences corresponding thereto. Accordingly, that man would also have to comply with, and conform to, the limited views and prejudices of the subject concerning the totality of things and the world. But even more! Not only as the result of the whole of my discussion so far are spirits seen through the dream-organ and in consequence of an influence that reaches the brain from within instead of the usual one through the senses from without, but also J. Kerner, firmly upholding the objective reality of appearing spirits, says the same thing in his frequently repeated statement that spirits 'are seen not with the somatic eye, but with the spiritual'. Accordingly, although the spirit apparition is brought about by an internal influence that springs from the being-in-itself of things and hence by a magic influence on the organism, which is transmitted to the brain by means of the ganglionic system, such an apparition is nevertheless perceived after the manner of objects that act on us from without by means of light, air, sound, impact, and odour. What a change a dead man's assumed influence must have undergone during such a transference, so complete a metamorphosis! Yet how can it be assumed that, during such transference and in such roundabout ways, an actual dialogue of statement and reply can take place, as is so often reported? Incidentally, here it may be remarked that the ludicrous, as well as the gruesome, element which attaches more or less to every assertion of an apparition of this kind and on account of which one hesitates to communicate it, arises from the narrator's speaking as of a perception through the external senses. But such a perception certainly did not exist since otherwise a spirit would necessarily be seen and perceived invariably and in the same way by all present. A perception which is only apparently external and has arisen as a result of an internal impression, but which is to be distinguished from the mere fantasy, does not happen to everyone. Therefore, with the assumption of an actual spirit apparition, these would be the difficulties to be found on the part of the subject perceiving it. Again, there are other difficulties to be found on the part of the dead man who is assumed to exert the influence. In consequence of my doctrine, the *will* alone has a metaphysical reality by virtue whereof it is indestructible through death. The intellect, on the other hand, as the function of a bodily organ, is merely physical and perishes therewith. And so the way in which a dead man could obtain knowledge of living persons, in order to act on them in accordance therewith, is highly problematical. Not less so is the nature of that action itself; for with corporeality the dead man has lost all ordinary, i.e. physical, means of influencing others as well as the physical world generally. Yet, if we wish to concede some truth to the incidents which are reported and asserted from so many different sources and definitely point to an objective influence of dead persons, then we must so explain the matter that, in such cases, the will of the dead man is still always passionately directed to mundane affairs. Now in the absence of physical means for influencing these, the will has recourse to that *magic* power which belongs to it in its original and hence metaphysical capacity and consequently in death as well as in life. I have already touched on this and have discussed in detail my ideas on the subject in the chapter 'Animal Magnetism and Magic' of my work *On the Will in Nature*. Therefore only by virtue of this *magic* power would it be capable, perhaps even now, of that whereof it may also have been capable in life, namely of exerting a real *actio in distans*, without the assistance of a body and accordingly of influencing others directly without any physical intervention, by affecting their organism in such a way that forms were bound to present themselves intuitively to their brain, just as they are usually produced there only in consequence of an external impression on the senses. Indeed, as this influence is conceivable only as magical, that is, as one to be produced by the inner essence of things which is identical in all and hence by the *natura naturans*,[30] we might perhaps venture to take the bold step of not limiting it to human organisms, but of conceding it also to inanimate and thus inorganic bodies that could therefore be moved by it, as not absolutely and utterly impossible. if the reputation of respectable reporters were to be vindicated solely in this way. This we could do to obviate the necessity of bluntly censuring as false certain very trustworthy narratives like those of Hofrat Hahn in the *Seherin von Prevorst*. For this is by no means an isolated case, but in older works and even in modern reports

[30] ['Creating nature', as distinct from *natura naturata* 'created nature'.]

there are many instances exactly similar to it. But here the matter certainly borders on the absurd; for, in so far as the magic way of acting is confirmed by animal magnetism and thus legitimately, even now it still offers only one feeble and questionable analogue for such an effect, namely the fact asserted in the *Mittheilungen aus dem Schlafleben der Auguste K.* . . . *zu Dresden*, 1843, pp. 115 and 318, that this somnambulist, by her mere will and without using her hands, repeatedly succeeded in diverting the magnetic needle. The same thing is reported by Ennemoser about a somnambulist named Kachler (*Anleitung zur Mesmerischen Praxis*, 1852): 'The clairvoyante Kachler moved the magnetic needle not only by holding out her fingers, but also by using her eyes. She directed her glance to the north point at a distance of about half a yard and after a few seconds the needle turned four degrees to the west. As soon as she withdrew her head and turned away her glance, the needle returned to its former position.' In London the same thing was done by the somnambulist Prudence Bernard at a public meeting and in the presence of selected competent witnesses.

The view, here expounded, of the problem in question explains first why, if we intend to admit as possible an actual influence of the dead over the world of the living, such could take place only extremely rarely and wholly by way of exception, since its possibility would be tied up with all the conditions stated which do not easily occur together. Moreover, if we do not wish to declare as purely subjective, as mere *aegri somnia*,[31] the facts narrated in the *Seherin von Prevorst* and the kindred writings of Kerner, the most detailed and authentic reports on spirit seeing that have appeared in print; if we are unwilling to be satisfied with the assumption previously discussed of a retrospective second sight to whose dumb show the clairvoyante from her own resources would have added the dialogue, but wish to establish our case on an actual influence of the dead, then it follows from what has been said that the world-order, so revoltingly absurd indeed so infamously stupid, that emerged from the statements and actions of these spirits would not thereby obtain any objectively real basis. On the contrary, such a world-order would have to be established entirely on the

---

[31] ['Dreams of the sick' (Horace, *Ars poetica*, 7).]

strength of the intuitively perceiving and thinking activity of an exceedingly ignorant clairvoyante who is thoroughly at home with her beliefs in the catechism, although such activity was awakened by an influence coming from outside nature, yet necessarily remaining true to itself.

In any case, a spirit apparition primarily and directly is nothing but a vision in the brain of the spirit seer. Experience has frequently testified to the fact that a dying man can from without give rise to such an apparition. That a living man can also do this has in several cases been confirmed on good authority. The question is merely whether one who is dead can also do it.

Finally, when explaining spirit apparitions, we might still refer to the fact that the difference between those who were formerly alive and those now alive is not absolute, but that one and the same will-to-live appears in both. In this way, a living man, going back far enough, might bring to light reminiscences that appear as the communications of one who is dead.

If in all these remarks I should have succeeded in throwing even a feeble light on a very important and interesting subject with regard to which two parties have faced each other for thousands of years, the one persistently assuring us that 'it is!', and the other as obstinately repeating that 'it cannot be', then I have achieved all that I promised to do, and in fairness the reader had a right to expect this.

APHORISMS ON THE
WISDOM OF LIFE

*Le bonheur n'est pas chose aisée: il est très difficile
de le trouver en nous, et impossible de le trouver ailleurs.*
                                                    Chamfort.

['Happiness is no easy matter; it is very difficult
to find it in ourselves and impossible to find it
elsewhere.']

Aphorisms on the Wisdom of Life

Introduction

Here I take the idea of wisdom of life entirely in the immanent sense, namely that of the art of getting through life as pleasantly and successfully as possible, the instructions to which might also be called eudemonology. Accordingly, they would be instructions on how to have a happy existence. Such might perhaps be again defined as one that, considered purely objectively or rather with cool and mature reflection (for here it is a question of a subjective judgement), would be definitely preferable to non-existence. From this conception of it, it follows that we should be attached to it for its own sake and not merely from the fear of death; and again from this that we would like to see it last for ever. Now whether human life does or ever can correspond to the conception of such an existence, is a question that, as we know, is answered in the negative by my philosophy; whereas eudemonology presupposes an answer in the affirmative. Now this is based on the inborn error which is censured by me in the forty-ninth chapter of the second volume of my chief work. However, to be able to work out such an answer, I have therefore had to abandon entirely the higher metaphysical ethical standpoint to which my real philosophy leads. Consequently, the whole discussion here to be given rests to a certain extent on a compromise, in so far as it remains at the ordinary empirical standpoint and firmly maintains the error thereof. Accordingly, its value can be only conditioned, for even the word eudemonology is only a euphemism. Moreover, this discussion makes no claim to completeness partly because the theme is inexhaustible and also because I should otherwise have to repeat what has already been said by others.

The only book I can recall which is written with the same purpose as are the present aphorisms is *De utilitate ex adversis capienda*[1] by Cardanus which is well worth reading and can, therefore, supplement what is given here. It is true that

---

[1] ['On the Use of Adversity'.]

Aristotle also introduced a brief eudemonology into the fifth chapter of the first book of his *Rhetoric;* yet it proved to be very stale and dry. As compilation is not my business, I have not made use of these predecessors, the less so as through it one loses coherence and continuity of view which are the spirit and soul of works of this kind. In general, of course, the sages of all times have always said the same thing and the fools, that is, the immense majority of all times, have always done the same thing, namely the opposite; and so will it always be. Therefore Voltaire says: *Nous laisserons ce monde-ci aussi sot et aussi méchant que nous l'avons trouvé en y arrivant.*[2]

---

[2] ['We shall quit this world as stupid and as bad as we found it when we came into it'.]

CHAPTER I

Fundamental Division

ARISTOTLE (*Nicomachean Ethics*, I. 8) has divided the good things of human life into three classes, those outside, those of the soul, and those of the body. Now retaining nothing of this except the number three, I say that what establishes the difference in the lot of mortals may be reduced to three fundamental qualifications. They are:

(1) What a man *is* and therefore personality in the widest sense. Accordingly, under this are included health, strength, beauty, temperament, moral character, intelligence and its cultivation.

(2) What a man *has* and therefore property and possessions in every sense.

(3) What a man *represents*; we know that by this expression is understood what he is in the eyes of others and thus how he *is represented* by them. Accordingly, it consists in their opinion of him and is divisible into honour, rank, and reputation.

The differences to be considered under the first heading are those established by nature herself between one man and another. From this it may be inferred that their influence on the happiness or unhappiness of mankind will be much more fundamental and radical than what is produced by the differences that are mentioned under the two following headings and result merely from human decisions and resolutions. Compared with *genuine personal advantages*, such as a great mind or a great heart, all the privileges of rank, birth, even royal birth, wealth, and so on, are as kings on the stage to kings in real life. Metrodorus, the first disciple of Epicurus, gave the title to a chapter: περὶ τοῦ μείζονα εἶναι τὴν παρ' ἡμᾶς αἰτίαν πρὸς εὐδαιμονίαν τῆς ἐκ τῶν πραγμάτων. (*Majorem esse causam ad felicitatem eam, quae est ex nobis, eâ, quae ex rebus oritur.*[1] Cf. Clement of Alexandria, *Stromata*, lib. II, c. 21, p. 362 of the Würzburg

[1] ['The cause of happiness which lies within us is greater than the cause that comes from things.']

edition of the polemical works). And it is certain that for man's well-being, indeed for his whole mode of existence, the main thing is obviously what exists or occurs within himself. For here is to be found immediately his inner satisfaction or dissatisfaction which is primarily the result of his feeling, his willing, and his thinking. On the other hand, everything situated outside him has on him only an indirect influence; and so the same external events and circumstances affect each of us quite differently; and indeed with the same environment each lives in a world of his own. For a man is directly concerned only with his own conceptions, feelings, and voluntary movements; things outside influence him only in so far as they give rise to these. The world in which each lives depends first on his interpretation thereof and therefore proves to be different to different men. Accordingly, it will result in being poor, shallow, and superficial, or rich, interesting, and full of meaning. For example, while many envy another man the interesting events that have happened to him in his life, they should rather envy his gift of interpretation which endowed those events with the significance they have when he describes them. For the same event that appears to be so interesting in the mind of a man of intelligence would be only a dull and vapid scene from the commonplace world when conceived in the shallow mind of an ordinary man. This is seen in the highest degree in many of Goethe's and Byron's poems which are obviously based on real events. Here it is open to the foolish reader to envy the poet the most delightful event, instead of envying him the mighty imagination that was capable of making something so great and beautiful from a fairly commonplace occurrence. In the same way, a man of melancholy disposition sees a scene from a tragedy, where one of sanguine temperament sees only an interesting conflict and someone phlegmatic sees something trifling and unimportant. All this is due to the fact that every reality, in other words, every moment of actual experience, consists of two halves, the subject and the object, although in just as necessary and close a connection as are oxygen and hydrogen in water. Therefore when the objective half is exactly the same, but the subjective is different, the present reality is quite different, just as it is in the reverse case; thus the finest and best objective half with a dull and inferior subjective half furnishes only an inferior reality, like a beautiful landscape in bad weather or in the reflected light of a bad *camera obscura*. In plainer language, everyone is confined to his consciousness as he is within his own skin and only in this does he really live; thus he cannot be helped very much from without. On the stage one man is a prince, another a councillor, a third a servant, a soldier, or a general, and so on. These differences, however, exist only on the outer surface; in the interior, as the kernel of such a phenomenon, the same thing is to be found in all of them, namely a poor player with his wants and worries. In life it is also the same. Differences of rank and wealth give everyone his part to play, but there is certainly not an internal difference of happiness and satisfaction that corresponds to that role. On the contrary, here too there is in everyone the same poor wretch with his worries and wants. Materially these may be different in everyone, but in form and thus in their essential nature they are pretty much the same in all, although with differences of degree which do not by any means correspond to position and wealth, in other words, to the part a man plays. Thus since everything existing and happening for man directly exists always in his own *consciousness* and happens only for this, the nature thereof is obviously the first essential and in most cases this is more important than are the forms that present themselves therein. All the pomp and pleasure that are mirrored in the dull consciousness of a simpleton are very poor when compared with the consciousness of Cervantes writing *Don Quixote* in a miserable prison. The objective half of the present reality is in the hands of fate and is accordingly changeable; we ourselves are the subjective half that is, therefore, essentially unchangeable. Accordingly, the life of every man bears throughout the same character in spite of all change from without and is comparable to a series of variations on one theme. No one can get outside his own individuality. In all the circumstances in which the animal is placed, it remains confined to the narrow circle, irrevocably drawn for it by nature, so that, for instance, our endeavours to make a pet happy must always keep within narrow bounds precisely on account of those limits of its true nature and consciousnessness. It is the same with man; the measure of his possible happiness is determined beforehand by his individuality. In particular, the limits of his mental powers have fixed once for all his capacity for pleasures of a higher order. (Cf. *World as Will and Representation*, vol. ii, chap. 7.) If those powers are small, all the efforts from without, everything done for him by mankind or good fortune, will not enable him to rise above the ordinary half-animal human happiness and comfort. He is left to depend on the pleasures of the senses, on a cosy and cheerful family life, on low company and vulgar pastimes. Even education, on the whole, cannot do very much, if anything, to broaden his horizon. For the highest, most varied, and most permanent pleasures are those of the mind, however much we may deceive ourselves on this point when we are young; but these pleasures depend mainly on innate mental powers. Therefore it is clear from this how much our happiness depends on what we *are*, our individuality, whereas in most cases we take into account only our fate, only what we *have* or *represent*. Fate, however, can improve; moreover, if we are inwardly wealthy we shall not demand much from it. On the other hand, a fool remains a fool, a dull blockhead a dull blockhead, till the end of his life, even if he were surrounded by houris in paradise. Therefore Goethe says;

> Mob, menial, and master
> At all time admit,
> The supreme fortune of mortals
> Is their personality alone.
> *Westöstlicher Diwan.*

Everything confirms that the subjective is incomparably more essential to our happiness and pleasures than is the objective, namely from the fact that hunger is the best sauce, hoary old age regards the goddess of youth with indifference, up to the life of the genius and the saint. In particular, health so far outweighs all external blessings that a healthy beggar is indeed more fortunate than a monarch in poor health. A quiet and cheerful temperament, resulting from perfect health and a prosperous economy, an understanding that is clear, lively, penetrating, and sees things correctly, a moderate and gentle will and hence a good conscience—these are advantages that no rank or wealth can make good or replace. For what a man is by himself, what accompanies him into solitude, and what no one can give him or take from him is obviously more essential to him than everything he possesses, or even what he may be in the eyes of others. A man of intellect, when entirely alone, has excellent entertainment in his own thoughts and fancies, whereas the continuous diversity of parties, plays, excursions, and amusements cannot ward off from a dullard the tortures of boredom. A good, moderate, gentle character can be contented in needy circumstances, whereas one who is covetous, envious, and malicious is not so, in spite of all his wealth. Indeed for the man who constantly has the delight of an extraordinary and intellectually eminent individuality, most of the pleasures that are generally sought after are entirely superfluous; indeed they are only a bother and a burden. Therefore Horace says of himself:

> *Gemmas, marmor, ebur, Tyrrhena sigilla, tabellas,*
> *Argentum, vestes Gaetulo murice tinctas,*
> *Sunt qui non habeant, est qui non curat habere;*[2]

and when Socrates saw luxury articles displayed for sale, he said: 'How many things there are I do not need!'

Accordingly, for our life's happiness, what we *are*, our personality, is absolutely primary and most essential, if only because it is operative at all times and in all circumstances. Moreover, unlike the blessings under the other two headings, it is not subject to fate and cannot be wrested from us. To this extent its value can be described as absolute in contrast to the merely relative value of the other two. Now it follows from this that it is much more difficult to get at a man from without than is generally supposed. Only the all-powerful agent, Time, here exercises its right; physical and mental advantages gradually succumb to it; moral character alone remains inaccessible to it. In this respect, it would naturally appear that the blessings which are enumerated under the second and third headings, of which time cannot directly deprive us, have an advantage over those of the first. A second advantage might be found in the fact, that, as such blessings lie in the objective, they are by their nature attainable and everyone has before him at least the possibility of coming into possession of them, whereas the

---

[2] ['Ivory, marble, trinkets, Tyrrhenian statues, pictures, silver plate, clothes dyed with Gaetulian purple, many do without such things, and some do not bother about them.' *Epistles*, II.2.180.]

subjective is certainly not given into our power, but has entered *jure divino*[3] and is unalterably fixed for the whole of life, so that here Goethe's words inexorably apply:

> As on the day that lent you to the world
> The sun received the planets' greetings,
> At once and eternally you have thrived
> According to the law whereby you stepped forth.
> So must you be, from yourself you cannot flee,
> So have the Sibyls and the Prophets said;
> No time, no power breaks into little pieces
> The form here stamped and in life developed.

The only thing that in this respect lies within our power is for us to take the greatest possible advantage of the given personality and accordingly to follow only those tendencies that are in keeping with it and to strive for the kind of development that is exactly suitable to it, while avoiding every other, and consequently to choose the position, occupation, and way of life that are suited to it.

A man of Herculean strength who is endowed with unusual muscular power and is compelled by external circumstances to follow a sedentary occupation, to carry out with his hands minute and intricate tasks, or to pursue studies and mental work that demand powers of quite a different order from those he possesses, and consequently to leave unused those powers in which he excels, will feel unhappy all his life. But even more unhappy will be the man whose intellectual powers are of a very high order, and who must leave them undeveloped and unused in order to pursue a common business that does not require them, or even some physical work to which his strength is not really adequate. Yet here, especially in youth, we have to avoid the precipice of presumption of attributing to ourselves an excess of powers which we do not possess.

From the decided superiority of the blessings of the first heading over those of the other two, it follows that it is wiser for us to aim at maintaining our health and at cultivating our faculties than at acquiring wealth. However, this must not be misinterpreted as meaning that we should neglect the acquisition of what is necessary and suitable. Wealth proper, that is, great

---

[3] ['By divine right'.]

superfluity, can do little for our happiness. Therefore many wealthy people feel unhappy because they are without any real mental culture, without any knowledge, and therefore without any objective interest that could qualify them for mental occupation. For what wealth can achieve, beyond the satisfaction of the real and natural needs, has little influence on our happiness proper; on the contrary, this is disturbed by the many inevitable worries that are entailed in the preservation of much property. Nevertheless, people are a thousand times more concerned to become wealthy than to acquire mental culture, whereas it is quite certain that what we *are* contributes much more to our happiness than what we *have*. Therefore we see very many work from morning to night as industriously as ants and in restless activity to increase the wealth they already have. Beyond the narrow horizon of the means to this end, they know nothing; their minds are a blank and are therefore not susceptible to anything else. The highest pleasures, those of the mind, are inaccessible to them and they try in vain to replace them by the fleeting pleasures of the senses in which they indulge at intervals and which cost little time but much money. If their luck has been good, then as a result they have at the end of their lives a really large amount of money, which they now leave to their heirs either to increase still further or to squander. Such a life, though pursued with a very serious air of importance, is therefore just as foolish as is many another that had for its symbol a fool's-cap.

Therefore what a man *has in himself* is most essential to his life's happiness. Merely because this is so very little as a rule, many of those, who are beyond the struggle with want, at bottom feel just as unhappy as those who are still engaged therein. The emptiness of their inner life, the dullness of their consciousness, the poorness of their minds drive them to the company of others which consists of men like themselves, for *similis simili gaudet.*[4] They then pursue pastime and entertainment in common which they seek first in sensual pleasures, in amusements of every kind, and finally in excess and dissipation. The source of the deplorable extravagance, whereby many a son of a wealthy family entering life with a large patrimony often gets through it in an incredibly short time, is really none

---

4 ['Birds of a feather flock together.']

other than the boredom that springs from the poorness and emptiness of his mind which I have just described. Such a young man was sent into the world outwardly rich but inwardly poor, and he then vainly endeavoured to make his external wealth compensate for his internal poverty by trying to obtain every-thing *from without*, somewhat like old men who try to strengthen themselves through the perspiration of young girls. And so in the end, inner poverty also produced a poverty in external things.

I need not stress the importance of those blessings of human life that are contained under the other two headings. For the value of possessions is nowadays so universally acknowledged that it is not in any need of a recommendation. Compared with the second heading, even the third has a very ethereal character, for it consists merely in other people's opinions. Yet everyone has to strive for reputation, in other words, a good name; rank is aspired to only by those serving the State, and fame by very few indeed. However, reputation is regarded as a priceless treasure and fame as the most precious of all the blessings that man can attain, the Golden Fleece of the elect; on the other hand, only fools will prefer rank to possessions. Moreover, the blessings under the second and third headings act and react on one another in so far as the maxim of Petronius *habes, habeberis*[5] is correct and, conversely, the favourable opinion of others in all its forms often helps us to obtain possessions.

[5] ['A man is worth what he has.']

CHAPTER II

What a Man is

WE have in general recognized that this contributes much more to a man's happiness than what he *has* or *represents*. It always depends on what a man is and accordingly has in himself; for his individuality always and everywhere accompanies him and everything experienced by him is tinged thereby. In everything and with everything he first of all enjoys only himself; this already applies to physical pleasures and how much truer is it of those of the mind! Therefore the English words 'to enjoy oneself'[1] are a very apt expression; for example, we do not say 'he enjoys Paris', but 'he enjoys *himself* in Paris.'[2] Now if the individuality is ill-conditioned, all pleasures are like choice wines in a mouth that is made bitter with gall. Accordingly, if we leave out of account cases of grave misfortune, less depends, in the good things as well as in the bad, on what befalls and happens to us in life than on the way in which we feel it, and thus on the nature and degree of our susceptibility in every respect. What a man is and has in himself, that is to say, personality and its worth, is the sole immediate factor in his happiness and well-being. Everything else is mediate and indirect and so the effect thereof can be neutralized and frustrated; that of personality never. For this reason, the envy excited by personal qualities is the most implacable, as it is also the most carefully concealed. Further, the constitution of consciousness is that which is permanent and enduring and individuality is at work constantly and incessantly more or less at every moment. Everything else, on the other hand, acts only at times, occasionally, temporarily, and in addition is subject to variation and change. Therefore Aristotle says: ἡ γὰρ φύσις βέβαιον οὐ τὰ χρήματα (*nam natura perennis est, non opes*).[3] *Eudemian Ethics*, VII. 2. To this is due the fact that we can bear with more composure a misfortune that has befallen us entirely

---

[1] [Schopenhauer's own words.]   [2] [Schopenhauer's own words.]
[3] ['For we can depend on nature, not on money.']

from without than one that we have brought upon ourselves, for fate can change, but our own nature never. Therefore subjective blessings, such as a noble character, a gifted mind, a happy temperament, cheerful spirits, and a well-conditioned thoroughly sound body, and so generally *mens sana in corpore sano*[4] (Juvenal, *Satires*, x. 356), are for our happiness primary and the most important. We should, therefore, be much more concerned to promote and preserve such qualities than to possess external wealth and external honour.

Now of all those qualities the one that most immediately makes us happy is cheerfulness of disposition; for this good quality is its own instantaneous reward. Whoever is merry and cheerful has always a good reason for so being, namely the very fact that he is so. Nothing can so completely take the place of every other blessing as can this quality, whilst it itself cannot be replaced by anything. A man may be young, handsome, wealthy, and esteemed; if we wish to judge of his happiness, we ask whether he is cheerful. On the other hand, if he is cheerful, it matters not whether he is young or old, straight or hump-backed, rich or poor; he is happy. In my youth, I once opened an old book in which it said: 'Whoever laughs a lot is happy, and whoever weeps a lot is unhappy', a very simple remark, but because of its plain truth I have been unable to forget it, however much it may be the superlative of a truism. For this reason, we should open wide the doors to cheerfulness whenever it makes its appearance, for it never comes inopportunely. Instead of doing this, we often hesitate to let it enter, for we first want to know whether we have every reason to be contented; or because we are afraid of being disturbed by cheerfulness when we are involved in serious deliberations and heavy cares. But what we improve through these is very uncertain, whereas cheerfulness is an immediate gain. It alone is, so to speak, the very coin of happiness and not, like everything else, merely a cheque on a bank; for only it makes us immediately happy in the present moment. And so it is the greatest blessing for beings whose reality takes the form of an indivisible present moment between an infinite past and an infinite future. Accordingly, we should make the acquisition and encouragement of this blessing our first endeavour. Now it is certain that nothing

4 ['A healthy mind in a healthy body'.]

contributes less to cheerfulness than wealth and nothing
contributes more than health. The lower classes or the workers,
especially those in the country, have the more cheerful and
contented faces; peevishness and ill-humour are more at home
among the wealthy upper classes. Consequently, we should
endeavour above all to maintain a high degree of health, the
very bloom of which appears as cheerfulness. The means to this
end are, as we know, avoidance of all excesses and irregularities,
of all violent and disagreeable emotions, and also of all mental
strain that is too great and too prolonged, two hours' brisk
exercise every day in the open air, many cold baths, and similar
dietetic measures. Without proper daily exercise no one can
remain healthy; all the vital processes demand exercise for their
proper performance, exercise not only of the parts wherein they
occur, but also of the whole. Therefore Aristotle rightly says:
ὁ βίος ἐν τῇ κινήσει ἐστί.[5] Life consists in movement and has its
very essence therein. Ceaseless and rapid motion occurs in every
part of the organism; the heart in its complicated double systole
and diastole beats strongly and untiringly; with its twenty-eight
beats it drives the whole of the blood through all the arteries,
veins, and capillaries; the lungs pump incessantly like a steam-
engine; the intestines are always turning in motus peristalticus;[6]
all the glands are constantly absorbing and secreting; even the
brain has a double motion with every heart-beat and every
breath. Now when there is an almost total lack of external
movement, as is the case with numberless people who lead an
entirely sedentary life, there arises a glaring and injurious dis-
proportion between external inactivity and internal tumult.
For the constant internal motion must be supported by something external. That want of proportion is analogous to the case
where, in consequence of some emotion, something boils up
within us which we are obliged to suppress. In order to thrive
even trees require movement through wind. Here a rule applies
which may be briefly expressed in Latin: omnis motus, quo
celerior, eo magis motus.[7] How much our happiness depends on
cheerfulness of disposition, and this on the state of our health,
is seen when we compare the impression, made on us by external
circumstances or events when we are hale and hearty, with that

[5] ['Life consists in movement.']   [6] ['Worm-like movement'.]
[7] ['The more rapid a movement is, the more it is movement.']

produced by them when ill-health has made us depressed and anxious. It is not what things are objectively and actually, but what they are for us and in our way of looking at them, that makes us happy or unhappy. This is just what Epictetus says: ταράσσει τοὺς ἀνθρώπους οὐ τὰ πράγματα, ἀλλὰ τὰ περὶ τῶν πραγμάτων δόγματα (commovent homines non res sed de rebus opiniones).[8] In general, however, nine-tenths of our happiness depend on health alone. With it everything becomes a source of pleasure, whereas without it nothing, whatever it may be, can be enjoyed, and even the other subjective blessings, such as mental qualities, disposition, and temperament, are depressed and dwarfed by ill-health. Accordingly, it is not without reason that, when two people meet, they first ask about the state of each other's health and hope that it is good; for this really is for human happiness by far the most important thing. But from this it follows that the greatest of all follies is to sacrifice our health for whatever it may be, for gain, profit, promotion, learning, or fame, not to mention sensual and other fleeting pleasures; rather should we give first place to health.

Now however much health may contribute to the cheerfulness that is so essential to our happiness, this does not depend solely on health; for even with perfect health we may have a melancholy temperament and a predominantly gloomy frame of mind. The ultimate reason for this is undoubtedly to be found in the original and thus unalterable constitution of the organism and generally in the more or less normal relation of sensibility to irritability and power of reproduction. An abnormal excess of sensibility will produce inequality of spirits, periodical excess of cheerfulness and prevailing melancholy. Now since a genius is conditioned by an excess of nervous force and hence of sensibility, Aristotle quite rightly observed that all people of superior eminence are melancholy: πάντες ὅσοι περιττοὶ γεγόνασιν ἄνδρες, ἢ κατὰ φιλοσοφίαν, ἢ πολιτικὴν, ἢ ποίησιν, ἢ τέχνας, φαίνονται μελαγχολικοὶ ὄντες[9] (Problemata, 30, 1, Berlin edn.). This is undoubtedly the passage that Cicero had in mind when he made the statement, often quoted: Aristoteles ait, omnes

---

[8] ['It is not things that disturb men, but opinions about things.']

[9] ['All who have distinguished themselves whether in philosophy, politics, poetry, or the arts, appear to be melancholy.']

ingeniosos melancholicos esse[10] (*Tusculanae disputationes*, I. 33). Shakespeare has given a fine description of the great and innate diversity of fundamental temperament generally which we are considering:

> Nature hath fram'd strange fellows in her time:
> Some that will evermore peep through their eyes,
> And laugh, like parrots, at a bag-piper;
> And others of such vinegar aspect,
> That they'll not show their teeth in way of smile,
> 'Though Nestor swear the jest be laughable.'
>
> *Merchant of Venice*, Act I, Sc. I.

This is precisely the difference described by Plato with the expressions δύσκολος and εὔκολος,[11] which is traceable to the very different susceptibility shown by different people to pleasant and unpleasant impressions, in consequence whereof one man laughs at what would drive another almost to despair. As a rule, the weaker the susceptibility is to pleasant impressions, the stronger is that to unpleasant ones, and vice versa. With the equal possibility of the fortunate or unfortunate end of an affair, the δύσκολος will be annoyed or grieved if the issue is unfortunate, but not pleased if it proves to be fortunate. On the other hand, the εὔκολος will not be annoyed or grieved if the affair goes wrong, but will be pleased if the outcome is fortunate. If the δύσκολος succeeds in nine schemes out of ten, he is not satisfied, but is annoyed that one of the schemes was a failure. On the other hand, the εὔκολος is able to find consolation and cheerfulness even in a single successful scheme. Now just as it is not easy to find an evil without some compensation, so even here we see that the δύσκολος and hence those of gloomy and nervous character will have to endure misfortunes and sufferings on the whole more imaginary but less real than those endured by the gay and carefree. For the man who sees everything with dark glasses, always fears the worst, and accordingly takes precautions, will not be wrong in his reckoning as often as the man who always paints things in bright colours with prospects. However, when a morbid affection of the nervous system or of the organs of digestion plays into the hands of an innate

---

[10] ['Aristotle says that all men of genius are melancholy.']
[11] ['Peevish and cheerful'.]

δυσκολία,[12] this can reach such a pitch that permanent dissatisfaction engenders a weariness of life and accordingly a tendency to suicide arises. Even the most trivial annoyances and vexations can then bring it about; in fact, when the evil reaches the highest degree, there is no need even for such annoyances. On the contrary, a man decides to commit suicide merely in consequence of a permanent dissatisfaction; and he then commits it with such cool deliberation and firm resolve that, often as a patient under supervision, he uses the first unguarded moment to seize without hesitation, without a struggle or recoil, the now natural and welcome means of relief. Detailed descriptions of this state of mind are given by Esquirol in *Des maladies mentales*. But even the healthiest and perhaps also the most cheerful can of course, in certain circumstances, decide to commit suicide, for example, when the magnitude of their sufferings or of the misfortune that is sure to arrive overcomes the terrors of death. The difference lies solely in the varying magnitude of the requisite motive which is inversely proportional to the amount of the δυσκολία. The greater this is, the less the motive need be, indeed in the end this may sink to zero. On the other hand, the greater the εὐκολία[13] and the health that sustains it, the more must there be in the suicide motive. Accordingly, there are innumerable cases between the two extremes of suicide, between that springing merely from a morbid intensification of the innate δυσκολία and that of the healthy and cheerful man for purely objective reasons.

Beauty is partly akin to health. Although this subjective good quality does not really contribute directly to our happiness, but only indirectly by impressing others, it is nevertheless of great importance even to a man. Beauty is an open letter of recommendation that wins hearts for us in advance; and so Homer's verse is here specially applicable:

Οὔτοι ἀπόβλητ᾽ ἐστὶ θεῶν ἐρικυδέα δῶρα,
Ὅσσα κεν αὐτοὶ δῶσιν, ἑκὼν δ᾽οὐκ ἄν τις ἕλοιτο.[14]
Iliad, iii.65.

The most general survey shows that pain and boredom are the two foes of human happiness. In addition, it may be

---

[12] ['Peevish frame of mind'.]   [13] ['Cheerful frame of mind'.]
[14] ['Not to be despised are the divine gifts of the gods which they alone bestow and which none can obtain at will.']

remarked that, in proportion as we succeed in getting away from the one, we come nearer to the other, and vice versa. And so our life actually presents a violent or feeble oscillation between the two. This springs from the fact that the two stand to each other in a double antagonism, an outer or objective and an inner or subjective. Thus externally, want and privation produce pain; on the other hand, security and affluence give rise to boredom. Accordingly, we see the lower classes constantly struggling against privation and thus against pain; on the other hand, the wealthy upper classes are engaged in a constant and often really desperate struggle against boredom.* But the inner or subjective antagonism between pain and boredom is due to the fact that in the individual a susceptibility to the one is inversely proportional to a susceptibility to the other since it is determined by the measure of his mental ability. Thus feebleness of mind is generally associated with dullness of sensation and a lack of sensitiveness, qualities that render a man less susceptible to pains and afflictions of every kind and intensity. On the other hand, the result of this mental dullness is that *inner vacuity and emptiness* that is stamped on innumerable faces and also betrays itself in a constant and lively attention to all the events in the external world, even the most trivial. This vacuity is the real source of boredom and always craves for external excitement in order to set the mind and spirits in motion through something. Therefore in the choice thereof it is not fastidious, as is testified by the miserable and wretched pastimes to which people have recourse and also by the nature of their sociability and conversation, and likewise by the many who gossip at the door or gape out of the window. The principal result of this inner vacuity is the craze for society, diversion, amusement, and luxury of every kind which lead many to extravagance and so to misery. Nothing protects us so surely from this wrong turning as *inner* wealth, the wealth of the mind, for the more eminent it becomes, the less room does it leave for boredom. The inexhaustible activity of ideas, their constantly renewed play with the manifold phenomena of the inner and outer worlds, the power and urge always to make

---

* The *nomadic life*, indicating the lowest stage of civilization, is again found at the highest in the *tourist life* which has become general. The first was produced by *want*, the second by *boredom*.

different combinations with them, all these put the eminent
mind, apart from moments of relaxation, quite beyond the
reach of boredom. On the other hand, this enhanced intelligence is directly conditioned by a heightened sensibility and is
rooted in a greater vehemence of will and hence of impulsive-
ness. From its union with these qualities, there now result a
much greater intensity of all the emotions and an enhanced
sensitiveness to mental and also physical pain, even greater
impatience in the presence of obstacles, or greater resentment
of mere disturbances. All this contributes much to an enhancement of the whole range of thoughts and conceptions, and so
too of repulsive ideas the liveliness of which springs from a
powerful imagination. This holds good relatively of all the
intermediate stages between the two extremes of the dullest
blockhead and the greatest genius. Accordingly, both objectively and subjectively, everyone is the nearer to the one source
of suffering in human life, the more remote he is from the other.
In keeping with this, his natural tendency will in this respect
direct him to adapt as far as possible the objective to the subjective and thus to make greater provision against *that* source of
suffering to which he is more susceptible. The clever and
intelligent man will first of all look for painlessness, freedom
from molestation, quietness, and leisure and consequently for a
tranquil and modest life which is as undisturbed as possible.
Accordingly, after some acquaintance with human beings so
called, he will choose seclusion and, if of greater intellect, even
solitude. For the more a man has within himself, the less does
he need from without and also the less other people can be to
him. Therefore eminence of intellect leads to unsociability.
Indeed if the quality of society could be replaced by quantity, it
would be worth while to live in the world at large; but unfortunately a hundred fools in a crowd still do not produce one
intelligent man. On the other hand, as soon as want and privation give a man from the other extreme a breathing-space, he
will look for pastime and society at any price and will readily
put up with anything, wishing to escape from nothing so much
as from himself. For in solitude, where everyone is referred
back to himself, he then sees what he has *in himself*. For the
fool in purple groans under the burden of his wretched individuality that cannot be thrown off, whereas the man of

great gifts populates and animates with his ideas the most dreary and desolate environment. What Seneca says is, therefore, very true: *omnis stultitia laborat fastidio sui*[15] (*Epistulae*, 9), as also the statement of Jesus ben Sirach: 'The life of the fool is worse than death.' Accordingly, we shall find on the whole that everyone is sociable to the extent that he is intellectually poor and generally common.* For in this world we have little more than a choice between solitude and vulgarity. The most sociable of all human beings are said to be the Negroes who intellectually are decidedly inferior. According to accounts from North America in the French paper (*Le Commerce*, 19 October 1837), the blacks shut themselves up in large numbers in the smallest space, free men and slaves all together, because they cannot see enough of their black flat-nosed faces.

Accordingly, the brain appears as the parasite or pensioner of the entire organism and a man's hard-won *leisure*, by giving him the free enjoyment of his own consciousness and individuality, is the fruit and produce of his whole existence that is in other respects only toil and effort. But what does the leisure of most men yield? Boredom and dullness, except when there are sensual pleasures or follies for filling up the time. How utterly worthless this leisure is, is seen by the way in which such people spend it; it is precisely Ariosto's *ozio lungo d'uomini ignoranti*.[16] Ordinary men are intent merely on how to *spend* their time; a man with any talent is interested in how to *use* his time. Men of limited intelligence are so exposed to boredom and this is due to their intellect's being absolutely nothing but the *medium of motives* for their will. Now if at the moment there are no motives to be taken up, the will rests and the intellect takes a holiday since the one, like the other, does not become active of its own accord. The result is a terrible stagnation of all the powers of the entire man, in a word boredom. To ward off this, men now present the will with trivial motives that are merely temporary and are taken at random in order to rouse it and thus bring into action the intellect that has to interpret them. Accordingly, such motives are related to real and natural ones as paper-money to silver, for their value is arbitrarily assumed. Now such

* The very thing that makes people sociable is their inner poverty.

[15] ['Stupidity suffers from its own weariness.']

[16] ['The boredom of the ignorant'.]

small motives are *games*, with cards and so on, which have been invented for this very purpose. And if these are wanting, the man of limited intelligence will resort to rattling and drumming with anything he can get hold of. For him even a cigar is a welcome substitute for ideas. And so in all countries the principal entertainment of all society has become card-playing; it is a measure of the worth of society and the declared bankruptcy of all ideas and thoughts. Thus since they are unable to exchange any ideas, they deal out cards and attempt to take one another's half-crowns. What a pitiful race! But not to be unjust here, I will not refrain from saying that, in defence of card-playing, it could at any rate be said that it is a preliminary training for life in the world of business in so far as in this way we learn to make clever use of the accidentally but unalterably given circumstances (cards in this case) in order to make therefrom what we can. For this purpose we become accustomed to showing a bold front by putting a good face on a bad game. But for this very reason, card-playing has a demoralizing effect since the spirit of the game is to win from another what is his and to do so in every possible way and by every trick and stratagem. But the habit, acquired in play, of acting in this way strikes root, encroaches on practical life, and we gradually come to act in the same way with respect to the affairs of mine and thine and to regard as justifiable every advantage we have in our hands whenever we are legally permitted to do so. Proofs of this are furnished by ordinary everyday life. And so, as I have said, *free* leisure is the flower, or rather the fruit, of everyone's existence, since it alone puts him in possession of himself. Therefore those are to be called happy who in themselves then preserve something of value; whereas for the majority leisure yields only a good-for-nothing fellow who is terribly bored and a burden to himself. Accordingly, we rejoice 'dear brethren that we are not children of the bondwoman, but of the free'. (Galatians 4:31.)

Further, just as that country is the best off which requires few or no imports, so too is that man the most fortunate who has enough in his own inner wealth and for his amusement and diversion needs little or nothing from without. For imports are expensive, make us dependent, entail danger, occasion trouble and annoyance, and in the end are only an inferior substitute for the products of our own soil. For on no account should we expect much from others or generally from without. What one man can be to another is very strictly limited; in the end, everyone remains alone and then the question is *who* is now alone. Accordingly, Goethe's general remarks (*Dichtung und Wahrheit*, vol. iii, p. 474) here apply, namely that in all things everyone is ultimately referred back to himself, or as Oliver Goldsmith says:

> Still to ourselves in ev'ry place consign'd,
> Our own felicity we make or find.
> *The Traveller*, ll. 431f.

Therefore everyone must himself be the best and most that he can be and achieve. Now the more this is so and consequently the more he finds within himself the sources of his pleasures, the happier he will be. Therefore Aristotle is absolutely right when he says: ἡ εὐδαιμονία τῶν αὐτάρκων ἐστὶ (*Eudemian Ethics*, vii. 2), which means that happiness belongs to those who are easily contented. For all the external sources of happiness and pleasure are by their nature exceedingly uncertain, precarious, fleeting, and subject to chance; therefore, even under the most favourable circumstances, they could easily come to an end; indeed this is inevitable in so far as they cannot always be close at hand. In old age almost all these sources necessarily dry up, for we are deserted by love, humour, desire to travel, delight in horses, aptitude for social intercourse, and even our friends and relations are taken from us by death. Then more than ever does it depend on what we have in ourselves, for this will last longest; but even at any age it is and remains the genuine and only permanent source of happiness. There is not much to be got anywhere in the world; it is full of privation and pain and for those who have escaped therefrom boredom lurks at every corner. In addition, baseness and wickedness have as a rule the upper hand and folly makes the most noise. Fate is cruel and mankind pitiable. In a world so constituted the man who has much within himself is like a bright, warm, cheerful room at Christmas amid the snow and ice of a December night. Accordingly, the happiest destiny on earth is undoubtedly to have a distinguished and rich individuality and in particular a good endowment of intellect, however differently such a destiny may turn out from the most brilliant. It was, therefore, a wise statement which the nineteen-year-old Queen Christina of Sweden made about Descartes with whom she had become acquainted merely through one essay and from verbal accounts and who at that time had for twenty years lived in Holland in the deepest seclusion. *Mr. Descartes est le plus heureux de tous les hommes, et sa condition me semble digne d'envie.*[17] (*Vie de Descartes*, par Baillet, Liv VII, chap. 10) Of course, as was the case with Descartes, external circumstances must be favourable to the extent of enabling a man to be master of his own life and to be satisfied therewith. Therefore Ecclesiastes 7:11 says: 'Wisdom is good with an inheritance; and by it there is profit to them that see the sun.' Whoever has been granted this lot through the favour of nature and fate will be anxious and careful to see that the inner source of his happiness remains accessible to him and for this the conditions are independence and leisure. And so he will gladly purchase these at the price of moderation and thrift, the more so as he is not, like others, dependent on the external sources of pleasure. Thus he will not be led astray by the prospects of office, money, favour, and approbation of the world into surrendering himself in order to conform to the sordid designs or bad taste of people.* When the occasion occurs, he will do what Horace suggested in his epistle to Maecenas (lib. 1, ep. 7). It is a great folly to lose the *inner* man in order to gain the *outer*, that is, to give up the whole or the greater part of one's quiet, leisure, and independence for splendour, rank, pomp, titles and honours. But this is what Goethe did; my genius has definitely drawn me in the other direction.

The truth, here discussed, that the chief source of human happiness springs from within ourselves, is also confirmed by the very correct observation of Aristotle in the *Nicomachean Ethics* (I. 7; and VII. 13, 14), namely that every pleasure presupposes some activity and hence the application of some power, and without this it cannot exist. This teaching of Aristotle that a man's happiness consists in the unimpeded exercise of his out-

---

* They achieve their welfare at the expense of their leisure; but of what use to me is welfare if for it I have to give up that which alone makes it desirable, namely my leisure?

[17] ['M. Descartes is the happiest and most fortunate of men and his condition seems to me to be most enviable.']

WHAT A MAN IS

standing ability, is also given again by Stobaeus in his description of the Peripatetic ethics (*Eclogae ethicae*, lib. II, c. 7, pp. 268–78), for example: ἐνέργειαν εἶναι τὴν εὐδαιμονίαν κατ᾽ ἀρετήν, ἐν πράξεσι προηγουμέναις κατ᾽ εὐχήν (the version in Heeren runs: *felicitatem esse functionem secundum virtutem, per actiones successus compotes*).[18] Generally in even briefer statements he explains that ἀρέτη is any supreme skill. Now the original purpose of the forces with which nature endowed man is the struggle against want and privation that beset him on all sides. When once this struggle is over, the unemployed forces then become a burden to him and so now he must *play* with them, that is, use them aimlessly, for otherwise he falls at once into the other source of human suffering, namely boredom. Thus the wealthy upper classes are primarily martyrs to this evil and Lucretius has given us a description of their pitiable condition. Even now in every great city we daily have instances of the aptness of this description:

> *Exit saepe foras magnis ex aedibus ille,*
> *Esse domi quem pertaesum est, subitoque reventat;*
> *Quippe foris nihilo melius qui sentiat esse.*
> *Currit, agens mannos, ad villam praecipitanter,*
> *Auxilium tectis quasi ferre ardentibus instans:*
> *Oscitat extemplo, tetigit quum limina villae;*
> *Aut abit in somnum gravis, atque oblivia quaerit;*
> *Aut etiam properans urbem petit, atque revisit.*[19]
>
> III. 1060–7.

In youth these gentlemen must have muscular strength and procreative power. In later years, we are left with only mental powers; but these they lack or the development thereof and the accumulated material for their activity; and their plight is pitiable. Now since the *will* is the only inexhaustible force, it is roused by a stimulation of passions, for example, by games of chance for high stakes, this truly degrading vice. But generally speaking, every unoccupied individual will choose a game for

---

[18] ['Happiness is a virtuous activity in those affairs which have the desired result.']

[19] ['Frequently he quits the large palace and hurries into the open, for the house disgusts him, until he suddenly returns because out of doors he feels no better off. Or else he gallops off to his country-house, as if it were on fire and he were hurrying to put it out. But as soon as he has crossed the threshold, he yawns with boredom or falls asleep and tries to forget himself, unless he prefers to return to the city.']

the exercise of those powers wherein he excels; it may be skittles or chess, hunting or painting, horse-racing or music, cards or poetry, heraldry or philosophy, and so on. We can even investigate the matter methodically by going to the root of all the manifestations of human force and thus to the *three physiological fundamental forces*. Accordingly, we have here to consider them in their aimless play wherein they appear as the sources of three kinds of possible pleasures. From these every man will choose the ones that suit him according as he excels in one or other of those forces. First we have the pleasures of the *power of reproduction* which consist in eating, drinking, digesting, resting, and sleeping. There are even whole nations in whom these are regarded as national pleasures. Then we have the pleasures of *irritability* which consist in walking, jumping, wrestling, dancing, fencing, riding, and athletic games of every kind, also in hunting and even conflict and war. Finally, we have the pleasures of *sensibility* which consist in observing, thinking, feeling, writing poetry, improving the mind, playing music, learning, reading, meditating, inventing, philosophizing, and so on. On the value, degree, and duration of each of these kinds of pleasure remarks of many kinds can be made which are left to the reader himself to supply. But it will be clear to everyone that, the nobler the nature of the power that conditions our pleasure, the greater this will be; for it is conditioned by the use of our own powers and our happiness consists in the frequent recurrence of our pleasure. Again no one will deny that, in this respect, sensibility, whose decided preponderance is man's superiority to the other animal species, ranks before the other two fundamental physiological forces which in an equal and even greater degree are inherent in animals. Our cognitive powers are related to sensibility; and so a preponderance thereof qualifies us for the so-called *intellectual* pleasures that consist in *knowledge*; and indeed such pleasures will be the greater, the more decided that preponderance.* A thing can gain the normal ordinary

---

* Nature advances continuously first from the mechanical and chemical action of the inorganic kingdom to the vegetable and its dull enjoyment of self, thence to the animal kingdom with the dawning of intelligence and consciousness. From feeble beginnings, she ascends by stages ever higher and in the final and greatest step reaches *man*. In his intellect, therefore, nature attains the pinnacle and goal of her productions and thus furnishes the most perfect and most difficult thing she is capable of producing. But even within the human species the intellect presents us

man's lively concern only by stirring his *will* and hence having
for him a personal interest. Now the constant excitement of the
will is at any rate not an unmixed blessing, and thus entails
pain. Card-playing, the usual occupation of 'good-society'
everywhere, is an intentional device for producing such excitement and indeed by means of such trivial interests that they can
give rise only to momentary and slight, not to permanent and
serious, pain and are accordingly to be regarded as a mere
tickling of the will.* On the other hand, the man of great
intellectual powers is capable, in fact in need, of the liveliest
interest on the path of mere *knowledge*, without any admixture
of the *will*. But this interest then puts him in a region to which

with many observable differences of degree and only extremely rarely does it
reach the highest, really eminent intelligence. This, then, in the narrower and
stricter sense is the most difficult and supreme product of nature and consequently
the rarest and most precious thing whereof the world can boast. In such an intelligence the clearest consciousness occurs and accordingly the world presents itself
more distinctly and completely than anywhere else. Therefore whoever is endowed
with such intelligence, possesses the noblest and choicest thing on earth and
accordingly has a source of pleasure compared with which all others are of little
value. From without he requires nothing but the leisure to enjoy this possession in
peace and to polish his diamond. For all other pleasures not of the intellect are of a
lower order; they all lead to movements of the will and hence to desires, hopes,
fears, and attainments, no matter in what direction. But here they cannot pass off
without pain; moreover, with attainment, disappointment more or less as a rule
occurs, whereas in the case of intellectual pleasures truth becomes ever clearer. No
pain reigns in the realm of intelligence, but all is knowledge. Now all intellectual
pleasures are accessible to everyone only by means, and thus to the extent, of his
own intelligence; for *tout l'esprit qui est au monde, est inutile à celui qui n'en a point.*
['All the intelligence in the world is useless to him who has none.' La Bruyère.]
But a real drawback which accompanies that advantage is that, in the whole of
nature, the capacity for pain is enhanced with the degree of intelligence, and thus
here reaches its highest.
  * At bottom, *vulgarity* consists in the fact that in consciousness willing so completely outweighs knowing that knowledge appears only in the service of the will.
Where such service does not demand knowledge and so when there are no motives
great or small, knowledge ceases entirely and consequently the result is a complete
absence of ideas. Now willing without knowledge is the commonest thing there is.
Every blockhead has it and shows it at any rate when he falls down. This state,
therefore, constitutes vulgarity in which are left only the organs of sense and the
small intellectual activity required for apprehending their data. In consequence of
this, the vulgar man is constantly open to every impression and thus instantly
perceives all that goes on around him, so that the least sound and every circumstance,
even the most trivial, at once rouses his attention, just as they do that of the animals.
This entire state of mind reveals itself in his face and the whole of his appearance;
and the result is that vulgar look whose impression is the more repulsive when, as is
often the case, the will that here completely occupies consciousness is base, egoistical, and thoroughly bad.

pain is essentially foreign; it places him so to speak, in the atmosphere where the gods live easily and serenely, θεῶν ῥεῖα ξωόντων.[20] Accordingly the life of the masses is passed in dullness since all their thoughts and desires are directed entirely to the petty interests of personal welfare and thus to wretchedness and misery in all its forms. For this reason, intolerable boredom befalls them as soon as they are no longer occupied with those aims and they are now thrown back on themselves, for only the fierce fire of passion can stir into action the dull and indolent masses. On the other hand, the existence of the man who is endowed with outstanding intellectual powers is rich in ideas and full of life and meaning. Worthy and interesting objects occupy him as soon as he is permitted to devote himself to them, and he bears within himself a source of the noblest pleasures. Stimulation from without comes to him from the works of nature and the contemplation of human affairs and then from the many and varied achievements of the most highly gifted of all ages and lands; only such a man is really capable of thoroughly enjoying those things for he alone can fully understand and feel them. Accordingly, for him those highly gifted men have actually lived; to him they have really appealed; whereas the rest as casual hearers only half-understand something or other. But naturally through all this, the man of intelligence has one need more than the others, namely to learn, to see, to study, to meditate, to practise, and consequently the need for leisure. But because, as Voltaire rightly remarks, *il n'est de vrais plaisirs qu'avec de vrais besoins*,[21] so is this need the condition for the accessibility to him of pleasures that are denied to others. Indeed, even when they are surrounded by the beauties of nature and art and by intellectual works of all kinds, such things at bottom are to them only what courtesans are to a greybeard. As a result of this, a man so gifted leads two lives, a personal and an intellectual. For him the latter gradually becomes the real end to which the former is regarded merely as a means, whereas for the rest this shallow empty and troubled existence must be regarded as an end in itself. The man mentally gifted will, therefore, prefer to concern himself with that intellectual life. Through a constant extension of his

---

[20] ['Of the gods who live lightly'.]
[21] ['There are no true pleasures without true needs.']

insight and knowledge, such a life obtains cohesion, steady enhancement, totality, and perfection, becoming ever more complete like a slowly maturing work of art. Compared with it, the merely practical lives of others cut a sorry figure, devoted as they are merely to personal welfare and capable of an increase in length but not in depth. Yet, as I have said, to those others such a life must be regarded as an end in itself, whereas to the man of intellect it is only a means.

When our real practical life is not moved by passions, it is tedious and humdrum; but when it is so moved, it becomes painful. Therefore they alone are fortunate to whom there has been granted an excess of intellect over that required in the service of their will. For with this they lead, in addition to their actual life, an intellectual one that always occupies and entertains them *painlessly* yet vividly. Mere *leisure*, that is, intellect *unoccupied* in the service of the will, is not sufficient; but an actual excess of *power* is required, for this alone enables a man to undertake a purely mental occupation that does not serve the will. On the contrary, *otium sine litteris mors est et hominis vivi sepultura*[22] (Seneca, *Epistulae*, 82). Now according as this excess is small or great, there are innumerable degrees of that intellectual life from the mere collection and description of insects, birds, minerals, or coins to the highest achievements of poetry and philosophy. Such an intellectual life, however, is a protection not only against boredom, but also against the pernicious effects thereof. Thus it becomes a safeguard against bad company and the many dangers, misfortunes, losses, and extravagances in which we land when we seek our happiness entirely in the outside world. Thus, for example, my philosophy has never brought me in anything, but it has spared me many a loss.

The normal man, on the other hand, as regards the pleasures of his life, relies on things that are *outside him* and thus on possessions, rank, wife and children, friends, society, and so on; these are the props of his life's happiness. It therefore collapses when he loses such things or is disillusioned by them. We may express this relation by saying that his centre of gravity lies *outside him*. For this reason his wishes and whims are always changing; if he has the means, he will buy country-houses or

[22] ['Leisure without literature is death; it is for man like being buried alive.']

horses, give parties, or travel; but generally speaking, he will indulge in great luxury, just because he seeks satisfaction *from without* in all kinds of things. He is like a man who is debilitated and hopes through soups and medicines to recover his health and strength whose true source is his own vital force. Before going at once to the other extreme, let us compare him with a man whose mental powers are not exactly outstanding, but yet exceed the normal narrow limit. We then see such a man as an amateur practising a fine art, or pursuing some branch of science such as botany, mineralogy, physics, astronomy, history, and so on, and immediately finding most of his pleasure and deriving recreation therefrom, when those outside sources dry up or no longer satisfy him. To this extent, we can say that his centre of gravity already lies partly *within himself*. Nevertheless, since mere dilettantism in art is still far removed from creative ability and mere scientific knowledge stops at the mutual relations of phenomena, the ordinary man is unable to become wholly absorbed therein; his whole nature cannot be thoroughly imbued with them and thus his existence cannot be so intimately associated with them that he would lose all interest in everything else. This is reserved only for supreme intellectual eminence which is usually described by the name of genius; for this alone takes existence and the nature of things entirely and absolutely as its theme. It will then endeavour to express its profound comprehension of these things in accordance with its particular tendency, either through art, poetry, or philosophy. And so only to such a man is the undisturbed preoccupation with himself, his ideas and works, an urgent necessity; solitude is welcome, leisure is the greatest blessing, and everything else is superfluous; in fact, when it exists it is often only a burden. Thus only of such a man can we say that his centre of gravity is *entirely within himself*. We can even explain from this why men of this nature, who are exceedingly rare, do not show, even with the best character, that intimate and immense interest in friends, family, and the community at large, of which many others are capable. For in the last resort, they can put up with the loss of everything else, if only they have themselves. Accordingly, there is in them an element of isolation which is the more effective, as others never really satisfy them completely. And so they cannot look on these as entirely their equals;

in fact, as the difference of each and all is always making itself felt, they gradually grow accustomed to moving among men as if they were beings of a different order, and, in their thoughts about people, to making use of the word *they* instead of *we*. Our moral virtues benefit mainly other people; intellectual virtues, on the other hand, benefit primarily ourselves; therefore the former make us universally popular, the latter unpopular.

Now from this point of view, the man who is richly endowed by nature in an intellectual respect, appears to be the happiest, so surely does the subjective lie nearer to us than the objective; for the effect of the latter, whatever its nature, is invariably brought about by the former and is therefore only secondary. This is also testified by the fine verse:

Πλοῦτος ὁ τῆς ψυχῆς πλοῦτος μόνος ἐστὶν ἀληθής,
T' ἄλλα δ' ἔχει ἄτην πλείονα τῶν κτεάνων.²³
Lucian, *Epigrams*, 12.

Such an inwardly wealthy man requires nothing from without except a negative gift, namely leisure to be able to cultivate and develop his intellectual faculties and to enjoy that inner wealth. Thus he wants permission simply to be entirely himself throughout his life, every day and every hour. If a man is destined to impress on the whole human race the mark of his mind, he has only one measure of happiness or unhappiness, namely to be able wholly to develop his abilities and to complete his works, or to be prevented from so doing. For him everything else is of no importance. Accordingly, we see eminent minds of all ages attaching the greatest value to leisure. For every man's leisure is as valuable as he is himself. Δοκεῖ δὲ ἡ εὐδαιμονία ἐν τῇ σχολῇ εἶναι (*videtur beatitudo in otio esse sita*)²⁴ says Aristotle (*Nicomachean Ethics*. x. 7), and Diogenes Laërtius (II.5.31) reports that Σωκράτης ἐπῄνει σχολήν, ὡς κάλλιστον κτημάτων (*Socrates otium ut possessionum omnium pulcherrimam laudabat*).²⁵ In keeping with this, Aristotle (*Nicomachean Ethics*, x. 7, 8, 9) declares the philosophical life to be the happiest. Even what he says in the *Politics* (IV. 11) is relevant: τόν εὐδαίμονα βίον εἶναι τόν κατ' ἀρετὴν ἀνεμπόδιστον, which properly translated states: 'To be able

²³ ['True wealth is only the inner wealth of the soul; Everything else brings more trouble than advantage.']
²⁴ ['Happiness appears to consist in leisure.']
²⁵ ['Socrates prized leisure as the fairest of all possessions.']

without hindrance to exercise his pre-eminent quality, whatever its nature, is real happiness' and thus agrees with Goethe's words in *Wilhelm Meister*: 'Whoever is born with a talent for a talent discovers therein his finest existence.' Now the possession of leisure is foreign not only to man's customary fate, but also to his usual nature, for his natural destiny is to spend his time providing what is necessary for his own and his family's existence. He is a son of want and privation, not a free intelligence. Accordingly, leisure soon becomes for him a burden and indeed ultimately a great affliction, if he is unable to employ his time by means of imaginary and fictitious aims of all kinds through every form of game, pastime, and hobby. For the same reason, it also brings him danger, since *difficilis in otio quies*[26] is a true saying. On the other hand, a measure of intellect that goes far beyond the normal is likewise abnormal and therefore unnatural. Nevertheless, when once it exists, then for the happiness of the man so gifted just that leisure is needed which others find either so burdensome or so pernicious, for without it he will be a Pegasus under the yoke and consequently unhappy. Now if these two unnatural circumstances, external and internal, coincide, then it is most fortunate, for the man so favoured will now lead a life of a higher order, that of one who is exempt from the two opposite sources of human suffering, want and boredom, from the anxious business of earning a living and the inability to endure leisure (i.e. free existence itself). A man escapes these two evils only by their being mutually neutralized and eliminated.

On the other hand, against all this, we must consider the fact that great intellectual gifts, in consequence of predominant nervous activity, produce a very much enhanced sensitiveness to pain in every form. Further, the passionate temperament that conditions such gifts, and at the same time the greater vividness and completeness of all images and conceptions inseparable therefrom, produce an incomparably greater intensity of the emotions that are thereby stirred, whilst in general there are more painful than pleasant emotions. Finally, great intellectual gifts estrange their possessor from the rest of mankind and its activities. For the more he has in himself, the less is he able to find in others, and the hundred things in which they take a great

[26] ['It is difficult to keep quiet when one has nothing to do.']

WHAT A MAN IS 343

delight are to him shallow and insipid. Perhaps in this way, the law of compensation which everywhere asserts itself, remains in force even here. Indeed, it has been often enough maintained, and not without plausibility, that the man of the most limited intelligence is at bottom the happiest, although no one may envy him his luck. I do not wish to forestall the reader in a definite decision on the matter, the less so as even Sophocles has made two diametrically opposite statements on the subject:

> Πολλῷ τὸ φρονεῖν εὐδαιμονίας πρῶτον ὑπάρχει.
> (*Sapere longe prima felicitatis pars est.*)[27]
>
> Antigone, 1328.

and again:

> Ἐν τῷ φρονεῖν γὰρ μηδὲν ἥδιστος βίος.
> (*Nihil cogitantium jucundissima vita est.*)[28]
>
> Ajax, 550.

The philosophers of the Old Testament are just as much at variance with one another. Thus: 'The life of a fool is worse than death!' τοῦ γὰρ μωροῦ ὑπὲρ θανάτου ζωὴ πονηρά, Jesus ben Sirach 12:12); and: 'In much wisdom is much grief; And he that increaseth knowledge increaseth sorrow.' (ὁ προστιθεὶς γνῶσιν, προσθήσει ἄλγημα, Ecclesiastes 1:18). However, I will not omit to mention here that the man who *has no intellectual needs* in consequence of the strictly normal and scanty measure of his intellectual powers, is really what is described as a *Philistine*. It is an expression exclusively peculiar to the German language and came from the universities; but it was afterwards used in a higher sense, although still always analogous to the original meaning as denoting the opposite of the son of the Muses. Thus a Philistine is and remains the ἄμουσος ἀνήρ.[29] Now it is true that, from a higher point of view, I should state the definition of Philistine so as to cover those who are always most seriously concerned with a reality that is no reality. But such a definition would be transcendental and not appropriate to the popular point of view which I have adopted in this essay; and so perhaps it would not be thoroughly understood by every reader. On the other hand, the first definition more readily

---

[27] ['To be intelligent is the main part of happiness.']
[28] ['The most agreeable life consists in a lack of intelligence.']
[29] ['A man forsaken of the Muses'.]

admits of a special elucidation and adequately indicates the essence of the matter, the root of all those qualities that characterize the *Philistine*. Accordingly, he is a man *without intellectual needs*. Now it follows from this that, *as regards himself*, he is left without any intellectual *pleasures* in accordance with the principle, already mentioned, *il n'est de vrais plaisirs qu'avec de vrais besoins.*[30] His existence is not animated by any keen desire for knowledge and insight for their own sake, or by any desire for really aesthetic pleasures which is so entirely akin to it. If, however, any pleasures of this kind are forced on him by fashion or authority, he will dispose of them as briefly as possible as a kind of compulsory labour. For him real pleasures are only those of the senses whereby he indemnifies himself. Accordingly, oysters and champagne are the acme of his existence, and the purpose of his life is to procure for himself everything that contributes to bodily welfare. He is happy enough when this causes him a lot of trouble. For if those good things are heaped on him in advance, he will inevitably lapse into boredom against which all possible means are tried, such as dancing, the theatre, society, card-playing, games of chance, horses, women, drinking, travelling, and so on. And yet all these are not enough to ward off boredom where intellectual pleasures are rendered impossible by a lack of intellectual needs. Thus a peculiar characteristic of the Philistine is a dull dry seriousness akin to that of animals. Nothing delights him, nothing excites him, nothing gains his interest; for sensual pleasures are soon exhausted and society consisting of such Philistines soon becomes boring; in the end card-playing becomes wearisome. At all events, he is still left with the pleasures of vanity to be enjoyed in his own way. These consist in his excelling in wealth, rank, or influence and power others by whom he is then honoured; or they consist in his going about at any rate with those who have a surplus of such things and thus in sunning himself in their reflected splendour (a snob). From the fundamental nature of the Philistine I have just mentioned, it follows that, *in regard to others*, as he has no intellectual but only physical needs, he will seek those who are capable of satisfying the latter not the former. And so of all the demands he makes on others the very smallest will be that of any outstanding intellectual abilities.

[30] ['There are no true pleasures without true needs.']

On the contrary, when he comes across these they will excite his antipathy and even hatred. For here he has a hateful feeling of inferiority and also a dull secret envy which he most carefully attempts to conceal even from himself; but in this way, it grows sometimes into a feeling of secret rage and rancour. Therefore it will never occur to him to assess his own esteem and respect in accordance with such qualities, but they will remain exclusively reserved for rank and wealth, power and influence, as being in his eyes the only real advantages to excel in which is also his desire. But all this follows from his being a man *without intellectual needs*.

A great affliction of all Philistines is that *idealities* afford them no entertainment, but to escape from boredom they are always in need of *realities*. Thus the latter are soon exhausted where, instead of entertaining, they weary us; moreover they entail all kinds of evil and harm. Idealities, on the other hand, are inexhaustible and in themselves harmless and innocuous.

In all these remarks about personal qualities that contribute to our happiness, I have been concerned mainly with those that are physical and intellectual. Now the way in which moral excellence also contributes directly to our happiness has already been discussed by me in my prize-essay 'On the Basis of Ethics', § 22, to which I therefore refer the reader.

CHAPTER III

What a Man has

EPICURUS, the great teacher of happiness, has correctly and finely divided human needs into three classes. First there are the natural and necessary needs which, if they are not satisfied, cause pain. Consequently, they are only *victus et amictus*[1] and are easy to satisfy. Then we have those that are natural yet not necessary, that is, the needs for sexual satisfaction, although in the account of Laërtius Epicurus does not state this; (generally I here reproduce his teaching in a somewhat better and more finished form). These needs are more difficult to satisfy. Finally, there are those that are neither natural nor necessary, the needs for luxury, extravagance, pomp, and splendour, which are without end and very difficult to satisfy. (See Diogenes Laërtius, lib. x, c. 27, § 149, also § 127, and Cicero, *De finibus*, lib. I, c. 14 and 16.)

It is difficult, if not impossible, to define the limit of our reasonable desires in respect of possessions. For a man's satisfaction in regard to this rests not on an absolute but a merely relative amount, namely the relation between his claims and his possessions. Therefore, to consider possessions alone is just as meaningless as to take the numerator of a fraction without the denominator. A man to whom it has never occurred to claim certain good things, does not miss them at all and is perfectly satisfied without them; whereas another, who possesses a hundred times more than he, feels unhappy because he lacks the very thing he is claiming. In this respect, every man also has his own horizon of what is possible and attainable for him and his claims extend as far as this. When any object lying within this horizon presents itself so that he can count on its attainment, he feels happy; on the other hand, he feels unhappy when difficulties appear and deprive him of the prospect. What lies beyond this horizon has no effect on him at all. Thus the great possessions of the rich do not worry the poor; on the other hand,

---

[1] ['Food and clothing'.]

if the wealthy man's plans fail, he is not consoled by the many things he already possesses. Wealth is like sea-water; the more we drink, the thirstier we become; and the same is true of fame. After the loss of wealth or position, our habitual frame of mind proves to be not very different from what is was previously, when once the first grief and sorrow are overcome. The reason for this is that, after fate has reduced the amount of our possessions, we ourselves now diminish to an equal extent that of our claims. In the case of a misfortune, however, this operation is really painful; after it has been performed, the pain becomes less and less and in the end is no longer felt; the wound has healed up. Conversely, in the case of good fortune, our claims are pressed ever higher and are extended; here is to be found the delight. But it lasts only until this operation is entirely performed. We become accustomed to the increased measure of our claims and are indifferent to the possessions that correspond to it. The passage from Homer, *Odyssey*, XVIII. 130–7, states this and the last two lines are:

Τοῖος γὰρ νόος ἐστὶν ἐπιχθονίων ἀνθρώπων,
Οἶον ἐπ' ἦμαρ ἄγῃσι πατὴρ ἀνδρῶν τε, θεῶν τε.[2]

The source of our dissatisfaction lies in our constantly renewed attempts to press the amount of our claims ever higher, whilst the other factor remains fixed and prevents this from happening.

With a race so destitute and full of needs as the human, it is not surprising that *wealth* is esteemed, indeed worshipped, more highly and sincerely than anything else, and even the power merely as a means to wealth. It should also not surprise us that, for the purpose of acquiring gain, everything else is pushed aside or thrown overboard, for example, as is philosophy by the professors of philosophy.

People are often reproached because their desires are directed mainly to money and they are fonder of it than of anything else. Yet it is natural and even inevitable for them to love that which, as an untiring Proteus, is ready at any moment to convert itself into the particular object of our fickle desires and manifold needs. Thus every other blessing can satisfy only *one* desire and *one* need; for instance, food is good only for the hungry, wine

---

[2] ['For the feelings of earthly mortals are like the day that was granted by the father of gods and men.']

for the healthy, medicine for the sick, a fur coat for winter, women for youth, and so on. Consequently, all these are only ἀγαθὰ πρός τι,[3] that is to say, only relatively good. Money alone is the absolutely good thing because it meets not merely one need *in concreto*, but needs generally *in abstracto*.

Means at our disposal should be regarded as a bulwark against the many evils and misfortunes that can occur. We should not regard such wealth as a permission or even an obligation to procure for ourselves the pleasures of the world. People who originally have no means but are ultimately able to earn a great deal, through whatever talents they may possess, almost always come to think that these are permanent capital and that what they gain through them is interest. Accordingly, they do not put aside a part of their earnings to form a permanent capital, but spend their money as fast as they earn it. But they are then often reduced to poverty because their earnings decrease or come to an end after their talent, which was of a transitory nature, is exhausted, as happens, for example, in the case of almost all the fine arts; or because it could be brought to bear only under a particular set of circumstances that has ceased to exist. Workmen may always act in the way I have mentioned, because their capacity for output is not easily lost and is replaced by the energy of their comrades, and because the things they make are objects in demand and always find a market; hence the proverb 'a trade in hand finds gold in every land' is quite right. However, such is not the case with artists and *virtuosi* of every kind and this is precisely the reason why they are better paid. Therefore what they earn should become their capital, whereas they recklessly regard it as mere interest and thus end in ruin. On the other hand, those who possess inherited wealth at least know at once and quite correctly what is capital and what interest. And so most of them will endeavour to secure their capital and in no case will they encroach on it; in fact, where possible, they will put by at least an eighth of the interest to meet future contingencies; thus they usually remain well off. All these remarks do not apply to business men for whom money itself is the means to further gain, the tools and implements, so to speak. Therefore even when the money is earned entirely through their own efforts, they try to preserve

[3] ['Good things for a definite purpose'.]

and increase it by making the best use thereof. Accordingly, in no class is wealth so thoroughly at home as in the commercial.

Generally we shall find as a rule that those who have already experienced real want and privation are much less afraid thereof and so are more inclined to extravagance than those who know poverty only from hearsay. The former are those who have passed fairly rapidly from poverty to affluence through some piece of good fortune or special talents, no matter of what kind; the latter, on the other hand, are those who have been born well off and have remained so, and who are usually more concerned about the future and are thus more thrifty than the former. From this it might be inferred that, when viewed from a distance, poverty is not so bad as it seems. Yet perhaps the true reason might be that, to the man born in a position of wealth, this appears to be something indispensable, the element of the only possible existence, like air. He therefore guards it as he guards his life and so is usually orderly, tidy, prudent, and thrifty. On the other hand, to the man born in poverty, this seems to be the natural state; but wealth, that is subsequently inherited in some way, is regarded as something superfluous, as merely useful to be enjoyed and squandered. For when it has gone, he manages just as well without it as he did previously, and he is rid of an anxiety. Then things are as Shakespeare says in *Henry VI*, Pt. III, Act I, Sc. 4:

> The adage must be verified
> That beggars mounted run their horse to death.

Moreover, there is the fact that such people carry in their hearts rather than in their heads a firm and excessive confidence partly in fate and partly in their own resources that have already rescued them from need and poverty. Therefore, unlike those who are born wealthy, they do not regard the shallows of poverty as bottomless, but think that, by kicking against the bottom, they will be again lifted up. From this peculiar human trait we can also explain why women who were poor girls are very often more pretentious and extravagant than are those who have brought their husbands a rich dowry. For in most cases wealthy girls not only bring a dowry, but also show more keenness and indeed hereditary tendency to preserve it than do poor girls. If, however, anyone wishes to assert the contrary, he will find authority for his view in Ariosto's first satire. On the other hand, Dr. Johnson agrees with my opinion: 'A woman of fortune being used to the handling of money, spends it judiciously; but a woman who gets the command of money for the first time upon her marriage, has such a gusto in spending it, that she throws it away with great profusion.' (Boswell, *Life of Johnson, ann.* 1776, *aetat.* 67.) In any case, however, I would like to advise those marrying poor girls to allow them to inherit not the capital but only an annuity, and to take special care that the children's fortune does not fall into their hands.

I certainly do not think that I am doing anything unworthy of my pen in here recommending that one should be careful to preserve what has been earned and inherited. For to possess at the outset so much that we can live comfortably, even if only for our own person and without a family, and can live really independently, that is, without working, is a priceless advantage. For it means exemption and immunity from the poverty and trouble attaching to the life of man, and thus emancipation from universal drudgery, that natural lot of earthly mortals. Only under this favour and patronage of fate is a man born truly free; for only so is he really *sui juris*,⁴ master of his own time and powers, and is able to say every morning 'The day is mine'. And for the very same reason, the difference between the man with a thousand a year and one with a hundred is infinitely less than that between the former and the man who has nothing. But inherited wealth attains its highest value when it has come to the man who is endowed with mental powers of a high order and who pursues activities that are hardly compatible with earning money. For then he is doubly endowed by fate and can now live for his genius; but in this way, he will pay a hundredfold his debt to mankind by achieving what no other could do and by producing something that contributes to the good of all and also redounds to their honour. Again, another in such a favourable position will deserve well of humanity through his philanthropic activities. On the other hand, the man with inherited wealth who achieves none of these things, even only partially or tentatively, and who does not even open up the possibility at least of advancing some branch of knowledge by thoroughly studying it, is a mere idler and a contemptible

⁴ ['His own master'.]

loafer. He will not be happy, for the exemption from want delivers him into the hands of boredom, that other pole of human misery, which torments him so much that he would have been much happier if povery and privation had given him something to do. But this very boredom will soon lead him into extravagances which rob him of that advantage whereof he was unworthy. Very many actually find themselves in want simply because they spent money when they had it, merely to procure for themselves momentary relief from the boredom that oppressed them.

Now it is quite another matter if our object is to reach a high position in the service of the State where favour, friends, and connections must be obtained so that we may thereby gain promotion step by step possibly even to the highest posts. Here at bottom it is better to be cast into the world without any money. If a man is an absolutely poor wretch, it will specially redound to his real advantage when he is not of noble birth, but is, on the other hand, endowed with some talent. For what everyone looks for and likes best is the inferiority of the other man, even in mere conversation, let alone in the service of the State. Now it is only a poor devil who is convinced of and impressed with his own complete, profound, positive, and general inferiority, and his utter insignificance and worthlessness to the extent that is here demanded. Accordingly, he alone keeps on bowing often enough and his bows reach a full ninety degrees; he alone puts up with and smiles at everything; he alone knows the entire worthlessness of merits; he alone in a loud voice or even in heavy type openly and publicly praises as masterpieces the literary amateurisms of those who are placed over him or are otherwise in a position of influence; he alone knows how to beg; consequently, he alone can become at times, and so in his youth, even an exponent of that hidden truth that is revealed to us by Goethe in these words:

> Let none complain
> Of what is base and mean;
> For 'tis this that sways the world
> Whatever may be said to you.
> *Westöstlicher Diwan.*

On the other hand, the man who originally has enough to live on will often have an independent turn of mind; he is accustomed to go about *tête levée*;[5] he has not learnt all those arts of the beggar. Perhaps he even boasts of a few talents, but he should realize how inadequate these are in face of the *médiocre et rampant*.[6] In the end, he is quite capable of observing the inferiority of those over him; and if in addition he now receives insults and indignities, he becomes refractory and shy. This is not the way to get on in the world. On the contrary, he may ultimately say with the bold Voltaire: *Nous n'avons que deux jours à vivre: ce n'est pas la peine de les passer à ramper sous des coquins méprisables*.[7] Incidentally, the term *coquin méprisable* is alas applicable to a devilish number of people in this world. We see, therefore, that Juvenal's words

> *Haud facile emergunt, quorum virtutibus obstat*
> *Res angusta domi*,[8]

apply more to the career of art and literature than to that of worldlings.

I have not included wife and family in *what a man has*, for they have him rather than he has them. Friends could be more readily included in what he has, yet even here the possessor must be to the same extent the possession of the other man.

[5] ['With head erect'.]
[6] ['Mediocre and cringing'.]
[7] ['We have only two days to live; it is not worth our while to spend them in grovelling before contemptible rogues.']
[8] ['It is difficult to rise where the cramped conditions in the house prevent the development of one's powers.' (*Satires*, iii.164.)]

CHAPTER IV

What a Man represents

THIS, in other words, what we are in the opinion of others, is generally much overrated in consequence of a peculiar weakness of our nature; although the slightest reflection could tell us that, in itself, it is not essential to our happiness. Accordingly, it is difficult to explain why everyone is at heart very pleased whenever he sees in others signs of a favourable opinion and his vanity is in some way flattered. If a cat is stroked it purrs; and just as inevitably if a man is praised sweet rapture and delight are reflected in his face; and indeed in the sphere of his pretensions the praise may be a palpable lie. Signs of other people's approbation often console him for real misfortune or for the scantiness with which the other two sources of our happiness, previously discussed, flow for him. Conversely it is astonishing how infallibly he is annoyed and often deeply hurt by every injury to his ambition in any sense, degree, or circumstance, and by any disdain, disrespect, or slight. In so far as the feeling of honour rests on this peculiar characteristic, it may have salutary effects on the good conduct of many as a substitute for their morality; but on the man's own *happiness* and above all on the peace of mind and independence essential thereto, its effect is more disturbing and detrimental than beneficial. Therefore, from our point of view, it is advisable to set limits to this characteristic and to moderate as much as possible, through careful consideration and correct assessment of the value of good things, that great susceptibility to the opinions of other people, not only where it is flattered, but also where it is injured, for both hang by the same thread. Otherwise we remain the slave of what other people appear to think:

> *Sic leve, sic parvum est, animum quod laudis avarum*
> *Subruit ac reficit.*[1]

Accordingly, a correct comparison of the value of what we are

---

[1] ['How trifling and insignificant is that which depresses or elates the man who thirsts for praise!' (Horace, *Epistles*, II. I. 179.)]

in and by ourselves with what we are in the eyes *of others* will
greatly contribute to our happiness. Belonging to the former is
everything that fills up the whole time of our existence, its
inner content and consequently every blessing that was considered by us in the two chapters 'what a man is' and 'what a
man has'. For the place wherein all this has its sphere of
activity is our own consciousness. On the other hand, the place
of what we are *for others* is their consciousness; it is the kind of
figure in which we appear in that consciousness together with
the notions and concepts that are applied to it.* Now this is
something that certainly does not directly exist for us but only
indirectly, namely in so far as the behaviour of others towards
us is thereby determined. And this is also taken into consideration only in so far as it influences anything whereby what
we are *in and by ourselves* can be modified. Besides, what goes on
in the consciousness of others is as such a matter of indifference
to us; and to it we shall gradually become indifferent when we
acquire an adequate knowledge of the superficial and futile
nature of the thoughts in the heads of most people, of the
narrowness of their views, of the paltriness of their sentiments,
of the perversity of their opinions, and of the number of their
errors. We shall also become indifferent to the opinions of
others when from our own experience we learn with what
disrespect one man occasionally speaks of another as soon as he
no longer has to fear him or thinks that what he says will not
come to the ears of the other man; but we shall become
indifferent especially after we have once heard how half a
dozen blockheads speak with disdain about the greatest man.
We shall then see that whoever attaches much value to the
opinions of others pays them too much honour.

In any case, that man is in a pretty poor way who does not
find his happiness in the two classes of blessings already considered, but has to look for it in the third, thus in what he is not
in reality but in the minds of others. For in general, the basis
of our whole being, and therefore of our happiness, is our
animal nature; and so health is the most essential factor for our
welfare and after it come the means for maintaining ourselves

---

* In their brilliance, their pomp and splendour, their show and magnificence
of every kind, the highest in the land can say: 'Our happiness lies entirely outside
ourselves; its place is in the heads of others.'

and thus for having a livelihood that is free from care. Honour, pomp, rank, and reputation, however much value many of us may attach to them, cannot compete with or replace those essential blessings for which, in case of necessity, they would unquestionably be given up. For this reason, it will contribute to our happiness if at times we reach the simple view that everyone lives primarily and actually within his own skin, not in the opinion of others, and that accordingly our real and personal condition, as determined by health, temperament, abilities, income, wife, family, friends, dwelling-place, and so on, is a hundred times more important to our happiness than what others are pleased to make of us. The opposite notion will make us unhappy. If it is emphatically exclaimed that honour is dearer than life itself, this really means that existence and well-being are nothing and the real thing is what others think of us. At all events, the statement can be regarded as a hyperbole whose basis is the prosaic truth that honour, that is, other people's opinion of us, is often absolutely necessary for us to live and make our way in the world. I shall later return to this. On the other hand, when we see how almost everything, assiduously sought by people throughout their lives with restless energy and at the cost of a thousand dangers and hardships, has as its ultimate object the enhancement of themselves in the opinion of others; thus when we see how they strive not only for offices, titles, and decorations, but also for wealth, and even science* and art, basically and mainly for the same reason, and how the greater respect of others is the ultimate goal to which they work, then this alas merely shows us the magnitude of human folly. To set too high a value on the opinion of others is an erroneous idea that prevails everywhere. Now it may be rooted in our nature itself or may have arisen in consequence of society and civilization. In any case, it exerts on all our actions an influence that is wholly immoderate and inimical to our happiness. We can follow it from the anxious and slavish regard for the *qu'en dira-t-on*[2] to the case where Virginius plunges the dagger into his daughter's heart, or where, for posthumous fame, a man is induced to sacrifice peace, wealth,

---

* *Scire tuum nihil est, nisi te scire hoc sciat alter.* ['What you know is worthless, unless others also know that you know it.']

[2] ['What will people say?']

health, and even life itself. This erroneous idea certainly offers a convenient handle to the man who has to control or otherwise direct people; and so, in every scheme for training humanity, instructions for maintaining and strengthening the feeling of honour occupy a prominent place. But it is quite a different matter as regards a man's own happiness that we intend here to consider; on the contrary, one should be dissuaded from placing too high a value on the opinion of others. Daily experience, however, tells us that this is done and that most people attach the highest importance precisely to what others think of them. They are more concerned about this than about what immediately exists for them because it occurs *in their own consciousness*. Accordingly, they reverse the natural order of things and the opinion of others seems to them to be the real part of their existence, their own consciousness being merely the ideal part. They therefore make what is derived and secondary the main issue and the picture of their true nature in the minds of others is nearer to their hearts than is this true nature itself. Consequently, this direct regard for that which certainly does not exist directly for us is that folly which has been called *vanity, vanitas,* in order to indicate the empty and insubstantial nature of this striving. It is also easy to see from the above remarks that vanity, like avarice, causes us to forget the end in the means.

In fact, the value we attach to the opinion of others and our constant concern in respect thereof exceed almost every reasonable expectation, so that it can be regarded as a kind of mania that is widespread or rather inborn. In everything we do or omit to do, almost the first thing we consider is the opinion of other people and, if we examine the matter more closely, we shall see that almost half the worries and anxieties we have ever experienced have arisen from our concern about it. For it is at the root of all our self-esteem that is so often mortified because it is so morbidly sensitive, of all our vanities and pretensions, and also of our boasting and ostentation. Without this concern and craze, there would be hardly a tithe of the luxury that exists. Pride in every form, *point d'honneur*, and *puntiglio*, however varied their sphere and nature, are due to this opinion of others, and what sacrifices it often demands! It shows itself even in the child and then at every age, yet most strongly in old age because when the capacity for sensual pleasures fails, vanity and pride have only to share their dominion with avarice. It can be most clearly observed in the French in whom it is quite endemic and often becomes the absurdest ambition, the most ludicrous national vanity, and the most shameless boasting. But then in this way they defeat their own efforts, for they have been made fun of by other nations and nicknamed *la grande nation.* Now to furnish a special illustration of the perverse nature of that excessive concern about the opinion of others, a really superlative example may here be given of that folly that is rooted in human nature. Through the striking effect of the coincidence of the circumstances with the appropriate character, it is suitable to a rare degree, for in it we are able wholly to estimate the strength of this very strange motive. It is the following passage that comes from a detailed report of the execution of Thomas Wix which had just taken place, and it appeared in *The Times* of 31 March 1846. Wix, a journeyman, had out of revenge murdered his master. 'On the morning fixed for the execution, the rev. ordinary was early in attendance upon him, but Wix, beyond a quiet demeanour, betrayed no interest in his ministrations, appearing to feel anxious only to acquit himself bravely before the spectators of his ignominious end.—This he succeeded in doing. In the procession Wix fell into his proper place with alacrity, and, as he entered the chapel-yard, remarked, sufficiently loud to be heard by several persons near him, "Now, then, as Dr. Dodd said, I shall soon know the grand secret." On reaching the scaffold, the miserable wretch mounted the drop without the slightest assistance, and when he got to the centre, he bowed to the spectators twice, a proceeding which called forth a tremendous cheer from the degraded crowd beneath.' This is an excellent example of a man with death in its most terrible form before his eyes and eternity behind it, not caring about anything except the impression he would make on a crowd of gapers and the opinion that would remain in their minds! And indeed, in the same year, Lecomte in France was executed for an attempt on the king's life. At the trial he was annoyed mainly because he could not appear in decent attire before the Chamber of Peers; and even at his execution his main worry was that he had not been allowed to shave beforehand. Even in former times, it was just the same, as is seen from what Mateo Alemán says in the introduction (*declaracion*) to his famous novel, *Guzman de Alfarache*, that many infatuated criminals used their last hours that should have been devoted exclusively to the salvation of their souls, for the preparation and committing to memory of a short sermon that they intended to deliver on the steps of the gallows. Yet in such characteristics we can see a reflection of ourselves, for extreme cases always give us the clearest illustration. The anxieties of all of us, our worries, vexations, bothers, troubles, fears, exertions, and so on, are really concerned with someone else's opinion, perhaps in the majority of cases, and are just as absurd as is the behaviour of those miserable sinners. For the most part, our envy and hatred also spring from the same root.

Now it is obvious that our happiness, resting as it does mainly on peace of mind and contentment, could scarcely be better promoted than by limiting and moderating these motives to reasonable proportions that would possibly be a fiftieth of what they are at present, and thus by extracting from our flesh this thorn that is always causing us pain. Yet this is very difficult, for we are concerned with a natural and innate perversity. Tacitus says: *Etiam sapientibus cupido gloriae novissima exuitur*[3] (*Historiae*, iv. 6). The only way to be rid of this universal folly is clearly to recognize it as such and for this purpose to realize how utterly false, perverse, erroneous, and absurd most of the opinions usually are in men's minds, which are, therefore, in themselves not worth considering. Moreover, other people's opinions can in most cases and things have little real influence on us. Again, such opinions generally are so unfavourable that almost everyone would worry himself to death if he heard all that was said about him or the tone in which people spoke of him. Finally, even honour itself is only of indirect not direct value. If we succeeded in such a conversion from this universal folly, the result would be an incredibly great increase in our peace of mind and cheerfulness, likewise a firmer and more positive demeanour, and generally a more natural and un-affected attitude. The exceedingly beneficial influence a retired mode of life has on our peace of mind is due mainly to the fact that we thereby escape having to live constantly in the

[3] ['The thirst for fame is the last thing of all to be laid aside by wise men.']

sight of others and consequently having always to take into consideration the opinions they happen to have; it restores to a man his true self. Similarly, we should avoid a great deal of real misfortune into which we are drawn simply by that purely ideal endeavour, or more correctly that incurable folly. We should also be able to devote much more attention to solid blessings and then enjoy them with less interruption. But as they say χαλεπὰ τὰ καλά.[4]

The folly of our nature, here described, puts forth three main offshoots, ambition, vanity, and pride. The difference between the last two is that *pride* is the already firm conviction of our own paramount worth in some respect; *vanity*, on the other hand, is the desire to awaken in others such a conviction, often accompanied by the secret hope of being able thereby to make it our own. Accordingly, pride is self-esteem that comes from *within* and so is direct; vanity, on the other hand, is the attempt to arrive at such esteem from *without* and thus indirectly. Accordingly, vanity makes us talkative, whereas pride makes us reserved and reticent. The vain man, however, should know that the high opinion of others which is coveted by him can be gained much more easily and certainly by persistent silence than by speech, even if he has the finest things to say. Anyone wishing to affect pride is not necessarily proud, but at most can be; yet he will soon drop this, as he will every assumed role. For only the firm, inner, unshakeable conviction of pre-eminent qualities and special worth makes us really proud. Now this conviction may be mistaken or rest on merely external and conventional advantages; that makes no difference to pride if only the conviction is present in real earnest. Therefore since pride is rooted in *conviction*, it is, like all knowledge, not within our *arbitrary power*. Its worst foe, I mean its greatest obstacle, is vanity which solicits the approval of others in order to base thereon our own high opinion of ourselves, wherein the assumption of pride is already quite firmly established.

Now however much pride is generally censured and decried, I suspect that this has come mainly from those who have nothing whereof they could be proud. In view of the effrontery and impudence of most men, anyone who has virtues and merits will do well to keep them in mind in order not to let

---

4 ['What is noble is difficult.']

them fall into oblivion. For whoever mildly ignores such merits
and associates with most men, as if he were entirely on their
level, will at once be frankly and openly regarded by them as
such. But I would like to recommend this especially to those
whose merits are of the highest order, that is to say, are real and
therefore purely personal, for, unlike orders and titles, such
merits are not brought to men's minds at every moment by an
impression on their senses; otherwise they will see often enough
exemplified the *sus Minervam*.[5] 'Joke with a slave, and he will
soon show you his backside' is an admirable proverb of the
Arabs, and the words of Horace should not be rejected: *sume
superbiam, quaesitam meritis*.[6] But the virtue of modesty is, I
suppose, a fine invention for fools and knaves; for according to
it everyone has to speak of himself as if he were a fool; and this
is a fine levelling down since it then looks as if there were in the
world none but fools and knaves.

On the other hand, the cheapest form of pride is national
pride; for the man affected therewith betrays a want of
individual qualities of which he might be proud, since he would
not otherwise resort to that which he shares with so many
millions. The man who possesses outstanding personal qualities
will rather see most clearly the faults of his own nation, for he
has them constantly before his eyes. But every miserable fool,
who has nothing in the world whereof he could be proud,
resorts finally to being proud of the very nation to which he
belongs. In this he finds compensation and is now ready and
thankful to defend, πὺξ καὶ λάξ,[7] all the faults and follies
peculiar to it. For example, of fifty Englishmen hardly more
than one will be found to agree with us when we speak of the
stupid and degrading bigotry of his nation with the contempt
it deserves; but this one exception will usually be a man of
intelligence. The Germans are free from national pride and
thus furnish a proof of the honesty that has been said to their
credit; but those of them are not honest who feign and ludi-
crously affect such pride. This is often done by the 'German
Brothers' and democrats who flatter the people in order to lead
them astray. It is said that the Germans invented gunpowder,

---

5 ['The swine (instructs) Minerva.' (Cicero.)]
6 ['Arrogate to yourself the pride you earned through merit.' (*Od.* III. 30. 14.)]
7 ['Tooth and nail'.]

but I cannot subscribe to this view. Lichtenberg asks: 'Why is it that a man who is not a German does not readily pass himself off as one, but usually pretends to be a Frenchman or an Englishman when he wants to give himself out as something?' For the rest, individuality far outweighs nationality and in a given man merits a thousand times more consideration than this. Since national character speaks of the crowd, not much good will ever be honestly said in its favour. On the contrary, we see in a different form in each country only human meanness, perversity, and depravity, and this is called national character. Having become disgusted with one of them, we praise another until we become just as disgusted with it. Every nation ridicules the rest and all are right.

The subject of this chapter, namely what we *represent* in the world, that is, what we are in the eyes of others, may now be divided, as already observed, into *honour, rank, and fame*.

For our purpose, *rank* may be dismissed in a few words, however important it may be in the eyes of the masses and of Philistines, and however great its use in the running of the State machine. Its value is conventional, that is to say, it is really a sham; its effect is a simulated esteem and the whole thing is a mere farce for the masses. Orders are bills of exchange drawn on public opinion; their value rests on the credit of the drawer. However, quite apart from the great deal of money they save the State as a substitute for financial rewards, they are a thoroughly suitable institution provided that they are distributed with discrimination and justice. Thus the masses have eyes and ears, but not much else, precious little judgement and even a short memory. Many merits lie entirely outside the sphere of their comprehension; others are understood and acclaimed when they make their appearance, but are afterwards soon forgotten. I find it quite proper through cross or star[8] always and everywhere to exclaim to the crowd: 'This man is not like you; he has merits!' But orders lose such value when they are distributed without justice or judgement or in excessive numbers. And so a prince should be as cautious in conferring them as a businessman is in signing bills. The inscription *pour le mérite* on a cross is a pleonasm; every order should be *pour le mérite, ça va sans dire*.[9]

---

[8] [i.e. decorations.]   [9] ['That goes without saying.']

The discussion of *honour* is much more difficult and involved than that of rank. First we should have to define it. Now if for this purpose I said that honour is external conscience and conscience internal honour, this might perhaps satisfy a number of people; yet it would be an explanation that is more showy than clear and thorough. And so I say that objectively honour is other people's opinion of our worth and subjectively our fear of that opinion. In the latter capacity, it often has in the man of honour a very wholesome, though by no means a purely moral, effect.

The feeling of honour and shame, inherent in everyone who is not utterly depraved, and the great value attributed to the former, have their root and origin in the following. By himself alone man is capable of very little and is like Robinson Crusoe on a desert island; only in the society of others is he a person of consequence and capable of doing much. He becomes aware of this state of affairs as soon as his consciousness begins to develop in some way and there at once arises in him the desire to be looked upon as a useful member of society, as one capable of playing his part as a man, *pro parte virili*, and thus as one entitled to share in the advantages of human society. Now he is a useful member of society firstly by doing what all are everywhere expected to do and secondly by doing what is demanded and expected of him in the particular position he occupies. But he recognizes just as quickly that here it is not a question whether he is useful in his own opinion, but whether he is so in that of others. Accordingly, there spring from this his keen desire for the favourable *opinion* of others and the great value he attaches to this. Both appear with the original nature of an innate feeling, called a feeling of honour, and, according to circumstances, a feeling of shame (*verecundia*). It is this that makes a man blush at the thought of having suddenly to fall in the opinion of others even when he knows he is innocent, or where the fault that comes to light concerns only a relative obligation and thus one arbitrarily undertaken. On the other hand, nothing stirs his courage and spirits more than does the attained or renewed certainty of other people's favourable opinion because it promises him the protection and help of the united forces of all which are against the evils of life an infinitely greater bulwark than his own forces.

From the different relations in which a man may stand to others, and in respect of which they must show him confidence and therefore have a certain good opinion of him, there arise several *kinds of honour*. These relations are mainly mine and thine, then the fulfilment of pledges, and finally the sexual relation. Corresponding to them we have civic honour, official honour, and sexual honour, each of which again has subspecies.

Civic honour has the widest sphere; it consists in the assumption that we respect absolutely the rights of everyone and therefore shall never use for our own advantage unjust or unlawful means. It is the condition for our taking part in all amicable intercourse. It is lost through a single action that openly and violently runs counter thereto and so through every criminal punishment, yet only on the assumption that this was just. In the last resort, however, honour always rests on the conviction that moral character is unalterable by virtue whereof a single bad action is a sure indication of the same moral nature of all subsequent actions as soon as similar circumstances occur. This is also testified by the English expression *character* for fame, reputation, honour. For this reason, honour once lost cannot be recovered unless the loss had rested on a mistake, such as slander or a false view of things. Accordingly, there are laws against slander, libel, and also insults; for an insult, mere abuse, is a summary slander without any statement of the reasons. This might be well expressed in Greek: ἔστι ἡ λοιδορία διαβολὴ σύντομος,[10] which, however, is nowhere to be found. The man who is abusive shows, of course, that he has no real and true complaint against the other man since he would otherwise give this as the premisses and confidently leave the conclusion to the hearers; instead of which he gives the conclusion and leaves the premisses unsaid. But he relies on the presumption that this is done merely for the sake of brevity. It is true that civic honour has its name from the middle classes, but it applies without distinction to all classes, even to the highest. No one can dispense with it and it is a very serious matter which everyone should guard against taking lightly. Whoever breaks trust and faith has for ever lost trust and faith, whatever he may do and whoever he may be, and the bitter fruits, entailed in this loss, will not fail to come.

[10] ['The insult is a summary slander.']

In a certain sense, *honour* has a *negative* character in contrast
to *fame* which has a *positive*. For honour is not the opinion of
particular qualities that belong to this subject alone, but only of
those which, as a rule, are to be assumed as qualities in which
he should not be wanting. Therefore honour asserts merely that
this subject is not an exception, whereas fame asserts that he is.
Thus fame must first be acquired; honour, on the other hand,
has simply not to be lost. According to this, want of fame is
obscurity and something negative; want of honour is shame and
something positive. This negativity, however, must not be
confused with passivity; on the contrary, honour has quite an
active character. Thus it proceeds solely from its *subject*; it rests
on *his* actions, not on what others do and on what befalls him;
it is therefore τῶν ἐφ᾽ ἡμῖν.[11] This is, as we shall see in a moment,
the mark of distinction between true honour and chivalry or
sham honour. Only through slander is an attack on honour
possible from without, and the only way to refute it is to give it
proper publicity and unmask the slanderer.

The respect shown to old age appears to be due to the fact
that the honour of young people is, of course, assumed but has
not yet been put to the test; it therefore really exists on credit.
But with older people it had to be shown in the course of their
lives whether through their conduct they could maintain their
honour. For neither years in themselves, which are also
attained by animals and even greatly exceeded by some, nor
even experience, as being merely a more detailed knowledge of
the ways of the world, are a sufficient ground for the respect that
the young are required everywhere to show to their elders.
Mere feebleness of old age would entitle a man to indulgence
and consideration rather than respect. But it is remarkable
that a certain respect for white hair is inborn and therefore
really instinctive in man. Wrinkles, an incomparably surer sign
of old age, do not inspire this respect at all. One never speaks
of venerable wrinkles, but always of venerable white hair.

The value of honour is only indirect; for, as already explained
at the beginning of this chapter, other people's opinion of us
can be of value only in so far as it determines or can at times
determine their behaviour to us. Yet this is the case so long as
we live with or among them. For, as in the civilized state we

[11] ['Part of what depends on us' (Term used by the Stoics).]

owe our safety and possessions simply to society and moreover we need others in all our undertakings and they must have confidence in us in order to have any dealings with us, their opinion of us is of great value, although this is always only indirect, and I cannot see how it can be direct. In agreement with this Cicero also says: *De bona autem fama Chrysippus quidem et Diogenes, detracta utilitate, ne digitum quidem, ejus causa, porrigendum esse dicebant. Quibus ego vehementer assentior.*[12] (*De finibus*, III. 17.) In the same way, Helvétius gives us a lengthy explanation of this truth in his masterpiece *De l'esprit* (Disc., Pt. III, chap. 13) the result of which is: *Nous n'aimons pas l'estime pour l'estime, mais uniquement pour les avantages qu'elle procure.*[13] Now as the means cannot be worth more than the end, the statement 'honour is dearer than life itself', of which so much is made, is, as I have said, an exaggeration.

So much for civic honour. *Official honour* is the general opinion of others that a man who holds an office actually has the requisite qualities and also in all cases strictly fulfils his official duties. The greater and more important a man's sphere of influence in the State and so the higher and more influential the post occupied by him, the greater must be the opinion of the intellectual abilities and moral qualities that render him fit for the post. Consequently, he has a correspondingly higher degree of honour, as expressed by his titles, orders, and so on, and also by the deferential behaviour of others to him. Now by the same standard, rank or status determines the particular degree of honour, although this is modified by the ability of the masses to judge of the importance of the rank. But greater honour is always paid to the man who has and fulfils special obligations than to the ordinary citizen whose honour rests mainly on negative qualities.

Official honour further demands that whoever holds an office will for the sake of his colleagues and successors maintain respect for it. This is done by the strict observance of his duties and also by the fact that he never allows to go unchallenged any attacks on himself or the office while he is holding it, in other

---

[12] ['But Chrysippus and Diogenes said of a good reputation that, apart from its being useful, one should not even raise a finger for its sake. I entirely agree with them.']

[13] ['We do not like esteem for its own sake, but simply for the advantage that it brings us.']

words, that he does not allow statements to the effect that he is not strictly carrying out his duties or that the office itself does not contribute to the public welfare. On the contrary, he must prove by legal penalties that such attacks were unjust.

Under official honour we have also that of the man serving the State, the doctor, the lawyer, every public teacher or even graduate, in short, everyone who has been declared publicly qualified for a certain kind of mental proficiency and has, therefore, promised to carry it out; in a word, the honour of all who, as such, have publicly undertaken to do something. Here, then we have true *military honour*; it consists in the fact that whoever has undertaken to defend his country actually possesses the requisite qualities, above all, courage, bravery, and strength, and that he is in fact ready to defend his country to the death, and will not for anything in the world desert the flag to which he has once sworn allegiance. Here I have taken *official honour* in a wider sense than the usual one, namely where it indicates the citizens' respect that is due to the office itself.

It seems to me that *sexual honour* calls for a more detailed consideration and a reference of its principles to their root. At the same time, this will confirm that all honour ultimately rests on considerations of expediency.

By its nature *sexual honour* is divided into that of women and that of men, and from both angles it is a well understood *esprit de corps*. The former is by far the more important of the two because in a woman's life the sexual relation is the essential thing. Hence female honour is the general opinion in regard to a girl that she has never given herself to a man and in regard to a wife that she has devoted herself solely to her husband. The importance of this opinion depends on the following. The female sex demands and expects from the male everything, thus all that it desires and needs; the male demands from the female primarily and directly one thing only. Therefore the arrangement had to be made whereby the male sex could obtain from the female that one thing only by taking charge of everything and also of the children springing from the union. The welfare of the whole female sex rests on this arrangement. To carry it out, this sex must necessarily stick together and show *esprit de corps*. But in its entirety and in closed ranks it then faces the whole male sex as the common foe who is in possession of all the good things of the earth through a natural superiority in physical and mental powers. The male sex must be subdued and taken captive so that the female sex, by holding it, may come to possess those good things. Now to this end the maxim of honour of the whole female sex is that all illicit intercourse is absolutely denied to the male so that every man is forced into marriage as into a kind of capitulation, and the whole female sex is provided for. This end can be completely attained, however, only by the strict observance of the above maxim; and therefore the whole female sex sees with true *esprit de corps* that that maxim is upheld by all its members. Accordingly, every girl who through illicit intercourse has betrayed the whole female sex, since its welfare would be undermined if this kind of conduct were to become general, is expelled by her sex and is branded with shame; she has lost her honour. No woman may have anything more to do with her; she is avoided like the plague. The same fate befalls the woman who commits adultery since for the husband she has not maintained the capitulation into which he entered; but through such an example men are discouraged from entering it; yet on such a capitulation depends the salvation of the whole female sex. Moreover, because of her gross breach of faith and of the deception of her deed, the adulteress loses not only her sexual honour but also her civic. Thus we may well excuse a girl by saying that she has 'fallen', but we never speak of a 'fallen wife'. In the former case the seducer can restore the girl's honour by marrying her, but this the adulterer cannot do after the wife has been divorced. Now if in consequence of this clear view, we recognize as the foundation of the principle of female honour an *esprit de corps* that is wholesome and indeed necessary but is also well calculated and based on interests, it will be possible for us to attribute to such honour the greatest importance for woman's existence and hence a value which is great and relative yet not absolute, not one that lies beyond life and its aims and is accordingly to be purchased at the price of this. And so there will be nothing to applaud in the extravagant deeds of Lucretia and Virginius which degenerate into tragic farces. Thus there is something so shocking at the end of *Emilia Galotti* that we leave the theatre in a wholly dejected mood. On the other hand, in spite of sexual honour, we cannot help sympathizing with Clara in *Egmont*. To push the principle of female honour too far is, like so many things, equivalent to forgetting the end for the means. For such exaggeration attributes to sexual honour an absolute value, whereas even more than any other it has a merely relative value. In fact it might be said that it has only a conventional value, when we see from Thomasius' *De concubinatu* how in almost all countries and at all times down to the Lutheran Reformation concubinage was a relation permitted and recognized by law in which the concubine retained her honour; not to mention the temple of Mylitta at Babylon (Herodotus, lib. I, c. 199) and other instances. Of course, there are also civil circumstances that render impossible the external form of marriage, especially in Catholic countries where no divorce occurs. In my opinion ruling sovereigns always act more morally when they have a mistress than when they contract a morganatic marriage whose descendants might one day raise claims if the legitimate descendants happen to die out. Thus however remote it may be, the possibility of civil war is brought about by such a marriage. Moreover, a morganatic marriage, that is, one contracted actually in defiance of all external circumstances, is at bottom a concession made to women and priests, two classes to whom we should be careful to concede as little as possible. Further, it should be borne in mind that everyone in the land may marry the woman of his choice except one to whom this natural right is denied; this poor man is the prince. His hand belongs to his country and is given in marriage for reasons of State, that is, for the good of the country. But yet he is human and wants one day to follow the inclinations of his heart. It is, therefore, as unjust and ungrateful as it is narrow-minded to prevent him from having a mistress, or to want to reproach him with this; it must always be understood, of course, that she is not permitted to have any influence on the government. As regards sexual honour, such a mistress is from her point of view to a certain extent an exception, as being exempt from the universal rule. For she has given herself merely to a man who loves her and whom she loves but could never marry. In general, however, the many bloody sacrifices which are made to the principle of female honour, such as the murder of children and the suicide of mothers, are evidence that this principle has not a purely natural origin. Of course a girl who surrenders illicitly thereby commits against her whole sex a breach of faith which is nevertheless only tacitly assumed and not affirmed on oath. And since in the usual case her own advantage suffers directly from this, her folly is here infinitely greater than her depravity.

The sexual honour of men is brought about by that of women as the opposite *esprit de corps*. This demands that everyone who has entered marriage, that capitulation so favourable to the opposite party, must now see that it is upheld so that not even this pact may lose its strength through any laxity in its observance and that men, by giving up everything, may be assured of the one thing for which they bargain, namely the sole possession of the woman. Accordingly, man's honour demands that he shall resent his wife's breach of the marriage tie and shall punish it at any rate by separating from her. If he tolerates it with his eyes open, he is discredited and disgraced by the entire community of men. Nevertheless, this shame is not nearly so grave as that of the woman who has lost her sexual honour; on the contrary, it is only a *levioris notae macula*[14] since with man the sexual relation is subordinate and he has many others that are more important. The two great dramatic poets of modern times have each twice taken as their theme man's honour in this sense; Shakespeare in *Othello* and *The Winter's Tale*, and Calderón in *El medico de su honra* (the Physician of his Honour) and *A secreto agravio secreta venganza* (for Secret Insult Secret Vengeance). For the rest, this honour demands only the woman's punishment not her lover's which is merely an *opus supererogationis*.[15] In this way is confirmed the statement that such honour originates from men's *esprit de corps*.

The honour, so far considered in its different forms and principles, is found to be universally accepted by all nations and at all times, although that of women may be shown to have undergone in its principles some local and temporary modifications. On the other hand, there is a species of honour entirely different from that which is universally and everywhere valid and of which neither Greeks nor Romans had any knowledge and even today the Chinese, Hindus, and Mohammedans know just as little. For it first arose in the Middle Ages

14 ['A blemish of less importance'.]
15 ['A piece of work going beyond what was required'.]

and became indigenous merely in Christian Europe; and even here only with a very small section of the population, the upper classes and those emulating them. It is *knightly honour* or *point d'honneur*. As its fundamental principles are quite different from those of the honour hitherto considered and, in some respects, are even opposed thereto, since the former produces the *honourable man* whereas the latter makes the *man of honour*, I will here specially lay down its principles as a code or mirror of knightly honour.

(1) Honour does *not* consist in other people's opinion of our worth, but simply and solely in the *expressions* of such an opinion, no matter whether the expressed opinion actually exists or not, let alone whether it has any grounds or reasons. Accordingly, in consequence of our way of life, others may entertain the worst opinion and may despise us as much as they please; but so long as no one ventures to express this aloud, no harm at all is done to our honour. But conversely, if through our qualities and actions we compel all others to think very highly of us (for this does not depend on their option or discretion), then as soon as anyone expresses his contempt for us, he might be utterly worthless and stupid, our honour is at once violated and indeed is lost for ever unless it is restored. Abundant proof of what I say, namely that it is certainly not what other people *think* but merely what they *say* that matters, is the fact that slanders and insults can be *withdrawn* or, if necessary, made the subject of an apology whereby the position is then as if they had never been made. Here it is quite immaterial whether the opinion that gave rise to the insults has also been altered and why this should have been done; only the expression is annulled and then everything is all right. Accordingly, here the object is not to merit respect, but to get it by threats.

(2) A man's honour depends not on what he *does*, but on what he *suffers*, on what happens to him. According to the principles of the honour first discussed which is everywhere applicable, this depends solely on what *he himself* says or does. Knightly honour, on the other hand, depends on what someone else says or does. Accordingly, it lies in the hands, indeed on the tip of the tongue, of everyone, and if such a man chooses to seize the opportunity, it can be lost for ever at any moment, unless the man who is attacked wrests it back again by a method to be

mentioned in a moment. Yet he can do this only at the risk of
losing his life, health, freedom, property, and peace of mind.
In consequence of this, a man's actions may be the noblest and
most righteous, his heart the purest, and his mind the most
eminent, and yet it is possible for his honour to be lost at any
moment, whenever anyone is pleased to *insult* him. Such a
reviler may not yet have violated these laws of honour, but in
other respects he may be the most worthless scoundrel, the
stupidest jackass, an idler, a gambler, a spendthrift, in short, a
person who is not worth the other man's consideration. In
most cases it will be just such a fellow who likes insulting
people because, as Seneca rightly remarks, *ut quisque con-
temtissimus et ludibrio est, ita solutissimae linguae est*[16] (*De constantia,*
11). Such a fellow will also be most easily irritated by the man
who was first described, because men of opposite tastes hate
each other and the sight of outstanding qualities usually breeds
the silent rage of worthlessness. Therefore Goethe says:

> Why do you complain of foes?
> Shall they ever become your friends,
> To whom your very nature is
> Secretly an eternal reproach?
> > *Westöstlicher Diwan.*

We see to what extent such worthless men are indebted to the
principle of honour, for it puts them on a level with those who
would otherwise be in every respect beyond their reach. Now if
such a fellow insults another, that is to say, attributes to him
some bad quality, this is considered for the time being to be a
well-founded and objectively true judgement, a decree with all
the force of law; indeed it remains true and valid for all time,
unless it is at once wiped out in blood. Thus the man who is
insulted remains (in the eyes of all 'men of honour') what the
reviler (who might be the most depraved of all mortals) has
called him; for he has 'swallowed the affront' (this is the
terminus technicus). Accordingly, 'men of honour' will then
utterly despise him and avoid him like the plague; for example,
they will publicly and vociferously refuse to go into any company where he is welcomed, and so on. I think I am able to

---

[16] ['The more contemptible and ridiculous a man is, the readier he is with his
tongue.']

trace with certainty the origin of this shrewd view to the fact
that in the Middle Ages up to the fifteenth century (according
to C. G. von Wächter's *Beiträge zur deutschen Geschichte, besonders
des deutschen Strafrechts*, 1845), in criminal cases it was not the
accuser who had to prove the guilt of the accused, but the
accused who had to prove his innocence. This could be done
through a compurgatorial oath which nevertheless still required
compurgators (*consacramentales*). These swore they were convinced that the accused was incapable of any perjury. If the
accused had no compurgators, or if the accuser did not admit
them, then judgement by God was introduced which usually
consisted in the duel. For the accused was now in disgrace
[*bescholten*] and had to clear himself. Here we see the origin of
the notion of being in disgrace and of the whole course of events
that even today takes place among 'men of honour', only with
the omission of the oath. Here too we have an explanation of the
usual deep indignation with which 'men of honour' accept the
reproach of the lie and in return for this demand vengeance in
blood. This seems to be very strange in view of the fact that lies
are of daily occurrence, but it has grown into a deep-rooted
superstition especially in England. (Actually everyone who
threatens to punish with death the reproach of the lie should
not have told a lie in his own life.) Thus in those criminal cases
of the Middle Ages, the form was shorter, namely the accused
retorted that the accuser was a liar, whereupon it was at once
left to the judgement of God. It is, therefore, written in the code
of knightly honour that the reproach of the lie must be at once
followed by an appeal to arms. So much as regards insult. But
now there is something even worse than the insult, so dreadful
that I must beg the pardon of all 'men of honour' for the very
mention of it in this code of knightly honour. For I know that
the mere thought of it makes their flesh creep and their hair
stand on end, since it is the *summum malum*, the greatest evil on
earth, and worse than death and damnation. Thus, *horribile
dictu*, one man may give another a slap or a blow. This is such a
dreadful incident and produces so complete an extinction of
honour that, although all other outrages on honour can be
healed by blood-letting, this demands for its thorough healing
the complete death-blow.

(3) Honour has nothing whatever to do with what a man may

be in and by himself, or with the question whether his moral nature can ever be altered and with all such pedantic inquiries. On the contrary, when it is violated or lost for the time being, it can be quickly and completely restored, if one acts speedily, by the one universal remedy, the duel. If, however, the aggressor is not from the classes that follow the code of knightly honour; or if he has once offended against it, we can engage in a safe operation, especially if the violation of our honour was a blow, but even if it should have been a mere matter of words, by striking him down, if we are armed, on the spot or at all events an hour later; whereby our honour is restored. But if we wish to avoid this step out of fear of any unpleasant consequences that may arise, or if we are merely uncertain whether the offender is or is not subject to the laws of knightly honour, we have a palliative in the *avantage*. This consists in our returning his rudeness with decidedly greater rudeness; if mere abuse is no longer practicable, we resort to blows and here indeed is a climax to the saving of our honour. Thus a box on the ears may be cured by blows with a stick and these by a thrashing with a dog-whip; even against this some recommend as a sovereign remedy that we should spit in the opponent's face. Only when these methods are no longer of any avail, do we have to resort at once to the operation of drawing blood. The reason for this palliative is really to be found in the following maxim.

(4) Just as to be insulted is a disgrace, so to insult is an honour. For example, my opponent has on his side truth, right, and reason; but I insult him and so these must yield and be off, and right and honour are on my side. For the time being, however, he has lost his honour, until he recovers it not by the exercise of right and reason, but by shots and stabs. Accordingly, rudeness is a quality which, in point of honour, is a substitute for every other, or outweighs them all. The rudest man is always right; *quid multa?*[17] However stupid, ill-bred, or bad a man may have been, all this as such is effaced by rudeness and made legitimate. If in some discussion, or otherwise in conversation, another man shows us that he has a more accurate knowledge of the subject, a stricter love of truth, a sounder judgement, and a better understanding than we have, or

[17] ['What more does one want?']

generally exhibits intellectual qualities that put ours in the shade, then we can at once eliminate all such superior qualities and also our own inferiority that is thereby revealed and can now in our turn be even superior by becoming offensive and rude. For rudeness defeats every argument and eclipses all intelligence. If, therefore, our opponent does not enter into the argument and retort with greater rudeness, thereby putting us into the noble contest of the *avantage*, we remain the victors and honour is on our side. Truth, knowledge, understanding, intellect, and wit must beat a retreat and are driven from the field by almighty rudeness. Therefore as soon as a man expresses an opinion that differs from theirs or shows more intelligence than they can muster, the 'men of honour' prepare to mount their chargers; and if in any controversy they lack a counter-argument, they search for some rudeness that serves the same purpose and is easier to find, and then quit the scene in triumph. Here we already see how right people are in crediting the principle of honour with ennobling the tone of society. This maxim again rests on the following that is the real and fundamental one and the soul of the entire code.

(5) The highest court to which we can appeal in all differences with others so far as honour is concerned, is that of physical force, in other words, brutality. For every case of rudeness is really an appeal to brutality since it declares as incompetent the contest of intellectual powers or moral right. In their place it puts that of physical force and in the case of the human species, defined by Franklin as a *tool-making animal*, this contest is fought with weapons that are peculiar to the species, namely in the duel, and produces an irrevocable decision. This fundamental maxim, as we know, is expressed by the words *right of might*, an expression analogous to that of *mock reasoning* and therefore, like this, ironical. Accordingly, the honour of the knight should be called the honour of might.

(6) If at the beginning we had found that civic honour was very scrupulous in the matter of mine and thine, of obligations entered into, and of the promise once made, the code we are now considering, on the other hand, displays in such matters the noblest liberality. Thus only *one* word must not be broken, the word of honour, that is, the one on which we have said 'on my honour!'—the presumption being that every other may be

broken. Even if the worst comes to the worst, we can break this word of honour and still save our honour by that universal remedy, the duel, that is by fighting those who maintain that we had given our word of honour. Further, there is only *one* debt that must be paid without question, that of gambling which is also called 'the debt of honour'. In all other debts we may cheat Jews and Gentiles alike, for this does not at all damage our knightly honour.*

At the first glance, the unprejudiced reader now sees that this strange, barbarous, and ridiculous code of honour has not sprung from the essence of human nature or from a healthy view of human relations. Moreover, this is confirmed by the exceedingly narrow sphere of its operation which is exclusively Europe, and indeed only since the Middle Ages, and even here only among the nobility, the army, and those who emulate

* This then is the code. When reduced to clear concepts and expressions, those principles cut so strange and grotesque a figure. Even at the present time in Christian Europe, all as a rule pay homage to them who belong to so-called good society with its so-called good manners. Indeed many of these in whom those principles have been instilled by word and example since early youth, more firmly believe in them than in any catechism. For them they cherish the profoundest and most genuine veneration, and are ready at any moment quite seriously to sacrifice to them their happiness, peace of mind, health, and life. They consider that those principles have their roots in the very nature of man and thus are innate, established *a priori*, and therefore above and beyond all investigation. However, I do not want to hurt their feelings, but it does little credit to their intelligence. These principles are, therefore, the least suited to that class which is destined to represent intelligence in the world and to become the salt of the earth; to the class that should prepare itself for that great mission and hence to the body of young students who, unfortunately in Germany more than any other class, pay homage to these principles. Now instead of impressing on this youth the drawbacks or immorality that attach to the consequences of such principles—this youth that was schooled in the works of Greece and Rome (as was done once, when I was still a member of it, by that worthless philosophaster J. G. Fichte in a *declamatio ex cathedra*, a man still regarded quite honestly by the German learned world as a philosopher), I have merely to say to them the following. You whose youth received the language and wisdom of Greece and Rome as a patroness and on whose minds such great trouble was taken to let fall at an early age the shafts of wisdom and nobleness of glorious antiquity, do you wish to begin by making this code of stupidity and brutality the standard of your conduct? Just consider it, as here seen before you in the clearest manner and in all its pitiable narrowness, and let it be the touchstone not of your heart but of your head. Now if your head does not reject it, then it is not capable of working in the field where the necessary requirements are an energetic power of judgement that breaks the bonds of prejudice, a thorough understanding that is capable of clearly separating the true from the false, even where the difference lies deeply concealed and is not palpably evident, as it is here. Therefore, my good men, try in this case to make a name for yourselves on a different path of honour; become soldiers or learn a trade that thrives in any soil.

them. For neither Greeks nor Romans, nor the highly civilized Asiatic peoples of ancient or modern times, know anything of this honour and its principles. The only honour they all know is the one first analysed by me. With all of them, therefore, a man is looked upon as what his actions proclaim him to be, not what any wagging tongue is pleased to say about him. With all of them what a man says or does may well ruin *his own* honour, but never that of another. With all of them a blow is just a blow and any horse or ass can deal out one more dangerous; according to circumstances, a blow will provoke anger and may well be avenged on the spot, but it has nothing to do with honour. Accounts were certainly not kept of blows or insulting words and of the 'satisfaction' for them that was demanded or left undemanded. In bravery and contempt of death they are certainly in no way inferior to the races of Christian Europe. The Greeks and Romans were indeed thorough heroes; but they knew nothing of *point d'honneur*. With them the duel was the business not of noblemen but of mercenary gladiators, abandoned slaves, and condemned criminals who, alternately with wild animals, were set to butcher one another for the people's amusement. With the introduction of Christianity, gladiatorial shows were abolished, but their place in Christian times was taken by the duel under the intervention of divine judgement. If gladiatorial shows were a cruel sacrifice made to the general desire for spectacles, the duel is a cruel sacrifice which is made to universal prejudice, yet not of criminals, slaves, and prisoners, but of the free and noble.

Many features that have been preserved for us are evidence that this prejudice was utterly foreign to the ancients. For instance, when a Teutonic chieftain had challenged Marius to a duel, this hero had a reply sent to the effect that if he were weary of life, he could go and hang himself; nevertheless he offered him a veteran gladiator with whom he could have a set-to (*Freinsh. suppl.*, Livy, bk. LXVIII, chap. 12). In Plutarch (*Themistocles*, 11) we read that Eurybiades, commander-in-chief of the fleet, while arguing with Themistocles, raised his stick to strike him. Yet the latter did not then draw his sword, but said: πάταξον μὲν οὖν, ἄκουσον δέ: 'strike, but hear me.' How shocked the reader 'of honour' must be at our having no information that the Athenian corps of officers at once declared their

unwillingness to continue to serve under such a Themistocles!
Accordingly, a modern French writer quite rightly says: *Si
quelqu'un s'avisait de dire que Démosthène fut un homme d'honneur, on
sourirait de pitié;—Cicéron n'était pas un homme d'honneur non plus.*[18]
(*Soirées littéraires*, by C. Durand, Rouen, 1828, vol. ii, p. 300.)
Further, the passage in Plato (*Laws*, ix, the last six pages,
likewise xi, p. 131, *ed. Bip.*) concerning αἰκία, that is, assault and
battery, shows clearly enough that in such matters the ancients
had no notion of a feeling of knightly honour. In consequence of
his frequent disputations, Socrates was often roughly treated
and bore this quite calmly. For instance when somebody once
kicked him, he patiently put up with it and said to the man who
showed surprise: 'Do you think I should resent it if an ass had
kicked me?' (Diogenes Laërtius, ii. 21). When, on another
occasion, someone asked him: 'Does not that fellow abuse and
insult you?' his reply was 'No; for what he says does not apply
to me' (ibid. 36). Stobaeus, (*Florilegium*, ed. Gaisford, vol. i,
pp. 327–30) has preserved for us a long passage of Musonius
from which we see what the ancients thought of insults. They
knew of no other satisfaction than that of the law, and prudent
men disdained even this. For a box on the ears the ancients
knew of no other satisfaction than that of the law, as is clearly
seen from Plato's *Gorgias* (p. 86, *ed. Bip.*), where Socrates'
opinion is also to be found (p. 133). The same thing is clear
from the account of Gellius (xx. 1) in respect of a certain
Lucius Veratius who, without any provocation, had the temerity
to box the ears of Roman citizens whom he met on the road.
But to avoid all complications, he arranged to be accompanied by a slave carrying a bag of money who at once paid
out to the astonished Romans the legal smart-money of twenty-
five pence. Crates, the famous Cynic, had received such a
severe box on the ears from the musician Nicodromus that his
face had swollen up and was covered with blood; whereupon
he put on his forehead a label with the inscription Νικόδρομος
ἐποίει (*Nicodromus fecit*).[19] This brought much disgrace on the
flautist (Apul. *Flor.*, p. 126, *ed. Bip.*) who had committed such
brutality on a man who was worshipped as a household god by

---

[18] ['If anyone took it into his head to say that Demosthenes was a man of
honour, one would smile indulgently;—nor was Cicero a man of honour.']
[19] ['Nicodromus did this.']

the whole of Athens. (Diogenes Laërtius, VI. 89.) In a letter to
Melesippus, Diogenes of Sinope says that he had been thrashed
by drunken sons of Athenians; but he pointed out that to him it
meant nothing. (Note by Isaac Casaubon on Diogenes Laërtius,
VI. 33.) In his book *De constantia sapientis*, from chapter 10 to the
end, Seneca considered in detail *contumelia*, insult or abuse, in
order to show that a wise man pays no attention to it. In
chapter 14 he says: '*At sapiens colaphis percussus, quid faciet?*'
*quod Cato, cum illi os percussum esset: non excanduit, non vindicavit
injuriam: nec remisit quidem, sed factam negavit.*[20]

'Yes', you say, 'these were wise men!' And you are fools, I
suppose? Quite so.

We see, therefore, that the whole principle of knightly
honour was utterly unknown to the ancients just because in
every respect they remained true to a natural and unprejudiced
view of things and so did not allow themselves to be influenced
by such sinister and arrant tomfoolery. Accordingly, the
ancients were unable to regard a blow in the face as anything
but a blow in the face, a trivial physical injury; whereas to the
moderns it has become a catastrophe and a theme for tragedies,
for example in the *Cid* of Corneille, or in a recent German
tragedy of ordinary civil life which is called *Die Macht der
Verhältnisse*,[21] but which ought to be called *Die Macht des
Vorurtheils*.[22] But if someone in the Paris National Assembly
were to receive a box on the ears, it would resound from one
end of Europe to the other. Now the classic instances and the
above-mentioned examples from antiquity are sure to upset
men 'of honour'; I therefore recommend that they read, as an
antidote, the story of M. Desglands in Diderot's masterpiece,
Jacques le fataliste. It is an exquisite specimen of modern
knightly honour which they may find enjoyable and edifying.[23]

---

[20] ['What is the wise man to do when he is struck?" What Cato did when he
had been struck in the face; he did not become angry or avenge the insult or even
condone it, but declared that it did not occur at all.']

[21] [The Force of Circumstances.]

[22] [The Power of Prejudice.]

[23] [The story of M. Desglands is given by Schopenhauer in the *Draft for a Short
Essay on Honour* as follows:

'Two men of honour, one of whom was named Desglands, were courting the
same woman. As they sat at table next to each other and opposite her, Desglands
tried to attract her attention by the liveliest conversation, whereas she was absent-
minded and did not appear to hear him but kept glancing at his rival. In his hand

From what has been said, it is clear enough that the principle of knightly honour cannot possibly be original and grounded in human nature itself. It is, therefore, artificial and its origin is not difficult to discover. It is obviously an offspring of that age when fists were more in use than heads, and priests held in chains the power of reason; it is thus a child of the lauded Middle Ages and their system of chivalry. In those days, people allowed the Almighty not only to care but also to judge for them. Accordingly, difficult cases were decided by ordeals or judgements of God and, with few exceptions, these consisted of duels, certainly not merely between knights, but also between ordinary citizens. There is a good example of this in Shakespeare's *Henry VI* (Part ii, Act ii, Sc. 3). From every judicial sentence an appeal could still always be made to the duel as a court of higher instance, namely the judgement of God. In this way, physical force and agility, and thus animal nature instead of the force of reason, were really on the seat of judgement and decided on matters of right and wrong not by what a man had done, but by what had happened to him, wholly in accordance with the principle of knightly honour that prevails even at the present day. Whoever still doubts this origin of duelling, should read that excellent work, *The History of Duelling*, by J. G. Mellingen, 1849. In fact even today, we find among those who conform to the principle of knightly honour and who, as we know, are not usually the best educated and the most thoughtful, some who actually regard the result of a duel as a divine decision of the dispute underlying it; this is certainly in accordance with a traditional and hereditary opinion.

Apart from this origin of the principle of knightly honour, its

Desglands was holding a fresh egg and a feeling of morbid jealousy caused him to crush the egg, whereupon it burst and its contents bespattered his rival's face. The rival made a movement with his hand, but Desglands seized it and whispered in his ear: "Sir, I take it as given." A profound silence then descended on the company. The next day, Desglands appeared with a large round piece of black plaster on his right cheek. The duel ensued and Desgland's opponent was severely, but not fatally, wounded. Desglands reduced somewhat the size of the piece of plaster. After the opponent's recovery, there was a second duel and once more Desglands drew blood and he again reduced the size of the plaster. This went on five or six times; after each duel, Desglands reduced the size of his plaster, until in the end the opponent was killed. O noble spirit of the old age of chivalry! But seriously speaking, whoever compares this characteristic story with the previous ones is bound to say here, as on so many occasions, how great the ancients were and how small the moderns are!']

tendency is primarily that, through the threat of physical force, a man wants to extort the outward marks of that respect which he considers to be either too onerous or too superfluous actually to gain. This is something like the man who warms in his hand the bulb of a thermometer and from the rising of the mercury attempts to show that his room is well heated. More closely considered, the heart of the matter is that, whereas civic honour, as aiming at amicable association with others, consists in their opinion of us that we merit perfect *confidence*, since we respect absolutely the rights of everyone, knightly honour, on the other hand, consists in the opinion that we are *to be feared*, since we mean to defend absolutely our own rights. The principle that it is more essential to be feared than to enjoy confidence would not be such a very false one, since little reliance can be placed on human justice, if we lived in a state of nature where everyone had to protect himself and directly defend his rights. But in civilization, where the State has undertaken the protection of our person and property, the principle is no longer applicable. It stands like the citadels and watch-towers from the times when might was right, useless and deserted between well-cultivated fields and frequented roads or even railways. Accordingly, knightly honour that sticks to that principle has seized on those infringements of the person which the State punishes only lightly or not at all in accordance with the principle *de minimis lex non curat*;[24] for they are slight vexations and sometimes mere pranks. But in regard to these, it has risen to an over-estimation of the value of the person which is quite inappropriate to the nature, constitution, and destiny of man.* It enhances this value to a kind of sanctity and accordingly regards as utterly inadequate the punishment the State gives for trivial vexations. It therefore undertakes to punish these itself, and always of course the life and limb of the offender. All this obviously rests on the most excessive arrogance and shocking insolence which entirely forget what man really is and claim for him absolute inviolability and blamelessness.† But whoever intends to carry

---

[24] "The law is not concerned with trifles.".

* What does it mean when we say to offend someone? It means to cause him to doubt the high opinion he has of himself.

† Knightly honour is an offspring of arrogance and folly. (Most sharply opposed to it is the truth expressed by Calderón's *Principe constante* with the words '*esa es la herencia de Adan*'—the lot of Adam is poverty.) It is striking that this superlative of

this out by force, and consequently proclaims the maxim: 'the man who insults me or strikes me shall die', really deserves to be banished from the country. For to palliate that rash arrogance, all sorts of excuses and pretences are made. If two intrepid individuals meet and neither will give way, a slight push may lead to insulting remarks, then to fisticuffs, and finally to a fatal blow. Accordingly, it would be better for the sake of decency to omit the intermediate steps and at once resort to arms. The more specific procedure has been developed into a rigid and pedantic system, with laws and rules, which is the most solemn farce in the world and stands as a true temple of honour to folly. But the principle itself is false; for in matters of small importance (those of greater are always dealt with by the courts), one of two intrepid individuals, of course, gives way, namely the more prudent, and they agree to differ. The proof of this is furnished by ordinary men or rather all the numerous classes who do not subscribe to the principle of knightly honour and who thus let disputes run their natural course. Among these a fatal blow is a hundred times rarer than with the class, amounting perhaps to only one in a thousand of the whole community, who pays homage to that principle; and even a thrashing is a rare event. Then it is asserted that the manners and customs of good society were ultimately based on that principle of honour which with its duels was the bulwark against outbursts of bad behaviour and brutality. But in Athens, Corinth, and Rome it was certainly possible to find good, indeed excellent, society and fine manners and customs

all arrogance is found solely and exclusively among the followers of that religion which enjoins on them the deepest humility; for neither previous ages nor other continents are acquainted with this principle of knightly honour. However, we must not attribute it to religion, but rather to the feudal system under which every nobleman regarded himself as a petty sovereign who acknowledged no human judge. He therefore came to attribute complete inviolability and sanctity to his person; and so every attack thereof, every blow and every word of abuse, seemed to him to be a heinous crime. Accordingly, the principle of honour and duels originally were only the business of the nobles and consequently in later times of officers who associated, now and again though not entirely, with the other upper classes in order not to be of less account. Although duels were a product of the old ordeals, these are not the reason, but rather the consequence and application, of the principle of honour. The man who acknowledges no human judge appeals to the divine. The ordeals themselves, however, are not peculiar to Christianity, but are found also in great force in Hinduism, especially in ancient times; yet even now there are still traces of them.

without the backing of that bugbear of knightly honour. But in ancient society, of course, women did not occupy a prominent position as they do with us. Such a situation imparts to a conversation a frivolous and puerile character and excludes all solid and serious discussion. It has certainly contributed a great deal to the preference, shown by the good society of our times, to personal courage over every other quality. Personal courage is, in fact, a very subordinate quality, a mere virtue of the rank and file wherein even the animals surpass us, and so we say, for example, 'as brave as a lion'. Contrary to the above assertion, the principle of knightly honour is often the sure asylum of dishonesty and wickedness in large matters as well as of rudeness, inconsiderateness, and incivility in small. For many cases of rudeness are suffered in silence just because no one feels inclined to risk his neck in censuring them. In keeping with all this, we see the duel carried to the highest pitch of bloodthirsty zeal in the very nation that has shown a want of real honesty in political and financial affairs. What it is like in its private and domestic intercourse can be ascertained from those who are experienced in such matters. But as regards its urbanity and social culture, these are conspicuous by their absence.

All those pretexts are, therefore, untenable. It can be urged with more reason that, when a dog is snarled at he snarls in return and when he is flattered he fawns, it also lies in man's nature to return hostility with hostility and to be embittered and irritated by signs of disdain or hatred. Therefore Cicero says: *habet quendam aculeum contumelia, quem pati pudentes ac viri boni difficillime possunt*;[25] for nowhere in the world (apart from a few pious sects) are insulting remarks or even blows taken calmly and with composure. Nevertheless, in no case does nature lead to anything more than a retaliation appropriate to the offence, certainly not to the death-penalty for the reproach of lying, being stupid, or being a coward. The old German principle of 'blood for a blow' is a revolting superstition of chivalry. In any case, the return or retaliation of insults is a matter of anger, certainly not of honour and duty, as the principle of knightly honour would have us believe. On the contrary, it is quite certain that every reproach can hurt only

[25] ['Insult and abuse leave behind a sting that even sensitive and tender-hearted men find most hard to bear.']

to the extent that it hits the mark, as can be seen also from the fact that the slightest hint that hits home wounds much more deeply than does the most serious accusation that is entirely without foundation. Therefore whoever actually knows that he does not deserve a reproach, can and will confidently treat it with contempt. On the other hand, the principle of honour demands that he shall show a susceptibility that he does not possess at all and shall take bloody vengeance for insults that do not harm him. But a man must have a poor opinion of his own worth if he hurries to suppress every offensive remark so that it may not be heard. Accordingly, in the case of insults, genuine self-esteem will make a man indifferent to them; but if he cannot remain indifferent, shrewdness and culture will help him to save appearances and conceal his anger. And so if only we could get rid of the superstition of the principle of knightly honour so that no one would any longer dare to imagine that he could, by being abusive, detract from the honour of another or restore his own; if only it were no longer possible for every wrong, every brutality, or every rudeness to be made legitimate at once by the readiness to give satisfaction, in other words, to fight for it, the view would soon become general that, in a case of rudeness and abuse, the vanquished in this contest is the victor, and that, as Vincenzo Monti says, insults are like church processions that always return to their starting-point. It would then no longer be enough, as at present, for a man to be rude in return in order to carry his point. Consequently, insight and understanding would have quite a different hearing from the one they obtain at present when they have always to consider first whether they are in some way offending the opinions of narrow-minded dullards who are alarmed and embittered even by their mere presence. For it is possible that the mind which contains insight and understanding may have to be gambled against the shallow pate wherein narrow-minded stupidity resides. In society intellectual superiority would then obtain its due precedence which is at present given to physical superiority and cavalier courage, although this fact is carefully concealed. The result of this would be that the most outstanding men would then have one reason less for withdrawing from society. A change of this sort would accordingly pave the way to *genuine* good manners and really good society, such as undoubtedly existed in Athens, Corinth, and Rome. Whoever wants to see a proof of this, is recommended to read Xenophon's *Banquet*.

But the last defence of the knightly code will undoubtedly say: 'Why, good gracious me, one man might pitch into another!'—to which I might briefly reply that this has been the case often enough with nine hundred and ninety-nine out of a thousand who do not recognize that code without one of them ever being killed, whereas with the followers of the code every blow as a rule becomes fatal. But I will go more closely into the matter. I have tried often enough, yet without success, to find some tenable, or at least plausible, reason, not merely consisting of fine phrases but reducible to clear conceptions, for the rooted conviction which is entertained by a section of human society that a blow is such a dreadful thing. I have looked for such in the animal as well as in the rational nature of man. A blow is and remains a minor physical evil that any man can inflict on another, showing thereby merely that he was stronger or more cunning, or that the other man was off his guard. An analysis of the problem does not give us any more than this. I then see the same knight, who regards a blow from the human hand as the greatest of evils, receive from his horse a blow ten times more severe, limp away in suppressed pain, and assure everyone that it is a matter of no consequence. And so I thought that the human hand must be to blame; but then I see our knight receive sword-thrusts and sabre-cuts in battle from this same hand and assure us that it is a trifling affair not worth mentioning. Then I hear that even blows with the flat of the sword are not nearly so bad as those with a stick; and hence that, a short time ago, cadets were liable to the former but not to the latter; and now indeed to be knighted with the blade of a sword is the greatest honour. Now I have come to the end of my psychological and moral reasons and there is nothing left for me but to regard the thing as an old, deep-rooted superstition, as one more of so many examples that show how men can be talked into anything. This is also confirmed by the well-known fact that in China blows with a bamboo are a very frequent form of punishment for ordinary citizens and even for officials of all classes since it shows us that human nature, and a highly civilized human nature at that, does not affirm the same thing in China.[26] But if we take an unprejudiced view of human nature, we even see that beating and flogging are as natural to man as is biting to beasts of prey and butting to horned animals. Man is simply a flogging animal. We are, therefore, shocked when in rare cases we hear that one man has bitten another, whereas it is a perfectly natural event of daily occurrence for him to give and receive blows. It is evident that, with more enlightenment and intelligence, we are glad to dispense with blows by the exercise of mutual self-restraint. But it is a cruel thing to make a nation, or even only a class, believe that a given blow is a terrible misfortune which must have death and murder as its consequence. In the world there are too many real evils to allow of our increasing them by imaginary evils that bring real ones in their train; but this is done by that stupid and iniquitous superstition. I am, therefore, bound to condemn governments and legislative bodies when they promote such a superstition by eagerly pressing for the abolition of all corporal punishment both civil and military. In this respect, they think they are acting in the interests of humanity, whereas the very opposite is the case since they are in this way helping to strengthen that unnatural and vicious folly to which so many have already been sacrificed. For all offences except the worst, caning or beating, is the punishment that first occurs to man and is therefore natural; whoever is not susceptible to reasons will be to floggings. It is as reasonable as it is natural for a man to receive moderate corporal punishment who cannot be fined because he has no possessions and cannot be profitably deprived of his freedom because his services are required. Against it there are no arguments at all except mere talk about the 'dignity of man'; and such is based not on clear conceptions, but simply on that pernicious superstition which was previously mentioned and lies at the root of the matter, as is confirmed by an almost ludicrous example. In the armies of many countries, flogging had recently been replaced by condemnation to a bed of laths which, just like flogging, causes

---

[26] *Vingt ou trente coups de canne sur le derrière, c'est, pour ainsi dire, le pain quotidien des Chinois. C'est une correction paternelle du mandarin, laquelle n'a rien d'infamant, et qu'ils reçoivent avec action de grâces.—Lettres édifiantes et curieuses,* 1819 edn. vol. ii, p. 454.
['Twenty or thirty strokes with the cane on the backside are, so to speak, the daily bread of the Chinese. It is a paternal correction of the mandarin which has nothing ignominious in it and which they receive with thanksgiving.']

bodily pain but is not supposed to be derogatory to honour and dignity.

By encouraging this superstition, however, one is playing into the hands of the principle of knightly honour and therefore of the duel; whereas attempts are made, or are supposed to be made, to abolish this.* As a result, we find that fragment of the right of might, which has drifted down from the crudest medieval times, still floating about as a public scandal in the nineteenth century. It is high time it was ignominiously cast out. Nowadays it is not permitted to set dogs or cocks at each other (at any rate in England such pastimes are punished); but men are set at each other in deadly conflict against their will through the ridiculous superstition of the absurd principle of knightly honour and its narrow-minded advocates and exponents who impose on them the obligation to fight like gladiators for the sake of any trifling thing. I therefore suggest to our German purists the word 'baiting' for the word 'duel' which probably comes not from the Latin *duellum*, but from the Spanish *duelo*, meaning suffering, nuisance, annoyance. The pedantic way in which this folly is carried on certainly affords material for laughter. It is, however, revolting that this principle and its absurd code establish a state within the State which acknowledges no other right than that of might. It tyrannizes the classes that come under its authority by keeping open a holy Vehmgericht[27] before which anyone can be

* The real reason why governments apparently strive to suppress the duel and, whilst this would obviously be a very easy matter especially at the universities, give one the impression of not wanting to succeed, seems to me to be this. The State is not in a position to pay cash in full for the services of its officers and civil officials and therefore arranges for the other half of their emoluments to consist in honour that takes the form of titles, uniforms, and orders. Now to maintain at a high level this ideal indemnification of their services, the feeling of honour must be fostered and intensified in every possible way; at all events it must become something fantastic and extravagant. As civic honour is not enough for the attainment of this end simply because it is shared by all alike, knightly honour is resorted to and upheld in the way I have described. In England where the emoluments for civil and military service are very much higher than on the Continent, this expedient is not necessary. Therefore the duel has been almost entirely eradicated in that country, especially during the last twenty years, and now occurs very rarely indeed. When it does occur, it is laughed at as a piece of folly. It is certain that the great Anti-Duelling Society, numbering many peers, admirals, and generals among its members, has largely contributed to this result. The Moloch must do without its victims.

[27] [A secret tribunal in late medieval Westphalia.]

charged on the flimsiest of pretexts as a myrmidon, to be tried on an issue of life and death. Now this naturally becomes the hiding-place whence any villain, if only he belongs to those classes, can menace and even exterminate the noblest and best of men who, as such, must inevitably be odious to him. Nowadays justice and the police have made it fairly difficult for any scoundrel in the street any longer to shout at us: 'Your money or your life'; and at last sound reason should be able to prevent any rogue from disturbing the peace by shouting: 'Your honour or your life'. The upper classes should be relieved of the burden that arises from the fact that anyone at any moment may become responsible, with his life and limb, for the rudeness, roughness, stupidity, and malice of anyone else who is pleased to visit these on him. It is outrageous and scandalous that, when two young hot-heads have words, they should atone for this with blood, their health, or their lives. The evil of the tyranny of that state within the State and the magnitude of the force of that superstition can be gauged from the fact that those who found it impossible to restore their wounded knightly honour because of the superior or inferior rank or of any other inappropriate peculiarity of the offender, took their lives in utter despair and thus came to a tragi-comic end. The false and absurd are in the end often disclosed by the fact that, at their culminating point, they blossom into a contradiction. Here too they ultimately appear in the form of the most glaring antinomy; thus an officer is forbidden to take part in a duel, but is punished with dismissal if, when challenged, he declines to take part.

While I am on the subject, I will be even more frank. Considered in the proper light and without prejudice, the important distinction, often insisted on, between our killing our enemy in fair fight with equal weapons and our lying in ambush for him rests merely on the fact, as I have said, that this state within the State recognized no other right than that of the stronger and thus of might, raised this to a judgement of God, and made it the basis of its code. For by killing our enemy in a fair fight, we have simply proved that we were the stronger or more skilful. Therefore the justification we seek when engaged in a fair fight, presupposes that the *right of the stronger* really is a *right*. But the truth is that, if the other man is unable to defend himself, this circumstance gives me the possibility, yet by no means the right, to kill him. On the contrary, this right and thus my *moral* justification can rest only on *motives* that I have for taking his life. Now if we assume that these actually existed and were sufficient, there is absolutely no reason for making this depend on whether I can shoot or fence better than he, but it is then immaterial how I kill him, whether I attack him from the front or from behind. For morally, the right of the stronger has no more weight than has that of the more skilful, which is employed by the treacherous murderer. Therefore right of might and right of skill here have equal weight; further, it should be observed that, even in the duel, both are brought to bear since every feint in fencing is treachery or deception. If I consider myself morally justified in taking a man's life, then it is stupid to let this depend on whether he can shoot or fence better than I; for in that case he will not only have wronged me, but will have taken my life into the bargain. It is Rousseau's opinion that insults should be avenged not by a duel, but by assassination. He cautiously hints at this in the very mysterious twenty-first note to the fourth book of *Émile* (p. 173, *ed. Bip.*). But he is here so much under the influence of knightly super-stition that he thinks he is justified in assassinating a man who has reproached him with lying; whereas he must have known that everyone, and he himself most of all, merited this reproach times without number. The prejudice that justifies the killing of the offender, on condition that this is done in an open contest with equal weapons, evidently regards the right of might as real and the duel as a judgement of God. On the other hand, the Italian who, in a fit of rage, falls on his opponent wherever he finds him, and stabs him without ceremony, at any rate acts consistently and naturally; he is more cunning, but not worse than the duellist. If it should be said that, in killing my opponent in the duel, I am justified by the fact that he is like-wise endeavouring to kill me, the retort is that, by challenging him, I put him under the necessity of having to defend himself. By intentionally putting themselves under such necessity, the two duellists are in effect seeking a plausible excuse for murder. Justification through the principle *volenti non fit injuria*[28] would be more plausible in so far as both have mutually agreed to

[28] ['No wrong is done to him who wishes to have it thus.' (Aristotle, *Nicomachean Ethics*, lib. v. c. 15.)]

stake their lives on this. But against this it can be said that the
volens is not necessarily in the right, for the myrmidon is the
tyranny of the principle of knightly honour and its absurd code
which drags both, or at any rate one of the two combatants,
before this bloody Vehmgericht.

On the question of knightly honour, I have gone into detail;
but I have done so with good intention, because philosophy is
the only Hercules against the moral and intellectual enormity
in the world. In the main there are two things that distinguish
the social conditions of modern times from those of antiquity
to the detriment of the former, since they have given these a
grave, dark, and sinister aspect, from which antiquity, bright
and ingenuous like the morning of life, is free. I refer to the
principle of knightly honour and venereal disease, *par nobile
fratrum!*[29] Together they have poisoned the νεῖκος καὶ φιλία[30] of
life. Venereal disease extends its influence much farther than
might appear at first glance since this is by no means merely
physical but moral as well. Since Cupid's quiver also contains
poisoned arrows, the relations between the sexes have assumed
a strange, hostile, and even diabolical element. In consequence
thereof, a sombre and fearful mistrust permeates such relations;
and the indirect influence of such a change in the foundation of
all human society even extends, more or less, to all other social
relations. But to enter into this would take me too far from my
subject. Analogous to this, although of quite a different nature,
is the influence of the principle of knightly honour, this solemn
farce which was foreign to the ancients but makes modern
society stiff, serious, and nervous because people scrutinize and
ruminate on every fleeting expression. But this is not all! This
principle is a universal Minotaur to which a good number of
the sons of noble houses must be brought as tribute every year,
not from one country, as of old, but from every country in
Europe. It is, therefore, time boldly to attack this bugbear, as
is being done here. May these two monsters of modern times
come to an end in the nineteenth century! We will not give up
hope that doctors will finally succeed in dealing with the first
by means of prophylactics. But to abolish the *bugbear* is the
business of philosophers by correcting conceptions, since

[29] ['A noble pair of brothers' (Horace, *Satires*, ii. 3. 243).]
[30] ['Quarrel and love' (Empedocles).]

governments by means of legislation have hitherto failed; moreover, only on the first path is the evil attacked at the roots. If, however, governments should really be in earnest about suppressing the duel and the small success of their efforts is really due merely to their inability to cope with the evil, then I will suggest to them a law whose success I guarantee; moreover, they can resort to it without any sanguinary operations, scaffold, gallows, or life imprisonment. On the contrary, it is quite a small, easy, homoeopathic expedient; thus the man who challenges another or adopts towards him a hostile attitude, should receive *à la chinoise* in broad daylight before the main guard twelve strokes from the corporal, whilst seconds and witnesses should each receive six. The ultimate consequences of a duel that has actually taken place should form the subject of ordinary criminal proceedings. Perhaps a man of knightly notions might object that, after the carrying out of such a punishment, many a 'man of honour' might possibly shoot himself. My answer is that it is better for such a fool to shoot himself than shoot others. At bottom, however, I know quite well that governments are not really in earnest about abolishing the duel. The salaries of civil officials and even more so those of officers (apart from the highest posts) are far less than the value of their services. The other half of their emoluments is, therefore, paid in honours that are represented primarily by titles and orders and generally in the wider sense by the honours of rank and position. Now for this honour of rank, the duel is a useful side-horse and so preliminary training in it is already given at the universities. Accordingly, its victims pay with their blood for the deficiency in their salaries.

For the sake of completeness, we have still to mention *national honour*. It is the honour of a whole nation that is a part of the community of nations. Now as there is in this no other forum than that of force and as therefore every member of that community has to protect its own rights, a nation's honour consists not only in the established opinion that it is to be trusted (credit), but also in the opinion that it is to be feared. Therefore it must never allow to go unpunished attacks on its rights; and thus it combines civic with knightly honour.

Reputation was the last thing previously mentioned under what a man *represents*, in other words, what he is in the eyes of the world; and so we have still to consider it. Reputation and honour are twins; yet they are like the Dioscuri of which Pollux was immortal whereas Castor was mortal; reputation is the immortal brother of mortal honour. This, of course, is to be understood only of reputation or fame of the highest order which is real and genuine; for there are certainly many kinds of ephemeral fame. Now honour concerns only those qualities that are demanded of all who are in the same circumstances; fame concerns those that cannot be demanded of anyone. Honour has to do with those qualities that everyone may publicly attribute to himself; fame with those that no one may so attribute. Whereas our honour reaches as far as the information about us, fame conversely hurries in advance of that information and carries this as far as it itself goes. Everyone has a claim to honour; only the exceptions have one to fame which is won only by extraordinary achievements. Again, these are either *actions* or *works*; and accordingly two paths are open to fame. A great heart is a special qualification for the path of *actions* and a great mind for that of *works*. Each of the two paths has its own advantages and drawbacks, and the main difference is that actions pass whereas works remain. Of actions there remains only the memory that becomes ever more feeble, distorted, and insignificant, and must gradually cease to exist, unless history takes it up and then hands it on to posterity in a petrified state. Works, on the other hand, are themselves immortal and, especially if they are in writing, can live throughout the ages. The noblest deed has only a temporary influence, whereas the work of genius lives and has a beneficial and ennobling effect for all time. Of Alexander the Great only the name and memory live; whereas Plato and Aristotle, Homer and Horace themselves still exist, live, and have an immediate effect. The *Vedas* and their *Upanishads* exist, but of all the actions that took place in their age no information whatever has come down to us.* Another disadvantage of actions is their

---

* Accordingly, it is a poor compliment when anyone, as is the fashion nowadays, imagines he is honouring works by calling them actions; for works are essentially of a higher order. An action is always something based on motive and consequently fragmentary and fleeting; and it appertains to the universal and original element of the world and hence to the will. A great or fine work, on the other hand, is something permanent because it is of universal significance. It has sprung from the intelligence, pure, spotless, and rising like a perfume from this world of the will.

dependence on the opportunity that must first afford the possibility of their occurrence. Connected with this is the fact that their fame is not directed solely to their intrinsic worth, but to the circumstances that impart to them lustre and importance. Moreover, if as in war the actions are purely personal, their fame depends on the statements of a few eyewitnesses who, however, are not always present and, even if they are, are not always just and impartial. On the other hand, actions have the advantage, as something practical, of lying within the sphere of the general ability to judge; and so if only the data are correctly transmitted to it, justice is at once done to them, unless their motives are correctly known and properly appreciated only later; for to understand any action, knowledge of its motive is required. With works it is just the opposite; their origin does not depend on chance but simply on their author, and as long as they last they remain what they are in and by themselves. In their case, on the other hand, there is difficulty in judging, and the higher their character, the greater is this difficulty; frequently there is a lack of competent critics and often there are no impartial and honest judges. However, their fame is not decided by *one* instance, but an appeal is made. For whereas, as I have said, only the memory of actions comes down to posterity and indeed only in the form furnished by contemporaries, works come down to us as they are, apart from a few missing fragments. Here, then, we have no distortion of the data, and also any unfavourable influence of environment at their origin later disappears. In fact it is often only after the lapse of time that the few really competent judges gradually appear who are already themselves exceptions and sit in judgement on even greater exceptions. Successively they give their weighty verdicts and then, sometimes of course only after centuries, we have a perfectly just appreciation that can no longer be set aside by future ages; so secure and inevitable is the

An advantage of the fame of actions is that it appears as a rule at once with a loud explosion, often so loud that it is heard all over Europe; whereas the fame of works appears slowly and gradually; at first it is slight; then it grows ever louder and often only after a hundred years does it reach its full force. But then it lasts because works remain, sometimes for thousands of years. On the other hand, after the first explosion is over, the fame of actions gradually becomes weaker and is known to fewer and fewer people until in the end it has only a ghostlike existence in history.

fame of works. On the other hand, it depends on external circumstances and chance whether their author lives to enjoy fame; the loftier and more difficult they have been, the more rarely will this be the case. In keeping with this, Seneca says with incomparable beauty (*Epistulae*, 79) that merit is followed by fame as infallibly as a body by its shadow; but like this, of course, it is sometimes in front of and sometimes behind it, and after making this clear, he adds: *etiamsi omnibus tecum viventibus SILENTIUM LIVOR INDIXERIT, venient qui sine offensa, sine gratia judicent.*[31] Incidentally, from this we see that the art of suppressing merit by malicious silence and by ignoring it in order to conceal from the public the good in favour of the bad, was practised even by the bunglers of Seneca's time as it is by our own, and that in both cases *envy tightened their lips*. As a rule, the longer fame has to endure, the later will it be in appearing, for everything that is excellent matures slowly. The fame that will become posthumous and permanent is like an oak that grows very slowly from its seed; easy ephemeral fame resembles the rapid-growing plant of one year, and false fame can be compared to the quick-sprouting weed that can be most readily uprooted. This state of affairs is really due to the fact that, the more a man belongs to posterity, i.e. actually to mankind generally, the more of a stranger he is to his age, since what he produces is not specially devoted to this as such, but only in so far as it is a part of mankind. And so his works are not tinged with the local colour of his times; but, in consequence of this, it may easily happen that he is allowed to pass away as a stranger. On the contrary, his age appreciates those who minister to the affairs of its own brief day, or who serve the mood of the moment and therefore belong entirely thereto, living and dying with it. Accordingly, the history of art and literature shows generally that the highest achievements of the human mind were, as a rule, not favourably received and remained out of favour until minds of a higher order came who were impressed by them and brought them into vogue. They then subsequently maintained themselves therein through the authority that was obtained in this way. But all this is due ultimately to the fact that everyone can really understand and

---

[31] ['Although *envy imposed silence* on all who lived with you, those men will come who will judge without ill-will and without favour.']

appreciate only what appeals to his nature. Now the dullard
will like what is dull, the common man what is common, the
vague person what is confused and indistinct, the brainless fool
what is nonsense, and everyone is pleased most of all with his
own works, as being thoroughly in keeping with his nature.
Therefore the ancient and legendary Epicharmus sang:

> Θαυμαστὸν οὐδέν ἐστί, με ταῦθ' οὕτω λέγειν,
> Καὶ ἀνδάνειν αὐτοῖσιν αὐτοὺς καὶ δοκεῖν
> Καλῶς πεφυκέναι· καὶ γὰρ ὁ κύων κυνὶ
> Κάλλιστον εἶμεν φαίνεται, καὶ βοῦς βοΐ,
> Ὄνος δὲ ὄνῳ κάλλιστον, ὗς δὲ ὑΐ.

which I will translate so that it will not be lost:

> It is no wonder that I speak according to my views,
> And they are pleased with themselves, and vainly imagine
> They are worthy of praise. For to the dog a dog
> Seems to be the finest thing, to the ox an ox,
> To the ass an ass, and to the pig a pig.

When even the strongest arm flings away a light body, it is
still unable to impart thereto any motion with which it might
fly far and violently hit the mark. On the contrary, such a body
soon falls to the ground because it lacked material substance
of its own for absorbing the outside force. It is the same with
fine and great ideas, in fact with the masterpiece of genius,
when for their reception there exist only puny, feeble, or queer
minds. The voices of the wise men of all ages have joined in the
chorus of deploring this. For instance, Jesus ben Sirach says:
'He that telleth a tale to a fool, speaketh to one in slumber;
when he hath told his tale, he will say, What is the matter?'
And Hamlet says: 'A knavish speech sleeps in a fool's ear.'
Goethe says:

> The most felicitous word is mocked,
> When it is heard by the dullard's ear.

Again:

> Your effect is nought, all is still so dull.
> Be of good cheer! No rings are formed,
> When a pebble is cast in the mire.

Lichtenberg says: 'If a head and a book collide and there is a
hollow sound, is it always the book?' Again: 'Such works are
mirrors; if an ape looks in, no apostle can look out.' Indeed,

Father Gellert's fine and touching lament is worth recalling once more:

> The best of all gifts are often the least admired.
> Most of the world regards the worst as the best.
> Daily is this evil seen, yet how to prevent this scourge?
> I doubt if it can be removed from our world.
> The sole remedy on earth is extremely hard.
> Thus fools must be wise, but this they will never be.
> They never know the worth of things. With their eyes they
> Judge, but not with their minds. The trivial is
> Eternally praised because they have never known the good.

To this intellectual incapacity of men in consequence whereof the excellent, as Goethe says, is rarely found and still more rarely perceived and appreciated, is now added the moral depravity of mankind which here appears as envy. Thus the fame that is won by a man again raises him above all those of his class who are, therefore, to that extent degraded; and so every outstanding merit acquires its fame at the expense of those who have none.

> When we pay honour to others,
> We must degrade ourselves.
> Goethe, *Westöstlicher Diwan*.

This explains why excellence, in whatever form it may appear, is at once confronted with the united mediocrity of the vast majority who are in league against it and are sworn to prevent it from appearing and, if possible, to suppress it. Their secret pass-word is: *À bas le mérite.*[32] But even those who themselves possess merit and have thus acquired fame, will not want to see the appearance of a new fame whose radiance will make theirs the less brilliant; and so even Goethe says:

> Had I lingered at my birth
> · Till I were granted life,
> I should still not be on earth.
> As you may know, when you see
> How they fain would ignore me
> Who give themselves such airs,
> To parade and show their wares.

Therefore, whereas *honour* as a rule meets with fair judges and

[32] ['Down with merit!']

is not attacked by envy, in fact everyone is even credited in advance with it, *fame* must be won after a struggle with envy and the laurel is awarded by a tribunal of decidedly unfair judges. For honour we can and will share with everyone; fame is curtailed and made more difficult by everyone who acquires it. Further, the difficulty of acquiring fame through works is inversely proportional to the number of those who form their public; and the reasons for this are easy to see. Therefore it is much greater with works that promise instruction than with those that promise entertainment; it is greatest of all with philosophical works because the instruction promised by them is doubtful and uncertain, on the one hand, and useless from a material point of view, on the other. Accordingly, such works make their appearance primarily before a public that consists of none but rivals and competitors. From the above-mentioned difficulties that oppose the attainment of fame, it is clear that if those who produce works of merit did not do so out of love for them and for their own enjoyment but needed to be encouraged by fame, mankind would have received few, if any, immortal works. In fact, the man who is to produce what is good and right and to avoid what is bad, must defy and thus disdain the judgement of the masses and their spokesmen. On this rests the correctness of the remark that is in particular stressed by Osorius (*De gloria*) that fame eschews those who seek it and follows those who pay it no heed; for the former adapt themselves to the tastes of their contemporaries whereas the latter defy them.

Accordingly, difficult as it is to acquire fame, it is easy to retain it. Here too it stands in contrast to honour with which everyone is even credited; for he has merely to defend it. But this is the problem, for by a single unworthy act honour is irretrievably lost. Fame, on the other hand, can never really be lost; for the deed or work whereby it was acquired is established for all time and its author retains his fame, even if he does nothing more. If, however, the fame actually dies away and has had its day, it was not genuine, that is, it was un-merited and arose from a temporary over-estimation; or it was even a fame such as Hegel enjoyed, and is described by Lichten-berg as 'trumpeted abroad by a clique of friendly candidates and resounding with the echo of empty heads;—but how posterity will smile when it one day knocks on the doors of brightly coloured word-edifices, of the nests of departed fashions, and of the dwellings of dead and defunct conventions, and finds everything empty, not even the smallest thought that could confidently say: *come in!*'

Fame really rests on what a man is in comparison with others. Accordingly, it is something essentially relative and so can have only a relative value. It would disappear entirely if others were to become what the famous man is. Absolute value can belong only to that which retains it under all circumstances and thus to what a man is directly and by himself. Consequently, the value and good fortune of a great heart and great mind must be found here. Therefore not fame but that whereby we merit it is the thing of value. For it is, so to speak, the substance, fame being only the accident; indeed, this affects the famous man mainly as an external symptom whereby he obtains confirmation of his own high opinion of himself. Accordingly, it might be said that, just as light is not visible at all unless it is reflected by a body, so every excellent quality becomes certain and positive only through its own reputation. But it is not even an infallible symptom, for we also have fame without merit and merit without fame; hence Lessing's clever remark: 'Some men are famous and others deserve to be.' Moreover, it would be a miserable existence whose worth or worthlessness depended on how it appeared in the eyes of others. But such would be the life of the hero and the genius if his worth consisted in fame, that is to say, in the approbation of others. On the contrary, every man lives and exists on his own account and, therefore, primarily in and by himself. What a man is, whatever his mode of existence, is first and foremost a matter for himself; and if in this respect he is not worth much, then he is not worth much in general. On the other hand, the image of his nature in the minds of others is something secondary, derived, and subject to chance, and refers only very indirectly to that nature. Moreover, other people's heads are too wretched a place for true happiness to have its seat; rather do we find there only an imaginary happiness. What a mixed company we meet in that temple of universal fame: generals, ministers, quacks, jugglers, dancers, singers, millionaires, and Jews! In fact, the excellent qualities of all these are much more sincerely appreciated in this temple, meet with much more *estime sentie*,[33] than do intellectual qualities, especially those of a higher order which with the great majority obtain only an *estime sur parole*.[33] Thus from the point of view of eudemonology, fame is nothing but the rarest and daintiest morsel for our pride and vanity. But in most men these exist to excess, though they are concealed; perhaps they are strongest in those who are in some way qualified to acquire fame. Such men, therefore, have to wait a long time in uncertainty regarding their outstanding worth before the opportunity comes for them to put this to the test and then experience its acknowledgement. Till then, they felt as though they had suffered a secret injustice.* But generally speaking, as was discussed at the beginning of this chapter, the value a man attaches to other people's opinion of him is unreasonable and out of all proportion. Hobbes expressed the matter very forcibly, it is true, but perhaps quite correctly when he said: *omnis animi voluptas, omnisque alacritas in eo sita est, quod quis habeat quibuscum conferens se, possit magnifice sentire de se ipso*[34] (*De cive*, lib. I, c. 5). From this one can easily appreciate the great value that is usually attached to fame and the sacrifices that are made in the mere hope of one day attaining it:

> Fame is the spur that the clear spirit doth raise
> (That last infirmity of noble mind)
> To scorn delights and live laborious days.
> Milton, Lycidas.

And again:

> How hard it is to climb
> The steep where Fame's proud temple shines afar!
> Beattie, The Minstrel.

Finally, we can also see why the vainest of all nations constantly talks about *la gloire* and regards this unquestionably as the main incentive to great deeds and works. But there is no doubt that fame is only something secondary, the mere echo,

---

* Our greatest pleasure consists in being *admired*; but the admirers, even if there is every cause, are not very keen to express their admiration. And so the happiest man is he who has managed sincerely to admire himself, no matter how. Only others must not cause him to doubt this.

[33] ['Felt esteem'; 'esteem on the strength of a remark'.]

[34] ['All the delights of the heart and every cheerful frame of mind depend on our having someone with whom we can compare ourselves and think highly of ourselves.']

reflection, shadow, or symptom of merit, and that in any case the thing admired must be worth more than the admiration. Therefore what makes a man really happy cannot be found in fame, but in that which enables him to acquire this and hence in merit itself, or to speak more precisely, in the disposition and abilities whence such merit has come, whether it be of a moral or intellectual order. For everyone must necessarily be for himself the best that he is; the reflection of this in the minds of others and their opinion of him is a secondary matter and for him can be only of subordinate interest. Accordingly, the man who *merits* fame without obtaining it possesses by far the greater thing, and what he forgoes is something about which he can console himsef with what he possesses. For it is not the fact that he is considered a great man by a crowd of deluded people without judgement, but the fact that he is so which makes him envied. His great happiness is not that posterity will know something about him, but that in him thoughts are engendered which merit preservation and consideration for hundreds of years. Moreover, this happiness cannot be wrested from him; it is $\tau\hat{\omega}\nu$ ἐφ' ἡμῖν, whereas fame is $\tau\hat{\omega}\nu$ οὐκ ἐφ' ἡμῖν.[35] If, on the other hand, admiration itself were the principal matter, the thing admired would not be worth it; this is actually the case with false, i.e. unmerited, fame. The possessor of such must live on it without actually having that whereof the fame should be the symptom or mere reflection. But even that fame itself must often become distasteful to him when at times, in spite of all the deception, born of self-interest, he feels giddy at heights he was never fit to climb, or feels as if he were a copper coin. The fear of being unmasked and rightly humiliated then seizes him, especially when he already reads the verdict of posterity on the brows of the more prudent. Accordingly, he is like a man who possesses property through a forged will. The most genuine fame, namely posthumous, is never heard of by the man who has acquired it, and yet he is considered fortunate. His good fortune, therefore, consisted in the great qualities themselves whereby he acquired fame and in the fact that he found the opportunity to develop them, and was granted to act in a way best suited to him or to do what he liked and enjoyed doing; for only works born of this acquire posthumous fame. Thus his

[35] ['Is in our power . . . is not in our power'.]

happiness consisted in his great heart or even in the wealth of a mind whose stamp receives in his works the admiration of the centuries to come. It consisted in the ideas themselves whose consideration became the business and pleasure of the noblest minds of an immeasurable future. Hence the value of posthumous fame is to be found in meriting it; and this is its own reward. Now whether works that acquired fame also enjoyed the praise of their author's contemporaries depended on chance circumstances and was not of great importance. For as people generally are unable to judge for themselves and are also absolutely incapable of appreciating noble and difficult achievements, they always follow here the authority of someone else; and reputation of a higher order rests on mere faith in the case of ninety-nine out of a hundred of those who praise. And so for those who think, the vociferous approbation of contemporaries can be only of little value since in it they always hear merely the echo of a few voices that are themselves only the product of a day. Would a musician feel flattered by the loud applause of his audience if it were known to him that, with the exception of one or two, it consisted entirely of deaf people who, to conceal from one another their infirmity, eagerly clapped as soon as they saw the one or two exceptions move their hands? And supposing that in addition he knew that those exceptions could often be bribed to obtain the loudest applause for the poorest violinist! From this it is easy to see why the praise of contemporaries is so rarely transformed into posthumous fame. Therefore in his exceedingly fine description of the temple of literary fame, D'Alembert says: 'The interior of the temple is inhabited by none but the dead who during their lifetime were not there, and by a few still living almost all of whom will be thrown out when they die.' Incidentally, it may be observed here that to erect a monument to a man during his lifetime is tantamount to declaring that, with regard to him, posterity is not to be trusted. If, however, a man lives to see his fame that is to become posthumous, this will rarely occur before he is old. Possibly among artists and poets there are a few exceptions to this rule; they are fewest among philosophers. A confirmation of this is furnished by the portraits of men who have become famous through their works, for in most cases they were taken only after their subjects had become celebrated. As a rule, they are depicted as old and grey, especially if they are philosophers. From the point of view of eudemonology, this is absolutely as it should be; since fame and youth at the same time are too much for a mortal. Our life is so poor that its good things must be sparingly allotted. Youth has enough and to spare in its own wealth and should rest content therewith. But when in old age joys and pleasures wither like trees in winter, the tree of fame most opportunely bursts forth as a genuine wintergreen. It can also be compared to winter pears that grow in summer but are eaten in winter. There is no finer consolation in old age than the feeling of our having embodied the whole force of our youth in *works* that will not grow old.

Now if we wish to consider somewhat more closely the paths by which we attain fame in those branches of knowledge with which we are immediately concerned, the following rule can be laid down. The intellectual superiority that is indicated by such fame is always brought to light by a new combination of some data. Now these can be of a very varied nature, yet the fame to be acquired through their combination will be the greater and more widespread, the more the data themselves are universally known and are accessible to everyone. For example, if they consist in numbers or curves, in some special fact of physics, zoology, botany, or anatomy, or else in some mutilated passages of ancient authors, in half-obliterated inscriptions, or in inscriptions whose alphabet is missing, or even in obscure points of history, the fame to be gained from their correct combination will not go much further than a knowledge of the data themselves; thus it will extend to a small number of those who often live retired lives and are jealous of their reputation in their particular branch of knowledge. If, on the other hand, the data are known to the whole of the human race; if, for example, they are the essential characteristics of the human mind or human heart common to everyone, or natural forces whose whole manner of operation is constantly before our eyes, or the universally known course of nature in general, then the fame of having shed more light on them by a new, important, and evident combination will extend in time to almost the whole of the civilized world. For if the data are accessible to everyone, so too will be their combination in most cases. Nevertheless, the fame here will always be in keeping only with the difficulties overcome; for the more generally known the data are, the more difficult will it be to combine them in a new and yet correct way since an exceedingly great number of minds have already tried their strength on them and have exhausted their possible combinations. On the other hand, data that are not accessible to the public at large, and are reached only in difficult and arduous ways, always admit of new combinations. If, therefore, a man approaches them with a clear understanding and sound judgement and thus with a moderate amount of intellectual superiority, it is quite possible for him to be fortunate enough to form a new and correct combination of them. But fame thus gained will be limited more or less in the same way as is a knowledge of the data. For the solution of such problems, no doubt, calls for much study and labour, merely in order to acquire a knowledge of the data; whereas with problems of the other kind wherein the greatest and most widespread fame is to be won, the data are given gratuitously without any study or labour. But in proportion as this type of problem calls for less labour, it requires more talent and even genius; and with these, as regards merit and value, no labour or study bears any comparison.

Now it follows from this that those who feel they have good understanding and sound judgement, without presuming to have the highest mental gifts, should not be afraid of much study and laborious work. For by means thereof they work themselves above the great mass of humanity who have the well-known data before their eyes; and they reach the remoter places that are accessible only to the activity and industry of scholars. For here the number of competitors is infinitely smaller, and a man of even only moderate intelligence will soon find an opportunity for a new and correct combination of the data. Indeed the merit of his discovery will even be based on the difficulty of arriving at them. But the applause of his colleagues which has been won in this way—for they are the only ones who are familiar with the subject—will be heard by the crowd only from a great distance. Now if we wish to pursue to the very end the path here indicated, a point will be reached where the data alone, without the necessity of their combination, suffice to establish fame because they are very difficult to obtain. This is the case as regards journeys to remote and rarely visited countries, where a man is famous for what he has seen and not for what he has thought. This way also has a great advantage in the fact that it is very much easier to communicate to others what we have seen than what we have thought, and it is just the same as regards people's comprehension. Accordingly, we shall find many more readers for the former than for the latter; for as Asmus says:

> When someone makes a journey,
> He has a tale to tell.[36]

But in keeping with all this, a personal acquaintance with famous travellers frequently reminds us of an observation by Horace:

> *Coelum, non animum, mutant qui trans mare currunt.*
> *(Epistles,* I. II. 27.)[37]

But as regards the man endowed with great intellectual ability who alone should venture to solve the most difficult problems, namely those dealing with the universal and total aspect of things, he will do well to extend his horizon as far as possible, yet always equally in all directions without ever going too far astray in some particular region that is known to only a few, in other words, without going too deeply into the intricacies of some special branch of knowledge, to say nothing of getting involved in minute details. It is not necessary for him to apply himself to subjects that are difficult of access in order to avoid a crowd of competitors. On the contrary, the very thing that everyone can see will supply him with material for new, important, and true combinations. Now according to this, it will be possible for his merit to be appreciated by all to whom the data are known and so by a great part of the human race. On this rests the immense difference between the fame that is won by poets and philosophers and that attainable by physicists, chemists, anatomists, mineralogists, zoologists, philologists, historians, and others.

[36] [Matthias Claudius.]

[37] ['Whoever travels overseas has a change of climate, not a change of tastes and ideas.']

CHAPTER V

Counsels and Maxims

MY object here is anything but an attempt to be complete; for otherwise I should have to repeat the many maxims, some excellent, which have been laid down by the thinkers of all ages from Theognis and Solomon to La Rochefoucauld; and in so doing it would be impossible to avoid many a well-worn commonplace. Moreover, an attempt at completeness entails for the most part the abandonment of any systematic arrangement. We may console ourselves for the loss of these two with the thought that, in things of this kind, they are almost inevitably attended with tediousness. I have given just what occurred to me, what seemed to be worth communicating, and, as far as I know, what has not yet been said, at any rate not entirely and in just this form. And so I have written only a supplement to what others have achieved in this immense field.

Yet to introduce some order into the great variety of opinions and advice that are relevant here, I intend to divide them into those that are general, those that concern our attitude to ourselves, to others, and finally to fate and the course of the world.

A. *General Views*

(1) I regard as the first rule of all wisdom of life a sentence, incidentally expressed by Aristotle in the *Nicomachean Ethics* (VII. 12): ὁ φρόνιμος τὸ ἄλυπον διώκει, οὐ τὸ ἡδύ (*quod dolore vacat, non quod suave est, persequitur vir prudens.* The Latin version is feeble; a better one might be somewhat as follows: 'The prudent man aims at painlessness not pleasure.') The truth of this rests on the fact that the nature of all pleasure and happiness is negative, whereas that of pain is positive. A detailed discussion of this will be found in my chief work, vol. i, § 58; however, I will here illustrate it by another fact that can be daily observed. If our whole body is healthy and sound except for some sore or painful spot, we are no longer conscious of the health of the whole, but our attention is constantly directed to

the pain of the injured spot and all the comfort and enjoyment of life vanish. In the same way, when all our affairs turn out the way we want them to go with the exception of one that runs counter to our intentions, this one affair constantly recurs even when it is of little importance. We often think about it and pay little attention to all the other more important things that are turning out in accordance with our wishes. Now in both cases, what is injuriously affected is the will, in the one case as it objectifies itself in the organism, in the other, as it is objectified in man's efforts and aspirations. In both we see that the satisfaction of the will always operates only negatively and therefore is not directly felt at all; but at most we become conscious of it when we reflect on the matter. On the other hand, what checks and obstructs the will is something positive which therefore makes its presence known. Every pleasure consists merely in the removal of this hindrance, on our liberation therefrom, and is in consequence of short duration.

This, then, is the basis of the above-mentioned rule of Aristotle which tells us to direct our aim not to what is pleasant and agreeable in life, but to the avoidance, as far as possible, of its numberless evils. If this were not the right way, then Voltaire's remark: *Le bonheur n'est qu'un rêve, et la douleur est réelle*[1] would of necessity be as false as it is in fact true. Accordingly, whoever wants to assess the result of his life in terms of eudemonology, should draw up the account to show not the pleasures he has enjoyed, but the evils he has escaped. Indeed, eudemonology must begin by informing us that its very name is a euphemism and that, when we say 'to live happily', we are to understand by this merely 'to live less unhappily' and hence to live a tolerable life. It is quite certain that life is not really given to us to be enjoyed, but to be overcome, to be got over. This is also seen in many expressions, such as *degere vitam, vita defungi,*[2] the Italian *si scampa cosi,*[3] the German *man muss suchen, durchzukommen,*[4] *er wird schon durch die Welt kommen,*[5] and others. In old age it is indeed a consolation to know that the business of life is behind us. Accordingly, the happiest lot is that

---

[1] ['Happiness is only a dream and pain is real.']
[2] ['To get through life, to overcome life'.]   [3] ['If only we get over it!']
[4] ['We must try to get along as well as we can.']
[5] ['He will get through the world.']

of the man who has got through life without any very great pain, bodily or mental, not that of the man who has experienced the keenest delights or greatest pleasures. Whoever tries to measure the happiness of life according to pleasures and delights, has taken a false standard. For pleasures are and remain negative; that they make us happy is an erroneous idea which is cherished by the envious to their own punishment. Pain, on the other hand, is felt positively; and so its absence is the standard of happiness. If in addition to a state of painlessness we have absence of boredom, we have really attained earthly happiness; for all else is a chimera. Now it follows from this that we should never purchase pleasures at the price, or even the risk, of pain, since we then pay what is positive and real for something that is negative and thus illusory. On the other hand, we are left with a gain when we sacrifice pleasures in order to avoid pain. In both cases, it is immaterial whether the pain follows or precedes the pleasure. It is really the greatest absurdity to try to turn this scene of woe and lamentation into a pleasure-resort and to aim at joys and pleasures, as do so many, rather than at the greatest possible freedom from pain. Whoever takes a gloomy view regards this world as a kind of hell and is accordingly concerned only with procuring for himself a small fireproof room; such a man is much less mistaken. The fool runs after the pleasures of life and sees himself cheated; the wise man avoids its evils. Yet even if he should fail to avoid them, this is the fault of fate not of his folly; but in so far as he succeeds, he is not duped, for the evils he avoided are indeed very real. Even if he should have gone too far in avoiding them and have unnecessarily sacrificed pleasures, nothing has really been lost; for all pleasures are illusory, and to grieve about having missed them would be frivolous and even ridiculous.

The failure to recognize this truth—a failure encouraged by optimism—is the source of much unhappiness. Thus while we are free from pain, restless desires show us in bright colours the chimera of a happiness that does not exist at all and we are seduced into pursuing them; but in this way we bring down on ourselves pain that is undeniably real. We then regret the loss of that painless state which, like a paradise thrown away, lies behind us and in vain do we desire to be able to undo what has been done. It seems as if an evil spirit with visions of desires always enticed us away from the painless state, from the greatest genuine happiness. The careless and thoughtless youth imagines that the world exists in order to be enjoyed; that it is the abode of a positive happiness; and that men miss this because they are not clever enough to take possession of it. He is strengthened in this view by novels and poems and also by hypocrisy which the world always and everywhere practises for the sake of appearance and to which I shall later return. Henceforth his life is a more or less deliberate pursuit of positive happiness and this, as such, is said to consist of positive pleasures. The dangers to which he is exposed in his hunt for happiness must be risked. This hunt for game that does not exist at all leads, as a rule, to very real and positive unhappiness that appears as pain, suffering, sickness, loss, care, poverty, disgrace, and a thousand other miseries. The undeceiving comes too late. On the other hand, if, by following the rule we are here considering, the plan of life is directed to the avoidance of suffering and hence to keeping clear of want, illness, and every kind of distress, the aim is a real one. Something may then be achieved which will be the greater, the less the plan is disturbed by striving after the chimera of positive happiness. This agrees also with the passage of Goethe's *Wahlverwandtschaften* where Mittler, who is always trying to make others happy, is represented as saying: 'Whoever tries to get rid of an evil always knows what he wants; but whoever desires something that is better than what he has, is quite blind.' This also reminds us of the fine French saying: *le mieux est l'ennemi du bien.*[6] In fact, even the fundamental idea of the Cynics can be deduced from this, as I have shown in my chief work, volume ii, chapter 16. For what was it that induced them to spurn all pleasures if not the thought that pain was more or less bound up with them? To avoid pain seemed to them to be much more important than to obtain pleasure. They were deeply imbued with the knowledge of the negative nature of pleasure and of the positive nature of pain. And so they consistently did everything to avoid evils; but for this purpose they considered it necessary to reject pleasures wholly and deliberately because in them they saw only snares that deliver us over to pain.

[6] ['Leave well alone!']

Of course, as Schiller says, we are all born in Arcadia; in other words, we come into the world full of claims to happiness and pleasure and cherish the foolish hope of making them good. As a rule, however, fate soon comes along, seizes us harshly and roughly, and teaches us that nothing belongs to *us* but everything to *it*, since it has the undisputed right not only to all our possessions and acquisitions, to wife and family, but even to our arms and legs, our eyes and ears, and to the very nose in the middle of our face. In any case, experience after a time teaches us that happiness and pleasure are a *fata Morgana* which is visible only from a distance and vanishes when we approach it. On the other hand, we are taught that suffering and pain are real which immediately make themselves felt and need no illusion or expectation. Now if this teaching bears fruit, we cease to run after happiness and pleasure, but rather are we more concerned to bar as much as possible the way to pain and suffering. We then recognize that the best the world has to offer is a painless, quiet, and tolerable existence to which we restrict our claims in order to be the more certain of making them good. For the surest way not to become very unhappy is for us not to expect to be very happy. Merck, the friend of Goethe's youth, recognized this truth for he wrote: 'Everything in this world is ruined by the excessive pretension to happiness and indeed in a measure that corresponds to our dreams. Whoever is able to get rid of this and desires nothing but what he has in hand can get along in the world' (*Briefe an und von Merck*, p. 100). Accordingly, it is advisable to reduce to very moderate proportions our claims to pleasures, possessions, rank, honour, and so on, just because it is this striving and struggling for happiness, brilliance, and pleasure that entail great misfortunes. Therefore reducing our claims is prudent and advisable simply because it is quite easy to be very unhappy, whereas to be very happy is not exactly difficult but absolutely impossible. Therefore the poet of the wisdom of life quite rightly sings:

> *Auream quisquis mediocritatem*
> *Diligit, tutus caret obsoleti*
> *Sordibus tecti, caret invidenda*
> *Sobrius aula.*

Saevius ventis agitatur ingens
Pinus: et celsae graviore casu
Decidunt turres: feriuntque summos
Fulgura montes.[7]

Whoever has fully accepted the teaching of my philosophy and thus knows that our whole existence is something which had better not have been, and to deny and reject which is the highest wisdom, will not cherish great expectations of anything or any condition; he will not ardently aspire to anything in the world, nor will he complain very much if he fails in any undertaking. On the contrary, he will be imbued with Plato's words: οὔτε τι τῶν ἀνθρωπίνων ἄξιον μεγάλης σπουδῆς (*Republic*, x. 604).[8] See the motto to Sadi's *Gulistan*, translated by Graf:

> If you have lost possession of a world,
> Be not distressed, for it is nought;
> And have you gained possession of a world,
> Be not o'erjoyed, for it is nought.
> Our pains, our gains, all pass away;
> Get beyond the world, for it is nought.
>   Anwari Soheili.

What makes it specially difficult for us to arrive at these wholesome views is the hypocrisy of the world which I have already mentioned and which should be made known to one at an early age. Most of the pomp and splendours are, like theatre decorations, mere show, and the very essence of the thing is missing. Ships festooned and dressed with pennants, salutes with cannon, illuminations, beating of drums and blowing of trumpets, shouting, applauding, and so on, all are the outward sign, the hint, the suggestion, the hieroglyphic of *gaiety or joy*. But this is just where joy is rarely found; it alone has declined to be present at the festival. Where it actually makes its appearance, it as a rule comes uninvited and unannounced, by itself and *sans façon*.[9] Indeed, it quietly slips in often on the most unimportant and trivial occasions, in the

---

[7] ['The chooser of the golden mean is certainly far removed from the squalor of the broken hovel and far enough from the envied splendours of the prince's palace.

Caught by the storm, the crown of the mighty pine sways in the wind, the tallest towers crash heavily down, and the mountain tops are struck by thunderbolts.' (Horace, *Odes*, II. 10. 5-12.)]

[8] ['No human affair is worth our troubling ourselves very much about it.']

[9] ['Unceremoniously'.]

most ordinary everyday circumstances; in fact, anywhere but where the company is brilliant or distinguished. It is scattered here and there, like the gold in Australia, by the whim of pure chance according to no rule or law, often only in tiny grains, and exceedingly rarely in large quantities. But the object of all the things just mentioned is to make others believe that joy had here put in an appearance; to produce this illusion in the minds of others is the intention. It is the same with mourning as with joy. How sad and melancholy is that long and slowly moving funeral procession! There is no end to the number of carriages. But look inside them; they are all empty and the deceased is escorted to the grave merely by the coachmen of the whole town. An eloquent picture of the friendship and esteem of this world! This, then, is the falsehood, hollowness, and hypocrisy of human affairs. Again, many guests in ceremonial dress and welcomed with much pomp and festivity afford another example; they are the signs of noble and exalted fellowship. But instead, the real guests, as a rule, are only compulsion, pain, and boredom; for where there are so many guests, it is already a rabble, even though they wear on their breasts all the stars. Thus genuinely good society is everywhere of necessity very small. Generally speaking, however, brilliant parties and noisy entertainments at bottom always have emptiness and even a jarring note because they flagrantly contradict the misery and barrenness of our existence and the contrast enhances the truth. Looked at from without, however, all this has its effect and this is precisely its purpose. Therefore Chamfort makes the excellent remark: *la société, les cercles, les salons, ce qu'on appelle le monde, est une pièce misérable, un mauvais opéra, sans intérêt, qui se soutient un peu par les machines, les costumes et les décorations.*[10] Now it is the same as regards academies and chairs of philosophy; these are the signs, the outward show, of *wisdom*; but she too has often declined to come and is to be found in quite a different place. The continual ringing of bells, the costumes of priests, pious attitudes, and grotesque antics are the outward sign, the false appearance, of devotional feeling, and so on. Thus almost everything in the world can be called a hollow nut; the kernel is in itself rare and

---

[10] ['Society, circles, salons, what is called high society, is a miserable play, a bad opera, without interest, which is kept going for a while by the stage effects, the costumes, and the decorations.']

even more rarely is it to be found in the shell. It must be sought in quite a different place; and frequently it is found only by accident.

(2) If we want to appraise a man's state as regards his happiness, we should ask not about the things that please him, but about those that trouble him; for the more trivial these are in themselves, the more fortunate he is. To be sensitive to trifles implies a state of well-being, since in misfortune we never feel them at all.

(3) We should guard against building the happiness of our life on a *broad foundation* by making many demands. For on such a basis happiness is very easily overthrown, since it offers many more opportunities for accidents, and these are always happening. Therefore, in this respect, the structure of our happiness is the very opposite of all those others that most securely rest on a broad foundation. Accordingly, the surest way to avoid great misfortune is to reduce as much as possible our claims in relation to our means of every kind.

Generally speaking, it is one of the greatest and commonest of follies to make *extensive preparations* for life, in whatever way this may be done. In the first place, such depend on a complete and full life that is attained by very few indeed. Even when men live long enough, the time proves to be too short for the plans that have been made, since to carry them out always requires very much more time than was at first assumed. Moreover, like all things human, such plans are exposed to so many failures and obstacles that they very rarely reach their goal. Finally, even when everything is ultimately attained, the changes that time produces in *ourselves* were ignored and left out of account. Thus we forgot that our capacities either to achieve or enjoy do not last a whole lifetime. The result is that we often work at things which, when finally achieved, are no longer suitable; and also that the years we spend on the preparations of a work imperceptibly rob us of the strength to carry it out. Thus it often happens that we are no longer able to enjoy the wealth we have acquired at so much effort and risk, and that we have laboured for others. Or again, we are no longer able to fill a post that has been finally obtained after many years of aspirations and exertions; for us things have come too late. Or, in the opposite case, we come too late with things; thus in the case of achievements or productions, the taste of the times has changed; a new generation has grown up which takes no interest in such things; others have taken short cuts and have got in front of us, and so on. Horace has all this in mind when he says:

quid aeternis minorem
Consiliis animum fatigas?[11]

The cause of this frequent mistake is the inevitable optical illusion of the mind's eye by virtue whereof life, when seen from the beginning, appears to be endless, but when reviewed from the end of the journey, seems to be very short. This illusion, of course, has its good point, for without it hardly anything great would ever be produced.

In life we are generally like the traveller for whom objects assume, as he progresses, forms that are different from those they exhibited at a distance; they are transformed, so to speak, by his approaching them. This is especially the case as regards our desires. We often find something quite different from, and even better than, what we were looking for. Also we often find the thing sought on a path quite different from the one we had first taken in our vain search for it. Moreover, where we were looking for pleasure, happiness, and joy, we often find instead instruction, insight, and knowledge, a lasting and real benefit in place of one that is fleeting and illusory. This is the idea that runs like a bass-note through Goethe's *Wilhelm Meister*; for this is an intellectual novel and is, therefore, of a higher order than all the rest, even Sir Walter Scott's, which are all ethical, that is to say, treat human nature merely from the side of the will. So too in the *Magic Flute*, this grotesque but significant and ambiguous hieroglyphic, the same fundamental idea is symbolized in large coarse lines as are those of theatre decorations. It would even be complete if, at the end, Tamino were cured of his desire to possess Tamina[12] and received, instead of her, only initiation into the temple of wisdom. On the other hand, it would be quite right for Papageno, his necessary counterpart, to get his Papagena. Noble and distinguished people soon become aware of that teaching of fate and gratefully submit to be moulded thereby. They see that possibly instruction but not

---

[11] ['Why do you wear out your soul that is too weak for eternal plans?']
[12] [i.e. Pamina.]

happiness is to be found in the world; and so they become
accustomed and content to exchange hope for insight, and in the
end say with Petrarch:

Altro diletto, che 'mparar, non provo.[13]
(*Trionfo d'Amore*, I. 21.)

It may even be that they still follow to a certain extent their
desires and aspirations merely as a trifle and for the sake of
appearance, but that really, in their heart of hearts, they
expect only instruction; an attitude which then gives them a
sublime, contemplative touch of genius. In this sense, it can
also be said that we are like the alchemists who, while looking
only for gold, discovered gunpowder, china, medicines, and
even the laws of nature.

B. *Our Attitude to Ourselves*

(4) The workman, assisting in the erection of a building, is
either unacquainted with the plan of the whole or does not
always have it in mind. Similarly, while a man is spinning
away the separate days and hours of his life, his attitude to the
whole of its course and character is the same. The worthier,
more important, systematic, and individual this is, the more
necessary and salutary it is for him occasionally to have in
mind a reduced sketch thereof, namely the plan. For this
purpose, of course, he should have made a start in γνῶθι σαυτόν;[14]
he should, therefore, know what he really wants principally
and primarily, what is the most essential thing for his happiness,
and thereafter what occupies second and third place. He should
also know generally what is his vocation, his role, and his relation to the world. Now if this is on important and grandiose
lines, a glance at his life's plan on a small scale will, more than
anything else, strengthen, uplift, and exalt him; it will encourage him to be active and keep him from going astray.

Just as the traveller gets a connected survey of the road he has
taken with all its turns and bends only when he has arrived at
the top of the hill, so it is only at the end of a period of our life or
even at the very end thereof that we recognize the true connection between our actions, achievements, and works, their
precise consistency and sequence, and even their value. For as

---

[13] ['No other happiness than learning do I feel.']   [14] ['Know thyself.']

long as we are preoccupied with all this, we always act only in
accordance with the fixed qualities of our character, under the
influence of motives, and within the limits of our abilities and
hence throughout with necessity, since at any particular moment we do simply what we deem to be right and proper at
the time. Only the sequel shows us what has transpired; and
only when we look back at the connected course of life do we
see the how and why thereof. And so while we are performing
the greatest deeds or creating immortal works, we are just not
conscious of them as such. On the contrary, we regard them as
something appropriate to our present aims, something in
keeping with our intentions of the moment, which is, therefore,
just the very thing to be done. But only from our life as a
connected whole do our character and abilities subsequently
emerge in their true light. We then see in the particular case
how, guided by our genius, we took, as though by inspiration,
the only right path out of a thousand devious tracks. All this
applies to the theoretical as well as the practical and in the
opposite sense to the worthless and unsuccessful. The importance
of the present moment is seldom recognized at the time, but
only much later.

(5) An important point in the wisdom of life consists in a
correct balance between the attention we give to the present
and to the future so that for us the one will not impair the other.
Many live too much in the present, namely the frivolous and
light-hearted; others live too much in the future, that is to say,
the nervous and faint-hearted. Rarely will a man hold the right
balance between the two. Those who by aspiring and hoping
live only in the future and always look ahead and impatiently
anticipate the things to come—things that are first to bring
them true happiness—while they let the present slip by un-
heeded and unenjoyed, are, in spite of their clever airs, comparable to those donkeys in Italy whose pace is quickened by
their having a stick with a truss of hay fastened to their heads.
They see this just in front of them and hope they will be able to
reach it. They defraud themselves of their whole existence
since they are always living only *ad interim*—until they are
dead. Therefore instead of being always and exclusively pre-
occupied with plans and troubles for the future or of indulging
in hankering over the past, we should never forget that the

present alone is real and certain, that the future, on the other hand, almost invariably turns out differently from what we think and that even the past was also different. In fact, on the whole, both are of less account than they appear to us. For distance that makes objects look small to the eye, causes them to appear large to the mind. The present alone is true and actual; it is the really filled time wherein our existence exclusively lies. And so we should always consider it worthy of a cheerful reception and thus consciously enjoy as such every hour that is bearable and free from immediate annoyance or pain. In other words, we should not cast a gloom over the present by looking peevish over the vain hopes of the past or over our anxiety for the future. For it is extremely foolish to reject the present hour that is good or wantonly to ruin it through annoyance at what is past or anxiety over what is to come. A definite time should, of course, be devoted to solicitude and even to regret; but after this we should think of what has happened:

$$\text{'Αλλὰ τὰ μὲν προτετύχθαι ἐάσομεν ἀχνύμενοί περ,}$$
$$\text{Θυμὸν ἐνὶ στήθεσσι φίλον δαμάσαντες ἀνάγκῃ}^{15}$$

and of the future:

$$\text{'Αλλ' ἤτοι μὲν ταῦτα θεῶν ἐν γούνασι κεῖται,}^{16}$$

but of the present: *singulos dies singulas vitas puta,*[17] and make this as agreeable as possible, for it is the only real time we have.

Only those future evils are entitled to disturb us which are certain to come, the time of their appearance being just as certain. But of these there will be very few; for evils are either merely possible, at all events probable, or they are indeed certain; the time of their occurrence, however, is wholly uncertain. Now if we yield to these two kinds of evil, we shall no longer have a moment's peace. And so if we are not to be deprived of all our peace through uncertain and indefinite evils, we must accustom ourselves to regard the former as never likely to happen and the latter as likely to happen though certainly not very soon.

---

[15] ['But however much it mortified us, we will let bygones be bygones; and hard as it may be for us, we will subdue the peevishness in our hearts.' (Homer, *Iliad*, XVIII. 112f.)]

[16] ['This lies in the lap of the gods.' (Homer, *Iliad*, XVII. 514.)]

[17] ['Regard each particular day as a special life.' (Seneca, *Epistulae*, 101, 10.)]

Now the less our peace is disturbed by fear, the more we are agitated by wishes, desires, and aspirations. Goethe's song that is such a favourite, 'Ich hab' mein' Sach auf nichts gestellt',[18] says in effect that only after a man has shaken off all possible pretensions, and has returned to bare existence, does he obtain that peace of mind which constitutes the basis of human happiness. For such peace is necessary if he is to find bearable the present moment and thus the whole of life. For this purpose, we should always bear in mind that today comes but once and never again. We imagine, however, that it comes again tomorrow; but tomorrow is another day that also comes only once. But we forget that every day is an integral and thus irreplaceable part of life and regard it rather as included under life just as are individual things under a common concept. We should also better appreciate and enjoy the present if in the good days when we are well we were always conscious of how in sickness or depression of spirits, our memory conjures up every hour that was free from pain and privation as something infinitely to be envied, as a lost paradise, as a friend we neglected and undervalued. But we live through the fine days without noticing them; only when we fall on evil ones do we wish to have back the former. With sour faces we let a thousand bright and pleasant hours slip by unenjoyed and afterwards vainly sigh for their return when times are trying and depressing. Instead of this, we should cherish every present moment that is bearable, even the most ordinary, which with such indifference we now let slip by, and even with impatience push on. We should always bear in mind that such moments are just now ebbing into the apotheosis of the past where, irradiated by the light of imperishableness, they are then preserved in the memory so that, when this lifts the curtain especially in bad times, they will present themselves as an object of our deepest longing.

(6) *All limitation makes us happy.* The narrower our range of vision, our sphere of action, and our points of contact, the happier we are; the wider these are, the more often do we feel anxious and worried. For with them our cares, desires, and terrors are increased and intensified. Therefore even the blind are not so unhappy as they must *a priori* appear to be; and this is

18 ['On nothing have I set my hopes.']

testified by that gentle and almost serene calm on their faces. This is due partly to the rule that the second half of life proves to be more melancholy than the first. For in the course of life, the horizon of our aims and connections becomes ever wider. In childhood it is restricted to the most immediate environment and the narrowest relations; in youth there is already a considerable widening of these; in manhood the horizon embraces the whole course of our lives and often extends to the most distant relations, to states and nations; in old age it embraces posterity. On the other hand, every limitation, even that of the mind, is conducive to our happiness; for the less the will is excited, the less we suffer; and we know that suffering is positive whereas happiness is merely negative. Limitation of the sphere of action removes from the will the external motives for excitation; limitation of the mind takes away the internal. But the latter has the disadvantage of opening the door to boredom that becomes indirectly the source of countless sufferings; for to banish it, men resort to everything, to dissipation, society, luxury, gambling, drinking, and so on which, however, entail all kinds of mischief, ruin, and unhappiness. *Difficilis in otio quies.*[19] On the other hand, *external* limitation is conducive, and even necessary, to human happiness in so far as it is possible for us to have this. We see this in the fact that the only kind of poetry, namely the idyll which undertakes to give a description of happy people, presents them invariably and essentially in an extremely restricted position and environment. This feeling in the matter underlies the pleasure we experience when looking at so-called genre-pictures. Accordingly, the greatest possible *simplicity* in our relations and even *monotony* in our way of living will make us happy, as long as they do not produce boredom. For they enable us to feel life itself as little as possible and consequently the burden that is essential thereto. It flows by like a stream without waves and whirlpools.

(7) With regard to our weal and woe, the question ultimately turns on what fills and engrosses our consciousness. Now here every purely intellectual occupation for the mind capable thereof will achieve, on the whole, far more than will practical life with its constant alternations of success and failure together with its shocks and vexations. But, of course, for such

[19] ['It is difficult to keep quiet when one has nothing to do.']

occupation pre-eminent intellectual abilities are required. Then in this connection it must be noted that, just as an outwardly directed active life distracts and diverts us from study and deprives the mind of the requisite quiet concentration, so, on the other hand, constant mental preoccupation renders us more or less unfit for the noisy pursuits of real life. It is, therefore, advisable to suspend mental work entirely for a while when circumstances arise which in some way demand energetic and practical activity.

(8) To live quite *prudently and judiciously* and draw from our own experience all the instruction it contains, it is often necessary to think back and recapitulate what we have done and experienced and what our feelings were, and to compare our former with our present judgement, our plans and aspirations with the success and satisfaction they have produced. This is a repetition of the private tuition that is given to everyone by experience. Our own experience may be regarded as the text, and reflection and knowledge as the commentary thereto. Much reflection and knowledge with little experience resemble those editions whose pages present us with two lines of text and forty lines of commentary. Much experience with little reflection and scanty knowledge is like the *editiones Bipontinae* which are without notes and contain much that is unintelligible.

The advice here given is also alluded to by the rule of Pythagoras that, every evening before going to sleep, we should review what we have done in the course of the day. The man who in the toil and moil of business or pleasure has no thought for the morrow, never ruminates on the past, but rather reels his life off like cotton, is devoid of prudence and reflectiveness. His feelings become a chaos and a certain confusion comes over his ideas, as is at once testified by the abrupt and fragmentary nature of his conversation that is like mincemeat. This will be all the more the case, the greater the excitement from without, the greater the mass of impressions, and the smaller the inner activity of his own mind.

Here it may be observed that, after the circumstances and environment that influenced us have in the course of some time passed away, we are unable to recall and renew the mood and feeling they stirred in us at the time. However, we are able to call to mind our own *observations* which they suggested at that time and which are now the result, expression, and measure of those circumstances. We should, therefore, carefully preserve the memory or record of such observations from important moments of our lives. For this purpose diaries are very useful.

(9) To be self-sufficient and all in all to oneself and to be able to say *omnia mecum porto mea*,[20] is certainly the most useful qualification for our happiness. Hence Aristotle's saying: ἡ εὐδαιμονία τῶν αὐτάρκων ἐστί (*felicitas sibi sufficientium est*,[21] *Eudemian Ethics*, VII. 2) cannot be too often repeated. (It is also essentially the same idea that is expressed in that exceedingly well-turned sentence of Chamfort. I have prefixed it as a motto to this essay.) For we cannot with any certainty count on anyone else except ourselves; moreover, the difficulties and disadvantages, the dangers and annoyances, that society entails are countless and inevitable.

There is no more mistaken path to happiness than social life, *high life*; for its object is to transform our miserable existence into a succession of joys, delights, and pleasures, a process in which disillusionment cannot fail to appear and which is on a par with its obligato accompaniment, the habit people have of lying to one another.*

In the first place, all society necessarily demands mutual accommodation and temperament; and so the greater it is, the more insipid it will be. Everyone can *be entirely himself* only so long as he is alone; and therefore whoever does not like loneliness, does not like freedom; for only when a man is alone is he free. Restraint and want of freedom are the inseparable companions of all society; and the sacrifices demanded by it will prove to be the heavier, the more eminent the man's own individuality. Accordingly, everyone will shun, endure, or like solitude exactly in proportion to this own worth. For in solitude the wretch feels the whole of his wretchedness, the great mind the full extent of his greatness; in short, everyone feels himself to be what he is. Further, the higher a man stands in nature's order of precedence, the more lonely he is; and this is essential

---

* Just as our body is covered with clothes, so is our mind with *lies*. Our words, our actions, our whole nature are deceitful; and only through this veil can our true sentiments sometimes be guessed, just as the shape of the body is guessed through the clothes.

[20] ['All my possessions I carry with me.']

[21] ['Happiness belongs to those who are easily contented.']

and inevitable. But it is beneficial to him if the physical solitude is in keeping with the mental, otherwise frequent association with others of a different nature has a disturbing and even adverse effect on him, robs him of himself, and, as compensation, has nothing to offer him. Then, whereas nature has established the widest difference, both morally and intellectually, between one man and another, society, regardless of all this, treats them all alike or rather sets up instead artificial differences and degrees of position and rank which are often the very opposite of nature's list of precedence. With this arrangement, those whom nature has placed low are in a very good position, but the few who are rated high by her come off badly. The latter, therefore usually withdraw from society where, as soon as it is numerous, vulgarity prevails. What in society offends great minds is an equality of rights that leads to one of claims and pretensions, in spite of the inequality of abilities, and consequently to an equality of (social) achievements. So-called good society admits merits of all kinds except those of the mind, which are even contraband. It puts us under the obligation of showing boundless patience with every kind of folly, stupidity, perversity, and dullness. Excellent personal qualities, on the other hand, should beg to be excused or conceal themselves; for intellectual superiority offends by its mere existence without any desire so to do. Accordingly, society that is called good not only has the drawback of offering us men whom we cannot praise and like, but also it will not allow us to be ourselves in harmony with our nature. On the contrary, it compels us, for the sake of agreeing with others, to shrivel up and even alter our shape. Intellectual talking and ideas are fit only for intellectual society; in ordinary society they are positively loathed, for here in order to go down well it is absolutely necessary to be dull and narrow-minded. In such society, therefore, we must practise great self-denial and give up three-quarters of our own individuality in order to become like other people. In return, we naturally have the others, but the more merit a man has, the more he will find that here the gain does not cover the loss and the business turns out to his disadvantage. For, as a rule, men are insolvent; in other words, when we associate with them, they have nothing that would compensate us for the boredom, annoyance, and disagreeableness of their company and for the self-denial it imposes on us. Accordingly, most society is so constituted that whoever exchanges it for loneliness makes a good bargain. Moreover, there is the fact that, in order to provide a substitute for genuine, i.e. intellectual, superiority that is intolerable and also hard to find, society has arbitrarily assumed a false conventional superiority. This rests on arbitrary principles, is traditionally handed down to the higher circles, and, like the password, can be altered. It is called *bon ton*,[22] *fashionableness*. When, however, it comes into collision with genuine superiority, it shows its weakness. Moreover, *quand le bon ton arrive, le bon sens se retire*.[23]

Generally speaking, every man can *be in the most perfect harmony* only with himself, not with his friend or even with his betrothed. For differences of individuality and temperament always produce a discord, although only slight. Therefore genuine tranquillity of the heart and perfect peace of mind, the highest blessings on earth after health, are to be found only in solitude and, as a permanent disposition, only in the deepest seclusion. If, then, a man's own self is great and rich, he enjoys the happiest state that can be found in this miserable world. Indeed, let us be frank; however intimately anyone may be tied by friendship, love, and marriage, in the end he *quite honestly* looks only to himself and at most to his child. The less a man is compelled, in consequence of objective or subjective conditions, to come in contact with others, the better off he is. *Loneliness* and solitude enable us, if not to feel all their evils at once, at any rate to survey them. Society, on the other hand, is *insidious*; it conceals great and often irreparable mischief behind the pretence of pastime, communication, social pleasure, and so on. A principal study for youth should be *learning how to put up with loneliness*, since it is a source of happiness and peace of mind. Now it follows from all this that he is best off who has depended on himself and can be all in all to himself. Even Cicero says: *Nemo potest non beatissimus esse qui est totus aptus ex sese, quique in se uno ponit omnia*[24] (*Paradoxa*, II). Again, the more a man has in himself, the less can others be to him. It is a certain feeling of

---

[22] ['Good form'.]

[23] ['When good form appears, good common sense retires.']

[24] ['It is impossible for anyone not to be perfectly happy who depends entirely on himself and possesses in himself alone all that he calls his.']

self-sufficiency which restrains those of intrinsic merit and wealth from making the considerable sacrifices that are demanded by intercourse with others, let alone from seeking such associations by obviously denying themselves. The opposite of this makes ordinary people so sociable and accommodating; since it is easier for them to put up with others than to tolerate themselves. In addition, it should be remembered that in this world what has real value is not esteemed and what is esteemed has no value. The proof and consequence of this is that seclusion of every man of eminence and distinction. In accordance with all this, it will be genuine wisdom of life in the man who in himself is worth anything if, in case of need, he limits his requirements in order to preserve or extend his freedom and, in consequence, he has as few dealings as possible with his fellow-men, for relations with them are unavoidable.

On the other hand, what makes people sociable is their inability to endure loneliness and their own company. It is inner vacuity, weariness, and boredom that drive them into society and into going abroad. Their minds lack resilience for imparting any movement of their own. They try to enhance this through wine and in this way many become drunkards. For this reason, they are always in need of excitement from without and indeed the strongest, i.e. that from creatures like themselves, without which their minds sink under their own weight and lapse into a grievous lethargy.* It might also be said that each of them is only a small fraction of the Idea of humanity and, therefore, needs to be greatly supplemented by others so that, to some extent, a whole human consciousness emerges. On the other hand, whoever is a complete human being, a human being

---

* It is well known that evils are alleviated by the fact that we bear them in common. People seem to regard boredom as one of these and therefore get together in order to be bored in common. Just as the love of life is at bottom only fear of death, so too the *urge to be sociable* is at bottom not direct. Thus it does not depend on love of society, but on the fear of *loneliness*, since it is not so much the pleasant company of others which is sought, as rather the dreariness and oppression of being alone, together with the monotony of one's own consciousness, that are avoided. Therefore to escape this, we put up with bad company and tolerate the burden and feeling of restriction that all society necessarily entails. If, on the other hand, a dislike of all this has triumphed and consequently a habit of solitude and an inurement to its immediate impression have arisen so that it no longer produces the effects previously described, then we can always be alone with the greatest ease and without hankering after society. For the need of society is not direct and, on the other hand, we are now accustomed to the wholesome virtues of solitude.

par excellence, represents a whole number, not a fraction, and therefore has enough in himself. In this sense ordinary society can be compared to that Russian horn music wherein each horn has only one note and the music is produced merely by all the horns coming together at the right moment. For the temperament and mentality of most people are as monotonous as is such a horn with its one note. Indeed, many of them look as if they always had only one and the same idea and were incapable of any other. It is easy to see from this not only why they are so bored, but also why they are so sociable and prefer most of all to go about in crowds: *the gregariousness of mankind*. It is the monotony of his own nature that becomes intolerable to everyone of them: *omnis stultitia laborat fastidio sui*:[25] only together and united are they anything at all; just like those horn players. The man of intelligence, on the other hand, is comparable to a virtuoso who performs his concert *alone*; or he is comparable to a piano. Just as such an instrument by itself alone is a small orchestra, so is the man of intelligence a small world; and what all those others are only by co-operation he presents in the unity of a single consciousness. Like the piano, he is no part of the symphony, but is suitable for the solo and for solitude. If he is to co-operate with them, he can do so only as the principal voice with accompaniment, like the piano; or for setting the tone in vocal music, like the piano. However, those who are fond of society may draw from this simile the rule that what their acquaintances lack in quality must to some extent be made up in quantity. One man of intelligence can be company enough; but if there are none to be found except the ordinary sort, it is a good thing to have quite a number of them so that something may result from their variety and co-operation—on the analogy of the aforesaid horn music; and for this may heaven grant you the patience!

But to that inner vacuity and barrenness of men is also attributable the fact that, when men of a better nature form a society for some noble and ideal purpose, the result is almost always that, of the crowds of people who like vermin cover all things and are always ready indiscriminately to seize on everything with the object of defeating their boredom or their defects in other circumstances, there are some who intrude or thrust

[25] ['Stupidity suffers from its own weariness.' (Seneca, *Epistulae*, 9.)]

themselves into that society. In a short time they either ruin the whole business, or so alter it that it becomes practically the opposite of the original intention.

Moreover, gregariousness can also be regarded as a kind of mutual mental warming of men similar to the bodily warmth which they produce by crowding together when it is very cold. But whoever has great mental warmth needs no such crowding. In the last chapter of the second volume of this work, the reader will find a fable devised in this sense by me. The result of all this is that a man's sociability is roughly in inverse ratio to his intellectual worth; and 'he is very unsociable' is tantamount to saying 'he is a man of great qualities.'

Solitude confers a twofold advantage on the man of intellectual eminence; first that of being by himself and secondly that of not being with others. The latter will be highly valued if we bear in mind how much want of freedom, annoyance, and even danger are entailed in all social intercourse. La Bruyère says: *tout notre mal vient de ne pouvoir être seuls.*[26] *Gregariousness or sociability* is one of the dangerous and even fatal tendencies, for it brings us into contact with people the great majority of whom are morally bad and intellectually dull or perverse. The unsociable man is one who does not need them; to have enough in oneself so that one does not need society is, therefore, a great piece of good fortune. For almost all our sufferings spring from society, and peace of mind, constituting next to health the most essential element of our happiness, is endangered by all society and therefore cannot really exist without a significant amount of solitude. The Cynics renounced all possessions in order to partake of the bliss of peace of mind; whoever with the same intention renounces society, has chosen the most prudent course. What Bernardin de St. Pierre says is fine and to the point: *La diète des alimens nous rend la santé du corps, et celle des hommes la tranquillité de l'âme.*[27] Accordingly, whoever at an early age is on friendly or even affectionate terms with solitude, has gained a gold-mine; but certainly not everyone is able to do this. For just as men are driven together originally by need and privation, so too are they by boredom, when these are removed.

---

[26] ['All our trouble comes from our not being able to be alone.']

[27] ['Abstemiousness in food guarantees the health of our body, and that in association with men secures the peace of our soul.']

Without privation and boredom, everyone would probably remain alone if only because in solitude the environment is in keeping with the exclusive importance and even uniqueness which everyone has in his own eyes and which is reduced to nought by the crowded events of the world, where at every step it receives a painful *démenti*. In this sense, loneliness is even the natural state of everyone; it reinstates him as Adam in the original happiness that is appropriate to his nature.

But, of course, Adam had no father or mother! And so again in a different sense, loneliness is not natural to man, in so far as he did not find himself alone when he came into the world, but had parents, brothers, and sisters, and was, therefore, in a community. Accordingly, love of solitude cannot exist as an original tendency, but arises only in consequence of experience and reflection; and this will occur to the extent that our own mental powers are developed, but at the same time with an increase in our age; and so, generally speaking, a man's urge to be sociable will be inversely proportional to his age. The small child utters a cry of fear and distress as soon as it is left alone for a few moments. For a boy to be alone is a great penitence. Young people readily herd together; only the more noble-minded among them occasionally seek solitude; yet it will still be difficult for them to spend a whole day by themselves. A man, on the other hand, can easily do so; and he is able to be alone for a longer period, the older he becomes. The old man who is the sole survivor of vanished generations and is too old or dead to the pleasures of life, finds his proper element in loneliness. But here in individuals an increase in the tendency to seclusion and solitude will always occur in proportion to their intellectual worth. For, as I have said, this tendency is not a purely natural one directly brought about by needs; it is rather only an effect of the experience we have had and of the reflection thereon, particularly of the insight gained into the miserable nature, morally and intellectually, of the great majority of men. The worst thing here is that in the individual moral and intellectual shortcomings conspire and work hand in hand, the result being extremely disagreeable phenomena of all kinds that make association with most people unpleasant and even intolerable. And so although there is in this world very much that is really bad, the worst thing in it is society, so that even Voltaire, the sociable Frenchman, had to say: *La terre est couverte de gens qui ne méritent pas qu'on leur parle.*[28] That gentle spirit Petrarch, so strong and constant in his love of solitude, also gives the same reason for this tendency:

> *Cercato ho sempre solitaria vita*
> *(Le rive il sanno, e le compagne e i boschi),*
> *Per fuggir quest' ingegni sordi e loschi,*
> *Che la strada del ciel' hanno smarrita.*[29]

In the same sense, he amplifies the matter in his fine book, *De vita solitaria*, which seems to have been Zimmermann's model for his noted work on solitude. It is this merely secondary and indirect origin of unsociability that is expressed in his sarcastic vein by Chamfort when he says: *On dit quelquefois d'un homme qui vit seul, il n'aime pas la société. C'est souvent comme si on disait d'un homme qu'il n'aime pas la promenade sous le prétexte qu'il ne se promène pas volontiers le soir dans la forêt de Bondy.*[30]* But even the gentle Christian Angelus Silesius says in his own mythical language exactly the same thing:

> Herod is a foe; Joseph is the mind
> In whose dream God makes known the peril.
> Bethlehem's the world, Egypt is *solitude.*
> Flee, my soul! else suffering and death are yours.

In the same sense, Giordano Bruno gives his opinion that *tanti uomini che in terra hanno voluto gustare vita celeste, dissero con una voce: 'ecce elongavi fugiens et mansi in solitudine.'*[31] In this sense, Sadi the Persian says of himself in the *Gulistan*: 'Disgusted with my friends in Damascus, I withdrew into the desert near Jerusalem to look for the companionship of animals.' In short,

---

* In this sense, Sadi says in the *Gulistan*: 'Since this time, we have taken leave of society, and have resolved to follow the path of seclusion. For *safety resides in solitude.*'

[28] ['The earth swarms with people who are not worth talking to.']

[29]   ['A lonely life have I always sought
(Stream, field, and wood can speak of this),
Fleeing from those dull and feeble spirits,
Through whom I cannot choose the path of light.'
                        (Sonnet 221.)]

[30] ['It is sometimes said of a man who lives alone that he does not like society. This is often as if one were to say of a man that he does not like going for a walk because he is not fond of walking at night in the forest of Bondy.']

[31] ['Many who on earth wished to enjoy a divine life, have said with one voice: "Lo, then would I wander far off, and remain in the wilderness."' (Psalms 55:7.)]

the same idea has been expressed by all whom Prometheus had formed of better clay. What pleasure can they derive from associating with those to whom they are related only through what is lowest and most ignoble in their own nature and thus what is commonplace, trivial, and vulgar? What can they find in those who form a community and for whom, because they cannot rise to a higher level, there is nothing left but to drag others down to theirs, which then becomes their aspiration? It is therefore, an aristocratic feeling that fosters the inclination to seclusion and solitude. All knaves are sociable; how pitiful. On the other hand, we see that a man is of a nobler nature primarily in his finding no pleasure in others; on the contrary, he ever more prefers solitude to their company. With the passing of the years, he gradually comes to see that, apart from rare exceptions, there is in the world only the choice between loneliness and vulgarity. However hard this may sound, even Angelus Silesius, notwithstanding his Christian gentleness and love, could not leave unsaid:

> Solitude is necessary; yet be not vulgar,
> For you can everywhere a desert find.

Now with regard to great minds, it is quite natural for these real teachers of the entire human race to feel as little inclined to frequent association with others as for schoolmasters to join in the games of the boisterous and noisy crowds of children who surround them. They have come into the world to lead mankind across the sea of error into the haven of truth and to draw it from the dark abyss of its coarseness and vulgarity up into the light of culture and refinement. It is true that they must live among men and women without, however, really belonging to them. From their early years they therefore feel that they are noticeably different from others, but only gradually and with the lapse of time do they come to a clear knowledge of the position. They then take care that their mental isolation from others is reinforced also by one that is physical, and no one is allowed to approach them, unless he himself is more or less exempt from the prevailing vulgarity.

And so from all this it follows that love of solitude does not appear directly and as an original impulse, but develops indirectly, preferably in nobler minds, and only gradually.

This development is not achieved without our overcoming the natural social urge and occasionally opposing the whispered suggestion of Mephistopheles:

> This nursing of the pain forgo thee,
> That, like a vulture, feeds upon thy breast!
> The worst society thou find'st will show thee
> Thou art a man among the rest.[32]

Solitude is the lot of all pre-eminent minds and this at times they will bemoan; but they always choose it as the lesser of two evils. In this respect, however, *sapere aude*[33] becomes ever easier and more natural; and when a man is past sixty the urge to be alone has become really natural and even instinctive, for everything now combines to favour it. The strongest inclination to be sociable, namely love of women and the sexual impulse, no longer has any effect; in fact, the sexless condition of old age lays the foundation to a certain self-sufficiency that gradually absorbs the urge to sociability. A thousand illusions and follies have been given up; active life is for the most part over. A man has nothing more to expect, no more plans and designs. The generation to which he really belongs exists no longer; surrounded by a strange new one, he already stands objectively and essentially alone. The flight of time has then become more rapid and he would like to use it intellectually. For if only the mind has retained its strength, the great amount of knowledge and experience we have acquired, the gradually perfected elaboration of all ideas, and the great skill in the use of our powers render study of all kinds more than ever easy and interesting. We clearly see a thousand things that were previously in a cloud of uncertainty; we reach results and feel a sense of complete superiority. From long experience we have ceased to expect much from men; for, on the whole, they do not belong to those who gain on closer acquaintance. On the contrary, we know that, apart from rare and fortunate exceptions, we shall come across nothing but very defective specimens of human nature which it is better to leave alone. We are, therefore, no longer exposed to the ordinary illusions of life, and from a man's appearance we judge what he is; rarely shall we feel any desire

---

[32] [Goethe's *Faust*, Bayard Taylor's translation.]
[33] ['Bring yourself to be reasonable.']

to enter into closer relations with him. Finally, the habit of isolation and our own company has supervened and become second nature, especially if solitude has been the friend of our youth. Accordingly, the love of solitude, which formerly had first to be wrested from the social impulse, is now quite natural and simple; in solitude we are like a fish in water. Therefore every individual of eminence who is thus unlike the rest and stands alone feels, through this isolation that is essential to his nature, oppressed when he is young, but relieved when he is old.

Of course, everyone always enjoys this real privilege of old age only to the extent that he has intellectual powers; and so the eminent mind enjoys it most of all, although everyone does so to a lesser extent. Only exceedingly inferior and common natures will still be as sociable in their old age as in their youth. To a society to which they are no longer suited they are tedious and at best succeed in being tolerated, whereas formerly they were in demand.

We can also discover a teleological side to this inverse proportion between our age and the degree of our sociability. The younger a man is, the more in every respect he has to learn. Now nature has relegated him to a system of mutual instruction which he receives when associating with people like himself and in respect of which human society may be called a large Bell–Lancaster educational establishment. For books and schools are artificial institutions because they are remote from nature's plan. It is, therefore, quite proper that he visits nature's educational institution with the greater keenness, the younger he is.

Nihil est ab omni parte beatum,[34] as Horace says; and 'No lotus without a stem' is an Indian proverb. So even solitude with its many advantages has its minor drawbacks and difficulties which are, however, small in comparison with those of society. And so whoever is in himself worth anything, will always find it easier to get on without rather than with people. Yet of those disadvantages, there is one that does not as readily come to our notice as do the others. Thus through our always remaining at home, our body becomes so sensitive to external influences that every little cool breeze morbidly affects it. In the same way, through continual seclusion and solitude our mood becomes so sensitive that we feel disturbed, mortified, or ruffled by the most

[34] ['For there is nothing perfect on earth.']

insignificant events, words, or even mere looks, whereas such things are entirely overlooked by those who remain always in the hurly-burly of life.

Now whenever a well-founded dislike of people has scared a man into solitude, he may not be able to endure for any length of time its bleakness, especially if he is young. I advise him to form the habit of taking into society some of his solitude, and thus learn to be alone to some extent even in company. Accordingly, he should not at once communicate to others what he is thinking; on the other hand, he should not take too literally what they say. On the contrary, he should not expect much from them, either morally or intellectually, and therefore, as regards their opinions, should strengthen in himself that indifference that is the surest way of always practising a praiseworthy tolerance. Although moving among them, he will then not be so entirely in their company, but his relations with them will be of a more purely objective character. This will protect him from too close a contact with society and thus from every contamination or even outrage. We possess even a very readable dramatic description of this restricted or entrenched sociability in the comedy *El Café o sea la comedia nueva*[35] by Moratin, especially in the character of D. Pedro in the second and third scenes of the first act. In this respect, society can also be compared to a fire where a prudent man warms himself at a proper distance, whereas the fool comes too close and then, after scorching himself, rushes out into the cold of solitude, loudly complaining that the fire burns.

(10) *Envy* is natural to man; yet it is simultaneously a vice and a misfortune.* We should, therefore, regard it as the enemy of our happiness and should try to stifle it as an evil demon. Seneca in fine words directs us to do this: *nostra nos sine comparatione delectent; nunquam erit felix quem torquebit felicior* (*De ira*, III. 30); and again: *quum adspexeris quot te antecedant, cogita quot sequantur*[36] (*Epistulae*, 15). We should, therefore, more often consider those who are worse off than we, for those who are

---

* People's *envy* shows how unhappy they feel. Their constant *attention* to the affairs of others shows how heavily time hangs on their hands.

[35] ['The Café or the New Comedy'.]

[36] ['We will find pleasure in what we have got without making comparisons. We shall never be happy if we are worried that someone else is luckier than we. . . . If you see many who are better off than you, think of how many who are worse off.']

better off only appear to be. Even when actual evils have befallen us, the most effective consolation, although flowing from the same source as envy, is afforded by the thought of greater sufferings than ours and then by association with those who are in the same situation, thus the *socii malorum*.[37]

So much for the active side of envy. As regards the passive, it should be remembered that no hatred is so implacable as that of envy. We should, therefore, not incessantly and assiduously endeavour to excite it; on the contrary, it would be better for us to renounce this pleasure, like many another, because of its dangerous consequences.

There are *three kinds of aristocracy*: (1) of birth and rank, (2) of money, and (3) of the mind or intellect. The last is really the most distinguished and is acknowledged as such if only it is given time. Even Frederick the Great said: *les âmes privilégiées rangent à l'égal des souverains*,[38] and this to his chamberlain who took umbrage at the fact that, whereas ministers and generals dined at the chamberlain's table, Voltaire should be given a place at the table where only monarchs and their princes sat. Each of these aristocracies is surrounded by a host of envious people who are secretly embittered towards any member thereof. If they are not under any obligation to fear him, they are at pains to let him know in a variety of ways that he is no better than they. But it is these very efforts on their part that show how convinced they are of the opposite. The method to be adopted by those who are exposed to envy consists in keeping at a distance the whole host of the envious and avoiding as much as possible all contact with them so that they remain separated by a wide gulf. If this is not possible, the best method is to bear their attacks with the greatest composure, for their very source neutralizes them. We see also the general application of this method. On the other hand, the members of one aristocracy will for the most part get on well with those of the other two without being envious, because each will match his advantages and privileges with those of the others.

(11) A plan should be given mature and repeated consideration before it is carried out; and even after everything has been thoroughly thought out, we should still make some concession

---

[37] ['Companions in misfortune'.]
[38] ['Privileged minds have equal rank with sovereigns.']

to the inadequacy of all human knowledge. For there may always be circumstances which we cannot possibly investigate or foresee and which might upset the whole calculation. This reflection will always affect the negative side of the balance and counsel us not to move unnecessarily in important matters: *quieta non movere.*[39] But when once we have come to a decision and have set to work so that everything has now to take its course and only the result is awaited, we should not worry ourselves by constant reflection on what has already been carried out and by repeated doubts about possible danger. On the contrary, we should now dismiss the matter entirely from our minds and regard as closed all thought of it, confidently convinced that at the proper time we gave everything mature consideration. This advice is also given by the Italian proverb: *legala bene, e poi lascia la andare,*[40] which Goethe translates: 'Saddle well and confidently ride.' Incidentally, many of his aphorisms that are given under the heading of 'proverbial' are proverbs from the Italian. If, however, the result is bad, this is because all human affairs are the sport of chance and error. Socrates, the wisest of mankind, needed a warning *genius* or δαιμόνιον to do the right thing in his own personal affairs, or at any rate to avoid false steps; and this proves that no human intellect is adequate for this purpose. Therefore the saying, originating ostensibly from one of the Popes, that we are to blame, at any rate to some extent, for every misfortune that befalls us, is not absolutely true in all cases, although it is so in the great majority. Even a feeling of this truth seems to be largely responsible for the fact that men try to conceal their misfortunes as much as possible and to put on them the best face they can. They are afraid that their guilt may be inferred from their suffering.

(12) In the case of a misfortune that has already occurred and therefore cannot be altered, we should not even permit ourselves to think that it might have been different; still less that it could have been prevented. For this simply intensifies the pain to the point of its becoming intolerable and we thus become ἑαυτοντιμορούμενος.[41] On the contrary, we should follow the example of King David who, so long as his son lay on a bed of

---

[39] ['Not to set in motion what is at rest.']
[40] ['Harness the horse and send him off!']   [41] ['Self-tormentor'.]

sickness, incessantly assailed Jehovah with supplications and entreaties, but who snapped his fingers and thought no more of it after the son had died. But whoever is not light-hearted enough for this should take refuge in fatalism since there is revealed to him the great truth that all that happens occurs necessarily and is therefore inevitable.

In spite of everything, this rule is one-sided. It is, of course, useful in misfortunes for our immediate relief and consolation; but if, as is often the case, our own negligence or rashness is at any rate partially responsible for them, the repeated and painful deliberation on how they could have been prevented is a wholesome and salutary self-discipline for our experience and improvement and so for the future. We should not try, as we usually do, to extenuate, palliate, or lessen faults that are obviously committed by us, but should confess them and bring them in all their enormity clearly before our eyes so that we may firmly make up our minds to avoid them in future. Here, of course, we have to undergo the self-inflicted pain of dis-satisfaction with ourselves; but ὁ μὴ δαρεὶς ἄνθρωπος οὐ παιδεύε-ται.[42]

(13) In all that concerns our weal and woe, we should *keep a tight rein on our imagination*. Above all, we should not build castles in the air since they are too expensive; for with a sigh we have to pull them down again immediately afterwards. But we should be still more on our guard against tormenting and distressing ourselves by depicting merely possible misfortunes. Thus if these were purely unfounded or indeed very far-fetched, we should know at once on waking up from such a dream that the whole thing had been only an illusion and should, therefore, be the more pleased with the better reality, and in any case see here a warning against quite remote, though possible, mis-fortunes. But our imagination does not readily play with such things; at best, it builds bright castles in the air in quite a leisurely fashion. The material for its sombre dreams are mis-fortunes that to some extent actually threaten us, although remotely. It magnifies them, brings their possibility much nearer than is actually the case, and paints them in the most terrible colours. On waking up, we cannot at once shake off

such a dream as we can a pleasant one; for reality instantly refutes and disproves this and at best leaves behind in the lap of possibility a faint hope. But if we have yielded to a fit of the blues,[43] images and figures are brought close to us which do not so readily vanish again; for the possibility of the thing generally is unshaken and we are not always able to estimate this. Possibility then easily becomes probability and so we have delivered ourselves into the hands of anguish and uneasiness. Therefore things that affect our weal and woe should be considered by us with reason and judgement and consequently with cool and dispassionate deliberation; thus we should operate with mere concepts in the abstract. Imagination should here be left out of the question, for it is not competent to judge. On the contrary, it conjures up mere images or pictures that agitate our feelings unprofitably and often very painfully. This rule should be most strictly observed in the evening; for just as darkness makes us timid and causes us to see everywhere terrifying shapes, so does obscurity or confusion of ideas have an analogous effect since every uncertainty gives rise to a feeling of insecurity. And so in the evening, when relaxation has enveloped our understanding and power of judgement in a shroud of subjective obscurity, the intellect is tired and θορυβούμενος,[44] and is incapable of going to the root of things. If the objects of our meditation concern our personal affairs, they can then easily assume a dangerous aspect and become terrifying pictures. This is often the case at night when we are in bed; for then the mind is wholly relaxed and therefore the power of judgement is no longer equal to its task, but the imagination is still active. For night imparts to everything its black colour. Therefore when we go to sleep or even wake up in the night, our thoughts are frequently almost as bad distortions and perversions of things as are dreams; moreover, if they concern our personal affairs, they are usually as black as possible and even frightful. In the morning all such terrible apparitions have like dreams vanished, as is expressed by the Spanish proverb: *noche tinta, blanco el dia* (the night is coloured, the day is white). But also in the evening when the candles are burning, the understanding, like the eye, does not see things

---

[43] [Schopenhauer uses the English expression 'blue devils' alongside the German *die schwarzen Phantasien*.]

[44] ['Agitated', 'confused', 'dazed', 'bewildered'.]

so clearly as it does during the day; therefore this time is not suited for meditating on serious and especially unpleasant affairs for which the morning is the right time, as it also is generally without exception for all work, whether mental or physical. For the morning is the youth of the day; everything is bright, fresh, and easy; we feel strong and have at our complete disposal all our faculties. We should not shorten it by getting up late, or even waste it in unworthy occupations or gossip; on the contrary, we should regard it as the quintessence of life and to a certain extent treat it as sacred. Evening, on the other hand, is the day's old age; at such a time we are dull, garrulous, and frivolous. Each day is a little life for which our waking up is the birth and which is brought to an end by sleep as death. Thus going to sleep is a daily death and every waking up a new birth. In fact to complete the simile, we could regard the discomfort and difficulty of getting up as labour pains.

But generally speaking, the state of our health, sleep, nourishment, temperature, weather, environment, and many other external circumstances powerfully influence our mood and hence our thoughts. Thus both our view of an affair and our capacity for any work are subject so much to time and even to place. Hence

> To the serious mood pay heed,
> For seldom does it come.
>   Goethe, *Generalbeichte*.

Not only must we await objective conceptions and original ideas as to whether they choose to come and when; but even a thorough deliberation of a personal matter does not always succeed at the time we have fixed for it in advance and when we have prepared ourselves to deal with it. On the contrary, it too chooses its own time and then the train of thought appropriate to it becomes active of its own accord; we then follow it up with all our interest.

The reining in of the imagination, which I have recommended, means also that we do not let it conjure up and depict for us injustices previously suffered, injuries, losses, insults, slights, humiliations, and so on; for in this way we again excite long-slumbering anger and resentment and all the hateful passions whereby our nature is polluted. According to a fine parable by

Proclus the Neoplatonist, there dwells in every town the mob (ὄχλος) as well as those who are noble and distinguished; so too in every man, even the noblest and most exalted, there exist, according to his disposition, the meanest and commonest elements of human and even of animal nature. This mob must not be allowed to revolt or peep out of the window, for it has an ugly appearance and its demagogues are the flights of imagination I have described. Here we might also mention that the smallest vexation, whether coming from people or things, can swell up into a hideous monster and put us at our wit's end through our constantly brooding over it and painting it in glaring colours on an enlarged scale. We should rather take an extremely prosaic and matter-of-fact view of everything unpleasant, so that we are able to accept it as easily as possible.

Just as small objects held close to the eyes restrict our field of vision and conceal the world, so the people and things of our *immediate environment*, however insignificant and unimportant, will often engross our attention and thoughts to excess and even unpleasantly, thus leaving no room for thoughts and matters of importance. We should work against such a tendency.

(14) When we look at something we do not possess, the thought readily occurs: 'Ah, if that were mine', and we are made sensible of our privation. Instead of this, we should say more often: 'Ah, if that were not mine'. I mean that we should endeavour sometimes to regard what we possess as it would appear to us after we had lost it. Indeed, we should do this with everything, whatever it may be; property, health, friends, those we love, wife, children, horse, and dog. For in most cases, the loss of things first tells us of their value. On the other hand, if we consider things in the way recommended by me, the result will be first that their possession will at once give us more pleasure than formerly, and secondly that we shall do everything to prevent their loss. Thus we shall not endanger our property, exasperate friends, expose a wife's faithfulness to temptation, fail to look after the health of children, and so on. We often try to brighten the gloom of the present by speculating on favourable possibilities and invent many different kinds of fanciful hopes. Every one of these is pregnant with a disappointment that never fails to appear when it is dashed by the hard facts of life. It would be better for us to make the many

unpleasant possibilities the theme of our speculation. For this would cause us to take steps to prevent their happening and also give us pleasant surprises in the event of their not being realized. Are we not always noticeably more cheerful after we have passed through some anxiety? In fact, it is even a good thing sometimes to picture to ourselves great misfortunes that might possibly befall us so that we can more easily endure the many minor actual ones that subsequently happen to us. For we then console ourselves by looking back at the great misfortunes that did not befall us. When, however, we consider this rule, we must not neglect the one that preceded it.

(15) The affairs and events that concern us turn up quite separately with no order or reference to one another, in the most glaring contrast, and with nothing in common except that they are simply our affairs. Therefore, to be in keeping with them, our thoughts and cares concerning them are bound to be just as abrupt. Accordingly, when we undertake anything, we must leave out of consideration everything else and dismiss the matter from our minds, in order to attend to each thing in its own time, to enjoy or endure it, and be wholly unconcerned about everything else. We must, therefore, have our thoughts in a chest of drawers, so to speak, one of which we open while all the others remain shut. In this way we prevent the heavy burden of an anxiety from spoiling every little pleasure of the present and depriving us of all peace; we see to it that the consideration of one thing will not supplant that of another, that the attention to an important matter will not result in the neglect of many affairs of small importance, and so on. But, in particular, whoever is capable of lofty and noble thoughts should never allow his mind to be so completely filled and engrossed with personal affairs and trivial worries that they bar the way to such thoughts; for this would really be *propter vitam vivendi perdere causas.*[45] Of course, self-restraint is necessary for this proper management of ourselves, as it is for so many other things. For this, however, we should be strengthened by the thought that everyone has to endure a great deal of severe outside control without which life would be impossible. Nevertheless, a little self-restraint applied at the right place afterwards prevents much restraint from without, just as a small section of

[45] ['To ruin the purpose of life in order to live.']

a circle close to the centre corresponds to one at the periphery that is often a hundred times greater. By our self-restraint, more than by anything else, we avoid that restraint from without; this is what Seneca says: *Si vis tibi omnia subjicere, te subjice rationi*[46] (*Epistulae*, 37). We also have self-restraint always in our power; and if the worst comes to the worst, or where it touches our tenderest spot, we can discontinue it. Restraint from without, on the other hand, is harsh, inconsiderate, unsparing, and merciless. It is, therefore, prudent to anticipate this through self-restraint.

(16) We should set a limit to our wishes, curb our desires, and subdue our anger, always mindful of the fact that the individual can attain only an infinitely small share of the things that are worth having whereas many evils must necessarily befall everyone. In other words, ἀπέχειν καὶ ἀνέχειν, *abstinere et sustinere*,[47] is a rule that must be observed, otherwise neither wealth nor power can prevent us from feeling wretched. This is the object of Horace's words:

> *Inter cuncta leges, et percontabere doctos*
> *Qua ratione queas traducere leniter aevum;*
> *Ne te semper inops agitet vexetque cupido,*
> *Ne pavor, et rerum mediocriter utilium spes.*[48]

(17) Ὁ βίος ἐν τῇ κινήσει ἐστί (*vita motu constat*)[49] says Aristotle, who is obviously right. Accordingly, our physical life consists in ceaseless motion; and also our inner mental life constantly demands occupation, occupation with something through thought or action. A proof of this is given by that tapping with the fingers or with anything that comes to hand, to which those men at once resort who have nothing to do or to think about. In other words, our existence is essentially restless and fidgety; and therefore complete inactivity soon becomes intolerable, since it gives rise to terrible boredom. Now this impulse should be regulated so that it may be methodically and thus better satisfied. Activity to do something, if possible

---

[46] ['If you want to subject everything to yourself, then subject yourself to reason.']
[47] ['Bear and forbear.']
[48] ['Always read between the lines of what you are doing, and ask the wise men how you may pass your life with an easy mind, so that you may not be tormented by desire, fear, or the hope for things that are of little use.' (*Epistles*, I. 18. 95–9.)]
[49] ['Life consists in movement.']

to make something, at any rate to learn something, is therefore absolutely essential to a man's happiness. He longs to make use of his powers and would like somehow to perceive the result thereof. The greatest satisfaction in this respect, however, is given when we *make* or manufacture something, whether it be a book or a basket; but we are at once pleased when we see a work every day grow in our hands and finally reach completion. This pleasure is afforded by a work of art, a manuscript, or even manual labour; and of course the nobler the work, the greater the pleasure. In this respect, the happiest are those highly gifted men who are aware of their ability to produce great works of significance and coherence. This gives their whole life an interest of a higher order and imparts to it a flavour that is lacking in the lives of others, which by comparison are, therefore, very dull and insipid. For such highly gifted men life and the world, together with everything common and material, have a second and higher interest, a formal interest, since these contain the theme of their works. As soon as the pressure of personal needs allows them time to breathe, they are assiduously engaged throughout their lives in the collection of material. To a certain extent, they have a double intellect; one for ordinary affairs (matters of the will) similar to that of everyone else; and one for the purely objective conception of things. Thus their lives are twofold, for they are simultaneously spectators and actors, whereas all the rest are merely actors. Nevertheless, everyone should do something according to the measure of his abilities. For on long pleasure-trips we see how pernicious is the effect on us of not having any systematic activity or work. On such trips we feel positively unhappy because we are without any proper occupation and are, so to speak, torn from our natural element. Effort, trouble, and struggle with opposition are as necessary to man as grubbing in the ground is to a mole. The stagnation that results from being wholly contented with a lasting pleasure would be for him intolerable. The full pleasure of his existence is in overcoming obstacles which may be of a material nature as in business and the affairs of life, or of an intellectual, as in learning and investigating. The struggle with them and the triumph make him happy. If he lacks the opportunity for this, he creates it as best he can; according to the nature of his individuality, he will hunt or play cup and ball; or, guided by the unconscious urge of his nature, he will pick a quarrel, hatch a plot, or be involved in fraud and all kinds of wickedness, merely in order to put an end to an intolerable state of repose. *Difficilis in otio quies.*[50]

(18) For the guiding star of our efforts we should take not *the pictures of our imagination*, but clearly thought-out *concepts*. But in most cases the opposite happens. Thus on closer examination, we shall find that what ultimately turns the scale in our resolves are often not concepts and judgements, but a picture of the imagination which represents one of the alternatives. In a novel by Voltaire or Diderot, I do not know which, to the hero standing as a young Hercules at the parting of the ways virtue always appeared in the form of his old tutor holding a snuff-box in his left hand and a pinch of snuff in his right and thus moralizing; vice, on the other hand, always appeared in the form of his mother's chambermaid. Especially in youth, the goal of our happiness is fixed in the form of a few pictures that hover before us and often persist for half our lives and sometimes till the very end. They are really taunting ghosts; for when we have acquired them, they fade away into nothing since we learn from experience that they achieve absolutely nothing of what they promised. Of the same nature are the individual scenes of domestic, private, and social life, pictures of our residence, environment, marks of honour, evidence of respect, and so on; *chaque fou a sa marotte.*[51] The picture of those we love is much the same. It is natural, of course, that for us things should go like this; for being something immediate, the thing intuitively perceived has a more direct effect on our will than has the concept or abstract thought. But this gives us merely the universal without the particular, and yet it is just the particular that contains reality. Therefore the concept can affect our will only indirectly; and yet it is only the concept that keeps its promise; and so it is education and culture to rely on it alone. Of course, it will sometimes need elucidation and paraphrase through some pictures, yet only *cum grano salis.*[52]

(19) The foregoing rule may be subsumed under the more universal that we should always be masters of the impression generally of what is present and intuitively perceived by us.

[50] ['It is difficult to keep quiet when one has nothing to do.']
[51] ['Every fool has his cap and bells.']   [52] ['With a grain of salt.']

Compared with what is merely thought and known, this impression is exceedingly strong by virtue not of its matter and substance which are often very limited, but of its form, perceptibility, and immediacy which forcibly invade the mind, disturb its peace, or shatter its resolutions. For what is present and intuitively perceived can be readily surveyed and always acts at once with all its force. On the other hand, ideas and reasons require time and leisure so that we can think them out one at a time; and so we cannot have them at every moment wholly before us. Consequently, the sight of something pleasant attracts us even though we have given it up as a result of careful thought. In the same way, we are annoyed by an opinion that we know to be wholly incompetent; we are angered by an offence whose contemptible nature is clear; and likewise ten reasons for thinking that there is no danger are outweighed by the false illusion of its actual presence. In all this we clearly see the fundamental and original irrationality of our true nature. Women will often succumb to a similar impression, and few men have such an excess of reasoning faculty that they would not have to suffer from its effects. Now where we are unable entirely to overcome that impression by means of mere ideas, the best thing to do is to neutralize it by the opposite impression; for example, to neutralize the impression of an insult by looking for those who hold us in high esteem and the impression of a threatening danger by considering what counteracts it. In the *Nouveaux essais*, Livre I, c. 2, § 11, Leibniz mentions an Italian who was able to withstand even the tortures of the rack. This he did by never for one moment allowing the picture of the gallows to vanish from his imagination, for this would have been his fate had he confessed. And so from time to time he called out: *io ti vedo*,[53] words that he afterwards explained in this sense. For the very same reason we are here considering, it is difficult for us not to be made irresolute when all around us are of a different opinion and behave accordingly, even when we are convinced of their error. For a fugitive king who is being pursued and is travelling strictly *incognito*, the secretly observed ceremonious and submissive attitude of his trusted attendant must be an almost necessary encouragement lest in the end he should have doubts about himself.

[53] ['I see thee.']

(20) After stressing in the second chapter the great value of *health* as the first and most important element of our happiness, I will here state one or two quite general instructions for strengthening and maintaining it.

We may harden ourselves by imposing on the body, as a whole as well as on each of its parts, many strains and burdens while we are healthy and by accustoming ourselves to withstand adverse influences of all kinds. On the other hand, as soon as an unhealthy state appears either in the whole body or one of its parts, the opposite course should be taken and the diseased body or part should be spared and nursed in every possible way; for that which is ailing and debilitated is incapable of being hardened.

The muscle is strengthened by vigorous use, whereas the nerves are weakened thereby. Thus we may exercise our muscles by every suitable exertion but should protect our nerves therefrom; and so the eyes should be protected from too bright a light, especially reflected light, from all straining in the dark, and also from the prolonged examination of exceedingly small objects. In the same way, the ears should be protected from too loud a noise. Above all the brain should not be exposed to exertions that are forced, incessant, or ill-timed. Accordingly, we should let it rest during digestion; for the very same vital force that forms ideas in the brain is hard at work in the stomach and intestines for the purpose of preparing chyme and chyle. For similar reasons, the brain should be protected from exertion during, or even after, strenuous muscular exercise. It is much the same with the motor nerves as with the sensory; and just as the pain felt by us in injured limbs has its real seat in the brain, so it is not actually the legs and arms that walk and work, but the brain, namely that part of it which, by means of the oblong cord and the spine, stimulates the nerves of those limbs and thereby sets them in motion. Accordingly, the fatigue felt in our legs or arms has its true seat in the brain; and for this reason only *those* muscles become fatigued whose movement is arbitrary and voluntary, in other words, comes from the brain, not those that work involuntarily, like the heart. Therefore the brain is obviously impaired if we force on it, simultaneously or even at short intervals, strenuous muscular activity and intellectual exertion. This is not at variance with the fact that, at the beginning of a walk, or generally during short strolls, we often feel enhanced mental activity; for no fatigue of the aforesaid parts of the brain has yet occurred. On the other hand, such light muscular activity and the respiration increased thereby assist the flow to the brain of blood that is arterial and now better oxygenated. But we should especially give the brain the full measure of sleep necessary to restore it; for sleep is to the whole man what winding up is to a clock. (Cf. *World as Will and Representation*, vol. ii, chap. 19.) This measure will vary according to the development and activity of the brain; yet to go beyond this would be a mere waste of time, since the sleep then loses in depth what it gains in length. (Cf. *World as Will and Representation*, vol. ii, chap. 19 at the end.)* In general, we should clearly understand that our thinking is nothing but the organic function of the brain and is accordingly, as regards exertion and rest, in a position analogous to every other organic activity. Just as excessive strain ruins the eyes, so does it damage the brain. It has been rightly said that just as the stomach digests, so does the brain think. The erroneous notion of a soul which is immaterial, simple, essentially and always thinking, consequently untiring and which is merely lodged in the brain and requires nothing in the world, has certainly misled many into senseless practices and a blunting of their mental powers. For example, Frederick the Great once tried to break himself entirely of the habit of sleeping. The professors of philosophy would do well not to encourage, through their old women's philosophy that tries to be so accommodating to the catechism, such an erroneous notion that is pernicious even from a practical point of view. We should accustom ourselves to regard our mental powers absolutely as physiological functions in order to treat them accordingly, to spare or apply them, and to remember that all physical suffering, malady, or disorder, in whatever part of the body it may be, affects the mind. We are enabled best to do this by Cabanis in his work *Des rapports du physique et du moral de l'homme*.

Neglect of the advice here given is the reason why many

---

* Sleep is a morsel of *death* which we borrow *anticipando* and for this we restore and renew the life that is exhausted by a day. *Le sommeil est un emprunt fait à la mort.* Sleep borrows from death for the maintenance of life; or it is the *provisional interest* of death, death itself being the paying off of the capital. The higher the rate of interest and the more regularly it is paid, the later is the paying off demanded.

great minds and also great scholars have in their old age become feeble-minded, childish, and even mad. For example, the famous English poets of the nineteenth century, such as Sir Walter Scott, Wordsworth, Southey, and others, became in their old age and even in their sixties mentally dull and incapable and lapsed into imbecility. The explanation of this is undoutedly the fact that all were tempted by high pay to treat literature as a trade and thus to write for money. This seduced them into unnatural exertions; and whoever puts his Pegasus to the yoke and drives his Muse with a whip will have to pay the penalty in the same way as the man who has abused his sexual powers. I suspect that even Kant overworked in the last years of his life, after he had finally become famous, and thus brought on the second childhood of his last four years. On the other hand, the gentlemen of the Weimar Court, Goethe, Wieland, Knebel, retained their mental powers and activity until they were very old because they were not hack-writers. It was precisely the same with Voltaire.

Every month of the year has a peculiar influence on our health, the state of our body generally, and even of our mind, an influence which is direct, that is to say, independent of the weather.

C. *Our Attitude to Others*

(21) To get through life, we shall find it expedient to have a great deal of *foresight* and *forbearance*; the former will protect us from injury and loss, and the latter from disputes and quarrels.

Whoever has to live with men and women should not absolutely condemn any individual, not even the worst, the most contemptible, or the most ridiculous, in so far as he is once produced and given by nature. On the contrary, such an individual has to be taken as something unalterable who, in consequence of an eternal and metaphysical principle, is bound to be as he is. In bad cases we should remember Goethe's words: 'there must be such queer birds, however.'[54] If we act otherwise, we commit an injustice and challenge the other man to a contest of life and death. For no one can alter his real individuality, that is, his moral character, intellectual powers, temperament, physiognomy, and so on. If we now condemn him absolutely, there is nothing for him but to treat us as a

---

[54] [From Goethe's *Faust*, Pt. i, Bayard Taylor's translation.]

mortal enemy; for we are willing to grant him the right to
exist only on condition that he becomes different from what
he invariably is. To be able to live among men and women, we
must, therefore, allow everyone to exist with his given individuality, whatever this may prove to be; and our only concern
should be to use it in the way permitted by its nature and
character. But we should not hope to change it or condemn it
out of hand for what it is. This is the true meaning of the maxim
'live and let live'; the task, however, is not so easy as it is
reasonable, and fortunate is the man who is able to avoid for
good and all very many individuals. To learn to put up with
people, we should exercise our patience on inanimate objects
that, by virtue of mechanical or other physical necessity,
stubbornly resist our actions; every day there is occasion for this.
Afterwards we learn to apply to people the patience gained in
this way in that we accustom ourselves to think that, whenever
they thwart us, they inevitably do so by virtue of a necessity
which arises from their nature and is just as strict as is that with
which inanimate objects operate. It is, therefore, as foolish to be
indignant over their actions as to be angry with a stone that
rolls on to our path. With many people our wisest thought is:
'I shall not change them, and so I will make use of them.'

(22) It is astonishing how easily and quickly homogeneity
or heterogeneity of mind and disposition between men shows
itself in conversation; it is noticeable in every trifle. Even if the
conversation is about the strangest and most insignificant things,
one of two essentially different natures will be more or less dis-
pleased by almost every sentence that is uttered by the other;
and in many cases he will be really annoyed. People of similar
temperament, on the other hand, at once feel a certain agreement in everything; and in the case of great similarity, such
agreement soon flows into perfect harmony and even unison.
From this is first explained why quite ordinary people are so
sociable and always so readily find really good company—those
dear, amiable, honest folk. With unusual people the reverse is
the case; and this is the more so, the more outstanding they are;
so that in their seclusion they may be at times really delighted
at having discovered in someone else a cord, however slender,
which is in tune with themselves. For each can be to another
only as much as that other is to him. Really great minds, like

eagles, build their nests in lofty solitude. In the second place, it is easy to see how men of similar disposition find one another so quickly just as if they were drawn together by magnetic force; kindred souls greet each other from afar. Of course, we shall have occasion to observe this most frequently in those with vulgar natures or inferior gifts, but only because their name is legion; whereas better and more distinguished natures are rare and this is their name. Accordingly, in a large company, for example, devoted to practical purposes, two downright scoundrels will recognize each other as quickly as if they wore a badge and will come together to plot some abuse or treachery. In the same way, *per impossibile*,[55] if we picture to ourselves a large company of very intelligent and clever men except for two blockheads who happen to be there, these two will feel drawn to each other by sympathy and each will soon be heartily pleased at having come across at least one sensible and rational man. It is really remarkable to witness how two such men, especially if they are morally and intellectually inferior, recognize each other at first sight, how keenly desirous they are of coming near to each other, how affably and gladly they hasten to greet each other, just as if they were old friends. It is so striking that we are tempted to assume, in accordance with the Buddhist doctrine of metempsychosis, that they had been friends in a former life.

Nevertheless, even in the case of great agreement and accord, what keeps people apart and also produces between them a temporary discord, is the diversity of the mood they have at the moment. For everyone this is almost invariably different, according to his present circumstances, occupation, environment, physical state, passing train of thought, and so on. From all this discords occur even between the most harmonious personalities. To be able always to make the necessary correction for the removal of this disturbance and to introduce a uniform temperature, would be an achievement of the highest culture. What uniformity of mood can do for a social gathering may be seen from the fact that even a large company is roused to lively communicativeness and sincere interest with a general feeling of pleasure as soon as something objective influences them all at the same time and in the same way, whether this be a danger,

---

[55] ['Indeed this is impossible.']

hope, piece of news, a rare spectacle, a play, some music, or anything else. For by overcoming all private interests, such things produce a general unity of mood. In the absence of such an objective influence, a subjective one is as a rule seized; accordingly, bottles of wine are the usual means for introducing into a party a communal spirit. Even tea and coffee serve the same purpose.

But that discord, so readily introduced into all society by the diversity of moods at the moment, also partly explains why everyone is idealized and sometimes appears almost transfigured in the memory that is released from this and all similar disturbing, though fleeting, influences. Memory acts like the convex lens of a *camera obscura*; it contracts everything and thus produces a much finer picture than the original. Through every absence we secure, to some extent, the advantage of being seen in this way. For although the idealizing memory requires plenty of time for the completion of its work, a beginning of this is at once made. It is, therefore, even prudent for us to see our friends and acquaintances only after considerable intervals of time; for then, on seeing them again, we shall note that memory has already been at work.

(23) No one can see *above himself*; by this I mean that everyone sees in someone else only as much as he himself is; for he can grasp and understand him only to the extent of his own intelligence. Now if this is of the lowest order, no intellectual gifts, not even the greatest, will have any effect on him; and he will see nothing in their possessor except the lowest elements in his individual nature, and thus only all his weaknesses and defects of temperament and character. That other man will, therefore, be to him of a composite nature; his higher intellectual abilities are just as non-existent as are colours to the blind. For all minds are invisible to him who has none; and any value attaching to a work is a product of the value of the work itself and of the range of knowledge of the man who is giving his opinion. It follows from this that we are reduced to the level of everyone with whom we speak, since all the advantages we may have over him disappear and even the self-denial necessary for this remains wholly unacknowledged. Now when we consider how utterly vulgar and inferior and so how thoroughly *common* most people are, we shall see that it is not possible to talk to

them without ourselves becoming *common* for the time being (on the analogy of electrical distribution). We shall then thoroughly understand the real meaning and point of the expression 'to demean ourselves'; yet we shall also be glad to avoid the society of all with whom we can communicate only by means of the *partie honteuse*[56] of our nature. We shall see also that with fools and blockheads there is only one way of showing our intelligence and that is by not talking to them. But then, of course, many in society will sometimes feel like a dancer who went to a ball where he met only lame people; with whom should he dance?

(24) That man gains my respect (and he is one in a hundred) who, when he has to wait for anything and is therefore sitting with nothing to do, does not at once rattle or beat time with the first thing that comes into his hands, whether it be his stick, a knife and fork, or anything else. He is probably thinking of something. On the other hand, it is evident that with many people seeing has completely taken the place of thinking. They try to become aware of their existence by making a noise, that is, when no cigar is handy which serves this very purpose. For the same reason, they are incessantly all eyes and ears for everything that is going on around them.

(25) La Rochefoucauld has made the pertinent remark that it is difficult to feel simultaneously for anyone veneration and great affection. Accordingly, we should have to choose whether we wanted to gain men's affection or their respect. Their affection is always selfish although in very different ways; moreover, the means whereby we earn it are not always calculated to make us feel proud. In the main, a man will be popular to the extent that he moderates his claims on the heads and hearts of others and indeed does so in earnest and without dissimulation not merely out of forbearance for them, which is rooted in contempt. If we recall here the very true saying of Helvétius: *le degré d'esprit nécessaire pour nous plaire, est une mesure assez exacte du degré d'esprit que nous avons;*[57] the conclusion follows from these premisses. With men's veneration, on the other hand, the case is the very opposite; for it is extorted from them only

---

[56] ['Pudendum'.]

[57] ['The degree of intellect necessary to please us is a fairly accurate measure of the degree of intellect that we possess.']

against their will and is for that reason often concealed. Therefore, at heart, it gives us a much greater satisfaction; it is connected with our worth, a fact that is not directly true of men's affection; for this is subjective, whereas veneration is objective. Affection, of course, is more useful to us.

(26) Most men are so subjective that at bottom nothing whatever but they themselves interests them. The result is that, with everything that is said, they at once think of themselves and every chance reference to anything personal, however remote, monopolizes and engrosses their whole attention. Thus they have no power left over for grasping the objective side of a discussion and with them no arguments are of any effect when once these are opposed to their interests or vanity. Thus they are so readily distracted, so easily insulted, offended, or annoyed, that in discussing with them anything objectively, we cannot be too careful to avoid any possible and perhaps derogatory reference of our remarks to the worthy and sensitive souls whom we have before us. This alone, and nothing else, worries them; and whereas they cannot feel or understand what is true and striking, or fine, beautiful, and witty in the words of someone else, they are most sensitive to everything that could hurt, even most remotely and indirectly, their petty vanity, or could in any way reflect prejudicially on their exceedingly precious selves. Thus in their touchiness, they are like the little dog on whose paws we inadvertently tread and whose yapping has then to be endured; or they resemble a patient covered with sores and boils with whom we must very carefully avoid all possible contact. Now with many men matters go so far that if intellect and understanding are brought to light, or in conversation with them are not sufficiently concealed, they feel these to be a positive insult; although for the time being they hide their feelings. But afterwards, the man who lacks experience of life reflects and ruminates in vain on these matters and asks how on earth he could have incurred their rancour and hatred. By virtue of the same subjectivity, they are also just as easily flattered and won. And so their judgement is in most cases corrupt and merely a statement in favour of their party or class, not something objective and impartial. All this is due to the fact that in them the will far outweighs knowledge and their meagre intellect is wholly in the service

of the will from which, even for one moment, it cannot free itself.

Astrology furnishes a splendid proof of the contemptible *subjectivity* of men in consequence whereof they refer everything to themselves and from every idea at once go straight back to themselves. Astrology refers the course of celestial bodies to the miserable ego; it also establishes a connection between the comets in heaven and the squabbles and rascalities on earth. But this has always been done even in the most ancient times. (See, for example, Stobaeus, *Eclogae*, lib. i, c. 22, § 9, p. 478.)

(27) When any absurdity is uttered in public or company, or is written in literature and well received, or at any rate is not refuted, we should not despair and think that that is the end of the matter. On the contrary, we should know and take comfort in the thought that afterwards the matter will gradually be scrutinized, elucidated, thought over, considered, discussed, and, in most cases, ultimately judged correctly. Thus after a time, the length of which will depend on the difficulty of the subject, almost everyone understands what a clear mind saw at once. Meanwhile, of course, we must be patient. For a man of correct insight among those who are duped and deluded resembles one whose watch is right while all the clocks in the town give the wrong time. He alone knows the correct time, but of what use is this to him? The whole world is guided by the clocks that show the wrong time; even those are so guided who know that his watch alone states the correct time.

(28) People resemble children in that they become naughty if we spoil them; and so we should not be too indulgent and ingratiating to anyone. As a rule, we shall not lose a friend by refusing him a loan, but may very easily do so if we grant him one. In the same way, we shall not readily lose a friend by proud and somewhat careless behaviour, but this is often possible if we show too much friendliness and courtesy, for these make him arrogant and unbearable, and thus a breach ensues. But in particular, the thought that we stand in need of men is positively too much for them; the inevitable consequences of this are arrogance and insolence. With some people rudeness to a certain extent occurs when we deal with them frequently or speak to them confidentially. Soon they will think that we ought to put up with anything from them and they will try to

transgress the limits of good manners. This is why so few are fit to become more intimately acquainted with us and why we should specially guard against becoming familiar with vulgar natures. Now if a man gets the idea that he is much more necessary to me than I am to him, he at once feels as if I had stolen something from him; he will try to have his revenge and get it back. *Superiority* in our dealings with men results solely from our not needing them at all and our letting them see this. For this reason, it is advisable from time to time to let everyone feel, whether man or woman, that we can very well manage without them. This strengthens friendship; in fact with most men it can do no harm if, now and then, in our attitude to them we insert a grain of disdain. They attach all the more value to our friendship: *chi non istima vien stimato* (who esteems not is esteemed) says a fine Italian proverb. If, however, a man is really of very great value to us, we must conceal this from him as if it were a crime. Yet this is not very gratifying, but for all that it is true. Indeed dogs can hardly stand too much kindness, let alone human beings.

(29) It is often the case that those who are of a nobler nature and more highly gifted betray, especially when they are young, a surprising lack of knowledge of men and of worldly wisdom and are, therefore, easily deceived or otherwise led astray. Vulgar natures, on the other hand, are able to get on in the world much better and more rapidly. The reason for this is that, with lack of experience, we have to judge *a priori* and that in general no experience comes up to what is *a priori*. Thus this *a priori* suggests to common people just their own selfish point of view; but it does not do this to those who are noble and eminent. For precisely as such are they so very different from the rest; and as they appraise the thoughts and actions of others in accordance with their own, their calculation does not prove to be correct.

Now even if such a noble character has finally learnt *a posteriori*, namely from the advice of others and from his own experience, what is to be expected generally from men, thus that five-sixths of them are so constituted morally or intellectually that whoever is not through circumstances brought into relation with them, had better avoid them in advance and remain as far as possible from all contact with them—still he will hardly ever obtain an *adequate* notion of their paltry and contemptible nature. On the contrary, as long as he lives, he will always have to extend and add to his notion of them, but in the meantime he is bound to make many miscalculations to his own detriment. Then again, after he has actually taken to heart the advice he has obtained, it will occasionally happen that, when he is in the company of those still unknown to him, he will be surprised to discover how thoroughly reasonable they all seem to be in their conversation and demeanour, how honest, sincere, virtuous, and trustworthy they are, as well as shrewd and clever. Yet this should not disturb him, for the reason is merely that nature is not like inferior poets who, when they present knaves or fools, go to work so clumsily and deliberately that we see the poet standing, as it were, behind all such characters, continually disavowing their sentiments and their words, and exclaiming in a tone of warning: 'This is a knave; that is a fool; do not attach any value to what he says.' Nature, on the other hand, goes to work as do Shakespeare and Goethe in whose dramas every character, even though he be the devil himself, carries his point while he stands before us and speaks. He is interpreted so objectively that we are drawn towards his interests and are forced to sympathize with him. For such a character, like the works of nature, is developed from an inner principle by virtue whereof what is said and done appears to be natural and thus necessary. Therefore whoever expects to see devils go through the world with horns and fools with jingling bells will always be their prey or plaything. Moreover, there is the fact that in intercourse with others people are like the moon and hunchbacks in that they always show only one side. Indeed everyone has an inborn talent for working his physiognomy up into a mask by way of mimicry. This portrays him exactly as he is really *supposed* to be, and since it is calculated exclusively for his own individual nature, it fits and suits him to perfection and the effect proves to be extremely deceptive. He puts on the mask whenever it is a case of ingratiating himself. We should attach as much value to it as if it were made of oilcloth, bearing in mind that admirable Italian proverb: *non è si tristo cane che non meni la coda* (no dog is so bad that he does not wag his tail).

In any case, we should carefully guard against forming a very favourable opinion of anyone with whom we have recently become acquainted, otherwise in the great majority of cases we shall be deceived to our shame or even our cost. Here the words of Seneca are also worth mentioning: *argumenta morum ex minimis quoque licet capere*[58] (*Epistulae*, 52). Precisely in trifles, wherein a man is off his guard, does he show his character; and then we are often able at our leisure to observe in small actions or mere mannerisms the boundless egoism which has not the slightest regard for others and in matters of importance does not afterwards deny itself, although it is disguised. We should never miss such an opportunity. If in the petty affairs and circumstances of everyday life, in the things to which the *de minimis lex non curat*[59] applies, a man acts inconsiderately, seeking merely his own advantage or convenience to the disadvantage of others; if he appropriates that which exists for everybody; then we may be sure that there is no justice in his heart, but that he would be a scoundrel even on a large scale if his hands were not tied by law and authority; we should not trust him across our threshold. Indeed, whoever boldly breaks the laws of his own circle will also break those of the State whenever he can do so without risk.*

To forgive and forget is equivalent to throwing away dearly bought experience. Now if anyone with whom we are connected or associated reveals an annoying or unpleasant trait, we have only to ask ourselves whether he is of so much value to us that we are willing to put up with the same thing from him repeatedly and frequently and in an even more aggravated form. If he is of value, there will not be much to say about it because talking is of little use. We must, therefore, let the matter pass with or without a reprimand; yet we should realize that we have in this way laid ourselves open to a repetition of the trouble. If, on the other hand, he is not of value, we have to break at once and for ever with our worthy friend, or if he is a servant, to dismiss him. For when the case occurs again, he will inevitably do exactly the same thing or something wholly

* If in men, as they are in most cases, the good outweighed the bad, it would be more advisable to rely on their justice, fairness, gratitude, fidelity, love, or compassion than on their fear. But since the bad outweighs the good, the opposite course is more advisable.

[58] ['We can obtain proofs of the nature of a man's character even from trifles.']
[59] ['The law is not concerned with trifles.']

analogous, even when he is now deep and sincere in his assurances of the contrary. A man can forget everything, absolutely everything, but not himself, his own true nature. For character is positively incorrigible because all man's actions flow from an inner principle by virtue whereof, under similar circumstances, he must always do the same thing and cannot do otherwise. The reader should peruse my prize-essay on the so-called freedom of the will and free himself from the erroneous idea. Therefore to make our peace with a friend, with whom we had broken, is a weakness for which we shall have to atone when at the first opportunity he again does the very same thing that had brought about the breach; indeed he does it again with more audacity and assurance because he is secretly aware of his being indispensable. The same thing holds good of servants whom we have dismissed and taken back into our service. For the same reason, we ought not to expect a man under *altered* circumstances to do the same thing as previously. On the contrary, people change their demeanour and sentiments just as rapidly as their interest changes; in fact their premeditated action draws a bill at so short a sight that one must be even more short-sighted not to let it go to protest.

Suppose, therefore, that we want to know how a man will act in a situation into which we are thinking of placing him; we should not build on his promises and assurances. For assuming that he were speaking sincerely, he is talking about a matter whereof he has no knowledge. Therefore we must estimate how he will act solely from a consideration of the circumstances in which he has to appear and of their conflict with his character.

To obtain generally a really necessary, clear, and thorough comprehension of the true and very melancholy nature of most people, it is very instructive to use their conduct and actions in literature as the commentary of their conduct and actions in practical life, and vice versa. This is very useful for avoiding mistaken ideas either about ourselves or about others. But no special trait of meanness or stupidity which we come across in life or literature should ever be the subject of anger and annoyance, but merely of knowledge, in that we see in it a new contribution to the characteristic qualities of the human race and accordingly bear it in mind. We shall then regard it in much the same way as the mineralogist who comes across a very characteristic specimen of a mineral. There are exceptions of course, inconceivably great exceptions, and the differences in individuals are enormous; and generally speaking, the whole world lieth in wickedness, as was said long ago. Savages eat one another and civilized folk deceive one another; and this is what is called the way of the world. What are states with all their elaborate machinery in home and foreign affairs and their measures of force—what are they but precautions for setting up barriers against the boundless iniquity of mankind? Do we not see in the whole of history how every king, as soon as he is firmly established and his country enjoys some degree of prosperity, uses these to lead his army, like a band of robbers, for the purpose of attacking neighbouring states? Are not almost all wars ultimately expeditions of plunder? In ancient times and to some extent in the Middle Ages, the conquered became the slaves of the conquerors, that is, ultimately they had to work for the latter. But the same thing has to be done by those who pay war contributions; they sacrifice the income from previous work. *Dans toutes les guerres il ne s'agit que de voler,*[60] says Voltaire and the Germans should be reminded of this.

(30) No man has such a character that he should be left to his own devices and be allowed entirely to go his own way; but everyone needs guidance through opinions and maxims. Now if we try to go too far in this direction and take on a character that has not sprung from our own inborn nature but merely from rational deliberation, a character that is really acquired and artificial, we shall very soon find a confirmation of the words of Horace:

Naturam expellas furca, tamen usque recurret.[61]

Thus we can very easily understand, and even discover and aptly express, a rule for our conduct towards others; and yet in real life we shall shortly afterwards violate it. Nevertheless, we should not be discouraged by this and think that it is impossible to guide our conduct in life in accordance with abstract rules and maxims, and that it is, therefore, best for us to indulge our own inclinations. On the contrary, here it is the same as with all

[60] ['In all wars it is only a question of stealing.']
[61] ['Expel nature with a pitchfork, she still comes back.' (*Epistles*, I. 10. 24.)]

theoretical rules and instructions for something practical; to understand the rule is the first thing, and to learn to practise it is the second. The former is gained at once by our faculty of reason, the latter gradually through practice. The pupil is shown the notes on the instrument or the parades and thrusts with the rapier; yet even with the best intentions, he at once makes a mistake and now imagines that it is absolutely impossible to observe them in the speed of reading the notes or in the heat of the duel. Nevertheless, he gradually learns through practice by stumbling, falling, and getting up again. It is the same with the rules of grammar in writing and speaking Latin. And so in no other way does a lout become a courtier, a hothead a subtle man of the world, a frank person reticent, or a man of noble birth ironical. Such self-training, however, the result of long habit, will operate as a restraint coming from without which nature never entirely ceases to resist and sometimes breaks through unexpectedly. For actions in accordance with abstract maxims are related to those that spring from an original innate tendency as a human work of art, such as a watch where form and movement are forced on to a substance foreign to them, is to a living organism wherein form and substance pervade each other and are one. A statement of the Emperor Napoleon is, therefore, confirmed by this relation between the acquired and inborn characters. He says: *tout ce qui n'est pas naturel est imparfait.*[62] In general, this is a rule that is applicable to everything whether in the physical or moral sphere; the sole exception that occurs to me is natural aventurine which is known to mineralogists but cannot compare with the artificial product.

Here is the place to utter a warning against any and every form of *affectation*. It always arouses contempt; firstly as deception which as such is cowardly because it is based on fear; and secondly as self-condemnation that is brought about by ourselves, since we try to appear to be what we are not and thus what we regard as better than what we are. To affect some quality, to plume oneself thereon, is a confession that one does not possess it. Whether it is courage, learning, intellect, wit, success with women, wealth, social position, or anything else of which a man boasts, we can conclude from this that it is

[62] ['Everything that is not natural is imperfect.']

precisely in this respect that he is rather weak. For it never occurs to anyone, actually in full possession of an aptitude, to parade and affect it since he is quite content with the thought of having it. This is also the meaning of the Spanish proverb: *herradura que chacolotea clavo le falta* (the clattering horseshoe lacks a nail). As I said at the beginning, naturally no one should unconditionally have his fling and show himself entirely as he is since the many bad and bestial elements of our nature need to be concealed. But this justifies merely something negative, dissimulation, not something positive or simulation. We should know also that affectation is recognized even before it is clear what a man really affects. Finally, it does not last for any length of time, but one day the mask falls off. *Nemo potest personam diu ferre fictam: ficta cito in naturam suam recidunt.*[63] (Seneca, *De clementia*, lib. I, c. I.)

(31) A man bears the weight of his own body without feeling it, yet he feels that of every other which he tries to move. In the same way, he does not notice his own shortcomings and vices, but only those of others. Instead of this, everyone has in others a mirror wherein he clearly sees his own vices, faults, bad manners, and offensive traits of all kinds. But in most cases, he is like the dog who barks at his own image because he does not know that he is looking at himself, but thinks he sees another dog. Whoever finds fault with others is working at his own reformation. And so those who have the inclination and are secretly in the habit of subjecting to a searching and *sharp criticism* other people's conduct in general, their commissions and omissions, are thus working at their own improvement and perfection. For they will possess enough justice or pride and vanity to avoid doing what they so often severely censure. The opposite holds good of those who are tolerant; thus *hanc veniam petimusque damusque vicissim.*[64] The Gospel moralizes prettily on the mote in the eye of one's neighbour and on the beam in one's own; but the nature of the eye consists in looking outwards and not at itself. Therefore to note and censure faults in others is a very suitable way of becoming conscious of our own. We need a mirror to improve ourselves.

[63] ['No one can wear a mask for long; sham and pretence rapidly return to their original nature.']

[64] ['We beg this freedom for ourselves and likewise grant it to others.' (Horace, *Ars poetica*, II.)]

The same rule also applies as regards style and the way to write. Whoever in these admires a new folly, instead of censuring it, will imitate it. Thus every piece of folly rapidly gains ground in Germany; the Germans are very tolerant; everybody can see this. Their motto is: *hanc veniam petimusque damusque vicissim*.

(32) In his youth the man of nobler nature thinks that the essential and decisive relations, and the associations arising therefrom, between men are *ideal*, in other words, are based on similarity of disposition, way of thinking, taste, intellectual powers, and so on. Later on, however, he discovers that they are *real*, that is to say, are based on some material interest. This is the foundation of almost all associations; indeed most people have no notion of any other relations. Consequently, everyone is considered from the point of view of his office, business, nation, family or generally of the position and role assigned to him by convention. In accordance with this, he is ticketed and treated like a factory article. On the other hand, what he is in and by himself and thus as a human being in virtue of his personal qualities, is mentioned only at random and therefore only by way of exception. It is set aside and ignored by anyone whenever it suits him, and thus in most cases. The more worth a man has in this respect, the less he will be pleased with the arrangements of convention and the more he will try to withdraw from their sphere. Such arrangements, however, are due to the fact that, in this world of want and need, the means for preventing these are everywhere what is essential and therefore paramount.

(33) Just as we have paper money instead of silver, so in the world, instead of true esteem and genuine friendship, there circulate outward demonstrations and mimic gestures thereof which are made to look as natural as possible. On the other hand, it may also be asked whether there are men who really deserve the true coin. In any case, I attach more value to an honest dog wagging his tail than to a hundred such gestures and demonstrations.

True genuine friendship presupposes a strong, purely objective, and wholly disinterested sympathy with another's weal and woe, and this again means our really identifying ourselves with our friend. The egoism of human nature is so much opposed to this that true friendship is one of those things which, like colossal sea-serpents, are either legendary or exist somewhere, we know not which. There are, however, many associations between men which, of course, rest mainly on concealed egoistical motives of different kinds, but nevertheless have a grain of that true and genuine friendship. In this way, they are ennobled to such an extent that, in this world of imperfections, they may with some justification be given the name of friendship. They stand far above the everyday liaisons whose nature is such that, if we heard what most of our good acquaintances said about us in our absence, we would never say another word to them.

Apart from the cases where we need serious assistance and considerable sacrifice, our best opportunity for testing the genuineness of a friend is at the moment when we tell him of a misfortune that has just befallen us. The expression of his features then reflects either true, sincere, and unalloyed grief, or confirms by its absolute composure or some other fleeting feature, the well-known maxim of La Rochefoucauld: *Dans l'adversité de nos meilleurs amis, nous trouvons toujours quelque chose qui ne nous déplaît pas.*[65] On such occasions, the ordinary so-called friends are barely able to suppress the trace of a slight smile of satisfaction. There are few things that so certainly put people in a good humour as when we tell them of a serious misfortune that has recently befallen us, or unreservedly reveal to them some personal weakness. How characteristic!

Distance and long absence are detrimental to every friendship, however unwilling we are to admit it. For those whom we do not see, even if they were our dearest friends, gradually in the course of years dry up into abstract notions and in this way our interest in them becomes more and more rational and even traditional. On the other hand, we retain a lively and deep interest in those who are before our eyes, even if they are only pet animals. Thus is human nature tied to the senses; and so Goethe's words here hold good:

The present moment is a powerful goddess.
(*Tasso*, Act IV, Sc. 4.)

House friends are often rightly so called, since they are more friends of the house than of the master, and so are more like cats than dogs.

[65] ['In the misfortune of our best friends we always find something that does not displease us.']

Friends say they are sincere; enemies are so. We should, therefore, use their censure as a bitter medicine for getting to know ourselves.

Are friends in need so rare? On the contrary; no sooner have we become friendly with a man than he too is in need and wants us to lend him money.

(34) What a novice indeed is the man who imagines that to show intellect and understanding is a way to make himself popular in society! On the contrary, with the immense majority of men such qualities excite hatred and resentment; and such rancour is the more bitter, as the man who feels it has no right to complain of its cause; in fact he conceals this from himself. What precisely happens is that one man observes and feels great intellectual superiority in another with whom he is speaking and concludes, secretly and without being clearly aware of so doing, that the other man observes and feels to the same extent his inferiority and limitations. This enthymeme excites his bitterest hatred, resentment and wrath. (Cf. *World as Will and Representation*, vol. ii, chap. 19, where I quote from Dr. Johnson and from Merck, the friend of Goethe's youth.) Therefore Gracián is quite right when he says: *para ser bien quisto, el unico medio vestirse la piel del más simple de los brutos.*[66] (See *Oraculo manual, y arte de prudencia*, 240. *Obras*, Amberes, 1702, Pt. II, p. 287) To display intellect and understanding is only an indirect way of reproaching others with their incapacity and stupidity. Moreover, the vulgar man is driven to revolt when he catches sight of his opposite nature, and the secret provoker of such revolt is envy. For, as we can daily see, the satisfaction of their vanity is for men a pleasure that exceeds all others; yet this is possible only by their comparing themselves with others. But there are no qualities whereof a man is so proud as those of the mind; for on these alone rests his superiority over the animals.* To show anyone decided superiority in this respect, and moreover in the presence of witnesses, is therefore exceedingly rash. In this way, he feels provoked to

---

* It can be said that man has given himself the *will*, for this *is* man himself. The *intellect*, however, is an endowment that he has obtained from heaven, in other words, from eternal and mysterious fate and its necessity whose mere instrument was his mother.

[66] ['The only way to be popular is for us to be clad in the skin of the stupidest of animals.']

take revenge and will often seek an opportunity for so doing by means of insult, whereby he steps from the sphere of intelligence to that of the will where we are all alike in this respect. Therefore, whereas in society rank and riches may always count on respect and esteem, intellectual ability can never expect such treatment. In the most favourable case such ability is ignored; otherwise it is regarded as a kind of impertinence, or as something which its possessor got illegally and with which he now dares to give himself airs. For this everyone secretly tries to humiliate him in some other way and merely watches for the opportunity so to do. Even the most humble demeanour will barely succeed in obtaining forgiveness for intellectual superiority. Sadi says in the *Gulistan* (p. 146 of Graf's translation): 'We should realize that with the foolish man a hundred times more aversion to the wise will be found than the dislike the latter feels of the former.' On the other hand, intellectual *inferiority* proves to be a real recommendation. For just as warmth is beneficial to the body, so is a feeling of superiority to the mind; and thus everyone approaches the object that promises him this feeling as instinctively as he comes near a stove or into the sunshine. Now such an object is only one who is decidedly inferior in intellectual qualities in the case of men, and in beauty in the case of women. Of course, it takes a lot to give proof of real and unfeigned inferiority to many people whom we meet. On the other hand, see with what cordial friendliness a fairly good looking girl will welcome one who is positively ugly! With men physical advantages do not enter into the question very much, although we feel more comfortable next to a shorter man than next to one who is taller. Accordingly among men the stupid and ignorant and among women the ugly are generally popular and in demand. They easily acquire the reputation of an exceedingly good heart because everyone needs an excuse or pretext for his affection in order to blind both himself and others. For this reason, mental superiority of every sort is a quality that isolates men; it is shunned and hated and, as an excuse for this attitude, all kinds of faults and vices are attributed to its possessor.* Beauty among women has

---

* *For getting on in the world*, friends and comrades are by far the most important means. *Great abilities*, however, make a man *proud* and thus little inclined to flatter those who have only limited ability and from whom indeed he should, therefore,

precisely the same effect; very pretty girls never find friends or even companions of their own sex. It is better for them never to apply for positions as lady-companions; for when they make their appearance, their prospective mistresses will scowl at them and will certainly not require such a foil either for themselves or their daughters. On the other hand, matters are quite different with the advantages of rank; for these do not, like personal qualities, work through contrast and difference, but through reflection, like the reflected light on our faces from the colours of our environment.

(35) Our trust in others is often very largely made up of laziness, selfishness, and vanity; laziness when we prefer to trust someone else instead of making inquiries ourselves and of being vigilant and active; selfishness when the need to talk about our own affairs leads us to confide a secret to someone; vanity when it is one of those things of which we are rather proud. Nevertheless, we expect our trust to be honoured.

On the other hand, we should not get angry at the distrust and suspicion of others; for here is to be found a compliment for honesty, namely the sincere admission that it is very rare, so rare, in fact, that it is one of those things whose existence is doubted.

(36) *Politeness*, this cardinal virtue of the Chinese, is based on two considerations, one of which I have stated in my *Basis of Ethics*, para. 14, and the other is as follows. Politeness is a tacit agreement that we shall mutually ignore and refrain from reproaching one another's miserable defects, both moral and intellectual. In this way, they do not so readily come to light, to the advantage of both sides.

Politeness is prudence and consequently rudeness is folly. To make enemies by being wantonly and unnecessarily rude is as crazy as setting one's house on fire. For politeness is admittedly false coin, like a counter; to be niggardly with it shows a want

conceal and never show his own. The consciousness of only limited ability has the opposite effect. It is admirably compatible with a humble, affable, and kindly nature and with a respectful attitude to what is bad, and therefore produces friends and supporters.

What has been said applies not only to the public service, but also to posts of honour and rank and indeed to fame in the learned world. Thus, for example, in the academies near mediocrity is always at the top, whereas men of merit enter at a late hour or never at all; and so it is with everything.

of intelligence, whereas to be generous with it is prudent. All nations end a letter with *votre très-humble serviteur, your most obedient servant*,[67] *suo devotissimo servo*. Only the Germans refrain from using the word 'servant', because, of course, it is not true! On the other hand, to carry politeness to the point of sacrificing one's interests is like giving gold coins instead of counters. Wax, by nature hard and brittle, becomes so pliable with a little warmth that it assumes any desired shape. In the same way, through some politeness and friendliness, even the peevish and malevolent can be made manageable and accommodating. Accordingly, politeness is to man what warmth is to wax.

Of course, politeness is difficult in so far as it requires us to show to everyone the greatest respect, whereas most people merit none. Again, we have to feign the liveliest interest in them, whereas we must be very glad not to have anything to do with them. To combine politeness with pride is a masterpiece.

We should be much less upset over insults, as being really always expressions of disrespect, if, on the one hand, we did not cherish a wholly exaggerated notion of our own value and dignity and thus an excessive haughtiness and, on the other, were quite clear as to what one man in his heart usually thinks of another. What a glaring contrast there is between the sensitiveness of most people over the slightest hint of any blame attaching to them, and what they would hear if the remarks of their friends about them came to their ears! On the contrary, we should bear in mind that ordinary politeness is only a grinning mask; we should then not raise an outcry when it is shifted a little or is removed for a moment. But when a man is positively rude, it is as if he had cast off all his clothes and stood before us *in puris naturalibus*.[68] Of course, like most people in this condition, he cuts a poor figure.

(37) For what we do or omit to do we should not take someone else as our model because position and circumstances are never the same and difference in character also gives to an action a different touch and tone. Hence *duo cum faciunt idem, non est idem*.[69] We must act in accordance with our own character after ripe reflection and clear thought. Therefore in practical

[67] [Schopenhauer's own English.]
[68] ['Naked'.]
[69] ['When two people do the same thing, it is not the same.']

affairs, originality is indispensable, otherwise what we do is not in keeping with what we are.

(38) We should not join issue with anyone's opinion, but must remember that, if we tried to talk him out of all the absurdities he believes, we might live to be as old as Methuselah without getting the better of him.

In conversation we should also refrain from correcting people, however well meant our remarks may be; for it is easy to offend but difficult, if not impossible, to make amends.

If the absurdities of a conversation we happen to hear begin to annoy us, we must imagine that it is a scene in a comedy between two fools. *Probatum est.*[70] Whoever has come into the world seriously to *instruct* it in the most important things, can count himself lucky if he escapes with a whole skin.

(39) Whoever wants his judgement to be believed, should express it coolly and dispassionately; for all vehemence springs from the will. And so the judgement might be attributed to the will and not to knowledge, which by its nature is cold. Now since the radical element in man is the will, whereas knowledge is merely secondary and additional, people will sooner believe that the judgement has sprung from the excited will than that the excitation of the will has arisen from the judgement.

(40) Even when we are fully entitled to do so, we should not be tempted to praise ourselves. For vanity is something so ordinary, but merit so unusual that whenever we appear to praise ourselves, although only indirectly, everyone will wager a hundred to one that ours is the language of vanity and that we have not enough sense to see the absurdity of the thing. Yet in spite of everything, Bacon may not be entirely wrong when he says that the *semper aliquid haeret* applies not only to slander but also to self-praise, and therefore recommends the latter in moderate doses. (Cf. *De augmentis scientiarum*, Leiden, 1645, lib. VIII, c. 2, pp. 644 *seq.*)[71]

(41) If we suspect that a man is lying, we should pretend to believe him; for then he becomes bold and assured, lies more vigorously, and is unmasked. If, on the other hand, we notice

[70] ['It is tested and proved.']

[71] [Schopenhauer refers to the passage in Bacon's work where it says: 'Just as it is usually said of slander that something always sticks when people boldly slander, so it might be said of self-praise (if it is not entirely shameful and ridiculous) that if we praise ourselves fearlessly, something will always stick.']

that he has let slip part of a truth he would like to conceal, we should look as though we did not believe him. Provoked by the contradiction, he may follow up with the rear-guard of the whole truth.

(42) We have to regard all our personal affairs as secrets and must remain complete strangers, even to our good friends, in respect of everything about us which they cannot see with their own eyes. For in the course of time and with changed circumstances their knowledge of the most harmless things about us may be to our disadvantage. In general, it is more advisable to show our discernment by what we refrain from saying than by what we say. The former is a matter of prudence, the latter of vanity. The opportunities for both occur equally often; but we frequently prefer the fleeting satisfaction afforded by the latter to the permanent advantage secured by the former. Even the feeling of relief which occurs to lively people, when they speak aloud to themselves, should not be indulged lest it become a habit. For in this way, thought establishes such friendly terms with speech that even speaking to others gradually becomes like thinking aloud. Prudence, on the other hand, requires that we maintain a wide gulf between what we think and what we say.

Occasionally we imagine that others cannot possibly believe something concerning us, whereas it does not occur to them at all to doubt it. Yet if, through our action, this does occur to them, they are no longer able to believe it. But we often betray ourselves merely because we think it impossible for people not to notice this; just as we throw ourselves down from a height on account of giddiness, in other words, because we think it is impossible here to stand firm; the agony of standing here is so great that we think it better to cut it short. This vain imagining is called vertigo.

On the other hand, we should realize that even those who do not display any acuteness and acumen in other respects are experts in the algebra of other people's affairs. Here by means of a single given quantity, they solve the most complicated problems. If, for example, we tell them about a former event, without mentioning any names or giving any other descriptions of persons, we should be careful not to introduce any absolutely positive and particular circumstance, however insignificant, such as a place, a point of time, the name of someone of secondary importance, or anything else even only indirectly connected with it. For in this way they at once have a quantity positively given whereby their algebraical acumen discovers all the rest. The enthusiasm of curiosity is here so great that, by virtue thereof, the will spurs on the intellect and thus drives it to the attainment of the remotest results. For however insusceptible and indifferent men are to *universal* truths, they are keen on those that are individual and particular.

In accordance with all this, all the teachers of wordly wisdom have most urgently and with many different arguments recommended reticence and reserve; and so I can let the matter rest with what has already been said. I will, however, give one or two Arabian maxims that are particularly striking and little known. 'Do not tell your friend what your enemy ought not to know.' 'If I maintain silence about my secret, it is my prisoner; if I let it slip from my tongue, I am its prisoner.' 'On the tree of silence hangs the fruit of peace.'

(43) No money is spent to better advantage than that of which we have allowed ourselves to be defrauded; for with it we have directly purchased prudence.

(44) If possible, we should not feel animosity for anyone; yet we should note and remember everyone's *procédés* or actions in order to estimate his worth, at any rate in regard to ourselves, and accordingly to regulate our conduct and attitude towards him, always convinced that character is unalterable. To forget at any time the bad traits of a man's character is like throwing away hard-earned money. But in this way, we protect ourselves from foolish familiarity and foolish friendship.

'Neither love nor hate' contains a half of all wordly wisdom; 'say nothing and believe nothing' contains the other half. But, of course, we shall be only too glad to turn our back on a world where such rules and the following are necessary.

(45) Hatred or anger in what we say or in the way we look is futile, dangerous, imprudent, ridiculous, and common. Therefore we must never show anger or hatred except in our actions. We shall be able to do the latter more effectively in so far as we have avoided the former. It is only cold-blooded animals that are poisonous.

(46) *Parler sans accent.*[72] The object of this old rule of the

---

[72] ['To speak without emphasis'.]

worldly wise is that we should leave to the intelligence of others to discover what we have said. Their intelligence is slow and before it has arrived at our meaning we are off. On the other hand, *parler avec accent* is equivalent to addressing their feelings, and everything turns out the very opposite. If we are polite in manner and friendly in tone, we can without immediate risk be really rude to many a man.

D. *Our Attitude to the Ways of the World and to Fate*

(47) Whatever form human life assumes, there are always the same elements and therefore it is esssentially the same everywhere, whether it is passed in the cottage or at court, in the cloister or the army. Its events, adventures, successes, and misfortunes may be ever so varied, yet it is with life as with confectionery; there is a great variety of things, odd in shape and diverse in colour, but all are made from the same paste; and what has happened to one man resembles much more what has befallen another than we think from hearing the different versions. The events of our life are like the pictures in a kaleidoscope wherein we see something different at every turn; yet in reality we have before us always the same thing.

(48) An ancient writer very pertinently remarks that there are three forces in the world: σύνεσις, κράτος, καὶ τύχη, prudence, strength, and luck. I believe the last to be the most powerful; for our life can be compared to the course of a ship. Fate, τύχη, *secunda aut adversa fortuna*,[73] plays the part of the wind in that it speeds us on our course or plunges us a long way back; against this our own efforts and exertions are of little avail. These play the part of the oars; if they have carried us forward some distance through long hours of toil, a sudden gust of wind can cast us back just as far. If, on the other hand, the wind is favourable, it can carry us so far forward that we do not need to use the oars. The power of luck is admirably expressed by a Spanish proverb: *Da ventura a tu hijo, y echa lo en el mar* (give your son luck and cast him into the sea).

Chance is indeed a malignant power to which we should leave as little as possible. Yet which of all the givers is the only one who, in giving, at the same time most clearly shows us that we have no claim or title to his gifts; that for them we have

---

[73] ['Favourable or adverse fortune'.]

certainly not to thank our merits and deserts but simply his goodness and grace; and that these alone permit us to cherish the joyful hope of receiving, in all humility, many another unmerited gift? Such a giver is chance. Chance understands the royal art of making clear to us that all merit is powerless and unavailing against his favour and grace.

When we look back at the course of our life; when we survey our 'labyrinthine way of error',[74] and now must see so many cases in which our luck failed, so many instances of misfortune, we can easily go too far in reproaching ourselves. For the course of our life is certainly not our own work, but the product of two factors, the series of events and that of our resolves, which are always acting on and modifying each other. Moreover, there is the fact that in both of these our horizon is always very limited, since we cannot state our resolves far in advance and still less are we able to foresee future events; but in reality only the resolves and events of the present are actually known to us. Therefore as long as our goal is still very remote, we cannot steer straight towards it, but must direct our course only approximately and by conjecture; and so we must often tack about and alter course. Thus all we can do is to make our decisions always in accordance with our present circumstances, hoping to be able to bring nearer to us the principal goal. Thus events and our chief aims can in most cases be compared to two forces that pull in different directions, their resultant diagonal being the course of our life. Terence has said: *In vita est hominum quasi cum ludas tesseris: si illud, quod maxime opus est jactu, non cadit, illud quod cecidit forte, id arte ut corrigas.*[75] Here he must have had in mind a kind of backgammon. More briefly we can say that fate shuffles the cards and we play. For the purpose of expressing my present remarks, the following simile would appear to be the most suitable. Life is like a game of chess; we draw up a plan, but this remains conditioned by what in the game the opponent, in life fate, will be inclined to do. The modifications that our plan thereby undergoes are often so great that when it is being carried out several of its fundamental features are scarcely recognizable.

[74] [Goethe's *Faust*, Pt. 1.]
[75] ['Human life is like a game of dice. If the dice does not turn up as you want it, then skill must improve what chance has offered.' (*Adelphi*, IV, 7; ll. 739–41.)]

Moreover, there is in the course of our lives something above and beyond all else, namely a trivial truth, only too frequently confirmed, that we are often more foolish than we think. On the other hand, we are often wiser than we ourselves imagine, a discovery made only by those who in the event have been so and even then have taken a long time to make it. There is in us something wiser than our head. Thus in the big moves of our life, in the important steps of its course, we act not so much from a clear knowledge of what is right as from an inner impulse, one might say instinct, that comes from the depths of our very being. If afterwards we criticize our actions in the light of clear conceptions that are inadequate, acquired, or even borrowed, in the light of general rules, of other people's examples, and so on, without sufficiently weighing the maxim 'what suits one need not suit all', then we shall easily do ourselves an injustice. But in the end, it is seen who was right and only the man who has luckily attained old age is capable of judging the matter both subjectively and objectively.

Perhaps that inner impulse is under the unconscious guidance of prophetic dreams that are forgotten when we are awake. In this way they give to our life an evenness of tone and dramatic unity such as could never be given to it by our conscious brain that is so often irresolute, unstable, rambling, and easily altered. In consequence of such dreams, for instance, the man who has a vocation for great achievements of a definite kind inwardly and secretly feels this from his youth up and works in this direction, just as do bees in the building of their hive. But for everyone it is this that Baltasar Gracián calls *la gran sindéresis*, the great instinctive protection of himself, without which he is lost. To act in accordance with *abstract principles* is difficult and succeeds only after much practice, and even then not invariably; moreover they are often inadequate. On the other hand, everyone has certain *innate concrete principles* that are in his very blood and marrow, since they are the result of all his thinking, feeling, and willing. Usually he does not know them in the abstract, but only when he looks back on his life does he become aware that he has always observed them and has been drawn by them as by an invisible thread. According as they are, so will they lead him to his good or adverse fortune.

(49) We should constantly bear in mind the effect of time

and the transient nature of things. Therefore in the case of everything now taking place, we should at once vividly picture to ourselves its opposite; thus in prosperity misfortune, in friendship enmity, in fine weather bad weather, in love hatred, in confidence and frankness betrayal and regret, and so also in the reverse case. This would give us a permanent source of true wordly wisdom, since we should always remain thoughtful and not be so easily deceived. In most cases we should thus have anticipated merely the effect of time. But possibly to no form of knowledge is experience so indispensable as to a correct appreciation of the instability and fluctuation of things. Just because every state or condition exists for the time of its duration necessarily and thus with absolute right, every year, every month, or every day looks as if it could now at last retain the right to exist to all eternity. But none retains it and change alone endures. The prudent man is he who is not deceived by the apparent stability of things and in addition sees in advance the direction that the change will first take.* On the other hand, men as a rule regard as permanent the state of things for the time being or the direction of their course. This is because they see the effects, but do not understand the causes; yet it is these that bear the seed of future changes, whereas the effect that exists solely for those men contains no such seed. They stick to the effects and assume that the causes unknown to them which were able to produce such effects will also be in a position to maintain them. Here they have the advantage that, if they err, they always do so in unison; and so the calamity that hits them as the result of their error is universal, whereas when the thinker has made a mistake, he stands alone. Here, incidentally, we have a confirmation of my principle that error is always the result of concluding from the consequent to the reason or ground. See *World as Will and Representation*, vol. i, § 15.

Nevertheless, we should *anticipate time* only theoretically and by foreseeing its effect, not practically and thus not so that we

---

* *Chance* has so great a scope in all things human that when we try through present sacrifices to prevent a danger that threatens from afar, it often vanishes through an unforeseen state which things assume; and then not only are the sacrifices wasted, but the change brought about by them, with the altered state of things, is now a positive disadvantage. Thus in our precautionary measures, we must not look too far into the future, but must also reckon on chance and boldly face many a danger, hoping that it will pass like many a dark thunder cloud.

forestall it and demand *prematurely* what only time can bring. For whoever does this will discover that there is no worse and more exacting usurer than time; and if time is forced to make advances, it will demand heavier interest than would any Jew. For example, by means of unslaked lime and heat, we can so force a tree that within a few days it will bear leaves, blossom, and fruit; but it will then wither away and die. If a youth tries now to exercise the procreative power of a man, even if only for a few weeks, and wants to do at nineteen what he could very easily do at thirty, time will at any rate give him the advance, but a portion of the strength of his future years, in fact of his life itself, will be the interest. There are illnesses from which we completely recover only by our letting them run their natural course, after which they automatically disappear without leaving a trace. But if we demand to be well now and at once, so too must time here make an advance; the disease is cured, but the interest will be weakness and chronic complaint for the rest of our lives. When in time of war or civil disturbances we need money here and now, we are obliged to sell landed property or government stock for a third of their value, or even less, which we should have received in full had we given time its due and had, therefore, been willing to wait a few years; but we force time to grant an advance. Or we require a sum of money for a long journey; in a year to two we could have set it aside from our income. But we are unwilling to wait; the sum is, therefore, borrowed or sometimes taken from capital; in other words, time must advance the money. The interest will then be a disordered state of our accounts, a permanent and growing deficit from which we shall never be free. This, then, is time's usury; its victims are all those who cannot wait. To try to force the measured pace of time is a most costly undertaking. We should, therefore, guard against owing any interest to time.

(50) A characteristic difference, frequently appearing in everyday life, between ordinary and prudent men is that, when considering and estimating possible dangers, the former merely ask and take into account what of a similar nature *has happened* already; whereas the latter reflect on what *might possibly happen* and thus have in mind the words of a Spanish proverb: *lo que no acaece en un año, acaece en un rato* (what does not happen within a year may happen within a few minutes). Of course, the

difference in question is natural; for to survey what *may* happen requires discernment, but to see what *has* happened needs only our senses.

Our maxim, however, should be: sacrifice to evil spirits! In other words, we should not be afraid to spend time, trouble, and money, to put up with formalities and inconvenience, and to go without things, in order to shut the door on the possibility of misfortune. And the greater this may be, the smaller, more remote, and more improbable may be the possibility. The clearest example of this rule is the insurance premium; it is a sacrifice publicly made by all on the altar of evil spirits.

(51) We should not give way to great rejoicings or great lamentation over any incident partly because all things change and this alters its form; and partly because our judgement concerning what is favourable or unfavourable is deceptive. Consequently, almost everyone has at some time lamented over something that afterwards turned out for the best, or rejoiced over something that became the source of his greatest sufferings. The attitude of mind, here recommended to combat this, has been finely expressed by Shakespeare:

> I have felt so many quirks of joy and grief
> That the first face of neither, on the start,
> Can woman me unto't.
> (*All's Well that Ends Well*, Act III, Sc. 2.)

But in general, whoever remains calm and unruffled in spite of every misfortune, shows that he knows how colossal and thousandfold are the possible evils of life; and therefore he regards what has now occurred as a very small part of what could happen. This is the temperament of the Stoic, in accordance with which we should never *conditionis humanae oblitus*,[76] but should always bear in mind what a woeful and wretched fate human existence is in general and how innumerable are the evils to which it is exposed. To be reminded of this insight into things, we need only cast a glance around us; wherever we are, we shall soon have before our eyes that struggling, tormenting, and floundering for a bare miserable existence that yields nothing. Accordingly we shall moderate our claims, learn to submit to the imperfection of circumstances and things, and

---

[76] ['Forget the condition of man.']

always look out for misfortunes in order to avoid or endure them. For misfortunes, great and small, are the element of our lives and we should, therefore, always bear this in mind. Nevertheless, we should not, for this reason, lament and like a δύσκολος[77] pull a long face with Beresford[78] over the hourly *Miseries of Human Life*, still less *in pulicis morsu Deum invocare*.[79] On the contrary, like a εὐλαβής,[80] we should practise caution by forestalling and averting misfortunes, whether they come from people or things, and should become so refined in this that, like a clever fox, we neatly slip out of the way of every misfortune, great or small (which is in most cases only an awkwardness in disguise.)

A misfortune is for us less hard to bear if we have previously regarded it as possible and, as the saying is, have prepared ourselves to meet it. The main reason for this may be that, if we calmly think over the case as a mere possibility before it has occurred, we survey the extent of the misfortune clearly and in all directions and thus recognize it, at any rate, as finite and visible at a glance. Consequently, when it actually hits us, it cannot affect us with more than its true weight. On the other hand, if we have not thought over the matter and are caught unawares, our terrified mind is unable in the first instance to make a precise estimate of the magnitude of the misfortune. We cannot survey its extent and it easily appears to be incalculable, or at any rate much greater than it really is In the same way, obscurity and uncertainty make every danger appear to be greater than it is in reality. And, of course, there is also the fact that, while we have anticipated the misfortune as possible, we have at the same time thought of measures for obtaining help and consolation or at any rate have accustomed ourselves to a conception of it.

But nothing will better enable us to bear with composure the misfortunes that befall us than the conviction of the truth I have derived and established from its ultimate grounds in my prize-essay 'On the Freedom of the Will'. There it says (Pt. III, at the

---

[77] ['Discontented person'.]

[78] [The full title of the work is: 'The Miseries of Human Life; or the last groans of Timothy Testy and Samuel Sensitive, with a few supplementary sighs from Mrs Testy'.]

[79] ['To invoke the Deity for every flea-bite'.]

[80] ['Prudent and thoughtful person'.]

end): 'Everything that happens, from the greatest to the smallest, happens *with necessity*.' For a man is soon able to reconcile himself to what is inevitably necessary; and that knowledge enables him to regard everything, even that which is brought about by the strangest chances, as just as necessary as that which ensues in accordance with the most familiar rules and in complete anticipation. I refer the reader to what I have said about the soothing effect of the knowledge that everything is inevitable and necessary (*World as Will and Representation*, vol. i, § 55). Whoever is imbued with this knowledge, will first of all willingly do what he can, but will then readily suffer what he must.

The petty misfortunes that vex us every hour may be regarded as intended to keep us in practice so that the strength to endure great misfortunes may not be wholly dissipated in prosperity. We must be a horny Siegfried[81] against the daily annoyances, the petty frictions and dissensions in human intercourse, trifling offences, the insolence of others, their gossip, scandal, and so on. In other words, we must not feel them at all, much less take them to heart and brood over them. On the contrary, we should not be touched by any of these things and should kick them away like stones that lie in our path. We should certainly not take them up and seriously reflect and ruminate on them.

(52) But what men usually call fate are often only their own stupid actions. Therefore we cannot too often take to heart the fine passage in Homer (*Iliad*, XXIII. 313ff.) where he recommends μῆτις, i.e. prudent reflection. For if wicked actions are atoned for only in the next world, stupid ones are already atoned for in this, although now and then mercy may be shown.

Not ferocity but cunning has a terrible and dangerous look; so surely is man's brain a more terrible weapon than the lion's claw.

The perfect man of the world would be the one who was never irresolute and never in a hurry.

(53) Next to prudence, however, courage is a quality essential to our happiness. Of course, we cannot give ourselves either the

---

[81] [A reference to Siegfried, the German mythical hero, who encountered many adventures in his youth. His cloak of invisibility gave him the strength of twelve men.]

one or the other, but inherit the former from our mother and
the latter from our father. Yet whatever exists of these qualities
may be helped by resolution and practice. In this world where
'the dice are loaded', we need a temper of iron, armour
against fate, and weapons against mankind. For the whole of
life is a struggle, every step is contested, and Voltaire rightly
says: *on ne réussit dans ce monde qu'à la pointe de l'épée, et on meurt
les armes à la main.*[82] It is, therefore, a cowardly soul who shrinks,
laments, and loses heart, when clouds gather or even only
appear on the horizon. On the contrary, our motto should be:

tu ne cede malis, sed contra audentior ito.[83]

So long as the issue of any dangerous affair is still in doubt and
there is still a possibility that it may turn out successfully, we
should not think of nervousness or hesitation, but only of
resistance; just as we should not despair of the weather so long
as there is still a blue patch in the sky. In fact we should be
induced to say:

Si fractus illabatur orbis,
Impavidum ferient ruinae.[84]

The whole of life itself, not to mention its blessings, is still not
worth such a cowardly trembling and shrinking of the heart:

Quocirca vivite fortes,
Fortiaque adversis opponite pectora rebus.[85]

And yet even here an excess is possible, for courage can
degenerate into recklessness. Even a certain amount of timidity
is necessary for our existence in the world and cowardice is
merely the transgression of this measure. Bacon has admirably
expressed this in his etymological explanation of the *Terror
panicus* which is far superior to the older one that is preserved
for us by Plutarch (*On Isis and Osiris*, c. 14). Thus he derives it
from *Pan*, the personification of nature, and says: *Natura enim*

---

[82] ['In this world we succeed only at the point of the sword and we die with
weapons in hand.']

[83] ['Do not give way to the evil, but face it more boldly.' (Virgil, *Aeneid*, VI. 95.)]

[84] ['Even if the world collapses over him, the ruins still leave him undismayed.'
(Horace, *Odes*, III. 3. 7–8.)]

[85] ['Therefore he lives bravely and presents a bold front to the blows of fate.'
(Horace, *Satires*, II. 2. 135–6.)]

rerum omnibus viventibus indidit metum, ac formidinem, vitae atque essentiae suae conservatricem, ac mala ingruentia vitantem et depellentem. Verumtamen eadem natura modum tenere nescia est: sed timoribus salutaribus semper vanos et inanes admiscet; adeo ut omnia (si intus conspici darentur) Panicis terroribus plenissima sint, praesertim humana.[86] (*De sapientia veterum*, lib. vi.) Moreover, the characteristic feature of the *Terror panicus* is that it is not clearly conscious of its reasons, but presupposes rather than knows them; in fact, if necessary, it urges fear itself as the reason of fear.

[86] ['For the nature of things has infused all living beings with fear and terror as the preserver of their lives and for avoiding and warding off the evils that overtake them. However, this nature is here unable to exercise moderation, but always mixes vain and empty misgivings with those that are wholesome so that all beings, especially human, are full of this panic terror (if we could see into their hearts).']

CHAPTER VI

On the Different Periods of Life

VOLTAIRE has made the very fine statement:

> *Qui n'a pas l'esprit de son âge,*
> *De son âge a tout le malheur.*[1]

At the conclusion of these observations on eudemonology it will, therefore, be appropriate for us to cast a glance at the changes that are produced in us by the periods of life.

Throughout the whole of our lives we always possess only the *present* and never anything else. What distinguishes this is merely that, at the beginning, we see before us a long future, but that, towards the end, we see behind us a long past. Then there is the fact that our temperament, although not our character, undergoes certain well-known changes whereby the present always assumes a different hue.

In my chief work, volume ii, chapter 31, I have shown why in *childhood* we behave much more like *knowing* than *willing* beings. This is the reason for that happiness of the first quarter of our life in consequence whereof that period subsequently lies behind us like a lost paradise. In childhood we have only few associations and limited needs and thus little stirring of the will. Accordingly, the greater part of our true nature is taken up with *knowledge*. The intellect, like the brain that attains its full size in the seventh year, is developed early, although it is not mature. It incessantly seeks nourishment in the entire world of an existence that is still fresh and new, where everything, absolutely everything, is varnished over with the charm of novelty. The result of this is that our years of childhood are a continuous poem. Thus the essential nature of the poem, as of all art, consists in comprehending in every particular thing the Platonic Idea, in other words, what is essential and therefore common to the whole *species*, whereby each thing appears as the

---

[1] 'Who has not the spirit of his age,
Has all the misfortune of his age.'

representative of its class or family and one case holds good for a thousand. Now although it seems that in the scenes of our childhood we are always concerned only with the individual object or event for the time being and indeed only in so far as it interests our will for the moment, this is not really the case. Thus in all its significance, life is for us still so new and fresh without its impressions being deadened by repetition that, in the midst of our childish pursuits, we are always secretly concerned, without any clear purpose, to grasp in the particular scenes and events the essential nature of life itself, the fundamental types of its shapes and forms. We see all things and persons *sub specie aeternitatis*,[2] as Spinoza expresses it. The younger we are, the more every particular thing represents its whole class or family. This constantly decreases from year to year and accounts for the very great difference between the impression made on us by things when we are young and that made on us by them when we are old. And so the experiences and acquaintances of childhood and early youth afterwards become the regular standing types and rubrics of all later knowledge and experience, their categories as it were, to which we subsume everything that comes later, although we are not always clearly conscious of so doing.* Accordingly, the solid foundation of our view of the world and thus its depth or shallowness are formed in the years of childhood. Such a view is subsequently elaborated and perfected, yet essentially it is not altered. Therefore in consequence of this purely objective and hence poetical view which is essential to childhood and is sustained by the fact that the will is still far from appearing with all its energy, as children we behave far more like purely knowing than willing beings. Hence the serious contemplative look of many children which Raphael has used so happily for his angels, especially for those of the Sistine Madonna. For this very reason the years of childhood are so blissful that their memories are always accompanied by longing. Now while we are so earnestly engaged in the first comprehension of things through *intuitive perception*, education, on the other hand, aims at instilling into us *concepts* which, however, do not furnish us with what is really essential; on the

---

* Ah, those years of childhood! when time still passes so slowly that things seem to be almost at a standstill and to want to stay as they are to all eternity.

² ['From the aspect of eternity'.]

contrary, this, namely the fund and substance of all our knowledge, lies in the comprehension of the world through *intuitive
perception*. But this can be gained only from ourselves; it cannot
be *instilled* into us in any way. Therefore our worth, both moral
and intellectual, does not come to us from without, but proceeds
from the very depths of our own nature; and no Pestalozzian
pedagogics can turn a born simpleton into a thinker: never! As a
simpleton is he born, and as a simpleton must he die. The deep
comprehension, here described, of the first outside world of
intuitive perception explains also why the surroundings and
experiences of our childhood make so firm an impression on our
memory. Thus we were completely absorbed in our surroundings
and here nothing distracted us, and we regarded the things
standing before us as if they were the only ones of their kind,
indeed were the only ones that existed at all. Later we lose our
courage and patience when we know how many objects there
are. Now if we recall what I explained in chapter 30 of the
above-mentioned volume of my chief work, namely that the
objective existence of all things, that is, their existence in our
mere *representation or mental picture*, is generally agreeable,
whereas their *subjective* existence, that consists in *willing*, is
steeped in pain and misery, we shall accept the following
sentence as a brief expression of the matter: all things are
delightful to *see*, but dreadful to *be*. Now in consequence of the
foregoing remarks, things in our childhood are far better known
to us from the side of *seeing* and thus of the representation, of
objectivity, than from the side of *being*, which is that of the will.
Now since the objective is the pleasant side of things, whereas
the subjective and terrible side is still unknown to us, the young
intellect regards all those forms that are presented to it by
reality and art as just so many blissful beings. It imagines that
they are so beautiful to see and are perhaps even more beautiful
to *be*. Accordingly, the world lies before such an intellect like
an Eden; and this is the Arcadia in which we are all born.
Somewhat later, there results from this the thirst for real life,
the urge to do and to suffer, which drives us into the hurly-
burly of the world. We then come to know the other side of
things, the side of being, i.e. of willing, which thwarts us at every
step. There then comes on gradually the great disillusion and
after it has made its appearance people say: *l'âge des illusions est*

passé;[3] and yet it continues to come on and becomes ever more complete. Accordingly, it can be said that in childhood life presents itself as a theatre decoration that is seen from a distance, whereas in old age it looks like the same decoration that is seen at very close quarters.

Finally, there is also the following circumstance that contributes to the happiness of childhood. Just as at the beginning of spring all leaves have the same colour and almost the same shape, so are we all in early childhood like one another and therefore admirably harmonize. But with puberty there begins a divergence that becomes ever greater like that of the radii of a circle.

Now what disturbs and renders unhappy the remainder of the first half of life, namely the age of youth that has so many advantages over the second half, is the hunt for happiness on the firm assumption that it must be met with in life. From this arise the constantly deluded hope and so also dissatisfaction. Deceptive images of a vague happiness of our dreams hover before us in capriciously selected shapes and we search in vain for their original. And so in the age of adolescence, we are often dissatisfied with our position and environment, whatever they may be, because we attribute to them what belongs to the emptiness and wretchedness of human life everywhere, with which we are now making our first acquaintance, after expecting something quite different. Much would have been gained if through timely advice and instruction young men could have had eradicated from their minds the erroneous notion that the world has a great deal to offer them. But the very opposite occurs through our becoming acquainted with life often through fiction rather than from fact. In the bright dawn of our youth the scenes depicted by the poetry of fiction are resplendent before our gaze and we are now tormented by the yearning desire to see them realized, to grasp the rainbow. The young man expects the course of his life to be in the form of an interesting novel; and so arises the disappointment, already described by me in the previously mentioned second volume, chapter 30. For what lends charm to all those images is just that they are merely imaginary and not real and we are thus in the peace and all-sufficiency of pure knowledge when we

---

[3] ['The age of illusions is past.']

intuitively perceive them. To be realized means to be pre-occupied with willing and this inevitably produces pain. The reader who is interested may also be referred to chapter 37 of the above-mentioned volume.

Accordingly, if the characteristic feature of the first half of life is an unsatisfied longing for happiness, that of the second is a dread of misfortune. For with it there has more or less clearly dawned on us the knowledge that all happiness is chimerical, whereas all suffering is real. Therefore we, or at any rate the more prudent among us, now aspire to mere painlessness and an undisturbed state rather than to pleasure. When in my young days there was a ring at the door, I was pleased, for I thought, 'now it might come'; but in later years on the same occasion my feelings were rather akin to dread and I thought 'here it comes'. For distinguished and gifted individuals who, precisely as such, do not really belong to the world of men and women and who, therefore, stand alone, more or less according to the degree of their merits, there are two opposite feelings as regards this world. In youth they frequently have the feeling of being *abandoned* by the world, whereas in later years there is the feeling of having *run away* from it. The first is unpleasant and is due to our not being acquainted with the world, whereas the second is pleasant and rests on our acquaintance with it. As a result of this, the second half of life, like the second half of a musical period, contains less push and ambition but more relief and restfulness than does the first. This is due generally to the fact that in youth we think there is to be had in the world a prodigious amount of happiness and pleasure which is merely difficult to attain, and that in old age, on the other hand, we know there is nothing to be got and so are perfectly at ease in the matter, enjoy a bearable present, and even delight in trifles.

What the mature man acquires through his life's experience, whereby he sees the world with eyes different from those of the boy or youth, is primarily *frankness or freedom from prejudice*. He then sees things quite simply and takes them for what they are; whereas for the boy and the youth the world of reality was disguised or distorted by an illusion that was made up of self-created whims and crotchets, inherited prejudices, and strange fancies. For the first thing that experience finds to do is to free us from dreams, visions, and false notions that have settled in us in our youth. To protect youth from these would certainly be the best, though only a negative, education; but it is very difficult. For this purpose, the child's horizon would at first have to be kept as narrow as possible and yet within such horizon none but clear and correct notions would have to be inculcated. Only after the child had correctly appreciated everything lying within that sphere could it be gradually enlarged, care always being taken that nothing obscure, or even half or wrongly understood, was left behind. In consequence of this, the child's notions of things and of human relations would still always be limited and very simple, but yet clear and correct, so that they would always need only extension, not correction; and thus right on into the age of adolescence. This method requires in particular that one is not permitted to read novels, but that these are replaced by suitable biographies, such as, for instance, that of Franklin, *Anton Reiser*⁴ by Moritz, and others.

When we are young, we imagine that the important persons and momentous events in our life will make their appearance with a flourish of trumpets and drums. Yet in old age we see, when we look back, that they all slipped in very quietly by the back-door and almost unnoticed.

Further, from the point of view so far considered, life can be compared to a piece of embroidered material of which everyone, in the first half of his time, comes to see the top side, but in the second half the reverse side. The latter is not so beautiful, but is more instructive because it enables one to see how the threads are connected together.

Intellectual superiority, even the greatest, will assert its decided ascendancy in conversation only after one is forty years of age. For maturity of years and the fruit of experience can in many ways be surpassed, yet never replaced, by mental superiority. But even to the most ordinary man they give a certain counterpoise to the powers of the greatest mind so long as this is still young. Here I mean merely what is personal, not works.

After his fortieth year, any man of merit, anyone who is not just one of five-sixths of humanity so grievously and miserably endowed by nature, will hardly be free from a certain touch of misanthropy. For as is natural, he has inferred the characters of

⁴ [This is written in the form of a novel, but is to all intents and purposes a biography.]

others from his own and has gradually become disappointed. He has seen that they are not on his level, but are far beneath him, either as regards the head or the heart, often even as regards both. He therefore willingly avoids having anything to do with them. For in general, everyone will love or hate solitude, his own company, to the extent that he is worth anything in himself. Even Kant discusses this kind of misanthropy in the *Critique of Judgement*, at the end of the general remark to § 29 of the first part.

In a *young man* it is from an intellectual and also a moral point of view a bad sign if, at an early age, he knows *how to deal with people*, is at once at home with them, and enters into their affairs prepared as it were; it betokens vulgarity. On the other hand, an attitude of astonishment, surprise, awkwardness, and waywardness in such circumstances points to a nature of a nobler sort.

The cheerfulness and buoyancy of our youth are due partly to the fact that we are climbing the hill of life and do not see death that lies at the foot of the other side. But when we have crossed the summit, we actually catch sight of death that was hitherto known only from hearsay; and, as at the same time our vital strength begins to ebb, this causes our spirits to droop. A doleful seriousness now supersedes the youthful exuberance of joy and is stamped even on the countenance. As long as we are young, people can say what they like to us; we regard life as endless and accordingly use our time lavishly. The older we grow, the more we economize in our time; for in later years every day lived through produces a sensation akin to that felt by the condemned criminal at every step on his way to the gallows.

Seen from the standpoint of youth, life is an endlessly long future; from that of old age it resembles a very brief past. Thus at the beginning life presents itself in the same way as do things when we look at them through opera glasses that are held the reverse way; but at the end, it resembles things that are seen when the opera glasses are held in the normal way. A man must have grown old and lived long in order to see how short life is. In our youth time itself has a much slower pace; and so the first quarter of our life is not only the happiest but also the longest, so that it leaves behind many more memories. If he were required to do so, everyone would be able to narrate more from that period than from two of the following. As in the spring of the year, so in that of life, the very days ultimately become of tiresome length; in the autumn of both they become short, but brighter and more uniform.

When life draws to a close, we do not know what has become of it. Now why in our old age do we discover that the life we have lived is so short? Because we regard it as being just as short as is our memory thereof. Thus everything unimportant and much that was unpleasant have been forgotten and therefore little is left. For just as our intellect is generally very imperfect, so too is our memory. We must practise what has been learnt from experience and should ruminate on the past if the two are not to sink gradually into the abyss of oblivion. Now we do not usually ruminate on what was unimportant and rarely on what was unpleasant; and yet this is necessary if their memory is to be preserved. What is unimportant is always being added to; for through frequent and finally endless repetition many different things that at first seemed to us important gradually become unimportant; and so we remember the earlier years better than we do the later. Now the longer we live, the fewer are the events that seem to us important or significant enough to be subsequently considered. But only in this way could they be fixed in the memory; and so they are forgotten as soon as they are past. Thus time always passes without a trace. Now we do not like ruminating on what is unpleasant, at least when it wounds our vanity as indeed is often the case, since few troubles have befallen us for which we are entirely blameless; therefore much that is unpleasant is also forgotten. Now it is both the unpleasant and the unimportant that make our memory so short and this always becomes proportionately shorter, the longer its material becomes. Just as the objects on the shore from which we are sailing become ever smaller and more difficult to recognize and distinguish, so do our past years with all their events and actions. Moreover, there is the fact that memory and imagination occasionally present us very vividly with a scene from our life long past as if it had occurred only yesterday; and it then stands quite near to us. The reason for this is that it is impossible for us to conjure up just as vividly the long interval of time that has elapsed between now and then. For it cannot be surveyed in one picture; moreover, the events in it are for the most part forgotten. Only a general knowledge of it in the abstract is left, a mere conception but not an intuitive perception. Therefore what is long past appears to us so near in the individual thing, as if it had happened only yesterday; the intervening time vanishes and the whole life appears to be inconceivably short. Sometimes in old age the long past behind us and with it our old age itself appear to us in an instant almost like a miracle. This is due mainly to the fact that we see before us primarily the same fixed and immovable present. Inner events of this nature, however, are ultimately due to the fact that not our true being-in-itself but only the phenomenal appearance thereof lies in time and that the present is the point of contact between object and subject. And again, why in our youth does the life we still have before us look so immeasurably long? Because we have to find room for the boundless hopes with which we cram it and for whose realization Methuselah would die too young. Another reason is that, for measuring it, we take the few years we have already lived whose memory is always rich in material and therefore long. For novelty makes everything seem important; and so we subsequently ruminate thereon and thus often repeat it in our memory, whereby it becomes impressed on the mind.

Occasionally we think we long to see once more a distant *place*, whereas we really long to have the *time* that we spent there when we were younger and fresher. Time then deceives us by wearing the mask of space. If we travel to the place, we shall become aware of the deception.

For reaching a great age, with a sound constitution as a *conditio sine qua non*, there are two ways that can be illustrated by the burning of two lamps. One burns for a long time because with little oil it has a very thin wick; the other also burns for a long time because it has plenty of oil for a thick wick. The oil is the vital energy, the wick the use thereof in every way and by every means.

As regards *vital force*, we can as far as the age of thirty-six be compared to those who live on their interest; what is spent today exists again tomorrow. But after that age our position is analogous to that of the man of independent means who begins to touch his capital. At first, he does not notice this at all; the greatest part of the expense is again automatically recovered and a small deficit is not seen. But this gradually increases, becomes noticeable, and the increase itself every day grows larger. It spreads more and more; every day is poorer than its yesterday and there is no hope of things coming to a standstill. The decline speeds ever more on its way, like the falling of bodies, until at last nothing more is left. It is very depressing when both the things here compared, namely vital force and property, are on the point of actually melting away together. For this reason, love of possessions increases with age. On the other hand, at the beginning till we come of age, and even for some time afterwards, we resemble, as regards our vital force, those who from their interest still add something to their capital. Not only are the expenses again made good, but the capital increases. And again, this too is sometimes the case with money through the care and thoughtfulness of an honest guardian. O happy youth! O sad old age! Nevertheless, we should take care of the strength of our youth. Aristotle observes (*Politics*, last book, chap 5) that, of the Olympic victors, only two or three had carried off the victory as boys and again as men because the early exertions required by preliminary practice so exhausted their strength that they failed later when they reached the age of manhood. Just as this applies to muscular energy, so does it even more to nervous, whose manifestations are all intellectual achievements. Therefore the *ingenia praecocia*, the youthful prodigies, the fruit of a hothouse education, who excite our astonishment when they are young, afterwards become very ordinary individuals. Indeed the early and enforced efforts to acquire a knowledge of the ancient languages may be responsible for the subsequent dullness and lack of judgement that are shown by so many scholars.

I have observed that the character of almost every man appears to be particularly appropriate to one period of his life, so that at this age he is seen to better advantage. Some are sweet-tempered when they are young, and this then passes. Others are strong and active men who are robbed of all value by old age. Many a man is seen to the best advantage in old age when he is more lenient and indulgent because he is more experienced, unruffled, and resigned. This is often the case with the French, and it must be due to the fact that the character itself has in it something youthful, manly, or elderly with which the particular age of our life harmonizes or counteracts as a corrective.

Just as our progress on a ship is observed only by the way in which objects on the shore recede and accordingly become smaller, so do we become aware of our advancing years by the fact that those who are even older seem to us to be young.

We have already discussed how and why all that we see, do, and experience leaves in the mind fewer traces, the older we grow. In this sense, it might be asserted that only in youth do we live with a full degree of consciousness and that in old age we are really only half-conscious. The older we become, the less consciously do we live; things hurry past us without making any impression, just as none is made by a work of art that has been seen a thousand times. We do what we have to do and afterwards do not know whether we have done it. Now since life becomes more and more unconscious, the more it rushes towards the point where all consciousness ceases, so does its course become ever more rapid. In childhood the novelty of objects and the incident make us aware of everything and thus the day is interminably long. The same thing happens when we travel and one month then seems longer than four spent at home. Yet this novelty of things does not prevent time, which seems longer in both cases, from often becoming actually more protracted for us than when we are old or at home. But through long habit of perceiving the same things, the intellect gradually becomes so rubbed down and exhausted that everything passes over it and produces less and less effect. In this way, the days then become ever less important and thus shorter. The boy's hours are longer than the old man's days. Accordingly, our time has an accelerated motion like that of a ball that is rolling down. Just as on a revolving disc each point moves more rapidly, the farther it lies from the centre, so time passes away for everyone ever more rapidly, the farther he is from the beginning of his life. Consequently, it may be assumed that, in the direct assessment of our attitude, the length of a year is inversely proportional to the number of times it will divide into our age. For example, when the year is one-fifth of our age, it seems to be ten times longer than when it is only one-fiftieth. The variation in the rapidity of time has the most decided influence on the entire nature of our existence at each period thereof. In the first place, it makes childhood, although embracing only about fifteen years, seem the longest period of life and so the richest in reminiscences. Then again, the younger we are, the more likely we are to be bored. Children constantly need some pastime, whether it be play or work; if this ceases they are instantly seized by a terrible boredom. Even youths are still very liable to this and view with alarm the prospect of hours in which they will have nothing to do. In the age of manhood boredom vanishes more and more. For old men time is always too short and the days fly past like arrows. Of course, it is obvious that I speak of human beings and not of old brutes. Through this acceleration in the flight of time, boredom in most cases ceases to exist as we get older. On the other hand, as the passions with their torments are also silenced, the burden of life is, on the whole, actually lighter than in youth, if only one's health has been preserved. And so the years that precede the appearance of the feebleness and infirmities of extreme old age are called our 'best years'. This they may actually be as regards our feeling of ease and comfort; yet the years of our youth, when everything makes an impression and we are vividly conscious thereof, still have the advantage of being for the mind the productive period, its blossom-setting spring. Thus deep truths may only be discerned but not worked out; in other words, their first knowledge is immediate and is called forth by the momentary impression. Consequently, such knowledge occurs only so long as that impression is powerful, vivid, and deep. Accordingly, in this respect everything depends on the way in which we have used the years of our youth. In later years, we can make more impression on others, in fact on the world, because we ourselves are finished and accomplished and are no longer a prey to influences; the world, however, has less effect on us. These years are, therefore, the time for action and achievement, whereas those of our youth are the time for original conception and knowledge.

In youth intuitive perception predominates; in old age reflection; thus youth is the time for poetry, whereas old age is more for philosophy. Also in practical affairs we allow ourselves to be determined in youth by what is intuitively perceived and by the impression thereof, and in old age only by what is thought. This is due partly to the fact that only in old age have cases from intuitive perception occurred often enough and have been classified into concepts for these to be given full significance, substance, and credit, and at the same time for the impression of intuitive perception to be moderated through usage and practice. On the other hand, in youth the impression of intuitive perception and hence of the external aspect of things, especially on lively and imaginative minds, is so powerful that they regard the world as a picture. And so their main interest is what kind of figure they cut in it rather than how they feel mentally and morally. This already shows itself in the personal vanity and great fondness for clothes which are characteristic of young people.

The greatest energy and highest tension of our mental powers undoubtedly occur in youth up to the age of thirty-five at the latest. From then on they decline, although very slowly. Nevertheless our later years and even old age are not without their intellectual compensation. Only then have experience and learning become really abundant; we have had time and opportunity to consider and weigh in our minds everything from every aspect. We have compared one thing with another and have discovered their points of contact and connecting links so that only now are their relations rightly understood. Everything is cleared up and thus we now have a much more thorough knowledge even of that which we already knew in our youth, since we have for each concept many more proofs. What we thought we knew in our youth we really know in old age; moreover, we actually know much more and possess a knowledge that has been explored in every direction and is, therefore, really quite coherent and consistent. In our youth, on the other hand, our knowledge is always defective and fragmentary. Only the *man who attains old age* acquires a complete and consistent mental picture of life; for he views it in its entirety and its natural course, yet in particular he sees it not merely from the point of entry, as do others, but also from that of departure. In this way, he fully perceives especially its utter vanity, whereas others are still always involved in the erroneous idea that everything may come right in the end. On the other hand, there is more conception in youth and we are thus able to make more out of the little we know; but in old age we have more judgement, penetration, and thoroughness. A gifted man is already acquiring in his youth the material of his own knowledge, of his original and fundamental views, and hence that which he is destined to present to the world; but only in his later years does he become master of his material. Accordingly, in most cases, we shall find that great writers produced their masterpieces when they were about fifty years of age. Nevertheless youth remains the root of the tree of knowledge, although only the top bears fruit. But just as every era, even the most contemptible, regards itself as much wiser than the one immediately preceding it, not to mention the earlier ones, so does every age in the life of man; yet in both cases we are often mistaken. In the years of physical growth when we are daily adding to our mental powers and knowledge, it becomes a habit for today to look down with contempt on yesterday. Such a habit takes root and remains even when our intellectual powers have begun to decline and when today should rather look up to yesterday with reverence and respect. Thus we often underrate not only the achievements, but also the judgements, of our early years.*

Here we should make the general remark that, although in its fundamental qualities, man's intellect or head as well as his character or heart is innate, yet the former by no means remains so unalterable as does the latter. On the contrary, it is subject to very many transformations which on the whole regularly appear. This is due partly to the fact that the head or intellect has a physical foundation and partly to its having empirical material. Thus its own power has its gradual growth until it reaches its acme, after which there is a gradual decadence down to imbecility. On the other hand, the material occupying these forces and keeping them active, and hence the subject-matter of thought and knowledge, is experience, intellectual achievements, practice and thus a perfection of insight, an ever-growing quantity until a decided weakness makes its appearance and everything is thrown over and abandoned. Man consists of one element that is absolutely unalterable and of another that is regularly alterable in a twofold and opposite way. This explains the difference in his bearing and importance at different periods of his life.

In a wider sense, it can also be said that the first forty years of our life furnish the text, whereas the following thirty supply the

---

* Yet in our youth, when time is most precious, we often spend it most lavishly, and only in old age do we begin to economize in it.

commentary. This first teaches us properly to understand the true sense and sequence of the text together with its moral and all its niceties and subtleties.

Towards the end of life, much the same happens as at the end of a masked ball when the masks are removed. We now see who those really were with whom we had come in contact during the course of our life. Characters have revealed themselves, deeds have borne fruit, achievements have been justly appreciated, and all illusions have crumbled away. But for all this time was necessary. The curious thing, however, is that only towards the end of our lives do we really recognize and understand even ourselves, our real aim and object, especially in our relations to the world and to others. Very often, but not always, we shall have to assign to ourselves a lower place than we had previously thought was our due. Sometimes we shall give ourselves a higher, the reason for this being that we had no adequate notion of the baseness of the world, and accordingly set our aim higher than it. Incidentally, we come to know what we have in ourselves.

We are accustomed to call youth the happy time of life and old age the unhappy. This would be true if the passions made us happy. Youth is torn and distracted by them and they afford little pleasure and much pain. Cool old age is left in peace by them and at once assumes a contemplative air; for knowledge becomes free and gains the upper hand. Now since this is in itself painless, we are happier, the more conscious we are that it predominates in our nature. In old age we are better able to prevent misfortune, in youth to endure it. We need only reflect that the nature of all pleasure is negative and that that of pain is positive in order to see that passions cannot make us happy and that old age is not to be deplored just because it is denied many pleasures. For every pleasure is always only the allaying of a need or want. Now that pleasure should come to an end when the need ceases is no more a matter of complaint than that we cannot go on eating after a meal and must remain awake after a good night's rest. In the introduction to the *Republic*, Plato more correctly considers that hoary old age is happy in so far as it has finally done with the sexual impulse which has incessantly disturbed and tormented us. It might even be asserted that the many different and endless whims and crotchets that are engendered by the sexual impulse and the emotions arising therefrom foster in man a perpetual mild madness so long as he is under the influence of that impulse or devil with which he is constantly possessed; so that he becomes rational only when the passion is extinguished. But it is certain that, in general and apart from every individual circumstance and situation, a certain melancholy and sadness are peculiar to youth, while a certain cheerfulness is characteristic of old age. The reason is simply that youth is still under the sway and even forced labour of that demon which hardly ever grants it an hour of freedom and is at the same time the direct or indirect author of almost every evil or misfortune that befalls or threatens man. But old age has the cheerfulness of one who has rid himself of a shackle long borne and who now freely moves about. On the other hand, it might be said that, after the sexual impulse has faded away, the real kernel of life has gone and only the shell remains. In fact, it is like a comedy which is begun by human beings but is afterwards played to the end by automata dressed up in their costumes.

However that may be, youth is the period of unrest, old age that of repose; and even from this the feeling of ease and comfort of both could be inferred. The child greedily stretches out its hands for all the things of every colour and shape that it sees; for it is charmed by them, its senses being still so young and fresh. The same thing happens with greater energy to the youth who is also charmed by the world in its many colours and by its variety of forms. His imagination conjures up from them more than the world can ever promise. He is, therefore, full of eager desire and longing for something vague and indefinite; and this robs him of that peace without which there is no happiness. Accordingly, whereas the youth imagines that a prodigious number of things is to be had in the world, if only he could discover where, the old man is convinced from Ecclesiastes that all is vanity and knows that all nuts are hollow, however much they may be gilded. For in old age everything has abated partly because the blood is cooler and the senses are not so readily stimulated; and partly because experience has enlightened us as to the value of things and the intrinsic worth of pleasures. In this way, illusions, chimeras, and prejudices have been gradually dispelled which previously concealed and distorted a free and correct view of things. Thus we now recognize everything more clearly and correctly, take it for what it is, and arrive more or less at an insight into the vanity and unreality of all earthly things. It is just this that gives almost every old man, even if he has only very ordinary faculties, a certain touch of wisdom which distinguishes him from younger men. But the principal result of all this is peace of mind which is a great element in happiness and is really the condition and essence thereof.

Further, it is thought that the lot of old age is sickness and boredom. The former is certainly not essential to this age, especially if a long span of years is to be attained; for *crescente vita, crescit sanitas et morbus*.[5] As regards boredom, I have already shown why old age is even less exposed to it than is youth. Moreover, it is by no means a necessary accompaniment of the loneliness to which we are certainly led by old age, for reasons that can easily be seen. On the contrary, it is only for those who have experienced no other pleasures than those of the senses and of society and who have left their minds unstocked and their powers undeveloped. It is true that in old age our mental powers also decline, but there will still always be enough left to combat boredom. Then, as I have already shown, an accurate insight into things increases through experience, knowledge, practice, and reflection; our judgement is keener and the sequence and connection of events becomes clear. In all things we obtain an ever more comprehensive survey of the whole. Through ever fresh combinations of accumulated knowledge and its occasional enrichment, our own real self-culture continues to make progress in every respect and our mind is thus occupied, satisfied, and rewarded. The above-mentioned decline is to a certain extent compensated by all this. Moreover, as I have said, time passes much more rapidly in old age and this counteracts boredom. The decline in physical strength does little harm unless we need it for earning our livelihood. Poverty in old age is a great misfortune; but if this is banished and we retain our health, old age can be a very endurable period of our life. Comfort and security are its principal requirements; hence in old age we are even fonder of money than we were in our youth because it provides a substitute for failing strength. Deserted by Venus, we shall gladly look for merriment and

[5] ['With increasing age health and sickness increase.']

diversion in Bacchus. The desire to teach and speak replaces the urge to see, travel, and learn. But it is a piece of good fortune if an old man still retains his love of study, music, the theatre, and generally a certain susceptibility to external things. For in the case of some old people this undoubtedly lasts into extreme old age.

Only in our later years do we really attain to Horace's *nil admirari*,[6] in other words, to the immediate, sincere, and firm conviction of the vanity of all things and the hollowness of all the world's splendours. The chimeras have vanished and we are no longer of the opinion that a special happiness dwells somewhere, either in a palace or a cottage, which is greater than the one we essentially enjoy everywhere when we are just free from bodily or mental pain. For us there is no longer in world-values any difference between great and small, high and low. This gives old people a special placidity and serenity with which they smilingly look down on the phantasmagoria of the world. They are completely disillusioned and know that, whatever may be done to adorn and deck out human life, its barren and paltry nature soon shows through all such finery and tinsel. However much it may be tinted and trimmed, it is everywhere essentially the same, an existence whose true value is always to be estimated only on the basis of an absence of pain, not on that of a presence of pleasures, still less of pomp and show. (Horace, *Epistles*, 1.12.1–4). The fundamental characteristic of old age is disillusionment; the illusions which hitherto gave life its charm and spurred us to activity have vanished. We have recognized the vanity and emptiness of all the splendours of the world, especially of the pomp, brilliance, and magnificent show. We have learnt that there is very little behind most of the things desired and most of the pleasures hoped for; and we have gradually gained an insight into the great poverty and hollowness of our whole existence. Only when we are seventy do we thoroughly understand the first verse of Ecclesiastes;[7] but it is also this that gives to old age a certain touch of peevishness and ill-humour. What a man 'has in himself' is never more to his advantage than in old age.

Most people, of course, who have always been dull and dense

---

[6] ['Not to allow ourselves to be disconcerted (in face of desire and fear). Not to lose our equanimity.' (Horace, *Epistles*, 1.6.1.)]

[7] ['Vanity of vanities, saith the Preacher, vanity of vanities; all is vanity.']

become more and more of automata as they grow old. They always think, say, and do the same thing; and no outside impression is any longer able to bring about in them any change or to evoke from them anything new. To talk to such old people is like writing in the sand, for the impression is effaced almost immediately afterwards. An old age of this kind is, of course, only the *caput mortuum*[8] of life. It seems that nature tries to symbolize the appearance of second childhood in old age by the cutting of a third set of teeth which then in rare instances occurs.

The disappearance of all our powers as we grow older is certainly very distressing; yet this is necessary and even beneficial, as otherwise death would be too hard for which it prepares the ground. Therefore the greatest gain that comes to us through the attainment of a great age is euthanasia. This is a very easy way of dying, which is not ushered in by any illness, is not accompanied by any convulsions, and is not felt at all. A description of this will be found in the second volume of my chief work, chapter 41.*

However long we live, we are never in possession of anything more than the indivisible present; but memory daily loses more through forgetfulness than it gains through accretion. The older we grow, the smaller human affairs seem to be, one and all;

---

* Human life cannot really be called either long or short since it is at bottom the standard whereby we measure all other lengths of time. In the *Upanishad* of the *Veda* (*Oupnekhat*, vol. ii, p. 53) *the natural duration of human life* is stated to be a hundred years. I think this is correct because I have noticed that only those who have passed their ninetieth year attain to *euthanasia*, that is to say, die without illness, apoplexy, convulsions, or rattles in the throat; sometimes they die without turning pale, often when seated and after a meal; or rather they do not exactly die, but simply cease to live. At any earlier age one dies merely of disease and hence prematurely. In the Old Testament (Psalms 90:10) the span of human life is given as seventy or at most eighty years; and what is more important, Herodotus says the same thing (lib. 1, c. 32 and lib. III, c. 22). But this is wrong and is merely the result of a crude and superficial interpretation of daily experience. For if the natural span were between seventy and eighty years, people would inevitably die between those years *of old age;* but this is by no means the case. They then die, like younger people, *of disease* which is something essentially abnormal; and so it is not a natural end. Only between ninety and a hundred years do people die, but then as a rule *of old age*, without sickness, death-struggle, death-rattles, or convulsions, sometimes without turning pale; this is called *euthanasia*. Therefore here also the *Upanishad* is right in putting the natural span of human life at a hundred years.

[8] ['Dead head' i.e. dead residue (expression from ancient chemistry for the dry residue from the heating of certain materials in retorts).]

life, which in our youth stood before us as something firm and stable, now seems to be like a rapid flight of ephemeral phenomena; the vanity and emptiness of the whole stand out.

The fundamental difference between youth and age will always be that the former has in prospect life, the latter death; thus the former possesses a short past and a long future, whereas the latter possesses the opposite. In the years of old age life is like the fifth act of a tragedy; we know that a tragic end is near, but do not yet know what it will be. When we are old, we certainly have in front of us only death, but when we are young we have life. The question is which of the two is more hazardous and whether on the whole life is not something that it is better to have behind us than in front of us. Indeed Ecclesiastes (7:1) says: 'The day of death is better than the day of one's birth.' To want to live very long is in any case rash; for the Spanish proverb says: *quien larga vida vive mucho mal vive.*[9]

It is true that the course of an individual's life is not traced out and indicated in the planets, as astrology would have us believe; yet a man's life generally is so in so far as one planet in turn corresponds to each period thereof, and his life is accordingly governed in succession by all the planets. *Mercury* rules in the tenth year; and like this the individual moves rapidly and lightly in the narrowest circle. He can be won over by trifles, but he learns much easily under the sway of the god of astuteness and eloquence. At twenty we have the dominion of *Venus*; love and women have us entirely in their possession. At thirty *Mars* reigns, and a man is now impetuous, strong, bold, warlike, and defiant. At forty the *four asteroids* rule and accordingly a man's life is broadened; he is *frugi*, in other words, serves what is useful and expedient by virtue of *Ceres*; he has his own hearth by the influence of *Vesta*; he has learnt what he needs to know through *Pallas*; and the mistress of his house, his wife, reigns as *Juno*.[10] But at fifty *Jupiter* holds the sway; a man has already outlived most people and feels himself superior to the present generation. Still in full enjoyment of his powers, he has a wealth of experience and knowledge; according to his indivi-

---

9 ['Whoever lives long experiences much evil.']

10 Some fifty asteroids since discovered are an innovation in which I am not interested. And so my attitude to them is like that of the professors of philosophy to me. I ignore them because they do not suit my purpose.

dual nature and position, he has authority over all those about him. Accordingly, he is no longer willing to take orders but to give them himself. He is now most fitted to guide and govern in his own sphere. Thus Jupiter culminates and with him the man who is fifty years of age. Then follows *Saturn* at the sixtieth year and with him the heaviness, slowness, and ductility of *lead*:

> But old folks, many feign as they were dead;
> Unwieldy, slow, heavy and pale as lead.
> *Romeo and Juliet*, Act ii, Sc. 5.

Finally *Uranus* comes and then, as they say, we go to heaven. Here I cannot take into account *Neptune* (unfortunately so dubbed through thoughtlessness) because I may not call it by its true name which is *Eros*. Otherwise I would show how beginning and end are connected together, namely how Eros is secretly related to death. By virtue of his relation, Orcus or Amenthes of the Egyptians (Plutarch, *On Isis and Osiris*, c. 29) is the λαμβάνων καὶ διδούς,[11] thus not only the taker but also the giver, and death is the great reservoir of life. Therefore everything comes from Orcus and everything that now has life has already been there. If only we were capable of understanding the conjuring trick whereby this is done, all would be clear.

[11] ['The taker and giver'.]